READINGS IN
Child Behavior and Development

SECOND EDITION

READINGS IN Child Behavior AND Development

SECOND EDITION OF
READINGS IN CHILD DEVELOPMENT

Celia Burns Stendler
UNIVERSITY OF ILLINOIS

HARCOURT, BRACE & WORLD, INC.
NEW YORK · CHICAGO · SAN FRANCISCO · ATLANTA

Library of Congress Catalog Card Number 64-15590

PRINTED IN THE UNITED STATES OF AMERICA

CONTENTS

PART IV
Socialization Processes in Family and School

PART V
Intellective Processes in Children

PART VI

Stability of Individual Personality and Behavior Through Time

PREFACE

THIS edition of *Readings in Child Behavior and Development* is a revision of the 1954 *Readings in Child Development* that I edited with William E. Martin. Since the appearance of the first edition, both the volume and content of research output have changed significantly. The amount of research has increased enormously, with much of it devoted to investigation of problems not emphasized a decade ago. The plan of organization of this book reflects these recent developments. The six topics under which the studies are grouped seem to this writer to be the major concerns of present-day specialists in the child development field.

Developments in theory are also reflected in this edition. In the first edition, the child was viewed as a product of his biology, his culture, and his individual life experiences, and the studies were selected to illustrate each of these categories. They are still the major forces shaping the child, but now we are beginning to see more clearly how these forces interact with each other in the day-to-day transactions that the child carries on with people or objects in his environment. It is one thing to talk in general terms about the fact that heredity and environment both influence development; it is another to study a specific animal, to see how individual differences, not so great at birth, become magnified as the animal is exposed to particular experiences. It is one thing to talk about the importance of early experiences; it is another to see the specific effects of a particular kind of deprivation upon the motor development of institutionalized children. Behavior has been put under a microscope with far greater powers of magnification than formerly, with the result that we can now spell out many of the details about the interaction of the various forces at work upon the child and, in so doing, refine theory.

It is within the framework of the organism-environment-interaction hypothesis that many of the studies included here have been selected. The underlying assumption is that development should not be viewed as a process whereby neural cells ripen with age, bringing concomitant changes in behavior. Instead, development should be seen to evolve as new experiences reshape existing structures. The baby trying to bring into his playpen a ruler that has fallen outside makes the discovery that the stick will only go through the bars when it is held in a vertical position. This discovery reshapes existing information stored in his gray cells about how an object relates to space, and the new structure forms the basis on which future decisions will be made. Parts I and II in particular reflect advances in thinking about organism-environment-interaction.

Refinements of motivation theory since the publication of the first edition are reflected in Part III. There continue to be the two major schools of thought—Freudian and learning theory—each of which makes a contribution to our understanding of what motivates the child. Learning theorists have revised their thinking to account for the human propensity to explore, to be curious, and to seek stimulation. White's paper provides the theoretical background for an understanding of this problem, while Piaget's describes some infant behaviors that illustrate the "effect" drive at work. In addition, papers are included on the effects of certain experiences upon drive systems in children—upon curiosity, achievement, aggression, and dependency motivation.

The situation with respect to Freudian psychology is somewhat different. There have been no major refinements of orthodox Freudian theory. Erikson, however, has revised his book *Childhood and Society,* and one of its chapters which is included here should not be missed by the student who wants deeper insight into the developmental process. The fact that Erikson combines talent in psychoanalysis with a knowledge of anthropology makes the reading of this selection especially rewarding. Bronfenbrenner's paper on the various interpretations of identification is a major contribution to clearing up confusion about this concept.

Since the first edition, child psychologists have been increasingly concerned with the intellective process, and so a section on this topic has been included here. Piaget's work on logical development has had a tremendous impact upon American psychology, and his work is well represented in this book. I have written a lengthy introduction to help students who have had difficulty in understanding his theory. Developments in the psycho-linguistics field are also reflected in this section, with several important papers on the relationship between thought and language.

It is a sign of the advanced age of the field of child development that it is now possible to include a section on stability of the personality. Longitudinal studies carried on at research centers over a period of many years are providing data on how children change and how they stay the same with the passage of time. Part VI is devoted to this topic.

I have written introductions to each section to make the book usable as a text. In each case the introduction reviews some of the major issues relating to the section's topic, so that the student can see the relevance of each paper to that topic. Some studies not included in this volume are discussed and listed under *References* at the end of the introduction. Thus, for each of the major topics, the student can get background information from the introduction, read some of the major contributions to that topic, and, it is hoped, deepen his understanding by further reading.

With few exceptions, abridgments of the papers have been minor. Many instructors of courses in child psychology and development want their students to know not only research findings but also research design. By reading research reports in their entirety, students grow in their sophistication. The wide variety of design represented in these readings should further such growth.

I have given credit to the authors and publishers of each of the papers in appropriate footnotes throughout the book; it is their generosity in granting permission to reprint the material that has made this collection possible. I have been fortunate in having the counsel of Robert R. Sears and Eleanor E. Maccoby of Stanford University in assembling the collection; their good judgment steered me toward some excellent papers I might have missed, and away from others of lesser quality I might have included. In addition, professors using the first edition have been most helpful in evaluating papers in that edition, thus making easier the task of deciding which studies to retain. I am particularly grateful to Freda Rebelsky of Boston University, who generously shared her own reading lists and commented on my choices. Special thanks are due to William E. Martin for the various kinds of help he gave in the preparation of this volume, and in particular for the contribution of his fine paper "Singularity and Stability of Profiles of Social Behavior." Lastly, to my niece, Maureen Burns, I express my heartfelt thanks for her patient, persistent, and painstaking assistance with library materials.

CELIA BURNS STENDLER

January, 1964

READINGS IN
Child Behavior and Development

PART I

Determinants of Infant Behavior

SPECIALISTS of child development in the nineteen twenties and thirties were prone to explain development in either-or terms. The extreme hereditarian attributed its course to the genes, while the extreme environmentalist searched the child's immediate surroundings. Although there were few 100 percenters in either camp, most thought it possible to assess quantitatively the relative responsibility of heredity and environment. Thus, in explaining individual differences in intelligence, special talent, or personality, the hereditarian might attribute 80 per cent of the variance to heredity and the remaining 20 to environment, while the explanation of the environmentalist might be the reverse. Both fixed the division on the basis of statistical analyses of the measurements they took.

Today's student of child development is likely to find less interest in attributing proportional importance and more interest in explaining development as *interaction* between organism and environment. Heredity is not, then, a straitjacket severely limiting the development of that organism, nor is environment a rigid mold. Rather, emphasis is placed upon an organism-environment-interaction process in which both heredity and environment play a role.

There is nothing very new about the idea that *both* heredity and environment influence development. Cultural anthropologists, sociologists, and psychologists have been investigating for years by case study and correlational techniques the impact of environment upon the organism. What is new, however, is that now studies are being carried out with more emphasis upon the neurological. Research is being conducted to identify both the intrinsic and the extrinsic factors in the development of early responses, to find out how an individual's transactions with things in the environment shape developing neural structures and so alter future development. Hunt's (1961) [1] statement of the interaction position is appropriate here:

> The encounters that the infant and child have with the environment in the course of development collaborate with the human genotype in determining the development of those structures and those organizations of central processes within the child's brain that mediate his intelligent behavior. Beginning at conception, the

1 Dates refer to articles cited at the ends of the introductory essays. These citations are offered only for articles that have not been reprinted in this volume. Such articles are referred to here for their contribution to an understanding of the topic, and were omitted chiefly because of space limitations.

> human organism, like all others, lives in the ever-moving now. It responds to the circumstances encountered with those structures, both somatic and neuropsychological, that it has already developed. In the course of maturation and in accommodating new variations in those circumstances, these structures change. Thus, at any given stage of development, the phenotypic intelligence of a child, to paraphrase the words of Dobzhansky . . . , depends on his genotype, on the diet he has ingested, and on the succession of circumstances that he has encountered [p. 42].

The earliest interactions of the newborn are between the repertoire of behaviors present at birth and the actions of the mother. The repertoire of neonatal behaviors is comprised of certain reflex activities. Perhaps one of the best known of these is the startle pattern. In response to a loud noise or other sudden neural excitation, the neonate closes his eyes, tilts his head upward, extends his arms upward and outward, clenches his fists, moves his trunk forward, and bends his knees. The response is much like that which adults experience when they come to with a start while dropping off to sleep. Not quite so well known is the orienting or rooting reflex. In this reflex the neonate will turn his head sideways in response to the stimulation of one side of his cheek, orienting himself toward the stimulus.

Reflex activities are modified by environmental stimuli. The rooting reflex has been the subject of some especially interesting experimental research. Blauvelt (1962) notes that maternal handling of the newborn provides a natural stimulation of the sensitive zone. As the mother lifts the infant from his crib, she slides her hand and forearm beneath his head for support. Since the head is turned on one side in the tonic-neck-reflex position, her hand and arm stimulate the cheek, and the baby orients his face toward the touch, moving to meet it and following after it. Stimulation of the zone continues after the baby is placed in a feeding position, resulting in his orientation toward the breast or bottle. The mother coordinates her movements with the baby's; her movements in turn are picked up by the infant's sense receptors. The infant organism assimilates the sensory messages into existing neural structures, thereby modifying the structures. This modification results in a modification of the original response, so that each new movement depends upon the mother's response to a previous movement. Since the human environment is not stereotyped, there is a variety of stimulation afforded the neonate, resulting in a corresponding variety of changes in reflex responses to the environment. In such a variety of interactions may be found the key to individual differences; we come back to this point again in the discussion of the Scott and Charles paper later in this section.

Part I includes papers on some of the factors today regarded as important in the interaction process. We begin with the prenatal period, for behavior and development exist before birth as well as the influence of the environment upon that behavior and development.

The Prenatal Period

PRENATAL BEHAVIOR

ONE of the most ingenious investigators of organism-environment interaction during the prenatal period has been Kuo. From his imaginatively designed experiments on infrahuman fetuses have come observations of the modifications of behavior that develop as relations between embryo and physical environment change. In one of these studies (1932), he treated the shells of fertilized chicken eggs so that the chick embryo could be visible during the embryonic period. He found changes in reflexive behavior as the growing organism adjusts to the confining walls of the eggshell. Jerking and wiggling replace lateral twisting as the embryo grows in size and twisting can no longer be accomplished in the limited space available. It appears that a kind of action and initiative for action come, at least partially, from pressures exerted by extrafetal membranes.

Certain mechanical factors associated with anatomical growth also initiate behavior. Rhythmic vibrations of the heart, for example, set in motion a rather mechanical up-and-down movement of the head. As the head changes in weight, this up-and-down movement becomes a sidewise movement, which is later inhibited as space in the yolk sac is filled by the growing embryo.

In Kuo's opinion, movement begets movement. Mechanical movements (such as heartbeats) seem to stimulate head activity which, in turn, stimulates still other kinds of activity, so that by the time the chick is born, almost every part of its muscular system has been exercised. These early movements provide the elements out of which later behaviors are constructed. Such activities as pecking do not spring full-blown into existence after birth, but appear, given the proper stimulus, as a result of many separate movements practiced by the embryo and organized into a pattern.

Comparable studies of interaction between human fetus and environment do not exist, although we do have studies of the development of behavior before birth. These are understandably limited in number; the researcher does not have subjects readily available to him, and he is limited to those fetuses that have to be removed surgically from the mother or that have spontaneously aborted. Upon these he performs certain experiments, applying stimuli to various parts of the body and noting the resultant behavior. Since his interest is in normal behavior, the difficulties are enormous. The fetus of the first few months is so immature that it has no source of oxygen once separated from the placenta; unless a supply can be furnished within a minute or two, oxygen deprivation will affect the behavior elicited. In addition, certain types of drugs administered to the mother will anesthetize the fetus so that its activity is affected. There is also the danger of damage in delivery.

Despite these difficulties, Davenport Hooker, working with Tryphena Humphrey (1954), was able to experiment on over one hundred fetuses, recording some of their behaviors on film. A chapter from his book, *The Prenatal Origin of Behavior,* is included here. From Hooker's painstaking work over a twenty-four-year period, the reader will be able to see that neonatal responses are part of a continuum of human behavioral development. Feeding behaviors do not begin at birth; in fact, as Hooker points out, sensitivity to a stimulus appears in a region around the mouth at seven and one-half weeks of menstrual age (figured from the first day of the last menstrual period of the mother). His work also illustrates the integrative nature of the nervous system; movement in response to stimulation of the mouth involves the neck and upper trunk as well as the mouth, then it gradually spreads to include the entire trunk and, finally, the lower extremities.

In the Hooker studies, the stimulation setting off the fetal movements originated in pressure from a hair held in the experimenter's hand. We do not know the nature of the stimulus that initiates the movement *in utero.* Stimuli originating within the growing organism probably account for most of the behavior of the fetus, although there may be some external stimulation, such as Kuo noted in the case of the chick, emanating from the pressure of the egg sac. However, Hooker's studies of how behavior develops do seem to illustrate Kuo's point that movement begets movement. The explanation may be that firing of nerve cells first begins in sufficiently mature cells, with this electrical activity stimulating other cells as they become mature.

DISTURBANCES OF PRENATAL ENVIRONMENT AND THEIR EFFECTS ON LATER DEVELOPMENT

The chemical environment in which the organism lives before birth provides the organism with the essentials of life. When this environment is disturbed or is inadequate, dramatically unfortunate modifications in development can occur. Research, as reviewed by Montagu (1950), shows that such factors as poor nutrition, drugs, infections, and endocrine disturbances may take their toll in infant mortality, stillbirths, congenital malformations, and constitutional defects. The taking of thalidomide by mothers during the first three months of pregnancy and the subsequent birth of babies with undeveloped arms and legs served as a sharp reminder in 1962 of the importance of Montagu's message.

The work of Pasamanick, Knobloch, and Lilienfeld (1956) substantiates the finding that environmental factors can affect human development before birth as well as after. These researchers argue that there has been an overemphasis upon genetic endowment as a cause of human variation and an underemphasis upon socioeconomic variables. It is well known, as they point out, that physical growth is affected by these latter variables. For example, Mexicans and Japanese born in the United States are taller than those born in Mexico and Japan. Pasamanick and his co-authors also point out that socioeconomic variables can influence neuropsychological functioning as well. Their studies show that serious complications of pregnancy increase as socioeconomic status decreases and that nonwhites have the highest rates. With such complications goes an increased amount of damage to the central nervous system which may show up in such neuropsychiatric disorders as cerebral palsy and mental deficiency, and—later in life—in lesser handicaps, such as behavior disorders, reading disabilities, and tics.

The Infancy Period

GENETIC FACTORS AND INDIVIDUAL DIFFERENCES

THE organism-environment-interaction hypothesis should not be presented to the reader in such a way as to overlook genetic factors in development. Hall's paper on hereditary influences upon temperament may help the reader to keep the genetic viewpoint in perspective. Through a process of interbreeding he was able to produce generations of rats that were increasingly emotional as judged by an operational definition. He concludes that temperamental differences observed in human beings have a foundation in constitutional differences, genetic in origin, and that these differences are not readily modified by social control.

While evidence for constitutional influences from human mating experiments does not, of course, exist, some evidence comes from observations of neonatal behaviors. Studies by Shirley (1933), Escalona and Leitch (1949), Aldrich and Aldrich (1954), and others have long been in the literature, and they have documented the fact that even at birth babies can be observed to differ in irritability, sensitivity to environmental stimulation, and activity level. But while such constitutional differences are presumed to exist, the behavior characteristics of a neonate, which must be delineated before individual differences can be established, are extremely difficult to assess. Escalona's recent research (1962) indicates that one should approach earlier studies with caution. Her point is that the state of the organism must be taken into account in assessing neonatal behavior. Consider, for example, activity level. A new baby is presented with a stimulus and reacts strongly to it. Does he have a different constitutional make-up from one who barely reacts to the same stimulus? Or, are the two babies in a different state due to some unknown physiological variable, such as an imminent bowel movement? Until some precise assessment of the state of the organism can be made, or until the state can be controlled, observations of infant behavior are not trustworthy as a method of describing individual differences and predicting a developmental pattern of behavior. The infant who is judged to be highly active in a test may not actually be a highly active individual; the state of his organism at the time of testing might have made him more prone to activity than his constitutional capacity would customarily warrant.

THE ROLE OF MATURATION

Arnold Gesell was perhaps the most outspoken advocate of the point of view that maturation was the most important determinant of infant behavior. According to Gesell, by virtue of one's inheritance as a member of the human race, certain behaviors appear at predictable times and in accordance with an innate design. He believed that one could describe rather precisely the social behavior and personality of, say, a typical three-year-old, because three-year-old behavior was the result of a gradual unfolding of the human pattern. The key concept in his theory was maturation, an innate process; with age, neural cells ripen or mature, bringing about changes in behavior, thus making possible descriptions of normative behavior at a given age level. Maturation performs a regulatory function, Gesell believed, essential for stability and balance in the growing organism. It was the maturational factor that determined what the child would use in his environment and how he would interact with it.

Those who belong to the interaction school of thought would not discard maturation as a factor in behavior, but would point out that functional maturity of the cerebral cortex *depends upon its actual functioning* (Simon, 1957). The stair-climbing behavior of the non-trained twin described in Gesell's paper was not due only to a ripening of nerve cells in accordance with a preconceived design; rather, other behaviors practiced earlier by the infant contributed the elements out of which stair-climbing behavior could be constructed. The behavior would appear at that time when the nervous system is mature enough to coordinate the elements. Seen in this light, Gesell's and other investigators' experiments on the role of maturation can be reinterpreted: new behaviors do not make their appearance as the result of an innate, fixed design, but are possible because other behaviors in which the infant engaged contribute to the functional maturity of his nervous system.

Organism-Environment Interaction in the Neonate • In its modern reformulation, the interaction hypothesis has proved exceedingly fruitful. It has resulted in a tremendous number of highly significant studies both at the infrahuman and the human level. Many animal behaviors formerly believed to be instinctive are now viewed as the result of an imprinting process occurring immediately after birth. The Hess paper deals with this important process.

As is well known, goslings, lambs, and some other baby animals will follow behind the mother beginning soon after birth. Hess's experiments show such behaviors to depend upon imprinting, a learning process that can occur only during a very short critical period immediately following birth. During this period, if suitable stimuli are provided, these animals can be taught to follow *any* moving object, and the learning is rigid and irreversible. Ducklings, for example, exposed to a moving decoy learned to follow after the decoy, even preferring the decoy to the mother duck when the latter was put into the field after imprinting had occurred. Hess describes the conditions under which imprinting takes place.

The fourth and fifth papers in this section are also studies done within the organism-environment-interaction framework. The Scott and Charles study done at the Roscoe B. Jackson Memorial Laboratory illustrates how genetic variability in dogs can be magnified as the result of habit formation. In the case of this investigation, different populations of dogs were exposed to a weighing-in process, and their behaviors were rated in terms of activity. The dogs were studied over a fifteen-week period, during which time the rather slight differences in activity noted during the first week after birth, and attributed to a genetic factor, became magnified as the puppies practiced the early-appearing behaviors.

The Kuo paper is a fascinating account of how animals can be immunized against innate antisocial tendencies by the appropriate control of environmental conditions. Granted the powerful genetic factor in such species-specific behaviors as antagonisms between dog and cat, and the preying upon birds and mice by cats, can tendencies to develop such behaviors be modified by early training? Readers who have raised a dog and cat in relative harmony know that it is possible. Kuo describes the experimental modification of these tendencies.

The last paper in this section is in an area that has intrigued and continues to intrigue investigators. In the organism-environment interaction, what extrinsic factors can stimulate intrinsic factors? In the Fantz paper, the specific question is, What are the characteristics of objects in the environment that stimulate visual activity in the newborn? Part of the answer is given in his report, showing that infants can discriminate between patterns of varying complexity and that they prefer the more complex. The need for stimulation, common to all biological organisms from plants to man, is apparently at work here. When the infant encounters stimulation in the environment (and a change in a visual object provides this stimulation), he fixes his vision to prolong the stimulation. Thus Gesell (1943) finds the fussy infant intrigued and consequently quieted when given a flowered sofa cushion to look at. A physiological need for stimulation may also explain the responsiveness of the infant to human beings. As Rheingold (1961) points out, human beings present a complex and ever-changing stimulus. The human face, in particular, very satisfactorily provides needed stimulation; it moves almost constantly, it produces sound, and it has contour and complexity. The infant responds to the face with cooing or movement of his body, the social object coos back, and a pattern of social responsiveness is eventually built up out of a myriad of such interactions. Once again we see a pattern of serial dependency, of the type noted by Blauvelt.

REFERENCES

ALDRICH, C. A., & ALDRICH, MARY M. *Babies are human beings.* (2nd ed.) New York: Macmillan, 1954.

BLAUVELT, HELEN. Capacity of a human neonate reflex to signal future response by present action. *Child Develpm.*, 1962, 33, 21–28.

CANNON, W. B. *The wisdom of the body.* New York: Norton, 1939.

DOBZHANSKY, T. Heredity, environment, and evolution. *Science,* 1950, **111**, 161–166.

ESCALONA, SIBYLLE K. The study of individual differences and the problem of state. *J. Amer. Acad. Child Psychiat.*, 1962, **1**, 11–37.

ESCALONA, SIBYLLE K., & LEITCH, MARY. The reactions of infants to stress. In Ruth S. Eissler *et al.* (Eds.), *The psychoanalytic study of the child.* Vol. 3/4. New York: International Universities Press, 1949. Pp. 121–140.

GESELL, A., & ILG, FRANCES L. *Infant and child in the culture of today.* New York: Harper, 1943.

HOOKER, D. *Evidence of prenatal function of the central nervous system in man.* James Arthur Lecture, "The Evolution of the Human Brain." New York: American Museum of Natural History, 1958.

HOOKER, D., & HUMPHREY, TRYPHENA. Some results and deductions from a study of the development of human fetal behavior. *Gaz. méd. port.*, 1954, 7, 189–197.

HUNT, J. McV. *Intelligence and experience.* New York: Ronald, 1961.

KUO, Z. Y. Ontogeny of embryonic behavior in aves: II. The mechanical factors in the various stages leading to hatching. *J. exp. Zool.*, 1932, **62**, 453–487.

MONTAGU, A. Constitutional and prenatal factors in infant and child health. In M. J. E. Senn (Ed.), *Conference on problems of infancy and childhood: symposium on the healthy personality.* New York: Josiah Macy, Jr. Foundation, 1950. Pp. 148–175.

PASAMANICK, P., KNOBLOCH, HILDA, & LILIENFELD, A. M. Socio-economic status and some precursors of neuropsychiatric disorder. *Amer. J. Orthopsychiat.*, 1956, **26**, 594–601.

Rheingold, Harriet L. The effect of environmental stimulation upon social and exploratory behavior in the human infant. In B. M. Foss (Ed.), *Determinants of infant behavior.* London: Methuen, and New York: Wiley, 1961.

Shirley, Mary M. *The first two years.* Vol. 3. *Personality manifestations.* Minneapolis: Univer. Minnesota Press, 1933.

Simon, B. (Ed.) *Psychology in the Soviet Union.* London: Routledge & Kegan Paul, and Stanford, Cal.: Stanford Univer. Press, 1957.

Wolff, P. Observations on newborn infants. *Psychosom. Med.*, 1953, **21**, 110–118.

DAVENPORT HOOKER

*The Sequence in Human Fetal Activity**

IN THE Pittsburgh studies [of human fetal activity] [1] 131 cases have been observed. The fetuses range in age from 6½ weeks of menstrual age to a postmature of 45 weeks. It is interesting to note that four of the 131 cases were twins, but, with one exception, only one twin of each pair was studied intensively. Of the 131 cases observed, two failed to exhibit movement probably because they were too young (6½ weeks), 14 failed to show responses because of deep anesthesia or injury, and 31 moved, but their activities were possibly reduced or modified by the administration of anesthetic or hypnotic drugs to the mother. The remaining 84 were secured by hysterotomy or hysterectomy under novocaine spinal or local anesthesia or, in the cases of older fetuses, were born spontaneously without the use of drugs. These 84 and the two which were probably too young to move may be considered entirely unanesthetized. The report is based on the 84.

The standard method of stimulation employed to test for reflexes is stroking restricted areas of the skin with a hair. The hairs used are calibrated to provide maximum pressures of 10, 25, 50, 100 mg., 2 and 5 gm. The 10 mg. hairs are human; those capable of exerting greater pressures are horsehairs of carefully selected diameters.

. . .

The determination of the age of a human embryo or fetus is very difficult. Many women, and especially those in a ward population, have only a hazy idea of the date of onset of the last menstrual period (L.M.P.). With some notable exceptions, patients will furnish a date—any date—for the L.M.P., when urged. Examination of the level of development of the embryo or fetus proves that little dependence can be placed upon the date given for that particular L.M.P. In consequence, some other means of staging embryos and fetuses by age must be used. There are innumerable formulas and tables for determining [menstrual] age from length. Only two seem to have value. The tables published by the late George L. Streeter in 1920 were used in these studies, partly because they were the only reliable ones available when these studies were begun and partly because experience has indicated that they fit the Pittsburgh population well. . . . Furthermore, we have used menstrual age throughout, as attempts to "correct" it to "actual" age merely confound confusion.

. . .

Until about the middle of the 7th week of menstrual age, the human embryo appears to be incapable of any type of reflex activity. There is certainly no area of integument sensitive to exteroceptive stimulation before this time. The musculature of the human embryo may be electrically stimulated to contraction beginning with the latter part of the 6th week, but contractions so produced are sharply localized at this or at any subsequent age. There appears to be no true myogenic activity [activity of muscular origin] in human embryos.

From approximately the middle of the 7th to just before the 8th week, when the embryo is between 20 and 23 mm. CR [i.e., crown rump] stimulation by lightly stroking the upper or lower lip or the alae of the nose with

1 Words in brackets are those of the editor.

* REPRINTED with abridgment by permission of the author and The University of Kansas Press from *The Prenatal Origin of Behavior* by Davenport Hooker. Copyright 1952 by the University of Kansas Press.

a hair exerting a maximum bending pressure of 10 or 25 mg. causes typically a contralateral flexion [movement in conjunction with the side of the body opposite the one stimulated] of the neck and uppermost trunk, with little or no participation of the upper extremities and none of any other portion of the body. Two such cases have been observed in the Pittsburgh studies. From one (93A, 20.7 mm. CR), only a single response without visible participation of the upper extremities was elicited. From the other (No. 131, 22.6 mm. CR), a large number of identical responses was secured. In these the upper extremities quivered slightly during the contralateral neck and upper trunk flexion, as though its musculature were attempting to contract. This quivering motion extended even to the fingers, but the upper extremities did not move otherwise. The skin area sensitive to stimulation was limited to the region immediately about the mouth. Although previously it was believed that some slightly older embryos (8+ to 8½ weeks) showed sensitivity in the area supplied by the maxillary [upper jawbone] division of the fifth cranial nerve a shade earlier than in that supplied by the mandibular [lower jawbone] division, this was not confirmed in either of the embryos here described.

. . .

There is no active or unanesthetized embryo of exactly 8 weeks in the Pittsburgh series, but there are six embryos of 8½ weeks (25 to 28 mm. CR) which moved, one of which is subject to suspicion of being possibly slightly anesthetized because morphine had been administered to the mother. The five unanesthetized cases all responded to unilateral exteroceptive stimulation in the mouth region by light stroking with a hair, and the responses were, in each case, practically identical with every other when repeated. They were, thus, stereotyped.

The typical response at 8½ weeks consists of the following elements: (1) chiefly contralateral flexion of the neck and trunk, though two ipsilateral flexions are recorded; (2) extension (backward movement) of the arms at the shoulder, without participation of the elbow, wrist, or fingers; (3) rotation of the pelvis toward the contralateral side, with no noticeable independent participation of the lower extremities. The neck-trunk flexion and the arm extension were simultaneous. The pelvic (rump) rotation, slight in the younger embryos, occurs with the trunk flexion in these younger cases but tends to have an extremely short period of delay in those of increasing length (and, presumably, older) when the rotation has become somewhat more pronounced.

The relaxation of the movement (return to posture) is accomplished first by the arms, then by the neck, trunk, and rump, which tend to hold their flexion-rotation posture momentarily. Because the body of the embryo rolls as a result of the trunk flexion, return to the exact position occupied before the response does not always occur. However, the difference is slight. A series of such reponses may be elicited at short intervals for as long as three to four minutes after beginning placental separation. Each response is, within relatively minute biological variations, identical with every other, hence these responses are also stereotyped. However, as the time interval between the response and beginning placental separation lengthens and the degree of anoxia increases, the threshold rises gradually, requiring increasingly higher "pressure value" hairs to evoke a response.

As the young fetus approaches the 9½-week age, centering around 34 mm. CR, the rump rotation becomes still more marked and tends to become separated from the usually contralateral trunk flexion and bilateral arm extension at the shoulder as a distinct phase of the response. Although the vigor of movement of the caudal end of the trunk has increased over that seen at 8½ weeks, the skin area sensitive to stimulation remains the same. Furthermore, spontaneously executed movements in the form of the typical response first to one side, then to the other, are clearly evident at 9 to 9½ weeks, but only for a very short time, limited to about one minutes after the beginning of placental separation.

. . .

At 9½ weeks, another method of exciting the typical response, consisting of lateral trunk flexion, bilateral arm extension, and rump rotation, was accidentally discovered. To center a fetus (No. 16) under the lens, it was rapidly rotated by the umbilical attachment of the membranes without any contact being made with the usual reflexogenic perioral area [region around the mouth sensitive to stimulation]. A very complete typical response resulted. This was formerly (1944 *et ante*) interpreted as a vestibular response [response originating from stimulation in vestibule of the inner ear]. It is absent in two 8½-week fetuses which were similarly rotated. So far as may be determined histologically, the vestibular apparatus appears complete at 9½ weeks. However, there is much evidence that vestibular function does not appear in cat or sheep until much later. Windle and Fish (1932), on the basis of their rotatory experiments with cat fetuses and ablation of the vestibular apparatus, present evidence that the vestibular righting reflex in this form does not appear earlier than the 54th day of gestation, although body-righting reflexes appear on the 50th day. Barcroft and Barron (1937, 1939*b*) state that vestibular responses do not appear in the sheep until the 43rd day after birth, although the "neck righting reflex," as they term it, can be evoked by the 50th day of gestation. In consequence, the post-rotation response in the human fetus would appear to be a body-righting reflex caused by the disturbance of head-body relations. However, Minkowski (1936) states that both "cervical tonic" [neck reflex] and "labyrinthine" reflexes [originating in the sense organs of the inner ear] appear in the human fetus during the fourth month. This age is, of course, far greater than that of the 9½-week fetus in which the response under discussion was found.

At the 9½-week level, passive extension of the fingers has caused flexion at the wrist, elbow, and shoulder. These appear to be typical stretch responses, proprioceptive [produced by stimulation originating in the muscles] in nature.

If the description so far given of responses from about 7½ to 9½ weeks has accomplished its purpose, it should be evident that the earliest responses secured were flexion, predominantly contralateral, of neck and upper trunk without participation of the extremities. This was followed by more complete trunk flexion with extension of both upper extremities at the shoulder-joint and a slight pelvic or rump rotation, without movement of the lower extremities as such. Next in turn came marked lateral flexion of the trunk, preponderantly contralateral, bilateral arm extension, and such complete rump rotation that the lower extremities appeared to participate, especially so in the body-righting response. Except for a short period around 8 weeks, every step in the caudal progression of the response has been observed. During the period from 7½ to about 10 weeks, the only skin area sensitive to a light stroking with a hair is limited to the perioral distribution of the maxillary and mandibular divisions of the fifth cranial nerve. These early responses would appear to constitute a continually expanding total pattern. No other explanation fits the observed phenomena.

From 9½ to 10½ weeks there is no change in the nature of the response to stimulation in the perioral region.[2] At about 10½ weeks the palms of the hands become sensitive to strokes with a light hair, partial closure of the fingers resulting. In the finger-closing response, the thumb frequently does not participate. Three to five days later, stimulation of the volar [palm] or lateral surfaces of the upper arm may cause independent arm extension at the shoulder; of the upper eyelid, contraction of the orbicularis oculi muscle; and of the sole of the foot, plantar flexion of the toes. These responses have so far appeared in the order given, although independent arm extension has only rarely been seen. It will become apparent that it is easier to evoke responses from fingers or toes than from brachia [upper arms],[3] forearms, thighs, or legs.

2 Later research (Hooker, 1958) indicates that repeated stimulation of both lips may sometimes, though rarely, cause a stuttering movement. [Ed.]

3 The brachia move only with the trunk, having no capacity for independent movement before 10½ weeks, and then only rarely. [Ed.]

At about 11 weeks, the previously typical response to perioral stimulation becomes modified by the appearance of an element of trunk extension, either alternating with or partially combined with the lateral flexion. Arm extension, which has hitherto accompanied the trunk flexion, is giving way to medial rotation of the brachia, which will reach its full development in another few days. There is also some slight rotation of the thighs in the total pattern response. Finger closure, still only partial and seldom accompanied by thumb flexion, follows palmar stimulation. Stimulation of the skin of the forearm may occasionally cause forearm pronation [rotation ending with palm downward]. Plantar flexion of the toes, with or without participation of the hallux [the great toe], follows stimulation of the sole of the foot. Contraction of the orbicularis oculi and of the corrugator muscles may be elicited by stimulation either of the upper eyelid or of the eyebrow region of the forehead.

It will be noticed that the skin area sensitive to stimuli has been expanding. No longer limited to the perioral region, it now includes all skin over the front of the face and the whole of the upper and lower extremities. However, stimulation of the region innervated by the maxillary and mandibular divisions of V [the fifth cranial nerve] gives rise to total pattern type activity, of other areas to local responses only. On the trunk, there is no sensitive skin evident at 11 weeks. Only light stimuli are necessary to evoke responses over the face, hands, and feet, and the fetuses are active in responding. The total pattern type of response is thus modified by the appearance of a number of specific responses.

At 11½ weeks, the reflexogenous zone (area sensitive to stimuli) gives evidence of spreading downward over the upper chest. At this age, activities already present have become further perfected and additional new ones appear. Extension of the trunk is increasingly, but by no means entirely, replacing the hitherto typical lateral flexion. Trunk extension is especially marked when stimulation is in the midline of the face, but also occurs on stimulation elsewhere on the face. As one approaches closer to the end of the period during which reflexes can be elicited from an individual specimen, the lateral flexion type of response tends to increase in incidence, probably because of increasing asphyxia, although the locus of stimulation plays an important role. At this age, the medial rotation of the brachia accompanying the trunk movement has increased to the point where the two hands approach one another, although only the fingers touch. Rotation of the face to the opposite side has appeared in response to stimulation of the side of the face, but midline facial stimulation causes head extension. Head rotation is usually accompanied by lateral trunk flexion, head extension by trunk extension, and it is with the latter type of response that the medial rotation of the brachia reaches its maximum. Arm abduction or wrist or forearm flexion may follow stimulation of various areas of the skin of the upper extremity. Stimulation of the sole of the foot causes plantar flexion of the toes, flexion of the knee and thigh, and then a quick knee extension, resulting in a kick.

By 12 to 12½ weeks, the reflexogenous areas of the skin have not appreciably increased, but unilateral facial stimulation in the perioral region causes marked extension of neck and trunk accompanied by a wide variety of movements at many of the joints in the upper extremities. The responses are still quite mechanical in their execution and the fetuses continue to be very active, but there is somewhat greater variety in the exact components of the responses, one differing from another in the accompanying movements. . . .

At this age there are several specific reflexes which may be evoked. In at least two cases, stimulation over one eyelid was accompanied by a downward rotation of the eyeballs, made evident by the shift in the highlights on the still fused lids. Lip closure follows stimulation of the lips and, when repeated, may result in swallowing. Digital closure is incomplete but is usually accompanied by wrist flexion or a combined flexion-abduction motion. In 12½-week specimens, stimulation of the sole of the foot may result in dorsiflexion of the hallux and toe-fanning, or in plantar flexion of hallux and toes, though flexion of the hallux is likely to be less complete than that of the other digits, if not entirely absent.

By 12½ weeks, in the majority of cases, the total pattern activity is rapidly fading, being replaced by an increasing number of specific reflexes. Coghill himself has called these "partial patterns." Within the next ten days, the total pattern has almost completely disappeared, to be evoked only by extremes of stimulation. Some human fetuses have reached this stage by 13 weeks of menstrual age. Others at presumably the same age level still exhibit a stereotyped total pattern. All below the age of 13½ to 14 weeks tend to return to a total pattern type of response before asphyxia and other causes blot out further activity.

Specifically, at 13 weeks, unilateral stimulation in the perioral region may result in any one of the following response types, in addition to a total pattern shown by a few: (1) ipsilateral arm extension, only; (2) flexion of the head, bilateral arm extension, and extension of the ipsilateral thigh; (3) head extension, contralateral arm extension, and ipsilateral thigh flexion, knee extension, and dorsiflexion of the foot; (4) trunk and neck extension, rotating into a contralateral trunk flexion, without extremity participation; (5) contralateral turning of the face and flexion of the head away from the stimulus; or (6) turning of the face toward the stimulus. Stimulation over the extremities with hairs having pressure values of from 25 to 100 mg. or of 2 gm., depending on the degree of anoxia, may result in purely local responses of the part touched or of the entire extremity. This incomplete listing of responses exhibited serves to illustrate the transition from total pattern with some specific reflexes to a manifestation of specific responses almost solely, found between 13 and 14 weeks.

By 13½ to 14 weeks, except for the back and top of the head, almost the entire surface of the body is sensitive to stroking with a light hair. As noted, the total pattern type of response has practically disappeared. Unilateral stimulation of the face causes contralateral turning of the face alone, an avoiding response, accompanied by elevation of the angle of the mouth and nasal ala on the same side, if the hair touches the side of the nose, or a contraction of the orbicularis oculi muscle, if the stimulus is applied over the eyelids. If the lips only are stimulated, they are pressed together, without head rotation. Touching the inside of the lips or mouth may cause tongue movements. Swallowing sometimes follows lip stimulation, but usually only on repetition of the stimulus. Finger closure is complete, the pollex [thumb] rarely entering into the formation of the resulting "fist," but the closure is relatively momentary, there being no sustained grasping response as yet. The quality of the responses is altered. Instead of the mechanical, stereotyped movement seen earlier, the various activities are graceful and "flowing." The fetus is very active.

The 13½- to 14-week period is an important one in the development of human fetal activity. During the period of 6 to 6½ weeks after exteroceptive responses began as a total pattern at about 7½ weeks, many of the specific reflexes of the neonate have appeared, replacing the total pattern which has practically ceased to exist as such. Those reflexes which have made their appearance are concerned primarily with trunk, extremities, head, and face. They are not all in the final form they will assume, but, with the addition of a number not yet present, they lay the framework for gradual development into the reflexes of postnatal life. Among those reflexes which have not as yet appeared are, primarily, grasp, respiration, and phonation (the latter being of course dependent on the former), the suctorial reflex, and the tendon reflexes. Furthermore, the fetal muscles are weak and ineffective. In the remaining weeks of the gestation period, the increase in volume and strength of the muscles, the development of additional neuromuscular mechanism, and the growth of the lungs will occur.

During the remaining period of gestation, there will be almost no change in the sensitive areas of the body, as the back and top of the head remain relatively incapable of evoking reflexes for some time to come. There will, however, be a marked maturation of already existing reflexes and certain ones, now absent and probably requiring new central and neuromuscular connections, will gradually emerge.[4]

By 15 weeks, there is definite evidence of maintained finger closure, sometimes, though rarely, noticeable several days earlier. This is the first appearance of grasping. At this time also the abdominal muscles are capable of sufficient contraction to provide a feeble sort of abdominal reflex when the stimulating hair is drawn across them. The fetus is active and the pre-existing reflexes are already becoming more vigorous as muscle maturation proceeds.

About a week later, the fetus begins to undergo a profound change in its reactivity. Periods of sluggishness tend to alternate with bursts of activity and the threshold for stimulation has increased. As age progresses, the periods of relative inactivity of the fetus become more prolonged and the bursts of activity more difficult to evoke. This is characteristic of the period beginning at about 17 to 18 weeks and continuing until the fetus may be caused to breathe at about 23½ weeks. Barcroft and Barron (1937) observed the same thing in sheep fetuses with intact placental connections. The cause is still undetermined. In the human fetuses observed, in which the placental connections had been interrupted, it is possible that the sluggishness may be due to accumulations of CO_2 which are eliminated by the ventilation of the lungs on resuscitation. Certain it is that the establishment of respiration soon abolishes any such sluggishness.

By 17 weeks, stimulation of the upper lip causes its protrusion. Similar gentle stroking of the lower lip at this age produces lip closure, as was the case with either lip at 12½ weeks.[5]

4 At 14 weeks, for example, Dr. Hooker (1958) has found it possible to elicit withdrawal of the tongue in response to tactile stimulation, thus providing evidence for the existence of a functional reflex arc by at least this time. [Ed.]

5 Hooker and Humphrey (1954) have pointed out that reflexes elicited by stimulation of the mucous membranes of the lips and tongue are successive phases in the development of the feeding responses. [Ed.]

Gasping, as a terminal agonal phenomenon without external stimulation, has been observed in fetuses as young as 13 weeks. This is accompanied by chest contractions, indicative of respiratory attempts, albeit ineffectual in causing breathing. By 18½ weeks, weak chest contractions, later to be accompanied by abdominal contractions and expansions, the latter proving diaphragmatic activity, have been observed in some cases in response to chest stimulation, or spontaneously, though these also are ineffectual in causing respiration. The earliest Pittsburgh case in which effective respiration, self-sustained for a brief period when once initated, was observed was 23½ weeks old, as just noted. At 18½ weeks also, weakly effective grasping is present. A thin, moist glass rod laid in the palm will be held by maintained finger closure, so that it is possible to draw the arm across the chest by pulling the stimulator in the direction of its long axis. The thumb is not constantly involved in this primitive grasping. The fetus is notably sluggish in responding at this age. However, when reflexes are elicited by 100 mg. or 2 gm. hairs, the activity is vigorous.

By 20 weeks, stimulation of either upper or lower lip causes its protrusion and by 22 weeks there is definite pursing of the lips as well as protrusion. This is a preliminary step in the development of the suctorial response, but no actual suction is exerted as yet.

Between 18½ and 23½ weeks, the chest and abdominal contractions and expansions increase in incidence and amplitude, until brief but effective respiration, especially after use of the respirator, occurs. It may be that some fetuses younger than 23½ weeks might be resuscitated, but so far it has not been possible in this series. Whenever respiration occurs, phonation—only a high-pitched cry, of course—accompanies its initiation and may be repeated at intervals following the establishment of breathing. The establishment of respiration for 20 minutes or more completely abolishes the sluggish nature of the fetus. As its color begins to improve, for most fetuses of this age have at first a slightly cyanotic [bluish] appearance even with intact placental connections, the fetus becomes more active than at any time heretofore. The arms and legs are very actively moved in all direction, the trunk is flexed and extended in all planes and it becomes possible to elicit various tendon reflexes—ankle clonus [flexion and extension], knee jerk, etc.—not hitherto obtainable. The change in activity following respiration is startling, although, except for the possibility of eliciting tendon reflexes, no new activities appear. Indeed, little new appears during the next two or three weeks. It is almost as though the fetus were developing its respiratory capacity at the expense of the appearance of other new responses. This may, at least in part, be the result of the explosive appearance of "spontaneous" activity which renders the eliciting of reflexes difficult of evaluation. As a rule, it is almost impossible to determine whether a movement following stimulation was caused thereby or would have occurred without it.

By 25 weeks, all previous reflexes have greatly matured and the muscular system is increasing in strength. Self-sustained respiration, once begun, may last for over 24 hours. Tendon reflexes have become stronger and more complete. The eyelids may be opened and closed without stimulation by the observer and conjugate movements of the eyes, especially in the lateral plane, are evident. At this age, also, a Moro reflex [startle reflex] was observed quite inadvertently. It may, therefore, be elicitable earlier. One fetus, lifted gently from the premature bed, in which it was being photographed, in order to change the underlying sheet which had been discolored by urination, was quickly lowered again. The almost clonic extension of arms and legs which resulted were typical of this "startle" reflex, which appears to have a vestibular origin.

Some obstetricians are of the opinion that a few 25-week premature infants may be viable. This is conceivably possible, although the youngest viable fetus observed in this series was 27 weeks of menstrual age. As previously noted all ages assigned in this study are menstrual ages. If by 25 weeks the so-called "corrected actual" age is intended, it would agree with 27 weeks of menstrual age. If 25 weeks of menstrual age is intended—and too often the exact kind of age used is not specified—it might still be possible, but not too probable in the light of the Pittsburgh observations. Possible viability at 27 weeks of menstrual age seems to agree with the majority opinion of obstetricians.

The 27-week fetus has greatly matured. The grasp of one was sufficiently strong to maintain with one hand practically its entire weight for a short period. In all examined at this or later ages the grasp is effective and the thumb participates most of the time, though feebly.

Little in the way of new responses appears from 27 weeks to birth, either at the usual 40 weeks or in such postmatures as have been observed. The suctorial response becomes matured into an active and audible sucking by 29 weeks. A definite cremasteric reflex [in the region of the testicle] has been observed by 32 weeks. At 33 weeks, the tongue may "search" the lower lip when that organ is lightly touched. For more details of the activities of the circumnatal period the reader is referred to the work of Arnold Gesell. . . . The number of fetuses observed in the Pittsburgh studies in this age range has been inadequate for final conclusions.

REFERENCES

Hooker, D. *Evidence of prenatal function of the central nervous system in man.* James Arthur Lecture, "The Evolution of the Human Brain." New York: American Museum of Natural History, 1958.

Hooker, D., & Humphrey, Tryphena. Some results and deductions from a study of the development of human fetal behavior. *Gaz. méd. port.,* 1954, **7,** 189–197.

CALVIN S. HALL

The Inheritance of Emotionality*

THE proposition that individuals differ in all aspects of conduct is universally accepted by psychologists, and the investigation of the causation of individual differences in various psychological traits is one of the more popular problems of contemporary psychology. Witness the interest in intelligence testing. People vary in temperamental traits, for example, the degree to which they become agitated and stirred up by emotional stimuli, as well as in intellectual abilities. It should be possible, therefore, to measure variations in this trait, emotionality, and ascertain by experiment and correlation the underlying causes for the differences found.

The importance of such investigations should be evident to those who recognize the major role that emotion plays in conduct, especially that conduct deviating from the normal. Emotional instability is believed to be a major symptom if not the principal cause of nervous conditions and functional disorders. If we are to control and modify abnormal behavior, extensive knowledge concerning the bases for temperamental differences is required. Why does one child have a temper tantrum when in the same situation another child remains composed? Why does a business reversal cause one man to undergo a nervous breakdown, while for another it is a stimulus to subsequent business success? Why does Miss Jones embarrass her instructor with a hysterical outbreak as a consequence of receiving a poor grade, whereas Miss Smith accepts failure all too philosophically? These are questions concerning the why of temperamental differences among people. They are important questions and ones which psychologists have left largely to the unprofitable speculation of pseudo- and anti-scientific psychologists. The human desire to cast out those ubiquitous trouble-makers, "nervousness," "worry," "fear," and "melancholia" is so strong that any crackpot system which promises to do just that is eagerly taken up by the maladjusted. It does little good for those of us who consider ourselves respectably scientific to condemn charlatans when we have no worthy substitute for charlatanry.

There are two major explanations usually given for differences in emotionality—the conditioning or learning theory and the hereditary predisposition theory. (We often have theories about phenomena concerning which we know little. It is unfortunate that a theory may be regarded as a fact by the uncritical.) An extreme proponent of the conditioning theory, for instance, the noted behaviorist John B. Watson, believes that disparity in the frequency and strength of emotional reactions results from environmental influences encountered early in life. It is a fact that infants react emotionally to overstimulation, for example, loud noises, physical restraint and loss of support. These are as native and inborn as the sucking reflex or sneezing. All infants manifest them without variation according to the learning theorist. Individual differences in emotional behavior develop as a result of disparity in the amount of emotional conditioning established. A child exposed to frequent overstimulation develops greater excitability because certain other non-emotional stimuli acting on him at the time of his agitation tend on their recurrence to evoke emotional behavior, even though the original cause of the excited condition is then absent. In other words, all sorts of substitute

* REPRINTED with abridgment by permission of the author and the publisher, The Society of the Sigma Xi, from *Sigma Xi Quart.*, 1938, **26**, 17–27.

stimuli gain the power to arouse emotion as a result of previous experiences. The harmless snake becomes a symbol of terror to the child who is present when his mother screams at the sight of a snake. The rabbit comes to arouse fear in the very young infant when a loud noise is made at the same time that the rabbit is presented to the baby. These are easily demonstrable facts and any observant parent can prove to his own satisfaction what John B. Watson spent months investigating at Johns Hopkins University.

We do indeed learn our fears, our hates, our angers, yes, even our loves. One person is afraid of moths, another of sharp-pointed objects, another of crossing the street, another of dirt, another of open spaces, another of closed spaces. A few rare souls are practically fearless. Others are relentlessly tormented by dread. And that is exactly the point in question. Why do some have so many, others so few fears, angers, hates and loves? Is it because of differences in the mere number of emotional situations encountered by people? Another hypothesis suggests itself. May it not be that we are born with dissimilar susceptibilities to emotional conditioning? Admitted that we learn to react emotionally to concrete situations, still may not the fact that one person learns to react emotionally to many more stimuli than another, be due to inborn differences? We do not know. I predict, however, that affirmative answers will be found to these questions.

The extreme proponent of the heredity side of this issue ascribes all temperamental disparity to differences in the germ plasm. The important genetic factors are very likely those which influence development of the nervous system, particularly the autonomic system and the thalamus, and the endocrine glands, since these are the organs most intimately related to emotional reactions. Although it is apparent that differences do exist in these bodily structures and in their functioning, it is not clear on the one hand whether the structure and function of these various organs are entirely a result of genetic determination or, on the other hand, whether individual differences in visceral structures are correlated with variation in emotionality. Our ignorance regarding the inheritance of temperament is even more profound than that pertaining to its modification.

It was in order to gain some fundamental knowledge concerning the causes of individual differences in emotionality that the present program of research was initiated. The first question to be settled was this: Is it possible by selective breeding to obtain two strains of animals, one an emotional strain, the other relatively unemotional and phlegmatic? Man is, unfortunately, not available for assortive mating experiments. Consequently, we must inflict our controlled matings upon a more docile species. For these experiments we have used that most convenient of laboratory animals, *rattus Norvegicus*—the rat. If two such strains could be obtained it would of course demonstrate that individual differences in emotionality are inheritable. Such an outcome would not, however, exclude the importance of learning as a determiner of differences in emotionality, for conditioning might very well either accentuate or minimize the native dissimilarities.

This investigation is not the first to make use of the selective breeding technique for psychological purposes. Dr. R. C. Tryon of the University of California has selectively bred two strains of rats for maze-learning ability. The maze is for the rat what the Stanford-Binet is for the child. One can therefore speak of his two groups as geniuses or morons or high IQ and low IQ. After nine generations of breeding Dr. Tyron has obtained two widely differing strains. It is anticipated that by a comparative study of these two groups the factors underlying intelligence may be more readily exposed. You may question, of course, whether rat intelligence is the same as human intelligence, but if you do put the question you are really not an evolutionist, and therefore your views deserve little serious consideration.

Dr. Rundquist of the University of Minnesota has selectively bred active and inactive strains of rats, and Dr. C. P. Stone at Stanford University has obtained early maturing rats and later maturing rats by this method.

Undoubtedly as time goes on an increasing number of psychologists will find the selective breeding technique useful in the investigation of psychologically important traits. Its value, apart from genetic analysis, is that it yields extreme manifestations of the trait in question. Hence the differences, magnified and exaggerated, can be more easily analyzed.

Although we recognize that individuals differ in emotionality, there are no very valid or objective emotional tests such as we possess for measuring intelligence, mechanical proficiency and musical abilities. Many physiological and biochemical changes associated with and resulting from purported emotional stimulation have been observed and much behavior reputed to be emotional in nature has been recognized and classified. In recent years questionnaires which presume to diagnose emotional instability have flooded the psychological literature. None of these physiological and psychological samples of emotionality constitutes, however, a suitable yardstick for measuring the relative intensity of agitation displayed by individuals.

After much experimentation we have discovered two valid, reliable and extremely objective measures of individual differences in emotional instability. Their use has been limited as yet to the rat but they could doubtless be adapted for other animals. Their value in human investigations is questionable. The measures are persistence of defecation and persistence of urination during successive exposures to an originally strange and novel situation. The exact procedure used will be considered later.

It is of course absurd to consider all voiding reactions emotional in character. But it has long been recognized that these responses may be precipitated by terrifying situations. Dr. Alverez, the authority on emotional indigestion, states that the earliest reference to the purging effects of fear and anxiety is found in an eyewitness account of a battle between two young kings of Persia. The historical account reads thus: "The vehemence of my battle line like a bow overwhelmed them. To save their lives they trampled over the bodies of their soldiers and fled. Like young captured birds they lost courage. With their urine they defiled their chariots and let fall their excrements." It is commonly known that the World War originated its full share of anecdotes centering around the cathartic action of strong emotion. Love, as well as fear, may release the emptying reflexes. Alverez recounts that a young woman consulted him about an infirmity which threatened to interfere with her ever finding a mate. He writes: "In her the slightest sign of affection on the part of a young man so increased the tone and activity of the digestive tract that she was promptly summoned by a call of nature so imperative that it could not be denied; she had to flee precipitately just when she would most like to have remained." Hamilton, in his classic study of marriage adjustment, reports that individuals subjected to rigorous questioning concerning their marital behavior repeatedly interrupted the interviews in order to go to the restroom. This behavior is even more common among the less inhibited lower animals. Koehler, in his book on the mentality of apes, tells how the sight of a teddy bear so frightened his chimpanzees that they were immediately and thoroughly purged.

Every investigator working with rats must surely have verified our observation that these animals defecate and urinate during rough handling or during the first days in a new apparatus. Yerkes and after him Stone have used these reactions as measures of wildness and savageness in the rat. I see no justification for labeling a rat which persistently defecates as either wild or savage. He is just an emotional animal. The use of these measures as indirect criteria of wildness and savageness is, however, probably justified, since the less docile and tame a rat is the more excited he will become under conditions of captivity and restraint. Neither of these investigators attempted to show that the emptying reflexes are valid tests of individual differences in excitability.

Further evidence that defecation and urination may be evoked by exciting conditions is obtained from Cannon's studies on the physiology of emotion. He has characterized the sacral autonomic as a group of mechanisms for emptying. It supplies fibers to the colon, rectum and bladder. The normal stimulus for the evacuation of these reservoirs is distension by accumulation of contents. But during intense emotional stimulation impulses may overflow from the sympathetic system into the sacral segment and result in a discharge of the contents of the colon and bladder. Defecation and urination are thus linked to that configuration of reactions set off by the activation of the sympathetic segment of the autonomic nervous system. Apparently these emptying reflexes accompanying strong emotion have no utility such as the responses normally resulting from activation of the sympathetic segment.

How can we differentiate between emotional and normal evacuation? The criterion I have used for identifying defecation and urination as emotional is the fact that they cease upon repetition of the situation which originally evoked them. The situation which will evoke this behavior is probably any strange one.

The exact device I have most often employed is a circular enclosure seven or eight feet in diameter, surrounded by a wall high enough to prevent the rat from escaping. The floor of the enclosure is smooth and there are no nooks and crannies in which the animal may hide. The rat is by nature a stereotropic or wall-following animal. He is also negatively phototropic, that is, he prefers darkness to light. Consequently he finds the open field situation mildly terrifying. We have proved without question that these responses disappear after a certain number of experiences in the enclosure. Moreover, we have evidence that as these reactions disappear other behavior which represents increasing adjustment to the apparatus, for example the eating of food, makes an appearance.

That defecation and urination may be truly emotional responses is indicated, therefore, by four lines of evidence: (1) they occur in situations recognized to be emotionally arousing in character, (2) they are linked with other reactions set off by impulses travelling over the autonomic nervous system, (3) they disappear as the originally strange situation becomes familiar, and (4) as the number of animals defecating and urinating decreases, the number of animals eating increases. However, this evidence does not prove that defecation and urination are valid measures of *individual differences* in emotionality. It is quite possible that group averages might not hold for individual cases, and that a rat which never voided during the period of observation was actually more upset than a rat which did defecate or urinate on one or more occasions. In fact, Alverez has proposed a theory that diarrhea is caused by mild excitement, constipation by more serious emotional stimulation. If this hypothesis should hold for animals other than man, then it might be said that rats which never defecated in the field situation were constipated and hence more emotionally upset than the easily purged animals. According to this hypothesis, two modes or peaks of emotional intensity would be expected, one occurring at zero defecations and urinations, and one occurring at the maximum number of defecations and urinations. Our initial task was, therefore, to validate these excretory reactions as tests of individual differences in emotionality.

A measure possesses validity if it actually measures that which it is said to measure. The expressions "validity" and "to validate" may be unfamiliar to some of you, although I am sure you are all acquainted with the concept to which those expressions refer. I may clarify its meaning by an example. The Wassermann test is recognized to be a valuable and convenient test of the presence or absence of syphilitic infection. We would say it was a very valid test. Its validity was established by demonstrating that a positive Wassermann was related to other more direct but less conveniently measured diagnostic signs of syphilis, and that a negative Wassermann was not so related to these symptoms. Its validity is not, however, perfect because occasionally a person giving a negative Wassermann does have syphilis.

In the present case we had to clearly demonstrate that variation in the persistence of defecation and urination was intimately related to variation in other manifestations of excitability. The problem of finding another measure of individual differences in emotionality was not easy and was finally solved by the following reasoning. It is a commonplace that emotional excitement may hinder the adjustment of the animal. For example, it may be an obstacle to the satisfaction of such a need as hunger. Hence it was argued that if a rat which ate in its usual living cage immediately upon the presentation of food, was placed in a strange enclosure, where food was readily obtainable, its failure to eat would be due to the excited state of the animal. The number of trials required before food was eaten in the enclosure could be taken as a measure of the rat's emotionality. Variation in this measure was used, therefore, as the second measure of emotional intensity against which to validate defecation and urination.

I cannot take the time to report in detail the results of the many experiments we performed to establish the validity of these measures. The general conclusion can be stated that defecation and urination are as valid, if not more valid, than most tests used in psychology. There is quite a sizeable relationship between the adjustment of the animal to the field situation as measured by the emptying reflexes and its adjustment as measured by food-eating. For example, animals that did not defecate on any trial in the field commenced to eat in the field on the second or third daily trial. Animals which evacuated on one or more occasions but less than ten (the total number of possible occasions) began to eat on the fifth or sixth day. Whereas those animals that voided every day in the field for ten days never did eat within the limits of the experiment.

Incidentally, these results do not confirm the theory of Alverez mentioned above. If constipation is a consequence of more intense emotional stimulation than diarrhea then we should expect those animals which did not defecate in the field situation to make a very poor adjustment to the eating of food. The zero defecating animals, however, were the best adjusted of all the rats as measured by our criterion. It is quite true that in man constipation often is a symptom of emotional maladjustment. It is my hunch, however, that this is a strictly human condition and results from man's ability to gain control over his sphincters. The natural response of the sphincters to emotional stimulation is dilation. Man has, however, found the consequences of impulsive dilation socially inept and disapproved. Hence he learns to avoid disastrous consequences by exercising "will power." He may, however, become so strongly inhibited that voiding under socially approved circumstances is made difficult. Thus, constipation.

We come now to the proper subject matter of this paper, the inheritance of emotionality.

The P_1 or parental generation consisted of 145 animals, 60 males and 85 females. These animals were obtained from various colonies maintained at the University of California by the department of psychology, the department of household science and the Institute of Experimental Biology, and from a colony maintained by the nutrition department at Oregon State College. The P_1 generation, therefore, was a very heterogeneous sample of the rat population on the Pacific coast.

The animals were tested for their emotionality in the field situation as described above. The enclosure was seven feet in diameter, with a solid tin wall two feet high. The floor of the field consisted of battleship linoleum. The linoleum was washed after removing the animal in order to prevent the accumulation of odors. A daily trial consisted of two minutes and the records taken were presence or absence of defecation and urination during that time.

The distribution of the number of days during which the rats either defecated or urinated ranged from none to twelve. Seven of the most emotional males and seven of the most emotional females were mated. Likewise seven of the least emotional males and females were mated. From these matings there resulted seventy-five offspring. Forty of these were the offspring of emotional parents, thirty-five were the offspring of relatively non-emotional parents. At the age of three months these animals were tested for their emotionality according to the same schedule as that imposed upon the P_1 generation. The results of the tests on the F_1 generation are striking. There were 139 occurrences of emotional defecation or urination. Of these 139 occurrences, 123, or 88 percent, of the total were made by the progeny of emotional parents, although these offspring constituted but 53 percent of the F_1 generation. Only 15 of the 139 occurrences or 12 percent were contributed by the progeny of the least emotional P_1 rats.

The results may be presented in another way. The male offspring of the emotional rats defecated or urinated on the average approximately four days out of the total twelve daily trials in the field. In contrast, the male offspring of the non-emotional P_1 rats averaged less than one day when excretory reactions occurred. The differences between these two averages is 3.2 and according to a rigorous statistical criterion it is quite unlikely that this difference could be due to a sampling error. Similar differences in the emotional measures for the female rats were found. The female offspring of emotional animals averaged 2.4 days during which defecation or urination occurred, whereas the progeny of non-emotional rats averaged .07 days when emotional responses were elicited. This difference of 2.3 is also a true difference and not a chance one. Combining the results of both males and females, it may be said that the offspring of the most emotional rats were nearly seven times more emotional than the offspring of the least emotional rats. The distribution curves for the two groups are shown in FIGURE 1. These preliminary results unquestionably indicate that two strains of rats markedly different in the frequency of emotional behavior can be produced by assortative mating. Differences in emotionality appear to be genetically determined.

It is hoped that as a result of successfully breeding an emotionally stable, well-adjusted race of rats and an emotionally unstable, neurotic strain of rats, fruitful experiments on the basic causes of emotional instability will be facilitated. We hope to learn just how neurotic rats differ from the more stable ones. Are there, for example, significant anatomical differences? Is there noticeable variation in the structure and function of the various endocrine glands? Are there dissimilarities between the strains with respect to other organs of the body? Will biochemical analyses yield any clues as to the why and wherefore of emotionality? Will neuro-

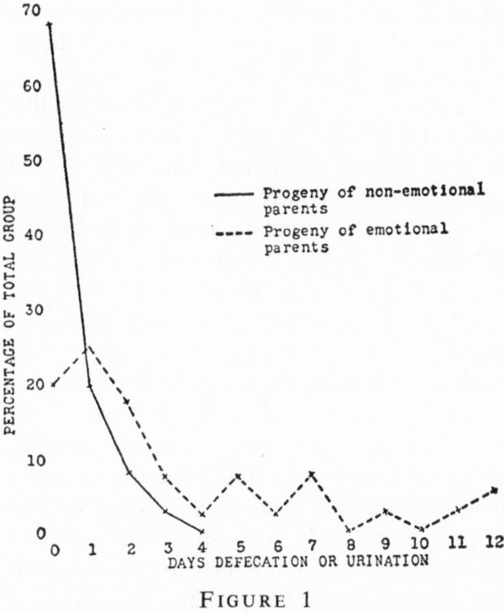

FIGURE 1

logical differences appear? It must be apparent that for these studies we will need much assistance from other biological scientists.

As a psychologist, I am primarily interested in the relationship of emotional instability to other aspects of behavior. Does the emotional animal, for example, learn with less efficiency than the non-emotional, that is, do emotional instability and feeblemindedness go together? We already have gathered some data on this point and the results so far indicate that the emotional animal is not handicapped in a learning situation. In conversation, however, with another investigator, Dr. E. E. Anderson of Harvard University, who has used our method of measuring emotional instability, he informs me that there is a small but significant relationship between emotionality and learning. The disrupted rats are slightly inferior in habit formation.

Is there any correlation between age and excitability, and, if so, is it negative or positive? Preliminary results indicate that young rats are less emotional than old ones. This may be due to the kind of living quarters provided for laboratory rats. They are kept in rather small cages and it might be expected that sudden exposure to an open field would be more of an emotional shock to staid old animals, accustomed to a set routine, than to young ones whose habits had not become so fixed.

Are there sex differences in emotionality? Rather extensive results indicate that the male is more emotional than the female. We do not even have a working hypothesis as to why this should be true, and I hesitate to state the bald fact in view of the conventional belief that females are more susceptible to fear-arousing stimuli. One convenience of using the lower animals as subjects for psychological experiments is the fact that they do not have culture patterns. Little girl rats grow up quite naturally without being admonished by their parents to act as little girls should. And thus growing up naturally these girl rats apparently develop greater stability in the face of danger than do their brothers. Or perhaps rat society is dominated by the weaker sex, and the males, as a result, are the ones who develop neuroses.

The relationship between emotionality and overt activity has been ascertained. Emotional rats are definitely less active than non-emotional ones. This suggests that caution is quite a primitive biological behavior pattern. We know, of course, that many animals go into a death feint when danger threatens. It is interesting to consider the inverse relationship between emotionality and activity with reference to the adjustment of the animal. You are all doubtless familiar with Cannon's emergency theory of the emotions, which states that the emotional pattern, consisting of a release of blood sugar, the counteraction of fatigue, a shift of blood volume to the peripheral muscles, increased activity of the heart, more rapid respiration and other changes, prepares the animal for either fight or flight. The freezing up behavior noted in excited rats does not appear on first thought to conform to this theory. It is quite likely, however, that a tense, crouching animal is more ready to flee when and if danger should strike. His cessation of activity is a preparation for danger which lurks in a strange environment. We cannot really know whether agitation will aid or hinder adjustment unless the total situation is considered. The student angered and frustrated by a difficult test is prepared by his emotion to fling the offending exam in the face of the instructor. That action would hardly constitute a good adjustment. Suppose, for example, that two animals differing in emotionality are placed in a food-seeking situation, and further suppose that the food objects are scattered rather sparsely throughout the environment. In this situation the less active, more emotional rat will be handicapped in locating food by the fact that he gets around in the environment to a lesser degree than the more active, non-emotional animal. Emotionality in this situation will prolong maladjustment. Consider an analogous situation in human behavior. We can predict that a timid, fearful person may fail to make an adequate adjustment because of the caution which accompanies his fear. He will be less likely to entertain novel ideas or undertake new ventures and thereby fail to improve his status. On the other hand he will avoid the maladjustments which often ensue from lack of caution.

. . .

I occupy a position somewhere between the conservative and the radical hereditarian. I believe in the importance of constitutional differences. I do not believe these differences are unalterable. On the other hand, I do not believe that they are readily modified by social control. I believe that individual differences in intelligence, temperament and character can be modified but not easily nor drastically. Finally, I believe that controlled breeding is man's most effective weapon against feeblemindedness, insanity, and psychopathic behavior.

ARNOLD GESELL

*Maturation and Infant Behavior Pattern**

THE influence of conditioning on the human infant has been so forcibly asserted from the standpoint of behaviorism, that it may be desirable to examine the influence of sheer maturation on his patterns of behavior.

The behavior of the infant, by nature, is obedient to pattern. Never does the picture of normal behavior become as diffuse and formless as a drifting cloud. Even the random movements of the month-old child are not utterly fortuitous. The closer one studies them the more configuration they assume. There is indeed no such thing as utter randomness in infant behavior. Accordingly the "random activity" of the two months infant is distinct from that of the month-old. It is distinctive because it has its own pattern.

Likewise with the fœtus. Its behavior is in no sense amorphous, but, as the studies of Minkowski have shown, manifests itself in fairly well-defined reflexes—long, short, diagonal, and trot reflexes; postural reflexes; rhythmical and inhibitive phenomena. These patterns of behavior follow an orderly genetic sequence in their emergence. Genetic sequence is itself an expression of elaborate pattern. And the relative stability of both prenatal and postnatal ontogenesis under normal and even unusual conditions must be regarded as a significant indication of the fundamental rôle of maturational factors in the determination of behavior.

Again take the fœtus. The uterus is the normal environment of the fœtus till the end of a gestation period of 40 weeks. But birth with survival, may exceptionally occur as early as 24 weeks and as late as 48 weeks, an enormous range of variation in natal age amounting to 6 lunar months. Variation with a range of 3 lunar months is common and yet this considerable variation does not impose a corresponding deviation on the complex of behavior. Our normative studies of both premature and postmature infants have shown repeatedly that the growth course of behavior tends to be obedient to the regular underlying pattern of genetic sequence, irrespective of the irregularity of the birth event. Refined studies will doubtless reveal that such irregularity does subtly modify many details of behavior; but as a point of departure for the discussion of maturation, nothing is more comprehensive in implication than the general stability of the trend and the tempo of development, in spite of precocious or postponed displacement of birth. The patterns of genetic sequence insure a basically similar growth career for full term, pre-term, and post-term infants. It is as though Nature had provided a regulatory factor of safety against the stress of extreme variations of environment. In the mechanisms of maturation this regulation operates.

The term *growth* may be construed to embrace the total complex of ontogenetic development. Maturation refers to those phases and products of growth which are wholly or chiefly due to innate and endogenous factors. It is our purpose to assemble in a summary manner, diverse evidences of behavior maturation, based upon our clinical, experimental and normative observations.

These evidences are drawn from several sources as follows:

(1) The development of prehension.

(2) Developmental correspondence in identical twins.

(3) The limitations of training.

* REPRINTED by permission of Gerhard A. Gesell and the American Psychological Association from *Psychol. Rev.*, 1929, 36, 307–319.

(4) The restricted influence of physical handicap.

(5) Developmental progression in emotional behavior.

1. *The Development of Prehension.*—The development of prehension throughout the first year of life displays significant progressive changes in behavior pattern. These changes raise searching doubts concerning the influence of experience and training upon these patterns. We have studied these changes with particular reference to a pellet 8 millimeters in diameter. The characteristic eye-hand reactions of an infant confronted with this tiny pellet may be recapitulated in the following which is a genetic order:

(*a*) No visual regard for the pellet.

(*b*) Transient regard for the pellet.

(*c*) More prolonged and definite fixation upon the pellet with slight postural changes (16 weeks).

(*d*) Visual fixation with crude bilateral or unilateral hand approach (20 weeks).

(*e*) Unilateral pronated hand approach with scratching in vicinity of the pellet (24 weeks).

(*f*) Pronated hand approach with occasional raking flexion resulting in palmar prehension (28 weeks).

(*g*) Pronated hand approach with extension of index finger and partial suppression of other digits resulting in poking or prehension by index finger with partial thumb opposition.

(*h*) Rotation of wrist in hand approach, with pincer-like prehension of pellet by index finger and thumb (40 weeks).

(*i*) Perfection and further delimitation of pincer-like response.

All these changes mature with subtle but significant accompanying changes in head posture, body posture, hand and arm attitude and associated visual behavior. It seems quite erroneous to say that the child learns to prehend the pellet in the traditional sense of the learning process. Crudely, but nevertheless effectively, he prehends the pellet by gross palmar approach as early as the age of 28 weeks. The refinement of his eye-hand behavior comes not by the alleged utilization of snatches of successful random activity, but by the progressive acquisition and consolidation of a hierarchy of behavior patterns which are the result of developmental decrements and increments rather than the stamping in or chaining of satisfying, successful reflexes. The defective child shows retardation in the acquisition of these patterns even though he may, in a durational sense, have a larger fund of prehensory experience. It is not improbable that many of these developmental changes in the pattern of prehension would be realized even if the prehensory hand were altogether swaddled and deprived of activity. When the prehensory mechanism is damaged by restricted birth injury to the brain, resulting in extensive athetosis,[1] the propensity to prehend or reach may still assert itself at the proper genetic level. Even though the propensity is aborted its presence is highly suggestive of the potency of maturational determination.

2. *Developmental Correspondence in Twins.*—During the past year we have gathered extensive detailed data on the development of prehension in a pair of identical infant twins. These twins were identical not only with regard to their skin patterns but also to a remarkable degree, with regard to their behavior patterns. Nowhere was this more objectively shown than in their prehensory reactions to cubes and pellets under controlled observational conditions. At 28 weeks both of these twins, being somewhat retarded in their development, were visually unheedful of the pellet, though they definitely regarded a cube. At 38 weeks they addressed themselves in an identical manner to the pellet. The hands were in full pronation, the fingers, spread apart in a fan-like manner, were fully extended. The thumb was fully extended almost at right angles. The photographic record of their attack upon the pellet, in the motion pictures, shows an almost uncanny degree of identity in the details of postural attitude, hand attitude and mecha-

1 Athetosis is a type of brain injury marked by slow, weaving movements of arms and legs, and by facial grimaces. [Ed.]

nism of grasp. Time does not permit the further specifications of these details.

At 40 weeks each twin made a crude raking attack upon the pellet, with occasional awkward but completed prehension in which the palm and all of the digits participated. The form of the prehension pattern was again remarkably similar in the two children. At 42 weeks they were again examined in the same situation. Although there had been no special instruction or conditioning in the interval, these 2 weeks imposed a palpable and strikingly similar change upon the prehension picture. Simultaneous flexion of the digits was very neatly displaced by a preferential flexion of the index finger. The raking approach was replaced by a poking with the tip of the index finger. Such an interesting inflection of the prehensory pattern surely could not have been induced so precisely and so simultaneously in both of these children without the presence of controlling factors of organic maturation. Of similar significance is the fact that comparable changes in prehension pattern appeared coincidentally throughout the course of their development.

The correspondences in behavior patterns in these twins were literally uncountable. However, the records of 13 developmental examinations were analyzed and 612 separate comparative ratings of behavior items were made from these records in order to determine items of correspondence and disparity. There were 99 items of minor disparity and 513 items of identical or nearly identical correspondence. The parity of behavior patterns was overwhelming.

Many convincing examples of behavior correspondence might be cited. We content ourselves with a few much abbreviated illustrations. Here is one which seems to us to have experimental control, even though it deals with nothing more than the reaction of two infants when placed in exactly the same manner upon a flat platform to observe their postural control in the sitting position. Both children showed precisely the same kind and degree of difficulty in equilibrium at the age of 28 weeks. In both there was a tendency to sway to the right; in both it was impossible, even by spreading the legs, to make the body lean forward sufficiently to establish a passive balance. In the case of each child there was an antagonistic tension which made the body rebound backward in an automatic manner resembling a sharp spring-like action of a knife blade snapping into position. We have never seen precisely this kind of reaction in an infant at this age. It is inconceivable that the response arose out of some identical conditioning factor in the environment. It is reasonable to suppose that this distinctive behavior pattern reflected a maturity level and a synchronous neural organization shared by both children because of their common genetic origin.

Within a week this reaction disappeared. Four days later the twins were placed upon a large blotter on the platform of a clinical crib and maintained the sitting position by leaning forward. Simultaneously they attacked the blotter with the hand in full pronation, and simultaneously, with vocalization, they continued to scratch the blotter, leaving visible marks. Here again was a dramatic bit of correspondence all the more impressive because displayed simultaneously. The complexity and nature of these two behavior patterns again suggest the determining rôle of maturation. If it is argued that extrinsic factors determine the form and the time incidence of these simultaneous patterns it is necessary to demonstrate in detail the cunning arrangements of environment and of conditioning stimuli which could design so precisely, and in duplicate, the configuration of behavior. How can the environment, even of twins, accomplish such architectonic miracles?

A brief example of behavior correspondence may be cited from the 44 weeks examination record. The twins were confronted with a test performance box with its three holes. The common method of approach of the two children, their preferred regard for the edge of the performance box, the fleeting regard for the holes, the exploitation of the vertical surface of the performance box by a scratching, simultaneous flexion of the digits, the failure to place a round rod into any of the holes, the brushing of the surface of the performance box with the rod, the transfer of the rod from one hand to the other, and finally an almost simultaneous peculiar, clicking vocalization in both twins—altogether constituted a very complicated behavior pattern, but one which bristled with numerous identities of spatial and dynamic detail. One can give due weight to the significance of this correspondence only by reflecting on the myriad of behavior exploitations of the situation which the twins *might* have adopted. But in spite of this multitude of exploitational possibilities, the twins were apparently under a common inner compulsion to adopt those very similarities of behavior which have been noted.

Still another, and very pretty example of identity was disclosed in the pellet and bottle test at 48 weeks. This test involved a bit of learning as well as perception and prehension. Three trials were made with each child. The examiner dropped a pellet into a small glass bottle and then gave the bottle to the child. Both children watched the dropping of the pellet with the same transfixed attention. Both children, on the first trial and on the second trial too, seized the bottle apparently heedless of the contained pellet. Both children on the third trial pursued the pellet by poking at it against the glass. Here the details of behavior pattern extended even into the marginal zone of adaptation through learning.

In passing it should be noted that although these observations on twins are comparative, they are objective. They have an objective, quantitative validity. It must be insisted that it would be very difficult to devise a more complicated and in some senses a more delicate instrument of behavior measurement than one twin used in juxtaposition with an identical co-twin as a standard of reference and comparative observation.

3. *Limitations of Training*.—While the positive results of training and conditioning have somewhat obscured the factors of maturation, the limitations of training may be adduced to show the existence of these factors. Such limitations were put to experimental study in the same pair of twins (Twin T and Twin C) whom we have just cited. At the age of 46 weeks, when the thorough-going mental and physical identity of the twins had been well established, it was decided to determine the influence of training confined to one twin, by using an experimental method which we have designated *the method of co-twin control*. T became the trained twin; C was reserved as a control.

Very briefly, Twin T was systematically trained for 20 minutes daily over a period of 6 weeks, in two fields of behavior, stair climbing and cube behavior, including prehension, manipulation and constructive play with a dozen one-inch red cubes. An experimental staircase arrangement of 5 treads was used, and for 10 minutes daily Twin T was put through her paces. At 48 weeks she scaled the stairs for the first time with slight assistance. At the conclusion of the 6 weeks training period (age one year) she was a relatively expert climber. At that age her untrained Co-twin C, would not yet scale the staircase, even with assistance. At the age of 53 weeks however, when C was again confronted with the staircase she climbed to the top without any assistance and without any previous training whatsoever. In this sense the form and the efficiency of her pattern of climbing were almost purely a function of the maturation of the appropriate neural counterparts.

Twin C was then given an experimental course of training in stair climbing, two weeks in length. At the end of this period (age 55 weeks) she approached Twin T in her climbing skill. By means of the motion picture it was possible to make a comparison of the climbing ability of C at 55 weeks (after 2 weeks of training) with that of T at 52 weeks (after 6 weeks of training). This comparison introduced an interesting form of relativity into the investigation and brought out the significant fact that although T had been trained three times longer and seven weeks earlier, this advantage was more than overcome by the three weeks of C's added age. Again the powerful influence of maturation on infant behavior pattern is made clear. Early training altered slightly the form of the pattern, and hastened the acquisition of facility, but left no considerable or decisive locomotor advantage in favor of Twin T.

In the field of cube play the experiment clearly showed that training had no significant effects upon the patterns of prehension, manipulation and constructive exploitation. Although Twin C had enjoyed no special opportunities in the handling of cubes, her cube behavior was fully equal to that of T after a 6 weeks training period. The similarity in temporal and spatial details of pattern was confirmed in this case by a time-space analysis of the behavior patterns by means of the cinema record. This does not mean, however, that there were no changes in the patterns of cube behavior during the training period from 46 weeks to 52 weeks. On the contrary, the records, when analyzed, show consistent and incontrovertible weekly increments. Indeed, a day by day analysis of the diurnal records of cube behavior satisfied us that there was a daily drift toward progressive changes in the cube performance patterns. These changes were developmentally achieved by steady processes of decrement and increment rather than by a saltatory or zigzag course. There may be spurts and plateaus and rhythms in the development of other fields of behavior, but at this stage of the life cycle there was a relatively constant trend toward daily change. This progressive daily changing apparently occurs by a process of continuous emergence which tends to lift the level of development slowly and steadily as though by tide action rather than by rhythmic spurt. We would explain the resistance of the patterns of cube behavior to the influences of training and conditioning by the fact that these patterns are basically under the stress and the regulation of the intrinsic organic factors of maturation. The very fact that there is a growth trend toward daily change of pattern makes the behavior less susceptible to stereotypy and to conditioning.

4. *The Restricted Influence of Physical Handicap.*—This subject opens up the vast field of experimental etiology in which the conditions of disease and environmental abnormality may be analyzed to determine the influence of extrinsic factors upon the complex of growth. In many instances these extrinsic factors seem to be much less powerful than one might suppose. Even grave degrees of malnutrition, correlated with excessive subnormality of weight, are usually incompetent to inflict any drastic changes upon the forms of fundamental behavior patterns and upon the genetic order of their sequence. While it must be granted that certain food deficiencies, for example in the field of calcium metabolism, may definitely influence the general picture of behavior, the nervous system itself is remarkably resistant to general adversity, even to malnutrition. When certain areas of the nervous system are actually damaged by disease or injury, maturation cannot make amends, but the maturation of the nervous system seems to proceed toward the optimum in the areas unimpaired, even though lacking the stimulus of exercise of the functions controlled by the impaired areas. It is for this reason that certain clinical types of profound motor disability attain none the less considerable approximation to normality in certain patterns of behavior.

In this context we may also mention the high degree of autonomy which the nervous system maintains even in extreme cases of *puberty præcox.* We have investigated one case in which there was a precocious displacement of puberty amounting to a whole decade. This girl became physiologically mature at the age of 3½ years. In spite of this extreme developmental alteration, the course of her behavior development in the fields of intelligence, language and locomotion has been relatively normal and stable.

Here, also, should be mentioned the general developmental course of the healthy infant born after an abnormally short or an abnormally long gestation period. A premature postnatal environment and a protracted uterine environment must be considered as drastic deviations from normal environmental influence. The relative immunity of the behavior patterns from these environmental deviations again bespeaks the potency of maturational factors.

5. *Developmental Progression in Emotional Behavior.*—The rôle of maturation in

the control of emotional behavior has had scant recognition. The primary emotions have been discussed as though they were elementary stable phenomena subject only to the changes of social conditioning. This is the implication in much that has been written concerning the emotion of fear. It seems to us that the problem has been over-simplified. Fear may be an original tendency, but it is subject to the genetic alterations of organic growth as well as to organization by environmental conditioning. Such conditioning may determine the orientation and reference of fears, but the mode of fearing undergoes change as a result of maturation. Fear is neither more nor less of an abstraction than prehension. It is not a simple entity. It waxes and alters with growth. It is shaped by intrinsic maturation as well as by experience, certainly during the period of infancy.

Consider for example the reactions of an infant to confinement in a small enclosed space, approximately 2 x 3 x 4 feet. In a physical sense the situation is entirely harmless. The space is ample in size, it is ventilated, it is illuminated, it is open at one end. In a personal sense however, the space may have elements of novelty and unusualness. The infant is not accustomed to lie in such a small space which shuts him off from his accustomed environment. What are his reactions, even when he is gently introduced into this enclosed chamber? At 10 weeks he may accept the situation with complete complaisance; at 20 weeks he may betray a mild intolerance, a dissatisfaction, persistent head turning and social seeking which we may safely characterize as mild apprehension; at 30 weeks his intolerance to the same situation may be so vigorously expressed by crying that we describe the reaction as fear or fright. Here then are three gradations of response: first, no disquietude; second, mild disquietude; third, robust disquietude. Is not this a genetic gradation of fear behavior which is based upon maturational sequence rather than upon an historical sequence of extrinsic conditioning factors? Such factors may account for specific aspects of fear behavior, but not for the organic pattern beneath such behavior. This pattern, we would suggest, is as much the product of organic growth as the various stages in the elaboration and perfection of prehension. Incidentally it may be said that the observation of duplicate twins will tend to substantiate the existence of maturational factors in the development of emotion. Although the tendency toward developmental divergence in identical twins is probably greater in the field of personality make-up than in any other sphere of behavior, there is, during infancy, an impressive tendency toward identity of emotional behavior. Twins T and C, already referred to, showed a highly significant degree of correspondence in their manifestations of initial timidity, in their responsiveness to social games, in their reactions to the mirror image, in their gestures of avoiding and refusing, in their seeking and begging gestures, in their laughter and crying. The relatively simultaneous and progressive nature of these changes in the field of emotional behavior suggests the influence of organic maturational factors as opposed to purely extrinsic factors in the determination of behavior pattern.

The extreme versions of environmentalist and conditioning theories suffer because they explain too much. They suggest that the individual is fabricated out of the conditioning patterns. They do not give due recognition to the inner checks which set metes and bounds to the area of conditioning and which happily prevent abnormal and grotesque consequences which the theories themselves would make too easily possible. Although it is artificial to press unduly a distinction between intrinsic and extrinsic factors, it must after all, be granted that growth is a function of the organism rather than of the environment as such. The environment furnishes the foil and the milieu for the manifestations of development, but these manifestations come from inner compulsion and are primarily organized by inherent inner mechanics and by an intrinsic physiology of development. The very plasticity of growth requires that there be limiting and regulatory mechanisms. Growth is a process so intricate and so sensitive that there must be powerful stabilizing factors, intrinsic rather than extrinsic, which preserve the balance of the total pattern and the direction of the growth trend. Maturation is, in a sense, a name for this regulatory mechanism. Just because we do not grant complete dichotomy of internal and external factors, it is necessary to explain what keeps the almost infinite fortuities of physical and social environment from dominating the organism of the developing individual.

The organismal concept requires that the individual shall maintain an optimum or normal integrity. The phenomena of maturation suggests the stabilizing and inexpugnable factors which safeguard the basic patterns of growth. Just as the respiration of the organism depends upon the maintenance of constant hydrogen-ion concentration, so probably on a vastly more intricate scale, the life career of the individual is maintained by the physiological processes of maturation—processes which determine in such large measure the form and the sequence of infant behavior pattern, that the infant as an individual is reasonably secure against extreme conditioning, whether favorable or unfavorable.

J. P. SCOTT *and* MARGARET S. CHARLES

*Genetic Differences in the Behavior of Dogs: A Case of Magnification by Thresholds and by Habit Formation**

A. Introduction

SOME years ago (Scott, 1944) it was pointed out that although hereditary differences in behavior were often small and insignificant, these differences could be magnified by thresholds in various ways so that very large differences could be obtained under special conditions.

Two of these situations are illustrated in FIGURE 1. In the first of these, two individuals, *A* and *B*, have slightly different thresholds of response which are genetically determined, but the same upper limit of response. Near the upper limit they show very small differences, but if a stimulus is set between the two thresholds, an all-or-none difference in response is obtained. This situation apparently applies to a case where large differences in response to light and vibration were obtained with stocks of fruit flies (Scott, 1943), and also to the more highly social situation involving differences in the behavior of dogs which is described in this paper.

In the second case (FIGURE 1b), two individuals are represented as having the same threshold, but a different response rate and upper limit of response, which are genetically determined. Under most conditions the observed differences in behavior are small, but grow larger as the upper limit is approached. If a threshold of success or failure is set between the two upper limits of response, an all-or-none difference can be obtained. This is the sort of situation which may be set in certain competitive games and in the so-called "power tests" of intelligence and performance. Of course, an actual case might involve both types of genetic differences.

An interesting and more complicated case of the first type may be found in connection with agonistic behavior of mammals. When an animal is attacked he has three principal ways of adapting to the situation: to fight back, to run away, or to remain passive. Which of these responses is chosen depends largely upon strength of stimulation. A mild attack will cause an animal to fight back whereas a very severe one may cause him to adopt a completely passive attitude (Scott, 1946). If animals have different genetically determined thresholds for stimulation it might be expected that a standard stimulation could cause one kind of animal to act passively and another to react with escape behavior or some form of mild or severe fighting.

This kind of interpretation appears to describe the results of a test situation in dogs in which an attempt was made to train puppies to stand still on the scales while being weighed. The methods used resulted in some animals becoming passive while others became more active, showing either escape behavior or playful aggressiveness.

The case is also interesting because the original differences observed became more definite and consistent as training proceeded. Apparently the original genetic differences, which probably act by producing different thresholds of stimulation, were still further

* REPRINTED by permission of J. P. Scott and The Journal Press from *J. genet. Psychol.*, 1954, 84, 175–188.

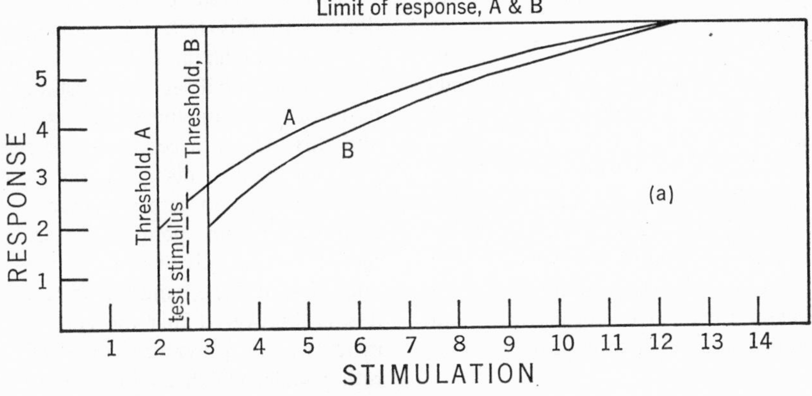

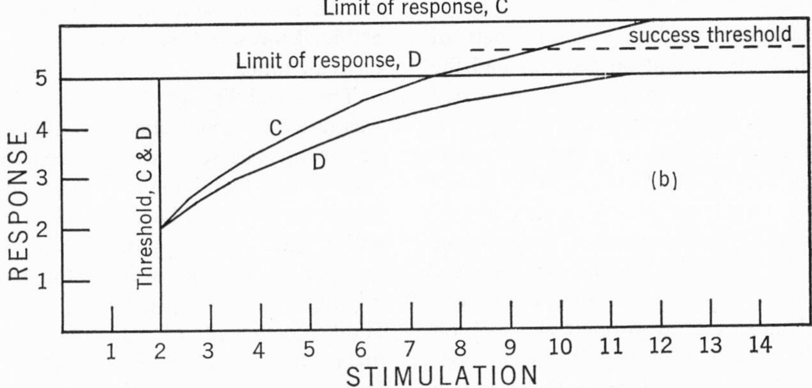

FIGURE 1

Graphic Representation of the Magnification of Genetic Differences by Thresholds

(a) Above their respective thresholds of stimulation individuals A and B, which have the same upper limit of response, show a response difference of only one unit, this decreasing rapidly as the response limit is approached. However, if a test stimulus is applied between values 2 and 3, which correspond to the thresholds of the two individuals, there is an absolute difference between response and no response.

In (b) is shown the theoretical situation in which the stimulus threshold is the same for both individuals, but the upper limit of response is different. The maximum difference in response is only one unit, but if a threshold of successful adjustment is set between the two upper limits, the result will be an absolute difference between failure and success. This is the kind of situation produced by so-called "power tests."

magnified by habit formation, an effect which may be explained as follows. A very mild sort of manual control was used so that either passivity or playful fighting was possible as an adjustment to the situation. If there should be an hereditary tendency in an individual for one of these reactions to occur more frequently than another because of the proximity of a threshold, habit formation would tend to fix the most frequent response. Two genetically different individuals may at first show considerable overlap in their behavior but, after exposure to the same training situation, begin to show consistent differences. Thus we have still another way in which originally small genetic differences may be magnified.

(For graphic illustrations of this effect, see later figures.)

This is an apparently paradoxical result which occurs fairly frequently in experiments with animals whose heredity is known. *A priori,* one would expect that young, naïve animals would show greater genetic differences in behavior than older and more experienced individuals. Actually, the behavior of naïve animals is usually quite variable and it is only after considerable training that such animals begin to behave consistently and clear-cut differences begin to appear.

B. Methods and Populations

THESE data were gathered as one part of the long-time experiment on genetics and the social behavior of dogs which is being carried out at the Jackson Laboratory (Scott & Charles, 1953; Scott & Fuller, 1950; Scott & Fuller, 1951). The dogs are raised as much as possible under the same environmental conditions, and during the first 16 weeks of life each litter is raised in a large nursery room, 18 x 13 feet in size. Once each week the animals are weighed in order to check on their health and growth and it was in connection with this procedure that these data were obtained.

The weighing is done inside the room with the scales placed on the nest-box. The puppy is first picked up by a handler and its heart rate taken by means of a stethoscope for 15 seconds. It is then placed upon a platform scale and weighed, being gently restrained with the hands if it tries to get off. Ordinarily no talking is done and sudden movements are avoided. An observer, sitting nearby, rates the amount of activity on the scale during a period of one minute. A rating of *quiet* means that the animal does not shift its feet after being placed on the scale although it may change its position; e.g., from sitting to lying. A rating of *partially active* means that the dog was seen to shift its feet at some time during the one-minute period, while a rating of *active* means that the dog is constantly shifting its feet, never being quiet as long as five seconds consecutively.

An experiment on observer reliability was done with this test, ratings being made by both the handler and observer. A tetrachoric correlation coefficient was estimated on the basis of reducing the ratings to two classes, and this yielded a coefficient of reliability of .96. The ratings disagreed on 14 out of 54 ratings but in no case was there a difference of more than one point in the scale. The observer consistently rated animals as more quiet than did the handler. After a conference it was discovered that the cause of disagreement was a difference in interpreting the rating scale, which could be easily corrected. The ratings used are therefore those of the one observer, and may be considered as artificial thresholds set by the observer on the basis of time.

The reliability of successive observations was tested by comparing the ratings at 15 and 16 weeks. The scale was reduced to two categories, first by adding the "quiet" and "partly active" groups, and later by adding the "partly active" and "active" groups. Tetrachoric correlation coefficients were estimated by the method of Jenkins (1950) and yielded reliability coefficients of .93 in both cases. This means that the animals are highly consistent in their behavior at this age, and that the observer was consistent in separating both the "quiet" and "active" groups from those labelled "partly active." On the other hand, the coefficient of reliability is much lower when the ratings at 5 and 6 weeks are compared, a fact which will be discussed in detail later.

When the general features of the test situation are analyzed it is found that from the viewpoint of social behavior we are dealing with a social interaction between an adult human being and an immature dog. The restraining movements of the handler may be classified as a mild form of agonistic behavior, and most of the responses of the puppy (escape behavior, crouching, sitting or lying posture, playful pawing and biting) may be included in the same category. Tail wagging and some hand licking are also observed. Dominance, or the habitual control of one individual by another by force, fighting, or threats, is obviously part of the situation.

From the viewpoint of adaptation (see Fuller's situational analysis, [1950]), directional interactions are only moderately strong or weak. Field impedance to effective reactions is set up so that only two of the possible responses, subordinate posture and playful aggressiveness, can take place, but neither of these is more than moderately difficult. The complexity of the field is not great, but it is set up in such a way that the animals have no reliable cues for cybernetic reactions, and should tend to choose responses on the basis of innate tendencies.

The animals used consisted of populations of purebred puppies taken from the Basenji, Beagle, Cocker Spaniel, and Wire-haired Terrier breeds, and included animals up to serial number 1673. The parent population of these puppies consisted of not more than 5 or 6 animals in each case and, therefore, cannot be considered an accurate random sample of the breed. This does not affect the results of the experiment, the object of which was to study and observe differences between these samples, but it does mean that it would be incorrect to generalize concerning the whole breeds from these small samples, even if the samples themselves did not indicate a great deal of overlap between breeds.

C. Results

THE ratings for each animal were added together for two six-week periods beginning respectively at 5 and 11 weeks and the results averaged for each breed. These are summarized in TABLE 1. No sex differences were found. It will be seen that the average rating at 5 to 10 weeks was almost exactly the same for all of the breeds except for the Cocker Spaniels, which falls much lower than the rest. At 11 to 16 weeks the situation has changed considerably. The Beagles are almost exactly the same as before, the Basenjis have fallen slightly in their activity, the Cocker Spaniels are even lower, and the Wire-haired Terriers have risen considerably. At 5–10 weeks three out of six interbreed comparisons are statistically significant, but at 11–16 weeks the number has risen to five.

The amount of variability is also interesting. At 5–10 weeks there are no significant

TABLE 1. *Activity ratings of puppies being taught to remain quiet on the scales*

Individual scores are expressed as the sum of 6 successive ratings, where 1 = Quiet, 2 = Partly Active, and 3 = Active. The scale used in the table therefore runs from 6 to 18.

POPULATION	*n*	MEAN 5–10 WEEKS	MEAN 11–16 WEEKS	*SD* 5–10 WEEKS	*SD* 11–16 WEEKS
Basenji	28	12.61 ± .4	11.04 ± .6	2.3 ± .3	3.2 ± .4
Beagle	36	12.61 ± .5	12.64 ± .7	2.7 ± .3	3.9 ± .5
Cocker Spaniel	44	9.82 ± .3	7.48 ± .2	2.2 ± .2	1.7 ± .2
Wire-haired Terrier	26	12.62 ± .6	14.65 ± .7	3.1 ± .4	3.3 ± .5
Total	134	11.59 ± .2	11.00 ± .4	2.9 ± .2	4.1 ± .2

TABLE 2. *Consistency of behavior as indicated by the percentage of duplicated ratings at various ages*

BREED POPULATION	AGE IN WEEKS 5–6	15–16	5–16
Basenji	46	64	29
Beagle	62	70	51
Cocker Spaniel	55	69	33
Wire-haired Terrier	50	70	40
Total	54	69	39

differences except between the extremes represented by the Cocker Spaniels and Basenjis on the low side and the Wire-haired Terriers on the high side. At 11 to 16 weeks variability has generally increased, most greatly in the animals which are nearest the middle of the distribution, and has gone down only in the Cocker Spaniels. The over-all picture (see FIGURE 2) shows a large increase in variability of the combined populations which may be considered as an effect of magnification of differences by habit formation.

The consistency of the behavior of individuals shows corresponding changes, as seen in TABLE 2. The measure used is the percentage of duplicated ratings, which is more accurate than using a tetrachoric correlation coefficient as the latter can be used only if the categories are reduced to two. (However, for purposes of rough comparison, the figure of 70 per cent in these data approximately corresponds to a tetrachoric *r* of .86 and a reliability coefficient of .93.)

It will be seen that the results within every breed population and also for the total show an increase in the consistency score when consecutive ratings at the beginning and end of the test period are compared. The Beagles appear to be different from the rest in that they show the least improvement of consistency between consecutive ratings and the greatest consistency between the early and late ratings. If training and habit formation is the essential factor involved, it would appear that the Beagles are either little affected by training, or are affected very rapidly. In any case, there is little change in this group from first till last.

This impression is borne out when the data are studied in more detail from the point of view of development. The graphs in FIGURES 2 and 3 show the percentage of animals which have crossed either threshold. In the case of the Cocker Spaniels the percentage of animals rated as quiet rises very steadily at a rate which is approximately 10 per cent of the animals which have not previously crossed the threshold, and the curve appears to be approaching 100 per cent as an asymptote. The same sort of thing is apparently occurring in the Basenjis at a slower rate and it does not appear that the asymptote will be much more than 70 per cent. In the Beagles the rise is very small indeed and in the Wire-haired Terriers it may even fall slightly.

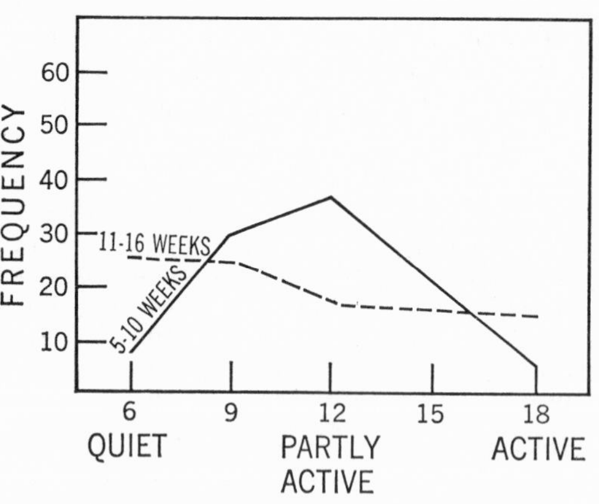

FIGURE 2

Distribution of scores of the combined breed populations. Note the greatly increased individual variability at 11–16 weeks, as compared with the earlier period.

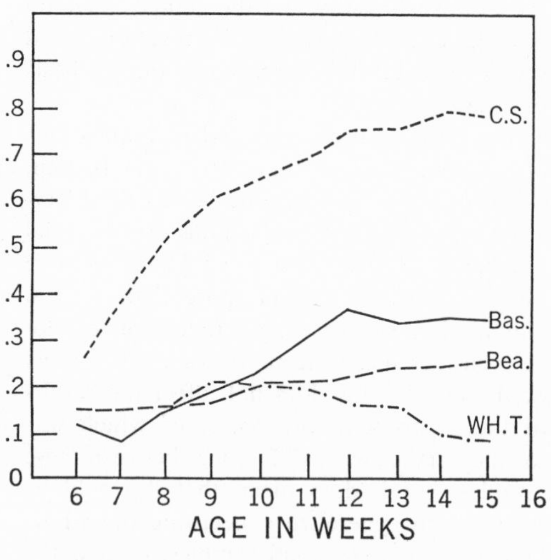

FIGURE 3

Curves showing the proportion of animals rated as "quiet" in the various breed populations. The curves have been smoothed by taking the average of each three successive points. Note that there is a tendency for the values to spread out further apart as the animals grow older.

We may now consider the animals which cross the other threshold toward the active side. Among the Cocker Spaniels this proportion starts out very low and falls off to 0. In the Basenjis it rises to a peak at eight weeks of age, falling off sharply at nine weeks and then rising slightly. In the Beagles there is a very slight rise. In the Wire-haired Terriers there is a steady and fairly rapid rise which might in time reach close to 100 per cent.

A more accurate estimate of these asymptotes might be achieved by fitting curves to the data, but since the last observations are near the points where the asymptotes should be reached, a more conservative estimate of the differences can be achieved by taking the percentage of animals falling above and below each threshold during the last four trials (see TABLE 3).

TABLE 3. *Average percentage of animals crossing either threshold, based on scores at* 13–16 *weeks*

BREED POPULATION	% QUIET	% ACTIVE
Basenji	35	20
Beagle	26	35
Cocker Spaniel	77	0
Wire-haired Terrier	11	56

When all possible comparisons are made between the populations in the quiet column, all but one, that between Basenjis and Beagles, are found to be significantly different from the rest. In the active column all but two of the comparisons (Basenji with Beagle and Beagle with Wire-haired Terrier) are significantly different. This compares very well with the results in TABLE 1 which showed that at 11 to 16 weeks all comparisons were significantly different except those between the Basenjis and Beagles.

D. Discussion

THE data present good evidence that genetic differences affecting this particular measurement do exist and that these differences tend to increase in time under the conditions given. Of the six possible comparisons between breeds only one does not show significant differences at the end of the test period.

It is also clear that the case involves two separate phenomena which tend to increase the importance of genetic differences. The first of these is the magnification of differences near a threshold. . . .

The second phenomenon is the fixation of genetic tendencies in behavior by habit formation, which tends to render behavior more consistent, and hence to magnify any original differences. This is well illustrated in FIGURES 3 and 4. Animals in the "Partly Active" category show inconsistent behavior, and the proportion of animals so classified tends to decrease with time. Likewise the consistency of behavior from one trial to the next tends to increase with time. The Beagles show more original consistency and less change than the rest.

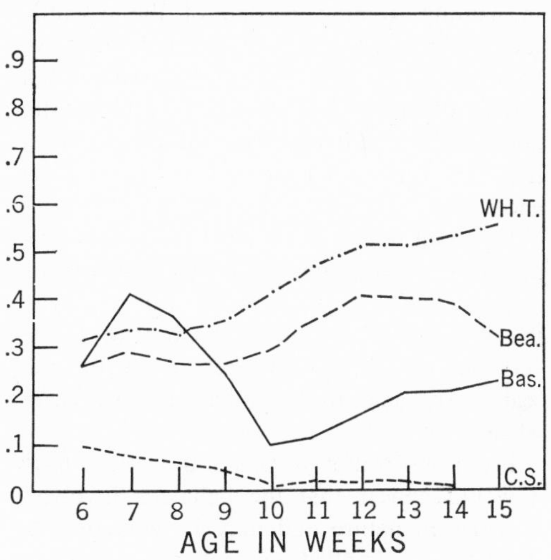

FIGURE 4

Smoothed curves for the proportion of animals rated as "active" in the 4 breed populations. Again note the tendency for differences to increase. For explanation of the irregularities in the Basenji curves, see text.

The point may be raised as to whether the increase in consistency observed is the result of training or the result of a simple maturation process. We have no control population which would test this point but other evidence would indicate that we are working with an effect of training. It has been shown that dogs are capable of habit formation at this age. During the time in which they are tested they undergo extensive handling during the other parts of the test program. Finally it has been found that animals which have been allowed to more or less run wild up to the age of 12 weeks tend to show the same or increasing amounts of escape behavior, in contrast to the increasing tameness of animals raised in the usual program.

If it may be assumed that we are correct in naming training as one of the essential factors involved we may conclude that we have an interesting case where an initial genetic difference is magnified by a threshold, and training and habit formation interact with it to still further magnify the original differences.

It should not be assumed that we are dealing with a simple unitary trait of activity or response to inhibitory training. For example, the Wire-haired Terriers, which tend to be very active while being restrained on the scales, are able to be quiet in most cases when restrained in a small cage.

From observation of this and of other tests it would appear that the behavior involved is social in nature and may be classified as agonistic, as implied in earlier paragraphs. In order that the scales may not be disturbed the handler has to touch the dogs quite gently, resulting in behavior which is apparently ambiguous as far as the puppies are concerned. The gentle restraint can be responded to as an attempt at enforcing dominance (which is the intention of the handler) or as an invitation toward playful fighting behavior. An attempt toward dominance can be responded to in at least three ways: assuming a subordinate attitude of crouching, attempting to escape, and by aggressiveness. Restraint is given in such a way that escape behavior is never effective (the puppies are never allowed to leave the scales), but the other two reactions are possible.

The Cocker Spaniels, as shown in other tests, have a strong tendency to crouch and remain still in response to human handling and this probably accounts for their quietness on the scales. The Basenjis in early life show a tendency toward escape behavior when handled but this disappears rapidly as they get older. This probably accounts for the peak in the activity rating seen in the early tests on the Basenjis. The [Wired-haired] Terriers on the other hand show two tendencies, to respond with escape behavior early in life (though not as strongly as Basenjis), and later on to respond with more and more aggressive behavior. Finally, the Beagles do not show any of these traits very strongly.

It is obvious that the tendency to escape will interfere with the tendencies to be subordinate or aggressive but there is no indication as yet that any of these traits form the opposite ends of one or more scales. Rather, they appear to be alternate ways of adjusting to a situation.

. . .

It would appear that in the higher animals genetic differences do not throw a straight-jacket around the behavior of an individual. Rather, each species seems to have several ways of adjusting to a given situation. Genetic differences do not ordinarily eliminate any of these responses but affect their frequency, so that a naïve animal may try out one solution to a problem more often than another. He can still give different responses when required, maintaining considerable initial flexibility of behavior, and it is only under certain conditions that genetic tendencies may result in consistent habits. However, the generality of this phenomenon must still be established.

Summary

1. The ways in which small hereditary differences in behavior may be magnified by special situations are discussed theoretically.

2. When puppies are trained to stand quietly while being weighed, hereditary differences are apparently magnified in two ways: different thresholds of response to minimal repressive stimulation tend to produce all-or-

none responses, and the process of habit formation tends to cause individuals to react consistently one way or the other, producing increasingly clear-cut differences.

3. The test situation is a social one involving dominance of the handler over the puppies. From the viewpoint of adaptation . . . directive (motivational) factors are weak, effective interactions are simple, and no reliable cues are available for cybernetic interactions, so that the animals tend to choose responses on the basis of innate tendencies.

4. The test consists of rating puppies as "active," "partly active," or "quiet," as they stand for one minute on the scales. Ratings are taken weekly from 5–16 weeks of age. A test of observer reliability gives a coefficient of reliability of .96, while a test of consistency between consecutive tests gives a figure of .93 at 15–16 weeks of age.

5. The populations tested consists of 28 Basenjis, 36 Beagles, 44 Cocker Spaniels, and 26 Wire-haired Terriers.

6. When analyzed, the results show that the Cocker Spaniels are at first significantly different from the other three populations and tend to become increasingly quiet, finally reaching a figure of 77 per cent quiet and 0 per cent active.

7. The Beagle population shows little change, either in average ratings or consistency, indicating that the animals are little affected by training of the sort given during the period of 5–16 weeks of age.

8. The majority of the Wire-haired Terriers become increasingly active, finally reaching a figure of 56 per cent active and 11 per cent quiet.

9. The Basenjis show approximately equal numbers of animals which tend to become quiet and active (final figures 35 and 20 per cent).

10. The effect on the total population is one of greatly increased variability from early to later tests, which may be interpreted as the result of habit formation increasing consistency and thus magnifying genetic variability.

11. Relevant data from other sources are discussed, and it is concluded that a tentative generalization may be drawn; namely, that hereditary differences in behavior of the higher animals tend to cause an individual to choose one of several alternate modes of behavior with greater frequency than others, this tendency becoming consistent with habit formation under certain situations. Thus identically treated animals may show smaller and less consistent differences before than after training.

REFERENCES

FULLER, J. L. Individual differences in the reactivity of dogs, *J. comp. physiol. Psychol.*, 1948, **41,** 339–347.

FULLER, J. L. Situational analysis: a classification of organism-field reactions. *Psychol. Rev.*, 1950, **57,** 3–18.

JAMES, W. T. Morphological form and its relation to behavior. In C. R. Stockard, *The genetic and endocrine basis for differences in form and behavior*. Philadelphia: Wistar Institute, 1941.

JENKINS, W. L. A single chart for tetrachoric *r*. *Educ. psychol. Measmt,* 1950, **10,** 142–144.

ROYCE, J. R. A factorial analysis of emotionality in the dog. Ph.D. thesis (MS), Univer. of Chicago, 1951.

SCOTT, J. P. Effects of single genes on the behavior of Drosophila. *Amer. Nat.*, 1943, **77,** 184–190.

SCOTT, J. P. The magnification of differences by a threshold. *Science,* 1944, **100,** 569–570.

SCOTT, J. P. Incomplete adjustment caused by frustration of untrained fighting mice. *J. comp. Psychol.*, 1946, **39,** 379–390.

SCOTT, J. P., & CHARLES, MARGARET S. Some problems of heredity and social behavior. *J. genet. Psychol.*, 1953, **48,** 209–230.

SCOTT, J. P., & FULLER, J. L. (Eds.). A manual of dog-testing techniques. Bar Harbor, Maine: R. B. Jackson Memorial Laboratory, 1950. (Mimeographed.)

SCOTT, J. P., & FULLER, J. L. Research on genetics and social behavior at the Roscoe B. Jackson Memorial Laboratory, 1946–1951—a progress report. *J. Hered.*, 1951, **42,** 191–197.

ZING YANG KUO

*Studies on the Basic Factors in Animal Fighting: VII. Inter-Species Coexistence in Mammals**

A. Problem

THE purpose of this study is twofold: (*a*) to prevent the formation of certain anti-social habits in the dog and cat such as prey and hunting and killing of smaller animals, antagonism between dogs and cats, and fighting between and domination over members of the same species. And (*b*) to extend or transfer certain sociable behavior patterns to other species. Our ultimate goal was, of course, to establish a peaceful and tranquil mammalian society not only without fighting, but also with the dominance orders or social ranks eliminated. Throughout this investigation the developmental or ontogenic methods were used.

B. The Experiments

THE subjects employed in these experiments were newly born puppies, kittens, albino rats, and rabbits. In addition, two species of very young birds, canaries, and cockatoos were included in this research. The subjects were divided into five main groups, each group was subdivided into nine pens, each pen consisting of one animal of one species and five of another species. Thus, in Group I Pen 1, one dog and five cats were reared together—see TABLE 1. The new born animals were put to live together in pens according to the plans of the study as soon as they were old enough to be hand-fed with cow's milk. The sexes of each group were, whenever possible, equally divided. Of the five groups, the first two were used as experimental subjects, the next two groups as controls, and Group V for the study of the effects of isolation on cats and dogs; other species were not involved in this group. Each pen in which six animals of two species lived together was placed in a wire net enclosure 18′ x 18′ x 10′ (high). The detailed arrangements of the four groups are presented

TABLE 1. *Species and number of the new born animals reared together in the same pen*

Species Pen No.		CATS (C) AND COCKATOOS (CO) Pen 9	CATS (C) AND CANARIES (CA) Pen 8	DOGS (D) AND CANARIES (CA) Pen 7	DOGS (D) AND COCKATOOS (CO) Pen 6	CATS (C) AND RABBITS (RB) Pen 5	CATS (C) AND RATS (R) Pen 4	DOGS (D) AND RABBITS (RB) Pen 3	DOGS (D) AND RATS (R) Pen 2	DOGS (D) AND CATS (C) Pen 1
GROUPS	I	1C 5Co	1C 5Ca	1D 5Ca	1D 5Co	1C 5Rb	1C 5R	1D 5Rb	1D 5R	1D 5C
	II	1Co 5C	1Ca 5C	1Ca 5D	1Co 5D	1Rb 5C	1R 5C	1Rb 5D	1R 5D	1C 5D
	III	1C 5Co	1C 5Ca	1D 5Ca	1D 5Co	1C 5Rb	1C 5R	1D 5Rb	1D 5R	1D 5C
	IV	5Co 5C	5Ca 5C	1Ca 5D	1Co 5D	1Rb 5C	1R 5C	1Rb 5D	1R 5D	1C 5D
	V	Ten dogs and ten cats reared in isolation								

* REPRINTED by permission of Leonard Carmichael (The Smithsonian Institution) and The Journal Press from *J. genet. Psychol.*, 1960, **97**, 211–225.

in TABLE 1. In the table, the letters *D, C, R,* etc. stand for dogs, cats, rats, etc. respectively. The figures preceding the letters indicated the number of animals reared together in a pen; thus, 1D 5C means one new born dog reared together with five new born cats.

All the dogs in this investigation were short haired Chinese chows, except in the experiments in connection with canaries and cockatoos when newly born Boston terriers were used. The cats belonged to the Chinese local breed. Whenever possible, [efforts] were made to equally divide the new borns from the same litter between Groups I and III on the one hand, and between II and IV on the other.

From our studies on the fighting of birds and our preliminary observations on the social behavior of various mammals we had come to the conclusion that competition over food and over sex, playing activities, hostility towards strangers, and living in isolation were among the major environmental factors leading to the development of such anti-social behavior patterns as mentioned above. In this study, therefore, special emphasis was placed on the control of these factors during development. In the control groups (III and IV) no attempt was made to interfere with the spontaneous development of eating and play activities of the subjects; these control animals were not allowed to see any strange animals until they were 10 months old. In Group V (dogs and cats reared in isolation) each subject was tested for its reactions to strange animals after [it was] 10 months old (dogs, cats, rats, rabbits, guinea pigs, canaries and cockatoos, as well as several other species of birds and mammals).

1. SOCIALIZING EATING HABITS

The object of this part of the investigation was to prevent competition over food by socializing the eating habits of the animals in Groups I and II. Only dogs, cats, and cockatoos were used. The cockatoos were included in this study because they could be brought up to become very fond of bread soaked in milk, which they could pick up from the food dish for dogs and cats. The procedure is briefly as follows:

When the dogs, the kittens, and cockatoos were about two months old, they were daily brought to eat by turn in the feeding platform the detailed ground plane of which is shown in FIGURE 1. All the partition walls and doors

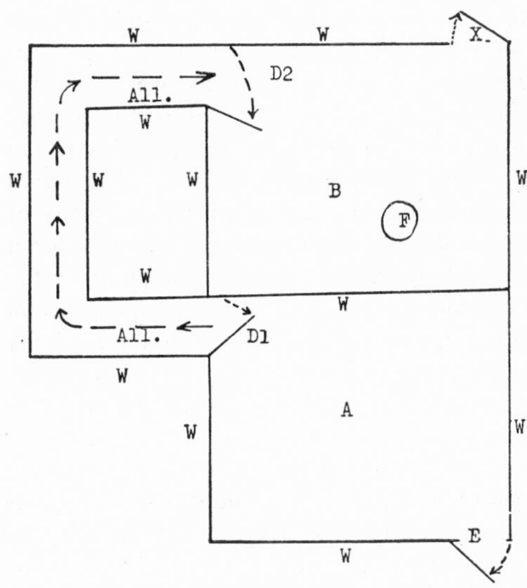

FIGURE 1
Ground Plan of Feeding Platform

E—entrance to the observation compartment.
A—observation compartment.
B—eating compartment.
F—food dish.
D1—glass door leading from A to alley way.
A11—alley way leading from D1 to D2.
D2—glass door from alley way to eating compartment.
X—exit from eating compartment.
W—glass walls.

were made of plate glass. The walls [were] moveable so that the two compartments, *A* and *B,* as well as the alley way could be widened or narrowed according to the sizes of the animals. There were several sets of doors which could be changed in accordance with the sizes of the two compartments and the alley way. Each door was fixed with a spring hinge and could be opened by pulling the string attached to it. When the string was released, the door closed immediately. Generally, Compartment *A* is so set as to have sufficient room for six animals to move and turn about. The alley way was set to allow only one animal to walk through at a time so that if a second animal attempted to overtake the first one, it could do so only by squeezing or crawling under the first animal in front. When all the six animals (or five dogs or five cats only in those pens where rabbits or canaries were their co-inhabitants) were brought into Compartment *A* through Entrance *E*, one of them was admitted through D1, the alley way, and D2 into Compartment *B* to eat in the food dish (F), and the other five animals were allowed to watch the first admitted animal in eating. If any of the watchers became impatient and began to bark or meow, or tried to jump at the partition wall between *A*, *B*, a black curtain was lowered to cover the wall until all the impatient movements and noises in the waiting compartment were quieted down. The animal in eating was allowed to finish his meal in 10 minutes. After 10 minutes the bell rang, and the animal must leave Compartment *B* by the exit (X). Otherwise, he was gently pushed out through X. This done, another animal in waiting was allowed in the same manner to take his meal while the rest of the animals had to wait for their turn. After all the animals in the pen had learned to wait quietly in Compartment *A* for their turns to be admitted to eat in Compartment *B*, the next step in the training was to open Door D1 and let the waiting animals in Compartment *A* file one by one into the alley way while one was already eating in Compartment *B*. At first, the experimenter had to push them one by one into the alley way when the Door D1 was opened. But later on, all learned to do this without help as soon as D1 was opened. While lining up in the alley way, if one of the animals attempted to overtake another either by squeezing through or by crawling under, the overtaker was immediately brought back to the end of the waiting line.

After all the subjects had learned to line up in the alley way instead of Compartment *A*, each waiting for its turn to be admitted to Compartment *B*, Door D2 was kept open. But if the animal in front of the waiting line rushed into Compartment *B* before the animal in eating had finished his meal and left the place, the door was immediately closed and the violator was taken up and replaced at the end of the waiting line. Through a number of trials, all the animals in the pen learned not to enter D2, though it was open, until Compartment *B* was clear of any animal.

One month after every animal in the pen had mastered "the dining car etiquette" (a nickname we used in the laboratory because the process resembled waiting in the dining car in a crowded American train), they were tested for their reactions to a food situation (not in the feeding platform) in which the other animals had either to wait beside the one in eating, or to push him away in order to occupy the food dish, which did not allow more than one animal to eat at the same time. Each subject was given three tests.

Since it is not our purpose in this report to analyse the learning process and due to space limitation, the records of the animals of these three species in learning the "dining car etiquette" will not be presented here. Suffice it to state that all the cockatoos, cats, and dogs in Groups I and II had eventually become "socialized" in their eating habits, and that the dogs were the quickest learners, the cats next, the cockatoos the slowest (three to 10 trials for the dogs, eight to 25 trials for the cats, 21 to 29 trials for the cockatoos).

In the three tests in a situation outside the feeding platform all the animals showed that the eating habits, that is, to wait, not to push, if the food dish [was] occupied, and not to compete with another while trying to reach the food dish which was just unoccupied, were preserved, even in a new environmental setting, although 56 per cent of the dogs, 42 per cent of the cats, and 33 per cent of the cockatoos often came so close to the food dish and made attempts to sniff at it, but neither the animal in eating objected to it, nor did the sniffer show any sign to join him in eating.

In the control groups (III and IV), no attempt was made to prevent fighting or domination in eating. The feeding plate was large enough for all the six animals in the pen to eat together. The phenomenon of food competition ended in domination without fighting, or as a result of one or at most two fightings was observed in the two groups: (66 per cent for dogs, 68 per cent for cats, 48 per cent for rats, and 72 per cent for cockatoos). A dominant dog occupying the food plate or having a piece of food in the mouth would growl to warn off the other animals. A dominant cat would snarl or hiss. A dominant rat would bite another rat. The dominant cockatoo would peck or chase other birds away. The non-dominant ones (dogs, cats, as well as cockatoos) learned to quietly steal a piece of food and run to eat in a corner. A non-dominant cockatoo would steal with its beak one piece of food and put it to one of its feet to hold it, and with the free beak steal another piece before it went away to eat the stolen food. All these happened when the dogs were about three to four weeks old, cats about four to eight weeks old, rats and cockatoos about two to three months old. All such behavioral phenomena were observed only during feeding time. At other times all the animals living in the same pen were friendly to each other, playing together, and even fondled or [were] attached to one another.

It would seem that there is a striking contrast in the behavioral patterns relative to the eating habit between the experimental and control groups.

2. PLAY

In the experimental groups, play of the animals was closely watched every day. The experimenter, with a water spray in hand (the kind commonly used in ironing clothes) would quickly spray water on the face of the animals as soon as fighting started during play. In the chow, puppies of three to four weeks would start to fight during play, or to bite at the handler, but with one to three sprays of water, fighting or biting would not occur again. We also employed water spray on a puppy carrying something in his mouth, who would growl or bite when another animal or the handler tried to snatch it from the mouth. However, in the case of play between cats, between cats and dogs, between dogs and cockatoos, and between cockatoos and cats, no fighting was ever observed. In the case of rabbits and canaries there are no acts which can be interpreted as play activities, except the preliminary and final sex acts.

In the two control groups, fighting between dogs during play was not stopped by the experimenter. But such fighting lasted often only for a few seconds, rarely resulting in bodily injury, but might end with the establishment of the dominance relationship in favor of the stronger puppy.

In play activities there is one significant fact which must be pointed out here. There was no species barrier in play. The same kind of play pattern of a dog was manifested in the play either between a dog and a cat or between a dog and a cockatoo. Five of the puppies in all the first four groups even attempted at sham coitus movements on the cats or cockatoos or rabbits. The kittens displayed cat-like play patterns with cockatoos or with dogs. The cockatoo in playing with cats or dogs would nod its head, ruffle its crest, flutter its wings, touching the floor with its beak, attempting billing movements with a dog or a cat, or gently touch the face or neck of the dog or cat with its beak, making tender sounds in the meantime.

In inter-species social life, while there is no species barrier in play as well as in attachment or fondling activities, nevertheless, there is still species preference. It will be noted that in the first four groups of animals in this investigation there [were] six animals of two different species living in one pen. Thus, in Pen 1 in Group I there [were] one puppy and five kittens living together; in Pen 9 Group I one cat to five cockatoos; in Pen 6 Group II five dogs to one cockatoo, etc. (see TABLE 1). Now, in the pen with one cockatoo and five dogs, all the attachment, fondling activities, and play of the cockatoo were built around the five puppies. When all the puppies were taken out from the pen, the cockatoo became restless, making loud noises, until one of the five puppies was returned to the pen. Even when a strange well-tamed cockatoo was put into this pen, instead of returning a puppy mate, the restless cockatoo adopted an indifferent attitude towards the stranger (or even hostile if the restless cockatoo belonged to Pen 6 Group IV instead of Pen 6 Group II). On the other hand, the attitude of the five puppies in the same pen towards this single avian pen mate can be described as "friendly, occasional playmate, but not indispensable." They did not play with the bird as much as they [did] among themselves. If four puppies were taken from [the] pen, leaving one of the five with the cockatoo, the lone little dog would become as restless and in great distress as if the avian pen mate were not there. The reversal of the same phenomena was observed in the case in which there were five cockatoos to one puppy in the same pen. In this case, the pup became attached almost solely to the cockatoos, acted as if they were his sole companions and play mates while [he remained] indifferent to other animals including dogs. On the other hand, the cockatoos reacted to this lone dog with a tolerant and indifferent attitude. When two or four cockatoos were paired, their love making activities were confined to their sex mate, becoming indifferent not only to the lone dog, but also to the other cockatoos. And this applies to the relationship between kittens and cockatoos and between kittens and puppies throughout this investigation. In other words, when one young animal grows up together with mates of its species as well as a different species, it is more attached to the mates of its own species than to the mates of another species. [However] when one lone young animal of one species is reared together with one or more young of a different species, after the critical time (two to three months), its attachment is in most cases entirely fixed with the mates not belonging to its own species, so that when it meets a stranger of its own species its attitude is either indifferent or hostile depending on its past experience with strange animals.

. . .

C. Prey on Small Animals, Hunting, Reaction to Strangers, and the Effects of Isolation

KITTENS and puppies in Group V naturally were not allowed to see any strange animal of whatever species during the period of isolation. From the tenth month on, each was tested bi-weekly for its reaction to strangers including dogs, cats, rats, rabbits, guinea pigs, [and many varieties] of parrots, canaries, and sparrows. Similarly, the control animals (Groups III, IV) had not seen any strange animal until they were 10 months old, and, thenceforth, each was given a bi-weekly test with the animals of those species used to test Group V. On the other hand, those animals in Groups I and II from the start of their collective life in the pens were allowed to spend 10 minutes every day with one strange animal of the various species used to test animals in Groups III, IV, and V. These testing animals had been trained to be very tame, having no fear [of] or hostility to strange animals of any species, birds or mammals, but in most cases [they] were very friendly to the animals in the pen they were introduced to visit. The reactions of the kittens and dogs of the five groups to the strange visitors are summed up . . . [as follows:] . . . (*a*) Those cats and dogs which received a strange visitor every day from the very start of the collective life in the pen showed neither [a] hostile nor attacking reaction to the strange animals of any species during the testing period. Gone were their preying and hunting tendencies. Their reaction to strange animals was either indifferent or friendly. Gone, too, was the antagonism or hostile attitude between dogs and cats. (*b*) But it is not the case with the cats and dogs in Groups III and IV [to] which no strange animals were allowed to pay visits. Upon tests, their reaction was by and large hostile or attacking. There were, however, a small number of cases in these two groups in which an indifferent or even friendly attitude was displayed by some of the dogs and cats. Our records show that these dogs or cats were the subjects which were brought up in the same pen with the animals which belonged to the same species as the testing animals used as strange visitors, to which the dogs and cats in question had displayed an indifferent or friendly attitude instead of a hostile or attacking reaction. (*c*) When we come to the dogs and cats brought up in isolation in the first 10 months, their reactions to strangers [were] predominantly hostile or attacking although there [were] a few cases in which the dogs or cats showed an attitude of indifference or a mild degree of friendliness. Our records show 10 cases in which small birds and rats were killed and eaten by the isolated cats, while the dogs chased and killed rats [and] guinea pigs, as well as rabbits and birds. (*d*) The antagonism between cats and dogs, between two dogs and between two cats [was] very strong as [could be seen in] the reaction of the animals in Group V to visiting cats and dogs. . . .

1. SUPPRESSION OF AGGRESSION

. . . There [were] 22 dogs in Groups III, IV, and V which would rush to attack strange dogs whenever they were introduced into their enclosure. We purposely selected as visitors to these enclosures, dogs of extreme timidity who [would] invariably run to escape whenever the resident or residents of the enclosure rushed out and, when an escape was blocked, they would lie down on their backs and let the attackers attack without resistance.

Now, as a last step in this investigation, we made use of 20 (all chows) of these 22 aggressive dogs (the other two, Boston terriers) as experimental subjects on suppression of aggression. The suppressor was a medium sized, short-haired chow with a broad muzzle and with a bodily make-up excellent for a fighter. When we employed this chow as the suppressor for the 20 chow aggressors, it was about three years old. For all the three years of its life this dog never initiated a fight, but when attacked, never failed to make a counter-attack and never lost a single combat. In any environmental setting, familiar or unfamiliar, whenever he met one or more strange dogs or whenever one or more dogs rushed to challenge him, his first and invariable reaction was to stand straight with his tail tightly bent forward to his back, making neither motion nor noise. Such a reaction pattern was in a majority of cases sufficient to send the challengers away without a fight. However, if he was attacked he always fought so well that, unless he was ordered to stop by his trainer, the fight was finished almost always with a very serious injury, or death to his opponent. We made this three-year-old chow pay visits to those 20 chows by turn. In case of some mild injury or fatigue, the suppressor was rested until full recovery. Results: 13 of them (65%) were sent away peacefully by his firm and steady stand, the other seven got him into battles which were ended with three cases of severe injury, two cases of light injury, and two cases of death. After the wounds were healed, all these dogs were given four more tests with the suppressor as the visitor and with other new visiting dogs. Results: of the 13 which did not have any fight with the suppressor, six tried to keep in some distance from him, the others got near him but soon left him alone. All the 13 continued to challenge or threatened to attack other visiting dogs. All the injured dogs had the typical reactions of an underdog in the presence of the suppressor. All those which continued to have hostile or attacking reactions to the other dog visitors did so with a milder degree than before.

It must be noted in passing that in Groups III and IV when a top dominant dog or cat was removed from the pen, the next dominant animal moved up to take its place as the top ranking animal. The hierarchy or rank order remained constant until one of the dominant animals was removed.

D. Summary and Conclusion

IN a number of experiments it has been demonstrated: (*a*) That in such anti-social behavioral patterns in dogs and cats as have been popularly known as prey on small animals, hunting, mutual antagonism between cats and dogs, aggressive or hostile reactions between two dogs, and hostility to or attacking strangers could be prevented from appearance if appropriate environmental situations were in force during development. (*b*) That sociable behavior patterns in mammals such as attachment to one another, fondling acts and courting could be brought to cross the species barrier and even extended from mammals to birds and vice-versa. This was accomplished also by the developmental or ontogenic methods. (*c*) That by adequate control of environmental conditions during development, eating habits in dogs and cats and even cockatoos could be socialized to resemble human etiquette. (*d*) That during development, by elimination of competition over food, by prevention of fighting during play, and by avoidance of competition over sex, a mammalian society could be immunized against not only fighting but also what has been supposed to be a normal phenomenon in vertebrate animals, namely, the so-called dominance-submission relationship. (*e*) That in mammals as well as in fish and birds, isolation during development has been found to be a major factor in developing hostile reaction to other animals, which reaction is a step leading to fighting. (*f*) That in dogs (cats, also, [but] the data concerning this are not presented in this paper) "standing firm," instead of running or submission, has a 65 per cent chance to stop or avoid an aggressive attack. This confirms our findings in fish and birds. (*g*) And that in dogs, too, we confirm the conclusions based on the results of our investigation on fish and birds that an aggressor could be suppressed or subdued by a stronger or more powerful aggressor. But the suppression is never complete nor permanent, and [is] rather costly as such a suppression may lead to severe injuries or even death. Here again, in mammals as in other classes of vertebrates, when the most aggressive animal is removed from the group, another moves up to take its place and establish itself as the top aggressor. It appears, then, that suppression of an aggressor or removal of a dominant animal from the group will not end social domination or fighting in an animal society.

Our observation on the behavior of animals towards strangers raised some doubt about the validity of the concept of defense of territory in animals. We are rather inclined to think that the so-called "territorial defence" is, after all, merely a fancy name for the reaction patterns to strangers flavored with anthropomorphism and the 19th century Darwinism. Further and more systemic experimental explorations are necessary to decide this issue.

. . .

As has been repeatedly pointed out in the previous reports of this series, fixation of behavioral patterns (habituation) during development plays an important role as a determinant of behavior. Its significance can not be overemphasized. It is an essential controlling factor not only in social domination and fighting but also in the development of behavior in general. . . .

In conclusion, let us restate that although social domination and fighting are very common phenomena in animal societies, and although our studies have demonstrated that once such behavior patterns are formed and once the social hierarchy is established it is extremely difficult, if not impossible, to stamp them out, there is no reason to accept the fatalistic view that such behavioral patterns are "necessary evils" in social life. Our hope for a peaceful and tranquil society without fighting and social domination lies in the prevention of the development of such behavior patterns. Our findings have demonstrated that by appropriate control of environmental conditions during development we can immunize against certain types of anti-social behavior patterns in animals. We seem to be able to accomplish such an immunization without resorting to such drastic measures as depriving the animals of the essential nutritional factors such as thiamin, or castration of the gonads. Our experimental attack on the various problems of the elimination of social domination and fighting is just beginning, and further and more extensive investigations are required in order to work out a detailed and systematic program for the prophylaxis of aggression in animal society. However, the developmental or ontogenic approach seems to have encouraged us to hope that the day may not be so far off when it will be just as feasible to immunize against social domination and fighting as [to immunize] against smallpox or poliomyelitis.

ECKHARD H. HESS

Imprinting*

STUDENTS of behavior generally agree that the early experiences of animals (including man) have a profound effect on their adult behavior. Some psychologists go so far as to state that the effect of early experience upon adult behavior is inversely correlated with age. This may be an oversimplification, but in general it appears to hold true. Thus, the problem of the investigator is not so much to find out *whether* early experience determines adult behavior as to discover *how* it determines adult behavior.

Three statements are usually made about the effects of early experience. The first is that early habits are very persistent and may prevent the formation of new ones. This, of course, refers not only to the experimental study of animals but also to the rearing of children. The second statement is that early perceptions deeply affect all future learning. This concept leads to the difficult question whether basic perceptions—the way we have of seeing the world about us—are inherited or acquired. The third statement is simply that early social contacts determine the character of adult social behavior. This is the phenomenon of imprinting.

At the turn of the century, Craig (1908), experimenting with wild pigeons, found that in order to cross two different species it was first necessary to rear the young of one species under the adults of the other. Upon reaching maturity the birds so reared preferred mates of the same species as their foster parents. Other interspecies sexual fixations have been observed in birds and fishes.

Heinroth (1910, 1924–33) and his wife successfully reared by hand the young of almost every species of European birds. They found that many of the social responses of these birds were transferred to their human caretaker. Lorenz (1935) extended these experiments, dealing especially with greylag geese.

Lorenz was the first to call this phenomenon "imprinting," although earlier workers had observed this effect. He was also the first to point out that it appeared to occur at a critical period early in the life of an animal. He postulated that the first object to elicit a social response later released not only that response but also related responses such as sexual behavior. Imprinting, then, was related not only to the problem of behavior but also to the general biological problem of evolution and speciation.

Although imprinting has been studied mainly in birds, it also has been observed to occur in other animals. Instances of imprinting have been reported in insects (Thorpe, 1944), in fish (Baerends & Baerends-van Roon, 1950), and in some mammals. Those mammals in which the phenomenon has been found—sheep (Grabowski, 1941), deer (Darling, 1938), and buffalo (Hediger, 1938)—are all animals in which the young are mobile almost immediately after birth. Controlled experimental work with mammals, however, has just begun.

The first systematic investigations of imprinting were published in 1951. Simultaneously in this country and in Europe, the work of Ramsay (1951) and Fabricius (1951) gave the first indication of some of the important variables of the process. Ramsay worked with several species of ducks and a variety of breeds of chickens. He noticed the importance of the auditory component in

* REPRINTED by permission of the author and the American Association for the Advancement of Science from *Science,* 17 July 1959, 130, 133–141.

the imprinting experiment and the effect of changes in coloring on parental recognition as well as on recognition of the parents by the young. His findings also showed that color is an essential element in recognition, while size or form seemed to be of less importance. Most of Ramsay's experiments dealt with exchange of parents and young and did not involve the use of models or decoys as imprinting objects, although he also imprinted some waterfowl on such objects as a football or a green box.

Fabricius carried on experiments with several species of ducklings and was able to determine approximately the critical age at which imprinting was most successful in several species of ducks. In some laboratory experiments he found it impossible to do imprinting in ducklings with a silent decoy—something which my coworkers and I were easily able to do a few years later in our Maryland laboratory. After the appearance of this pioneer work by Ramsay and by Fabricius, no relevant papers appeared until 1954. At that time Ramsay and Hess published a paper on a laboratory approach to the study of imprinting. The basic technique was modified slightly the following year and then was continued in the form described below. Papers [in 1953] by Margaret Nice and [in 1956] by Hinde, Thorpe, and Vince include most of the pertinent materials published up to 1956 since Lorenz's classic statement of the problem.

Since 1956, however, there has been an increasing number of papers on imprinting in a variety of journals. However, most investigators report experiments which are primarily designed to look for ways in which imprinting can be likened to associative learning and are not primarily carried out to investigate the phenomenon itself. Later we shall return to a consideration of these experiments; for the present we shall concern ourselves mainly with the program carried out since 1951 at McDonogh and at Lake Farm Laboratory, Maryland, and at our laboratories at the University of Chicago.[1]

Experimental Studies

OUR laboratory in Maryland had access to a small duck pond in which we kept relatively wild mallards. The birds laid their eggs in nesting boxes, so the eggs could be collected regularly. After storage for a few days, the eggs were incubated in a dark, forced-air incubator. About two days before hatching, the eggs were transferred to a hatching incubator. Precautions were taken to place the newly hatched bird into a small cardboard box (5 by 4 by 4 inches) in such a way that it could see very little in the dim light used to carry out the procedure.

Each bird was given a number, which was recorded on the box itself as well as in our permanent records. The box containing the bird was then placed in a still-air incubator, used as a brooder, and kept there until the bird was to be imprinted. After the young bird had undergone the imprinting procedure, it was automatically returned to the box, and the box was then transferred to a fourth incubator, also used as a brooder, and kept there until the bird was to be tested. Only after testing was completed was the duckling placed in daylight and given food and water.

The apparatus we constructed to be used in the imprinting procedure consisted of a circular runway about 5 feet in diameter. This runway was 12 inches wide and 12½ feet in circumference at the center. Boundaries were formed by walls of Plexiglas 12 inches high. A mallard duck decoy, suspended from an elevated arm radiating from the center of the apparatus, was fitted internally with a loud-speaker and a heating element. It was held about 2 inches above the center of the runway. The arms suspending the decoy could be rotated by either of two variable-speed motors. The speed of rotating and intermittent movement could be regulated from the control panel located behind a one-way screen about 5 feet from the apparatus. The number

1 The work described in this article was supported in part by grant No. M-776 of the National Institutes of Health, Public Health Service, Department of Health, Education, and Welfare, Bethesda, Md.; by the Wallace C. and Clara A. Abbott Memorial Fund, of the University of Chicago, Chicago, Ill.; and by the Wallace Laboratories, New Brunswick, N.J.

of rotations of both the decoy and the animal were recorded automatically. Tape recorders with continuous tapes provided the sound that was played through the speaker inside the decoy. A trap door in the runway, operated from the control panel, returned the duckling to its box.

IMPRINTING PROCEDURE

The young mallard, at a certain number of hours after hatching, was taken in its box from the incubator and placed in the runway of the apparatus (FIGURE 1). The decoy at this

FIGURE 1

The apparatus used in the study of imprinting consists primarily of a circular runway around which a decoy duck can be moved. In this drawing a duckling follows the decoy. The controls of the apparatus are in the foreground.

time was situated about 1 foot away. By means of a cord, pulley, and clip arrangement, the observer released the bird and removed the box. As the bird was released, the sound was turned on in the decoy model, and after a short interval the decoy began to move about the circular runway. The sound we used in the imprinting of the mallard ducklings was an arbitrarily chosen human rendition of "*gock*, gock, gock, gock, gock." The decoy emitted this call continually during the imprinting process. The duckling was allowed to remain in the apparatus for a specified amount of time while making a certain number of turns in the runway. At the end of the imprinting period, which was usually less than 1 hour, the duckling was automatically returned to its box and placed in an incubator until it was tested for imprinting strength at a later hour.

TESTING FOR IMPRINTING

Each duckling to be tested was mechanically released from its box halfway between two duck models placed 4 feet apart. One of these was the male mallard model upon which it had been imprinted; the other was a female model which differed from the male only in its coloration. One minute was allowed for the duckling to make a decisive response to the silent models. At the end of this time, regardless of the nature of the duckling's response, sound was turned on simultaneously for each of the models. The male model made the "gock" call upon which the duckling had been imprinted, while the female model gave the call of a real mallard female calling her young.

Four test conditions followed each other in immediate succession in the testing procedure. They were: (i) both models stationary and silent; (ii) both models stationary and calling; (iii) the male stationary and the female calling; (iv) the male stationary and silent and the female moving and calling. We estimated these four tests to be in order of increasing difficulty. The time of response and the character of the call note (pleasure tones or distress notes) were recorded. Scores in percentage of positive responses were then recorded for each animal. If the duckling gave a positive response to the imprinting object (the male decoy) in all four tests, imprinting was regarded as complete, or 100 percent.

Determination of the "Critical Period"

To determine the age at which an imprinting experience was most effective we imprinted our ducklings at various ages after hatching. In this series of experiments the imprinting experience was standard. It consisted in having the duckling follow the model 150 to 200 feet around the runway during a period

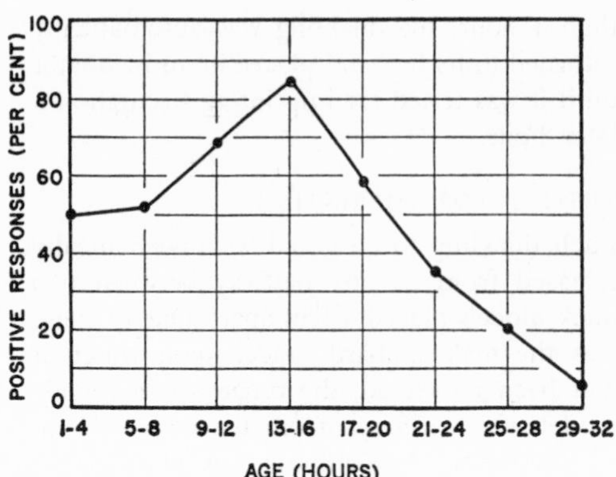

FIGURE 2

The critical age at which ducklings are most effectively imprinted is depicted by this curve, which shows the average test score of ducklings imprinted at each age group.

of 10 minutes. FIGURE 2 shows the scores made by ducklings in the different age groups. It appears that some imprinting occurs immediately after hatching, but a maximum score is consistently made only by those ducklings imprinted in the 13- to 16-hour-old group. This result is indicated in FIGURE 3, which shows the percentage of animals in each age group that made perfect imprinting scores.

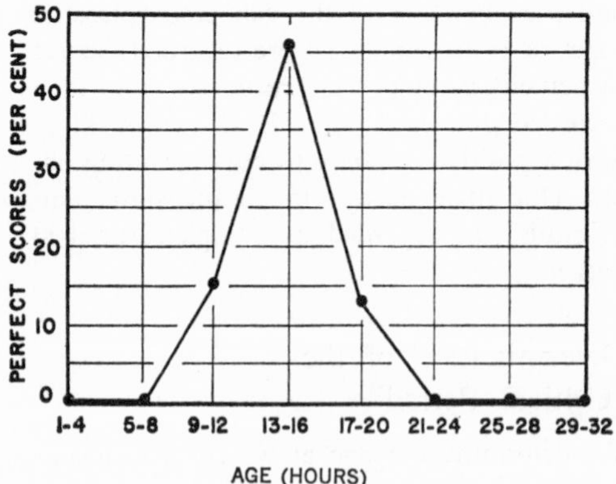

FIGURE 3

Another way of showing the critical age is by plotting the percentage of animals in each age group that made scores of 100 percent in testing.

SOCIAL FACILITATION IN IMPRINTING

In order to find whether imprinting would occur in those ducklings which were past the critical age for imprinting—that is, over 24 hours of age—we attempted to imprint these older ducklings in the presence of another duckling which had received an intensive imprinting experience. Ducklings ranging in age from 24 to 52 hours were given 100 feet of following experience during a period of 30 minutes. The average score for the ducklings was 50 percent; this shows that some imprinting can occur as a result of social facilitation. Two conclusions can be drawn. (i) Social facilitation will extend the critical age for imprinting. (ii) The strength of imprinting in these older ducklings is significantly less than that when the animal is imprinted alone at the critical age under the same time and distance conditions; under the latter circumstances the average score made is between 80 and 90 percent. A further indication of this dissipation of imprintability with increasing age is obtained when we average the scores for those animals which were between 24 and 32 hours old. The average score for these animals was 60 percent, while the score made by older animals ranging in age from 36 to 52 hours was 43 percent. One last item points to the difference; even when the time and distance were increased during imprinting of the older ducklings there were no perfect scores. With such a large amount of distance to travel during the imprinting period, approximately 40 percent of the animals would be expected to make perfect scores if they were imprinted during the critical period.

Field Tests of Imprinting

IN this same exploratory vein we have also carried out some studies under more normal environmental conditions. To do this we took animals imprinted in our apparatus and placed them in the duck-pond area, where they could either stay near a model placed at the water's edge or follow the model as it was moved along the surface of the duck pond, or go to real mallards which had just hatched their ducklings. Imprinted ducklings did not follow the live mallard females who had young of an age similar to that of the experimental animals. In fact, they avoided [them] and moved even closer to the decoy. Naive mallards, about a day old, from our incubator, immediately joined such live females and paid no attention to the decoys. These records, which we captured on motion-picture film, offer proof that what we do in the laboratory is quite relevant to the normal behavior of the animals and is not a laboratory artifact.

Color and Form Preferences in Imprinting Objects

AN examination of the importance of the form and color of an imprinting object is relevant to any inquiry concerning factors contributing to the strength of imprinting (Schaefer & Hess, 1959).

Eight spheres approximately 7 inches in diameter in the colors red, orange, yellow, green, and blue, and in achromatic shades of near-black, near-white, and neutral grey were presented to 95 young Vantress broiler chicks as imprinting objects. The imprinting procedure was essentially the same as that described above in the duckling experiments. All the animals were exposed to one of the spheres during the critical period. Each imprinting experience lasted for a total of 17 minutes, during which time the imprinting object moved a distance of 40 feet.

Twenty-four hours after imprinting, each animal was tested in a situation where the object to which it had been imprinted was presented, together with the remaining four colored spheres, if the animal had been imprinted to a colored sphere, or with the remaining two acromatic spheres, if the animal had been imprinted to one of the achromatic spheres.

It was found that the stimuli differed significantly in the degree to which they elicited the following-reaction. The stimuli, ranked in their effectiveness for eliciting following during imprinting, from the highest to the lowest, are: blue, red, green, orange, grey, black, yellow, white. These colors, in the same order, were increasingly less effective in terms of the scores made during the testing period. We concluded from this that the coloring of a stimulus is more important than its reflectance.

In order to determine also form preferences in imprinting objects, we took the same spheres we used in determining color preferences and added superstructures of the same coloring, so that the spheres had heads, wings, and tails (FIGURES 4 and 5).

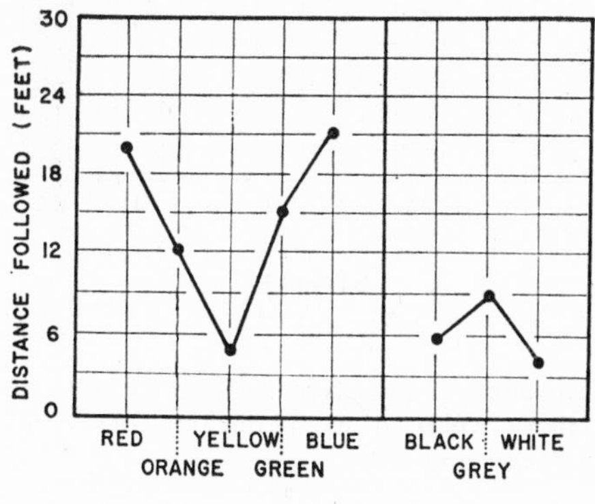

FIGURE 4

Mean distance, in feet, traveled in the course of following-response, by eight groups of animals, to eight different stimuli differing in color or reflectance.

The addition of superstructures had a definite effect on the ease with which the following-reaction could be elicited: the plain ball was found to be the most efficient; the ball with wing- and tail-like superstructures, less so; and the ball to which wings, tail, and head had been added, least efficient. We even presented a stuffed brown Leghorn rooster to the chicks, and it was found to be the least efficient model of all in eliciting the following-response.

Auditory Imprinting in the Egg

SOME investigators of imprinting have felt that vocalization of the incubating parent might cause imprinting to that vocalization even before the young fowl hatched. This

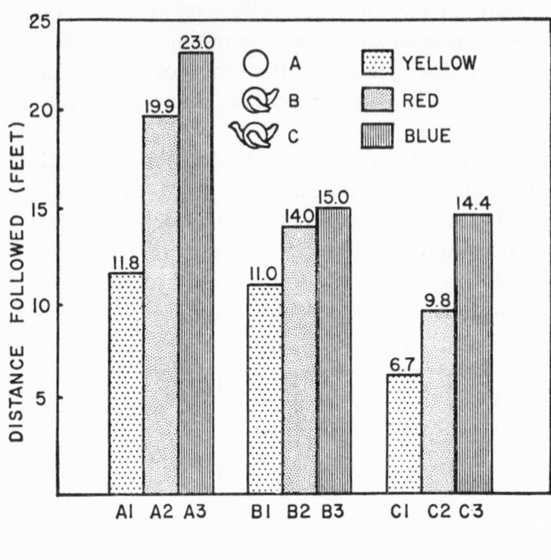

FIGURE 5

Effectiveness of models in eliciting the following-reaction, expressed as a function of stimulus complexity and color.

seemed a likely hypothesis, so we carried out the following experiment. About 30 mallard eggs were incubated in an incubator with a built-in loud-speaker. For 48 hours before hatching these mallards were exposed to a constantly played taped recording of a female mallard calling her young. Eggs were removed just before hatching and placed in a different incubator. Later, when tested, these young made no significantly greater choice of this source of sound than of the "gock" call used in our normal imprinting procedure. [A preliminary experiment was reported earlier (Ramsey & Hess, 1954).] Auditory imprinting, while the mallard is still in the egg, is therefore considered to be unlikely.

Law of Effort

WE decided to vary independently the factors of time of exposure and the actual distance traveled by the duckling during the imprinting period. Since previous results had indicated that a 10-minute exposure period was sufficient to produce testable results, we decided to run a series of animals, varying the distance traveled but keeping the time constant at 10 minutes. We therefore used one circumference of the runway (12½ feet) as a unit and ran groups of animals for zero, one, two, four, and eight turns. This resulted in imprinting experiences in which the ducklings moved about 1 foot, 12½ feet, 25 feet, 50 feet, and 100 feet, respectively. All ducklings were imprinted when they were between 12 and 17 hours of age, in order to keep the variable of critical period constant. The results showed that increasing the distance over which the duckling had to follow the imprinting object increased the strength of imprinting. A leveling-off of this effect appears to occur after a distance of about 50 feet. These results are shown in FIGURE 6.

In order to determine the effect of length of exposure time on imprinting strength, we chose a distance that could be traversed by ducklings in periods of time as short as 2, 10, and 30 minutes. The scores made by animals imprinted for 2, 10, and 30 minutes, respectively, while traveling a distance of 12½ feet were essentially identical. Moreover, there is no significant difference between the findings for ducklings allowed to follow for a distance of 100 feet during a 10-minute period and those allowed 30 minutes to cover the same distance. These results are shown in FIGURE 7.

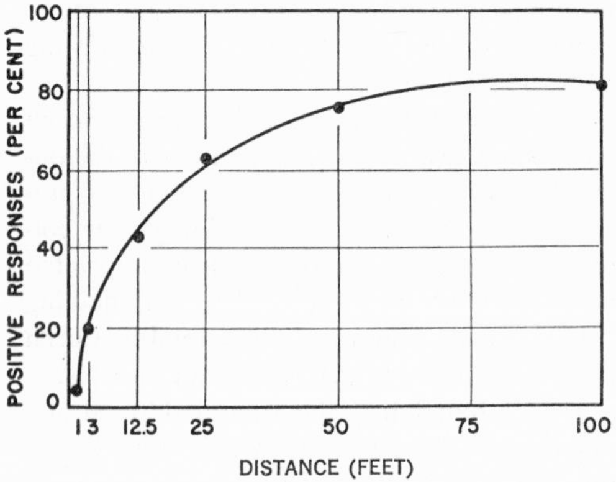

FIGURE 6

Strength of imprinting as a function of distance traveled by ducklings, with exposure time held constant.

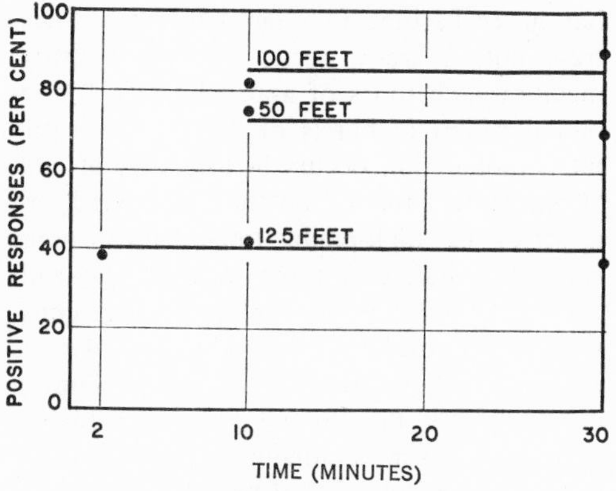

FIGURE 7

Strength of imprinting as a function of duration and exposure in minutes. Time had little effect on the test scores of the ducklings when the distance traveled was held constant.

The strength of imprinting appeared to be dependent not on the duration of the imprinting period but on the effort exerted by the duckling in following the imprinting object. To confirm this notion we tried two supplementary experiments (Hess, 1958). In the first, we placed 4-inch hurdles in the runway so that the ducklings not only had to follow the model but also had to clear the obstacles. As we suspected, the birds which had to climb the hurdles, and thus expend more effort, made higher imprinting scores than those which traveled the same distance without obstacles. In the second experiment we allowed the duckling to follow the decoy up an inclined plane, with similar results. After further experiments we came to the conclusion that we could write a formula for imprinting: the strength of imprinting equals the logarithm of the effort expended by the animal to get to the imprinting object during the imprinting period, or $I_s = \log E$.

Previous accounts in the literature on imprinting have made the following of a moving object a necessary condition of imprinting. Our results, as formulated in the law of effort, indicate that the amount of walking done by the animal during the imprinting period is of primary significance. The following experiment was therefore carried out. Two identical decoys were spaced 3 feet apart. A light over each decoy could be turned on and off so that only the model giving the "gock" call was illuminated in the darkened experimental apparatus, and the illumination was made to coincide with the call. When the duckling reached the lighted and calling model, the light and sound were turned off in that model and turned on in the other, which was 3 feet away. In this manner we could shuttle the animal back and forth and have it cover a distance similar to that used in the normal imprinting situation, where it walks behind a moving object.

Animals were run at four shuttles and 16 shuttles. The results show scores similar to those obtained previously for the 12½-foot and 50-foot distances (see FIGURE 6). They indicate, again, that imprinting strength is a function of the distance walked by the duckling, regardless of whether or not the more complex perception of *following* a moving object is involved.

Fear Behavior and Locomotory Ability

IN the light of the "critical period" results, the question arises as to what developmental changes might be taking place that would account for the limits of the critical period.

During the very early hours of their lives, animals show no fear. We conducted an experiment with 137 White Rock chicks of different ages (Hess, 1959) and found that there is no fear up to 13 to 16 hours after hatching. Afterwards, the proportion of animals from age group to age group begins gradually to increase up to the age of 33 to 36 hours, when all animals show fear. Fear responses will prevent an animal from engaging in the kind of social behavior necessary for imprinting to take place, since a fearful animal will avoid rather than follow a potential imprinting object.

On the other hand, fear behavior cannot account for the limitation of imprinting before the peak of maximum effectiveness. Since the strength of imprinting is dependent on locomotor activity, we postulated that the ability to move about might thus be an important factor. The ability to move about is a growth function and would limit the onset of the critical period. Hence, we tested 60 Vantress broiler chicks of White Rock stock of different ages to determine the development of increasing locomotor ability.

The two curves we obtained from these two experimental studies—one for increasing locomotor ability and one for increasing incidence of fear behavior with increasing age—were found to be in substantial agreement with the limits of the critical period. In fact, in plotting these two curves together, we obtained a hypothetical "critical period" for imprinting which strongly resembled the empirical one obtained for that breed.

It seems likely that all animals showing the phenomenon of imprinting will have a critical period which ends with the onset of fear. Thus, we can predict in a series of animals, knowing only the time of onset of fear, the end of imprintability for that species. Even in the human being one could thus theoretically place the end of maximum imprinting at about 5½ months, since observers have placed the onset of fear at about that time (Bridges, 1932; Spitz & Wolf, 1946).

Innate Behavior Patterns and Imprinting

MOST commonly the following-reaction to a certain model has been taken as a means of observing the progress of imprinting during the first exposure to the imprinting object and also as an indicator of the effectiveness of this exposure. However, the following-reaction is always accompanied by other innate behaviors which may also be observed and recorded. For the present purpose, the emission of "distress notes" or "contentment tones," maintenance of silence, and fixation of an object were checked for individual animals for a 2-minute period at the beginning of an imprinting session (Hess & Schaefer, 1959).

To differentiate between the "distress notes" and the "contentment tones" of chickens is comparatively easy, even for the layman who has never become familiar with them. "Distress notes" are a series of high-intensity, medium-pitch tones of approximately ¼-second duration in bursts of five to ten. Little pitch modulation occurs in this kind of call. "Contentment tones," on the other hand, are a series of high-pitch, low-intensity notes emitted in bursts of three to eight and with considerable pitch modulation during emission. The duration of the individual tones is much shorter, 1/12 of a second or less. During distress notes the animal usually holds its head high; during contentment tones it holds its head beak down. The designations *distress notes* and *contentment tones* are merely labels and should not necessarily be taken literally.

The subjects were 124 Vantress broiler chicks which had never experienced light until the time of the experiment. The experimental situation was much like the first 2 minutes of an imprinting experiment.

We found that the behavior of the animals changed markedly with age. The younger the animals were, the more pronounced was their striving to move under the cover of the nearby model. FIGURE 8 reflects the way in which this behavior diminished with age. FIGURE 9 shows that the proportion of animals fixating, or orienting toward, the model also diminished with increasing age. Although it was considerably more difficult for the younger

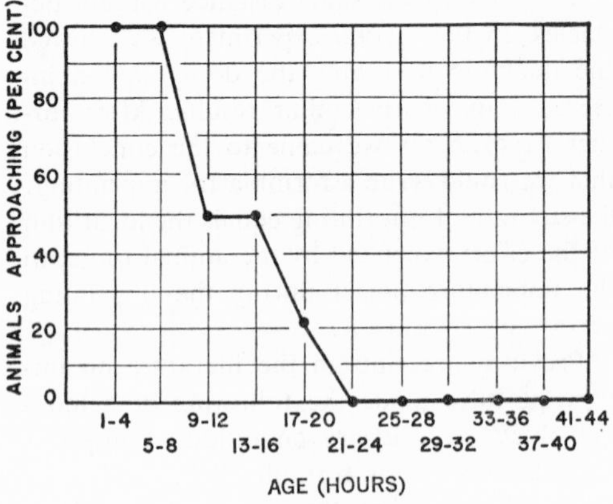

FIGURE 8

Percentage of 124 chicks that approached the stimulus objects at different ages.

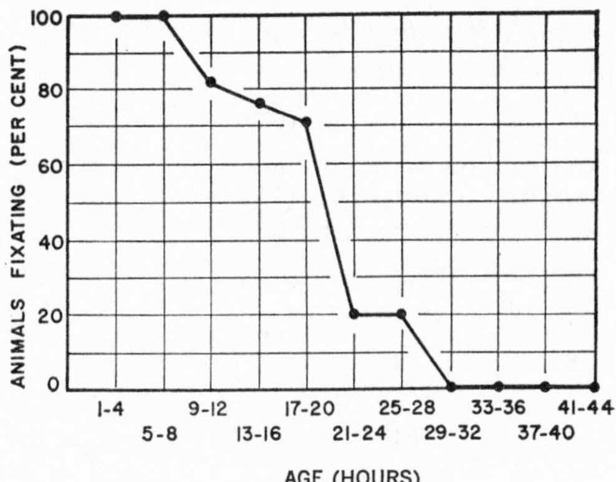

FIGURE 9

Percentage of 124 chicks that fixated the stimulus object at different ages.

animals to cover even the short distance between their original location and the model because of their poor locomotor ability, the time it took these younger animals to reach the model was much shorter than the time it took the older animals. However, the mode of locomotion for these younger animals was not walking but, rather, a kind of tumbling; they used both feet and wings as supports, and this left them exhausted after reaching the model a few inches away.

These results concerning behavior patterns during imprinting offer still further corroborating evidence for the location of the critical period as empirically determined. The emission of distress notes by animals older than 17 hours, even in the presence of an object that offers warmth and shelter, may be taken as an indication that a new phase of the animals' perception of their environment has set in. This behavior obstructs imprinting under the conditions of our laboratory arrangement. The high incidence of animals emitting contentment tones in the presence of the model is gradually replaced by an increasing number of animals emitting distress notes. No similar displacement occurs in animals remaining silent. The emission of contentment tones decreased as the animals became older, and the emission of distress notes increased at the same time.

The most important interpretation of these findings is that elicitation of following-behavior by various means after the critical period may not touch upon imprinting phenomena at all. Conventional training methods may be employed to overcome the fear response which the animals show after 17 hours, and it is not impossible to induce them, for example, to follow human beings. However, during the critical period, habituation or learning proper need not be considered as far as lowering of fear behavior is concerned, since at that time there is little or no fear present in the animals.

Drug Studies

THE rapid drop in imprinting, then, appears to be coupled with the developing emotional response of fear—a response that makes imprinting impossible. To examine this aspect of imprinting, reduction of the emotional response by means of a tranquilizing drug (Hess, 1957) seemed a logical step. Meprobamate was chosen because of evidence that it would reduce emotionality without markedly influencing motility or coordination. Preliminary experiments with dosages of meprobamate showed clearly that the emotionality of the ducklings was markedly reduced. In fact, the ducklings showed no fear of strange objects or persons, even though they were at an age where marked fear is normally a certainty.

To obtain the maximal information from this experiment, we then decided to test animals under the following four conditions: (i) drug at 12 hours of age, imprinting at 24 hours of age when the effect of the drug had worn off; (ii) drug at 12 hours of age, imprinting at 14 to 16 hours of age, test when the drug effect had worn off; (iii) imprinting at 16 hours, test under drug later; and (iv) drug at 24 hours, imprinting at 26 hours, test when the drug effect had worn off.

In general, the procedure for imprinting and testing was the same as that which has been described. Control animals were given distilled water, and chlorpromazine and Nembutal were used to obtain additional information. The results are shown in TABLE 1.

TABLE 1. *Percentage of positive responses made by ducklings under different conditions of testing and drug administration.*

CONDITIONS	CONTROL H_2O	MEPRO-BAMATE (25 MG/KG)	NEMBUTAL (5 MG/KG)	CHLOR-PROMAZINE (15 MG/KG)
Drug at 12 hr, imprinting at 24 hr	14	54	31	57
Drug at 12 hr, imprinting at 14–16 hr	62	8	28	63
Imprinting without drug at 16 hr, test under drug	61	65	61	58
Drug at 24 hr, imprinting at 26 hr	19	17	16	59

It is obvious that, while meprobamate reduces fear or emotional behavior, it also makes imprinting almost impossible. It does not, however, interfere with the effects of imprinting. This is clear from the results of test (iii). Chlorpromazine allows a high degree of imprinting under all conditions, whereas Nembutal reduces imprintability at all points except under the conditions of test (iii).

From the data, it appears that we might interpret the action of the drugs as follows. If we assume that meprobamate and chlorpromazine reduce metabolism, then we could expect the high imprinting scores found at 24 hours of age [test (i)], because metabolism had been slowed and we had thus stretched out the imprinting or sensitive period. This did not occur when we used Nembutal or distilled water. The second point deals with the reduction of emotionality. In test (iv) we had little evidence of emotionality in the meprobamate and the chlorpromazine groups. Emotionality did occur in the control and in the Nembutal group. Thus far, the only way we can interpret this former result is to consider the law of effort. Here we had found that the strength of imprinting was a function of effort or of distance traveled. It may be that, since meprobamate is a muscle relaxant, these effects of meprobamate cut into the muscular tension or other afferent consequences and thus nullify the effectiveness of the imprinting experience. Since, under the same circumstances, we attain perfectly good imprinting in all cases with chlorpromazine, this notion becomes even more tenable.[2]

Cerebral Lesions

IN addition to drug effects we also studied the results of cerebral lesions on the imprinting behavior of chicks. This was done partly because we had noticed a loss of the fear response in some chicks that had undergone operations—chicks which were old enough to have this response fully developed.

Chicks with a type 1 lesion showed good imprinting at the age of 3 days. This is considerably better than the finding for the control chicks, which only occasionally show this behavior so late in their first few days. Even with this lesion, chicks at 5 and at 7 days showed no imprinting.

Chicks with type 2 lesion showed no imprinting, although some that had been prepared earlier gave no evidence of fear reponses to strange objects.

Completely decerebrate animals were run only at 2 days of age, and they followed well, but the tests were inconclusive insofar as imprinting strength was concerned. Diagrams of the various lesions are shown in FIGURE 10.

Although the number of animals used in this study is still small, this seems to be a fruitful avenue of approach. Control ani-

2 Further studies are in progress following up this hypothesis.

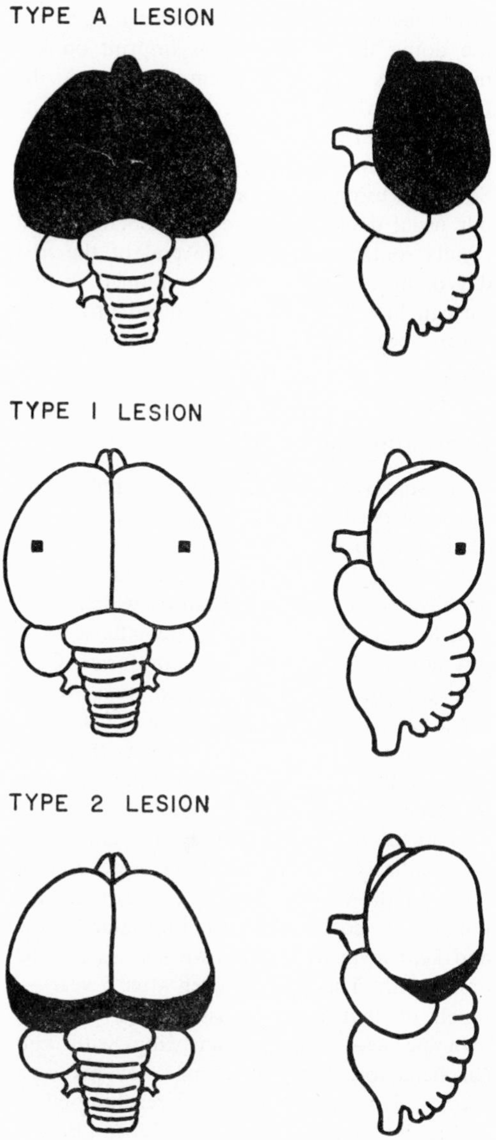

TYPE A LESION

TYPE 1 LESION

TYPE 2 LESION

FIGURE 10

Three types of lesions in the chick brain, used to study the effect of extirpation on imprintability.

mals that have had sham operations act essentially like normal chicks. Other experiments involving electrical stimulation are being undertaken, since such stimulation may reinforce imprinting behavior.

Genetic Studies

WE have also considered the genetic side of imprinting. We kept ducklings which were highly imprintable and bred them separately from ducklings which showed very little imprinting response. We thus had two groups of offspring, those produced by "imprinters" and those produced by "non-imprinters." There was a clear and significant difference in the imprinting behavior of the two groups, even in the first generation. The offspring of imprintable parents were easily imprinted; those of less imprintable parents were difficult to imprint. The "imprinter" ducklings had imprinting test scores more than three times better than those of the "non-imprinter" ducklings. Similar results were also obtained in a study of bantam chicks. We are also following up those animals which have had experimental imprinting experiences to determine what influence, if any, these experiences have on their behavior as adults. So far the results are inconclusive, but they do suggest that experimental imprinting of mallards affects their behavior as adults, particularly with respect to courtship patterns.

Birds of various species show differing degrees of imprintability. Domestic fowl do show imprinting responses, but the results are not as clear as for wild birds. We have had good success in imprinting some breeds of chicks, and the best imprinters among them are the Vantress broilers. Leghorns, on the other hand, appear to be too highly domesticated to give clear results. Other animals we have used in our experimentation are two kinds of geese, black ducks, wood ducks, turkeys, pheasants, quail, Peking ducks, and Rouens. The various breeds we have so far used in our work and the degree of imprintability found in each are shown in TABLE 2.

Imprinting in Mammals

THE guinea pig is similar to the chick and the duckling in that it is mobile and reasonably self-sufficient soon after birth. For this reason we used it in exploratory work. We first developed a method of obtaining the young

TABLE 2. *Number and imprintability of different experimental animals. Most of the animals were imprinted in runway and mallard decoy situations. Some of the Vantress broilers were imprinted on colored spheres, and the sheep were imprinted on human beings.*

ANIMAL	NO.*	IMPRINTABILITY †
Ducks		
Wild mallard	3500	E+
Domesticated mallard	150	E
Peking	200	G
Rouen	100	F
Wood	50	P
Black	50	G
Total	4050	
Geese		
Canada	30	E+
Pilgrim	50	G
Total	80	
Chickens		
Jungle fowl	100	G
Cochin bantam	300	G
New Hampshire Red	100	G
Rhode Island Red	100	G
Barred Rock	200	G
Vantress broiler	500	G+
White Rock	100	F
Leghorn	200	P
Total	1600	
Other Fowl		
Pheasant	100	P
Eastern bobwhite quail	50	G
California valley quail	20	E
Turkey	30	F
Total	200	
Mammals		
Sheep	2	G
Guinea pig	12	G
Total	14	
Total	5944	

* Estimated for fowl, actual for mammals.
† E, excellent; G, good; F, fair; P, poor.

from the mother with minimal parental contact. This was done by Caesarean section. However, further work showed that it was sufficient to obtain the young within an hour after they were born, and for the moment we are doing this. Guinea pigs imprint on human beings and follow them about as do the fowl with which we have been working. The maximum effectiveness of the imprinting experience seems to be over by the second day. So far, in using our imprinting apparatus with our usual duck decoy we have obtained best results sometime before the end of the first day of age. Work is being continued so that we can have a more standardized procedure before beginning a major program in this area.

Imprinting and Learning

THE supposed irreversibility of imprinting has been particularly singled out by some investigators to show that imprinting is nothing but "simple learning"—whatever that is. We do have some isolated instances which point to a long-range effect, but systematic work is just now beginning in our laboratories. Canada goslings, imprinted on human beings for a period of a week or two, will from that time on respond to their former caretaker with the typical "greeting ceremony," as well as accept food out of his hand. This occurs in spite of the fact that they normally associate entirely with the Canada geese on our duck pond. A more striking case is that of a jungle fowl cock which was imprinted by me and kept away from his own species for the first month. This animal, even after 5 years—much of that time in association with his own species—courts human beings with typical behavior, but not females of his own species. This certainly is a far-reaching effect and is similar to the finding of Räber (1948), who reported on a male turkey whose behavior toward human beings was similar. An increased amount of homosexual courtship in mallards has been observed with some of our laboratory imprinted animals, which, while not a statistically valuable finding, perhaps points also to long-range, irreversible effects.

Imprinting is currently receiving much attention, and papers on the subject are being published at an impressive rate. Unfortunately, most experimenters appear to be certain that imprinting is identical with simple association learning and design their experiments as studies in association learning. In many instances the animals are too old when used in the experiments to fall within the critical age for imprinting, with the result that only association learning can occur. Papers falling into this category are those of Jaynes (1956, 1957, 1958), Moltz & Rosenblum (1958), and James (1959).

Our own experiments on the relation between association learning with food as a reward and imprinting during the critical period show four distinct differences.

In the first place, learning a visual discrimination problem is quicker and more stable when practice trials are spaced by interspersing time periods between trials than when practice trials are massed by omitting such intervening time periods. With imprinting, however, massed practice is more effective than spaced practice, as shown by our law of effort. Secondly, *recency* in experience is maximally effective in learning a discrimination; in imprinting, *primacy* of experience is the maximally effective factor. The second difference is illustrated by the following experiment. Two groups of 11 ducklings each were imprinted on two different imprinting objects. Group 1 was first imprinted on a male mallard model and then on a female model. Group 2, on the other hand, was first imprinted on a female model and subsequently on a male model. Fourteen of the 22 ducklings, when tested with both models present, preferred the model to which they first had been imprinted, showing primacy. Only five preferred the model to which they had been imprinted last, showing recency, and three showed no preference at all.

In addition, it has been found that the administration of punishment or painful stimulation increases the effectiveness of the imprinting experience, whereas such aversive stimulation results in avoidance of the associated stimulus in the case of visual discrimination learning.

Finally, chicks and ducklings under the influence of meprobamate are able to learn a color discrimination problem just as well as, or better than, they normally do, whereas the administration of this drug reduces imprintability to almost zero.

Imprinting, then, is an obviously interesting phenomenon, and the proper way to approach it is to make no assumptions. To find out its characteristics, to explore its occurrence in different organisms, and to follow its effects would seem a worth-while program of study.

What can we say in conclusion about the general nature of imprinting? Our best guess to date is that it is a rigid form of learning, differing in several ways from the usual association learning which comes into play immediately after the peak of imprintability. In other words, imprinting in our experiments results in the animal learning the rough, generalized characteristics of the imprinting object. Its detailed appreciation of the *specific* object comes as a result of normal conditioning—a process which in the case of these animals takes a much longer time and is possible days after the critical period for imprinting has passed. It is an exciting new field and is certainly worthy of study.

REFERENCES

BAERENDS, G. P., & BAERENDS-VAN ROON, J. M. *Behaviour* (Suppl.), 1950, **1,** 1.

BRIDGES, K. M. B. *Child Develpm.,* 1932, **3,** 324.

CRAIG, W. *Amer. J. Sociol.,* 1908, **14,** 86.

DARLING, F. F. *Wild country.* London: Cambridge Univer. Press, 1938.

FABRICIUS, E. *Acta Zool. Fennica,* 1951, **68,** 1.

GRABOWSKI, U. *Z. Tierpsychol.,* 1941, **4,** 326.

HEDIGER, H. *Wild animals in captivity.* London: Butterworth, 1938.

HEINROTH, O. *Verhandl. 5th Int. Ornithol. Kong.,* 1910. Pp. 589–702.

HEINROTH, O., & HEINROTH, M. *Die Vögel Mitteleuropas.* Berlin: Lichterfelde, 1924–33.

HESS, E. H. *Ann. N.Y. Acad. Sci.,* 1957, **67,** 724.

HESS, E. H. *Scient. Amer.,* 1958, **198,** 81.

HESS, E. H. *J. comp. physiol. Psychol.*, in press.
HESS, E. H., & SCHAEFER, H. H. *Z. Tierpsychol.*, 1959, **16,** 155.
HINDE, R. A., THORPE, W. H., & VINCE, M. A., *Behaviour,* 1956, **9,** 214.
JAMES, H. *Canad. J. Psychol.*, in press.
JAYNES, J. *J. comp. physiol. Psychol.*, 1956, **49,** 201; *ibid.* 1957, **50,** 6; *ibid.* 1958, **51,** 234, 238.
LORENZ, K. *J. Ornithol.* 1935, **83,** 137, 289.
MOLTZ, H., & ROSENBLUM, L. A. *J. comp. physiol. Psychol.*, 1958, **51,** 580.
NICE, MARGARET M. *Condor,* 1953, **55,** 33.
RÄBER, H. *Behaviour,* 1948, **1,** 237.
RAMSAY, A. O. *Auk,* 1951, **68,** 1.
RAMSAY, A. O., & HESS, E. H. *Wilson Bull.*, 1954, **66,** 196.
SCHAEFER, H. H., & HESS, E. H. *Z. Tierpsychol.*, 1959, **16,** 161.
SPITZ, R. A., & WOLF, K. M. *Genet. Psychol. Monogr.*, 1946, No. 34, 57–125.
THORPE, W. H. *Proc. Linnean Soc. London,* 1944, **156,** 70.

ROBERT FANTZ

Pattern Vision in Newborn Infants*

It is usually stated or implied that the infant has little or no pattern vision during the early weeks or even months, because of the need for visual learning or because of the immature state of the eye and brain, or for both reasons.[1] This viewpoint has been challenged by the direct evidence of differential attention given to visual stimuli varying in form or pattern.[2] This evidence has shown that during the early months of life, infants: (i) have fairly acute pattern vision (resolving ⅛-inch stripes at a 10-inch distance); (ii) show greater visual interest in patterns than in plain colors; (iii) differentiate among patterns of similar complexity; and (iv) show visual interest in a pattern similar to that of a human face.

The purpose of the present study was to determine whether it was possible to obtain similar data on newborn infants and thus further exclude visual learning or postnatal maturation as requirements for pattern vision. It is a repetition of a study of older infants which compared the visual responsiveness to patterned and to plainly colored surfaces.[3] The results of the earlier study were essentially duplicated, giving further support for the above conclusions.

The subjects were 18 infants ranging from 10 hours to 5 days old. They were selected from a much larger number on the basis of their eyes remaining open long enough to be exposed to a series of six targets at least twice. The length of gaze at each target was observed through a tiny hole in the ceiling of the chamber and recorded on a timer. The fixation time started as soon as one or both eyes of the infant were directed towards the target, using as criterion the superposition over the pupil of a tiny corneal reflection of the target; it ended when the eyes turned away or closed.[4] The six targets were presented in random order for each infant, with the sequence repeated up to eight times when possible. Only completed sequences were included in calculating the percentage of total fixation time for each target.

The targets were circular, 6 inches in diameter, and had nonglossy surfaces. Three contained black-and-white patterns—a schematic face, concentric circles, and a section of newspaper containing print $\frac{1}{16}$ to ¼ inch high. The other three were unpatterned—white, fluorescent yellow, and dark red. The relative luminous reflectance was, in decreasing order: yellow, white, newsprint, face and circles, red. Squares containing the patterns or colors were placed in a flat holder which slid horizontally into a slightly recessed portion of the chamber ceiling to expose the pattern or color to the infant through a circular hole in the holder. The chamber and underside of the holder were lined with blue felt to provide a contrasting background for the stimuli, and to diffuse the illumination (between 10

1 See, for example: Dewey, Evelyn. *Behavior development in infants.* New York: Columbia Univer. Press, 1935; Pratt, K. C., in L. Carmichael (Ed.), *Manual of child psychology.* New York: Wiley, 1954; Spock, B. *Baby and child care.* New York: Pocket Books, 1957.

2 Fantz, R. L., Ordy, J. M., & Udelf, M. S. *J. comp. physiol. Psychol.,* 1962, **55,** 907; Fantz, R. L. *Psychol. Rec.,* 1958, **8,** 43.

3 Fantz, R. L. *Scient. Amer.,* 1961, **204,** 66.

4 High reliability of a similar technique, using the same criterion of fixation, was shown with older infants (see Footnote 1). Since eye movements are less coordinated and fixations less clear-cut in newborn infants, a further check of the response measurement is desirable; I plan to do this by photographic recordings.

TABLE 1. *Relative duration of initial gaze of infants at six stimulus objects in successive and repeated presentations*

AGE GROUP	N	MEAN PERCENTAGE OF FIXATION TIME						P *
		Face	*Circles*	*News*	*White*	*Yellow*	*Red*	
Under 48 hours	8	29.5	23.5	13.1	12.3	11.5	10.1	.005
2 to 5 days	10	29.5	24.3	17.5	9.9	12.1	6.7	.001
2 to 6 months †	25	34.3	18.4	19.9	8.9	8.2	10.1	.001

* Significance level based on Friedman analysis of variance by ranks.
† From an earlier study (see Footnote 2).

and 15 ft-ca) from lights on either side of the infant's head. The subject was in a small hammock crib with head facing up directly under the targets, 1 foot away.

The results in TABLE 1 show about twice as much visual attention to patterns as to plainly colored surfaces. Differences in response to the six stimulus objects are significant for the infants both under and over 2 days of age; results from these groups do not differ reliably from each other, and are similar to earlier results from much older infants. The selectivity of the visual responses is brought out still more strikingly by tabulating the longest-fixated target for each newborn infant: 11 for face, 5 for concentric circles, 2 for newsprint, and 0 for white, yellow, and red. For comparison, the first choices of infants 2 to 6 months were distributed as follows: 16, 4, 5, 0, 0, 0.

Three infants under 24 hours could be tested sufficiently to indicate the individual consistency of response. Two of these showed a significant (.005 and .05) difference among the targets in successive sets of exposures, one looking longest at the face pattern in 7 of 8 exposures, the other looking longest at the "bull's-eye" in 3 of 6 exposures. The third infant 10 hours after birth looked longest at the face in 3 of 8 exposures.

It is clear that the selective visual responses were related to pattern rather than hue or reflectance, although the latter two variables are often thought to be primary visual stimuli. Specification of the prepotent configurational variables is unwarranted at this time. The results do not imply "instinctive recognition" of a face or other unique significance of this pattern; it is likely there are other patterns which would elicit equal or greater attention.[5] Longer fixation of the face suggests only that a pattern with certain similarities to social objects also has stimulus characteristics with considerable intrinsic interest or stimulating value; whatever the mechanism underlying this interest, it should facilitate the development of social responsiveness, since what is responded to must first be attended to.

Substantiation for the visual selection of patterned over unpatterned objects is given in an independent study of newborn infants in which more visual attention was given to a colored card with a simple figure, when held close to the infant, than to a plain card of either color.[6]

The results of TABLE 1 demonstrate that pattern vision can be tested in newborn infants by recording differential visual attention; these and other results call for a revision of traditional views that the visual world of the infant is initially formless or chaotic and that we must learn to see configurations.

5 I chose the targets for their expected attention value for the older infants of the earlier study; this may be different for newborn subjects: response to the newsprint may be decreased by less acute vision (although some patterning would be visible without resolution of individual letters); "bull's eye" elicited strong differential attention only over 2 months of age in another study (see Footnote 3); and blue is preferred to red and yellow by newborns. The face pattern might for these reasons have a relative advantage for newborns.

6 Stirnimann, F. *Ann. Paediat.*, 1944, 163, 1.

PART II

Early Experiences and Later Development

PART II continues the examination of the process of child development within the organism-environment-interaction framework. It takes the child beyond the infancy period, to consider the impact of experiences both in infancy and early childhood upon later development.

That early experiences do have a very important impact upon later development is a generalization widely accepted during the last two decades. In that period of time, there has been considerable success in spelling out the variables in infant experience that might conceivably alter development and the direction that alteration might take. We now know a great deal more than we did about what conditions affect later development and about how social relationships and intellective processes are affected by what happens to the child in his early years.

One of the basic variables affecting later development is the amount of stimulation the infant organism receives. Unless stimulation is adequate, organisms will not develop normally. Infant animals reared in isolation and deprived of the opportunity to interact with the world show mental deficiency and behavior disorders later in life as a result of inadequate stimulation. A study by Thompson and Melzack (1956) showed that dogs reared in families and subjected to the barrage of stimulating experiences available in such an environment evidenced normal responses to test situations later in life, in sharp contrast to their littermates reared in separate cages and deprived of stimulation. Restricted animals, kept in darkness and without contact with other living things (even the caretaker), were deficient in problem-solving ability and were slower to develop normal emotional responses to strange phenomena.

Included here is a paper by Levine which emphasizes that there are positive effects even from noxious stimulation. This experimenter discovered that administering electric shock to rats in infancy did not begin to have such adverse effects upon later behaviors as was evidenced in rearing a control group without any handling whatsoever. In fact, rats shocked in infancy were able to handle stressful situations later in life, whereas the nonmanipulated animals evidenced abnormal behaviors. Levine explains his findings in terms of organism-environment interaction; handling and stress apparently stimulate certain physiological processes that hasten the maturation of the central nervous system, thereby resulting in a more rapid rate of development.

The *quality* of infant experience as a variable affecting later development has also received attention in the literature. Does it make a difference if the infant animal has one type of stimulating experience rather than another? The next paper, by Forgus, sheds some light on this interesting question. Readers who think of themselves as better able to learn through one sensory channel than another, as "visual-minded" or "auditory-minded," will be especially interested in this investigation of the influence of early visual and motor experience upon maze-learning ability in adult rats. Whether or not a particular kind of early experience has an impact apparently depends, at least in part, upon the demands of the problem-solving task.

The first papers in this section report on research using animal subjects to investigate the effects of early experiences. The question is inevitably raised as to whether the findings from animal experimentation are applicable to human beings. However, as Levine points out, the effects of early experiences have been studied in a variety of animals, including many mammals. There are also available some studies using human subjects. These investigations, of course, have to use already existing situations. Where infants have been discovered being reared under adverse circumstances, such as foundling homes, it has been possible to contrast their development with that of infants being raised in more favorable circumstances.

During the nineteen thirties and forties published papers consistently reported that babies reared in psychologically inadequate institutions suffered serious defects in both the cognitive and emotional aspects of development. The reader is undoubtedly familiar with the research of René Spitz (1945, 1946), who contrasted the development of infants living in a foundling home with those reared in a prison nursery. While physical care was excellent in the foundling home, babies were kept in curtained cribs with no opportunity to establish warm contact with an adult human being. Infants living in the prison nursery, on the other hand, spent some time each day with their mothers, receiving considerable affection and care. The reader will recall that Spitz found that infants in the foundling home suffered severe emotional upsets, to the point where an infant occasionally went into a state of "anaclitic depression," characterized by mourning, negative emotions, inability to act, and actual physical deterioration. Eventually, loss of appetite and sleep tended to make the infant susceptible to disease, which even resulted in an occasional premature death.

It was Spitz's belief that lack of mother-love was the adverse factor in institution care; to him, the mother-child relationship was so important that an infant might languish and die without it. Other writers, notably Bowlby, have emphasized the importance of the continuous presence of the mother, particularly in early childhood, for satisfactory emotional adjustment. Bowlby (1952) reviewed the literature on maternal deprivation, a condition which he defined as existing when a young child is deprived of its mother for an extended period of time. Such deprivation might result from hospitalization of either mother or child, death of the mother, divorce, or even a prolonged visit by the mother outside the home. The time-span roughly from six months of age to four years was deemed the most critical. Deprivation of the mother during this time, as would be true in the case of institutionalized children, resulted in a typical pattern of behavior that included lying, stealing, inability to relate to others, and a curious lack of emotional response to situations where such a response would be normal.

More recently, however, research by Bowlby and others has resulted in some modification of these views regarding the effects of deprivation. In a study (1956) of sixty children, aged seven to thirteen years, who, as tubercular patients, had been separated from their parents before the age of four, it was found that the contrast between "deprived" children and a control group was not as great as had been anticipated. Bowlby concluded that: ". . . Statements implying that children who experience institutionalization and similar forms of severe . . . deprivation in early life *commonly* develop psychopathic or affectionless characters are incorrect."

Support for the position that children reared in psychologically inadequate institutions do not fare, as a rule, as well as children in foster homes is brought out in the Goldfarb paper reprinted here. Goldfarb describes the child brought up under conditions of psychological privation as flighty, craving affection yet having little capacity for love, hyperactive and undirected, and having a marked inability to form concepts or to think abstractly.

While "psychologically inadequate" was originally defined in terms of maternal deprivation, the term has been more recently defined in terms of lack of stimulation. In other words, institution care may be bad, not because the mother is missing, but because busy caretakers cannot supply enough stimulating experiences. However, the amount of stimulation as a variable may encompass too much ground to be meaningful. As the fourth paper shows, Rheingold and Bayley found the level of stimulation in institutions at least adequate to develop and maintain interest and skills in infants of three months. Their paper demonstrates the need to study the dimensions of early experiences in a highly specific manner under controlled conditions.

From the Dennis paper included here we begin to get some clues as to specific variables in handling institution children that result in retardation and faulty development. Dennis used as his sample Iranian children reared in institutions. He contrasted the development of infants brought up in three types of institutions, which differed mainly in the number of infants assigned to a particular caretaker and in the kind of stimulation available to the babies. He attributed the extreme motor retardation of the babies in the first two institutions to the restriction of specific kinds of learning opportunities. If a baby is to walk at the normal age, he must have opportunities for such experiences as lying prone on a firm surface (rather than on a soft mattress) to encourage head-raising and other movements, and being propped up before he can sit up by himself; maturation alone does not suffice. It is the interaction between the child and his environment that helps to develop his nervous system and prepares him for more advanced behaviors.

The age at which certain experiences or deprivations occur is also being studied as a variable. In one study, the age of separation of kittens from their mothers appeared to be significant. Seitz (1959) found that kittens separated from their mothers at two weeks of age were more disturbed by intense stimulation and more fearful and aggressive than a second group separated at weaning age and a third group separated at twelve weeks of age. Seitz discussed the findings in terms of a need for physical closeness and contact, which, when not satisfied, can lead to lack of "confidence" in the adult animal. He also pointed out that the kittens separated at two weeks of age had an early "expectancy of danger" and "readiness for action."

We might hypothesize, on the basis of the Seitz findings, that kittens left longer with their mothers are exposed to more stimuli than are other kittens and thus that they have a chance to learn to discriminate what is truly dangerous. Like Levine's rats, these kittens would be subjected to a variety of stresses and to more handling than the early separated kittens; these interactions could conceivably lead to the development of effective ways of dealing with stress. A kitten under its mother's care might learn to accept certain noxious stimuli, such as a sharp clout from the mother's paw, knowing that disaster would not ensue from the blow. Kittens separated very early from their mothers and not provided with suitable mother-substitutes would be deprived of such opportunities to learn.

The papers included here on maternal deprivation and institutionalization represent the various hypotheses that have been explored by investigators. For a thorough review of the research on these factors, the reader is referred to the monograph by Casler (1961), too lengthy to be reprinted here. Casler's summary of his findings is comparable with the conclusions reached in this book.

> 1. Emotional, physical, and intellectual malfunctioning is known to occur with frequency among children in many institutions.
>
> 2. Some authors have alleged that this malfunctioning is attributable to the deprivation of maternal love.
>
> 3. It is more likely, however, that deprivation of maternal love can have ill effects only after specific affective responsiveness has been achieved by the child (usually at about the age of six months). Ill effects found in children maternally deprived before this age probably have some other cause.
>
> 4. Evidence is accumulating, both on the human and the animal level, that this "other cause" is perceptual deprivation—the absolute or relative absence of tactile, vestibular, and other forms of stimulation.
>
> 5. Those forms of social stimulation necessary for proper language development, etc., can be provided within an institutional setting.
>
> 6. Recent neuroanatomical findings, especially those concerning the reticular formation, help to explain why perceptual stimulation is so important for normal development [p. 49].

The papers mentioned so far are empirical in nature; they present experimental evidence on the effects of early experiences and explore such variables as timing and quality of experiences. The remaining papers deal with the theory of how early experiences might conceivably affect later development. Two schools are represented, that of learning theory, and that of Freudian theory.

Investigators working today within the framework of learning theory have rejected the early S-R approach, which held that a response appeared *directly* after the presentation of a stimulus and that the response was directly under the control of the stimulus. Instead, there is agreement for the most part on the existence of central processes that mediate responses. A frequently used model to explain cortical activity is that of the electronic computer. Just as a computer stores programs, so does the brain store strategies for information-processing that have been built up as a result of experiences. When a stimulus reaches the brain, a search is made among the strategies to find one that is congruent with the input. Where an incongruity appears, it must be resolved before output can be effected.

According to Hebb (1949), the mediating process occurs in a "cell-assembly," a group of neurons arranged as a set of closed pathways. These cell-assemblies store information from sensory inputs. Connections are made between assemblies that are repeatedly active at the same time. Sensory stimulation may fire one or more assemblies, with fresh combinations always possible. A particular behavior, then, is not seen as a fixed response to a particular stimulation, but is the result of a series of assembly activities.

The theory that central or mediating processes draw upon information stored in the cortex as a result of early experiences helps to explain why early experiences can have such an impact upon later development. Learning theorists, however, are not unique in emphasizing the significance of early experiences; Freudian psychologists have long made this one of their major tenets. But Freudians, as the reader well knows, have a different view of how the child will be affected. They see the process of development as biological, occurring in fixed stages; at each stage the child's energy is directed toward a love object and his satisfaction is attained through a particular organ of his body. At one of these stages the Oedipus complex occurs. The love-energy of the boy is directed toward his mother; at the same time he experiences guilt over masturbation. Castration-fears result and the dilemma must be resolved through the process of identification. As the boy identifies with his father, he can possess his mother.

The term "identification," however, has several meanings, even in the work of Freud himself. The Bronfenbrenner paper included here performs a very useful service to students of child development by critically examining the theory of identification both as it appears in Freud's own work and in later modifications.

The Freud and Dann paper discusses in Freudian terms the impact of some tragic early experiences on a group of young displaced children who, during and after World War II, had been buffeted about from refugee camp to refugee camp before being transported to a treatment home in England. The authors examine what happens to the developmental process in a situation where children are raised without parents, but with a long and continuous association with age-mates. While the set of early experiences described in the paper is, fortunately, unique, the authors help us to understand how a Freudian would explain the effects of these early experiences on child development.

REFERENCES

BOWLBY, J. *Maternal care and mental health.* Geneva: World Health Organization, 1952. (Monograph Series, No. 2.)

BOWLBY, J., AINSWORTH, MARY, BOSTON, MARY, & ROSENBLUTH, DINA. The effects of mother-child separation: a follow-up study. *Brit. J. med. Psychol.*, 1956, **29**, 211–244.

CASLER, L. Maternal deprivation: a critical review of the literature. *Monogr. Soc. Res. Child Develpm.*, 1961, **26**, No. 2.

HEBB, D. O. *The organization of behavior.* New York: Wiley, 1949.

SEITZ, P. F. D. Infantile experience and adult behavior in animal subjects: II. Age of separation from the mother and adult behavior in the cat. *Psychosom. Med.*, 1959, **21**, 353–378.

SPITZ, R. A. Hospitalism: an inquiry into the genesis of psychiatric conditions in early childhood. In Ruth S. Eissler *et al.* (Eds.), *The psychoanalytic study of the child.* Vol. 1. New York: International Universities Press, 1945. Pp. 53–74.

SPITZ, R. A. Hospitalism: a follow-up report on investigations described in Vol. 1, 1945. In Ruth S. Eissler *et al.* (Eds.), *The psychoanalytic study of the child.* Vol. 2. New York: International Universities Press, 1946. Pp. 113–117.

THOMPSON, W. R., & MELZACK, R. Early environment: with biographical sketches. *Scient. Amer.*, 1956, **194**, 20–21; 38–42.

SEYMOUR LEVINE

*Stimulation in Infancy**

WHEN the Emperor of Lilliput accepted Lemuel Gulliver into favor, His Most Sublime Majesty first secured Gulliver's solemn oath upon an agreement to observe certain rules of etiquette. The fourth article of the agreement stipulated that Gulliver should not take any Lilliputian subjects into his hands without their consent. Gulliver learned later to appreciate the sentiments behind this article in an intensely subjective way. In the country of Brobdingnag he was himself picked up in the huge hand of a Brobdingnagian. He recalled his reactions: "All I ventured was to raise my eyes towards the sun, and place my hands together in a supplicating posture, and to speak some words in an humble melancholy tone, suitable to the condition I then was in."

What Jonathan Swift describes here is the essence of an experience that befalls children and small animals every day. It happens whenever a parent picks up a baby, or a child tussles with his puppy. Almost all experiences of infancy involve some handling by a parent or some other larger and supremely powerful figure. Even the tenderest handling must at times be the occasion of emotional stress. Perhaps the only children insulated from such experience are those reared in orphanages and other institutions, and the only animals those that live in laboratories. Certainly the laboratory animal must find a minimum of stress and little stimulation of any other kind in an environment controlled for temperature, humidity, light and so on. In the ordinary world the infant must grow under the changing pressures and sudden challenges of an inconstant environment. One may well wonder how the stressful experiences of infancy affect the behavior and physiology of the adult organism later on.

When in 1954 we began our investigations into the broad area defined by this question, we naturally turned first to the presumably more obvious effects of early painful or traumatic experience. We subjected a group of infant rats to mild electric shocks, scheduled at the same hour each day. For control purposes we routinely placed the members of another group in the shock cage for the same length of time each day but did not give them shocks. A third group of infant rats was left in the nest and not handled at all. We expected that the shocked rats would be affected by their experience, and we looked for signs of emotional disorder when they reached adulthood. To our surprise it was the second control group—the rats we had not handled at all—that behaved in a peculiar manner. The behavior of the shocked rats could not be distinguished from that of the control group which had experienced the same handling but no electric shock. Thus the results of our first experiment caused us to reframe our question. Our investigation at the Columbus Psychiatric Institute and Hospital of Ohio State University has since been concerned not so much with the effects of stressful experience—which after all is the more usual experience of infants—as with the effects of the absence of such experience in infancy.

We have repeated our original experiment many times, subjecting the infant animals to a variety of stresses and degrees of handling. Invariably it is the nonmanipulated "controls" that exhibit deviations of behavior and physiology when they are tested as adults. Signif-

* REPRINTED by permission of the author from *Scient. Amer.*, 1960, 202, 80–86. Reprinted with permision.

icantly these deviations involve the organism's response to stress, and they show up in most of the diverse aspects of that response. In a standard behavioral test, for example, the animal is placed in the unfamiliar, but otherwise neutral, surroundings of a transparent plastic box. The nonmanipulated animals crouch in a corner of the box; animals that have been handled and subjected to stress in infancy freely explore the space. The same contrast in behavior may be observed and recorded quantitatively in the "open field": an area three feet square marked off into smaller squares. In terms of the number of squares crossed during a fixed time period, shocked and manipulated animals show a much greater willingness to run about and explore their surroundings. In both situations the nonmanipulated animals, cowering in a corner or creeping timidly about, tend to defecate and urinate frequently. Since these functions are largely controlled by the sympathetic nervous system, and since certain responses to stress are principally organized around the sympathetic nervous system, this behavior is a sure sign of reactivity to stress.

Another objective and quantitative index of stress response is provided by the hormones and glands of the endocrine system. Under stress, in response to prompting by the central nervous system, the pituitary releases larger quantities of various hormones, one of the principal ones being the adrenal-cortico-trophic hormone (ACTH). Stimulation by ACTH causes the outer layer, or cortex, of the adrenal gland to step up the release of its several steroids; distributed by the bloodstream, these hormones accelerate the metabolism of the tissues in such a way as to maintain their integrity under stress. The activity of the endocrine system may be measured conveniently in a number of ways: by the enlargement of the adrenal glands, by the volume of adrenal steroids in circulation or by the depletion of ascorbic acid (vitamin C) in the adrenals. By some of these measurements the nonstimulated animals showed a markedly higher reactivity when subjected to a variety of stresses, including toxic injection of glucose, conditioning to avoid a painful stimulus and swimming in a water maze.

The conclusion that these animals are hyperactive to stress is, however, an oversimplification that conceals an even more important difference in their stress response. Recently we measured the steroids in circulation in both stimulated and nonstimulated animals during the period immediately following stress by electric shock. Whereas the two groups showed the same volume of steroids in circulation before shock, the animals that had been exposed to stress in infancy showed a much higher output of steroids in the first 15 minutes after shock. The nonstimulated animals achieve the same output but more slowly, and appear to maintain a high level of steroid secretion for a longer period of time. There is thus a distinct difference in the pattern of the stress response in the two kinds of animal.

This observation acquires its full significance when it is considered in the light of the biological function of the stress response. The speed and short duration of the response in the stimulated animal obviously serve the useful purpose of mobilizing the resources of the organism at the moment when it is under stress. The delay in the endocrine response of the nonstimulated animal is thus, by contrast, maladaptive. Moreover, the prolongation of the stress response, as observed in these animals, can have severely damaging consequences: stomach ulcers, increased susceptibility to infection and eventually death due to adrenal exhaustion.

The maladaptive nature of the stress response in the nonmanipulated animal is further manifested in the fact that it may be elicited in such a neutral situation as the open-field test. The animal that has been manipulated in infancy shows no physiological stress response in this situation although it exhibits a vigorous and immediate endocrine response when challenged by the pain and threat of an electric shock.

In this connection we have made the interesting discovery that stimulation by handling and stress hastens the maturation of the stress response in the infant animal. Although the adrenal glands begin to function shortly after birth and the pituitary appears to contain ACTH early in the course of development, the nerve mechanism that controls the release of ACTH does not seem to come into operation until the rat is about 16 days of age. When we exposed infant rats that had been handled from birth to severe cold stress, however, they showed a significant ACTH response as early as 12 days of age. This four days' difference represents a considerable acceleration of development in the rat, equivalent to several months in the growth of a human infant. The manipulated animals, moreover, reached an adult level of response considerably earlier than their untreated litter mates.

From the evidence it may be inferred that stimulation must have accelerated the maturation of the central nervous system in these animals. We have direct evidence that this is so from analysis of the brain tissue of our subjects. The brains of infant rats that have been handled from birth show a distinctly higher cholesterol content. Since the cholesterol content of the brain is related principally to the brain's white matter, this is evidence that in these animals the maturation of structure parallels the maturation of function.

In all respects, in fact, the manipulated infants exhibit a more rapid rate of development. They open their eyes earlier and achieve motor coordination sooner. Their body hair grows faster, and they tend to be significantly heavier at weaning. They continue to gain weight more rapidly than the

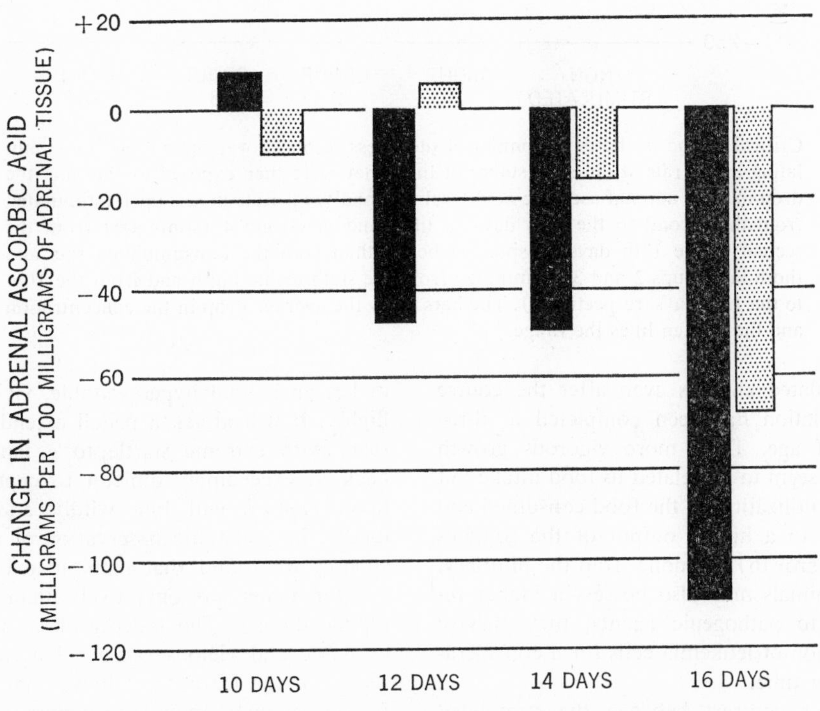

Exposure to cold produced a marked drop in the ascorbic acid (vitamin C) concentration in the adrenal glands of stimulated rats more than 10 days old (black bars), but produced no significant effect on the nonstimulated rats until they were 16 days old.

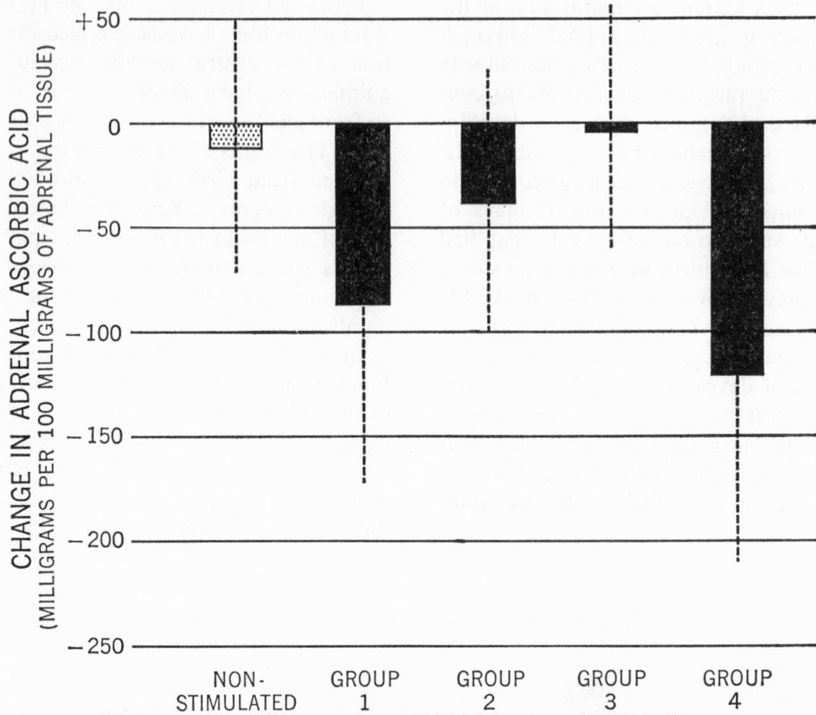

Critical period in the development of the stress response was determined by stimulating infant rats at different stages of life. They were then exposed to cold and the drop in their adrenal ascorbic acid level was analyzed. Rats in Group 1 (stimulated from the second to the fifth days of life) and in Group 4 (stimulated from the second to the 13th days) responded better than both the nonstimulated rats and those in Groups 2 and 3 (stimulated from the sixth to the ninth and from the 10th to the 13th days, respectively). The bars show the average drop in the concentration and the broken lines the range.

nonstimulated animals even after the course of stimulation has been completed at three weeks of age. Their more vigorous growth does not seem to be related to food intake but to better utilization of the food consumed and probably to a higher output of the somatotrophic (growth) hormone from the pituitary. These animals may also possess a higher resistance to pathogenic agents; they survive an injection of leukemia cells for a considerably longer time.

Another contrast between the stimulated and unstimulated animals developed when we electrically destroyed the septal region of their brains, the region between and under the hemispheres of the midbrain. Such damage makes an animal hyperexcitable, vicious and flighty. It will attack a pencil extended to it, react with extreme startle to a tap on the back, is exceedingly difficult to capture and upon capture will bite wildly and squeal loudly. In systematic observation of these responses we found that manipulated animals are far tamer postoperatively than nonmanipulated ones. The latter rank as the most excitable and vicious rats we have ever observed in the laboratory; it was not unusual for one of these animals to pursue us around the room, squealing and attacking our shoes and pants legs.

At the very least our experiments yield an additional explanation for the variability among laboratory animals that so often confuses results in experimental biology. This has been attributed to genetic differences, unknown factors and sometimes to experimental error. It is apparent that the character of early infant experience is another important determinant of individual differences in animals.

The same consideration leads to the broader question of "nature *v.* nurture," that is, the contribution of genetic factors as opposed to the influence of the environment. Both sets of factors are essential and they interact to give rise to the individual organism. The basic patterns of development are most likely determined by heredity. But the genetic determinants do not find expression except in interaction with various aspects of the environment. In the normal course of events the environment provides the substance, energy and milieu for the unfolding of the organism's potentialities; in the extreme, environmental influences can determine whether the process of development will continue and produce an organism. In other words, organisms do not grow in a vacuum. This is true even of our nontreated animals: litter mates and the routine laboratory procedures furnish stimulation of all kinds. Such stimulation does not compare, however, with that provided by our experimental treatments. We have dealt with only a limited range of effects, and have focused primarily on the physiological and behavioral responses to stress. But our results clearly indicate that stimulation of the infant organism has quite universal consequences

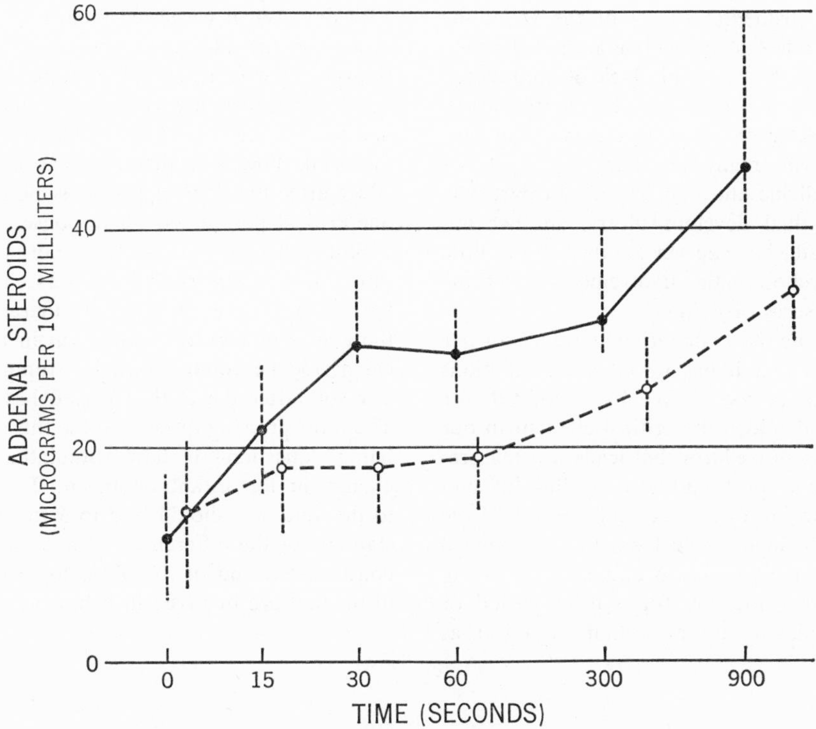

Sluggish response to an electric shock is indicated by the slow rise in the concentration of circulating steroid hormones in previously nonstimulated rats (broken line). In the stimulated animals (solid line) the level increases rapidly for about 15 minutes. The points on the curve indicate the average level and the vertical broken lines the range of values.

upon the behavior and physiology of the adult.

One must be careful in attempting to bridge the gap between animal experimentation and human biology. The effects of early experience have proved to be significant, however, in many species of mammal, including the monkey, dog, cat, guinea pig and mouse, and in such nonmammals as fish and fowl. It cannot be said that the phenomenon is species-limited. A great deal of clinical evidence, moreover, clearly indicates that infant experience in humans has a profound effect in shaping the character and constitution of the adult. Investigators concerned with maternal deprivation report that children raised in foundling homes develop at a retarded rate and are more susceptible to disease. These observations are similar to those we have made in our animal experiments. It may be that the detrimental effects of the foundling home have less to do with maternal deprivation than with the simple lack of stimulation that is inevitable in most such environments. The character of early experience may thus also underlie many problems in psychosomatic medicine and may explain in part why one individual develops ulcers, another migraine headaches and yet another shows little or no psychosomatic involvement under the same pressures of living.

One of the most encouraging aspects of our research is that it has raised more questions than it has answered. We have not yet, for example, identified the critical element in our stimulation procedures that leads to such predictable and profound effects. Painful and extreme forms of stimulation seem to have effects indistinguishable from those produced by merely picking up an animal and placing it in another location for a brief period of time. Is picking up an infant organism as casual and insignificant a procedure as it appears? Or is the experience of the infant closer to that of Gulliver in Brobdingnag? Mere handling may, in fact, constitute a stimulation as compelling and severe as the more obviously traumatic forms of stimulation. It may be that some degree of stressful experience in infancy is necessary for successful adaptation of the organism to the environment it encounters in later life.

Another important question is whether there is a critical infantile period (or periods) during which stimulation is most effective. The evidence so far points to a period following immediately after birth. In one study we handled the animals in three separate groups for four days each, from the second through the fifth day, from the sixth through the ninth day and from the 10th through the 13th day. When we tested them for stress response on the 14th day, only the first group showed any evidence that they were capable of an endocrine response. Other investigators have had similar results. This should not be taken to mean, however, that stimulation has no effect after the critical period is past or that one critical period sets all responses.

Still other questions have not yet been satisfied by even partial answers. There is, for example, the question of therapy: Can the effects of lack of stimulation in the critical period be counteracted by stimulation of any sort after the critical period has passed? The most pressing question—the most "stimulating" question—is how stimulation causes change in the infant organism. The answer to this question should lead to a fuller understanding of the differences between individual constitutions and of the physiological mechanisms that are involved in behavior.

RONALD H. FORGUS

*Early Visual and Motor Experiences as Determiners of Complex Maze-Learning Ability Under Rich and Reduced Stimulation**

IN A RECENT paper (Forgus, 1954) the writer reported evidence which he interpreted as indicating that early experience can be a hindrance or an aid to problem solving depending on the nature of the experience and its relationship to the problem. This interpretation is an extension of the theory of Hebb since in the work published so far by Hebb (1949) and his collaborators, Forgays (1952) and Hymovitch (1952), they have stated that the "freer" the early experience of an animal is, the better it will be in solving a variety of problems. Up to now, however, most of the studies of these psychologists have dealt with performance on the Hebb-Williams intelligence test for rats.

In the paper referred to above we reported, among other facts, that a group of rats which had had extensive visual experience with inanimate objects learned to discriminate visual forms faster than another group of rats which also had had extensive visual experience with the same objects, but which had also been permitted to explore these objects physically. This result appears, at first sight, to be contradictory to Hebb's theory. However, it must be remembered that Hebb has dealt only with the gross aspects of perceptual experience and has not, as yet, dealt with the effect of varying the complexity of experience in different sensory channels. We have hypothesized that animals which had a varied experience, both visually and physically, with inanimate objects, would attempt various methods of solving the problem; e.g., they would respond to position and response cues as well as to visual cues. The animals whose motor experience with inanimate objects was relatively restricted, as compared with complex visual experience with the same objects, should have a greater probability of responding exclusively to the visual cues earlier, and therefore should learn to discriminate visual forms more quickly. The longer learning time taken by the first group can be attributed to the time it takes these animals to abolish their wrong responses to the "irrelevant" cues. This "explanation" seems all the more plausible since there was no difference in form generalization after both groups had learned the discrimination. This hypothesis is consistent with Witkin's (1941) inference from his study that rats appear to display rather stable "reaction sets" when attempting to solve a problem.

The present study was performed to test further the hypothesis which was offered, viz., that whether a group of animals with more varied early experience will be superior in problem solving to a group with less varied early experience depends on the relationship of the experience to the requirements of the problem. We are arguing that the group of animals whose early experience was qualitatively more complex would be superior in solving a problem when external stimuli are reduced, i.e., they are able to change their reaction sets more readily when the solution

* REPRINTED with abridgment by permission of the author and the American Psychological Association from *J. comp. physiol. Psychol.,* 1955, 48, 215–220.

requires such a change. We therefore specifically tested the following hypothesis: *If two groups of animals, one reared in a complex visual and motor environment and the other reared in a complex visual but relatively simple motor environment were to learn, partially, a complex open maze with visual cues present and were then tested for complete learning with the visual cues greatly reduced, then the first group would be superior in performance on the second test.*

Method

REARING

Two groups of male hooded rats were reared under two different conditions from the age of 25 days until they were 85 days old. There were 16 rats in each group. The rearing conditions were almost identical with those reported in the author's previous study (Forgus, 1954). The cage which housed group 1 was 5 ft. long, 5 ft. wide, and 15 in. high. The walls were painted a flat black, and the white objects were within 15 in. from the wall all around the sides of the cage. Group 1 was called the complex visual-motor group since the animals had complex visual as well as complex motor experience with the inanimate objects in their cage. They learned to explore and climb over the objects quite easily.

The cage which housed group 2 had the same dimensions as those of the cage that housed group 1, and the white objects were in the same relative position. However, these animals were permitted to live only in the inner 900 sq. in. of their cage. This was accomplished by inserting a plastic cage, 30 in. long, 30 in. wide, and 15 in. high, inside a large box, identical with that of group 1. Thus, these animals could only see the inanimate objects but were never permitted to traverse them. For this reason group 2 was called the complex visual but relatively simple motor group. Food and water were in the same relative positions in both cages. Both cages had very good lighting during the day.

Before we continue with the procedure we should point out certain limitations of this design. Because of the practical limitations imposed on us by the amount of laboratory space, cages, etc., we had to rear these animals in groups. Thus, it is incorrect to say that the animals of group 2 had restricted kinesthetic experience as such. Any differences in maze learning found between these groups cannot be attributed to differences in "kinesthetic learning" per se. The kinesthetic experience which the animals in group 2 derived from playing with their cage mates was probably comparable to the kinesthetic experience of the animals in group 1. The animals in both groups should have been equally good in reacting to internal postural, sequential stimuli. There is also no reason to believe that the visual learning of the two groups was significantly different, especially since the objects in the second cage were well within the rats' field of clear vision.

The experiences of the two groups were very different in one important respect, however. The animals in group 1, living in a complex, object-filled environment, had much motor experience in learning to negotiate elevated platforms, alleys, and blinds, etc. This kind of experience should improve their ability to solve complex mazes when visual cues are reduced since they had ample experience in exploring these kinds of environments in the dark.

In spite of the limitations of the design, it seems justifiable to state two things about the rearing conditions: First, the two groups were reared under similar conditions, especially with respect to visual experiences with inanimate objects. Second, the greatest difference in the rearing conditions was that the animals in group 1 had more opportunity for motor experience in negotiating a complex physical environment.

. . .

Discussion

First, we may conclude that the hypothesis we set out to test has been confirmed. In this study the animals of group 1 were reared in a cage which afforded much opportunity for visual experience with inanimate objects and which also permitted physical exploration of this complex, object-filled environment. The animals of group 2 were reared under similar conditions with respect to breadth of visual experience but were not permitted physical exploration of the complex, object-filled environment which they saw. The problem is to explain why group 1 was poorer on the preliminary test but superior on the critical test. To interpret this fact, we will discuss three alternative explanations which immediately seem possible.

The first explanation is based on the assumption that the two groups had different emotional reactions to the task situation. Thus it might be argued that the group 2 animals, having little experience with elevated objects, are more frightened when they have to turn around after entering a blind on the elevated maze. Consequently they are more cautious not to re-enter the blinds, and thus avoid making errors more quickly in the preliminary test performed in the light. Furthermore, the animals in group 1 were quite used to falling off, climbing up, and turning around on elevated platforms since they presumably had much of this kind of experience in their living cage during the night when the lights were turned out. Group 2 animals were not. Thus it could be said that the group 2 animals were much more emotionally disturbed by the necessity of finding their way around a strange place, like the elevated maze, in the dark. This disturbance would account for their poorer performance in the dark. There are two reasons why this interpretation is not very plausible. The first is that we previously found no difference between two similar groups when we tested their emotionality on an elevated maze by using fairly standard emotionality tests (Forgus, 1954, pp. 332–333). Second, it seems difficult to believe that darkness per se would produce such startling differences since rats are normally dark adapted. We might add that the group 2 animals did not exhibit such disturbances. For example, there was not an obvious increase in defecation when the rats ran the maze in the dark. Moreover, no animal in either group ever fell off the maze.

The second alternative would assume that the animals in group 1 developed greater exploratory tendencies because of dealing with more varied inanimate objects. This greater exploratory behavior masks their learning in the preliminary test. But since they explored the maze more fully, they knew more about it. Thus they were better able to cope with the problem presented in the dark. This possibility is more appealing than the first, but again there is evidence which casts doubt on its validity. In our previous study (1954, pp. 332–333) we also found no differences in variability of behavior between two groups which were similar to the ones used in this study. Exploratory tendencies are usually revealed in variability of behavior.

We thus feel that the first two explanations taken alone are not adequate. We would like to suggest a more general type of explanation which probably includes aspects of the first two alternatives. This interpretation is based on the obvious fact that the animals in group 1 were more familiar with traversing elevated platforms. Thus they were less cautious when they ran on the elevated maze. This is supported by the fact that they ran much faster than group 2 animals. One of the reasons that the group 2 animals took a longer time per trial was the fact that they hesitated more at the bifurcation points on the maze. Now the arms of the maze were very short (15 in.) and the next T could vaguely be seen from the bifurcation point. Since the group 2 animals hesitated more frequently, they eliminated errors earlier and thus performed better during the preliminary test. We mentioned earlier that Ritchie *et al.* (1950) consider that the initial stage of maze learning is based primarily on visual cues. Because group 1 animals ran so much faster, they were not utilizing these cues as well as the animals in group 2. When the lights were turned out, however, both groups were forced to rely on nonvisual cues. Since group 1 animals had much experience in this kind of situation in their living cage, they were better able to negotiate the maze during the critical test.

In conclusion we wish to stress what we said in the introduction: In examining the effects of early experience on adult problem-solving behavior it seems to be the relationship between the kind of early experience and the demands of the problem task which is the important factor.

Summary

THIS paper reported a study which investigated the influence of early visual and motor experience on the maze-learning ability of adult rats. Two groups of rats were reared under different conditions from weaning until they were 85 days old. Group 1 was reared in a large complex environment which offered much opportunity for visual and motor experience whereas the environment of group 2 offered much opportunity for visual experience but relatively little opportunity for motor experience with inanimate objects. As adults these rats were tested for maze-learning ability under conditions of rich and reduced visual cues. Group 2 was superior when many cues were present whereas group 1 was superior when the visual cues were reduced. Three alternative explanations of the results were considered. It was concluded that results such as these point to the fact that the important theoretical issue in these developmental studies seems to be the relationship between the quality of early experience and the nature of task to be solved. Only in this light will we arrive at a clear idea of the effect of early experience on adult problem-solving ability.

REFERENCES

FORGAYS, D. G., & FORGAYS, JANET W. The nature of the effect of free-environmental experience in the rat. *J. comp. physiol. Psychol.,* 1952, **45,** 302–312.

FORGUS, R. H. The effect of early perceptual learning on the behavioral organization of adult rats. *J. comp. physiol. Psychol.,* 1954, **47,** 331–336.

HEBB, D. O. *The organization of behavior.* New York: Wiley, 1949.

HONZIK, C. H. The sensory basis of maze learning in rats. *Comp. Psychol. Monogr.,* 1936, **13,** No. 64.

HYMOVITCH, B. The effects of experimental variation on problem solving in the rat. *J comp. physiol. Psychol.,* 1952, **45,** 313–326.

RITCHIE, B. F., AESCHLIMAN, B., & PEIRCE, P. Studies in spatial learning: VIII. Place performance and the acquisition of place dispositions. *J. comp. physiol. Psychol.,* 1950, **43,** 73–85.

WITKIN, H. A. "Hypotheses" in rats: an experimental critique: II. The displacement of responses and behavior variability in linear situations. *J. comp. Psychol.,* 1941, **31,** 303–336.

WILLIAM GOLDFARB

Psychological Privation in Infancy and Subsequent Adjustment*

An attempt has been made to clarify the problem of infant deprivation through a series of controlled investigations of children whose infant rearing had been in an institution (institution children). These children had been in the infant home from the earliest months to about the age of 3 years, at which time they were transferred to foster homes. In each of the investigations the institution children were compared with children whose major life experience from early infancy had been in foster homes (foster home children).

The investigations have involved comparisons of the following groups of institution and foster home children:

(a) 15 equated pairs of children observed at the mean age of 3 years, and again at 3 years, 7 months (Goldfarb, 1945).
(b) 20 equated pairs at the mean age of 6 years, 7 months (Goldfarb, 1944a).
(c) 20 equated pairs at the mean age of 8 years, 5 months (Goldfarb, 1944a).
(d) 15 equated pairs at the mean age of 12 years, 2 months (Goldfarb, 1943a, 1943b, 1944b).

The studies varied in the investigative tools employed but the results were congruent and mutually confirmatory. Psychological data have thus been gathered on a group of institution children while still in the institution and following a period of placement, and of three successively older groups of institution children. This has made it possible to deal with the question of trait permanence in the considerations of the psychodynamic effect of infant deprivation. Carefully controlled experimental investigation permits one to speak with a fair degree of certainty of the personality trends to be anticipated with extreme infant deprivation. The life histories of the institution children assume meaning because of these focused investigations. Yet, there is also much to be gained from a review of the individual histories of the institution children in order to seek out the living analogues of the experimental data.

Fifteen institution children, 8 boys and 7 girls, at a mean age of 12 years and 2 months, have been contrasted with 15 foster home children equated in terms of age and sex (Goldfarb, 1943b, 1944b, 1945). The institution children and foster home children were undiscriminated insofar as subjective and objective aspects of the foster home were concerned. The true mothers of the institution children were superior to those of the foster home children. The experimental data showed clear-cut differences between both groups. Following the experimental studies, we made intensive investigations of the life histories of the 15 adolescent institution children. We found this procedure to be of value, inasmuch as it was thus possible to see each child as a growing unit going through progressive, positive adaptation. We should like to present impressions regarding the life histories of the institution children, and to relate these to the conclusions based on the experimental findings.

---

* Reprinted by permission of the author from *Amer. J. Orthopsychiat.*, 1945, 15, 247–255.

Intellectual Trends

INTELLECT

The experimental evidence has tended to verify that inferior intellectual performance is characteristic of the institution children at all ages studied. In spite of the fact that in individual cases in our experience we have been able to see conspicuous improvement in intellect with continued community contact, this has not been observed as a general rule. There is the obvious need to study the same group of institution children longitudinally over a long period of time. This has already been initiated for a small group of institution children studied before and after placement in foster homes. However, it has been possible to gather relevant psychometric data on 11 of the 15 institution children whose histories have been examined for the present report. Table 1 presents the median ages of first and second examinations, the difference in time of examination, and relevant intelligence test data. Since the Revised Stanford Binet (Form L) was employed during the first series of examinations, and the Wechsler Bellevue Intelligence Scales during the second examination, each child's test IQ was translated into a sigma score as follows:

Table 1

TEST	MEDIAN AGE	MEDIAN IQ	MEDIAN SIGMA SCORE
First Test, Revised Stanford Binet (L)	6–11	75	3.1
Second Test, Wechsler Bellevue	11–8	74	3.1
Difference	4–9	1	0.0

$$\text{Sigma Score} = \frac{\left\{\begin{array}{l}\text{Child's IQ minus Mean IQ} \\ \text{for his year group}\end{array}\right\}}{\left\{\begin{array}{l}\text{IQ Standard Deviation for} \\ \text{his year group}\end{array}\right\}}$$

A score of 5 was added to each child's sigma score in order to make all ratings positive. A final score of 5 is thus equivalent to the average IQ of the child's age group in the standardization population. A score below 5 indicates an IQ below the average of the standardization group, while a score above 5 indicates an IQ above the average IQ of the standardization group.[1]

It is apparent that the institution group maintained its status in intellectual performance relative to the mean performance of the standardizing populations. It might be stated parenthetically that there was no consistent difference between the two test IQ's. Six of the children had Binet IQ's which were higher than their later Wechsler IQ's, while five had higher Wechsler IQ's.

This evidence is in accord with the findings of the infant study where no improvement in relative intellectual status was observed following the first seven months of placement in the foster home. This is also in accord with the experimental demonstration of academic inferiority and the observation that all 15 of the institution children had had a consistent history of school difficulty.

CONCEPT FORMATION

One of the more important observations in the experimental study was the unusually defective level of conceptualization that was typical of the institution group. It became apparent that the children had difficulty in organizing a variety of stimuli meaningfully, and in abstracting relationships from them. It was hypothesized that this inability to think along the lines of abstraction and generalization reflected (a) volitional defect as expressed in a generalized state of intellectual and emotional passivity and impoverishment; (b) an absence of normal personality maturation and differentiation. This, of course, had contributed to the observed retardation in learning. On the other hand, the conceptual deficiency is in the nature of a primary thinking impediment with direct effect on all the rest of the children's behavior.

1 This procedure assumes equivalence in the standardization population of both tests.

EXPRESSIONS IN CONCEPT DEFICIENCY

1. The children consistently had difficulty in learning songs, rhymes, and stories. They were also late in grasping number concepts, eventually learning the computation tables by drill rather than understanding. Similarly, all learning based on insight or the sizing up of a situation was difficult.

2. Of particular interest was their difficulty in achieving time and space concepts, and consequent disregard of time and space limitations. This was a major cause of social maladjustment, for it led to disregard for school and family rules of behavior. There were constant complaints by foster parents of related kinds of behavioral maladjustment illustrated by the child's persistent running off the sidewalk in spite of punishment and warnings. The children could not be left alone in the street because they "tended to wander away." At school they had to be watched during recess or they would wander off; they were unable to observe when recess time was over. On returning from school it was also common for some of them to meander aimlessly through the streets and come home hours later than expected. The deficiency in time concepts was without doubt a factor in their limited foresight and in an inability to envision the consequences of their acts. This may explain the frequent complaint by foster parents of the inefficacy of punishment or reward. The children were found to be unmanageable and unresponsive to normal motivation.

3. Even as late as adolescence, these children [are] unable to remember or recall the past in any clear, focused fashion, have difficulty in anticipating and grasping the future, and are completely at the mercy of the immediate to which their response is unorganized and ineffectual. They are likely to respond to details of their environment rather than to its generalized import. Overt trial and error experimentation rather than controlled reflective sizing up of the situation is typical. This may explain in part the restlessness, hyperactivity, unusual curiosity, and flightiness of thinking that is typical during the preschool and latency periods. In some of the children this persists through adolescence. In other words, motility disturbance and social aggression are not necessarily secondary aspects of anxiety or hostility, but may actually be primary and positive modes of adaptation in the face of a lack which typifies the whole of the institution child's being. This may also explain the frequent reference to the syndrome of personality traits, hyperactivity, uncontrollability, lack of initiative, passivity, and "unwillingness" to learn.

Emotional Trends

THERE can be no doubt that their extremely concretistic, primitive modes of perception and conception have [a] signal effect on their emotional relationships. Emotional trends are consequently artificially separated from intellectual trends for purposes of discussion, and it is clear that the behavior deficiencies of the institution children involve the whole of their personalities.

1. *Absence of a Normal Inhibitory Pattern.* In 14 of the 15 cases there is a history of extremely difficult behavior. The problem appears to have been not so much one of focused hostility or conflict as of crippled or defective maturation and a primitivization of the total personality. Hyperactivity and disorganization are the major symptoms. The children are described as unmanageable and undisciplined, with no control over their actions, frequently flighty in their association, and unable to concentrate. Some are enuretic through the latency and adolescent periods. Severe temper tantrums are common. In the early years of school, a majority of the group is regarded as among the most unmanageable in their respective classes. Teachers were particularly impressed with disregard for rules, inability to sit in one place, and general lack of organization. There is a diffuse, random discharge of body energy. When strong external controls are introduced, strange body movements and grimaces appear.

John frequently showed twitching of mouth and nose. When reprimanded, Irving would stand in one place with twitching features and fixed stare, as though in a spell. Morris would shake his head in his sleep, and when awake would either shake his head or continuously move his legs back and forth. His twin sister indulged in grimaces or sat for long periods twisting her fingers, staring into space. Albert would scratch his whole body, twitch his face or parts of his body. It is of interest that in each of these children there was first a tendency to inhibition of hyperactivity and aggression as a result of firm handling by a strong mother-person with whom they had been placed for long periods.

There was extreme curiosity regarding the environment, yet an inability to grasp its meaning so that there was a constant unsatisfied drive to test and try out. The result was continuous movement and distractibility. During psychological examinations administered in the preschool and preadolescent periods, behavioral descriptions mentioned that children opened and closed drawers and closet doors constantly, had difficulty in keeping their hands off psychological materials, and were easily distracted by everything about them. Some asked innumerable questions but paid no attention to the answers.

The above description, while it discriminates social aggression from hostility, does not imply the complete absence of hostility. In fact, feelings of hostility were present and developed quickly and strongly in the face of minor blocking. The inability to grasp the totality of a living adjustment, the uninhibited, unreflective, unselective response to particularized ego-centered frustrations and the absence of an anticipatory capacity predisposed the children to impulsive reactions, marked temper displays, even feeling of persecution. Incomprehensible cruelty to other children, foster parents and animals was frequently observed. These feelings and expressions, while energetic, were also unpredictable, brief, and contradictory. What is probably of most significance is that the hostilities represented the unreasoned reaction to frustration feelings but were exaggerated by lack of ability to understand the total meaning of a specific adjustment or sequence of experiences.

2. *Affect Hunger.* In these children one observes exaggerated illustrations of the outcomes of unmitigated affect hunger. All indiscriminately demanded affection and attention. Irving was excessively demanding and never had enough of what affection was given to him. He carried this over into his food habits. On one occasion, when given an apple, he immediately ran to the refrigerator for another apple before he had finished the one in his hand. When the foster mother suggested that he finish the apple he was eating before taking another, he threw it on the ground, began to stamp his feet and scream. The same occurred in regard to desserts and other foods served to him. Foster mother stated that Irving made such demands constantly and was excessively demanding of affection. "All he wants is to hug and kiss." Constance's teacher felt that her outstanding characteristic was her demand for attention. If, in a particular period, the teacher happened to be too busy to give her attention, Constance would cease working and attempt to attract attention by misconduct. At 11 years of age Frances preferred the role of baby when playing house with other children. She once burst into tears when she observed the foster mother coaxing another foster child to eat. When asked what was the matter, she said that she wanted to eat. Asked if she were hungry, she said "no." During one period, when about 8 years of age, she would go to her room alone and engage in whining. Similarly, in several other children, the desire to be fed, dressed, and cared for as a baby was common in the school age even though these same children had previously been trained in the institution to do some of these very things for themselves.

The need for physical expression of affection was paramount, particularly in the preschool and early school periods. One worker commented, "James continues to be one of the most overtly affectionate children I ever visited. He spends half his time in the foster mother's lap kissing and hugging her and asking to be kissed in return." Irving would hurl himself on the foster mother and attempt to pull her down to the floor. This exaggerated display of sensuality in these children appears to parallel a state of infantilism. It coincides with the hypothesis that their love drives are concentrated at the very early autoerotic level where the need for physical stimulation is regnant.

3. *Emotional Imperviousness and Superficiality of Relationship.* The insatiable demand for affection did not significantly enrich the capacity of the children to form ties. In adolescence, most were described by their case workers as removed, emotionally isolated, and cold. In their previous histories, this trend was reflected in easy-going response to change in foster home or to threat of removal from foster homes where they had been completely accepted. In several situations, the adolescents, without feeling, were ready to precipitate change from homes where they had been reared almost from the point of transfer from the institution and where they had been completely assimilated by the foster family.

4. *Absence of Normal Tension and Anxiety Reaction.* This tendency to meagerness of feeling for other humans is complemented by the absence of normal anxiety display following acts of hostility, cruelty, or unprovoked aggression. In addition, focused tension in specific situations normally calling for tension responses are frequently not observed. This has been demonstrated experimentally but is also reflected in the complacent manner with which most of the children accept, for example, school failure. For this reason guardians and teachers were often dismayed by their inability to find a means of motivating controlled behavior. In several situations, neither physical punishment nor even the threat of removal from the foster home had any effect on the children's behavior.

5. *Social Regression.* The institution adolescents have been shown to be inferior to the foster home adolescents in social maturity (Goldfarb, 1943a). In one investigation it was noted that in the institution, the children showed normal social maturity but that shortly afterwards, there was a significant decline in their ability to do things for themselves (Goldfarb, 1945). This phenomenon of specific decline in social maturity was also observed in the life histories of our adolescent group. It is generally one aspect of the stubbornly maintained pattern of infantilism and passivity that has already been described.

Summary

THE life histories tend to confirm the previous conclusion that infant deprivation results in a basic defect of total personality. This defect manifests itself in the spheres of intellect and feeling in a manner suggesting that the institution child's personality is congealed at a level of extreme immaturity. The strong affective need is never fully met. In addition, this is complicated by the emaciated relatedness both to material reality and to people, and [by] the inability to adjust in organized, planful, understanding fashion. The defect in concept formation is accompanied by an attitude of passivity and emotional apathy so that normal growth does not follow the typical family and community experiences which are introduced following the institutional experience.

At the same time, there does appear to be a temporal sequence of adaptive response. The child comes to the foster home lacking in normal language skills and information, but with a more significant deficiency in his way of thinking and feeling. He is apathetic and impoverished in his intellectual life, weak in will or drive to understand and reorganize external experience. In a negative sense, he adjusted within the institution, [was] no problem, slept well, gave no indication of nightmares, fed himself, and strove to dress himself. He recognized his nurse, had known several adults, but had no constant, intimate experience with any single adult.

At about the age of 3 years he goes to his foster home without difficulty or display of feeling. There is some bewilderment at the new world of a family though this is not marked. He is given a great deal of affection and attention. He begins to seek this affection for himself, needs constant demonstration of love, but his affection is indiscriminate and he will go off with strangers. His initial picture of apathy soon develops into one of hyperactivity and disorganization; he is prone to run rather than walk, abrupt in his movements, and very distractible. He is unable to attend for more than brief periods, is flighty, and avoids difficult adjustments. He is destructive, disorganized, stubborn, has severe temper outbursts when crossed, though these pass quickly if disregarded. He cannot get along with children, hits them and provokes fights even if likely to be hurt. He cannot be left alone in the street, persists in running off into the gutter, and will wander off and get lost. He is very appealing to adults as a result of his attention-seeking and even his flightiness. Because of this or because of their own internal needs, some foster parents are likely to accept him into the family completely in spite of the many problems involved in his rearing. However, some foster parents are soon forced to seek replacement. The child is likely to accept this replacement calmly. A quick adjustment to the new foster home may impress his new foster parents; but he soon again demonstrates the patterns described above.

His aggressive behavior does not represent goal-seeking behavior. It is formless, diffuse, and consequently disorganized. He cannot be taught as readily as other children [because of both] the attention deficiency and the concept lack. In addition, he is passive in attitude and his distractibility reflects in part his inability to deal with his environment with normal reflective will and comprehension.

From the start there is the dual problem of meeting his need for love and of molding his impulses and drives in accord with social requirements. His appetite for affection is insatiable and there is no appreciable development of the capacity for identifying with and loving others. It is likely that the foster family experience is more successful in controlling his overt social behavior than in meeting his love-starved need for attention and affection, and creating a capacity for a normal, reciprocating relationship with others. Beyond the preschool period, the child learns that he must control some of the more unacceptable aspects of his behavior or he will become completely undesirable to the family and community. This problem of control continues to be a matter of concern to himself and his guardians as late as adolescence, while it is usually resolved in the preschool years by most children. However, an adaptation does occur. During the school period, a dominating family atmosphere is likely to cause the child to give up the constant activity and the aggressive testing out of the environment without ever understanding it. He becomes overtly removed, isolated, and apathetic, whereas previously emotional bluntness existed in conjunction with a pattern of overt hyperactivity and aggression. As indicated, strange body grimaces and tics may begin to appear at this point. In addition, while generally apathetic, there may still be occasional outbursts of rage.

There has been a tendency to confuse the deprivation experience of the institution children with that of rejected children in families. The rejected child ordinarily grows up in an atmosphere of hostility directed toward him by one or both parents. He is made to feel unwanted and despised by those adults on whom he must depend and with whom he consequently identifies. On the other hand, the parental rejection is more likely to express itself in cruelty and severe handling rather than in a lack of stimulation. The chances are that the parental feelings are mixed rather than clearly rejecting. Consequently, the child's capacity and desire for relationship do develop though they may be blocked by suspicion or distrust as the result of traumatic experience. Similarly, his abilities and intellect may also be stimulated to develop though his practical capacity to meet and solve problems may be distorted by his defensive need to hurt as he himself has been hurt. In a positive sense, he has experienced personal engagement with other adults and has thus been able to develop a full even if conflicted emotional existence.

This rejection pattern differs from that of infant deprivation as we have defined it. In an atmosphere of deprivation there is an extreme meagerness of stimulation. One would hardly describe the institution regimen as brutal or aggressively cruel. Its major defect lies in the bare and narrow horizons of experience it offers. This lack applies both to the world of things and to the world of people. The institution child thus establishes no specific identifications and engages in no meaningful reciprocal relationships with other people. The basic motivations to normal maturation and differentiation of personality are absent. Paucity in content and organization of both intellect and feeling follow. The ego structure is primitive and undeveloped. Its passivity is further exaggerated by the thoroughgoing adjustment to the routine demands of a group life in which individual volition is neglected. Both the "I" of the inner life, and the "IT" of the outer life, are crippled.

Thus the major points of difference between children with a deprivation experience, and children with a rejection experience are:

1. Institution children show a primary thinking defect characterized particularly by extremely limited capacity for abstract performance. Indeed, the defect in the abstract attitude involves the whole of the personality, inasmuch as it is reflected in the absence of goal striving, of self-conscious awareness of the implications of behavior, and of active remaking of experience.

The rejected child belongs to a more heterogeneous group in which his reaction patterns vary with the specific forms of parental rejection. In any case, a qualitative limitation in mentality is not an essential symptom. The pathological concretivity of the institution child's thinking is not observed.

2. The rejected child's personality is nearer to that of the normal. (a) Though suspicious, he has identifications and a developed capacity for relationship, which the institution child does not. (b) The rejected child's behavior is more ambitiously purposeful and goal-seeking. The institution child's behavior is passive, random, and undirected. (c) The rejected child shows more tension and anxiety, particularly in response to his aggressive acts. The institution child is less tense and anxious; his hostile acts do not necessarily produce anxiety reactions. The rejected child is a child in conflict. The institution child is an undeveloped child. His feelings and conflicts are meager. (d) The rejected child has greater capacity for self-insight. Treatment is thus more effective in altering behavior. The institution child has little self-insight. The institution child needs the stimulated growth of a normal ego structure rather than the amelioration of conflict or anxiety. Direct treatment is commonly ineffective, particularly at the adolescent level.

REFERENCES

GOLDFARB, W. The effects of early institutional care on adolescent personality. *J. exp. Educ.*, 1943, **12,** 106–129. (a)

GOLDFARB, W. The effects of early institutional care on adolescent personality. (Graphic Rorschach Data.) *Child Develpm.*, 1943, **14,** 213–223. (b)

GOLDFARB, W. Infant rearing and problem behavior. *Amer. J. Orthopsychiat.*, 1943, **13,** 249–266. (a)

GOLDFARB, W. The effects of early institutional care on adolescent personality. *Amer. J. Orthopsychiat.*, 1944. **14,** 441–447. (b)

GOLDFARB, W. The effects of psychological deprivation in infancy and subsequent stimulation. *Amer. J. Psychiat.*, 1945, **102,** 18–33.

HARRIET L. RHEINGOLD *and* NANCY BAYLEY

*The Later Effects of an Experimental Modification of Mothering**

An extensive literature in psychology attests to the effect of early experience upon later behavior. For the human infant an important determiner of early experience is maternal care. Some of the dimensions of maternal care thought to be of consequence are amounts and kinds of care, interruptions of care, the number of persons giving care, as well as their attitudes. There is not yet, however, any considerable *experimental* literature on the effects of these variables upon the later behavior of children. The present study reports an attempt to discover the presence, a year later, of a change in behavior brought about in a group of infants by an experimental modification of maternal care (Rheingold, 1956).

Sixteen children, living in an institution for approximately the first nine months of life, were the original subjects of study. From the sixth through the eighth month of life, half of them, the experimental group, were cared for by one person alone, the experimenter, for 7½ hours a day. They thus received more attentive care than the control subjects who were completely reared under institutional routine; and of course the number of different persons from whom they received care was markedly reduced. As a result the experimental babies became more responsive to the experimenter almost at once, while with time they became more responsive to other persons as well. They did not however do reliably better than the control subjects on the Cattell Infant Intelligence Scale or on tests of postural development and cube manipulation. At the conclusion of the study the experimental subjects returned to the full-time care of the institution. Details of the institutional care, of its experimental modification, of the tests used, and of the results may be found in the report referred to above.

One by one, all but one of both the experimental and the control subjects were placed outside the institution—in their own homes, or in adoptive or boarding homes. Approximately a year after the conclusion of the study, the children, then about 18 months of age, were seen again, in an attempt to detect the effects of the earlier treatment. Since the only clear difference between the groups at the time of the study had been an increase in social responsiveness among the experimental babies, it would be here that one would expect a difference, if any, to persist. Still, the possibility existed that differences might appear later as new functions matured. On the other hand, the subsequent, and more recent, experience of several months' duration in different life situations might reduce the chance of finding a difference.

The effects of experimental treatment were sought in two areas of behavior, the social and the intellectual. Would the experimental subjects be more socially responsive, that is, more friendly and outgoing than the control group to two examiners who visited the home? Would the experimental subjects, in addition, be more responsive to the original experimenter than to another person? If not, the variable under test is really their responsiveness to strangers. Second, would the experimental subjects now do better on a test of developmental progress?

* Reprinted by permission of the authors and the Society for Research in Child Development from *Child Develpm.*, 1959, 30, 363–372.

It was planned, in addition, to use the retest data to explore the effect of type of home placement, as well as to evaluate the performance of the whole group considered as a sample of institutionalized children.

Procedure

SUBJECTS

FOURTEEN of the original 16 children were located and tested; one from the experimental group and one from the control group could not be found.[1]

The mean age of the experimental group was 19.8 months (range, 17.6–22.1), of the control group, 20.1 months (range, 17.5–21.7). The experimental group had spent an average of 9.2 months in the institution before being placed in homes (range, 4.0–13.6); for the control group the mean time was 10.4 months (range, 6.5–18.1). If the control subject who was still in the institution was omitted from the calculations, the average stay for the control group became 9.2 months (range, 6.5–12.2). In respect, then, to age and to duration of stay in the institution both groups were similar.

The children left the institution at different ages. Two experimental subjects left after only three weeks of treatment. One control subject left in the sixth week of the study, another in the seventh week. All the other subjects stayed at least through the eight weeks of treatment.

The home placements were varied. Three experimental and two control subjects returned to their own homes. With one exception, the own parents of these five subjects were of foreign birth and the homes were marked by poverty. Two of the experimental and four of the control subjects were in adoptive homes which, in general, were superior to the own homes in socioeconomic status. Two experimental subjects were living in boarding homes, pending a release for adoption. And one control subject, a Negro boy, remained in the institution only because a home could not be found for him. Furthermore, there was no difference between the experimental and the control groups in the intellectual stimulation provided by the homes or in the friendliness of the mothers, according to ratings made by the Experimenter and the Examiner after each visit. In type of home placement, therefore, there appeared to be no major difference. Rather, the difference between homes within each group appeared to be larger than any difference between the groups.

THE TESTS

Each child was seen in his own home. The homes were scattered widely through Chicago, its suburbs and neighboring cities, with one home in another state. Two persons, the original Experimenter and an Examiner, visited the homes together, with one exception: the child who lived out of the state was examined by the Experimenter alone. The Experimenter knew all the children but, of course, had been especially familiar with the experimental subjects. She served *only* as a stimulus person in the social tests. The Examiner had no previous acquaintance with any of the children and did not know which had been the experimental subjects. She also served as a stimulus person in the social tests, but it was she alone who recorded the children's responses to both the Experimenter and herself, and who administered the test of developmental progress.

The social test resembled those reported in the first study, but was made more suitable for older children. It was composed of three parts, each of which set up a rather natural situation between adult and child, with an easy transition between the parts. In the first part, the responses to the stimulus person in the first few minutes after her entrance into the home were recorded. During this time the stimulus person did not talk to or approach the child but sat at some distance from him and talked to the mother, occasionally smiling at the child. The Examiner recorded the child's responses to whichever stimulus person happened first to engage his attention, then to the other person. At an appropriate mo-

1 We are grateful to Father Bernard Brogan, Director of the Catholic Home Bureau of Chicago, for his generous cooperation.

ment one of the persons smiled and spoke warmly to the child, saying, "Hi (child's name) come to me," accompanying her words by stretching out her arms in invitation. This constituted the second situation. In the third situation, the stimulus person actually approached the child, smiling, talking, and gesturing as in the second situation. After the child's responses had been recorded, the other stimulus person presented herself to the child similarly. The order of stimulus persons was determined by the convenience of the moment: whoever was closer to the child or was receiving more glances was the first stimulus person.

The child's responses were recorded on a checklist under these categories: *positive facial expression,* which included seven items of behavior ranging from "stares with expression" to "laughs"; *physical approach* with nine items ranging from "shows toy" through "makes physical contact" to "makes social overtures while in the stimulus person's lap"; *vocalizations* for which a child received a score of one for each part of the test in which he vocalized, whether he said discrete sounds, jargon, or words; *negative facial expression,* which included eight items ranging from "a fleeting sober expression" to "cries"; *physical retreat* with six items ranging from "hangs head" to "leaves room"; and *response to mother* (during the social test period) which included a series of six items, from "turns toward mother" to "stays in contact with mother."

Within each category, items of behavior were thus arranged in what seemed a reasonable progression in terms of duration or amplitude of response. Each item within a category was arbitrarily assigned a value of one. Because the items were arranged in ascending order, the score for any item was one plus the value of all other items below it in that category. The scores for the categories of positive facial expression, physical approach, and vocalizations were summed to yield a measure of *positive social responsiveness.* Similarly, the sum of both negative categories gave a measure of *negative social responsiveness.* The sum of these two measures was the measure of *total social responsiveness.* The category of *response to mother* was calculated separately and not included in the other measures.

After the social tests, the Cattell Infant Intelligence Scale (1940) was administered by the Examiner, with the Experimenter *not* present. Lastly, the number of words in the child's vocabulary was calculated from his performance on the language items of the Cattell and from the mother's report.

Results

THE EFFECT OF TREATMENT

TABLE 1 shows that both the experimental and the control subjects responded similarly to the Experimenter and to the Examiner. The close agreement of all means, and of the ranges, is apparent in the part, as well as in the total, scores. The only difference of any size between the two stimulus persons appeared in the experimental group's response to mother. But since only one subject of the seven gave a response to the mother when the Experimenter was the stimulus person, and only three subjects of the seven, when the Examiner was the stimulus person, this difference, as all the others, was not statistically significant. From the results we conclude that the experimental subjects did not appear to remember the Experimenter.

Furthermore, since the experimental and the control groups gave similar scores to both persons, it was assumed that they were of approximately equal stimulating value. Therefore, a combined score for each subject (the average of a subject's responses to both stimulus persons) was used in the analyses which follow. This procedure made it possible to add to the control group the subject who was seen by the Experimenter alone. If every other subject responded similarly to both stimulus persons, it may be assumed that this subject would too. (It will be seen in TABLE 1 that the addition of this subject to the control group made the combined means slightly different from the separate means.)

The combined scores showed that the experimental subjects were more responsive to

TABLE 1. *Means and ranges of the social test*

Subjects	EXPERIMENTER *Mean*	EXPERIMENTER *Range*	EXAMINER *Mean*	EXAMINER *Range*	COMBINED SCORE *Mean*
Experimental Group *					
Total Social Responsiveness	32.1	27–39	30.9	27–38	31.6
Positive	17.4	2–30	16.0	2–37	16.7
Negative	14.7	1–37	14.7	3–29	14.7
Response to Mother	2.3	0–16	5.7	0–19	4.0
Control Group †					
Total Social Responsiveness	28.0	14–39	28.3	22–44	28.4
Positive	19.8	5–32	20.2	4–37	20.1
Negative	8.2	3–12	8.2	2–18	8.0
Response to Mother	4.5	0–11	4.8	0–10	5.4

* *N* is 7.
† *N* is 6 for responses to Experimenter and to Examiner, but 7 for Combined Score. See text for explanation.

both persons than the control subjects, but the difference was not statistically significant. The part scores, further, revealed that the control group gave more positive responses, the experimental group, more negative responses. Again, the differences were not statistically reliable. Moreover, inspection of the data revealed that the negative responses of only two of the seven experimental subjects were responsible for the difference between the groups. The findings therefore do not warrant the conclusion that the experimental subjects were either more or less responsive to the stimulus persons, positively or negatively.

Because some of the subjects made no response to their mothers during the social tests, the means for this category of behavior were not subjected to test. Only three of the seven experimental subjects and five of the control subjects made some contact with the mother during social stimulation by one or the other of the stimulus persons, a difference which permits no conclusive statement of difference.

Although vocalizations had been included in the measure of positive social responsiveness (as explained above), a measure which did not differentiate the groups, they were also analyzed separately. Inspection showed that five of the seven experimental subjects vocalized to one or the other of the stimulus persons but only one of the control subjects did. The difference was significant by the Fisher exact probability test at $p = .051$ (one-sided), a finding in agreement with the original study in which, at the end of the experimental treatment, the experimental subjects also vocalized more than the control subjects.

On the Cattell Infant Intelligence Scale the mean IQ for the experimental group was 97.4 (range, 82–110); for the control group it was 95.4 (range, 83–122). More attentive care given during a limited period in the first year of life therefore appeared to produce no difference in IQ on retest a year later.

The experimental subjects had a larger spoken vocabulary than the control subjects (17.9 and 13.7 words), but the difference was again not statistically significant.

THE EFFECT OF HOME PLACEMENT

It early became clear that the adoptive homes were of a higher socioeconomic level than the the own homes, and therefore it seemed desirable to look for differences in the performance of the children in these two types of home placement. The adoptive homes were also ranked higher than the own homes by the investigators on the basis of the friendliness of the mother during the visit and of the intellectual stimulation the home seemed to offer the child.

On the social test the children in adoptive homes gave more positive responses than those in own homes; the means were 21.6 and 15.6, respectively, but the difference was not statistically significant. It should be noted, however, that one subject in a boarding home and the subject still in the institution made higher positive scores than the mean of the adoptive home group.

Similarly, the mean IQ of the children living in adoptive homes was higher (98.8) than that of those living in own homes (95.4), but the difference was not reliable. The two children living in boarding homes had IQs of 95 and 102. And, while the child still in the institution obtained an IQ of only 83, two children in own homes had lower IQs, one of 79 and one of 82, and one child in an adoptive home had an IQ of 84.

Finally, the children in adoptive homes had a larger vocabulary than the children in own homes (means were 18.6 and 13.4, respectively), although again the difference was not significant.

In summary, there was no reliable evidence that the children in adoptive homes were more socially responsive or more developmentally advanced than those in own homes.

THE GROUP AS A WHOLE

We may now evaluate the performance of the group as a whole ($N = 14$), representing as it does a sample of children who spent approximately nine months of the first year of life in the care of an institution and who then experienced a major change in life situation.

In general, the group was marked by a friendliness which seemed warm and genuine. Eleven of the 14 *S*s not only approached the stimulus persons but also allowed themselves to be picked up and held. Only two subjects, both boys, presented a different social response: they clung to their mothers and cried when the stimulus persons approached them. No comparable data are available for children who have lived all their lives in own homes, but in preliminary testing of the social test on three such children not one approached the examiners. Instead, they looked at the examiners from behind their mothers' skirts and retreated whenever the examiners moved in their direction.

On the Cattell Infant Intelligence Scale the mean IQ of the group was 96.4. At six months of age the mean IQ for these 14 children was 93.8; at eight months it was 94.3. They continue therefore to score in the normal range. Furthermore, the mean number of words in their vocabulary was 15.5, which compares favorably with Gesell's (1941) norms of 10 words at 18 months and 20 words at 21 months. Certainly, the group showed no sign of mental dullness or of language retardation.

No child, furthermore, showed the marked apathy or attention-seeking behavior believed by some to characterize the behavior of children reared in institutions. Differences there were, to be sure, between the children, but none seemed to depart markedly from the normal in temperament or personality. In fact, several of the mothers spontaneously commented upon how easy these children were to handle in comparison with their other children. They mentioned, specifically, their good eating and sleeping habits and their ability to amuse themselves.

Discussion

THE discussion will take up three separate points: (a) the effect of the experimental treatment, (b) the effect of own home versus adoptive home placement, and (c) the characteristics of the whole group considered as a sample of institutionalized children.

On the basis of the changes in social behavior produced at the time of treatment, one might have expected that the experimental subjects on retest would have been more responsive to the Experimenter than to the Examiner. Instead, no reliable difference was found in their responses to either person. The Experimenter was not remembered. Further, we did not find, except in the vocalizing of the children, any evidence that the experimental subjects were more responsive than the control subjects. It seems, therefore, that the experiences provided by the more attentive mothering were not great enough to maintain the experimentally produced difference over a year's time, except in one class of behavior.

The findings give rise to several speculations. First, it is possible that the verbal behavior of young children is more sensitive to changes in the environment than are other classes of behavior. In this connection, the responsiveness of vocalizations to conditioning in the three-month-old infant has already been demonstrated (Rheingold, Gewirtz, & Ross, 1959). Second, differences between the experimental and control groups may well have existed but in some untested area of behavior. Third, the expected (or some other) differences may make their appearance in the future in some more complex behavior incorporating the experiences of treatment. Finally, serious limitations to the study were imposed by the small number of subjects and by the diversity of home placements within each group. Differences would have to be very large indeed to surmount these limitations.

That no difference was found between the experimental and control groups in developmental status is not surprising, considering that no difference was found at the end of treatment. Some of the speculations about the course of social responsiveness may apply here, too.

We turn now to a consideration of the effect of home placement. The adoptive homes in general were of a higher socioeconomic level, the mothers were more sociable, and the homes were judged to offer more intellectual stimulation. For these reasons we would have expected the children in adoptive homes to be more socially responsive and more advanced in developmental status. But significant differences were not found. Possible explanations are that the differences between the two groups of home may have been not as great as they seemed, or that the number of cases was too small.

Lastly, the characteristics of the group as a whole may be assessed for the effects of a life experience usually thought of as deprived. All the children had been cared for in an institution for the first half of their lives, all but one had experienced a major "separation" in going from one life situation to another, and, furthermore, three children were now living in depressed socioeconomic environments, two were in boarding homes, and one was still in the institution. Yet, as a group, the children were healthy, of normal intelligence, and they appeared to be making a satisfactory adjustment. In addition, they seemed to be more friendly to strangers than children who have lived all their lives in own homes and, according to mothers' reports, were more adaptable than their other children. In no way, then, did they resemble the emotionally disturbed and mentally retarded children described in studies of the effect of institutional or hospital life or of separation from the mother.[2] They did not show apathy or the inability to form relationships or make excessive bids for attention. Even earlier, at the beginning of the study when the infants were still in the institution, they were physically robust, mentally alert, and socially responsive.

It is true that in kind and duration of experience they resemble exactly no other group of children reported in the literature. There is a tendency among workers, however, to lump together studies of children who actually differ in age and experience and to generalize from them to all children who have experiences which may be similar in only one of many possible respects. It is to be hoped that as more prospective (in contrast to retrospective) studies are carried out, the dimensions of deprivation and of its effects can be clarified. Certainly, we may expect to find that the effects will depend upon the age of the child, the nature and duration of the deprivation, and the experiences prior to and subsequent to it (Ainsworth & Bowlby, 1954). The present study of the effects of early experience, limited as it is, emphasizes the need for more precise measurement both of deprivation and of its effects.

2 Glaser and Eisenberg (1956) present a recent review of studies on maternal deprivation.

Summary

THE present study reports an attempt to discover the presence, a year later, of a change in behavior brought about in a group of infants by an experimental modification of maternal care.

Sixteen babies, living in an institution for approximately the first nine months of life, were the original subjects of study. Half of them, the experimental subjects, received more attentive care by one person, the Experimenter, from the sixth through the eighth month of life. As a result they became more socially responsive than the control group who were cared for under the usual institutional routine. They did not, however, do better upon tests of developmental progress.

Subsequently all but one of the children were placed in homes. A year later, when the children were about 19 months old, 14 of the original 16 subjects were located, and tested for their social responsiveness and developmental progress.

The results did not reveal any statistically significant differences between the experimental and the control groups except that more of the experimental subjects vocalized during the social tests. It is concluded therefore that the experience provided by the more attentive mothering, while great enough to produce a difference at the time of study, was not great enough to maintain that difference over time, except in one class of behavior. It is possible that the verbal behavior of young children is more sensitive to changes in the environment than are other classes of behavior.

No statistically significant differences in social responsiveness and developmental status were found between children living in own homes and in adoptive homes, although the adoptive homes were of higher socioeconomic status.

Finally, the group as a whole was friendly, of normal intelligence, and apparently was making a satisfactory adjustment. They did not resemble the emotionally disturbed and mentally retarded children described in studies of the effects of institutional life or of separation from the mother.

REFERENCES

AINSWORTH, MARY D., & BOWLBY, J. Research strategy in the study of mother-child separation. *Courrier of the Centre International de l'Enfance,* 1954, **4,** 105–131.

CATTELL, PSYCHE. *The measurement of intelligence of infants and young children.* New York: Psychological Corporation, 1940.

GESELL, A., & AMATRUDA, CATHERINE S. *Developmental diagnosis.* New York: Hoeber, 1941.

GLASER, K., & EISENBERG, L. Maternal deprivation. *Pediatrics,* 1956, **18,** 626–642.

RHEINGOLD, HARRIET L. The modification of social responsiveness in institutional babies. *Monogr. Soc. Res. Child Develpm.,* 1956, **21,** No. 2 (Serial No. 63).

RHEINGOLD, HARRIET L., GEWIRTZ, J. L., & ROSS, HELEN W. Social conditioning of vocalizations in the infant. *J. comp. physiol. Psychol.,* 1959, **52,** 68–73.

WAYNE DENNIS

Causes of Retardation Among Institutional Children: Iran*

A. Introduction

CONSIDERABLE interest has recently been shown in the fact that in some institutions for children there occurs a decided retardation in behavioral development. The observations of Spitz (1945, 1946a, 1946b) in particular have received much notice, chiefly because of the interpretations which Spitz has placed upon his data. In our opinion, the primary importance of these observations lies in their challenge to the theory that infant development consists largely of the maturation of a motor sequence which is little affected by learning.

Aside from the investigations of Spitz, studies of behavioral retardation among institutional children have been few in number. The scarcity of such studies is due in large part to the fact that institutions in which conditions comparable to those described by Spitz can be found are not numerous. In many countries institutional care has been replaced by other methods of caring for dependent children. However, institutions in which behavioral development is retarded can still be found in countries which are "underdeveloped" not only in regard to modern technology but also in respect to newer methods for the care of foundlings and other homeless infants.

The present paper reports studies of development in three institutions in Tehran, the capital of Iran. In two of these institutions, children are exceedingly retarded in their motor development. In the third little retardation is present. It is believed that comparisons of child care in these institutions, and of behavioral development in them, will throw considerable light upon the nature of the environmental factors which influence motor development. This paper supplements a recent report on behavioral retardation in a Lebanese institution by Dennis and Najarian (1957). In the earlier report attention was directed primarily to motor development in the first year of life, whereas in the present instance the period from one year to four years of age is the one with which we are mainly concerned. Preliminary observations indicated that development during the first year in the two Iranian institutions in which retardation occurs is essentially the same as in the Lebanese institution described in the previous paper. For this reason in the present study attention is given chiefly to the age period to which little attention was directed in the earlier report.

B. Description of the Institutions

THE two institutions in which marked retardation occurs, which will be called Institutions I and II, are supported chiefly by public funds; the third institution, to be labeled III, is supported by private funds. Several other children's institutions both public and private, exist in Tehran. The present report should not be taken to imply that retardation prevails in the majority of Iranian institutions.

It is worthy of note that the number of children to be found in institutions in Tehran is quite large. This number is explained by several factors. For one thing, Tehran is a large city, having approximately two million inhabitants. The recent growth of Tehran has

* REPRINTED by permission of the author and The Journal Press from *J. genet. Psychol.,* 1960, **96**, 47–59.

taken place in the main through migration from villages. This has led to a considerable amount of social disorganization which has increased the number of illegitimate children, foundlings, abandoned children, orphans and half-orphans. Furthermore in Tehran at the present time, provisions for the care of dependent children, other than by institutionalization, are quite inadequate. Consequently, almost all children not living with parents or relatives are to be found in institutions.

1. INSTITUTION I

Institution I feels obligated to accept all foundlings and all abandoned children under three years of age who are brought to it. The population of the institution varies from day to day because of departures and admissions. During the time of the present study (September, 1958) the average daily population was about 600; of these about 275 were between birth and one year of age, 135 were between one and two years of age, and about 110 were between two and three years of age. While children above three years are generally transferred to other institutions, a few remain in Institution I beyond this age.

The excess of younger children over older children in Institution I may be due to several causes, including an increased intake rate in recent years, a higher death rate during the first year than in later years, return of older children to relatives, and transfer of older children to other institutions. The data at our disposal do not permit an assignment of relative weights to these factors.

More than nine-tenths of the children in Institution I are recorded as having been under one month of age at the time of their admission. When the actual date of birth is not known, an estimate of age at admission, based on weight, size, and appearance is made and placed in the child's record.

The mother never accompanies the child to Institution I nor sees him after admission.

In general children are placed in individual cribs, although at times, because of overcrowding, two infants temporarily occupy the same crib. In such instances, the heads of the two babies are placed at opposite ends of the bed.

A child is bathed on alternate days. Except when being bathed, the younger children spend practically their entire time in their cribs. They are given milk and other liquids while lying in bed, the bottle being supported by a small pillow. When semi-solid foods are introduced, infants are sometimes held by an attendant and sometimes fed in bed. The children are placed in bed in the supine position. They are never placed prone and seldom get themselves into this position.

The paucity of handling is due primarily to the attendant-child ratio. On the average there were eight children per attendant. In addition to feeding the children, bathing them, and changing clothing and diapers, the attendants are also responsible for changing the bed-linen and cleaning the rooms, and have some responsibilities for preparing food. Each attendant is on duty 12 hours per day. In general there are 32 children and four attendants to a room, although this varies somewhat according to the size of the room. There is no assignment of attendants to particular children. The attendants have no special training for their work and are poorly paid. The emphasis on the part of the supervisors seems to be on neatness in the appearance of the rooms, with little attention to behavioral development.

In his crib the child is not propped up, and is given no toys. The child who can pull himself to sitting, and hence is in some danger of falling from his shallow crib, is placed, when awake, on a piece of linoleum on the composition stone floor of the room. Until he himself achieves the sitting position he remains in bed. In two rooms some of the children who can sit are seated in a row on a bench which has a bar across the front to prevent falling. Aside from these two benches and the frames for the cribs, the rooms have no children's furniture and no play equipment of any kind.

2. INSTITUTION II

This institution accepts children over three years of age. The children in this institution come mainly from Institution I. Child care practices in II are a continuation of the practices existing in I, but sanitation and cleanliness are poorer and the appearance of the children suggests that nutrition and health are poorer. However, in neither I nor II are there any records of growth in height or weight, and it was not possible for us to obtain any objective assessment of nutritional status.

3. INSTITUTION III

Institution III was established only one year prior to the present study. It was started primarily to demonstrate improved methods of institutional care. The children in III come from Institution I but are selected for transfer in the early months of life. It seems likely that those sent to Institution III are chosen from among the more retarded children. They remain in III until three years of age unless adopted before that date. The number of children per attendant is 3–4. Children are held in arms while being fed, are regularly placed prone during part of the time they are in their cribs, are propped up in a sitting position in their cribs at times and are placed in play pens on the floor daily when above four months of age. Numerous toys are provided. Attendants are coached in methods of child care, and supervisors emphasize behavioral development as well as nutrition and health.

Individual growth charts are available for each child in Institution III and show without exception that these children are much below prevailing weight norms on arrival but attain normal weight within a few months.

C. Types of Behavioral Data

QUANTITATIVE observations on the behavioral status of the groups described above were made only with regard to motor coordinations. Some general observations on social and emotional behavior will be presented after motor behavior has been discussed.

In respect to motor development, each child who was a subject of this study was classified with regard to his ability to meet each of the following behavioral criteria:

1. *Sit alone*. The child was placed in a sitting position on the floor. He was scored as sitting alone if he maintained this position for one minute. However, if a child could maintain this position at all he ordinarily could maintain it indefinitely.

2. *Creep or Scoot*. The child was placed sitting on the floor and was encouraged to locomote by having the attendant hold a cookie, or extend her arms, toward the child at a distance of about six feet. He was scored as passing the test if he covered the distance in any manner. If he locomoted, his mode of progression was recorded. The modes of locomotion will be discussed at a later point.

3. *Stand by holding*. The child was held under the arms and placed adjacent to the horizontal bars of a child's bed. It was observed whether or not he grasped the bars and maintained a standing position.

4. *Walk by holding*. The child who could stand by holding was observed for some minutes to determine whether he took steps while holding. He was urged to walk by the attendant.

5. *Walk alone*. The child who could walk by holding objects was placed standing without support and was encouraged to walk to the outstretched arms of the attendant. The child was scored as walking alone if he took at least two steps without support.

In the above tests one of the attendants with whom the child was familiar was coached to make the tests while the experimenter remained at a distance of six feet or more from the child and somewhat behind him. This procedure was followed because it was found that the child's unfamiliarity with the experimenter often inhibited the child's behavior if he was tested by the examiner himself. Communication between the attendant and the examiner was conducted via an Iranian interpreter. Tests were conducted among the children of a given room only after the experimenter and the interpreter had made several visits to the room and somewhat decreased the children's shyness. If a child failed a test, the attendant was asked whether or not he could usually perform the required response. If the answer was positive, renewed efforts were made to elicit a successful performance. The experimenter is convinced that subjects who were scored as failing a test were actually unable to perform the required task.

The numbers of children tested at each age level in each institution are shown in TABLE 1. In Institutions I and II the total number of children tested was 123. In selecting children to provide this sample, the children of appropriate ages were selected at random from each of several rooms, the rooms so far as we could determine not being unusual in any respect. However, we excluded from testing any child who had sensory or motor defects, who was ill or who had recently been ill. In Institution III all children between age one and three were tested. They totaled 51.

D. Results of Tests

TABLE 1 shows the per cent of each group which passed each test. The reader is asked to direct his attention first to the retardation which is evident in Institutions I and II. Among those children in Institution I who were between 1.0–1.9 years of age, fewer than half could sit alone and none could walk alone. In normative studies, of home-reared children, such as those conducted by Jones (1926), Gesell (1928), Dennis and Dennis (1937) and others, it has been found that by nine months of age all normal non-institutional American children can sit alone. By two years of age nearly all can walk alone. A majority of the children of Institution I cannot perform these responses at ages at which almost all home-reared children can perform them. It will be noted that even between 2.0–2.9 years of age only 8 per cent of the children in Institution I are able to walk alone and only 15 per cent of those children in Institution II who are 3.0–3.9 years of age are able to walk alone. We are not aware that any groups so retarded as Groups I and II have previously been reported.

In Institution III the picture is different. Of those children between 2.0–2.9 years of age nearly every child is able to walk unaided. While these children do not equal the performance of home-reared children, their motor behavior is much superior to that of children in Institutions I and II. In other words it is not institutionalization per se which handicaps Groups I and II since Group III children who are also institutionalized are but slightly retarded in motor development. The records of Group III also show that motor retardation is not a general characteristic of Tehran children.

Of special note is the difference in types of pre-walking locomotion between Institutions I and II on the one hand and Institution III on the other.

Of the 67 children in Institutions I and II who engaged in creeping or scooting, only 10 did so by creeping, i.e., going on hands and knees or on hands and feet. All others progressed by "scooting," i.e., their locomotion took place in the sitting position, the body being propelled forward by pushing with the arms aided by propulsion from the legs. Many children who could not walk were quite adept at scooting.

TABLE 1. *Per cent of each group passing each test*

INSTITUTIONS	I	I	II	III	III
N	50	40	33	20	31
Ages	1.0–1.9	2.0–2.9	3.0–3.9	1.0–1.9	2.0–2.9
Sit alone	42	95	97	90	100
Creep or Scoot	14	75	97	75	100
Stand holding	4	45	90	70	100
Walk holding	2	40	63	60	100
Walk alone	0	8	15	15	94

Since tests for creeping or scooting were made when the child was in a sitting position, it might seem that the frequency of scooting was due to the nature of the starting position. To test the effect of starting position, many subjects who were "scooters" were placed prone and offered a cookie at some distance, a powerful incentive for locomotion in these children. In each case the child first pushed himself to a sitting position and then scooted. Scooting was definitely the preferred mode of locomotion even when the child was placed prone. So far as we could determine, the majority of the scooters were completely unfamiliar with creeping.

In Institution III, the reverse situation prevailed. Of 15 children who were observed to creep or scoot, all progressed by creeping. No scooting whatsoever was seen in this institution, yet tests were made from the sitting position as with Groups I and II. When placed sitting and encouraged to locomote, the children leaned forward, got themselves on hands and knees, and crept.

E. Interpretative Comments on Motor Development

LET us examine now the probable reasons why the children in Institutions I and II were so severly retarded relative to home-reared children and why they were so much more retarded than children in Institution III. Several different possibilities need to be considered.

Attention should first be directed to malnutrition as a possible cause of retarded motor development. As noted earlier there can be no doubt that many of the children in Group I were much smaller and lighter than noninstitutional children and children of the same age in Group III. There can be no doubt, too, that malnutrition can be so severe as to interfere with motor performance and motor progress. But the question at stake is not whether malnutrition can affect motor functions but whether malnutrition was in fact a major cause of the retardation of Groups I and II.

We are inclined to think that undernourishment was not the major factor. The following considerations have led us to this interpretation: In the first place, Groups I and II were not entirely listless and inactive. In this connection we need to bring out a fact that we have not noted in earlier sections, namely that these children engaged to a considerable extent in automatisms such as head shaking and rocking back and forth. In many cases, these actions were quite vigorous. These activities tend to indicate that these children were not slow in motor development simply because of motor weakness.

The second consideration is somewhat similar to the first, namely, that the locomotor activities in which the children in Groups I and II engaged seem to require as much as or more energy than the locomotor activities which are usual at their respective ages, but in which they did not engage. For example, while few two-year-olds in Group I walked, three-fourths of them locomoted, chiefly by scooting. No physiological data are available, but it seems likely that the metabolic cost of covering a certain distance by scooting is as great as, or even greater than, the effort required to go the same distance by walking. Certainly this would be true for an adult, but of course one cannot argue from the adult to the child. At any rate the possibility exists that the reason that these children scooted was because this was the only form of locomotor skill which they had learned, not that they were too weak to walk.

This interpretation seems to be borne out by the fact that the pre-walking methods of locomotion were different in different groups. The retarded groups scooted. It is difficult to believe that malnutrition can lead to scooting rather than creeping. It is far from obvious that scooting is "easier" than creeping. If it is, why should not all children choose the easier method? In other words, the differences between groups seem to us to be due to the outcome of different learning situations rather than to differences in nutritional status.

What were the differences in the situations faced by Groups I and II and Group III which may account for the development of two different types of locomotion and different degrees of retardation? We suggest the following:

In Group III and in many homes infants are propped up in a sitting position, or held in a sitting position. In this position the child can raise his head and can partially raise his shoulders for short periods and can relax these efforts without falling. He can thus practice some elements of sitting. On the other hand, the child who remains on his back has no such opportunities to learn to sit. In some respects it is surprising that children who are never propped up or held on the lap are able to learn to sit at all. But it will be remembered that in Groups I and II some children could not sit until they were more than two years of age. Until they could sit alone, all forms of locomotion were impossible for them, because they were not placed in a position in which creeping was possible.

This is not true in Group III. In this group and in many homes, the child is frequently placed prone in bed or on the floor. In this position he can raise his head from the surface, push with his arms, raise his chest, pull his arms and legs beneath his body—in other words, he can practice acts which are employed in creeping. The child who lies on his back nearly every moment of the day is denied such practice. Thus one specific item of child care, i.e., occasionally placing the child face downward, may well contribute to the development of creeping in most children and its absence may account for the lack of creeping in Groups I and II.

The question may be raised as to why children in Institutions I and II did not get themselves into the prone position in their cribs. Repeated observations of these infants in their cribs showed that few ever attained the prone position. The probable reasons are the small size of the cribs and the softness of the beds, both of which made turning over very difficult.

It is likely that this item, i.e., absence of placement in the prone position, may lead to delayed development not only in regard to creeping but also in respect to walking. The child who can creep can go to a piece of furniture, grasp it and pull to his knees. This may lead to walking on his knees while holding furniture. Many children go from knee walking to walking by holding to furniture and thence to walking alone. In contrast to the child who creeps, the child who scoots to a piece of furniture is sitting when he arrives at his goal and can attain a higher position only by lifting his entire weight by his arms. In our opinion, the lack of creeping accounts in large measure for the retardation in walking of Groups I and II.

We are well aware that some persons have interpreted the behavioral retardation of institutional infants to emotional factors rather than to a paucity of learning opportunities. Some have even suggested that under certain conditions institutional infants simply "waste away" from psychological, not from medical causes, a process called marasmus.

If marasmus actually exists, it has somehow been escaped by several hundred children in Iranian institutions living under conditions which are supposed to foster it. Although the prevailing emotional tone of children in Institutions I and II is dysphoric, it is difficult to conceive of mechanisms whereby their unhappiness retards their motor development and causes them to scoot rather than to creep.

There remains the necessity of relating the results of the present study to certain findings reported earlier by the present author. We refer to a study which found no apparent effect of cradling upon the motor development of Hopi children (Dennis, 1940) and a study which indicated that infant development can proceed normally under conditions described as "minimal social stimulation" (Dennis, 1941). On the surface these results seem contradictory to those here reported, because the former studies found that environmental deprivations had but little effect whereas the present study reports that major consequences can ensue from them. In fact, however, the studies are not contradictory but complementary. To bring the results of these studies into harmony, one needs only to examine the kinds of deprivation which were involved and their severity. Certain differences among these studies seem to us to be crucial. The Hopi children were limited in regard to learning opportunities only *while on the cradleboard*. As we pointed out in our original report, they were on the cradleboard chiefly during these sleeping hours, when in any case little learning is expected to occur. When awake they were handled, held upright against the mother, placed sitting on her lap, and placed prone. Their deprivation of learning opportunities was much less than that encountered by the children in Institution I who 24 hours per day for many months remained in a supine position.

A similar contrast exists between Rey and Del, the subjects of an experiment in environmental deprivation, and children in Institutions I and II. Rey and Del were not deprived to the same degree nor in the same manner as the institutional children described above. As the original report shows (Dennis, 1941), Del and Rey, beginning at nine months, were regularly placed in a prone position on a pad on the floor. After it was found that they could not sit alone they were given special practice in sitting. Del and Rey were also given special training in supporting their weight when held upright. Such training was not given in Institutions I and II.

These experiences with special training given to Del and Rey suggest that the retardation of the institutional children could be fairly rapidly remedied if intensive specialized practice were given them. Unfortunately it was not possible for us to undertake such experiments while we were in Tehran. The speed with which delayed skills can be developed remains an important problem for future researches with institutional children.

So far as the permanency of motor deficiencies is concerned it should be noted that Institution II had many children between ages 6 and 15 years who presumably were as retarded at ages two and three as were the children whose behavior was described above. Yet these children were attending school, playing games, doing chores, and being trained in difficult skills, such as the weaving of Persian rugs. There was nothing in their general behavior to suggest that any permanent consequences issued from the extreme retardation in motor development during the early years. To be sure, we have no direct evidence that these children were retarded at two and three years of age, but so far as we could ascertain there has been no change in the child care offered by Institutions I and II and no reason to suppose that their early development was different from that of their counterparts in the present study.

Finally let us note that the results of the present study challenge the widely-held view that motor development consists in the emergence of a behavioral sequence based primarily upon maturation. Shirley's chart of the motor sequence is a textbook favorite. It shows sitting alone at 7 months, creeping at 10 months, and walking alone at 15 months. The present study shows that these norms are met only under favorable environmental conditions. Among the children of Institution I not only was sitting alone greatly retarded but in many cases creeping did not occur. Instead, an alternate form of locomotion was employed. These facts seem to indicate clearly that experience affects not only the ages at which motor items appear but also their very form. No doubt the maturation of certain structures, which as yet cannot be identified, is necessary before certain responses can be learned, but learning also is necessary. Maturation alone is insufficient to bring about most post-natal developments in behavior. This is also the conclusion which we reached in the Del-Rey experiment, but the present study supports this position more dramatically because the limitations of learning in Institutions I and II are more drastic and more long-continued than were those in the Del-Rey study.

F. Social and Emotional Behavior

ONLY incidental observations were made relative to social and emotional behavior. Several of these had to do with the infants' reactions to visitors.

In the weeks preceding our tests, it appears that Institution I seldom had visitors. The children of Institution II formerly had few visitors but several weeks before our arrival a volunteer social service group, aware of the isolation of these children, began to make periodic visits to them, taking them from their beds, holding them, and carrying them about. Institution III also had several visitors, partly because of the demonstration nature of this orphanage.

Children in Institution I, probably because of their unfamiliarity with visitors, were somewhat afraid of us during our first visit. They did not smile with us and, in most cases, would cry if we picked them up. On repeated visits, however, they became more friendly, smiled at us, and before our work was completed some of them would hold out their arms to be carried.

Most of the children in Institution II were positive to visitors at the beginning of our work. Several employed attention-seeking devices before visitors and cried if other children were selected for attention. In contrast in Group III, probably because of the greater time spent with attendants and because of their familiarity with visitors, there was little fear of strangers and only limited attention seeking.

Eagerness for food appeared to be greatest in Institution II. In this institution there was much crying before meal time. Children of this group handled cups and spoons quite well. In general there was very little wasting of food on the part of these children. Cups of milk were reached for eagerly, handled carefully, and drunk rapidly. There were attempts, sometimes successful, on the part of those who had finished eating to obtain the food of others, and hitting, pinching, and biting were sometimes the outcomes of such clashes. Children who could not walk could nevertheless manage to attack others and to defend themselves with considerable skill. After feeding they became much more jovial and nearly every child could be made to smile or laugh by an adult who shook him lightly or tickled him.

G. Summary

THIS paper has presented data concerning behavioral development among 174 children, aged one year to four years, in three Iranian institutions. In Institutions I and II infant development was greatly retarded. The behavioral progress of children in the third institution was much less retarded. The interpretations offered for these differences in behavior among the children of different institutions are as follows: the extreme retardation in Institutions I and II was probably due to the paucity of handling, including the failure of attendants to place the children in the sitting position and the prone position. The absence of experience in these positions is believed to have retarded the children in regard to sitting alone and also in regard to the onset of locomotion. The lack of experience in the prone positions seems in most cases to have prevented children from learning to creep; instead of creeping, the majority of the children in Institutions I and II, prior to walking, locomoted by scooting. In Institution III, in which children were frequently handled, propped in the sitting position, and placed prone, motor development resembled that of most home-reared children. The retardation of subjects in Institutions I and II is believed to be due to the restriction of specific kinds of learning opportunities. This interpretation was found to be congruent with the results of other studies in environmental deprivation. In the light of these findings, the explanation of retardation as being due primarily to emotional factors is believed to be untenable. The data here reported also show that behavioral development cannot be fully accounted for in terms of the maturation hypothesis. The important contributions of experience to the development of infant behavior must be acknowledged.

REFERENCES

DENNIS, W. The effect of cradling practices upon the onset walking in Hopi children. *J. genet. Psychol.*, 1940, **56,** 77–86.

DENNIS, W. Infant development under conditions of restricted practice and of minimum social stimulation. *Genet. Psychol. Monogr.*, 1941, **23,** 143–189.

DENNIS, W., & DENNIS, Marsena G. Behavioral development in the first year as shown by forty biographies. *Psychol. Rec.,* 1937, **1,** 349–361.

DENNIS, W., & NAJARIAN, P. Infant development under environmental handicap. *Psychol. Monogr.,* 1957, **71,** 1–13.

GESELL, A. *Infancy and human growth.* New York: Macmillan, 1928.

JONES, Mary C. The development of early behavior patterns in young children. *Ped. Sem.,* 1926, **33,** 537–585.

SHIRLEY, MARY M. *The first two years.* Vol. 1. *Postural and locomotor development.* Minneapolis: Univer. Minnesota Press, 1933. (*Inst. Child Welf. Monogr. Ser.,* No. 6.)

SPITZ, R A. Hospitalism: an inquiry into the genesis of psychiatric conditions in early childhood. In Ruth S. Eissler *et al.* (Eds.), *The psychoanalytic study of the child.* Vol. 1. New York: International Universities Press, 1945. Pp. 53–74.

SPITZ, R. A. Hospitalism: a follow-up report. In Ruth S. Eissler *et al.* (Eds.), *The psychoanalytic study of the child.* Vol. 2. New York: International Universities Press, 1946. Pp. 113–117. (a)

SPITZ, R. A. Anaclitic depression. In Ruth S. Eissler *et al.* (Eds.), *The psychoanalytic study of the child.* Vol. 2. New York: International Universities Press, 1946. Pp. 313–342. (b)

URIE BRONFENBRENNER

Freudian Theories of Identification and Their Derivatives*

Two years ago, prior to embarking on a program of research on parental roles and personality development, the writer was faced with the necessity of reviewing the literature on theories of identification. The task proved a difficult one on several counts. First, although current theory in this sphere derives almost exclusively from the work of one man —Sigmund Freud—the references to the topic are scattered *passim* through numerous books and papers written over half a lifetime. Second, when one finally views Freud's writings on this subject as a whole, it becomes abundantly clear that he often uses the same terms to refer to what are basically quite different concepts. Third, the above confusion becomes still further confounded in the later developments and modifications of Freud's theories by contemporary writers, who typically apply the same terminology in still other ways and introduce new names for concepts and processes discussed by Freud himself.

Having had to come to terms with these protean problems, the writer felt it might be useful to summarize in a single document the development of Freud's ideas and their elaboration by others and to make explicit the several levels of phenomena with which these theorists are concerned. Specifically, in addition to dealing with Freud's extensive discussion of the topic, this paper will treat with the criticisms and modifications of Freud's theory of identification by Stoke (1950), Mowrer (1950), Sanford (1955), Sears (1957), and Parsons (1955). In the course of our examination, we shall attempt to clarify ambiguities and, where relevant data are available, to examine and evaluate theoretical ideas in the light of existing knowledge.

Freud's Theory of Identification

We begin our exposition with an analysis of the ever-changing notions of identification appearing in Freud's writings. Throughout these transformations one constant feature is discernible. Identification, however described, is invariably based on "an emotional tie with an object," typically the parent. Freud's conception of the precise nature of this emotional tie appears to have shifted somewhat over the course of the years. For the most part, the tie has as its context the attachments and antagonisms of the Oedipus conflict, but in his first exposition of this complex, published in 1900, Freud makes no mention of identification either explicitly or implicitly. We are told only that "we are destined to direct our first sexual impulses toward our mothers, and our first impulses of hatred and violence toward our fathers" (1938, p. 308). As yet, there is no way out of this classic dilemma through identification. To the writer's knowledge, Freud's first extended discussion of the latter mechanism does not occur until fourteen years later in his essay "On Narcissism" (1925b). Although he does not refer to identification by name, he introduces here for the first time his theory of the development of the ego ideal and of conscience—the precursors of what he later called the superego.

It would not surprise us if we were to find a spe-

* Reprinted by permission of the author and the Society for Research in Child Development from *Child Develpm.*, 1960, 31, 15–40.

cial institution in the mind which performs the task of seeing that narcissistic gratification is secured from the ego-ideal and that, with this end in view, it constantly watches the real ego and measures it by that ideal. If such an institution does exist, it cannot possibly be something which we have not yet discovered; we need only to recognize it, and we may say that what we call our conscience has the required characteristics . . . [1925b, p. 52].

For that which prompted the person to form an ego-ideal, over which his conscience keeps guard was, the influence of parental criticism (conveyed to him by the medium of the voice), reinforced as time went on, by those who trained and taught the child. . . . The institution of conscience was at bottom an embodiment, first of parental criticism, and subsequently of that of society [1925b, p. 53].

The essay on narcissism has import for Freud's theory of identification in two other respects as well. It is here that he develops for the first time the notion of an attachment to another person based on other than direct sexual impulse and desire. He refers to this type of attachment as *anaclitic object choice;* that is, an object choice which is essentially presexual in character and based on a "leaning" or dependency relationship with the mother or the person having to do with "the feeding, care, and protection of the child." This anaclitic relationship is important for our purposes since it later becomes the primary basis of one of the two mechanisms of identification which for a long time remain fused in Freud's thinking but are eventually distinguished. The first of these mechanisms involves identification as a function of loss of love, the second as a function of fear of the aggressor. We shall refer to the former as *anaclitic identification* and to the latter by Anna Freud's (1946) classic phrase *identification with the aggressor,* or, more briefly, *aggressive identification.*

The first explicit discussion of identification appears in Freud's essay "Mourning and Melancholia" (1925a) published in 1917. In an attempt to explain the development of extreme self-criticism and feelings of worthlessness in patients who had recently lost a parent or other loved person, Freud proposed a developmental process involving three phases. The first phase, occurring in early childhood, consists in a "preliminary" form of identification in which ego and object are fused in a single undifferentiated pattern. Out of this there develops object choice, that is, the attachment of the libido to a person, typically the parent. Finally,

. . . owing to a real injury or disappointment concerned with the loved person, this object relationship was undermined. . . . The object cathexis proved to have little power of resistance and was abandoned; but the free libido was withdrawn into the ego and not directed to another object. It did not find application there, however, in any of several possible ways, but served simply to establish an *identification* of the ego with the abandoned object [1925a, p. 159].

It is essentially this same three-phase sequence which forms the basis of Freud's extended discussion of identification four years later in *Group Psychology and the Analysis of the Ego* (1948). Here, for the first time, the process is represented explicitly as a mechanism for resolution of the Oedipus complex. As before, the child begins with preliminary identifications with both parents but, in the case of the boy, the identification develops into

a straightforward sexual object-cathexis toward his mother. . . . The little boy then notices that his father stands in his way with the mother. His identification then takes on a hostile coloring and becomes identical with the wish to replace his father in regard to his mother as well. Identification, in fact, is ambivalent from the very first; it can turn into an expression of tenderness as easily as into a wish for someone's removal [1948, p. 61].

Here again, we may note that, as in Freud's earlier discussion, the notions of identification with a loved vs. a hated object are inextricably fused. Does the child identify with the father to recapture a lost loved and loving object or to defend himself against paternal threat and aggression, or both? The preceding quotation would seem to emphasize the obstructive and hostile aspects of the object with whom the child identifies. Yet, only a few paragraphs later Freud cites as an example of identification *par excellence* the instance of a young boy who, unhappy over the loss of a kitten, "declared straight out that now he himself was the kitten, and accordingly crawled about on all fours, would not eat at the table, etc."

It is in this essay that Freud states what is, in effect, his first formal definition of identification:

> It is easy to state in a formula the distinction between an identification with the father and the choice of the father as an object. In the first case, one's father is what one would like to *be,* and in the second he is what one would like to have. The distinction, that is, depends upon whether the tie attaches to the subject or the object of the ego. The former is therefore already possible before any sexual object choice has been made. It is much more difficult to give a clear metapsychological representation of the distinction. We can only see that identification endeavours to mould a person's own ego after the fashion of one that has been taken as a "model" [1948, pp. 62–63].

Freud's subsequent discussions of identification involve no new basic elements beyond those contained in the above early formulations, but his conception of the balance of forces making for identification shifts appreciably and culminates in a theory which is, in effect, differential for the two sexes. Specifically, in successive papers, Freud gives increasingly more emphasis to the fear of the punitive, castrating father as the primary force which brings about the resolution of the Oedipus complex and the development of identification. Witness the following passages from the essay on "The Passing of the Oedipus Complex" (1924):

> The Oedipus complex offered the children two possibilities of satisfaction, an active one replacing the father and a passive one replacing the mother. . . . But now the acceptance of the possibility of castration, the recognition that women are castrated, makes an end of both possibilities. If the gratification desired in consequence of the love is to cost the child his penis, a conflict must arise between the narcissistic interest in this part of the body and the libidinal cathexis of the parent objects. Normally, in this conflict the first of these forces triumphs; the child's ego turns away from the Oedipus complex [p. 272].

> Analytic observation enables us to perceive or to infer in these connections between the phallic organization, the Oedipus complex, the threat of castration, the formation of the superego and the latency period. They justify the statement that the Oedipus complex succumbs to the threat of castration [p. 273].

As Freud is quick to recognize, the above line of argument has crucial implications for the development of the female. Since she is already "castrated," she presumably would have no incentive for identifying with the "aggressor" and thence developing a superego. This is precisely Freud's conclusion, which he elaborates, albeit somewhat apologetically, in his essay on "Some Psychological Consequences of the Anatomical Distinction between the Sexes" (1950b).

> In girls the motive for the destruction of the Oedipus complex is lacking. Castration had already had its effect, which was to force the child into the situation of the Oedipus complex. Thus the Oedipus complex escapes the fate which it meets with in boys; . . . I cannot escape the notion (though I hesitate to give it expression) that for women what is ethically normal is different from what it is in men. Their superego is never so inexorable, so impersonal, so independent of its emotional origins as we require it to be in men. Character traits which critics of every epoch have brought up against women—that they show less sense of justice than men, that they are less ready to submit to the great necessities of life, that they are more often influenced in their judgments by feelings of affection and hostility—all these would be amply accounted for by the modification in the formation of their superego which we have already inferred. We must not allow ourselves to be deflected from such conclusions by the denials of feminists, who are anxious to force us to regard the two sexes as completely equal in position and worth; but we shall, of course, willingly

agree that the majority of men are also far behind the masculine ideal [pp. 196–197].

Perhaps more than any other Freudian assertions we have examined thus far, certain statements in the foregoing paragraph are subject to empirical verification. Also, we have probably gone far enough in our exposition of Freud's basic theory to begin to consider questions of fact. Despite their partisan character, Freud's views on psychological differences between the sexes are not entirely without scientific support. Witness the following summary statement from what is probably the most comprehensive and careful study of sex differences in personality carried out to date—that of Terman and Miles (1936):

The compassion and sympathy of the female . . . appears from the evidence personal rather than abstract, less a principled humanitarianism than an active sympathy for palpable misfortune and distress. In disgust, aesthetic judgment, and in moral censure, the evidence is rather for the influence of fashion and feeling than of principle or reason [p. 448].

But where do qualities of compassion and sympathy in the female come from? The absence of castration fears in the woman, though it may deprive her of the incentive to identify with the father, can hardly account for her identification with the mother. In his search for an alternative theory of identification for the female, one which does not rely primarily on identification with the aggressor, Freud returns to a conception implicit in his earlier thinking—namely, what we have called *anaclitic identification* or identification through loss of a loved object. In his own words:

Fear of castration is naturally not the only motive for repression; to start with, it has no place in the psychology of women; they have, of course, a castration complex, but they cannot have any fear of castration. In its place, for the other sex, is found fear of the loss of love, obviously a continuation of the fear of the infant at the breast when it misses its mother. You will understand what objective danger-situation is indicated by this kind of anxiety. If the mother is absent or has withdrawn her love from the child, it can no longer be certain that its needs will be satisfied, and may be exposed to the most painful feelings of tension [1933, p. 121].

The above formulation takes on prophetic qualities in the light of a series of recent research findings obtained independently by two groups of investigators. Working within a framework of learning theory rather than psychoanalysis, Sears, Maccoby, and Levin (1957), in a study of child rearing practices in Boston suburbia, found that discipline techniques involving "withdrawal of love" were more frequently used with girls than with boys; whereas the reverse was true for methods involving physical punishment, threat, or deprivation of property and privileges. Moreover, the former techniques were appreciably more effective, in both sexes, for achieving socialization of the child and the "development of conscience." Children exposed to love followed by its conditional withdrawal tended to show less aggression and more guilt (as evidenced by confessions and "feeling sorry"); in contrast, the more the child was threatened with or subjected to physical punishment, the more aggressive was his behavior.

Striking confirmation for this same finding comes from the psychoanalytically-oriented research of Miller, Swanson, and their students (1960). Working with families in the Detroit area, they found that boys whose mothers used psychological punishment (appeals to guilt, reasoning, or acting hurt) showed appreciably stronger evidence of guilt (as measured by a projective test) than boys who were punished directly by spanking or slapping. The latter, however, revealed more aggression both behaviorally and in projective tests.

The preceding studies have several important theoretical implications. First, they suggest that the two major mechanisms of identification proposed by Freud have relevance for differences in personality not only between the sexes but within the sexes as well. Such an inference is altogether consistent with Freud's own thinking. Thus, he points out (1950a) that the severity of the superego in the boy is a direct function of the degree to which "the father was hard, violent, and cruel." Moreover, even in his later formulations of the operation of the Oedipus complex in boys, he allows for the possibility of "an identification of an affectionate sort with the boy's father" (1950b) which presumably could lead to some measure of anaclitic identification. Analogously, the girl's identification is to some extent influenced by the Oedipus complex even though this influence is subordinated to the anaclitic relationship.

> The mother-identification of the woman can be seen to have two levels, the pre-oedipal, which is based on the tender attachment to the mother and which takes her as a model, and the later one, derived from the Oedipus complex. . . . But the phase of pre-oedipal tender attachment is the decisive one; it paves the way for her acquisition of those characteristics which will later enable her to play her part in the sexual function adequately, and carry out her inestimably social activities [1933, p. 183].

Although the findings of Sears and his colleagues, on the other hand, and those of Miller, Swanson, and their students, on the other, are consistent with some aspects of Freud's later theories of identification, they appear to contradict others. For example, Freud's hypothesis of the more complete development of superego in men would seem to imply that guilt should be a more frequent and pronounced phenomenon in men than in women. Yet, both groups of investigators report exactly the opposite result. These findings suggest that it is anaclitic identification involving withdrawal of love which fosters the development of the superego whereas identification with the aggressor leads rather to the adoption of the aggressor's hostile outlook not only toward the self but toward the environment at large. Such an interpretation is consistent with Anna Freud's description of the mechanism as one in which the child attempts to defend himself against aggression and power by emulating the characteristics of the person wielding power. Similarly, Bettelheim's dramatic report (1943) describing how the prisoners in Nazi concentration camps gradually adopted the dress, manner, and, above all, the sadistic methods of their guards and persecutors, as well as Sarnoff's study (1951) of the operation of the mechanism of identification with the aggressor among anti-semitic Jews, lends empirical support to the inference that it is hostility rather than guilt which is learned as the consequence of this mechanism.

At the same time, aggressive identification appears to require for its fulfillment a situation in which, to quote Sarnoff, "the victim is dependent upon the aggressor" and "cannot escape his influence." Thus, the prisoners in the concentration camp were not only unable to get away, but depended for their very survival on the whims of their captors, whether they gave food or withheld it, condemned one to the cremation chamber or not. In this same sense a child can be at the mercy of a hostile, punitive parent. Indeed, it is possible that neither kind of identification can occur unless the child is, in some sense, dependent on the parent. If the child comes to be dependent on love, then separation or withdrawal of love can lead to anaclitic identification and superego formation. If his dependence is one on survival and freedom from pain, then identification with the aggressor becomes the mechanism of choice. Finally, there is the possibility, indeed, the likelihood, that both processes operate simultaneously. The child is both loved and hated, and the balance between the two determines the course and character of identification. Perhaps, it is when love and hate are both maximized that there develops the extreme, self-punishing superego which Freud was so fond of describing as the virtually inevitable outcome of the boy's Oedipal conflict with his father. Such a conclusion would seem to be consistent with Freud's brilliant analysis of the self-destroying superego in his essay on "Dostoyevski and Parricide" (1950a).

One feature remains to be noted regarding Freud's theory of identification and superego formation. Although, even in his later writings, Freud continues to speak of identification as involving imitation of a model (1933,

1949), he now takes pains to emphasize that this model is not the immediate image which the parent presents to the child, but the ideal standard reflecting the parent's aspirations rather than his actual behavior. In Freud's words:

> In general, parents and similar authorities follow the dictates of their own super-egos in the up-bringing of children. Whatever terms their ego may be on with their super-ego, in the education of the child they are severe and exacting. They have forgotten the difficulties of their own childhood, and are glad to be able to identify themselves fully at last with their own parents, who subjected them to such severe restraints. The result is that the superego of the child is not really built upon the model of the parents, but on that of the parents' super-ego . . . [1933, p. 95].

In the light of this statement, some research findings by Helper (1955) are of interest. Working with a sample of high school pupils and their parents, this investigator compared the child's self-description with the parent's description of himself and the parent's ideal for the child ("Describe your child as you would most like him to be"). Helper found that the child's self-description was as similar to the parent's ideal for the child as it was to the parent's self-description. In other words, the child comes to resemble not only what the parent is but what the parent wants the child to be.

In concluding our presentation of Freud's theory—or perhaps more properly, theories—of identification, we are faced with the problem of summarizing views which—in part because they are ambiguous, in part because they have changed over the years—are not always consistent with each other. One way of resolving the dilemma is to treat these views as alternative formulations. This is what we propose to do.

We may begin by distinguishing between two uses of the term identification in Freud's writing. Most often, as in his discussion of the Oedipus complex, Freud treats identification as a process—the sequential interplay of forces internal and external which impel the child to take on the characteristics of the parent. It is in this sense of process that the term identification is used when we speak of anaclitic or aggressive identification. In other words, these represent alternative developmental mechanisms derivable from Freudian theory.

But, on occasion, Freud also uses the term identification to describe the *product* or outcome of the process—the resultant similarity in the characteristics of the child and the model. Moreover, there is the further question of what aspects of the model are being emulated. At times, as in the example of the boy who identifies with a kitten by crawling about on all fours, refusing to eat at the table, etc., it is the overt behavior of the model which is being adopted. In other instances, as when Freud speaks of moulding "one's ego after the fashion of one that has been taken as a model," identification would appear to include internalization of the motives as well as the overt behavior of another. Finally, as we have seen, in his later writings it is not the parent's ego with which the child identifies but his superego, his idealized standards for feeling and action. In short, there are three aspects of the parent after which the child may pattern himself, the parent's *overt behavior,* his *motives,* or his *aspirations* for the child. Which aspect of the model is in fact identified with becomes, from our point of view, an empirical question. It seems probable that all three aspects are involved at one time or another. Or it may be that one process, such as anaclitic identification, is more likely to result in the emulation of standards, while another, such as identification with the aggressor, leads to the adoption of parental motives and acts. Still other possibilities will emerge once we consider subsequent elaborations of Freud's original theories.

Psychological Variants of Freud's Theory of Identification

CRITICISMS and modifications of Freud's theory of identification have been proposed by a number of present-day psychologists—

notably Stoke (1950), Mowrer (1950), Sanford (1955), and, most recently, Sears (1957). For the most part, we find that these theorists underscore points with which we are already familiar. Thus, Stoke, in a searching analysis of factors influencing identification, points to the importance of distinguishing between "behavioral identification," in which the child exhibits the same overt behavior as the parent, and "emotional identification," which refers to the emotional tie (for Stoke, always positive) between the child and the parent. Stoke also raises the question, as we have, "whether fear of physical punishment alone can build up an adequate super-ego," and relies on what we have called anaclitic identification to explain the development of conscience and guilt. Nevertheless, he explicitly rejects Freud's theorizing on the grounds that,

> it is not scientifically verifiable, is inconsistent in its applicability to boys and girls, fails to account for differences as well as similarities, . . . does not explain the discrepancies between the emotional and behavioral aspects of identification, . . . emphasizes organic causes to the virtual exclusion of others, and is not very useful in child guidance [Stoke, 1950, p. 239].

A more charitable and optimistic view of the Freudian theory of identification is taken by Mowrer (1950), who views it as an appropriate point of departure for the formulation of research hypotheses (1953). On the basis of a comprehensive analysis of the treatment of identification by both Sigmund and Anna Freud, Mowrer, utilizing suggestions from the work of two of his students (Courtney, 1949; Lair, 1949), distinguishes two mechanisms of identification, *developmental* and *defensive;* "the one is powered mainly by biologically given drives ('fear of loss of love' in the analytic sense) and the other by socially inflicted discomforts ('castration fear' or, less dramatically, simply fear of punishment)" (Mowrer, 1950, p. 592). In short, here once again is the distinction between anaclitic and aggressive identification. Mowrer, however, regards the former as considerably less anxiety-provoking, and, therefore, less consequential for the formation of character. He states:

> Developmental identification, we may suppose, is a milder and simpler experience than is defensive identification, which has a violent, crisis-like nature. . . . The first presumably involves little conflict; but in the latter case, conflict and attendant anxiety are outstanding. . . . If a child were cared for but never disciplined, he would presumably show only developmental identification and would develop skills but no character [1950, pp. 592–593].

At first glance, this view is somewhat surprising, particularly in the light of Freud's conclusion, in his essay on *The Problem of Anxiety* (1936), that "The most basic anxiety of all . . . arises in connection with separation from the mother" (p. 76). Mowrer's position becomes more comprehensible, however, in the light of a subsequent exposition of "defensive identification."

> If a child has never known a normal degree of love during the infantile period, parental discipline produces comparatively little conflict. . . . But the case of the normally-loved child is different: the disciplinary demands of the parents cause him first of all to attack his parents (since their discipline frustrates him and he is too dependent to retreat from them), and when this behavior meets with still further punishment, he is likely to be thrown into *intolerable anxiety*.
>
> At this point, a most remarkable thing normally occurs. At the height of his conflict, the child discovers that he can satisfy his parents and at the same time, still his own inner turmoil if he will only do one thing: accept the standards of conduct and social values which his parents are holding up to him and make them *his* standards and *his* values. . . . In common parlance, we say that the child now has a conscience or that, in the language of psychoanalysis, his *superego* has begun to function. . . . the induction stands that character, conscience, or superego (the term is not important) is forged as a solution to the unbearable conflict generated during the period of "intensive" socialization by the great love for and equally great fear (and/or hatred) of the parents [Mowrer, 1953, p. 72].

As Sanford has so aptly pointed out in a recent paper (1955), Mowrer's "defensive identification" is actually "developmental"; that is, it is impelled by that "fear of the loss of love" which Mowrer designates as the hallmark of "developmental identification." Sanford himself prefers the term "introjection" for the latter mechanism and reserves identification for describing, among other phenomena, what we have called aggressive identification. Sanford argues that the lasting effects of this latter type of mechanism are "frequently overestimated" and that "the process by which figures of the environment become models for response readiness in the deeper layers of the personality, as in superego formation, is not defensive identification but introjection . . ." (1955, p. 112). From our point of view, the question of which mechanism is the more powerful cannot be settled by *a priori* argument. As we have indicated, the theoretical issue, which is an important one, can ultimately be resolved only through empirical investigation.

Both Mowrer and Sanford, then, though they employ their own terminology, may be said to follow Freud in postulating two different mechanisms of identification. Both these theorists, however, depart from Freud's thinking in other respects. Thus, Mowrer takes issue with Freud's basic notion that sexual object choice precedes rather than follows identification. Mowrer writes:

> Freud is correct in noting the difficulties connected with his view of psychosexual development, but he never made what would seem to have been a most natural alternative assumption, namely, that the love a child first develops for his parents is such as to lead to identification and that object choice *follows as a secondary result*. Thus, when a little boy begins to experience libidinal impulses he will, if already he has become firmly aligned with his father and with men in general, be strongly disposed to direct these impulses toward women, in keeping with the model provided by his father; and the little girl, in identifying with her mother, will tend, like mother, to take men as sex objects [1950, p. 607].

Mowrer's reversal of the traditional Freudian sequence is of particular interest since it leads him to a theoretical position, which, as we shall see, is very similar to that of the sociologist Parsons. For purposes of subsequent comparison, we quote the relevant portions of Mowrer's exposition of his "alternative view":

> . . . Because Freud assumed that object choice is primary and identification derived therefrom, he believed that the psychosexual development of boys is simpler than that of girls, since boys can at an early date take women as sex objects and retain them as such throughout life; but girls, Freud conjectured, having, like the boys, taken the mother as the first sex object, must later abandon this object choice in favor of men and assume instead an identification relationship with the mother and with women generally. The alternative hypothesis here suggested holds that the situation is the reverse. Because the infant's first experiences of care and affection are with the mother, we infer . . . that there will be a tendency for children of *both* sexes . . . to identify with the mother. This provides a path of development which the female child can follow indefinitely; but the male child must, in some way, abandon the mother as a personal model and shift his loyalties and ambitions to his father. Once the boy and the girl are securely aligned with the mother and the father, respectively, *in terms of their basic character structure,* then, as specific sexual needs arise, they can be handled along lines prescribed as correct and proper for members of their particular sex.
>
> However, we must not neglect to consider the question of how it is that the boy, whose primal identification is ordinarily with the mother—for example, mothers almost certainly play a greater role in their infant's learning to walk and talk than do their fathers—how it is that the boy eventually abandons the mother as his personal guide and takes instead the father. Here we have few facts to guide us, but we may plausibly conjecture that the first identification which infants make with mother figures is *undifferentiated*. By this I mean that the small child probably first comes to perceive the mother, not as a woman who is distinct from men, but simply as a human being, different in no systematic way from other adult figures in the environment. The personal characteristics which are acquired through identification with, or imitation of, the mother during this period are characteristics or accomplishments which are appropriate to all persons, male and female alike. It is only at a later stage, presumably, that the

child becomes aware of the partition of mankind into two sexes; and it is then that the father, who has played a somewhat subsidiary role up to this point, normally comes forward as the boy's special mentor, as his proctor, guide, and model in matters which will help the boy eventually to achieve full adult status in his society, not only as a human being, but also in the unique status of a *man*. This, we note, involves two things: (1) being a man in the sense of being honorable, reliable, industrious, skilful, courageous, and courteous; and (2) being a man in the sense of being masculine, i.e., sexually oriented toward members of the opposite sex [1950, pp. 607–608].

In short, Mowrer suggests that the series of identifications through which the child passes involves the progressive differentiation of social objects first with respect to age, and then to sex. It is this notion of sequential differentiation (apparently arrived at quite independently) which becomes the core of Parsons' theory of identification.

Sanford departs from the classical Freudian position in still another direction. He emphasizes the possibility—indeed, the likelihood—that the parental love or punishment need not necessarily result in "internalization" of the parent's attitudes; rather they may simply reinforce behavior directly, in accordance with familiar learning principles. He states:

. . . We should consider that normal character development can be largely explained, without benefit of either identification or introjection, on the basis of common forms of learning. A child learns which of his actions please, and which displease, his parents, which win him love, which disapproval, he learns what reactions are effective in inhibiting those impulses which if allowed free rein would lead to catastrophe, he learns how to regard himself from the way others regard him, and in building his ego system and his self-conception he learns what to keep and what to discard [1955, p. 117].

In other words, Sanford proposes yet another, at once more simple and more general mechanism to account for the child's adoption of parental characteristics. The process is the familiar one of learning through reinforcement by punishment and reward. The classic theoretical treatment of the role of reinforcement in inducing one person to behave like another in response to similar cues is that of Miller and Dollard (1941). These authors, however, make only passing reference to the concept of identification. Having defined copying as behavior in which "one person learns to model his behavior on that of another" and "knows that his act is an acceptable reproduction of the model act," Miller and Dollard state tentatively:

It is possible that a [more] detailed analysis would show that the mechanisms involved in copying are also involved in that aspect of character, or super-ego, formation which the Freudians have described as "identification" [1941, p. 164].

They then suggest, in a footnote, that identification is likely to vary as a function of the degree to which the model (e.g., the parent) is a "loved or prestigeful person."

This suggestion is, in effect, followed up in the previously mentioned research by Helper (1955). Working in the framework of reinforcement theory, Helper found, for example, that a boy is more likely to describe himself as similar to his father (and to aspire to his father's ideals for him) if the mother approves of the father as a model for the child. Both sexes were also more likely to emulate characteristics of the mother when the mother approved of herself as a model.[1]

In short, in addition to its other meanings, the term identification has been equated, theoretically and empirically, with "common forms of learning." Under these circumstances, one may legitimately ask whether the concept has any scientific utility and whether it might not better be abandoned. This is precisely the conclusion reached by Sanford, who writes:

A term that can be employed in so many different ways and that . . . has been accepted by most psychologists and sociologists, could hardly mean

1 The father's approval of the mother or of himself, however, showed no relation to the child's perceived similarity with the characteristics or ideals of either parent. We shall consider the implication of this parental difference in our discussion below of Parsons' theory of identification.

anything very precise. It might be proposed, quite seriously, that we give up the term "identification" altogether. When we are describing social behavior and have the impulse to say "identification" we must in any case specify "what kind"; if we go a step further and say just what we mean, it will almost always turn out that other words are available, and that they are, in fact, more accurate. . . . In other words, why not agree that identification is not an explanatory concept, and that as a descriptive one it is too vague to be useful [1955, p. 107]?

The argument is persuasive, but—in this writer's judgment—nevertheless mistaken. Admittedly, one could speak of the child's learning of parental behavior, motives, or standards without invoking the term identification. And, if a concept is needed to describe the product of such learning, one could employ some simple but noncommittal expression as "acquired similarity." It would also be possible to examine the effects of parental aggression, withdrawal of love, or direct punishment and reward on the child's learning of parental characteristics. What would be lost by a recasting of the problem in such more specific terms?

In this author's view, we would risk losing sight of an important psychological phenomenon, as well as an intriguing theoretical issue —a phenomenon and issue first recognized, howeved dimly, by Sigmund Freud. In concerning himself with identification, Freud was not asking why and how a child might learn an isolated piece of behavior from his parent. He was interested in what he felt to be a more sweeping and powerful phenomenon—the tendency of the child to take on not merely discrete elements of the parental model but a total pattern. Moreover, as Freud saw it, this acquisition was accomplished with an emotional intensity which reflected the operation of motivational forces of considerable power. These features of pattern and power are reflected in his use, as virtual synonyms for identification, such terms as introjection and incorporation—words which connote a sudden and somewhat desperate "swallowing whole" of the parent figure.

In short, psychoanalytic conceptions of identification should not simply be equated with any acquisition by the child, through ordinary learning, of characteristics of his parent. Freud's formulations have at least two distinguishing features which, though they may be expressible in terms of learning theory, are hardly conventional attributes of it. First, these conceptions clearly imply the existence of *a motive in the child to become like the parent.* Second, this motive functions in relation not to isolated elements but to a total pattern or Gestalt.

Similar conclusions regarding the defining properties of identification have been reached by at least one learning theorist. Sears (1957) has recently published a theoretical paper in which he defines identification as "a secondary motivational system for which 'acting like the mother' is the goal response" (p. 154). This motive gives rise to behavior in which the individual acts "like another person," but such learned activity can be distinguished from conventional learning by the absence of specific training. In Sears' words:

Children of two years and older have a tendency to act in a number of ways like their parents. They adopt parental mannerisms, play parental roles, and in the later preschool years seem to incorporate in their own value systems many of the values, restrictions, and ideals of the parents. That is to say, they develop a conscience. It is the apparent "absorption" of these characteristics without specific training, either by direct guidance or by reward and punishment, that leads to the hypothesis of a process (identification) that short-cuts the direct training process. It is as if the child had learned a general principle "to be like my father and mother." He then incorporates many of their psychological properties without, in each instance, appearing to receive overt rewards for doing so [1957, p. 152].

Though the language is that of behavior theory rather than psychoanalysis, Sears' views strike us as highly consistent with Freud's original conceptions. The parallelism is even more marked in Sears' exposition of the antecedents of identification. He begins with the familiar argument that the child's initial biological dependence on the mother inevitably becomes psychological—or, in his terminology, it "produces, in the infant, a secondary drive system of dependency-on-the-mother." Then,

> . . . since it is being assumed that the child does not discriminate between himself and his mother, the perception of *her* actions becomes an integral part of *his* action sequences just as much as his own actions do.
>
> If the mother is absent on some occasion when drive stimuli occur and start off one of the child's action sequences, he will attempt to perform those parts of the total sequences for which his mother was normally responsible. . . .
>
> . . . occurrence (of imitation) in a child with dependency drive for which the mother's actions are the appropriate rewards will permit the child to reward himself. That is, when he is motivated to secure the mother's nurturing responses, he can imitate her affectionate attitudes and gestures himself and hence secure at least partial gratification of his dependency drive.
>
> One consequence suggested by this formulation is that the degree of identification of the child with his mother should bear a curvilinear relationship to the amount of affectionate nurture the mother gives. If she is universally present and always plays a part in the dyadic mother-child sequence, the child will never have occasion to perform mother-acts, i.e., to establish identification. On the other hand, if she is continuously punitive, and is rarely associated with the satisfying completion of the child's goal striving, her acts will have no part in his action sequence, and there will be no initial instigation to act like her [1957, pp. 154–155].

Clearly, what Sears has ingeniously accomplished here is to restate in the language of learning theory Freud's theory of anaclitic identification. Does this mean that in our review of psychological variants of Freudian theory we have merely come the full circle? Not altogether, for we have achieved new clarity on a number of points. Most notably, among the many phenomena to which the term identification has been applied, we have found one which cannot readily be subsumed under more conventional or simple rubrics: this is the notion of a generalized motive on the part of one person to take on the characteristics of another as a total pattern. To this new insight, we can now apply generalizations reached earlier in this analysis. Thus, we have at least two theories, both Freudian in origin, to account for the existence of such a mechanism: the first involves defense against an aggressor by emulating his characteristics; the second, a response to an absent or depriving loved person by seeking to replace him, as it were, in one's own behavior. We have seen that the second of these developmental processes, and probably the first as well, can be restated in terms of present-day learning theory. Finally, taking a cue from Miller and Dollard's theory and Helper's research findings, we can conceive of still another mechanism, derivable from learning theory, which could account for the development of a general motive to become like another. If the parent is a "loved and prestigeful person" whom the child is rewarded for emulating, such emulation could become a need in its own right through secondary reinforcement.

In one important respect we have yet to modify our earlier reasoning. If the core of the concept of identification is a *motive* to become like another person, then the presence of similarity is, at best, only a by-product rather than an essential feature of the phenomenon. Indeed, as the writer has argued elsewhere (Bronfenbrenner, 1958), one could take the position that the stronger the desire to become like another, the more one is likely to exaggerate or distort the characteristics of the model. Perhaps Freud had this possibility in mind in asserting that the child's superego is modeled not after the parent as he is but after the "parental imagos," the child's exaggerated and distorted perceptions of his parents. Here again we find ourselves confronted with the still unsettled question of the *content* of identification. Granted that the child is motivated to acquire some patterned aspects of the parent, just what aspects are involved? How are they organized both in form and content? Although some light can be thrown on this issue from the perspective of psychological theories of identification, it is Parsons' sociological formulation which casts it into sharpest relief.

Parsons' Sociological Theory of Identification

PARSONS admittedly takes Freudian theory as his point of departure. Accordingly, before examining Parsons' elaborations of the now familiar psychoanalytic position, we take note briefly of the major points of convergence in the two approaches. First, the generalized motive to become like another stands, with Parsons as with Freud, at the core of the concept of identification. Thus, in *Toward a General Theory of Action* (Parsons & Shils, 1951), the following distinction is drawn between identification and imitation: [2]

> The two major mechanisms for the learning of patterns from social objects are *imitation,* which assumes only that alter provides a model for the specific pattern learned without being an object of generalized cathectic attachment; and *identification,* which implies that alter is the object of such an attachment and therefore serves as a model not only with respect to a specific pattern in a specific context of learning but also as a model in a generalized sense. Alter becomes, that is, a model for general orientations, not merely for specific patterns [p. 129].

Similarly, if we interpret it correctly, Parsons' theory of the antecedents of identification is a restatement, in still another and even more esoteric language, of the now familiar stages of the anaclitic process. He takes as his point of departure the four-phase "paradigm of social control" originally proposed in *The Social System* (Parsons, 1951, pp. 300–326) and further elaborated in the *Working Papers* (Parsons, Bales, & Shils, 1953, pp. 238–245). Applying his conceptual scheme primarily to the therapeutic process, Parsons distinguishes four sequential stages: *permissiveness* ("allowing the patient to express himself"); *support* ("to tolerate the excessive demands of the patient and 'accept' him as a human being"); denial of *reciprocity* ("the denial of response-reward, including . . . gratification in being duly punished for an aggressive act"); and *manipulation of rewards* ("a process of reinforcing 'reality oriented' adaptive instrumental performance"). In the volume on the family (Parsons & Bales, 1955), Parsons offers this same four-phase sequence as the basic foundation for his theory of socialization and, more specifically, identification. Thus, he asserts that in her treatment of the child, the mother begins with permissiveness and support which develop in the child "a diffuse attachment to *her,* a *dependency on her*" (italics Parsons').

> We may presume that once dependency in this sense has come to be well established, the demands for attention, and for specific acts of care expands. The child manifests what, from the point of view of the mother's standards of child care, are illegitimate positive wishes. He is waked up at certain times though he would rather be allowed to sleep, he is given only so much to eat, less than he wants, he is put down when he would like her to continue to fondle him, etc. Whereas his dependency in general is welcomed and rewarded, excessive manifestations are pruned off by denial of reciprocity. . . . The balance between denial of reciprocity and positive reward gradually leads to the establishment of a stable "orientation" or expectation system in the child the organization of his behavior both around the relation to the mother as an object and involving certain *standards* of what are and are not legitimate expectations of his own gratification and of her behavior. When this process has reached a certain stage we can speak of the internalization of the mother as an object as having taken place. . . . This internalization is what Freud meant by ego's primary identification [1955, p. 65].

Where then does Parsons diverge from Freud? Principally on the question of content, of what is internalized. The specific issues are raised in Parsons' essay on the superego (1953, pp. 13–29). The sociologist differs with the psychoanalyst on three major counts: First, Parsons criticizes Freud for failing to recognize that identification results in the internalization not only of moral standards (the superego) but also the cognitive and expressive features of the parent and through him of the culture as a whole.

2 The same distinction is made in *The Social System* (Parsons, 1951, p. 211).

The general purport of this criticism is that Freud, with his formulation of the concept of superego, made only a beginning at an analysis of the role of common culture in personality. The structure of his theoretical scheme prevented him from seeing the possibilities for extending the same fundamental analysis from the internalization of moral standards—which he applied to the superego—to the internalization of the cognitive frame of reference for interpersonal relations and for the common system of expressive symbolism; and similarly it prevented him from seeing the extent to which these three elements of the common culture are integrated with each other [1953, pp. 20–21].

In a second and derivative challenge, Parsons takes exception to what he regards as an exclusively constitutional basis for Freud's theory of sexuality.

. . . Freud speaks of the original "bi-sexuality" of the child. The presumption is that he postulated a constitutionally given duality of orientation. In terms of the present approach, there is at least an alternative hypothesis possible which should be explored. This hypothesis is that some of the principal facts which Freud interpreted as manifestations of constitutional bisexuality can be explained by the fact that the categorization of human persons—including the actor's categorization of himself as a point of reference —into two sexes is not, except in its somatic points of reference, biologically given but, in psychological significance, must be learned by child. It is fundamental that children of both sexes start life with essentially the same relation to the mother, a fact on which Freud himself rightly laid great stress. It may then be suggested that the process by which the boy learns to differentiate himself in terms of sex from the mother and in this sense to "identify" with the father, while the girl learns to identify with the mother, is a learning process. One major part of the process of growing up is the internalization of one's own sex role as part of the self-image. It may well be that this way of looking at the process will have the advantage of making the assumption of constitutional bisexuality at least partly superfluous as an explanation of the individual's sex identification. In any case it has the great advantage of linking the determination of sex categorization directly with the role structure of the social system in a theoretical as well as an empirical sense [1953, pp. 21–22].

In the light of our own analysis of Freud's theories of identification, we are inclined to doubt Parsons' contention that Freud overlooked the possibility of learning as a mechanism in the development of sex identity. But, by now, the reader is in a position to judge the merits of the case for himself. Parsons' final contention in the above quotation, however, can hardly be challenged. Certainly Freud has not linked "the determination of sex categorization directly with the role structure of the social system." Parsons' third and major criticism of Freud focuses around this very issue and becomes the major theme of the sociologist's complex revision and extension of Freudian theory in the volume on *Family, Socialization and Interaction Process* (Parsons & Bales, 1955). Here Parsons states:

Freud was clearly very much on the right track, and in fact gave us the foundations of the present view. But what Freud lacked was a systematic analysis of the structure of social relationships in which the process of socialization takes place. It is this which we are attempting to supply [1955, p. 104].

A prolonged effort on the part of this writer to extract the elements of the Parsonian analysis convinces him that the word "systematic" in the above quotation is being used in a truly Pickwickian sense. Adding to the usual difficulties of Parsonian prose (indeed it must be parsed to be understood) is the fact that the theory is stated at considerable length not once, but twice—once by Parsons alone (Chapters II and III); and again by Parsons and Olds jointly (Chapter IV), employing a somewhat different set of concepts. The basic features of the two formulations, however, are highly similar. The fundamental notion is that the child passes through not one but a series of identifications. The nature of these successive identifications is determined by the reciprocal roles being taken by parent and child at successive stages of the child's development. To understand these stages, however, we must first take cognizance of the familiar Parsonian polarity of expressive vs. instrumental function. The former, associated primarily with the mother, involves being "affectionate, solicitous, warm, emotional to the children" and serving as "the mediator and conciliator of the family." In contrast, instrumental activity refers primarily to "establishing the desired relations to external goal objects" (e.g., working at a job) and acting as "the final judge and executor of punishment, discipline, and control over the children of the family." Parsons' distinction between parental roles seems to parallel fairly closely Freud's descriptions of the nurturing mother and the punitive father. But one important difference may be discerned. The father's role, while involving discipline and control, is not predominantly hostile; it is also, and perhaps primarily, adaptive and directed at manipulation of the environment.

To return to the problem of developmental stages, Parsons emphasizes that at the outset the young child cannot respond to the parental roles in their fully differentiated form. Moreover, the parental behaviors to which the child is exposed are segmental and not representative of the full role-repertoire of each parent. For example, in the beginning the mother's function is primarily instrumental; she gives the child physical *care*. Since care is not always forthcoming, this "denial of reciprocity" leads the child to his first identification—"the internalization of the mother . . . *in her role as a source of care*." Parsons emphasizes that "it is not the mother as a total personality as seen by adults that has been internalized, but that aspect of her with which ego has stood in a meaningful relationship of interaction" (Parsons & Bales, 1955, p. 65). Moreover, since for Parsons a role always implies a reciprocal relationship, the denial of reciprocity leads to an identification not only with the mother as an agent of care but also with a primordial image of the child himself as "the object of care."

Herein lies the crux of Parsons' theory of the content of identification. At any given stage, the child identifies not with the parent as a total person but with the reciprocal role-relationship that is functional for the child at a particular time. Parsons stipulates a specific sequence of such role-relationships. Following his identification with the mother as a source of care, the child enters the stage of "love dependency" in which the mother's expressions of affection become rewarding in and of themselves; in other words, the child becomes responsive to the "expressive" aspects of the mother's function. Since "a mother's love . . . is always conditional," the denial of reciprocity at this level leads to internalization of the mother as a giver of love and of himself as a loved object.

Identification at the third or Oedipal stage reaches a new level of complexity. It is important to recognize, Parsons asserts, that at both earlier levels of identification the mother is still undifferentiated with respect to sex. It is only in the Oedipal phase that the child first recognizes and internalizes the distinction between male and female, again simultaneously both in relation to his parents and himself.

> . . . the crucial event of this phase is the first stage of the assumption by the child of his sex role. The pre-Oedipal child is, we assume, in the sense of fundamental personality constitution, sexless—as is in literal terms the "mother," since we assume that *for the child* the differentiation of the two parents as objects by sex has not yet on the requisite level been internalized. . . . In the earlier phases there was only *one* ascribed role the child could assume—more or less satisfactorily. Now he must "choose" between *two*—though the pressure to choose the ascriptively right one is overwhelmingly great [Parsons & Bales, 1955, p. 78].

Once more the differentiation occurs because of a shift in the parental role pattern presented to the child. Specifically, the expressive and instrumental functions are now divided between the parents with the mother specializing in the former and the father in the latter.

> . . . In the mother-child system it was the mother who played the predominantly instrumental role, whereas in the wider family system, of which the mother-child is, it will be remembered, a sub-system, it is the father. . . . This is to say that the father is, symbolically at least, the primary source of the new "demands" for

conformity and autonomous performance. The mother, on the other hand, this time as distinct "person," remains the primary source of "security" or "acceptance" in the love-relationship [Parsons & Bales, 1955, pp. 79–80].

Before he has internalized the father as an object the child cannot be fully sensitive to his attitudes as sanctions. He can, however, be motivated to do things which please *both* mother and father and be rewarded by mother's love and nurturance. By some such process he comes to cathect the father—because mother loves father and backs him up—and from the generalized parental object then a qualitatively different object can be differentiated out [Parsons & Bales, 1955, p. 81].

The above view is nicely in accord with the previously-cited finding of Helper that it was approval of the parental model by the mother, and not by the father, that predicted the extent to which the school-age child accepted this model for himself.

Although the division of expressive-instrumental functions between mother and father provides the child with a basis for differentiating the parents with respect to sex, it does not account for the selection of the appropriate sex-role by the child. Having minimized the influence of constitutional factors, Parsons relies for an explanation on what is, in effect, a theory of differential reinforcement for the two sexes. He states, "The new 'demands' of course this time are differentiated by sex. They consist in the appropriate forms of behavior for a 'big boy' and a 'big girl' respectively . . ." [Parsons & Bales, 1955, p. 80].

As Parsons describes it, identification at the Oedipal level is analogous to but nevertheless different from its manifestations at earlier stages. First, although the point is not made explicit, we may note that, while at earlier levels the child was described as internalizing the parent's overt behavior, at the Oedipal stage he is seen as motivated to identify not so much with what the parent himself does as what the latter regards as "appropriate." Implicit in this shift over successive developmental levels is an answer to the hitherto unresolved problem of whether identification refers to the parent's actual behavior or to his aspirations for the child. Parsons would seem to be suggesting that both are involved, but at different stages of development. At an early age level the child is able to identify only with the most concrete actions of the parent directly relevant to the child's well-being, and even then the identification is of a diffuse and relatively undifferentiated type. Later, with increasing capacity to abstract and discriminate, the child becomes capable of internalizing patterns which are at once more subtle and symbolic. Accordingly, if the parent "denies reciprocity" and "manipulates rewards" in relation to the symbolic aspects of the parent-child relationship (such as the child's conformity with parental standards), then it is this more abstract reciprocal role pattern which becomes internalized.

To put it in another way, Parsons' successive levels of identification represent a progressive differentiation of ever more complex role-relationships between the self, parent, and, ultimately, society. As in classical developmental psychology, the earlier differentiations are more diffuse, less stable—the later more specific and enduring. It follows that even though the same objective person serves as the model, the mother with whom, say, the girl identifies in infancy is quite different—both in her formal and substantive properties—from the mother internalized as an outcome of the Oedipal conflict. It was Freud's failure to recognize this distinction, Parsons asserts, which accounts for much of the ambiguity in the former's theory of identification.

Returning to problems closer to the field of socialization, we may next raise again some of the questions involved in the concept of "identification." This has of course been a notably ambiguous and controversial concept in the literature of the field. Perhaps we can suggest some of the sources of the difficulties and a constructive way out of them. Freud, it will be remembered, introduced the concept in connection with what, above, we have called the "mother-child identity." The principal difficulty seems to arise from the attempt to use the same concept in relation to the processes which go on in the Oedipal period, above all with reference to sex-role assumption. Thus a boy is often said to "identify" with his father at this period and a girl with her mother.

In our opinion the trouble comes from sticking to the attempt to deal only with the relation to *one* role-personality in a situation where multiple role-relations are already involved. In the case of "primary" identification there was only one object, the nurturing or "caring" mother. Identification with this object could be treated as an adequate focus of the total internalization process. From the child's point of view, in the significant sense, he and the mother become one.

When it comes to the Oedipal period, on the other hand, for the boy his father is only one of four basic types of object. . . .

What happens, then, is the reorganization of the total personality as a system. This involves the addition, *by fission,* of two new object-units, the father as discriminated from mother and the discrimination of ego from sibling of opposite sex. There is also a differentiation of the collectivity structure from the simple mother-child "we" to a familial "we" with six potential elementary sub-collectivities. The focus of a son's identification with his father is his self-categorization as belonging to the "we-males" sub-collectivity—which is the same thing as saying that he and father share the category of "maleness." It means that this we is set over against a "they" of the females to which he *cannot* belong. But there is another they to which he also cannot belong, namely that of the "parents"—in *this* nuclear family—and his father does belong to this one. In this sense the boy cannot identify with, i.e., play the role of, his father, but only with his brother if any, and with respect to generation, not sex, his sister. It is, however, profoundly true that in this process *both* boy and girl internalize the father as an object. *This* aspect is strictly parallel with internalization of the mother in the primary identification but the others clearly are not parallel, for the simple reason that in a one-unit system there are no analogies to many features of a four-unit system. . . .

We suggest that the term identification has tended to be used to designate a variety of these different aspects of the total complex, but that the complex as a whole has not been adequately analyzed. We can suggest a usage of the term which is free of ambiguity, namely that identification should designate the process of internalization of any common collective "we-categorization" and with it the common values of the requisite collectivity. In this meaning of the term, in the Oedipal phase of development a child undergoes not one but *three* new identifications. Two of them are common to members of both sexes, namely internalization of the familial we-category, and of the sibling category, namely "we children." The third, by sex, differs for children of each sex, in this third sense the boy identifies with his father, the girl with her mother [Parsons & Bales, 1955, pp. 91–93].

As the reader may have already recognized, Parsons' reformulation of Freud's theory of identification is remarkably similar to the previously-cited revision by Mowrer. The parallelism is even more clearly apparent in Parsons' views on the differences between the sexes in the resolution of the Oedipus complex (Parsons & Bales, 1955, pp. 98–99). Like Mowrer, he argues that Freud was wrong in believing that the resolution is more difficult for the girl than for the boy.

Parsons goes beyond Mowrer, however, in one important respect. He points out that the child in identifying with the parent of the same sex begins to exhibit behavior which is sex-typed but by no means identical with behavior of the adult parent. The discrepancy, Parsons asserts, is more marked for the boy and is related to two factors—the clarity of the role model and the degree of anxiety generated by the very conflict which motivates the child to seek a new identity.

The boy . . . tends to attempt to act out what are symbolic representatives of the instrumental aspects of adult masculine roles. These are notably nonfamilial in content. He plays with trains, cars, airplanes. He more or less explicitly assumes relatively tangible adult masculine roles such as fireman or soldier. He puts great emphasis on physical prowess. But his play is a less exact copy of the specific father role than his sister's is of the mother. This may well be explained, partly at least, by two facts. First the mother role is far more uniform than the masculine occupational role; the girl has a rather specific role-model stereotype. Secondly, being, as we have suggested, under less acute strain, the girl is less driven to the kinds of symbols which

> tangibly express compulsively tinged sex-qualities. Thus both the difficulty of understanding many middle-class occupations—their remoteness, and the fact that not involving physical prowess or skills, they do not patently symbolize masculinity—may prevent the urban middle-class boy from so directly emulating his father as the girl does her mother. . . [Parsons & Bales, 1955, p. 100].

Here Parsons' argument is reminiscent of Freud's statement that the child identifies not with the parent as he actually is but with the parental *imago,* an image distorted in part by the child's own anxieties and needs. Indeed, taking Parsons' writings on identification as a whole, it is difficult to discern much that is fundamentally new beyond the terminology. Although he points emphatically to the need for revising and expanding Freud's theory in several directions, his own efforts in these directions fall far short of the expectations he creates; for, either he restates in even less precise language ideas that are already familiar in the writings of others or he offers conceptions which, though provocative, are so diffuse that the basic tasks of theory construction have to be performed by the reader himself. Accordingly, it is perhaps merely a reflection of this author's limitations as a theorist that after earnest and repeated perusal of Parsons' writings on identification, he has had little success in deriving formulations that substantially modify or clarify existing theories in this sphere. Specifically only two ideas emerged from this analysis which, to the writer's knowledge, are not found in earlier treatments of identification. Both of these derive from Parsons' distinction between instrumental and expressive functions and the differential allocation of these two functions between the parents. If, as Parsons suggests, withdrawal of love can be used as a technique for motivating the child to identify with the instrumental pattern of moving out into and manipulating the environment, then perhaps we have an explanation for the apparent contradiction, noted earlier, between Freud's thesis of superior development of the superego in men (together with the partially supporting data of Terman and Miles) and the finding from two independent studies of child rearing practices that guilt feelings are more common in females than in males. The crucial factor may lie in the sphere of activity with which the superego is concerned. Both studies of child training dealt with guilt in a context of intimate interpersonal relationships, one being concerned with mother-child relationships and the other with relationships within the family and between a child and his teacher. In contrast, Terman and Miles based their conclusions on items dealing with general behavior (e.g., discourtesy, laziness) and broader social issues (e.g., "being an atheist"). Perhaps male morality is more concerned with general principles of conduct in relation to the outside world, while female morality centers about personal feelings and intimate interpersonal relationships. Such variation in the content or focus of the superego could be produced through the use of withdrawal of love in two somewhat different contexts. Thus, with girls this technique might be employed principally with reference to intimate family relationships, with boys more in regard to performance and achievement both within and outside the home. Finally, since the fathers, who are presumably instrumentally and externally oriented, are likely to have closer associations with sons than with daughters, boys would be more likely to develop a principled and objective (situation-oriented) superego. In contrast, girls—who, according to the findings of Sears, Macoby, and Levin, are particularly likely to be subjected to withdrawal of love by the mother—would tend to develop a superego highly susceptible to guilt over interpersonal matters rather than broader issues.

Parsons' picture of the father as executive rather than punitive suggests also a variant of Freud's theory of identification with the aggressor. The fact that the father exercises power and control over the environment may in itself invite emulation. To the extent that an exploratory or activity drive exists (perhaps differentially for the two sexes), a living example of patterns of action for expressing this drive may be sufficient to motivate the child to adopt an analogous pattern in his own behavior. Given the possibility of such a mechanism, a child whose father, or mother, was especially active in the manipulation of the environment, either through direct activity, or through the exercise of power (e.g., making plans, decisions, etc.) might be expected to emulate the parent's behavior, even without reinforcement through "denial of reciprocity" and "manipulation of rewards."

But we have wandered far from the Parsonian orthodoxy, if such there be, and must return to our consideration of his own explicit views. Staying at the very general level at which he has chosen to couch his formulations, we may summarize the major tenets of his position as follows:

First, Parsons makes explicit the thesis that the type of identification is a function of the developmental capacities of the child. Early identifications are more diffuse and related to concrete behavior; later ones are more differentiated and organized around symbolic role-entities. Second, Parsons stresses repeatedly that identification involves not only motivational but cognitive elements; the cathected pattern is determined in part by the substantive and formal properties of the model. To put it in another way, what the child strives to internalize will vary with the content and clarity of the reciprocal role relationship in which he is a participant.

From Theory to Research

We have now concluded our analysis of Freudian theories of identification and their psychological and sociological derivatives. Where does this analysis leave us? We have hardly achieved any new theoretical insights. Nor can we offer a synthesis of the diverse conceptions that have emerged from our survey. Perhaps the most we can hope to have achieved is a clarification of concepts and a clearing of the way for empirical work.

Specifically, our analysis calls attention to the importance of distinguishing three broad classes of phenomena to which the term identification has been applied, on occasion by one and the same theorist.

1. *Identification as behavior.* Here the emphasis is on overt action: A behaves in the manner of B. But even within this restricted context, the concept is used in at least three different ways. Most commonly, identification implies actions of A learned through taking as a model the overt actions of B. Less frequently, the term is used more loosely to refer to similarity of A to B without regard to whether B's behavior had actually served as a model (e.g., A is reinforced for acquiring aspects of his father's behavior which he himself never sees). Finally, there is identification in overt behavior with an ideal standard never actually exhibited ("Don't do as I do; do as I say.").

2. *Identification as motive.* When employed in this sense, identification refers to the *disposition* to act like another. Again the model may be overt behavior or an idealized standard, but there is no necessary correspondence between the actual behaviors of A and B, since, in his efforts to emulate, A may exaggerate or distort the characteristics of the model.

3. *Identification as process.* For the most part, Freudian theory and its derivatives deal with identification neither as behavior nor as motive but as a mechanism through which behavior and motives are learned; that is, theories of identification deal primarily with the psychological forces that impel the child to emulate a model. In the course of this analysis, we have distinguished or derived at least four such processes. Specifically, in addition to the basic Freudian mechanisms of *anaclitic* and *aggressive* identification, we have called attention to two additional possibilities. First, from Miller and Dollard's theory and Helper's research results, we extracted the simple hypothesis that conventional reward and punishment, without the necessity of specific reliance on frustrations implicit in either the *anaclitic* or *aggressive* mechanisms, might be sufficient to impel the child to emulate the parent. Finally, from Parsons' conception of an "instrumental" rather than "punitive" father role, we arrived (admittedly by an un-Parsonian chain of reasoning) at the notion that exposure to a

model who exhibits effective mastery of the environment might, through capitalizing on an already existent activity or exploratory drive, stimulate the child to adopt the father's "adventurous" pattern of activity.

When the theoretical conceptions outlined above are examined in the light of available research data, the conclusion is inescapable that the theories have grown all out of proportion to the facts. They offer elaborate and intricate explanations for phenomena presumed to be common if not universal; yet, the evidence for the prevalence or even the sheer existence of these phenomena is extremely sparse. Thus, to the writer's knowledge, there have as yet been no attempts to investigate empirically the presence of a generalized motive in the child to become like one or the other parent. Similarly, at the level of process, although existing theories assume that boys and girls are treated differently by the parent of each sex and that this differential treatment has markedly diverse effects on the child of each sex, actually very little is known about the extent of variation in the behavior of fathers and mothers toward sons and daughters, and even less about the possible effects of such differential treatment. All in all, it would seem that, before indulging in still further proliferation or even clarification of theory in this sphere, behavioral scientists would do well to follow the precedent of their colleagues in the natural sciences and to concentrate first on the more modest and at once more challenging task of discovering what phenomena do in fact exist that require theoretical explanation.

REFERENCES

BETTELHEIM, B. Individual and mass behavior in extreme situations. *J. abnorm. soc. Psychol.,* 1943, **38,** 417–452.

BRONFENBRENNER, U. The study of identification through interpersonal perception. In R. Tagiuri & L. Petrullo (Eds.), *Person, perception and interpersonal behavior.* Stanford, Cal.: Stanford Univer. Press, 1958. Pp. 110–130.

COURTNEY, P. D. Identification and learning: a theoretical analysis. Unpublished doctoral dissertation, Harvard Univer., 1949.

FREUD, ANNA. *The ego and the mechanisms of defense.* New York: International Universities Press, 1946.

FREUD, S. The passing of the Oedipus-complex. In *Collected papers.* Vol. 2. London: Hogarth, 1924. Pp. 269–282.

FREUD, S. Mourning and melancholia. In *Collected papers.* Vol. 4. London: Hogarth, 1925. Pp. 152–170. (a)

FREUD, S. On narcissism; an introduction. In *Collected papers.* Vol. 4. London: Hogarth, 1925. Pp. 30–59. (b)

FREUD, S. *New introductory lectures in psychoanalysis.* New York: Norton, 1933.

FREUD, S. *The problem of anxiety.* New York: Norton, 1936.

FREUD, S. The interpretation of dreams. In *The basic writings of Sigmund Freud.* New York: Random House, 1938. Pp. 181–549.

FREUD, S. *Group psychology and the analysis of the ego.* London: Hogarth, 1948.

FREUD, S. *An outline of psychoanalysis.* New York: Norton, 1949.

FREUD, S. Dostoyevski and parricide. In *Collected papers.* Vol. 5. London: Hogarth, 1950. Pp. 222–242. (a)

FREUD, S. Some psychological consequences of the anatomical distinction between the sexes. In *Collected papers.* Vol. 5. London: Hogarth, 1950. Pp. 186–197. (b)

HELPER, M. M. Learning theory and the self-concept. *J. abnorm. soc. Psychol.,* 1955, **51,** 184–194.

LAIR, W. S. Psychoanalytic theory of identification. Unpublished doctoral dissertation, Harvard Univer., 1949.

MILLER, D. R., & SWANSON, G. E. *Inner conflict and defense.* New York: Holt, Rinehart & Winston, 1960.

MILLER, N. E., & DOLLARD, J. *Social learning and imitation.* New Haven: Yale Univer. Press, 1941.

MOWRER, O. H. Identification: a link between learning theory and psychotherapy. In *Learning theory and personality dynamics.* New York: Ronald, 1950. Pp. 573–616.

MOWRER, O. H. Neurosis and psychotherapy as interpersonal process: a synopsis. In O. H. Mowrer (Ed.), *Psychotherapy: theory and re-*

search. New York: Ronald, 1953. Pp. 69–94.

PARSONS, T. *The social system*. New York: Free Press, 1951.

PARSONS, T., & BALES, R. F. *Family, socialization and interaction process*. New York: Free Press, 1955.

PARSONS, T., BALES, R. F., & SHILS, E. A. *Working papers in the theory of action*. New York: Free Press, 1953.

PARSONS, T., & SHILS, E. A. (Eds.) *Toward a general theory of action*. Cambridge, Mass.: Harvard Univer. Press, 1951.

SANFORD, N. The dynamics of identification. *Psychol. Rev.,* 1955, **62,** 106–117

SARNOFF, I. Identification with the aggressor: some personality correlates of anti-semitism among Jews. *J. Pers.,* 1951, **20,** 199–218.

SEARS, R. R. Identification as a form of behavior development. In D. B. Harris (Ed.), *The concept of development*. Minneapolis: Univer. Minnesota Press, 1957. Pp. 149–161.

SEARS, R. R., MACCOBY, ELEANOR E., & LEVIN, H. *Patterns of child rearing*. New York: Row, Peterson, 1957.

STOKE, S. M. An inquiry into the concept of identification. *J. genet. Psychol.,* 1950, **76,** 163–189.

TERMAN, L. M., & MILES, C. C. *Sex and personality*. New York: McGraw-Hill, 1936.

ANNA FREUD *and* SOPHIE DANN

*An Experiment in Group Upbringing**

Introduction

THE experiment to which the following notes refer is not the outcome of an artificial and deliberate laboratory setup but of a combination of fateful outside circumstances. The six young children who are involved in it are German-Jewish orphans, victims of the Hitler regime, whose parents, soon after their birth, were deported to Poland and killed in the gas chambers. During their first year of life, the children's experiences differed; they were handed on from one refuge to another, until they arrived individually, at ages varying from approximately six to twelve months, in the concentration camp of Tereszin.[1] There they became inmates of the Ward for Motherless Children, were conscientiously cared for and medically supervised, within the limits of the current restrictions of food and living space. They had no toys and their only facility for outdoor life was a bare yard. The Ward was staffed by nurses and helpers, themselves inmates of the concentration camp and, as such, undernourished and overworked. Since Tereszin was a transit camp, deportations were frequent. Approximately two to three years after arrival, in the spring of 1945, when liberated by the Russians, the six children, with others, were taken to a Czech castle where they were given special care and were lavishly fed. After one month's stay, the 6 were included in a transport of 300 older children and adolescents, all of them survivors from concentration camps, the first of 1000 children for whom the British Home Office had granted permits of entry. They were flown to England in bombers and arrived in August 1945 in a carefully set-up reception camp in Windermere, Westmorland, where they remained for two months. When this reception camp was cleared and the older children distributed to various hostels and training places, it was thought wise to leave the six youngest together, to remove them from the commotion which is inseparable from the life of a large children's community and to provide them with peaceful, quiet surroundings where, for a year at least, they could adapt themselves gradually to a new country, a new language, and the altered circumstances of their lives.

This ambitious plan was realized through the combined efforts of a number of people. A friend of the former Hampstead Nurseries, Mrs. Ralph Clarke, wife of the Member of Parliament for East Grinstead, Sussex, gave the children a year's tenancy of a country house with field and adjoining woodland, "Bulldogs Bank" in West Hoathly, Sussex, containing two bedrooms for the children, with adjoining bathrooms, a large day nursery, the necessary staff rooms, a veranda running the whole length of the house and a sun terrace.

The Foster Parents' Plan for War Children, Inc., New York, who had sponsored the Hampstead Nurseries during the war years 1940–1945, took the six children into their plan and adopted Bulldogs Bank as one of their colonies. They provided the necessary equipment as well as the financial upkeep.

The new Nursery was staffed by Sisters Sophie and Gertrud Dann, formerly the head nurses of the Baby Department and Junior

1 Theresienstadt in Moravia.

Nursery Department of the Hampstead Nurseries respectively. A young assistant, Miss Maureen Wolfison, who had accompanied the children from Windermere was replaced after several weeks by Miss Judith Gaulton, a relief worker. Cooking and housework was shared between the staff, with occasional outside help.

The children arrived in Bulldogs Bank on October 15, 1945. The personal data of the six, so far as they could be ascertained, are given in TABLE 1.

Meager as these scraps of information are, they establish certain relevant facts concerning the early history of this group of children:

(i) That four of them (Ruth, Leah, Miriam, Peter) lost their mothers at birth or immediately afterward; one (Paul) before the age of twelve

TABLE 1

NAME	DATE AND PLACE OF BIRTH	FAMILY HISTORY	AGE AT ARRIVAL IN TERESZIN	AGE AT ARRIVAL IN BULLDOG BANK
John	18.12.1941 Vienna	Orthodox Jewish working-class parents. Deported to Poland and killed.	Presumably under 12 months	3 years, 10 months
Ruth	21.4.1942 Vienna	Parents, a brother of 7 and a sister of 4 years were deported and killed when Ruth was a few months old. She was cared for in a Jewish Nursery in Vienna, sent to Tereszin with the Nursery.	Several months	3 years, 6 months
Leah	23.4.1942 Berlin	Leah and a brother were illegitimate, hidden from birth. Fate of mother and brother unknown. Brother presumed killed.	Several months	3 years, 5 months. Arrived 6 weeks after the others, owing to a ringworm infection.
Paul	21.5.1942 Berlin	Unknown.	12 months	3 years, 5 months
Miriam	18.8.1942 Berlin	Upper middle-class family. Father died in concentration camp, mother went insane, was cared for first in a mental hospital in Vienna, later in a mental ward in Tereszin where she died.	6 months	3 years, 2 months
Peter	22.10.1942	Parents deported and killed when Peter was a few days old. Child was found abandoned in public park, cared for first in a convent, later, when found to be Jewish, was taken to the Jewish hospital in Berlin, then brought to Tereszin.	Under 12 months	3 years

months, one (John) at an unspecified date;

(ii) that after the loss of their mothers all the children wandered for some time from one place to another, with several complete changes of adult environment (Bulldogs Bank was the sixth station in life for Peter, the fifth for Miriam, etc. John's and Leah's and Paul's wanderings before arrival in Tereszin are not recorded.);

(iii) that none of the children had known any other circumstances of life than those of a group setting. They were ignorant of the meaning of a "family";

(iv) that none of the children had experience of normal life outside a camp or big institution.

Behavior Toward Adults on Arrival

ON LEAVING the reception camp in Windermere, the children reacted badly to the renewed change in their surroundings. They showed no pleasure in the arrangements which had been made for them and behaved in a wild, restless, and uncontrollably noisy manner. During the first days after arrival they destroyed all the toys and damaged much of the furniture. Toward the staff they behaved either with cold indifference or with active hostility, making no exception for the young assistant Maureen who had accompanied them from Windermere and was their only link with the immediate past. At times they ignored the adults so completely that they would not look up when one of them entered the room. They would turn to an adult when in some immediate need, but treat the same person as nonexistent once more when the need was fulfilled. In anger, they would hit the adults, bite or spit. Above all, they would shout, scream, and use bad language. Their speech, at the time, was German with an admixture of Czech words, and a gradual increase of English words. In a good mood, they called the staff members indiscriminately *Tante* (auntie), as they had done in Tereszin; in bad moods this changed to *blöde Tante* (silly, stupid auntie). Their favorite swear-word was *blöder Ochs* (the equivalent of "stupid fool"), a German term which they retained longer than any other.

Group Reactions

CLINGING TO THE GROUP

THE children's positive feelings were centered exclusively in their own group. It was evident that they cared greatly for each other and not at all for anybody or anything else. They had no other wish than to be together and became upset when they were separated from each other, even for short moments. No child would consent to remain upstairs while the others were downstairs, or vice versa, and no child would be taken for a walk or on an errand without the others. If anything of the kind happened, the single child would constantly ask for the other children while the group would fret for the missing child.

This insistence on being inseparable made it impossible in the beginning to treat the children as individuals or to vary their lives according to their special needs. Ruth, for instance, did not like going for walks, while the others greatly preferred walks to indoor play. But it was very difficult to induce the others to go out and let Ruth stay at home. One day, they actually left without her, but kept asking for her until, after approximately twenty minutes, John could bear it no longer and turned back to fetch her. The others joined him, they all returned home, greeted Ruth as if they had been separated for a long time and then took her for a walk, paying a great deal of special attention to her.

It was equally difficult to carry out measures for the children's health, so far as they did not apply to everybody. When the children arrived, they were in fairly good physical condition, though somewhat pale, flabby, with protruding stomachs and dry, stringy hair, cuts and scratches on their skin tending to go septic. All the children were given cod-liver oil and other vitamins which were taken easily and liked by everybody. But it was nearly impossible to keep individual children in bed for small ailments, or for instance to give Miriam and Peter, who needed it, an afternoon nap while the others had no wish to rest. Sometimes those two children would fall asleep exhaustedly in the middle of the noise made by the others. At night, all children were restless sleepers, Ruth being unable to fall asleep, Paul and Peter waking up in the night crying. Whoever was awake, naturally disturbed the sleep of the others. The upset about separation was so great that, finally, children with colds were no longer kept upstairs. The only child who was in bed once, for two days with a slight bronchitis, was Paul. Another time three children had to be isolated for several days with stomatitis. The only other child in need of individual physical treatment was Leah. She had a bad squint, her eyes were treated daily but the operation was postponed for six months to give her time for better adjustment to a renewed separation.

Inability to be separated from the group showed up most glaringly in those instances where individual children were singled out for a special treat, a situation for which children crave under normal circumstances. Paul, for example, cried for the other children when he was taken as the only one for a ride in the pony cart, although at other times such rides were a special thrill to him as well as to the others. On another, later, occasion the whole group of children was invited to visit another nursery in the neighborhood. Since the car was not large enough to take everybody, Paul and Miriam were taken earlier by bus. The other four, in the car, inquired constantly about them and could not enjoy the trip nor the pleasures prepared for them, until they were reunited.

TYPE OF GROUP FORMATION

When together, the children were a closely knit group of members with equal status, no child assuming leadership for any length of time, but each one exerting a strong influence on the others by virtue of individual qualities, peculiarities, or by the mere fact of belonging. At the beginning, John, as the oldest, seemed to be the undisputed leader at mealtimes. He only needed to push away his plate, for everybody else to cease eating. Peter, though the youngest, was the most imaginative of all and assumed leadership in games, which he would invent and organize. Miriam too played a major role, in a peculiar way. She was a pretty, plump child, with ginger hair, freckles and a ready smile. She behaved toward the other children as if she were a superior being, and let herself be served and spoiled by them as a matter of course. She would sometimes smile at the boys in return for their services, while accepting Leah's helpfulness toward herself without acknowledgment. But she, too, did not guide or govern the group. The position was rather that she needed a special kind of attention to be paid to her and that the other children sensed this need and did their best to fulfill it. The following are some recorded examples of this interplay between Miriam and the group:

> November 1945.—Miriam, on a walk, has found a tiny pink flower, carries it in her hand but loses it soon. She calls out "flower!" and John and Paul hurry to pick it up for her, a difficult task since they wear thick gloves. Miriam drops the flower again and again, never makes an attempt to pick it up herself, merely calls "flower!" and the boys hurry to find it.
>
> March 1946.—From the beginning Miriam liked to sit in comfortable chairs. In the winter she would drag such a chair to the fireplace, put her feet on the fire guard and play in that position. When outdoor life began again, Miriam had a chair in the sandbox. She even helped weed the garden while sitting in a chair. But it did not happen often that she had to fetch a chair herself, usually the other children carried it into the garden for her. One day, Miriam and Paul played in the sandbox after supper. Suddenly Paul appears in the house to fetch Miriam's chair. When told that the evening was too cold already for outdoor play and that they had better both come in, he merely looks bewildered and says: "But Miriam wants chair, open door quickly."

May 1946.—Miriam drops her towel, turns around and says: "Pick it up, somebody." Leah picks it up for her.

August 1946.—Ruth is found in Miriam's bed in the morning and is asked to get up. Miriam replies instead of Ruth: "Oh, no, she much better stays here. She has to wait to fasten Miriam's buttons."

August 1946.—Miriam bangs her hand on the table and says to John: "Can't you be quiet when I want to talk?" John stops talking.

The children's sensitiveness to each other's attitudes and feelings was equally striking where Leah was concerned. Leah was the only backward child among the six, of slow, lower average intelligence, with no outstanding qualities to give her a special status in the group. As mentioned before, Leah's arrival in Bulldogs Bank was delayed for six weeks owing to a ringworm infection. During this period the five other children had made their first adaptation to the new place, had learned some English, had established some contact with the staff and dropped some of their former restlessness. With Leah's coming, the whole group, in identification with her, behaved once more as if they were all newcomers. They used the impersonal *Tante* again instead of first names for the members of staff. They reverted to talking German only, shouted and screamed and were again out of control. This regression lasted approximately a week, evidently for the length of time which Leah herself needed to feel more comfortable in her new surroundings.

POSITIVE RELATIONS WITHIN THE GROUP: ABSENCE OF ENVY, JEALOUSY, RIVALRY, COMPETITION

The children's unusual emotional dependence on each other was borne out further by the almost complete absence of jealousy, rivalry and competition, such as normally develop between brothers and sisters or in a group of contemporaries who come from normal families. There was no occasion to urge the children to "take turns"; they did it spontaneously since they were eager that everybody should have his share. Since the adults played no part in their emotional lives at the time, they did not compete with each other for favors or for recognition. They did not tell on each other and they stood up for each other automatically whenever they felt that a member of the group was unjustly treated or otherwise threatened by an outsider. They were extremely considerate of each other's feelings. They did not grudge each other their possessions (with one exception to be mentioned later), on the contrary lending them to each other with pleasure. When one of them received a present from a shopkeeper, they demanded the same for each of the other children, even in their absence. On walks they were concerned for each other's safety in traffic, looked after children who lagged behind, helped each other over ditches, turned aside branches for each other to clear the passage in the woods, and carried each other's coats. In the nursery they picked up each other's toys. After they had learned to play, they assisted each other silently in building and admired each other's productions. At mealtimes handing food to the neighbor was of greater importance than eating oneself.

Behavior of this kind was the rule, not the exception. The following examples merely serve the purpose of illustration and are in no way outstanding. They are chosen at random from the first seven months of the children's stay in Bulldogs Bank:

October 1945.—John, daydreaming while walking, nearly bumps into a passing child. Paul immediately sides with him and shouts at the passer-by: "Blöder Ochs, mein John, blöder Ochs Du!" ("Stupid fool, my John, you stupid fool!")

November 1945.—John refuses to get up in the morning, lies in his bed, screams and kicks. Ruth brings his clothes and asks: "Willst Du anziehen?" ("Don't you want to put them on?") Miriam offers him her doll with a very sweet smile. John calms down at once and gets up.

November 1945.—John cries when there is no cake left for a second helping for him. Ruth and Miriam offer him what is left of their portions. While John eats their pieces of cake, they pet him and comment contentedly on what they have given him.

December 1945.—Paul has a plate full of cake crumbs. When he begins to eat them, the other children want them too. Paul gives the two biggest crumbs to Miriam, the three middle-sized ones to the other children, and eats the smallest one himself.

December 1945.—Paul loses his gloves during a walk. John gives him his own gloves, and never complains that his hands are cold.

January 1946.—A visitor gives sweets to the children in the kitchen. Peter and Leah immediately demand a sweet for Miriam who is alone in the nursery.

March 1946.—Sister Gertrud opens a door and knocks it against John who stands behind it. When she enters the room next time, Ruth and Peter throw bricks at her and shout: "You naughty boy hit John!"

March 1946.—John has a temper tantrum when a ladybird, which he has caught, flies away. Leah hurries to him, strokes his hair, picks up his basket and all the carrots which he dropped out. She carries both John's and her own full baskets on the way home.

March 1946.—A dog approaches the children who are terrified. Ruth, though badly frightened herself, walks bravely to Peter who is screaming and gives him her toy rabbit to comfort him. She comforts John next by lending him her necklace.

April 1946.—On the beach in Brighton, Ruth throws pebbles into the water. Peter is afraid of waves and does not dare to approach them. In spite of his fear, he suddenly rushes to Ruth, calls out: "Water coming, water coming," and drags her back to safety.

DISCRIMINATION BETWEEN GROUP MEMBERS: ANTIPATHIES AND FRIENDSHIPS

Although the positive reactions of the children extended to all members of the group, individual preferences or their opposite were not lacking. There was a certain discrimination against Leah on the part of the other girls, as the following recordings indicate:

February 1946.—When Miriam cries, Leah runs immediately to comfort her, although Miriam each time screams: "Not Leah," and then accepts comfort from the other children.

April 1946.—Ruth is very helpful toward Leah, looks after her on walks and helps her to dress and undress. But her behavior indicates that these actions are duties, imposed by Leah's comparative clumsiness, rather than acts of friendship.

There were, further, close and intimate friendships between individual children, as for example between Paul and Miriam.

October 1945.—On his first evening in Bulldogs Bank, Paul goes to bed, saying with a deep sigh: "My Miriam."

October 1945.—Paul is very fond of Miriam. He gives her toys and serves her at mealtimes. Sometimes he takes her doll, walks with it around the room and returns it to her.

October 1945.—Paul loves eating corn flakes. He has just started eating when Miriam—who is not sitting next to him—drops her spoon. Paul at once stops eating and picks up the spoon for her before continuing.

November 1945.—On her third day in Bulldogs Bank, Miriam had been given a doll from which she became inseparable in day- and nighttime. No other child was allowed to touch it except Paul who sometimes took it for a walk around the room.

On November 11, Miriam gives the doll to Paul when saying good night and goes to sleep without it.

On November 12, she gives him the doll again in the evening but later cries in her bed. Paul, who has the doll in bed with him, gets up and calls through the closed door: "Miriam, dolly!" Miriam gets her doll and Paul goes to sleep without it.

December 1945.—After having had Miriam's doll for a few evenings and twice for a whole night, Paul takes it as his own possession. Now he is inseparable from the doll as Miriam has been before. The children call it now "Paul's dolly."

AGGRESSIVE REACTIONS WITHIN THE GROUP

With the exception of one child the children did not hurt or attack each other in the first months. The only aggressiveness to which they gave vent within the group was verbal. They quarreled endlessly at mealtimes and on walks, mostly without any visible provocation. The following is a sample of these word battles, as they raged between October and January:

> December 1945.—
> John: "Is hot."
> Ruth: "Is nicht (not) hot."
> John: "Is hot."
> Ruth (shouting): "Is nis hot."
> John (triumphantly): "Is hot."
> Paul: "Is nis hot, blöder Ochs" (Stupid fool").
> John: "Blöder Ochs, Paul."
> Paul: "Nicht blöder Ochs Paul, blöder Ochs John."
> John (shouting): "Blöder Ochs, Paul!"
> John shouts so loud that the other children begin to laugh; he joins in the laugh.

The disputes ended sometimes in a general uproar, sometimes in a concerted attack on any adult who had tried to interfere and appease the quarrel; mostly the quarrel merely petered out when some new event distracted the children's attention.

After the children had entered into more normal emotional relationships with the adults and had become more independent of each other, word battles diminished and were replaced to some degree by the fights normal for this age. This second phase lasted approximately from January to July, when the relations between the children became peaceful again on a new basis.

The only child whose reactions did not fit in with the general behavior of the group was Ruth. She behaved like the others so far as being inseparable from the group was concerned, did not want to be left alone and worried about absent children. She also did her share of comforting others or of helping Leah, the latter especially after Leah began to call her "my Ruth." But apart from these reactions, she was moved by feelings of envy, jealousy and competition, which were lacking in the other children and which made her actions stand out as isolated instances of maliciousness or spitefulness. In this connection it is interesting to remember that Ruth is the only child among the group who has a recorded history of passionate attachment to a mother substitute. The evidence is not sufficient to establish with certainty that it is this past mother relationship which prevented her from merging completely with the group, and which aroused normal sibling rivalry in her. On the other hand, the difference between her and the other children's behavior together with the difference in their emotional histories seems too striking to be a mere coincidence.

The following are instances of Ruth's negative behavior in the group. Between October and January these instances were daily events. They lessened considerably after she had formed a new attachment to Sister Gertrud and they disappeared almost altogether after June.

> October 1945.—Ruth hurts other children secretly, by kicking or pinching them underneath the table.
>
> October 1945.—Ruth takes other children's toys, shows a very pleased, triumphant expression.
>
> October 1945.—Peter has to wear a bonnet to protect a bandage where he has cut his head. Ruth takes off his bonnet repeatedly.
>
> November 1945.—Peter gets soap in his eyes at bathtime and cries. Ruth watches him. When he has almost ceased crying, her watchful expression changes suddenly to a malicious one. She snatches the piece of soap and tries to put it into Peter's eye.
>
> November 1945.—Ruth takes Paul's plate away while he is eating.
>
> November 1945.—Each child receives

a sweet. Ruth keeps hers until the others have finished eating theirs. Then she offers her sweet to one child after the other, withdrawing it as soon as the child touches it. Repeats this for twenty minutes and again later until the children stop paying attention to her.

November 1945.—Paul and Peter have fun at lunch by pretending to bite each other. When they stop, Ruth encourages them to continue and while they do so, she eats Peter's lunch with her fingers, although her own plate is still full.

December 1945.—Ruth breaks everybody's colored pencils.

January 1946.—Ruth kicks Peter under the table. This had not happened for some time.

January 1946.—John, Miriam and Peter are isolated with stomatitis. Ruth cannot stand the extra care given to them and takes out her jealousy on Paul and Leah by hitting and biting them. Her aggressiveness ceases again when the patients recover.

May 1946.—Ruth cries for her doll which Peter has taken and refuses to return. Leah takes it from Peter and hands it back to Ruth. Ruth, with a malicious expression, gives it once more to Peter and immediately begins to cry for it.

May 1946.—The children pick flowers which grow behind high nettles. They are warned to avoid being stung. John continues but moves and picks carefully. After a while he cries out as he gets stung: "Die Ruth, die Ruth push." Ruth stands behind him, pushing him into the nettles with a malicious expression on her face.

Aggressiveness Toward the Adults

As reported above, the children behaved with strong and uncontrolled aggression toward the adults from their arrival. This aggression was impersonal in its character, not directed against any individual and not to be taken as a sign of interest in the adult world. The children merely reacted defensively against an environment which they experienced as strange, hostile and interfering.

On arriving it was striking that the form of aggressive expression used by the children was far below that normal for their age. They used biting as a weapon, in the manner in which toddlers use it between eighteen and twenty-four months. Biting reached its peak with Peter, who would bite anybody and on all occasions when angry; it was least pronounced with Leah who showed very little aggression altogether. For several weeks John and Ruth would spit at the adults, Ruth also spitting on the table, on plates, on toys, looking at the adults in defiance. Similarly, Peter, when defying the staff, urinated into the brick box, on the slide, into the toy scullery, or wetted his knickers.

After a few weeks, the children hit and smacked the adults when angry. This happened especially on walks where they resented the restrictions imposed on them in traffic.

Shouting and noisy behavior was used deliberately as an outlet for aggression against the adults, even though the children themselves disliked the noise.

Toward spring these very infantile modes of aggressiveness gave way to the usual verbal aggressions used by children between three and four years. Instead of hitting out, the child would threaten to do so, or would say: "Naughty boy, I make noise at you," and then shout at the top of their voices. Other threats used by the children were: "Doggy bite you." Paul once used: "Froggy bite you." After a visit to Brighton in April, where Peter had been frightened of the waves, a new threat was used by them: "You go in a water." They sometimes tried to find a water so as to carry out the threat.

From the summer 1946 onward, the children used phrases copied from the adults to express disapproval: "I am not pleased with you."

The following samples of aggressive behavior are chosen from a multitude of examples of similar or identical nature during the first three months.

October 1945.—Mrs. X from the village returns the clean laundry. Both John and

Peter spit at her when she enters the nursery.

October 1945.—A painter works in the nursery with a high ladder. Peter, who climbs on the ladder, is lifted down by Sister Gertrud. He spits at her and shouts: "Blöde Tante, blöder Ochs!" ("Stupid auntie, stupid fool.")

October 1945.—John hits Mrs. Clarke repeatedly.

November 1945.—Paul does not like the sweet given by Sister Sophie in the evening, but does not ask for a different one. He wakes up in the night and without seeing Sister Sophie says: "Blöde Sophie." He says it again when waking up in the morning.

November 1945.—Sister Gertrud polishes shoes and tells Ruth not to play with the shoe polish. Ruth spits at her, throws the box with polish down the stairs and runs through the house, shouting: "Blöder Ochs, Gertrud."

First Positive Relations with the Adults

THE children's first positive approaches to the adults were made on the basis of their group feelings and differed in quality from the usual demanding, possessive behavior which young children show toward their mothers or mother substitutes. The children began to insist that the members of the staff should have their turn or share; they became sensitive to their feelings, identified with their needs, and considerate of their comfort. They wanted to help the adults with their occupations and, in return, expected to be helped by them. They disliked it when any member of staff was absent and wanted to know where the adults had been and what they had done during their absence. In short, they ceased to regard the adults as outsiders, included them in their group and, as the examples show, began to treat them in some ways as they treated each other.

SHARING WITH THE ADULTS

Christmas 1945.—The children are invited to a Christmas party in Mrs. Clarke's house. They receive their presents with great excitement. They are equally thrilled when they are handed presents for the staff, they call out: "For Gertrud," "For Sophie" with great pleasure, and run back to Mrs. Clarke to fetch more presents for them.

December 1945.—The children are given sweets in the shop and demand a "sweet for Sophie." After leaving the shop, they want to make sure that she has received the sweet. Sister Sophie opens her mouth for inspection and, in so doing, loses her sweet. The children are as upset as if they had lost one of their own sweets. John offers his but Sister Sophie suggests that she can wait to get another on returning home. When they reach home after an hour's walk with many distracting events, Peter runs immediately to the box of sweets to fetch one for Sophie.

CONSIDERATENESS FOR THE ADULTS

November 1945.—When the children are told that one of the staff has a day off and can sleep longer in the morning, they try to be quiet. If one or the other forgets, the others shout: "You quiet, Gertrud fast asleep."

November 1945.—Sister Sophie has told the children that the doctor has forbidden her to lift heavy weights. Paul asks: "Not too heavy?" whenever he sees her with a tray or bucket.

May 1946.—Leah, though a noisy child, tries hard to keep quiet when her Judith is tired.

EQUALITY WITH THE ADULTS. HELPFULNESS

December 1945.—The children become keen on fetching from the kitchen what is needed. They carry logs, set chairs and tables. They help to dress and undress themselves and to tidy up.

January 1946.—Ruth sees a woman with a shopping bag in the street. She approaches her and takes one handle silently to help carry it.

April 1946.—The children are alone in

the nursery after breakfast. Ruth and Peter each take a broom and sweep up the rubbish. When Sister Sophie enters, they call to her: "We tidy up nicely."

May 1946.—Miriam begins to help Sister Sophie in the kitchen when the latter is called away. When she returns Miriam has dried four big dishes, twelve bowls, sixteen spoons and has placed them tidily on a tray.

On a similar occasion Miriam is found on a chair in front of the sink, her arms up to the elbows in soapy water, with most of the washing-up done.

SENSITIVENESS TO ADULTS. IDENTIFICATION

March 1946.—Ruth and John lag far behind on a walk. When they reach the others eventually, Peter calls to them: "You naughty boys, you dragging behind; Sophie calling and calling and calling. You not coming, Sophie cross and sad!" Then he turns to Sister Sophie and says in a low voice: "You still cross and sad?" When she nods, he repeats his speech.

May 1946.—While the children are picking bluebells, Sister Sophie listens intently to the calling of birds. Paul suddenly puts his hand into hers and says: "You cross with everybody?" Though she assures him that she is not cross, merely absent-minded, he leaves his hand in hers to comfort her.

Second Phase of Positive Relations with Adults: Personal Relationships

SEVERAL weeks after arrival in Bulldogs Bank the first signs of individual personal attachments to adults appeared, alongside with and superimposed on the relationships based on community feelings. These new attachments had many of the qualities which are well known from the relationship of young children to their mothers or mother substitutes. Attitudes such as possessiveness, the wish to be owned, exclusive clinging, appeared, but they lacked the intensity and inexorability which is one of the main characteristics of the emotional life at that age. During the year's stay at Bulldogs Bank these ties of the children to the adults in no way reached the strength of their ties to each other. The children went, as it were, through the motions and attitudes of mother relationships, but without the full libidinal cathexis of the objects whom they had chosen for the purpose.

EXAMPLES OF OWNING AND BEING OWNED

Miriam was the first to say "Meine Sophie, my Sophie" at the end of October.

Peter, the youngest, was the next to show a personal attachment. At the end of November he cried on several occasions when Sister Gertrud left the room. He began to say: "Meine Gertrud" and shortly afterward called himself "Gertrud's Peter." He picked flowers for her and liked her to bathe him. But his attachment was in no way exclusive and he did not mind being with somebody else. He was fond of Sister Sophie too and disliked her going away.

Ruth very soon afterward showed a first preference for Mrs. Clarke. She began showing pleasure in seeing her, kissed her once spontaneously and said on another occasion: "Is bin (I am) Mrs. Clarke's Ruth."

Leah was a clinging child who made advances to every visitor and even to people passing in the street. She became attached to the assistant Judith, would hold her hand on walks, picked flowers for her and sang sometimes all day long: "My Judith bathes me all the time!" But the apparent warmth of this relationship was belied by the fact that she continued to attach herself to every stranger.

John called the young assistant "his" Maureen. His attachment showed more warmth than those of the others but was broken again, unluckily, by Maureen's leaving.

EXAMPLES OF CONFLICTING RELATIONSHIPS

Several children had considerable difficulties in choosing their mother substitutes, their positive feelings wavering uncertainly between the adult figures. John, after being left by Maureen, attached himself to Sister Gertrud, and shortly afterward became fond of Sister Sophie. Neither relationship was exclusive or very passionate and consequently he seemed to have no difficulties in maintaining both simultaneously. In contrast to this, Miriam, who was attached equally to Sisters Sophie and Gertrud, suffered badly from the consequent conflict of feeling. She lived in a constant state of tension without finding relief and satisfaction in her relationships. During Sister Sophie's absence, she "wrote" and dictated long letters to her and she was full of happiness on Sister Sophie's return. But the preference for Sister Sophie, which seemed established at the time, gave way once more to a preference for Sister Gertrud in the course of a few weeks.

EXAMPLES OF RESENTMENT OF SEPARATIONS

Even though the children's attachments to their mother substitutes took second place in their emotional lives, they deeply resented the absences or the leaving of the adults.

> January 1946.—Sister Sophie has left the house together with Mrs. Clarke. When she returns a few hours later, Peter refuses to say goodnight to her. He turns to the other side and says: "You go, you go to a Mrs. Clarke."
>
> March 1946.—When Sister Sophie returned to Bulldogs Bank after an absence of two months, Peter refused to let her do anything for him for a week, would not even take bread or sweets from her. Whenever she left the house, he asked: "You go in a London?"
>
> He regained his affection for her through a process of identification with her interests. Five weeks after her return the children played that they took a bus ride to London. When asked what they wanted to do there, Peter said: "Go in a Miss X's house." Peter saying: "Miss X all better?" From then onward, he called the patient "Peter's Miss X," cuddled and kissed Sister Sophie and held her hand on walks although the children usually preferred to walk on their own.

EXAMPLE OF FULL CATHEXIS OF A MOTHER SUBSTITUTE

The only child to choose a real mother substitute was Ruth, an exception which is easily explainable on the basis of her former attachment to the superintendent of the Children's Ward in Tereszin. She chose as her object Sister Gertrud, and developed toward her the same demandingness, aggressive possessiveness and wish for exclusive attention which had characterized her earlier relationship, a mixture of emotions which is well known from children in the toddler stage and at later ages from those who have gone through the experience of loss, separation, rejection and disappointments in their earliest object relationships. Ruth's lack of satisfaction and insecurity expressed itself with regard to Sister Gertrud in the constantly repeated phrase: "And Ruth? And Ruth?"

EXAMPLE OF A PASSIONATE FATHER RELATIONSHIP

The only child to form a passionate relationship to a father figure was Miriam. Since Miriam arrived in Tereszin at the age of six months, her father having been killed sometime previously, it cannot be presumed that what she went through was a past father relationship transferred to a new object, rather that it was the need for a father which found a first outlet in this manner:

> January 1946.—Mr. E., a neighbor, visits the Nursery for a whole afternoon and teaches the children songs. At the time, Miriam seems more interested in his picture book than in his person. But in the evening she begins to cry for him. She wakes up in the night twice and cries

for him and keeps asking for him during the next two days.

March 1946.—Miriam has seen Mr. E. more often lately. He has brushed her hair once in the evening and she insists on his doing it again. On evenings when he does not come, her hair is not brushed at all since she will not allow anybody else to touch it.

She blushes whenever she sees him. About twenty times a day she says: "Mein Mr. E.—meine Sophie."

March 1946.—Mr. E. says about Miriam: "I have never seen anything like her. That girl is puffing and panting with passion."

Oral Erotism, Masturbation

THERE was a further factor which accounted for the children's diminished capability to form new object relationships. As children for whom the object world had proved disappointing, and who had experienced the severest deprivations from the oral phase onward they had had to fall back to a large degree on their own bodies to find comfort and reassurance. Therefore oral-erotic gratifications persisted with each child in one form or another. Ruth, besides, had a habit of scratching herself rhythmically until she bled, and of smearing with the blood. One child, Paul, suffered from compulsive masturbation.

Peter, Ruth, John and Leah were all inveterate thumb-suckers, Peter and Ruth noisily and incessantly during the whole day, John and Leah more moderately, gradually reducing it to bedtime only. Miriam sucked the tip of her tongue, manipulating it with her teeth until she fell asleep. With Peter, sucking changed in spring to "smoking" carried out with match sticks, twigs, grass blades, then again to sucking his thumb when cross, angry, or at bedtime only. With Ruth sucking persisted even while she was carrying out interesting activities such as threading beads or playing with plasticene.

Since the children's sucking was noisy and obvious they often heard remarks from passers-by or in shops that they should stop or that "their thumbs would be cut off." Contrary to their usual oversensitiveness they remained completely indifferent on such occasions, not even needing reassurance. Sucking was such an integral and indispensable part of their libidinal life that they had not developed any guilt feelings or conflicting attitudes concerning it.

That the excess of sucking was in direct proportion to the instability of their object relationships was confirmed at the end of the year, when the children knew that they were due to leave Bulldogs Bank and when sucking in daytime once more became very prevalent with all of them.

This persistence of oral gratifications, more or less normal under the circumstances, which fluctuated according to the children's relations with the environment, contrasted strongly with Paul's behavior, where compulsive sucking and masturbation manifested themselves as a complicated and, at the time, inaccessible symptom.

Paul, in his good periods, was an excellent member of the group, friendly, attentive and helpful toward children and adults, and capable of friendship. Though not aggressive himself, he was always ready to come to another child's rescue and take up arms against an aggressor. But when he went through one of his phases of compulsive sucking or masturbating, the whole environment, including the other children, lost their significance for him. He ceased to care about them, just as he ceased to eat or play himself. He did not bother to take part in his favorite communal activities such as sorting the laundry or lighting fires. He did not defend himself, or anybody else, merely cried passively when something or somebody made him unhappy. These spells attacked him at any time of the day, while playing, when eating at the table, and during work. He was only free of masturbation on walks, when he sometimes sucked his thumb but otherwise showed a completely changed, cheerful and interested attitude.

In masturbating Paul used his hands, soft toys, picture books, a spoon; or rubbed himself against furniture or against other people.

When sucking, his whole passion was concentrated on face flannels or towels which he sucked while they were hanging on their hooks. He also used a corner of his dungarees, of his coat and the arms of a doll, which he sucked while it was hanging from his mouth. For a period of several weeks he treated the children's used bibs or feeders as so many fetishes, rubbing them rhythmically up and down his nose while sucking, treasuring all six feeders in his arms, or pressing one or more between his legs. When on a walk, he sometimes looked forward to these ecstasies with passionate excitement, rushing into the nursery on coming home with the joyous exclamation "Feeder—feeder!" Since he was indifferent to the same feeders when they were freshly laundered, it may be concluded that his erotic excitation was connected with the smell belonging to a feeding situation.

. . .

Toilet Habits

ACCORDING to the report from Tereszin, all the children had undergone, and successfully completed, an elaborate process of toilet training while in the Ward for Motherless Children. Martha Wenger attributed the length and difficulty of this procedure, which included taking up some of the children two or three times every night, to the "watery diet." The present authors recognize this protracted battle for cleanliness as characteristic for institutional children who do not acquire bowel and bladder control on the basis of an exclusive relationship with their mothers or with a stable mother substitute. According to Martha Wenger, the six children were finally completely and reliably clean and dry during day and night from the spring of 1945 until their liberation.

It bears witness to the disturbing effect of their subsequent changes of environment that with four of the children the result of this toilet training was wholly or partially undone. As usual, there was no simple direct correspondence between the extent of emotional disturbance and the loss of cleanliness. The two most deeply disturbed children, Paul and Ruth, remained clean, without relapses, manifesting their conflicts and abnormalities through other channels. John, Leah and Peter wetted regularly at night with frequent accidents in daytime; Leah and Peter even regressed to soiling for short periods. Miriam merely lost her reliability in toilet matters and had frequent accidents.

The close connection of wetting with the relationship to the adult world was demonstrated most convincingly by Peter's behavior. He used urination quite deliberately in defense against and in defiance of the staff, and as the expression of emotions such as anger, or a feeling of frustration. Characteristically enough for children with this type of wetting, a decisive turn in his toilet habits followed a present of new trousers with braces from his American foster parents. He was very excited about this personal gift, was very careful not to wet these trousers and, on the basis of these positive feelings, reacquired his lost bladder control.

Deviations from the Norm in Ego Attitudes

IN TERESZIN, i.e., up to the ages of three to three and one half, the children had led the existence of inmates of a Ward, within a restricted space, with few or no toys, with no opportunities for moving about freely, for contact with animals, for observing nature. They had not shared or observed the lives of ordinary people and, in the absence of strong emotional ties to the people who looked after them, they had lacked the normal incentives for imitating the adults and for identifying with them. Consequently, their knowledge of the external world, their ability to understand and to deal with it, were far below the level of their ages and of their intelligence.

INDOOR AND OUTDOOR ACTIVITIES

During their first weeks in Bulldogs Bank, the children were unable to use play material. The only toys which attracted their attention from the start were the soft toys, dolls and teddy bears which were adopted as personal possessions and not so much played with as used for autoerotic gratification (sucking, masturbation), or in replacement of it. All the children without exception, took their dolls or teddy bears to bed with them. When a child failed to do so in the evening, it would invariably wake up in the middle of the night, crying for the missing object.

The first play activity, which the children carried out with passionate eagerness, was the pushing of furniture, the usual favorite occupation of toddlers who have just learned to walk. They began their day in the morning with pushing chairs in the nursery and returned to this activity at intervals during the day, whenever they were free to do so. After they had learned to play in the sandpit, they used sand for the same purpose, pushing a supply of it along the whole front of the veranda by means of an inverted chair. They would revert to pushing furniture even on coming home from long walks, or when tired.

Gradual progress in their physical ability to handle objects and to manage their own possessions coincided with the growth of the children's emotional interest in the adult world. This led to the wish to "help," to share the work of the adults and, as described above, to fetch and carry, to set chairs and tables, etc., activities which were carried out surprisingly well. For a short while, the wish to be equal to the adults in these matters led to a frenzy of independence, as the following example shows:

> In November, the children are taken for their first bus ride. The situation has been explained to them beforehand, also that the ride will be short and that they will have to get out quickly at the bus stop. They have promised to co-operate, and they leave their seats without protest at the appointed time. But when the conductor and a passenger try very kindly to help them down the steps, they push them away, and shout and scream that they want to do it alone. Finally Miriam lies on the road, her face almost blue with fury, Paul sits next to her, kicking and screaming, the others cry and sob.

While such a phase of independence brought marked increases in the skill and range of the children's activities, in periods of an opposite emotional nature the advances seemed to be lost once more. In January all the children went through a phase of complete passivity, and dependence on the adults, corresponding to the change of their relationships with them from the more impersonal community feelings to warmer personal attachments. During this time they refused to do anything for themselves, wanted to be fed, dressed, etc., and did not co-operate in work. Their ambivalent attitude toward the adults, the outgoing and withdrawal of emotion toward them, was reflected in the sphere of activities by violent demands to be helped and looked after like a helpless infant, coupled with an equally violent refusal to accept the care. In such moods the children would run away from being dressed, push the tables and chairs away when they had been set for a meal, refuse to carry even their own belongings, etc.

After approximately six months' stay in Bulldogs Bank, these violent upheavals gave way to more ordinary and stable modes of progress.

In March 1946 the children began to lose interest in their soft toys and took picture books to bed with them for "reading." For some time each child was content to have any book. From April onward the children demanded books in which they were particularly interested.

When Miriam received her postcard from Mr. E. and "wrote" her answer on it before going to sleep in the evening, "reading" came to an end and "writing" took its place. Several children had received letters and parcels from their American foster parents and "wrote" to them in bed. At first they used pencils indiscriminately, after a while they chose their colors. The imaginary letters written at that time dealt with matters such as Sister Sophie's absence, news about animals, flowers, etc., i.e., interests in the external world which had taken the place of the exclusive autoerotic activities of the bedtime hour.

In the second half of their year in Bulldogs Bank, the children became increasingly interested in the usual nursery school occupations. At the end of the year they had become able to concentrate on an occupation for as much as an hour. They had become able to handle scissors, pencils, paint brushes, blunt needles, and enjoyed painting, cutting out, doing puzzles and threading beads. Even then they preferred "grownup work" to nursery occupations and carried it out very efficiently.

After the beginnings, which had showed the children to be backward in their play by as much as eighteen months or two years, it was all the more impressive to watch the speed with which they passed through consecutive stages of play activity making up for development which had been missed.[2]

Absence of adequate experience with consequent backwardness in understanding and behavior was even more striking outdoors than indoors. The children lacked both the city child's knowledge of traffic, shops, busy streets, etc., and the country child's familiarity with animals, trees, flowers and all types of work. They knew no animals except dogs, which were objects of terror. They did not know the name of a single plant and had never picked or handled flowers. They seemed to know no vehicles and were completely oblivious of the dangers of the road. Consequently their walks on the country road, through the village or the lanes and paths were exciting events during which innumerable new impressions crowded in on them.

2 See in this respect the paper by Lotte Danzinger and Lieselotte Frankl (1934) on the test results with Albanian infants who, according to custom, spend their first year tied down in their cradle. The authors watched some of these infants being taken out of the cradle and allowed to play with toys. While they at first appeared extremely backward in comparison with other children, they nearly caught up with them (though not completely), when they had played with the toys for some hours only. As explanation, the authors suggest that inner processes of maturation had taken place and progressed in spite of deprivations.

See also Phyllis Greenacre's comprehensive article on "Infant Reactions to Restraint" (1948).

Parallel to the speed of their development in the sphere of play, the children passed rapidly through the various stages of experience and behavior with regard to outdoor events, which are usually gone through between the ages of two and four. Their interest in animals, once awakened, was accompanied by the usual animal play, identification with animals and observations of animals. Interest in cars went from an initial terror of being "made too-too by a car" to a pride in being able to manage crossings, to admonish others to do so, and to distinguish between the types of car. Before they left Bulldogs Bank the children had acquired the experience normal for country children of their age. They knew most trees and practically all the common flowers by name and asked for information when meeting new specimens. They distinguished weeds from plants; they picked flowers with long stems instead of tearing their heads off as at first. They were greatly helped in making up for lost time by the interest of the village people who showed them their animals, permitted them to come into their gardens, gave them flowers, explained their tools, allowed them to look inside their vans or behind counters, all of it new experiences of unique importance for the children.

RETARDATION IN MODES OF THINKING

In dealing with the mass of experience which crowded in on them, the children revealed, during the first weeks, some characteristic peculiarities which are worth noting in individuals of their ages.

A first perception of an object, or the experiencing of an event, together with the naming of it, left an impression on their minds far overriding all later ones in strength and forcefulness. This was clearly demonstrated on several occasions.

A pony in the field had been introduced to the children as a donkey by mistake, and the first ducks which they met had been misnamed geese. In both cases it took several weeks to undo the wrong connection between object and word. In spite of repeated efforts at correction, the children clung to the names connected with their first image of the animal.

The first leaf shown to the children was an ivy leaf. For a whole month every green leaf was called ivy leaf.

When the children noticed a plane overhead for the first time and asked where it was going, they were told that it was going to France. "Going to France" remained a fixed attribute of every plane from then onward. During the whole year they called out: "Aeroplane going to France," whenever they heard a plane overhead.

The first time that letter writing had come into the children's lives was on the occasion of Sister Sophie's absence. All later letters, imagined or dictated by them, retained the opening phrases which they had used then: "Dear Sophie in a London in a Miss X's house. Miss X all better," regardless of the fact that Sister Sophie had returned long ago and that the letters were addressed to other people.

The first English song which the children learned in Bulldogs Bank was "Baa, baa, black sheep." Though they learned and sang many other nursery rhymes during their stay, "Baa, baa, black sheep" remained in a class of its own. They would sing it when cheerful or as a treat for somebody on special occasions.

When talking of people the children would name them according to their most interesting attribute or possession, or would name these objects after them. Mrs. Clarke, for example, had two small dogs which were the first friendly dogs known to the children and played an important role in helping them to overcome their terror of dogs. In December all children called Mrs. Clarke: "Miss Clarke's doggies." Objects given by her to the children were called by the same name. A big electric stove which came from her house was called by Peter: "Miss Clarke's doggies." Green porridge bowls given by her as a Christmas present were called Mrs. Clarke by everybody.

> December 1945.—When washing up, John says: "You wash Mrs. Clarke. I dry Mrs. Clarke. Look at that, Mrs. Clarke all dry."
>
> January 1946.—Ruth throws Peter's green bowl on the floor. Three children shout: "Mrs. Clarke kaputt, poor Mrs. Clarke all kaputt."

The examples quoted in this chapter reveal primitive modes of thinking which are shown by children in their second year of life. The overwhelming strength of a first link between an object or event and its name is characteristic for the time when children first learn to speak, or—to express it in metapsychological terms—when word representations are first added to the images (object representations) in the child's mind. The inability to distinguish between essential and nonessential attributes of an object belongs to the same age (see example of aeroplanes). Instances of naming where this is directed not to a single limited object but to a whole idea related to it (see example of "Miss Clarke's doggies") are forms of "condensation," well known from the primary processes which reveal themselves normally in dream activity, and continue in the second year of life as a mode of waking thought.

That these infantilisms in the sphere of thinking were not based on a general mental retardation with the children under observation was borne out by their adequate, adapted reasoning and behavior in situations with which they felt familiar (such as household tasks, community affairs, etc.); that they were not merely a function of the reversal in their emotional development is suggested by the fact that they overcame them before their libidinal attachments had changed decisively. That the rapid growth of life experience brought about an equally rapid advance in the modes of dealing with it mentally, suggests rather that it was the extreme dearth of new perceptions and varied impressions in their most impressionable years which deprived the children of the opportunity to exercise their mental functions to a normal degree and consequently brought about a stunting of thought development.

. . .

Conclusion

"EXPERIMENTS" of this kind, which are provided by fate, lack the satisfying neatness and circumscription of an artificial setup. It is difficult, or impossible, to distinguish the action of the variables from each other, as is demonstrated in our case by the intermingled effects of three main factors: the absence of a mother or parent relationship; the abundance of community influence; and the reduced amount of gratification of all needs, from the oral stage onward. It is, of course, impossible to vary the experiment. In our case, further, it proved impossible to obtain knowledge of all the factors which have influenced development. There remained dark periods in the life of each child, and guesswork, conclusions and inferences had to be used to fill the gaps.

Under such circumstances, no claim to exactitude can be made for the material which is presented here and it offers no basis for statistical considerations. Though an experiment staged by fate, in the sense that it accentuates the action of certain factors in the child's life (demonstrated through their absence or their exaggerated presence), it has little or nothing to offer to the experimental psychologist. What it helps to do is to create impressions which either confirm or refute the analyst's assumptions concerning infantile development—impressions which can be tested and in their turn confirmed or rejected in detailed analytic work with single individuals.

According to the results of child analysis and reconstruction from the analyses of adults, the child's relationship to his brothers and sisters is subordinated to his relationship to the parents, is, in fact, a function of it. Siblings are normally accessories to the parents, the relations to them being governed by attitudes of rivalry, envy, jealousy, and competition for the love of the parents. Aggression, which is inhibited toward the parents, is expressed freely toward brothers and sisters; sexual wishes, which cannot become manifest in the oedipal relationship, are lived out, passively or actively, with elder or younger brothers and sisters. The underlying relationship with siblings is thus a negative one (dating from infancy when all siblings were merely rivals for the mother's love), with an overlay of positive feelings when siblings are used for the discharge of libidinal trends deflected from the parents. Where the relations between the children of one family become finally manifestly positive, they do so according to the principles of group formation, on the basis of their common identification with the parents. The rival brother is tolerated as belonging to the mother; in special cases the rival brother even becomes an object of identification as the mother's favorite. The child's first approach to the idea of justice is made during these developments of the brother-sister relationship, when the claim to be favored oneself is changed to the demand that no one should be favored, i.e., that there should be equal rights for everybody. Since contemporaries outside the family are treated like the siblings, these first relationships to the brothers and sisters become important factors in determining the individual's social attitudes.

It is well in line with these views when our material shows that the relations of the Bulldogs Bank children to each other were totally different from ordinary sibling attitudes. The children were without parents in the fullest sense of the word, i.e., not merely orphaned at the time of observation, but most of them without an early mother or father image in their unconscious minds to which their earliest libidinal strivings might have been attached. Consequently, their companions of the same age were their real love objects and their libidinal relations with them of a direct nature, not merely the products of laborious reaction formation and defenses against hostility. This explains why the feelings of the six children toward each other show a warmth and spontaneity which is unheard of in ordinary relations between young contemporaries.

It merely bears out this theory to find that attachments to a mother figure in single instances disturb these positive relations, such as in Ruth's case. Or when John, in his mourning for Maureen, turned against his companions and began to hurt them. In these instances the positive libidinal attachment was directed toward the adult; the other children were thereby changed from the position of friends and love objects to that of enemies and rivals.

When working with the children of the Hampstead Nurseries (Freud & Burlingham, 1944), one of the authors has described certain attitudes of helpfulness, co-operation, identification and friendship which appeared in a group of toddlers (between fifteen months and two and one half years of age) who had been temporarily deprived of their mother's care. The six Bulldogs Bank children, as the observations prove, show these attitudes in excess, the quantitative difference between them and the Hampstead Nursery group corresponding to the difference between total and partial absence of a parent relationship.

The high degree of identification with each other's needs is known from one other relationship in early years, that of identical twins to each other. In a recent study of the subject, Dorothy Burlingham (1951) demonstrates the emotional importance of twins to each other, the way in which the twin is treated as an extension of the self, cathected with narcissistic as well as object love. Identification with the twin prospers on the basis of common needs, common anxieties, common wishes, in short, on the similar reactions of two beings of the same age living in close proximity under the same external conditions. While in the case of twins the twin relationship conflicts with and has to adapt itself to the parent relationship, the attitude to the companion within our age group of orphans reigned supreme.

That the children were able to attach their libido to their companions and the group as such, bypassing as it were the parent relationship which is the normal way to social attitudes, deserves interest in relation to certain analytic assumptions. In recent analytic work the experiences of the first year of life, the importance of the relationship to the mother during the oral phase and the linking of these experiences with the beginnings of ego development have assumed great significance. Explorations in these directions have led to the belief, held by many authors, that every disturbance of the mother relationship during this vital phase is invariably a pathogenic factor of specific value. Grave defects in ego development, lack or loss of speech in the first years, withdrawnness, apathy, self-destructive attitudes, psychotic manifestations, have all been ascribed to the so-called "rejection" by the mother, a comprehensive term which includes every disturbance within the mother relationship from loss of the mother through death, permanent or temporary separation, cruel or neglectful treatment, down to lack of understanding, ambivalence, preoccupation or lack of warmth on the mother's part.

The six Bulldogs Bank children are, without doubt, "rejected" infants in this sense of the term. They were deprived of mother love, oral satisfactions, stability in their relationships and their surroundings. They were passed from one hand to another during their first year, lived in an age group instead of a family during their second and third years, and were uprooted again three times during their fourth year. A description of the anomalies which this fate produced in their emotional life and of the retardations in certain ego attitudes [3] is contained in the material. The children were hypersensitive, restless, aggressive, difficult to handle. They showed a heightened autoerotism and some of them the beginning of neurotic symptoms. But they were neither deficient, delinquent nor psychotic. They had found an alternative placement for their libido and, on the strength of this, had mastered some of their anxieties, and developed social attitudes. That they were able to acquire a new language in the midst of their upheavals, bears witness to a basically unharmed contact with their environment.

The authors hope that further contact with

3 —though much of these have to be ascribed to the additional material deprivations—

these children, or those of similar experience, will give indications as to how such emotional anomalies of early life influence the shaping of the Oedipus phase, superego development, adolescence and the chances for a normal adult love life.

REFERENCES

BURLINGHAM, DOROTHY T. *Twins.* London: Imago, 1951.

DANZINGER, LOTTE, & FRANKL, LIESELOTTE. Zum Problem der Funktionsreifung, *Z. f. Kinderforschung,* 1934, **43**.

FREUD, ANNA, & BURLINGHAM, DOROTHY T. *Infants without families.* New York: International Universities Press, 1944.

GREENACRE, PHYLLIS. Infant reactions to restraint. In C. Kluckhohn & H. A. Murray (Eds.), *Personality in nature, society, and culture.* New York: Knopf, 1948.

PART III

Motivation and Learning

THE first papers in this section deal with the question of what motivates child behavior, of what energizes the constant stream of activity that is characteristic of human beings. The traditional position of many learning theorists has been a belief in drive reduction: that behavior occurs to reduce the state of excitement aroused in the organism by either a primary or a secondary drive and that reduction of the state reinforces the behavior. Hunger, thirst, pain, and sex have been considered the primary drives, since they satisfy an organic need, while drives acquired through a conditioning process have been considered secondary and have often been grouped into certain large categories such as aggression, dependency, anxiety, and achievement.

The difficulties inherent in the traditional picture have become increasingly apparent in recent years. First, a number of observers have pointed out that there are some kinds of behavior that cannot be explained by drive-reduction theory. The fact that human beings *seek* excitement, in some cases even slightly fearful or painful excitement, does not seem to fit in with a homeostatic conception of behavior. How can one explain the fact that a child seeks out scary TV programs, climbs to precarious positions in trees, explores physically dangerous places, shoots off firecrackers, begs to ride on roller coasters, and exposes himself to other noxious stimuli, by a theory that the organism acts to reduce or avoid painful stimuli? It is hard, too, to account for the energy of movement in these activities by any one of the traditional primary needs: oxygen, water, food, avoidance of pain, or need to maintain body temperature. Nor do such learned drives as achievement (defined usually as the need to compete with some standard of excellence) serve as satisfactory explanations. Readers who remember carrying on dangerous activities as children will agree that the intense excitement they felt in lighting a firecracker and the fear and trembling they felt while waiting for the loud explosion could hardly be described as the result of an achievement drive, or even a drive for prestige.

The literature contains descriptive research on behaviors difficult to explain by drive-reduction. One such group of behaviors involves seemingly unmotivated repetition. Monkeys, it seems, will work for a long time on simple mechanical puzzles when there is no reward (as usually defined) involved (Harlow, Harlow, & Meyer, 1950). They will work to undo a door clasp, fastened by a hook and pin, and will repeat the activity over and over again, although undoing the clasp is the end in itself, since the clasp does not fasten anything but is simply installed on the wall of their cage. Apparently merely discovering the means that made it possible to obtain an "interesting" result was motivating for the monkeys.

Excerpts from a chapter by Piaget included in this section reveal that he finds such behavior patterns peculiar to a sensorimotor stage of intelligence in the human infant. In his theory, active experimentation leads to discovery of new means to control external events, which initiates a circular reaction; that is, each performance produces stimuli that evoke a repetition of that performance, resulting in circularity. Jacqueline, one of Piaget's infant daughters, would repeat many times each new movement that she had discovered produced an "interesting" effect. If Piaget held her cheeks in his hands and then let them go, Jacqueline put her cheek back into the hand, or grasped her father's hand in order to press it against her cheek. On another occasion, she bumped her head hard on a table, and, although she had obviously suffered pain, she picked up a stick and struck her forehead in the same place. Deprived of the stick, she knocked herself intentionally, although prudently, against the arm of a chair. Piaget discusses how the infant acquires an expectation of outcome through the processes of assimilation and accommodation, conforming his new perceptions to those he has previously experienced and adapting his behavior repetoire to the facts of the new situation.

While the infant's actions described by Piaget are simpler than the monkey's actions in undoing the clasp, we see in both cases that means and ends are inseparable from one another; both the child and the monkey are motivated to act by a desire to rediscover the movement or movements which by chance produced a certain noticeable effect. Yet, according to drive-reduction theory, in the case of the bumped head, Jacqueline should have wanted to avoid the pain of further bumps; and the monkey, upon discovering that its activity got him nowhere and nothing, should have wanted to discontinue the task.

Still another group of behaviors difficult to explain by a homeostatic theory involves the seeking out of *complex* situations in preference to simple ones. Rats when offered a short, simple pathway to food and one that is longer, more indirect, or more "interesting," tend to choose the more complex one (Havelka, 1956). A bright six-year-old brought in for testing complains that the tests are too simple and asks to sit at a "harder" table where older children are being tested. Human beings as well as rats seem to want to avoid monotony; thus, they appear to be motivated to seek out complex and novel tasks. The Smock and Holt paper is an experimental study of such motivation.

Here we have a seeming inconsistency: in one situation, a child wants to repeat a seemingly monotonous task, and in another, a child appears motivated to seek complex tasks. One way that psychologists have sought out of the dilemma is to postulate additional primary drives. In particular, exploratory, manipulatory, and curiosity drives have been advanced as explanations of the behaviors discussed above. To explain why the monkeys repeatedly unclasped a hook, the opening of which led to nothing, Harlow and his associates maintained that there is also a manipulatory drive, that certain external stimuli arouse this drive which is then reduced by changing the external pattern. They propose adding such a drive to the list of primary drives.

Harlow (1958), has also postulated a primary need for contact-comfort as the basis of the secondary need of love or affection. He worked with two kinds of inanimate "mother"-monkeys (one providing contact-comfort and the other, a wire monkey, providing food). The experiment was designed to test the hypothesis that affection develops through conditioning to contact-comfort rather than to food. Recent research by Harlow (1962) indicates certain modifications in his earlier findings: monkeys raised on a wire monkey did, indeed, learn to seek out that figure for comfort; however, as adult monkeys, their sexual behavior was not normal. In addition, the females turned out to be very poor mothers.

To explain why living things avoid monotony and seek more complex tasks, Berlyne (1960) has proposed an exploratory or curiosity drive. According to this theory, perceptual novelty in a situation is an important factor; novel stimuli arouse the drive to explore which is reduced as the stimuli cease being novel. Complexity of stimuli, too, is a factor. The reader will recall the Fantz paper in Part I at this point. Presumably, the more complex stimuli offer greater novelty. Gesell (1943) observed that even at as young as four weeks the infant stares at lights and windows and may become angry if turned away from brightness. He appears interested in bright-colored cretonne pillows and particularly in the colors red and orange. He seeks out the perceptual novelty afforded by brightness and colors. Here the factor of *intensity* or contrast may be the contributing factor.

It is easy to see that more and more primary drives could be added to the traditional list in an attempt to explain certain behaviors otherwise difficult to understand. But proliferation of independent motives defeats the psychologist's quest for parsimony. The next paper on this topic takes a fresh look at motivation theory and attempts to resolve the dilemma in a different way. White's paper develops the thesis that these new drives (exploratory, manipulative, etc.) may be subsumed under the one category of competence, and that the urge that makes for competence has motivating effects. However, in addition to making this *rapprochement,* White also casts a critical eye on theories of motivation which make reinforcement dependent upon drive reduction. His paper is an important contribution to motivation theory.

Hebb (1955) also offers some possible solutions to problems in motivation theory. He sees man as an active animal *by his nature* and suggests a kind of general drive state resulting from arousal of the reticular activating system. Once this system is alerted, the conceptual nervous system takes over. While Hebb's (1955) paper offers some difficulty for the reader because the author is still formulating his theory, it sheds many interesting lights on motivational problems.

From the research, two tentative findings are emerging. One is that the list of primary drives will have to be revised to take into account the child's tendency to explore, investigate, manipulate, and in other ways seek stimulation. The second finding is that the drive-reduction principle of reinforcement will have to be modified to account for the fact that even when primary appetitive drives are satisfied, the child is still active, and the fact that sometimes an *increase* in tension rather than a decrease can be reinforcing.

Research by Gewirtz and Baer (1958) sheds some light on this latter point. This team investigated the reinforcing effects of deprivation and satiation of reinforcers (in this case, adult approval and social contacts) upon children's behavior while playing a game. In the one case children were deprived of the presence of the experimenter and approving remarks, while in the other case they were presumably satiated with both social contact and approval. It appears that when children are temporarily deprived of the opportunity for reinforcement, they try harder for it when the opportunity is restored than when they are satiated continuously with it.

The next three papers in this section deal with three important secondary drives: aggression, dependency, and achievement. Aggression is a drive learned through a conditioning process, typically in connection with frustration. As Sears, Maccoby, and Levin showed in their 1957 report, punishment of young children by the mother (which is, of course, frustrating) was positively correlated with aggression in the child, but so was permissiveness for aggression. Punishment for aggression resulted in more anxiety over the aggression than permissiveness. In the follow-up study included here, Sears reports on changes in these same children between five and twelve years of age.

The dependency drive has also been the subject of considerable discussion in the literature. A dependency drive is said to exist when the child is motivated to resolve tension by turning to another for affection, nurturance, or help. Like aggression, the strength of a dependency drive can vary. Frustration of dependency needs and inconsistent gratification appear to strengthen the drive. The Hartup paper included here presents evidence to this effect.

In the Rosen and D'Andrade paper, the achievement drive is considered. Beginning with the work of McClelland *et al.* (1953), investigators have considered the need for achievement to be related to training in independence. Presumably if a child is to learn to want to compete with standards of excellence, he must learn to perform certain tasks *by himself.* The earlier Winterbottom (1953) study showed that fourth grade boys who were given independence training also had a stronger achievement drive as measured by responses to selected T.A.T. pictures. Rosen and D'Andrade consider two other socialization variables: achievement training and sanctions. They investigate how parental behavior affects the strength of the achievement drive in preadolescent boys, and they include the behavior of fathers as well as mothers.

Erikson's "Eight Ages of Man" represents one of the most systematic modifications of Freudian theory that has yet been attempted. Here, while working within a psychoanalytic framework, he attempts to apply insights gained from cultural anthropology. In every culture there are conflicts to be faced at each of the different stages through which individuals proceed in the course of their socialization. As each conflict is resolved satisfactorily, a new factor is incorporated into the ego. If a particular conflict in unsatisfactorily resolved, specific damage to the ego results. Erikson's special concern is ego development, for he sees the acquiring of ego identity as an important developmental task. A strong and healthy ego identity is acquired only as the child receives wholehearted and consistent recognition of accomplishment that has meaning in his culture.

REFERENCES

Berlyne, D. E. The influence of the albedo and complexity of stimuli on visual fixation in the human infant. *Brit. J. Psychol.*, 1958, **49**, 315–318.

Gesell, A., & Ilg, Frances L. *Infant and child in the culture of today.* New York: Harper, 1943.

Gewirtz, J. L., & Baer, D. M. Deprivation and satiation of social reinforcers as drive conditions. *J. abnorm. soc. Psychol.*, 1958, **57**, 165–172.

Harlow, H. F. The nature of love. *Amer. Psychologist*, 1958, **13**, 673–685.

Harlow, H. F. The heterosexual affectional system in monkeys. *Amer. Psychologist*, 1962, **17**, 1–9.

Harlow, H. F., Harlow, Margaret K., & Meyer, D. R. Learning motivated by a manipulation drive. *J. exp. Psychol.*, 1950, **40**, 228–234.

Havelka, J. Problem-seeking behavior in rats. *Canad. J. Psychol.*, 1956, **10**, 91–97.

Hebb, D. O. Drives and the c. n. s. (conceptual nervous system). *Psychol. Rev.*, 1955, **62**, 243–254.

McClelland, D. C., Atkinson, J. W., Clark, R. A., & Lowell, E. L. *The achievement motive.* New York: Appleton-Century-Crofts, 1953.

Sears, R. R., Maccoby, Eleanor E., & Levin, H. *Patterns of child rearing.* New York: Row, Peterson, 1957.

Winterbottom, M. R. The relation of childhood training in independence to achievement motivation. Unpublished doctoral dissertation, Univer. of Michigan, 1953. (Abstract in Univer. Microfilms, Publication No. 5113.)

JEAN PIAGET

*Making Interesting Sights Last**

EDITOR'S INTRODUCTION

IN THE preceding chapters of this volume, Piaget has described how an infant exercises his innate reflexes (sucking, grasping, orienting) in the period immediately following birth; he has shown that each exercise is not the mere repetition of the original automatic response but is apparently dependent upon and develops from earlier episodes. Through processes of assimilation (utilizing something from the environment and incorporating that event into a pattern consistent with previous experience), and accommodation (the process of coping with environmental conditions through modification of behavior), the infant develops a repertoire of activities described as primary circular reactions. During this stage he seeks to prolong the use of the reflex; he sucks for the sake of sucking (not just to get food) and looks for the sake of looking.

In the excerpts reproduced below, Piaget is describing a third stage in infant development: the stage of secondary circular reactions. At this stage the infant repeats actions he has first tried out on his own body on phenomena in the external world. He repeats for the sake of creating again an interesting result in the environment. He *anticipates* an interesting result; his action is the means to this end. This progress in his behavior is accomplished first through assimilation and then through accommodation.

[PRIMARY circular reactions] consist in simple organic movements centered on themselves (with or without intercoördination) and not destined to maintain a result produced in the external environment. So it is that the child grasps for the sake of grasping, sucking, or looking, but not yet in order to swing to and fro, to rub, or to reproduce sounds. Moreover the external objects upon which the subject acts are one with his action which is simple, the means being confused with the end. On the other hand, in the circular reactions which we shall call "secondary" and which characterize the present stage, the movements are centered on a result produced in the external environment and the sole aim of the action is to maintain this result; furthermore it is more complex, the means beginning to be differentiated from the end, at least after the event.

. . .

First here are some examples of circular reactions relating to the movements the child gives to his bassinet and to the hanging objects:

Observation 94.—At 0;3 (5) [1] Lucienne shakes her bassinet by moving her legs violently (bending and unbending them, etc.), which makes the cloth dolls swing from the hood. Lucienne looks at them, smiling, and recommences at once. These movements are simply the concomitants of

1 Age in years, months, and days. [Ed.]

* The selection from Jean Piaget, *The Origins of Intelligence in Children.* From Chapter 3: "The Third Stage: The 'Secondary Circular Reactions' and the Procedures Destined to Make Interesting Sights Last."

joy. When she experiences great pleasure Lucienne externalizes it in a total reaction including leg movements. As she often smiles at her knick-knacks she caused them to swing. But does she keep this up through consciously coördinated circular reaction or is it pleasure constantly springing up again that explains her behavior?

That evening, when Lucienne is quiet, I gently swing her dolls. The morning's reaction starts up again, but both interpretations remain possible.

The next day, at 0;3 (6) I present the dolls: Lucienne immediately moves, shakes her legs, but this time without smiling. Her interest is intense and sustained and there also seems to be an intentional circular reaction.

At 0;3 (8) I again find Lucienne swinging her dolls. An hour later I make them move slightly: Lucienne looks at them, smiles, stirs a little, then resumes looking at her hands as she was doing shortly before. A chance movement disturbs the dolls: Lucienne again looks at them and this time shakes herself with regularity. She stares at the dolls, barely smiles and moves her legs vigorously and thoroughly. At each moment she is distracted by her hands which pass again into the visual field: she examines them for a moment and then returns to the dolls. This time there is definite circular reaction.

At 0;3 (13) Lucienne looks at her hand with more coördination than usually. In her joy at seeing her hand come and go between her face and the pillow, she shakes herself in front of this hand as when faced by the dolls. Now this reaction of shaking reminds her of the dolls which she looks at immediately after as though she foresaw their movement. She also looks at the bassinet hood which also moves. At certain times her glance oscillates between her hand, the hood, and the dolls. Then her attention attaches itself to the dolls which she then shakes with regularity.

At 0;3 (16) as soon as I suspend the dolls she immediately shakes them, without smiling, with precise and rhythmical movements with quite an interval between shakes, as though she were studying the phenomenon. Success gradually causes her to smile. This time the circular reaction is indisputable. Same reaction at 0;3 (24). Same observations during the succeeding months and until 0;6 (10) and 0;7 (27) at sight of a puppet and at 0;6 (13) with a celluloid bird, etc.

. . .

Accommodation and Organization of the Schemata

UNTIL the present behavior patterns—that is, during the entire stage of the pure primary reactions—accommodation remained relatively subordinated to assimilation. Sucking, looking, grasping, consisted in incorporating observed objects into corresponding schemata of assimilation, free to accommodate these schemata to a variety of things. So it is that the movements and positions of hands, eyes, and mouth vary as a function of the objectives, in a continuous accommodation concomitant to assimilation, although of opposite direction. At the other extreme of sensorimotor behavior patterns . . . we shall see, on the contrary, that accommodation precedes assimilation, in a sense. Confronted by new objects the child intentionally seeks to find out in what way they are new and so experiments upon them before assimilating them to a schema constructed on their effect. Hence accommodation evolves from the simple differentiation of schemata, peculiar to the primary reactions, to the search for the new, peculiar to the tertiary reactions. What of the secondary circular reaction?

In its point of departure the latter reveals no accommodation other than that of the primary reactions: a simple differentiation of schemata as function of the object. So it is that Laurent discovers the possibility of hitting a hanging doll, simply while trying to grasp it, and that Lucienne and Laurent learn to rub a toy against the side of the bassinet simply while swinging it. But, contrary to that which occurs in the primary reactions, this initial differentiaton of the schema does not, without adding something, lead to its application to new objects, precisely since Laurent does not succeed in grasping the doll nor in moving the rattle as he intends to, but discovers an unforeseen phenomenon due to this very defeat: the doll swings when one strikes it and the rattle rubs the wood of the bassinet. It is then that the specific accommodation of the secondary circular reaction is produced: the child tries to rediscover the movements which lead to the result observed. As we have previously demonstrated, the child begins, in effect, by trying to assimilate this new result while limiting himself to looking at it, etc. (primary schemata). Then, as soon as he has discovered, through reciprocal assimilation of the schemata, that this result depends on his manual activity, he tries to reproduce it by assimilation to this activity. But, as it is just in differentiating the latter that the subject has by chance obtained the new result, the question is to establish this differentiation intentionally and it is in this that the accommodation peculiar to the secondary reaction consists: rediscovering the movements which have given rise to the result observed. This accommodation, without preceding assimilation as is the case in the tertiary reaction, or simply doubling it, as is the case in the primary reaction, consists, then, in completing it at the moment when the new schema is formed. Therefore accommodation is no longer an almost automatic differentiation of the schemata, nor yet an intentional search for novelty as such, but it is a voluntary and systematic fixation of the differentiations imposed by new realities which arise by chance. A concrete example will enable us to understand:

Observation 105.—Laurent, from 0;4 (19) . . . knows how to strike hanging objects intentionally with his hand. At 0;4 (22) he holds a stick; he does not know what to do with it and slowly passes it from hand to hand. The stick then happens to strike a toy hanging from the bassinet hood. Laurent, immediately interested by this unexpected result, keeps the stick raised in the same position, then brings it noticeably nearer to the toy. He strikes it a second time. Then he draws the stick back but moving it as little as possible as though trying to conserve the favorable position, then he brings it nearer to the toy, and so on, more and more rapidly.

The dual character of this accommodation may be seen. On the one hand, the new phenomenon makes its appearance by simple fortuitous insertion in an already formed schema and hence differentiates it. But, on the other hand, the child, intentionally and systematically, applies himself to rediscovering the conditions which led him to this unexpected result.

It goes without saying that the use of the stick described in this example was only episodical: it has nothing to do with the "behavior pattern of the stick" which we shall describe in connection with the fifth stage.

. . .

As we have just seen, each of the secondary circular reactions which appear in the child is derived by differentiation from a primary circular reaction or a secondary reaction grafted upon a primary reaction. Everything thus goes back to movements of legs or feet, arms or hands, and it is these "circular" movements of prehension which become differentiated in movements directed at pulling, shaking, swinging, displacing, rubbing, etc. When Lucienne, at 3 to 4 months, shakes her bassinet and her dolls she limits herself to moving feet and legs, in conformity to a primary schema. When Laurent at 0;2 (24)–0;3 (0) shakes a rattle attached to his arm before knowing how to grasp, he is only prolonging the spontaneous circular movements of that arm. And when at 0;3 (13) he learns to shake the rattle by means of a chain, this is simply because he uses his nascent schema of prehension. The same applies to all the secondary circular reactions: each is the prolongation of an already existing schema. With regard to "procedures to make interesting sights last" of which we shall speak later on, they in turn prolong these circular reactions. The only difference between the secondary reactions and the primary reactions is, therefore, that henceforth the interest is centered on the external result and no longer only on the activity as such. But that is not contradictory to the conservative character of this function: in effect, the external result, arising suddenly at the very center of the child's activity, interests him at one and the same time inasmuch as it is related to his essential schemata and inasmuch as it is unforeseen and baffling. If it were only new it would merely deserve momentary attention; but on the contrary, it appears to the subject as being connected with his most familiar acts or with his schemata in actual use. Moreover this unforeseen result leads astray all that of which these schemata habitually admit. The attention is, therefore, perforce centered on the exterior and no longer only on the function. In short, the secondary circular reactions are essentially conservative and assimilatory since they prolong without adding anything to the primary reactions and, if the child's interest is displaced and externalized on the material result of the acts, it is simply because this result is [the] function of an increasingly rich assimilatory activity.

. . .

Recognitory Assimilation and the System of Meanings

THE facts hitherto studied constitute essentially phenomena of reproductive assimilation: through repetition rediscovering a fortuitous result. Before seeing how this behavior is extended into generalizing assimilation and thus gives rise to "procedures to make interesting sights last," let us once more emphasize a group of facts, which no longer constitute circular reactions in themselves but which are derived from secondary reactions, in the capacity of recognitory assimilations. What happens, in effect, is that the child, confronted by objects or sights which habitually set in motion his secondary circular reactions, limits himself to outlining the customary movements instead of actually performing them. Everything takes place as though the child were satisfied to recognize these objects or sights and to make a note of this recognition, but could not recognize them except by working, rather than thinking, the schema helpful to recognition. Now this schema is none other than that of the secondary circular reaction corresponding to the object in question.

Here are some examples:

Observation 107.—At 0;5 (3) Lucienne tries to grasp spools suspended above her by means of elastic bands. She usually uses them in order to suck them, but sometimes she swings them while shaking herself when they are there (see Obs. 94). She manages to touch but not yet to grasp them. Having shaken them fortuitously, she then breaks off to shake herself a moment while looking at them (shakes of the legs and trunk), then she resumes her attempts at grasping.

Why has she broken off in order to shake herself a few seconds? It was not in order to shake the spools because she did not persevere and was busy with something else at the moment when she made this movement: neither was it in order to facilitate her attempts at grasping. Is it a question of a purely mechanical movement started by the sight of their chance swinging? It would seem so, but the rest of the observation shows that this behavior pattern was renewed too often to be automatic: it therefore certainly has a meaning. Neither is it a question of a sort of ritual analogous to those we shall study in connection with the beginnings of play because the child, far from seeming to amuse herself, was perfectly serious. Everything transpires as though the subject, endowed for a moment with reflection and internal language, had said to [herself] something like this: "Yes, I see that this object could be swung, but it is not what I am looking for." But, lacking language, it is by working the schema that Lucienne would have thought that, before resuming [her] attempts to grasp. In this hypothesis, the short interlude of swinging would thus be equivalent to a sort of motor recognition.

Such an interpretation would remain completely hazardous when confronted by a single fact. But its probability increases along with the following observations. For instance at 0;5 (10) Lucienne again relapses into states identical to those vis-à-vis a rattle. So also, at 0;6 (5) she shakes herself several times in succession, very briefly each time, as soon as she has caught sight of her hand (which comes out of her mouth or by chance enters the visual field, etc.). One cannot see what this movement might mean if not that it is the outline of some action suggested by this sight.

. . .

Observation 107 repeated.—Laurent, too, at 0;4 (21) has an object in his hands when, in order to distract him, I shake the hanging rattles which he is in the habit of striking. He then looks at the rattles without relinquishing his toy and outlines with his right hand the movement of "striking." From 0;5 I often note such outlines of acts when confronted by familiar objectives; they are similar to Lucienne's.

It may be seen how such behavior patterns constitute a separate class. It is no longer a question of a simple secondary circular reaction, since the child reveals no effort to arrive at a result. It is true that there might be a simple automatization of earlier reactions. But, on the one hand, the child's expression does not give the impression that he acts mechanically and, on the other hand, we do not see at all why an automatic reproduction of useless acts would last so long (we have only chosen one or two examples from among innumerable ones). In the second place, these behavior patterns cannot be identified with the "procedures to make an interesting spectacle last," of which we shall speak presently. These "procedures . . ." appear at the moment when a sight contemplated by the child is interrupted, and their purpose is to act upon the things themselves, while the present behavior patterns arise at simple contact with an object, regardless of whether this is immobile or mobile, and without an attempt at acting upon it. In the third place, neither is it possible to reduce these behavior patterns to "explorations" and "tertiary circular reactions" of which we shall speak subsequently. The latter relate to new objects whereas the present behavior patterns are set in motion by familiar objects.

We therefore only see one interpretation for Observations 107–107 (repeated): they are acts of recognitory assimilation. Confronted by a familiar object or event, but whose sudden appearance was not foreseen by the child, the latter needs to adapt himself to the unexpected. This is what occurs, for example, when Lucienne sees a spool swing at the moment she wishes to grasp it, or perceives her hand, the parrots, etc., at a moment and in a place she did not expect them, etc. To adapt oneself means, in such cases, simply noting the event, in so far as it is known and of no use at present: it is then, without adding anything, a matter of recognizing and classing the thing. The subject will subsequently do this in enunciated words or in internal language but, due to his present lack of such symbolic instruments, the child is limited to outlining the gestures of the corresponding schema, used thus in the capacity of a recognitory schema. In other words, instead of saying: "Oh! the spool is swinging," or: "There is my hand. . . . There is the parrot. . . . There is the bassinet which is moving," the child assimilates these facts by means of motor concepts, not yet verbal, and, by shaking his own legs or hands, so indicates to himself that he understands what he perceives.

The existence of this recognitory assimilation might seem doubtful if it had not been prepared by all the reproductive assimilation of the secondary circular reaction. Two circumstances show that reproductive assimilation brings with it at the outset the formation of a sensorimotor recognition. In the first place, the very fact of rediscovering an interesting result—that is, the definition of secondary circular reaction—entails an increasingly accurate recognition. In the second place, once the schema has been constituted, it is reactivated by each new contact with the objects due to which it arose. Each time, for example, the child sees the doll hanging he is in the habit of swinging by shaking himself or striking it, etc., of his own accord he resumes shaking himself, striking, etc. This activation of the schema by immediate assimilation of the object to its function is simultaneously a recognitory and reproductive fact of assimilation, these two aspects of the assimilatory process being as yet undifferentiated during this initial phase. It is therefore very natural that simply recognitory assimilation should dissociate itself at a given moment from reproductive or purely active assimilation. At first, as revealed by the beginning of Observation 107, it can happen that the child finds himself incited by external facts to activate a schema at the exact moment when his interest is elsewhere and is already acting there according to a different schema. In this case the schema which interferes with the main action will simply be outlined whereas the activity in progress will be pursued normally. Then, it can happen, as revealed by the end of the same Observation 107, that the schema excited by the external events is too familiar to give rise to a real action and so is again limited to a short and simple indication of it. In both cases the outline of activity, replacing real activity, is consequently equivalent to a step which is more contemplative than active; in other words, to an act of simple recognition or simple classification rather than to effective action. So it may be seen that recognitory assimilation, at first involved in reproductive assimilation, detaches itself from it little by little, to remain in the half-active, half-verifying state which is the state nearest to the pure judgment of verification of which the sensorimotor intelligence is capable.

. . .

Generalizing Assimilation and the Constitution of "Procedures to Make Interesting Spectacles Last"

THE generalization of secondary schemata is produced when the child is confronted by new objects. In such cases the child from the outset makes use of his usual behavior patterns and assimilates the unfamiliar to their schemata, without adding anything. It is a remarkable thing that the younger the child, the less novelties seem new to him. Unfortunately, it is impossible to compare in this respect secondary with primary reactions in the presence of unfamiliar objects for there is no appreciable common gauge for them. But if the reactions of the present stage are compared to those of the following one and above all to the "tertiary circular reactions" of the fifth stage, the difference is all the more striking as the situations become more homogeneous. In the face of a new phenomenon, the child in the fifth stage is capable of adopting the attitude of experimentation (this does not mean that he necessarily adopts it, but he is apt to do so). He seeks novelty and varies the conditions of the phenomenon in order to examine all of its modalities. The child in the fourth stage, without reaching these true "experiments to see," is also interested in the new object in itself. But, in order to "understand" it, he tries to apply to it in turn the whole of the known schemata in order to find which one in particular will be most suitable to it. On the other hand, the child at the present stage, while sometimes feeling surprise in the presence of an unknown object, nevertheless from the outset treats it as a familiar object and employs it in the use of his habitual schemata. Thereafter one has the impression that the child, far from still being interested in the thing in itself and far from appreciating its novelty as such, merely tries to use his secondary schemata by pure functional assimilation, as he did hitherto by means of the primary schemata. Consequently there exists a simple generalization of secondary schemata.

Here are examples of this elementary generalizing assimilation:

Observation 110.—At 0;3 (29) for the first time Laurent sees the paper knife. . . . He grasps and looks at it, but only for a moment. Afterward he immediately swings it with his right hand as he does all the objects grasped. He then rubs it by chance against the wicker of the bassinet and tries to reproduce the sound heard, as though it were a rattle. It then suffices that I place the object in his left hand for him to shake it in the same way. He ends by sucking it. The novelty of the object has therefore in no way interested the child, except for the brief glance at the beginning: the paper knife from the outset was used as aliment for the habitual schemata.

At 0;4 (8) I place a large rubber monkey in front of Laurent; the mobile limbs and tail as well as its expressive head constitute an absolutely new entity for him. Laurent reveals, in effect, lively astonishment and even a certain fright. But he at once calms down and applies to the monkey some of the schemata which he uses to swing hanging objects; he shakes himself, strikes with his hands, etc., gradating his effort according to the result obtained.

Likewise, at 0;5 (25) and the days following, Laurent looks at an unfolded newspaper which I place on the hood of his bassinet. He immediately begins to pull the strings hanging from the hood, to shake himself or his feet and arms. He bursts out laughing on seeing the movements of the newspaper just as he frequently does when the rattles shake.

At 0;6 (0) Laurent at once grasps a big box of lozenges which is unfamiliar to him. He hardly looks at it but immediately uses it to rub against the sides of the bassinet, then he passes it from one hand to the other and rubs the object against the opposite side of the bassinet.

At 0;6 (1) he grasps a new rattle made of three parts: the handle, a middle ball of medium size and the end ball, a large one. Laurent looks at the object quite a long time while passing it from one hand to the other and even seems to palpate the surface which foretells the behavior patterns of the following stage. But he quickly desists in order to move the object in the air, at first slowly, then more and more rapidly, and finally he shakes it, rubs it against the sides of the bassinet, etc.

At 0;6 (7) I offer him various new objects to see if he will resume his attempts at spatial exploration which seemed to appear in connection with the last object. This does not occur; the child utilizes the new object as aliment for his habitual schemata. So it is that a penguin with long feet and a wagging head is only looked at briefly: at first Laurent strikes it, then rubs it against the side of the bassinet, etc., without paying attention to the end by which he grasped it. Several knick-knacks receive the same treatment: he grasps them with one hand and strikes them with the other.

At 0;6 (14) he takes hold of a new doll, looks at it for a moment without investigating either its shape or clothing; he strikes it, rubs it against the wicker, shakes it in the air, etc.

At 0;6 (18) a pipe holds his attention more but is subsequently utilized in the same way. At 0;6 (16) a new swan, encircled by a ring and with a handle is looked at with curiosity and immediately struck, shaken, rubbed, etc. At 0;6 (26) a series of unfamiliar objects (a rattle with a bell, a bear, a lamb, etc.) are barely examined before being struck, shaken, etc.

At 0;7 (2) he only looks a little at an unfamiliar bird of complicated shape mounted on a plank with wheels. He limits himself to shaking and striking it, and rubbing it against the side of the bassinet.

Observation 111.—At 0;5 (3) Lucienne only has one schema at her disposition which she employs in the course of her circular reactions and attempts to make interesting spectacles last: that of shaking her foot or entire body to cause swinging. Furthermore, of course, she knows how to grasp, suck, etc. When a new object is presented to her there ensues the curious result that she tries in turn the schemata of prehension and of shaking the feet, but applying the first chiefly to immobile and near objects and the second mainly to objects in motion or hanging before her. Here is the series of attempts:

First of all, before a cross of Malta

which hangs above her, Lucienne immediately moves her feet only. Then she slows down her movements and begins empty sucking while looking at the object; after this she grasps it and brings it in front of her eyes in order to examine it.

A pipe, motionless: attempts at prehension, sucking at a distance and foot movements, all simultaneous.

An eraser: surprise, sucking at a distance and prehension. Once the eraser has been grasped, Lucienne looks at it briefly, in her hand, then immediately begins to move her feet.

Again the cross of Malta: immediate and sustained foot movements. Then Lucienne's hand having knocked against the object, there is an attempt at prehension, but this second reaction is obviously due to a fortuitous cause.

A hanging puppet: she grasps it and pulls but, not succeeding in drawing it to her, she periodically desists in order to give hard shakes of the feet. She then resumes, grasping, then moves her legs again: there is constant alternation between these two activities.

A slide rule: exclusive attempts at prehension. No movement of the feet.

A strap which I swing slowly: shakes of the feet, then attempts at prehension.

A stick of sealing wax: only prehension.

A watch placed very near her face: first prehension, then when I raise it too high, shakes of the feet.

This observation consequently shows us how much the new object is immediately assimilated to a schema; that is to say, generically recognized as being able to give rise to a familiar behavior pattern, even when the habitual schemata are very limited in number. In what follows it goes without saying that the more these schemata are multiplied the more the new object is subjected to various attempts.

It may be seen in what such behavior patterns consist. When confronted by new objects the child does not yet try to find out in what way they are new, he limits himself, at the outset or after a short pause, to using them as aliments for his habitual behavior patterns. He therefore generalizes, without adding anything for their use, the schemata he possesses.

But the generalizing assimilation belonging to this stage is not limited to this elementary form. It sometimes happens that the novelty presented to the child does not consist in a particular object but in an event, in an actual spectacle on which the subject has no direct influence. What occurs then? The child, desirous of seeing the spectacle prolonged, also utilizes his habitual schemata which he generalizes without adding anything to this effect. That is what is revealed by Observation 110. When Laurent, at 0;4 (8) and 0;5 (25) cannot grasp the monkey or the newspaper which he sees from afar, he at once applies to them the schemata related to hanging objects and thus seeks to act upon them from a distance. From that to trying to act upon any phenomenon whatever, independently of any real contact, is only a step.

This step is taken as a result of the following behavior pattern: It is a transitional behavior pattern which stems from secondary circular reaction but whose higher forms foretell the combinations of the fourth stage. It is the activity by means of which the child tries to make last the interesting spectacles of which he has just been witness without himself having provoked their first appearance (for example, prolonging the swinging of a watch seen from afar, etc.). Such behavior patterns still partake of circular reaction, since it is simply a matter of conserving and reproducing, but they generalize its principle, since the schemata hitherto inserted in actual circular reactions are henceforth applied to entirely new circumstances. Here are some examples of these behavior patterns:

Observation 112.—The first example will make us understand how the secondary circular reaction is prolonged in procedures to make an interesting spectacle last. . . . At 0;3 (20) I make the following experiment on Laurent. I give him a rubber doll, unfamiliar to him and attached to the usual rattle by a string sufficiently loose so that the doll's movements do not shake the rattle. As soon as Laurent sees the doll, he grasps it in his right hand and sucks it. This preliminary phase lasts ten minutes during which the rattle has neither moved nor made a noise. After this Laurent lets his arm drop to the side while keeping the doll in his hand. I then shake the rattle without shaking the string or Laurent's hand; moreover, he did not look at the rattle at this time. Then, as soon as he hears the rattle, he looks at it and stretches out his right arm, while holding the doll in his hand, then he shakes this doll in a perfectly adapted way.

But a moment later Laurent's right hand is in contact with the doll, without holding it. I then shake the rattle again. He immediately moves his right arm, his hand remaining empty and not attempting to grasp the doll.

Thus it may be seen how, as soon as circumstances are changed, the schema becomes dissociated and the efficacious gesture (grasping, and shaking the arm, or simply shaking the arm) is advanced to the rank of procedure to make the interesting spectacle last, in the very absence of the usual intermediaries (of the chain).

The rest of the observation well shows, in effect, that this arm movement has become, for Laurent, a constant "procedure" and has not simply consisted in an episodic effort. At 0;3 (5) for example, Laurent practices grasping my hand when it is within his direct reach; but, when I put it at a distance of 50 cm. or more, he looks at it and then swings his arms rapidly just as he does when confronted by his usual rattle.—At 0;3 (23), I present him (at a distance of 50 cm.) with an unfamiliar doll (in costume) which I swing for a moment. As long as it moves, he looks at it, motionless, but as soon as it stops, he shakes his arm. Same reaction with respect to my watch and my wallet. The same day I saw him behave spontaneously in this way while looking at his hanging doll.

At 0;3 (29) I shake his arm as soon as I stop swinging a paper knife 100 cm. away from him.—At 0;4 (18) he shakes his arm in order to make me continue when I shake his feet. He laughs and waves his arms more and more vigorously until I resume. At 0;5 (26) he does the same as soon as a grating sound stops, a sound which I had made without his seeing me. He definitely gradates his movement according to the variations of the waiting time.

At 0;6 (27) again, he shakes his arm when he does not succeed in grasping a distant object or in order to make an object move at a distance (a sheet of paper placed on a cupboard, at a distance of 150 cm. from him, etc.). Same observation at 0;7 (5).

At 0;7 (7) he looks at a tin box placed on a cushion in front of him, too remote to be grasped. I drum on it for a moment in a rhythm which makes him laugh and then present my hand (at a distance of 2 cm. from his, in front of him). He looks at it, but only for a moment, then turns toward the box; then he shakes his arm while staring at the box (then he draws himself up, strikes his coverlets, shakes his head, etc.; that is to say, he uses all the "procedures" at his disposition). He obviously waits for the phenomenon to recur. Same reaction at 0;7 (12), at 0;7 (13), 0;7 (22), 0;7 (29) and 0;8 (1) in a variety of circumstances.

It therefore seems apparent that the movement of shaking the arm, at first inserted in a circular schema of the whole, has been removed from its context to be used, more and more frequently, as a "procedure" to make any interesting spectacle last.

CHARLES D. SMOCK *and* BESS GENE HOLT

*Children's Reactions to Novelty: An Experimental Study of "Curiosity Motivation"**

Casual observation of the activities of children and adults is sufficient to establish the power of novel features of the environment to evoke and direct behavior. Unusual or unfamiliar objects have considerable potency for attracting attention, while monotony and routine appear to arouse, in many individuals, an active striving to encounter new aspects of their environment. The apparent independence of these behavior tendencies from primary needs and "social influences" have led a number of psychological theorists to consider an explanation of curiosity and exploratory behavior essential to our understanding of human motivational processes. Since MacDougall's instinct theory, personality theorists have introduced such concepts as "effort after meaning" (Bartlett, 1959), need cognition (Cohen, Stotland, & Wolf, 1955), and competence motivation (White, 1959) to account for individual variation in the tendency to seek and maintain contact with environmental and/or psychological novelty. More recently the research of Harlow (1953) and others (cf. review by Glanzer [1958]) based on the concept of exteroceptively elicited drives has produced extensive data indicating that rats, raccoons, and monkeys, as well as men, *under certain conditions* tend to behave so as to maximize knowledge of an unfamiliar or novel environment. However, the environmental and psychological conditions that facilitate the development and maintenance of curiosity motivation during the various stages of ontogenetic development have received little attention. The investigation presented below is a preliminary step designed to provide information for the systematic study of curiosity motivation during early stages of childhood.

Curiosity motivation is generally inferred from instrumental actions that function to increase the organism's contact with new or different environmental objects. These actions may be such as to: (a) increase the level or quantity of sensory input; (b) increase the perceptual clarity, or number, of objects perceived; (c) increase verbal behavior that elicits information from others; (d) increase avoidance of familiar objects or environmental situations (Berlyne, 1960).[1] Theoretical explanations of the tendency for individuals to seek contact with "novel" aspects of their environment must, however, take into account the substantial experimental evidence that novelty (environmental ambiguity or uncertainty) also may evoke behavioral avoidance; psychological processes that reduce informational input (Callaway & Dembo, 1958; Jones, 1959; Smock, 1955a); or perceptual transformations to the "familiar" (Binder, 1958; Frenkel-Brunswick, 1949; Smock, 1955). It is apparent from these findings that the motivational properties of "novelty" are not always "positive," nor does the postulation of a special type of drive offer more than a description of the behavior to be explained (Mowrer, 1960).

One alternative is to assume that motivational properties of novelty or ambiguity are

1 This study was formulated and completed prior to the publication of Berlyne's recent book (1960). However, the authors' debt to prior work by Dr. Berlyne is obvious and gratefully acknowledged.

* Reprinted by permission of Charles D. Smock and the Society for Research in Child Development from *Child Develpm.*, 1962, 33, 631–642.

derived from the arousal of incompatible perceptual or cognitive processes (Hebb, 1946, 1949; Hunt, 1960). Substantial empirical support for this "incongruity-dissonance" hypothesis (Hunt, 1960) may be derived from earlier investigations concerned with children's reaction to "novelty." Arsenian (1943), for example, demonstrated that the presence of the mother (with the child) in a strange room tended to have "security value" in that symptoms of fearful reaction to the novel situation decreased. Mueller, Hesser, and Mabel (cited by Hebb [1949]) report more negative and fear reactions to partially strange stimulus patterns (e.g., a distorted voice paired with a familiar face or a mask over the face of a familiar figure speaking in a normal voice) than to completely strange patterns of stimulation. The developmental changes in the intensity of fear reactions to "strangers" (Heathers, 1954; Shirley, 1942) also is consistent with Hebb's hypothesis that the degree of perceptual conflict aroused by "novelty" is a primary factor determining the child's behavioral adjustments.

According to this analysis, exploratory behavior (manifest curiosity) may be conceived as *one* alternative behavioral consequence of the tendency for cognitive structures (schemata) to move toward, and maintain, organization and consistency (Festinger, 1957; Frenkel-Brunswick, 1949; Hebb, 1949; Hilgard, 1951; Hunt, 1960). Confrontation with environmental events that fail to "match" prevailing "schemata" evokes tendencies to develop new, or modify existing, perceptual cognitive structures by *maximizing information input from environmental sources*. This discrepancy between cognitive structure and environmental-event processes, then, constitutes the motivational basis for "curiosity." The major purpose of this investigation was to determine the relation between qualitatively different types of environmental uncertainty ("novelty") and curiosity in young children.

A second purpose of the study was to obtain data on the relation of modifiability of perceptual-cognitive structures to individual differences in degree of curiosity motivation. If "curiosity" is assumed to be some function of the degree of perceptual conflict, then personality factors affecting the *degree of conflict* associated with a particular type of stimulus novelty should modify the tendency to maximize perceptual input. Previous research has demonstrated that degree of perceptual rigidity and speed of closure (Binder, 1958; Smock, 1955a, 1957, 1958) are related to the amount of informational input. These findings suggest the hypothesis that relative nonmodifiability (rigidity) of perceptual schemata would, as a consequence of the reduction in amount of information assimilated, generate less conflict and thus be associated with relatively less "curiosity."

The specific hypotheses of the study may be reformulated as follows:

1. Environmental events that induce perceptual conflict ("novelty") will tend to evoke behavior that maximizes additional perceptual contact.

2. Variations in perceptual rigidity will be negatively related to the tendency to seek and maintain contact with novel stimuli.

Method

SUBJECTS

SUBJECTS for the study were obtained from the first grade of a rural elementary school.[2] Twenty-two boys and 22 girls (71 to 91 months CA) completed all phases of the experiment reported here.

APPARATUS

Two film strips, each containing a different order of presentation of the sets of stimuli for three of the tasks (SA, PC, and CC described below) were constructed. An equal number of boys and girls were administered each series. *S*s faced a mock TV set on which there was a response panel containing a button and a lever. Each time *S* pressed the "repeat" button a picture was projected on the TV screen for 250 milliseconds. Prior to

2 Appreciation is extended to the principal and teachers of the Delphi, Indiana elementary school system for their cooperation in this study.

beginning the experiment the examiner (B. G. Holt) explained and demonstrated that the function of the button was to repeat the "same" picture while the lever permitted *S* to "change" the picture. The essential instructions were:

We are trying to find out how interesting different kinds of pictures are for boys and girls. When you press this button, you can see a picture on the screen. You may look at the same picture as many times as you want. When you do not wish to see it again, pull this lever and that will make the next picture ready for you.

EXPERIMENTAL TASKS

Set SA: Stimulus Ambiguity [3] • Complexity of forms may be defined (Attneave, 1954) in terms of the absence of redundancy in visual "information"; e.g., homogeneity of dispersion in the visual field and number of changes in the contour of an object. The greater the complexity, the greater the relative difficulty in achieving clarity of perceptual structuring; thus the greater the ambiguity. Two sets of stimuli, representing both types of ambiguity (homogeneity of object dispersion and number of contour changes in forms), were included in this study (FIGURE 1). Sets SA-H$_1$ (homogeneity) contained one picture with nine crosses arranged in a square pattern (PX) and a second picture with crosses placed randomly (RX). Set SA-H$_2$ contained one picture with five straight lines (L$_1$) while the second contained wavy and dotted lines (L$_4$). Set SA-P$_1$ (points) contained four figures ranging from a circle (C) to a form with a highly irregular contour (IF). Set SA-P$_2$ contained six randomly generated nonsense forms (Attneave, 1954) containing either four or 24 points. An index of curiosity motivation was obtained on each of the four sets, for each individual, by subtracting the frequency of self-controlled exposures to the less complex from the more complex figure.

Set PC: Perceptual Conflict • Two sets of stimuli (animals and birds) containing in-

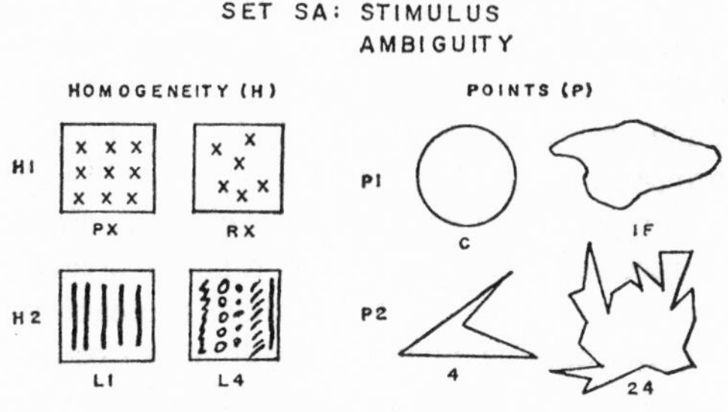

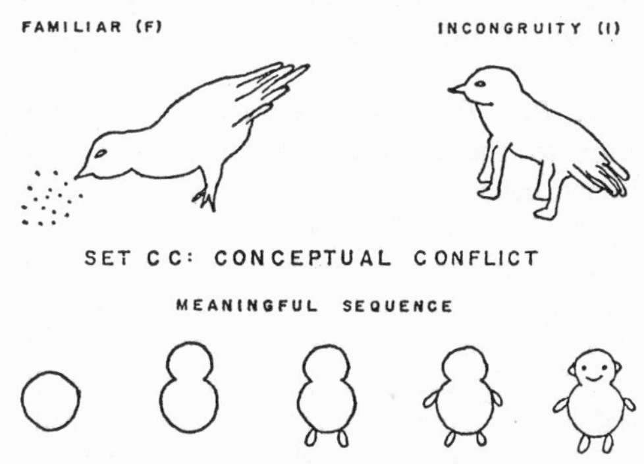

FIGURE 1

Sample of novel and nonnovel stimulus materials.

congruous and nonincongruous pictures were utilized for determining the effect of perceptual conflict on responsiveness. Two pictures in each series (e.g., number[s] 2 and 4 of the animal series) were incongruous (i.e., cues were added that were incompatible with prior perceptions of the object) while five were "familiar." The difference in frequency of response to incongruous (I) as compared to nonincongruous (F) pictures, for the sets combined, was used as the index of preference for novelty.[4]

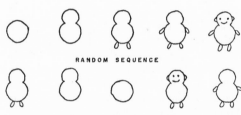

Set CC: Absence of Support for Schematizing • The failure of informational input to permit formation of "schemata" for an-

3 Many of the stimulus materials were taken from Berlyne's (1958) study of human curiosity.

4 Analysis of the data indicated no difference in frequency of self-controlled exposures between the birds and animal series.

ticipating subsequent events represents more conceptual, than perceptual, conflict. Two series, of six pictures each, were utilized. Each series began with a circle and, by the progressive addition of details, ended with a complete picture (bear or clown). Each *S* received one (balanced random assignment) of the series of stimuli in a meaningful (M) and the other in a random (R) order. The measure of curiosity was the difference in total frequency of self-controlled exposures to the pictures in the random as compared to the meaningful series.

Set PU: Preference for the Unknown • Prior to the beginning of the experiment proper, each child was introduced to 25 toys balanced for sex-appropriateness. The subject ranked the toys in order of preference by selecting the five most preferred toys for each of five trials until no toys remained. *E* recorded the order of selection within each trial so that a complete ranking was obtained.

Following the tasks described above, *S*s were administered the Preference for the Unknown task. *E* presented *S* with two toys on each of seven trials. On each trial, one toy (known toy, K) was hidden in a box while *S* watched. An identical box was shown to *S* and then concealed behind a screen while *E* explained that another toy (Unknown, U) was being placed there. The position of K and U varied in a predetermined random order. *E* reminded *S* of the identity and position of K and reassured him that the other box also contained a toy. *S* was then instructed to choose the box containing the toy he most wanted to play with after the test.

In the first four trials, both K and U were of medium preference value. On trials 5 and 6, K was of high preference value and U was of low preference value. On trial 7, both toys were of high preference value. The choice of K or U was recorded on each trial.

Perceptual Rigidity • The Blum Transition Test (Blum, 1959) was used to obtain an index of rigidity. The task consists of a series of five cards in which the picture of a cat (card 1) is successively modified so that a picture of a dog appears on card 5. *S* was shown one card at a time and asked to report what he "saw" on each card. The number of response shifts was used as the index of rigidity, no shifts indicating highest rigidity.

PROCEDURE

Each *S* was individually administered the toy preference test; the series of perceptual conflict tasks (SA, PC, CC); the preference for the unknown (PU) task; and then the transition task. The instructions for each task were presented in the appropriate section above.

Results

RESPONSE TO NOVELTY

A MAJOR concern of this study was to determine the effect of qualitatively different types of environmental novelty on children's tendency to maintain or seek perceptual contact with objects. The mean frequency of self-controlled exposures (button presses) to each of six tasks designed to measure the tendency to maintain perceptual contact are presented in FIGURE 2.[5] Analysis of variance of these data (TABLE 1) indicated that novel stimuli elicited significantly more responses than nonnovel pictures ($F = 22.27$, $p < .001$) on all tasks. The qualitative differences in novelty (novelty × tasks, $F = 2.34$) and the interaction of sex category and response to novelty ($F = 2.64$) were statistically significant at the .05 and .10 levels, respectively.

The mean number of choices of the "Unknown" toy, on the seven trials, was 4.37 which is in the predicted direction. A test of the significance of differences between the obtained (63 per cent) and expected (50 per cent) proportion of choice yielded a CR of 4.56 which is significant beyond the .01 level of confidence.

CURIOSITY MOTIVATION

The interaction of novelty and tasks, while of borderline statistical significance, supports

5 Analysis of variance yielded no difference attributable to order of task presentation.

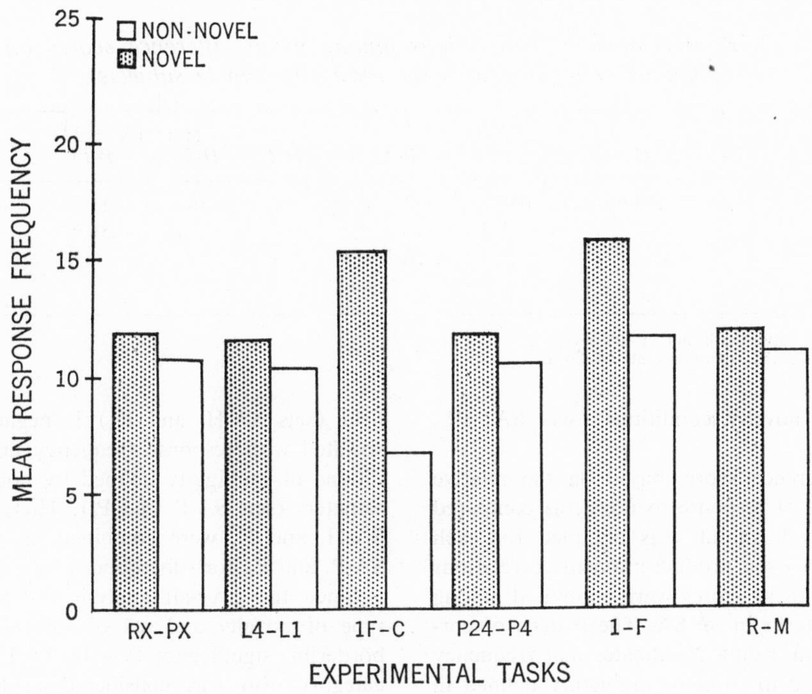

FIGURE 2

Mean frequency of self-controlled stimulus exposures as a function of type of novelty.

the original presumption of qualitatively different types of "novelty." Four of these tasks had been selected as representative of the "stimulus ambiguity" type of novelty (set SA). Examination of the data suggested that a further check on the validity of this classification should be completed prior to considering the relations among the original four

TABLE 1. *Analysis of variance of mean frequency of self-controlled exposure to novel and nonnovel stimuli on six tasks*

SOURCE	*df*	*MS*	*F*	*p*
Between *S*s	43			
Sex	1	840.94	1.02	*ns*
Residual (b)	42	822.84		
Within *S*s	484			
Novelty	1	1340.78	22.27	<.001
Tasks	5	107.23	1.80	*ns*
Novelty × Tasks	5	139.27	2.34	<.05
Novelty × Sex	1	157.24	2.64	.10
Tasks × Sex	5	75.79	1.27	*ns*
Novelty × Tasks × Sex	5	11.11	.19	*ns*
Residual (w)	462	59.55		
Total	527			

TABLE 2. *Product-moment correlations among mean difference scores on four stimulus ambiguity tasks for male and female subjects*

	FEMALE ($N = 22$)				MALE ($N = 22$)			
	H-1	*H-2*	*P-1*	*P-2*	*H-1*	*H-2*	*P-1*	*P-2*
H_1	. .	.59 **	.05	.22	. .	.36	−.11	−.27
H_2		. .	−.77 **	.16		. .	−.54 **	−.25
P_1			. .	.58 **			. .	.40 *
P_2				. .				. .

* $r > .40$, significant at .05 level.
** $r > .52$, significant at .01 level.

types of novelty conditions (sets SA, PC, CC, PU).

A difference score, based on the relative frequency of response to novel, as compared to nonnovel, stimuli was obtained for each subject. Pearson product-moment correlations based on these scores were computed among the four tasks in set SA. The pattern of correlations in TABLE 2 indicates that frequency of response to stimulus ambiguity defined in terms of homogeneity of pattern in the visual field (sets SA-H_1 and H_2) is negatively associated with response frequency under conditions of ambiguity defined by contour parameters (sets SA-P_1 and P_2). Therefore, sets SA-H_1 and H_2 were combined, as were sets SA-P_1 and P_2, for subsequent analysis of data.

Since the over-all analysis indicated that type of novelty and sex of subject were of borderline significance (*see* TABLE 1), the sex category also was considered in the more detailed analysis. FIGURE 3 graphically il-

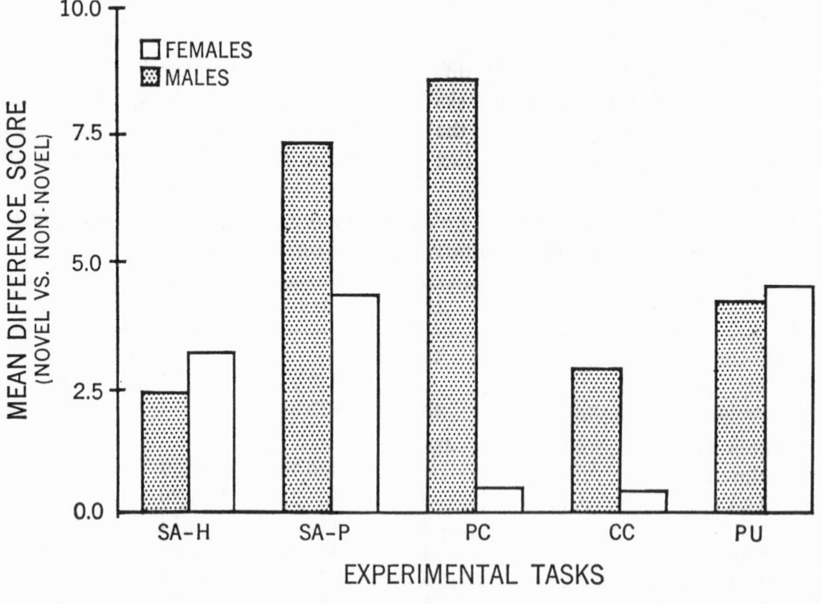

FIGURE 3

Mean difference scores in frequency of response of males and females to novel and nonnovel stimuli.

TABLE 3. *Analysis of variance of mean difference scores in frequency of self-controlled exposures to five types of novelty*

SOURCE	*df*	*MS*	*F*	*p*
Between *S*s	43			
Sex	1	381.48	4.59	<.05
Residual (b)	42	83.04		
Within *S*s	176			
Tasks	4	127.23	4.15	<.01
Tasks × Sex	4	119.12	3.89	<.01
Residual (w)	168	30.65		
Total	219			

lustrates the relative response frequency of male and female subjects to each of the five types of novelty. As indicated in TABLE 3, the different types of novelty arouse differential curiosity ($F = 4.15$, $p < .01$). The significant task-sex interaction ($F = 3.89$, $p < .01$) reflects the fact that female *S*s were relatively more responsive to the absence of environmental structure (set SA-H), and manifested a higher preference for the unknown (set PU); whereas males were more curious under conditions of stimulus complexity (set SA-P), incongruity (set PC), and meaningfulness of the sequence of information (set CC). Further analysis (*see* TABLE 4) is suggestive of the nature of these sex differences. It is noted that, for female subjects, Complexity (SA-P), Meaningful Sequence (CC), and Preference for the Unknown (PU) were positively correlated, whereas Perceptual Conflict (PC) was negatively correlated with the latter two tasks. These data indicate the females did not "respond" to incongruous stimulus events, but rather maximized environmental contact in the absence of information necessary to complete a spatial or temporal structure of events. Possible reasons for this differential behavior of the boys and girls will be discussed in a later section.

TABLE 4. *Product-moment correlations among mean difference scores on five measures of curiosity motivation*

	SA-H	*SA-P*	*PC*	*CC*	*PU*
FEMALES ($N = 22$)					
SA-H	..	.13	.16	.02	.25
SA-P		..	.23	.22	.66 **
PC			..	−.19	−.60 **
CC				..	.41 *
PU					..
MALES ($N = 22$)					
SA-H	..	−.03	.08	.05	−.07
SA-P		..	.14	.28	.72 **
PC			..	.76	.36 *
CC				..	.53 **
PU					..

* $r > .40$, significant at .05 level.
** $r > .52$, significant at .01 level.

RELATION OF CURIOSITY MOTIVATION TO PERCEPTUAL RIGIDITY

It was predicted that curiosity motivation would be negatively related to perceptual rigidity. The number of shifts in response on the rigidity task was taken as the index of rigidity. The scores ranged from 0 to 3 shifts on the five card series. Individuals were categorized as low (2 to 3) and high (0 to 1) on rigidity and low, medium, and high on each of the curiosity motivation tasks. Chi-square analysis indicated that rigidity was significantly associated with frequency of response to incongruity (set PC, $p < .01$) and stimulus ambiguity (set SA-P, $p < .05$) and moderately associated with responsiveness to meaningful sequence (set CC, $p < .15$). On each of these tasks the hypothesized negative relation between degree of curiosity and rigidity was obtained. Females, as a group, tended to manifest a higher degree of rigidity than the males ($p < .10$).

Discussion

THESE findings confirm the results of previous studies that novelty generally evokes "positive" approach behavior. However, it is clear that the motivational properties of novelty vary among individuals and that different types of novelty evoke varying degrees of positive and negative approach tendencies. The absence of environmental-event structuring (stimulus ambiguity), for example, generally elicited less curiosity in these children than stimuli inducing perceptual conflict (object incongruity). At the same time, the females were "curious" when confronted with an environment lacking in information necessary to complete a spatial or temporal pattern of events, but were relatively unresponsive when "familiar" alternative perceptual structuring was possible (i.e., incongruous objects). Such variation in "information seeking" as a function of qualitative differences in type of novelty and individual characteristics implies, according to the "incongruity-dissonance" hypothesis of motivation (Hunt, 1960), that the tasks produced differential degrees of perceptual-cognitive conflict. The investigation of ontogenetic factors that contribute to the differential motivational properties (conflict producing) of these different patterns of stimulation has important implications for understanding both cognitive and motivational development.

The negative relation between perceptual rigidity and curiosity motivation under conditions of stimulus ambiguity, incongruity, and meaningfulness of event sequence lends support to the hypothesis that reduction of informational input associated with perceptual rigidity would generally lessen the degree of conflict aroused by novelty and, therefore, decrease information seeking. The fact that females tended to be more rigid than the males, then, partially explains the finding that girls were relatively less "curious" than the boys.

One might speculate that the sex differences in response to novelty arise from the differential child-training practices affecting the course of sex-role development. Parental expectancies and demands tend to be more restrictive for girls during early stages of psychological development (Sears, Maccoby, & Levin, 1957). The more highly structured environment might be expected to limit tendencies to resolve conflict through seeking information (exploratory behavior). Such an interpretation is consistent with other recent findings relevant to sex differences in intellectual processes. For example, females tolerate less deviation from prior learned criteria for classifying objects (Wallach & Caron, 1959). The same relative dominance of prior formed "schemata" was noted in this study in that females manifested curiosity only where there was an absence of sufficient stimulus information to achieve a familiar perceptual or conceptual structure.

Summary

THE purpose of this study was to test the hypotheses that environmental events which induce perceptual conflict will evoke behavior that maximizes perceptual contact with these "novel" objects and that individual variation in perceptual rigidity will be negatively related to curiosity under these conditions. Forty-four first grade children (22 boys and 22 girls) were administered four tasks representing different types of perceptual conflict, stimulus ambiguity, stimulus incongruity, absence of stimulus support for conceptual structuring, and relative preference for the unknown, in addition to a measure of rigidity. Results generally supported both hypotheses.

REFERENCES

ARSENIAN, J. M. Young children in an insecure situation. *J. abnorm. soc. Psychol.*, 1943, **38,** 225–249.

ATTNEAVE, F. Some informational aspects of visual perception. *Psychol. Rev.* 1954, **61,** 183–193.

BARTLETT, F. C. *Thinking.* London: Methuen, 1959.

BERLYNE, D. E. The influence of complexity and novelty in visual figures on orienting responses. *J. exp. Psychol.*, 1958, **55,** 289–296.

BERLYNE, D. E. *Conflict, arousal and curiosity.* New York: McGraw-Hill, 1960.

BINDER, A. Personality variables and recognition response level. *J. abnorm. soc. Psychol.*, 1958, **57,** 136–142.

BLUM, A. The relationship between rigidity-flexibility in children and their parents. *Child Develpm.*, 1959, **30,** 297–304.

CALLAWAY, F., & DEMBO, D. Narrowed attention. *A.M.A. Arch. Neurol. Psychiat.*, 1958, **79,** 74–90.

COHEN, A., STOTLAND, E., & WOLF, M. An experimental investigation of need for cognition. *J. abnorm. soc. Psychol.*, 1955, **51,** 291–294.

FESTINGER, L. *Theory of cognitive dissonance.* New York: Row, Peterson, 1957.

FRENKEL-BRUNSWICK, ELSE. Intolerance of ambiguity as an emotional and perceptual variable. *J. Pers.*, 1949, **18,** 108–143.

GLANZER, M. Curiosity, exploratory drive, and stimulus satiation. *Psychol. Bull.*, 1958, **55,** 302–315.

HARLOW, H. F. Mice, monkeys, men, and motives. *Psychol. Rev.* 1953, **60,** 23–32.

HEATHERS, G. The adjustment of two year olds in a novel situation. *Child Develpm.*, 1954, **25,** 147–158.

HEBB, D. O. On the nature of fear. *Psychol. Rev.*, 1946, **53,** 259–276.

HEBB, D. O. *The organization of behavior.* New York: Wiley, 1949.

HILGARD, E. R. The role of learning in perception. In R. R. Blum & G. V. Ramsey (Eds.), *Perception: approach to personality.* New York: Ronald, 1951.

HUNT, J. McV. Experience and the development of motivation: some reinterpretations. *Child Develpm.*, 1960, **31,** 489–504.

JONES, A. The efficiency of utilization of visual information and the effects of stress. *J. exp. Psychol.*, 1959, **58,** 428–432.

MOWRER, O. H. *Learning theory and behavior.* New York: Wiley, 1960.

SEARS, R. R., MACCOBY, ELEANOR E., & LEVIN, H. *Patterns of child rearing.* New York: Row, Peterson, 1957.

SHIRLEY, MARY M. Children's adjustment to a strange situation. *J. abnorm. soc. Psychol.*, 1942, **37,** 201–217.

SMOCK, C. D. The influence of psychological stress on the "intolerance of ambiguity." *J. abnorm. soc. Psychol.*, 1955, **50,** 177–182. (a)

SMOCK, C. D. The influence of stress on the perception of incongruity. *J. abnorm. soc. Psychol.*, 1955, **50,** 354–356. (b)

SMOCK, C. D. The relationship between "intolerance of ambiguity," generalization and speed of perceptual closure. *Child Develpm.*, 1957, **28,** 27–36.

SMOCK, C. D. Perceptual rigidity and closure phenomena as a function of manifest anxiety in children. *Child Develpm.*, 1958, **29,** 237–247.

WALLACH, M. A., & CARON, A. J. Attribute criteriality and sex-linked conservatism as determinants of psychological similarity. *J. abnorm. soc. Psychol.*, 1959, **59,** 43–50.

WHITE, R. W. Motivation reconsidered: the concept of competence. *Psychol. Rev.*, 1959, **66,** 297–333.

ROBERT W. WHITE

*Motivation Reconsidered: The Concept of Competence**

When parallel trends can be observed in realms as far apart as animal behavior and psychoanalytic ego psychology, there is reason to suppose that we are witnessing a significant evolution of ideas. In these two realms, as in psychology as a whole, there is evidence of deepening discontent with theories of motivation based upon drives. Despite great differences in the language and concepts used to express this discontent, the theme is everywhere the same: Something important is left out when we make drives the operating forces in animal and human behavior.

The chief theories against which the discontent is directed are those of Hull and of Freud. In their respective realms, drive-reduction theory and psychoanalytic instinct theory, which are basically very much alike, have acquired a considerable air of orthodoxy. Both views have an appealing simplicity, and both have been argued long enough so that their main outlines are generally known. In decided contrast is the position of those who are not satisfied with drives and instincts. They are numerous, and they have developed many pointed criticisms, but what they have to say has not thus far lent itself to a clear and inclusive conceptualization. Apparently there is an enduring difficulty in making these contributions fall into shape.

In this paper I shall attempt a conceptualization which gathers up some of the important things left out by drive theory. To give the concept a name I have chosen the word *competence,* which is intended in a broad biological sense rather than in its narrow everyday meaning. As used here, competence will refer to an organism's capacity to interact effectively with its environment. In organisms capable of but little learning, this capacity might be considered an innate attribute, but in the mammals and especially man, with their highly plastic nervous systems, fitness to interact with the environment is slowly attained through prolonged feats of learning. In view of the directedness and persistence of the behavior that leads to these feats of learning, I consider it necessary to treat competence as having a motivational aspect, and my central argument will be that the motivation needed to attain competence cannot be wholly derived from sources of energy currently conceptualized as drives or instincts. We need a different kind of motivational idea to account fully for the fact that man and the higher mammals develop a competence in dealing with the environment which they certainly do not have at birth and certainly do not arrive at simply through maturation. Such an idea, I believe, is essential for any biologically sound view of human nature.

As a first step, I shall briefly examine the relevant trends of thought in several areas of psychology. From this it will become clear that the ideas advanced in this paper have already been stated, in one way or another, by workers in animal behavior, child development, cognitive psychology, psychoanalytic ego psychology, and the psychology of personality. If there is novelty in this essay, it lies in putting together pieces which are not in themselves new. They already lie before

* Reprinted by permission of the author and the American Psychological Association from *Psychol. Rev.,* 1959, **66,** 297–333.

us on the table, and perhaps by looking once more we can see how to fit them into a larger conceptual picture.

The Trend in Animal Psychology

ONE of the most obvious features of animal behavior is the tendency to explore the environment. Cats are reputedly killed by curiosity, dogs characteristically make a thorough search of their surroundings, and monkeys and chimpanzees have always impressed observers as being ceaseless investigators. Even Pavlov, whose theory of behavior was one of Spartan simplicity, could not do without an investigatory or orientating reflex. Early workers with the obstruction method, such as Dashiell (1925) and Nissen (1930), reported that rats would cross an electrified grid simply for the privilege of exploring new territory. Some theorists reasoned that activity of this kind was always in the service of hunger, thirst, sex, or some other organic need, but this view was at least shaken by the latent learning experiments, which showed that animals learned about their surroundings even when their major needs had been purposely sated. Shortly before 1950 there was a wave of renewed interest not only in exploratory behavior but also in the possibility that activity and manipulation might have to be assigned the status of independent motives.

EXPLORATORY BEHAVIOR

In 1953 Butler reported an experiment in which monkeys learned a discrimination problem when the only reward was the opening of a window which permitted them to look out upon the normal comings and goings of the entrance room to the laboratory. The discriminations thus formed proved to be resistant to extinction. In a later study, Butler and Harlow (1957) showed that monkeys could build up a series of four different discriminations solely for the sake of inspecting the entrance room. Butler concluded that "monkeys—and presumably all primates—have a strong motive toward visual exploration of their environment and that learning may be established on the basis of this motive just as it may be established on the basis of any motive that regularly and reliably elicits responses." Montgomery, in 1954, reported a study with rats in which the animals, their major organic needs satiated, learned to avoid the short arm of a **Y** maze and to take the path which led them into additional maze territory suitable for exploration. Similar findings have been described by Myers and Miller (1954), whose rats learned to press a bar for the sake of poking their heads into a new compartment and sniffing around. Zimbardo and Miller (1958) enlarged upon this study by varying the amount of novelty in the two compartments. In their report "the hypothesis advanced is that opportunity to explore a 'novel' environment or to effect a stimulus change in the environment is the reinforcing agent."

These experiments make a strong case for an independent exploratory motive. The nature of this motive can be more fully discerned in situations in which the animals are allowed a varied repertory of behavior. In 1950 Berlyne published a searching paper on curiosity, a theme which he further developed in subsequent years (1955, 1957, 1958). The rats in his experiments were confronted with an unfamiliar space and later with various novel objects placed in it. Approaching, sniffing, and examining were readily elicited by each novelty, were fairly rapidly extinguished, but were restored nearly to original strength when a fresh novelty was added. Exploration on the part of chimpanzees has been studied by Welker (1956), who put various pairs of objects before the animals and observed the course of their interest. The objects were often first approached in a gingerly manner, with signs of uneasiness, then examined and handled quite fully, then discarded. Introducing a new pair of objects promptly reproduced the whole sequence, just as it did with the rats in Berlyne's experiments. Welker used pairs of objects to find out whether or not the chimpanzees would have common preferences. Bigness and brightness evoked more interest, and greater time was spent upon objects which could be moved, changed, or made to emit sounds and light.

Recent reviews by Butler (1958) and Cofer (1959) shows that a great deal of similar work is going on in animal laboratories, generally with similar results.

EXPLORATION AS A DRIVE

The designers of these experiments have favored the idea that exploration should be listed as an independent primary drive. In all cases the experimental plan calls for the elimination of other primary drives by satiation. It is recognized, however, that a confirmed advocate of orthodoxy might bring up two objections to the proposed enlargement of the list of primary drives. He might claim that exploratory behavior could be explained as a consequence of secondary reinforcement, or he might contend that it is reinforced by reduction of anxiety.

The first argument meets an immediate difficulty in Butler's finding that discriminations learned on the basis of visual exploration are resistant to extinction. When reinforcement of primary drive never takes place in the experimental situation, it is to be expected that secondary reinforcement will not prevent extinction (Miller, 1951). But even in those cases where extinction is rapid, as it was with Berlyne's rats and Welker's chimpanzees, serious problems are raised by the quick recovery of exploratory behavior when a novel stimulus is introduced (Berlyne, 1950). In order to sustain the idea that secondary reinforcement accounts for this fact, we should have to suppose that primary rewards have often been connected with the exploration of novelties. It would have to be assumed, for instance, that the securing of food by young animals occurred with considerable frequency in connection with the investigation of novel objects. This image may seem to fit mature animals who search the environment for their food, but it certainly cannot apply to young mammals before they are weaned. Here the learning process can do virtually nothing to reinforce an interest in novelties. Gratification comes from following the same old cues to the same old consummatory responses, and the animal whose attention strays to some novel variation of the breast will only find himself frustrated. One can say that the whole mammalian pattern of infancy works in the opposite direction. The mother is more active than the young in providing gratifications, and the babies must be pursued and retrieved if they stray from the scene of her ministry. However one looks at it, the hypothesis of secondary reinforcement seems to me to demand improbable assumptions about the relationship in the lives of young animals between exploration and primary need gratification.

The hypothesis that exploratory behavior is related to fear and receives its reinforcement from the reduction of anxiety is at first glance considerably more plausible. It seems justified by the observation that Welker's chimpanzees showed uneasiness on first contact with novel objects, and it fits the behavior of rats in a new maze, as reported by Whiting and Mowrer (1943), where initial terror gave place to an exploration so feverish that the food reward was not eaten. Montgomery and Monkman (1955) have undertaken to challenge this hypothesis by a direct experimental attack. They showed that fear induced in rats before entering a novel situation did not increase exploratory behavior, and that fear induced within the novel situation decreased exploration to an extent correlated with the intensity of the fear. They find it more reasonable to suppose that fear and exploration are conflicting forms of behavior, and this view can also be defended on purely logical grounds. Fear shows itself in either freezing or avoidance, whereas exploration is clearly an instance of approach. There is hardly a more perfect example of conflict between incompatible responses than that of an animal hesitating between investigation and flight. It is clear that exploration can sometimes serve to reduce anxiety, but the proposition that it comes into existence only for this purpose cannot be so easily accepted.

What assumptions have to be made to support the thesis that exploration is motivated by anxiety reduction? It has to be assumed that certain characteristic stimuli arouse anxiety and that exploration of these stimuli is then found to reduce the anxiety. If the characteristics in question are those of novelty and unfamiliarity, we must heed Berlyne's reminder that for the infant all experience is novel and unfamiliar. Berlyne (1950) proposes that the exploratory reaction "may be one that *all* stimuli originally evoke, but which disappears (becomes habituated) as the organism becomes familiar with them." But if all stimuli at first arouse anxious tension, we would have to deduce that all response would consist of avoidance in the interest of reducing that tension. Approaching a stimulus and taking steps to increase its impact could not occur. An exploratory tendency must be there in the first place before it can achieve the function of reducing anxiety. As Woodworth (1958) expresses it, "if there were no exploratory drive to balance and overbalance the fear drive, an animal would be helpless in a novel situation." I find it hard to believe that creatures so liberally endowed with fear could ever achieve a working mastery of the environment if they were impelled toward it only by the pressure of organic needs.

Both hypotheses thus far examined—secondary reinforcement and anxiety reduction—require us to make improbable assumptions. There remains the possibility that exploration should simply be added to the list of primary drives and otherwise treated in orthodox fashion. Myers and Miller (1954) suggest that this is the appropriate course, provided the new drive shows the same functional properties as those already known. "If an exploratory tendency can produce learning like other drives such as hunger, and also show a similar pattern of satiation and recovery, these functional parallels to already known drives would help to justify its classification in the same category." Logically the problem can be dealt with in this way, but we must consider very carefully what happens to the category of drive if we admit this new applicant to membership.

Using hunger as the chief model, the orthodox conception of drive involves the following characteristics: (*a*) there is a tissue need or deficit external to the nervous system which acts upon that system as a strong persisting stimulus; (*b*) this promotes activity which is terminated by a consummatory response with consequent reduction of need; (*c*) the reduction of need brings about the learning which gradually shapes behavior into an economical pursuit of suitable goal objects. In this scheme the tension of an aroused drive is interpreted as unpleasant, at least in the sense that the animal acts in such a way as to lower the drive and becomes quiescent when it is lowered. There are probably no living champions of so simple an orthodoxy, yet the scheme remains pervasive, and it is therefore worth while to observe that the proposed exploratory drive hardly fits it at all.

In the first place, the exploratory drive appears to bear no relation whatever to a tissue need or deficit external to the nervous system. It is, of course, clearly related to certain characteristics of stimulation from the external environment, a source of motivation which Harlow (1953) would like to see restored to a serious place in contemporary psychology; but it certainly cannot be correlated with a visceral need comparable to hunger, thirst, or sex. Considering the pattern of satiation and recovery shown by Welker's chimpanzees, Woodworth (1958) remarks that "what becomes satiated is not the exploratory tendency in general, but the exploring of a particular place or object." It is possible, as Hebb (1955) has pointed out, that the so-called "reticular activation system" in the brain stem creates a kind of general drive state, and this mechanism might indeed be flexibly responsive to changes in sensory stimulation. This interesting suggestion, however, is still a far cry from viscerogenic drives; it commits us instead to the novel idea of a neurogenic motive, one in which the state of the nervous system and the patterns of external stimulation conspire to produce motivated behavior. There is even a good deal of trouble in supposing that the adequate stimuli for exploration are either strong or persistent. Novelty certainly cannot be equated with strength or persistence, and animals seem readily able to disregard the stimuli to exploration when they are weary.

In the second place, exploratory behavior cannot be regarded as leading to any kind of consummatory response. It is usual for the animal's investigation to subside gradually. If the animal at some point turns away and leaves the once novel object we may say that its curiosity is "satisfied," but we do not mean by this that the equivalent of a consummatory response has just taken place. The sequence suggests rather that curiosity wears out and slowly falls to a level where it no longer guides behavior, at least until a fresh novelty comes into view.

Finally, in the case of exploratory behavior there is real difficulty in identifying reinforcement with need reduction. Montgomery (1954), describing the learning of the Y maze, points out that the short arm, essentially a dead end, would tend to reduce the exploratory drive, whereas the long arm, itself a complex maze, would increase it—but the long arm is chosen. If the long arm functions as a reinforcing agent, "the mechanism underlying this reinforcement is an *increase,* rather than a decrease, in the strength of the exploratory drive." In this experiment, as in their natural habitat, animals do not wait to have novelty thrust upon them, nor do they avoid situations in which novelty may be found. Such behavior can be most readily conceptualized by admitting that under certain circumstances reinforcement can be correlated with an increase in arousal or excitement rather than a decrease. A drive which has no consummatory climax seems almost to require this formulation. It is distinctly implausible to connect reinforcement with the waning of an agreeable interest in the environment or with a general progress from zestful alertness to boredom.

If we admit exploration to the category of drive we are thus committing ourselves to believe that drives need have no extraneural sources in tissue deficits or visceral tensions, that they are not necessarily activated by strong or persistent stimuli, that they do not require consummatory responses, and that drive increase can sometimes be a mechanism of reinforcement.

ACTIVITY AND MANIPULATION

Exploration is not the only motive proposed by critics of drive orthodoxy, and novelty is not the only characteristic of the environment which appears to incite motivated behavior. Some workers have suggested a need for activity, which can be strengthened by depriving animals of their normal opportunities for movement. Kagan and Berkun (1954) used running in an activity wheel as the reward for learning and found it "an adequate reinforcement for the instrumental response of bar pressing." Hill (1956) showed that rats will run in an activity wheel to an extent that is correlated with their previous degree of confinement. It is certain that the activity wheel offers no novelty to the animals in these experiments. Nevertheless, they seem to want to run, and they continue to run for such long times that no part of the behavior can readily be singled out as a consummatory response. Perhaps an unpleasant internal state created by inactivity is gradually worked off, but this is certainly accomplished by a tremendous increase of kinaesthetic stimulation and muscular output which would seem to imply increased excitation in the system as a whole.

Harlow and his associates (Harlow, 1953; Harlow, Harlow, & Meyer, 1950) maintain that there is also a manipulative drive. It is aroused by certain patterns of external stimulation and reduced by actively changing the external pattern. The experiments were done with rhesus monkeys, and they involve the solving of a mechanical problem which, however, leads to no further consequences or rewards. The task might be, for instance, to raise a hasp which is kept in place by both a hook and a pin; all that can be accomplished is to raise the hasp, which opens nothing and leads to no fresh discoveries. When the hasp problem is simply installed in the living cages, the monkeys return to it and solve it as many as 7 or 8 times over several days. It seems unlikely that novelty can be postulated as the essential characteristic of the stimulus which evokes this repeated behavior. The simplest interpretation is rather that value lies for the animal in the opportunity, as Zimbardo and Miller (1958) express it, "to effect a stimulus change in the environment." This formulation suggests something like the propensities toward mastery or power that have often been mentioned in discussions of human motivation.

The addition of activity and manipulation to the list of primary drives can only make more serious the difficulties for the orthodox model that resulted from admitting exploration. But recent research with animals has put the orthodox model on the defensive even on its home grounds. It has become increasingly clear that hunger, thirst, and sex cannot be made to fit the simple pattern that seemed so helpful 40 years ago.

CHANGING CONCEPTIONS OF DRIVE

In a brief historical statement, Morgan (1957) has pointed out that the conception of drive as a noxious stimulus began to lose its popularity among research workers shortly after 1940. "On the whole," he says, "the stimulus concept of drive owed more to wishful thinking than to experimental fact." When technical advances in biochemistry and brain physiology made it possible to bring in an array of new facts, there was a rapid shift toward the view that "drives arise largely through the internal environment acting on the central nervous system." One of the most influential discoveries was that animals have as many as a dozen specific hungers for particular kinds of food, instead of the single hunger demanded by Cannon's model of the hunger drive. If an animal's diet becomes deficient in some important element such as salt, sugar, or the vitamin-B complex, foods containing the missing element will be eagerly sought while other foods are passed by, a selectivity that obviously cannot be laid to contractions of the stomach. Similarly, a negative food preference can be produced by loading either the stomach or the blood stream with some single element of the normal diet. The early work of Beach (1942) on sexual behavior brought out similar complications in what had for a time been taken as a relatively simple drive. Hormone levels appeared to be considerably more important than peripheral stimulation in the arousal and maintenance of the sex drive. Further work led Beach (1951) to conclude that sexual behavior is "governed by a complex combination of processes." He points out that the patterns of control differ tremendously from one species to another and that within a single species the mechanisms may be quite different for males and females. Like hunger, the sex drive turns out to be no simple thing.

New methods of destroying and of stimulating brain centers in animals have had an equally disastrous effect on the orthodox drive model. The nervous system, and especially the hypothalamus, appears to be deeply implicated in the motivational process. Experimental findings on hypothalamic lesions in animals encourage Stellar (1954) to believe that there are different centers "responsible for the control of different kinds of basic motivation," and that in each case "there is one main excitatory center and one inhibitory center which operates to depress the activity of the excitatory center." As research findings accumulate, this picture may seem to be too cleanly drawn. Concerning sexual behavior, for example, Rosvold (1959) concludes a recent review by rejecting the idea of a single center in the cerebrum; rather, the sex drive "probably has a wide neural representation with a complex interaction between old and new brain structures and between neural and humoral agents." Nevertheless, Miller's (1958) careful work seems to leave little doubt that motivated behavior in every way similar to normal hunger and normal pain-fear can be elicited by electrical stimulation of quite restricted areas of the hypothalamus. It is clear that we cannot regress to a model of drives that represents the energy as coming from outside the nervous system. Whatever the effects of peripheral stimulation may be, drives also involve neural centers and neural patterns as well as internal biochemical conditions.

What sort of model becomes necessary to

entertain these newly discovered facts? In 1938 Lashley expressed the view that motivation should not be equated with disturbance of organic equilibrium but rather with "a partial excitation of a very specific sensorimotor mechanism irradiating to affect other systems of reaction." Beach (1942) postulated that there must be in the nervous system "a condition analogous to Sherrington's central excitatory state." Morgan, in 1943, undertook to capture the facts in a systematic theory which seems to have been well sustained by subsequent research (Morgan, 1957). He distinguished two types of process which he called *humoral motive factors* and *central motive states.* The humoral factors consist of chemical or hormonal constituents of the blood and lymph, and they are conceived to influence behavior chiefly by a direct sensitizing action on neural centers. The central motive states have several properties: They are partly self-maintaining through neural circuits, they tend to increase the organism's general activity, they evoke specific forms of behavior not strongly controlled by the environment, and they prime or prepare consummatory responses which will occur when adequate stimulation is found. This is a far cry from the orthodox model, but we must nowadays admit that the orthodox model is a far cry from the facts.

In view of this radical evolution of the concept of drive, it is not surprising to find the drive reduction hypothesis in serious difficulties. The earlier identification of reinforcement with drive reduction has been directly attacked in a series of experiments designed to show that learning takes place when drive reduction is ruled out.

In 1950 Sheffield and Roby showed that instrumental learning would take place in hungry rats when the reward consisted not of a nutritive substance but of sweet-tasting saccharine in the drinking water. This finding appeared to be "at variance with the molar principle of reinforcement used by Hull, which identifies primary reinforcement with 'need reduction.'" The authors naturally do not question the vital importance of need reduction, but they point out that need-reducing events may accomplish reinforcement through a mechanism more direct and speedy than the reduction of the need itself. They think that "stimulation and performance of a consummatory response appears to be more important to instrumental learning—in a primary, not acquired, way—than the drive satisfaction which the response normally achieves." Their findings are in line with an earlier experiment with chickens by Wolfe and Kaplon (1941), who used different sizes of food pellets so that the number of pecks and the amount of food received could be thrown out of their usual close connection. The chickens, we might say, would rather peck than eat; learning was more strongly reinforced when four pecks were necessary than when one peck was enough to take the same amount of food.

The substitution of the consummatory response for need reduction as the immediate reinforcing mechanism is a step in advance, but it soon turns out that another step is required. Can it be shown that an aroused need which does not reach consummation has a reinforcing effect? To test this possibility Sheffield, Wulff, and Backer (1951) provided male rats with the reward of copulating with a female, but not enough times to produce ejaculation. This reward was favorable to instrumental learning even though there was no need reduction and no performance of the final consummatory act. The results were supported by Kagan (1955), whose animals showed substantial learning under the same conditions, though learning was still faster when ejaculation was permitted. Sheffield, Roby, and Campbell (1954) have proposed a *drive-induction* theory according to which the property of reinforcement is assigned to the excitement of an aroused drive. We have already seen that some such assumption is essential if exploration is to be assigned the status of a drive. Here it can be added that the whole theory of pregenital sexuality involves motivation without consummatory acts and without any but the most gradual need reduction. And as a final blow to the orthodox hypothesis comes the finding by Olds and Milner (1954) that positive reinforcement can be brought about by direct electrical stimulation of certain areas of the brain. Once again we learn that neural centers are deeply implicated in the plot of motivation. The simple mechanics of need reduction cannot possibly serve as the basis for a theory of learning.

Twenty years of research have thus pretty much destroyed the orthodox drive model. It is no longer appropriate to consider that drives originate solely in tissue deficits external to the nervous system, that consummatory acts are a universal feature and goal of motivated behavior, or that the alleviation of tissue deficits is the necessary condition for instrumental learning. Instead we have a complex picture in which humoral factors and neural centers occupy a prominent position; in which, moreover, the concept of neurogenic motives without consummatory ends appears to be entirely legitimate. Do these changes remove the obstacles to placing exploration, activity, and manipulation in the category of drives?

Perhaps this is no more than a question of words, but I should prefer at this point to call it a problem in conceptual strategy. I shall propose that these three new "drives" have much in common and that it is useful to bring them under the single heading of competence. Even with the loosening and broadening of the concept of drive, they are still in important respects different from hunger, thirst, and sex. In hunger and thirst, tissue deficits, humoral factors, and consummatory responses retain an important position. The mature sex drive depends heavily on hormonal levels and is sharply oriented toward consummation. Tendencies like exploration do not share these characteristics, whatever else they have in common with the better known drives. It is in order to emphasize their intrinsic peculiarities, to get them considered in their own right without a cloud of surplus meanings, that I prefer in this essay to speak of the urge that makes for competence simply as motivation rather than as drive.

The Trend in Psychoanalytic Ego Psychology

RATHER an abrupt change of climate may be experienced as we turn from the animal laboratory to the psychoanalytic treatment room, but the trends of thought in the two realms turn out to be remarkably alike. Here the orthodox view of motivation is to be found in Freud's theory of the instincts—they might be known to us as drives if an early translator had been more literal with the German *Trieb*.

FREUD'S THEORIES OF INSTINCT AND EGO

In his final work, Freud (1949) described instincts as "somatic demands upon mental life" and as "the ultimate cause of all activity." He wrote further:

> It is possible to distinguish an indeterminate number of instincts and in common practice this is in fact done. For us, however, the important question arises whether we may not be able to derive all of these instincts from a few fundamental ones. . . . After long doubts and vacillations we have decided to assume the existence of only two basic instincts, *Eros* and the *destructive instinct* [Freud, 1949, p. 20].

The history of Freud's long doubts and vacillations has been lucidly related by Bibring (1941). Up to 1914 Freud used a twofold classification of sexual instincts and ego instincts. The ego instincts made their appearance in his case histories in a somewhat moral character, being held responsible for the disastrous repression of sexual needs, but in systematic usage they were conceived as serving the goal of self-preservation, and hunger was generally taken as an appropriate model. In 1914, when he evolved the concept of narcissism and saw that it threatened to blur the line between sexual and ego tendencies, Freud (1925b) still expressed himself as unwilling to abandon an idea which followed the popular distinction of love and hunger and which reflected man's dual existence "as reproducer and as one who serves his own ends." Various facts, particularly those of sadism and masochism, served to overcome his reluctance, so that he finally united self-preservation and preservation of the species under the heading of Eros or life instincts, establishing destructiveness or the death instinct as the great antagonist in a profound biological sense (Freud, 1948). This highly speculative step proved to be too much for some of his otherwise loyal followers, and the earlier orthodoxy did not become entirely extinct.

It is easier to follow Freud's reasoning when we bear in mind the simultaneous development of his ideas about the mental apparatus. Bibring (1941) points out that even in his early thinking a sharp contrast was always drawn between instinct and mental apparatus. Instinct supplied the energy in the form of powerful, persisting internal stimuli; the apparatus guided it into channels which produced organized behavior and eventually put a stop to the persisting stimulation. In 1915 Freud wrote:

> The nervous system is an apparatus having the function of abolishing stimuli which reach it or of reducing excitation to the lowest possible level; an apparatus which would even, if this were feasible, maintain itself in an altogether unstimulated condition. . . . The task of the nervous system is—broadly speaking—*to master stimuli* [Freud, 1925c, p. 63].

During the next decade there was a considerable growth in his ideas about the mental apparatus, culminating in the well known division into id, ego, and superego. The activities of the ego now received much fuller recognition. Freud (1927) assigned to it "the task of self-preservation," which it accomplished through its several capacities of perception, memory, flight, defense, and adaptive action. One can see Freud's thought moving from a mechanical analogy—an engine and its fuel—toward a much more adaptational conception of the mental apparatus. Ego instincts did not wholly disappear, but the decline in their systematic importance was compensated by the insight that self-preservative tendencies were to some extent built into the whole living system. It is significant that as he took this course he came to question the earlier tension-reduction theory. In the last year of his life he declared it to be probable "that what is felt as pleasure or unpleasure is not the *absolute* degree of the tensions but something in the rhythm of their changes" (Freud, 1949).

Freud's tendency to revise his thinking makes it difficult to pin down an orthodox doctrine, but most workers will probably agree that his main emphasis was upon somatically based drives, a mental apparatus which received its power from the drives, and, of course, the multitude of ways in which the apparatus controlled, disguised, and transformed these energies. His treatment of the ego was far from complete, and it was not long before voices were raised against the conception that so vital and versatile a part of the personality could be developed solely by libidinal and aggressive energies.

AN INSTINCT TO MASTER

In 1942 Hendrick proposed that this difficulty be met by assuming the existence of an additional major instinct. "The development of ability to master a segment of the environment," he wrote, and the need to exercise such functions, can be conceptualized as an "instinct to master," further characterized as "an inborn drive to do and to learn how to do." The aim of this instinct is "pleasure in exercising a function successfully, regardless of its sensual value." The simpler manifestations are learning to suck, to manipulate, to walk, to speak, to comprehend and to reason; these functions and others eventually become integrated as the ego. "The central nervous system is more than a utility," Hendrick declared. The infant shows an immediate desire to use and perfect each function as it ripens, and the adult secures gratification from an executive function efficiently performed regardless of its service to other instincts.

Hendrick's procedure in this and two supporting papers (1943a, 1943b) is quite similar to that of the animal psychologists who propose listing exploration as an additional primary drive. The instinct to master has an aim—to exercise and develop the ego functions—and it follows hedonic principles by yielding "primary pleasure" when efficient action "enables the individual to control and alter his environment." It is to this extent analogous to the instincts assumed by Freud. But just as an exploratory drive seemed radically to alter the whole conception of drive, so the instinct to master implied a drastic change in the psychoanalytic idea of instinct. Critics were quick to point out that Freud had always conceived of instincts as having somatic sources external to the ego apparatus, a condition not met by the proposed instinct to master. There was nothing comparable to erogenous zones, to orgasm, or to the sequence of painful tension followed by pleasurable release. Mastery, the critics agreed, could not be an instinct, whatever else it might be.

It is of interest that Fenichel (1945), who definitely rejected Hendrick's proposal, gives us another close parallel to the animal work by attributing mastering behavior to anxiety-reduction. He argued that mastery is "a general aim of every organism but not of a specific instinct." He agreed that there is "a pleasure of enjoying one's abilities," but he related this pleasure to cessation of the anxiety connected with not being able to do things. "Functional pleasure," he wrote, "is pleasure in the fact that the exercise of a function is now possible without anxiety," and he contended that when anxiety is no longer present, when there is full confidence that a given situation can be met, then action is no longer accompanied by functional pleasure. We must certainly agree with Fenichel that anxiety *can* play the part he assigns it, but the proposal that all pleasure in ego functions comes from this source raises the same difficulties we have already considered in connection with exploratory behavior. That we exercise our capacities and explore our surroundings only to reduce our fear of the environment is not, as I have already argued, an assumption that enjoys high probability on biological grounds.

HARTMANN ON THE EGO

A less radical change in the orthodox model is proposed by Hartmann, who, in a series of papers since 1939, often in conjunction with Kris and Loewenstein, has been refining and expanding Freud's views on the ego and the instincts. While the ego is conceived as a "substructure" of the personality, this term is somewhat metaphorical because in practice the ego has to be defined by its functions. The list of functions, which includes grasping, crawling, walking, perceiving, remembering, language, thinking, and intention, covers much the same ground that was indicated by Hendrick, but Hartmann does not attribute their growth to an instinct. On the other hand, Hartmann (1950) early came to the conclusion that development could not be explained, as Freud had seemed to conceive it, simply as a consequence of conflict between instinctual needs and frustrating realities. The instincts alone would never guarantee survival; they require mediation by the innate ego apparatus if they are to meet "the average expectable environmental conditions." He therefore proposed that we conceive of an autonomous factor in ego development, an independent maturation of functions taking place in a "conflict-free ego sphere." Functions such as locomotion ripen through maturation and through learning even when they are not caught up in struggles to obtain erotic and aggressive gratification or to avoid anxiety. As Anna Freud (1952) has pointed out, walking becomes independent of instinctual upheavals a few weeks after its beginning; thereafter, it serves the child impartially in situations of conflict and those that are free from conflict.

Hartmann's idea of autonomous ego development has of course been assumed all along by workers in child psychology, but it is an important step to relate it to Freud's disclosures concerning unconscious motivation. In what now looks like an excess of enthusiasm for his own concepts, Freud (1925a) undertook to explain the outgrowing of the pleasure principle and the substituting of the reality principle as a simple and direct consequence of the frustration of instinctual needs. However, the reality principle contained the idea of postponing an immediate gratification in favor of a future one, and Hartmann (1956) properly notes that the capacities for postponement and anticipation cannot be conjured into existence simply by the collision of frustrating reality and ungratified need. Important as frustrations may be, these capacities must already be available, "some preparedness for dealing with reality" must already exist, before the frustration can produce its momentous educative effect. It can be seen from this example that Hartmann's analysis opens the way for profitable commerce between developmental psychologies inside and outside of psychoanalysis.

Hartmann's emphasis on adaptation permits him to perceive much more that is autonomous about the ego than was ever seriously included in Freud's systematic thought. He allows, for instance, that aims and interests which develop in the beginning as defenses against instincts may later become part of conflict-free spheres of activity—become interests in their own right—and thus achieve "secondary autonomy," a concept very close to Allport's (1937) functional autonomy of motives (Hartmann, 1950). He deals with the possibility that adaptive skills developing in the conflict-free sphere may have a decisive influence on the handling of conflicts. These skills have a history of their own, shaped jointly by the child's abilities and by the responses evoked from parents. As Monroe (1955) has expressed it, they have "a very important role in the development of the conscious and semiconscious psychological self." They may thus have a direct influence upon the outcome when a child becomes involved in conflict. Rapaport (1958) sees Hartmann's ideas on the autonomy of the ego as vital to the proper understanding not only of healthy development but also of psychopathology itself.

In explaining the autonomous growth of the ego, Hartmann makes generous use of the concept of maturation, but he naturally does not exclude learning. Hartmann (1950) entertains the possibility, mentioned casually from time to time by Freud (1916, 1949), that ego functions are supplied with their own sources of energy independent of instincts, and that there is pleasure connected with their mere exercise. However, he makes little systematic use of this idea, relying instead upon a concept more central in Freud's thinking, that of the neutralization of drive energies. Freud (1927) found that he could "make no headway" in accounting for the varied activities of the ego without assuming "a displaceable energy, which is in itself neutral, but is able to join forces either with an erotic or with a destructive impulse, differing qualitatively as they do, and augment its total cathexis." He speculated that the neutral energy came from Eros and could be conceived as desexualized libido. Hartmann, Kris, and Loewenstein (1949) carried the idea forward a logical step by proposing that the energies of aggressive instincts could similarly be neutralized and placed at the disposal of the ego. Neutralized energy contributes to the development of the ego and makes possible a continuing interest in the objects of the environment regardless of their immediate relation to erotic or aggressive needs. Hartmann (1955) finds this concept particularly helpful in unscrambling the confusions that have arisen over the concept of sublimation.

The doctrine of neutralized instinctual energies is a curious one, and we should bear in mind the complex clinical findings that perhaps suggested it. Freud was an unquestioned genius in detecting the subtle operation of erotic urges and aggressive fantasies, along with elaborate mechanisms of defense, behind the seemingly objective or "neutral" activities of everyday life. Remarkable transformations of interest could sometimes be observed in the course of development. For example, a patient's childhood erotic rivalry and aggressive competition with his father might later disappear beneath a strong objective interest in running the family business; then suddenly, on the brink of success, this interest might come to a total halt, paralyzed by anxiety because the underlying instinctual goals came too close to symbolic fulfilment. The reappearance of instinctual preoccupations in such a case lends a certain color to the idea that they have somehow been driving the behavior all the time, even though the daily pursuit of business goals seems utterly remote from instinctual gratifications.

It is worth noticing that Freud's procedure in making the assumption of neutralized instinctual energy is similar to the one followed by orthodox behaviorists in connection with primary drives. These theorists started from the assumption that all behavior was powered by a limited number of organic drives, and then, in order to protect this assumption, they developed further hypotheses, such as secondary reinforcement, to account for motivated behavior that bore no obvious relation to primary goals. At the point where he could "make no headway" without postulating neutralization, Freud could conceivably have made a good deal of headway if he had been willing to assume that neutral energy, neither sexual nor aggressive, was available as a natural endowment in the first place. But he preferred to protect his assumption of two primary drives and to interpret other energies as transformations of these drives. Even so, the concept seems superfluous if we take Freud at his word about the nature of the life instincts. Freud (1949) made it clear that Eros included more than instincts having a sexual aim; its larger goal was "to establish even greater unities and to preserve them thus—in short, to bind together." Under this formula, it would seem possible to include energies inherently directed toward building up the integrated functions of the ego. But Freud did not exploit the full range of his theory of Eros and proposed only that neutral energies should be conceived as desexualized.

The concept of neutralization has in some respects had a good effect on psychoanalytic ego psychology. In Hartmann's writings, as we have seen, and in Rapaport's (1951, 1954) work on thinking, it has encouraged a strong interest in autonomous ego functions and a fresh analysis of their place in personality. Nevertheless, it seems to me an awkward conceptualization, one which in the end is likely to lead, as Colby (1955) has expressed it, to a "metapsychological snarl." The theory requires that instinctual energies can completely change their aims, which makes one wonder what purpose was served in the first place by defining them as having aims. It preserves an image of mobility of energies that seems much out of line with recent research on animal motivation, where energy is being conceived in a constantly closer relation to specific structures. To my mind it thus compares unfavorably with its quite straightforward alternative, which is that the alleged neutralized energies are there in the first place as part of the natural make-up of an adaptive organism. I shall later develop this possibility by means of the concept of competence in its motivational aspect, and I believe that this concept gains support from certain other lines of work in the psychoanalytic tradition.

MOTILITY AND A SENSE OF INDUSTRY

The trend away from instinct orthodoxy is illustrated by the work of Kardiner (1947) on what he calls "the development of the effective ego." Kardiner's reflections arose from his work on the traumatic neuroses of war. In these disorders the main threat is to self-preservation, and some of the most important symptoms, such as defensive rituals and paralyses, are lodged in the action systems that normally bring about successful adaptive behavior. It thus becomes pertinent to study the growth of action systems, to discover how they become integrated so as to maintain "controlled contact" with the environment and "controlled exploitation of objects in the outer world," and to work out the conditions which either favor or disrupt this acquired integration. Thinking along these lines, Kardiner is led to conclusions just about the opposite of Freud's: It is the successful and gratifying experiences, not the frustrations, that lead to increasingly integrated action and to the discrimination of self from outer world. Frustration produces chiefly disruptions and inhibitions which are unfavorable to the early growth of the ego. Children are gratified when they discover the connection between a movement executed and the accompanying and subsequent sensations. They are still more gratified when they carry out actions successfully; this "gives rise to the triumphant feeling of making an organ obedient to the will of the ego." Such experiences build up "a definite self- or body-consciousness which becomes the center and the point of reference of all purposeful and coördinated activity." Growth of the ego, in short, depends heavily upon action systems and the consequences of action. The course and vicissitudes of this development have to be studied in their own right, and they cannot be understood as side effects of the stages of libidinal development.

A similar theme is pursued to even more radical conclusions by Mittelmann (1954) in his paper on motility. Mittelmann regards motility, which manifests itself most typically in skilled motor actions such as posture, locomotion, and manipulation, as an "urge in its own right" in the same sense that one speaks of oral, excretory, or genital urges. From about 10 months of age it has a distinctly "driven" character, and there is restlessness and anger if it is blocked. During the second and third years the motor urge "dominates all other urges," so that it is proper to "consider this period the motor level of ego and libido development." The child makes tremendous efforts to learn to walk, and to walk well, and he exhibits joyous laughter as he attains these ends. Restrictions of motility may occur because the parents are anxious or because the child's assertiveness troubles them, and a lasting injury to the parent-child relationship may result. Clumsiness in motor or manipulative accomplishments may lead to self-hatred and dependence, for "the evolution of self-assertiveness and self-esteem is intimately connected with motor development." Motility is of central importance in many of the most characteristic functions of the ego. Partly by its means the infant differentiates himself from other objects, and the child's knowledge of objects depends on an extensive activity of manipulation and examination. "Thus motility becomes one of the most important aspects of reality testing." Because it is an element in all cognitive behavior, it can also be considered "the dominant integrative function." Mittelmann bases motor development, in short, on an independent urge, and he sees this urge as the really crucial motive behind the development of the ego.

Like Kardiner, Mittelmann does not attempt to formulate in detail the nature of the motility urge. It is likened not to an instinct but to a "partial instinct," and this seems to place it somewhere between Hendrick's instinct to master and Hartmann's dimly sketched independent energies of the ego. This indefiniteness may irk the systematic theorist, but Mittelmann's account of the part played by motility in ego development easily stands as a significant contribution. Even more influential in this respect is the work of Erikson (1953), who has given a highly detailed timetable of ego development. Erikson stays with the libido theory as far as it will go, but he passes beyond its reach in his account of the latency period and some of the later crises of growth. It is clear that something more than the orthodox instincts is involved in the "enormous value" with which the child in the second year "begins to endow his autonomous will." Something more would seem to be implied in the expanding imagination and initiative of the "phallic" child. Certainly more is involved during the school years, when children address themselves to motor, manual, and intellectual achievements and need "a sense of being able to make things and make them well and even perfectly: this is what I call the *sense of industry*." Erikson's (1950) theory of play is also influenced by the idea that learning to deal with the animate and inanimate worlds is an important preoccupation of childhood: "the playing child advances forward to new stages of real mastery." Action systems, motility, and a sense of industry all direct our attention to behavior which can scarcely be contained in the old bottle of instinct theory.

Glancing back over these trends in psychoanalytic ego psychology, we cannot fail to be impressed by striking similarities to the trend in animal work. Using Reik's familiar metaphor, we might say that those who listen with their two ears and those who listen with the third ear have apparently been hearing much the same sounds. In both realms there is discontent with drive orthodoxy. In both there is persistent pointing to kinds of behavior neglected or explained away by drive orthodoxy: exploration, activity, manipulation, and mastery. Similar theories have been proposed to account for the energies in such behavior: (*a*) they are derived or transformed in some way from the primary drives or instincts (secondary reinforcement, neutralization of drive energies); (*b*) they are powered by the need to reduce anxiety; (*c*) they can be accounted for only by postulating a new primary drive (exploratory drive, instinct to master). When these explanations are considered to have failed, the one remaining course is to work out a different idea of motivation. In his study of action systems, Kardiner prefers to leave the question of energy sources unanswered, but Erikson's sense of industry and Mittelmann's motility urge point to a motivational base which is only remotely analogous to primary drives or fundamental instincts. I believe that the difficulties in this undertaking can be greatly reduced by the concept of competence, to which we shall shortly turn.

Related Developments in General Psychology

If a systematic survey were in order, it would be easy to show a parallel drift of opinion in other parts of the psychological realm. Among theorists of personality, for example, something like drive orthodoxy is to be found in the work of Dollard and Miller (1950), who have translated the main concepts of Freud's psychoanalysis, including processes such as repression and displacement, into the language of reinforcement theory. With them we might put Mowrer (1950), whose searching analysis of fear as an acquired drive has led him to postulate anxiety-reduction as the master motive behind the development of the ego. Discontent with drive orthodoxy has long been expressed by Allport (1937, 1946), who not only argues for a functional autonomy of motives from their infantile roots in primary drives but also seriously questions the law of effect, the very cornerstone of reinforcement theory. Little comfort for the orthodox can be found in Murray's (1938) detailed taxonomy of needs, especially when it comes to needs such as achievement and construction, which can be tied to primary drives only by conceptual acrobatics. Murray and Kluckhohn (1953), moreover, have made a case for pleasure in activity for its own sake, reviving the *Funktionslust* proposed many years ago by Karl Bühler (1924) and recently developed in some detail by French (1952). They also argue for intrinsic mental needs: "the infant's mind is not acting most of the time as the instrument of some urgent animal drive, but is preoccupied with *gratifying itself*." Murphy (1947) takes the view that all tissues can become seats of tension and thus participants in drive; in addition to visceral drives, he postulates two independent forms, activity drives and sensory drives. Then there are workers such as Goldstein (1939) who approach the whole problem with a holistic philosophy which precludes the dictatorship of any isolated or partial drives. Goldstein (1940) assumes one master tendency, that toward self-actualization, of which the so-called visceral drives are but partial and not really isolated expressions, and which can find expression also in an urge toward perfection—toward completing what is incomplete, whether it be an outside task or the mastery of some function such as walking. It has been shown by the Ansbachers (1956) that Adler, never a friend of instinct orthodoxy, in his later years reached an idea very similar to the urge toward perfection. Maslow (1954, 1955), too, belongs with the heterodox. He insists that we should take account of growth motivation as well as the deficiency motivation implied in the visceral drives, and he offers the valuable idea of a hierarchy of motives, according to which the satisfaction of "lower" needs makes it possible for "higher" needs to emerge and become regnant in behavior.

Mention of these names must suffice here to show that the trends observed in animal psychology and psychoanalytic ego psychology are pervasive in contemporary psychological thought. Doubtless the same controversies and problems could be pointed out in child development, in cognitive psychology, and in other fields. But in order to advance to my main theme, I shall select only certain developments which bear directly on the concept of competence.

NEEDS FOR EXCITEMENT AND NOVELTY

Human experience provides plentiful evidence of the importance of reducing excessive levels of tension. Men under wartime stress, men under pressure of pain and extreme deprivation, men with excessive work loads or too much exposure to confusing social interactions, all act as if their nervous systems craved that utterly unstimulated condition which Freud once sketched as the epitome of neural bliss. But if these same men be granted their Nirvana they soon become miserable and begin to look around for a little excitement. Human experience testifies that boredom is a bad state of affairs about which something must be done. Hebb (1949) has been particularly insistent in reminding us that many of our activities, such as reading detective stories, skin-diving, or driving cars at high speeds, give clear evidence of a need to raise the level of stimulation and excitement. Men and animals alike seem at times bent on increasing the impact of the environment and even on creating mild degrees of frustration and fear. Hebb and Thompson (1954) reflect upon this as follows:

> Such phenomena are, of course, well known in man: in the liking for dangerous sports or roller coasters, where fear is deliberately courted, and in the addiction to bridge or golf or solitaire, vices whose very existence depends upon the level of difficulty of the problems presented and an optimal level of frustration. Once more, when we find such attitudes toward fear and frustration in animals, we have a better basis for supposing that we are dealing with something fundamental if a man prefers skis to the less dangerous snowshoes, or when we observe an unashamed love of work (problem solving and frustration included) in the scientist, or in the business man who cannot retire. Such behavior in man is usually accounted for as a search for prestige, but the animal data make this untenable. It seems much more likely that solving problems and running mild risks are inherently rewarding, or, in more general terms, that the animal will always act so as to produce an optimal level of excitation [Hebb & Thompson, 1954, p. 551].

The concept of optimal stimulation has been developed by Leuba (1955), who sees it as helpful in resolving some of the problems of learning theory. Believing that most theorizing about motivation has been based upon "powerful biological or neurotic drives," Leuba bids us look at the much more common learning situations of nursery, playground, and school, where "actions which increase stimulation and produce excitement are strongly reinforced, sometimes to the dismay of parents and teachers." He proposes that there is an optimal level of stimulation, subject to variation at different times, and that learning is associated with movement toward this optimal level, downward when stimulation is too high and upward when it is too low. A similar idea is expressed by McReynolds (1956) concerning the more restricted concept of "rate of perceptualization." Monotonous conditions provide too low a rate, with boredom; excessive stimulation produces too high a rate, with disruptive excitement; the optimal rate yields the experience of pleasure. These ideas are now amply supported by recent experimental work on sensory deprivation (Lilly, 1956; Hebb, 1958).

In recent papers Young (1949, 1955) has argued for an hedonic theory of motivation, one in which affective processes "constitute a form of primary motivation." According to Young's theory, "an organism behaves so as to maximize positive affective arousal (delight, enjoyment) and to minimize negative arousal (distress)." McClelland (1953) has offered a version of hedonic theory which is of particular value in understanding the significance of novelty. Affective arousal occurs when a stimulus pattern produces a discrepancy from the existing adaptation level. Small discrepancies produce pleasant affect and a tendency to approach; large ones produce unpleasantness and a tendency toward avoidance. The child at play, like the young chimpanzee and the exploring rat, needs frequent novelty in the stimulus field in order to keep up his interest—in order to maintain pleasant discrepancies from whatever adaptation level he has reached. Hebb's (1949) theory of the neurological correlates of learning also deals with novelty, though in a somewhat different way. He equates sustained interest with a state of neural affairs in which "phase sequences" are relatively complex and are growing, in the sense of establishing new internal relations. Such a state follows most readily from a stimulus field characterized by difference-in-sameness; that is, containing much that is familiar along with certain features that are novel. If the field is entirely familiar, phase sequences run off quickly, are short-circuited, and thus fail to produce sustained interest. Hebb's theory, which has the engaging quality of being able to explain why we enjoy reading a detective story once but not right over again, expresses in a neurological hypothesis the familiar fact that well-learned, habituated processes do not in themselves greatly interest us. Interest seems to require elements of unfamiliarity: of something still to be found out and of learning still to be done.

It seems to me that these contributions, though differing as to details, speak with unanimity on their central theme and would force us, if nothing else did, to reconsider seriously the whole problem of motivation. Boredom, the unpleasantness of monotony, the attraction of novelty, the tendency to vary behavior rather than repeating it rigidly, and the seeking of stimulation and mild excitement stand as inescapable facts of human experience and clearly have their parallels in animal behavior. We may seek rest and minimal stimulation at the end of the day, but that is not what we are looking for the next morning. Even when its primary needs are satisfied and its homeostatic chores are done, [an] organism is alive, active. and up to something.

DEALING WITH THE ENVIRONMENT

If we consider things only from the viewpoint of affect, excitement, and novelty, we are apt to overlook another important aspect of behavior, its effect upon the environment. Moving in this direction, Diamond (1939) invites us to consider the motivational properties of the sensorineural system, the apparatus whereby higher animals "maintain their relations to the environment." He conceives of this system as demanding stimulation and as acting in such a manner as to "force the environment to stimulate it." Even if one thinks only of the infant's exploring eyes and hands, it is clear that the main direction of behavior is by no means always that of reducing the impact of stimulation. When the eyes follow a moving object, or when the hand grasps an object which it has touched, the result is to preserve the stimulus and to increase its effect. In more elaborate explorations the consequence of a series of actions may be to vary the manner in which a stimulus acts upon the sense organs. It is apparent that the exploring, manipulating child produces by his actions precisely what Hebb's theory demands as a basis for continuing interest: he produces differences-in-sameness in the stimulus field.

In a critical analysis of Freud's views on the reality principle, Charlotte Bühler (1954) makes a strong case for positive interests in the environment, citing as evidence the responsiveness and adaptiveness of the newborn baby as well as the exploratory tendencies of later months. The problem is worked out in more detail by Schachtel (1954) in a paper on focal attention. Acts of focal attention are characteristically directed at particular objects, and they consist of several sustained approaches "aimed at active mental grasp" while excluding the rest of the field. These qualities can be observed even in the infant's early attempts to follow a moving object with his eyes, and they show more clearly in his later endeavors to learn how objects are related both to himself and to one another. Such behavior bespeaks "a relatively autonomous capacity for object interest." Schachtel makes the proposal that this interest is pursued precisely at those times when major needs are in abeyance. High pressure of need or anxiety is the enemy of exploratory play and is a condition, as every scientist should know, under which we are unlikely to achieve an objective grasp of the environment. Low need pressure is requisite if we are to perceive objects as they are, in their constant character, apart from hopes and fears we may at other times attach to them. Schachtel doubts that "the wish for need-satisfaction alone would ever lead to object perception and to object-oriented thought." Hence an autonomous capacity to be interested in the environment has great value for the survival of a species.

Being interested in the environment implies having some kind of satisfactory interaction with it. Several workers call attention to the possibility that satisfaction might lie in having an effect upon the environment, in dealing with it, and changing it in various ways. Groos (1901), in his classical analysis of play, attached great importance to the child's "joy in being a cause," as shown in making a clatter, "hustling things about," and playing in puddles where large and dramatic effects can be produced. "We demand a knowledge of effects," he wrote, "and to be ourselves the producers of effects." Piaget (1952) remarks upon the child's special interest in objects that are affected by his own movements. This aspect of behavior occupies a central place in the work of Skinner (1953), who describes it as "operant" and who thus "emphasizes the fact that the behavior *operates* upon the environment to generate consequences." These consequences are fed back through the sense organs and may serve to reinforce behavior even when no organic needs are involved. A rat will show an increased tendency to press a bar when this act produces a click or a buzz. A baby will continue to investigate when his efforts produce rattling or tinkling sounds or sparkling reflections from a shiny object. The young chimpanzees in Welker's experiment spent the longest time over objects which could be lighted or made to emit sounds. Skinner finds it "difficult, if not impossible, to trace these reinforcing effects to a history of conditioning." "We may plausibly argue," he continues, "that a capacity to be reinforced by any feedback from the environment would be biologically advantageous, since it would prepare the organism to manipulate the environment successfully before a given state of deprivation developed."

WOODWORTH'S BEHAVIOR-PRIMACY THEORY

The most far-reaching attempt to give these aspects of behavior a systematic place in the theory of motivation is contained in Woodworth's recent book, *Dynamics of Behavior* (1958). Woodworth takes his start from the idea that a great deal of human behavior appears to be directed toward producing effects upon the environment without immediate service to any aroused organic need. "Its incentives and rewards are in the field of behavior and not in the field of homeostasis." This is illustrated by exploratory behavior, which is directed outward toward the environment.

> Its long-range value as the means of making the child acquainted with the world he has to deal with later, and so equipping him through play for the serious business of life, can scarcely lie within the little child's horizon. His goals are more limited and direct: to see this or that object more closely, to find what is behind an obstacle, to hear the noise an object makes when it strikes the floor, to be told the name of a thing or person [Woodworth, 1958, p. 78].

More complex play, such as building with blocks, illustrates the same outgoing tendency and reveals more plainly the element of finding out what one can and cannot do with objects. Even social play falls into the pattern. Playmates do not chiefly supply affection or satisfy organic needs; rather, they "afford the opportunity to do something interesting in the environment."

Woodworth draws a contrast between *need-primacy* theories of motivation and the *behavior-primacy* theory. The latter holds that "all behavior is directed primarily toward dealing with the environment." It is to be noted that "dealing with the environment" means a good deal more than receiving stimuli and making responses. Stimuli must be taken as indicators of objects in space, and responses must be adapted to produce effects upon these objects. Even the so-called "mental" capacities, such as memory and ideational thinking, become in time high-level methods of dealing with the environment. Woodworth leaves no doubt as to what he considers basic in motivation. "We are making the claim that this direction of receptive and motor activity toward the environment is the fundamental tendency of animal and human behavior and that it is the all-pervasive primary motivation of behavior." Organic drives have to break into this constantly flowing stream of activity and turn it in a special direction. But the goals of drives cannot be achieved without effective action upon one's surroundings. The ever-present, ever-primary feature of motivation is the tendency to deal with the environment.

It may appear to some workers that Woodworth has overshot the mark by making primary what has commonly been regarded as secondary, and by reducing the familiar drives to what sounds a little like a subordinate station. Woodworth's theory, however, like Goldstein's concept of self-actualization, probably should be construed not as an attempt to down-grade the drives but rather as an insistence that they be kept in the context of a whole living organism which during its waking hours is more or less constantly active. Woodworth's emphasis on dealing with the environment makes his theory a point of culmination for many of those driftings away from drive orthodoxy which we have found to be persistent in so many different areas of psychology. It will soon appear that the concept of competence, to which I now turn, represents in many respects a similar way of thinking. It emphasizes dealing with the environment, and it belongs in the trend away from drive *orthodoxy,* but it is not intended to supplant, or even to subsume, such dynamic forces as hunger, sex, aggression, and fear, which everyone knows to be of huge importance in animal and human nature.

Competence and the Play of Contented Children

A BACKWARD glance at our survey shows considerable agreement about the kinds of behavior that are left out or handled poorly by theories of motivation based wholly on organic drives. Repeatedly we find reference to the familiar series of learned skills which starts with sucking, grasping, and visual exploration and continues with crawling and walking, acts of focal attention and perception, memory, language and thinking, anticipation, the exploring of novel places and objects, effecting stimulus changes in the environment, manipulating and exploiting the surroundings, and achieving higher levels of motor and mental coordination. These aspects of behavior have long been the province of child psychology, which has attempted to measure the slow course of their development and has shown how heavily their growth depends upon learning. Collectively they are sometimes referred to as adaptive mechanisms or as ego processes, but on the whole we are not accustomed to cast a single name over the diverse feats whereby we learn to deal with the environment.

I now propose that we gather the various kinds of behavior just mentioned, all of which have to do with effective interaction with the environment, under the general heading of competence. According to Webster, competence means fitness or ability, and the suggested synonyms include capability, capacity, efficiency, proficiency, and skill. It is therefore a suitable word to describe such things as grasping and exploring, crawling and walking, attention and perception, language and thinking, manipulating and changing the surroundings, all of which promote an effective —a competent—interaction with the environment. It is true, of course, that maturation plays a part in all these developments, but this part is heavily overshadowed by learning in all the more complex accomplishments like speech or skilled manipulation. I shall argue that it is necessary to make competence a motivational concept; there is a *competence motivation* as well as competence in its more familiar sense of achieved capacity. The behavior that leads to the building up of effective grasping, handling, and letting go of objects, to take one example, is not random behavior produced by a general overflow of energy. It is directed, selective, and persistent, and it is continued not because it serves primary drives, which indeed it cannot serve until it is almost perfected, but because it satisfies an intrinsic need to deal with the environment.

No doubt it will at first seem arbitrary to propose a single motivational conception in connection with so many and such diverse kinds of behavior. What do we gain by attributing motivational unity to such a large array of activities? We could, of course, say that each developmental sequence, such as learning to grasp or to walk, has its own built-in bit of motivation—its "ailment," as Piaget (1952) has expressed it. We could go further and say that each item of behavior has its intrinsic motive—but this makes the concept of motivation redundant. On the other hand, we might follow the lead of the animal psychologists and postulate a limited number of broader motives under such names as curiosity, manipulation, and mastery. I believe that the idea of a competence motivation is more adequate than any of these alternatives and that it points to very vital common properties which have been lost from view amidst the strongly analytical tendencies that go with detailed research.

In order to make this claim more plausible, I shall now introduce some specimens of playful exploration in early childhood. I hope that these images will serve to fix and dramatize the concept of competence in the same way that other images—the hungry animal solving problems, the child putting his finger in the candle flame, the infant at the breast, the child on the toilet, and the youthful Oedipus caught in a hopeless love triangle—have become memorable focal points for other concepts. For this purpose I turn to Piaget's (1952) studies of the growth of intelligence from its earliest manifestations in his own three children. The examples come from the first year of life, before language and verbal concepts begin to be important. They therefore represent a practical kind of intelligence which may be quite similar to what is developed by the higher animals.

As early as the fourth month, the play of the gifted Piaget children began to be "centered on a result produced in the external environment," and their behavior could be described as "rediscovering the movement which by chance exercised an advantageous action upon things" (1952, p. 151). Laurent, lying in his bassinet, learns to shake a suspended rattle by pulling a string that hangs from it. He discovers this result fortuitously before vision and prehension are fully coordinated. Let us now observe him a little later when he has reached the age of three months and ten days.

> I place the string, which is attached to the rattle, in his right hand, merely unrolling it a little so that he may grasp it better. For a moment nothing happens. But at the first shake due to chance movement of his hand, the reaction is immediate: Laurent starts when looking at the rattle and then violently strikes his right hand alone, as if he felt the resistance and the effect. The operation lasts fully a quarter of an hour, during which Laurent emits peals of laughter [Piaget, 1952, p. 162].

Three days later the following behavior is observed.

> Laurent, by chance, strikes the chain while sucking his fingers. He grasps it and slowly displaces it while looking at the rattles. He then begins to swing it very gently, which produces a slight movement of the hanging rattles and an as yet faint sound inside them. Laurent then definitely increases by degrees his own movements. He shakes the chain more and more vigorously and laughs uproariously at the result obtained [Piaget, 1952, p. 185].

Very soon it can be observed that procedures are used "to make interesting spectacles last." For instance, Laurent is shown a rubber monkey which he has not seen before. After a moment of surprise, and perhaps even fright, he calms down and makes movements of pulling the string, a procedure which has no effect in this case, but which previously has caused interesting things to happen. It is to be noticed that "interesting spectacles" consist of such things as new toys, a tin box upon which a drumming noise can be made, an unfolded newspaper, or sounds made by the observer such as snapping the fingers. Commonplace as they are to the adult mind, these spectacles enter the infant's experience as novel and apparently challenging events.

Moving ahead to the second half of the first year, we can observe behavior in which the child explores the properties of objects and tries out his repertory of actions upon them. This soon leads to active experimentation in which the child attempts to provoke new results. Again we look in upon Laurent, who has now reached the age of nine months. On different occasions he is shown a variety of new objects—for instance a notebook, a beaded purse, and a wooden parrot. His carefully observing father detects four stages of response: (*a*) visual exploration, passing the object from hand to hand, folding the purse, *etc.;* (*b*) tactile exploration, passing the hand all over the object, scratching, *etc.;* (*c*) slow moving of the object in space; (*d*) use of the repertory of action: shaking the object, striking it, swinging it, rubbing it against the side of the bassinet, sucking it, *etc.*, "each in turn with a sort of prudence as though studying the effect produced" (1952, p. 255).

Here the child can be described as applying familiar tactics to new situations, but in a short while he will advance to clear patterns of active experimentation. At 10 months and 10 days Laurent, who is unfamiliar with bread as a nutritive substance, is given a piece for examination. He manipulates it, drops it many times, breaks off fragments and lets them fall. He has often done this kind of thing before, but previously his attention has seemed to be centered on the act of letting go. Now "he watches with great interest the body in motion; in particular, he looks at it for a long time when it has fallen, and picks it up when he can." On the following day he resumes his research.

He grasps in succession a celluloid swan, a box, and several other small objects, in each case stretching out his arm and letting them fall. Sometimes he stretches out his arm vertically, sometimes he holds it obliquely in front of or behind his eyes. When the object falls in a new position (for example on his pillow) he lets it fall two or three times more on the same place, as though to study the spatial relation; then he modifies the situation. At a certain moment the swan falls near his mouth; now he does not suck it (even though this object habitually serves this purpose), but drops it three times more while merely making the gesture of opening his mouth [Piaget, 1952, p. 269].

These specimens will furnish us with sufficient images of the infant's use of his spare time. Laurent, of course, was provided by his studious father with a decidedly enriched environment, but no observant parent will question the fact that babies often act this way during those periods of their waking life when hunger, erotic needs, distresses, and anxiety seem to be exerting no particular pressure. If we consider this behavior under the historic headings of psychology we shall see that few processes are missing. The child gives evidence of sensing, perceiving, attending, learning, recognizing, probably recalling, and perhaps thinking in a rudimentary way. Strong emotion is lacking, but the infant's smiles, gurgles, and occasional peals of laughter strongly suggest the presence of pleasant affect. Actions appear in an organized form, particularly in the specimens of active exploration and experimentation. Apparently the child is using with a certain coherence nearly the whole repertory of psychological processes except those that accompany stress. It would be arbitrary indeed to say that one was more important than another.

These specimens have a meaningful unity when seen as transactions between the child and his environment, the child having some influence upon the environment and the environment some influence upon the child.

Laurent appears to be concerned about what he can do with the chain and rattles, what he can accomplish by his own effort to reproduce and to vary the entertaining sounds. If his father observed correctly, we must add that Laurent seems to have varied his actions systematically, as if testing the effect of different degrees of effort upon the bit of environment represented by the chain and rattles. Kittens make a similar study of parameters when delicately using their paws to push pencils and other objects ever nearer to the edge of one's desk. In all such examples it is clear that the child or animal is by no means at the mercy of transient stimulus fields. He selects for continuous treatment those aspects of his environment which he finds it possible to affect in some way. His behavior is selective, directed, persistent—in short, motivated.

Motivated toward what goal? In these terms, too, the behavior exhibits a little of everything. Laurent can be seen as appeasing a stimulus hunger, providing his sensorium with an agreeable level of stimulation by eliciting from the environment a series of interesting sounds, feels, and sights. On the other hand we might emphasize a need for activity and see him as trying to reach a pleasurable level of neuromuscular exercise. We can also see another possible goal in the behavior: the child is achieving knowledge, attaining a more differentiated cognitive map of his environment and thus satisfying an exploratory tendency or motive of curiosity. But it is equally possible to discern a theme of mastery, power, or control, perhaps even a bit of primitive self-assertion, in the child's concentration upon those aspects of the environment which respond in some way to his own activity. It looks as if we had found too many goals, and perhaps our first impulse is to search for some key to tell us which one is really important. But this, I think, is a mistake that would be fatal to understanding.

We cannot assign priority to any of these goals without pausing arbitrarily in the cycle of transaction between child and environment and saying, "This is the real point." I propose instead that the real point is the transactions as a whole. If the behavior gives satisfaction, this satisfaction is not associated with a particular moment in the cycle. It does not lie solely in sensory stimulation, in a bettering of the cognitive map, in coordinated action, in motor exercise, in a feeling of effort and of effects produced, or in the appreciation of change brought about in the sensory field. These are all simply aspects of a process which at this stage has to be conceived as a whole. The child appears to be occupied with the agreeable task of developing an effective familiarity with his environment. This involves discovering the effects he can have on the environment and the effects the environment will have on him. To the extent that these results are preserved by learning, they build up an increased competence in dealing with the environment. The child's play can thus be viewed as serious business, though to him it is merely something that is interesting and fun to do.

Bearing in mind these examples, as well as the dealings with environment pointed out by other workers, we must now attempt to describe more fully the possible nature of the motivational aspect of competence. It needs its own name, and in view of the foregoing analysis I propose that this name be *effectance.*

Effectance

THE new freedom produced by two decades of research on animal drives is of great help in this undertaking. We are no longer obliged to look for a source of energy external to the nervous system, for a consummatory climax, or for a fixed connection between reinforcement and tension-reduction. Effectance motivation cannot, of course, be conceived as having a source in tissues external to the nervous system. It is in no sense a deficit motive. We must assume it to be neurogenic, its "energies" being simply those of the living cells that make up the nervous system. External stimuli play an important part, but in terms of "energy" this part is secondary, as one can see most clearly when environmental stimulation is actively sought. Putting it picturesquely, we might say that the effectance urge represents what the neuromuscular system wants to do when it is otherwise unoccupied or is gently stimulated by the environment. Obviously there are no consummatory acts; satisfaction would appear to lie in the arousal and maintaining of activity rather than in its slow decline toward bored passivity. The motive need not be conceived as intense and powerful in the sense that hunger, pain, or fear can be powerful when aroused to high pitch. There are plenty of instances in which children refuse to leave their absorbed play in order to eat or to visit the toilet. Strongly aroused drives, pain, and anxiety, however, can be conceived as overriding the effectance urge and capturing the energies of the neuromuscular system. But effectance motivation is persistent in the sense that it regularly occupies the spare waking time between episodes of homeostatic crisis.

In speculating upon this subject we must bear in mind the continuous nature of behavior. This is easier said than done; habitually we break things down in order to understand them, and such units as the reflex arc, the stimulus-response sequence, and the single transaction with the environment seem like inevitable steps toward clarity. Yet when we apply such an analysis to playful exploration we lose the most essential aspect of the behavior. It is constantly circling from stimulus to perception to action to effect to stimulus to perception, and so on around; or, more properly, these processes are all in continuous action and continuous change. Dealing with the environment means carrying on a continuing transaction which gradually changes one's relation to the environment. Because there is no consummatory climax, satisfaction has to be seen as lying in a considerable series of transactions, in a trend of behavior rather than a goal that is achieved. It is difficult to make the word "satisfaction" have this connotation, and we shall do well to replace it by [the] "feeling of efficacy" when attempting to indicate the subjective and affective side of effectance.

It is useful to recall the findings about novelty: the singular effectiveness of novelty in engaging interest and for a time supporting persistent behavior. We also need to consider the selective continuance of transactions in which the animal or child has a more or less pronounced effect upon the environment—in which something happens as a consequence of his activity. Interest is not aroused and sustained when the stimulus field is so familiar that it gives rise at most to reflex acts or automatized habits. It is not sustained when actions produce no effects or changes in the stimulus field. Our conception must therefore be that effectance motivation is aroused by stimulus conditions which offer, as Hebb (1949) puts it, difference-in-sameness. This leads to variability and novelty of response, and interest is best sustained when the resulting action affects the stimulus so as to produce further difference-in-sameness. Interest wanes when action begins to have less effect; effectance motivation subsides when a situation has been explored to the point that it no longer presents new possibilities.

We have to conceive further that the arousal of playful and exploratory interest means the appearance of organization involving both the cognitive and active aspects of behavior. Change in the stimulus field is not an end in itself, so to speak; it happens when one is passively moved about, and it may happen as a consequence of random movements without becoming focalized and instigating exploration. Similarly, action which has effects is not an end in itself, for if one unintentionally kicks away a branch while walking, or knocks something off a table, these effects by no means necessarily become involved in playful investigation. Schachtel's (1954) emphasis on focal attention becomes helpful at this point. The playful and exploratory behavior shown by Laurent is not random or casual. It involves focal *attention* to some object—the fixing of some aspect of the stimulus field so that it stays relatively constant—and it also involves the focalizing of *action* upon this object. As Diamond (1939) has expressed it, response under these conditions is "relevant to the stimulus," and it is change in the *focalized* stimulus that so strongly affects the level of interest. Dealing with the environment means directing focal attention to some part of it and organizing actions to have some effect on this part.

In our present state of relative ignorance about the workings of the nervous system it is impossible to form a satisfactory idea of the neural basis of effectance motivation, but it should at least be clear that the concept does not refer to any and every kind of neural action. It refers to a particular kind of activity, as inferred from particular kinds of behavior. We can say that it does not include reflexes and other kinds of automatic response. It does not include well-learned, automatized patterns, even those that are complex and highly organized. It does not include behavior in the service of effectively aroused drives. It does not even include activity that is highly random and discontinuous, though such behavior may be its most direct forerunner. The urge toward competence is inferred specifically from behavior that shows a lasting focalization and that has the characteristics of exploration and experimentation, a kind of variation within the focus. When this particular sort of activity is aroused in the nervous system, effectance motivation is being aroused, for it is characteristic of this particular sort of activity that it is selective, directed, and persistent, and that instrumental acts will be learned for the sole reward of engaging in it.

Some objection may be felt to my introducing the word *competence* in connection with behavior that is so often playful. Certainly the playing child is doing things for fun, not because of a desire to improve his competence in dealing with the stern hard world. In order to forestall misunderstanding, it should be pointed out that the usage here is parallel to what we do when we connect sex with its biological goal of reproduction. The sex drive aims for pleasure and gratification, and reproduction is a consequence that is presumably unforeseen by animals and by man at primitive levels of understanding. Effectance motivation similarly aims for the feeling of efficacy, not for the vitally important learnings that come as its consequence. If we consider the part played by competence motivation in adult human life we can observe the same parallel. Sex may now be completely and purposefully divorced from reproduction but nevertheless pursued for the pleasure it can yield. Similarly, effectance motivation may lead to continuing exploratory interests or active adventures when in fact there is no longer any gain in actual competence or any need for it in terms of survival. In both cases the motive is capable of yielding surplus satisfaction well beyond what is necessary to get the biological work done.

In infants and young children it seems to me sensible to conceive of effectance motivation as undifferentiated. Later in life it becomes profitable to distinguish various motives such as cognizance, construction, mastery, and achievement. It is my view that all such motives have a root in effectance motivation. They are differentiated from it through life experiences which emphasize one or another aspect of the cycle of transaction with environment. Of course, the motives of later childhood and of adult life are no longer simple and can almost never be referred to a single root. They can acquire loadings of anxiety, defense, and compensation, they can become fused with unconscious fantasies of a sexual, aggressive, or omnipotent character, and they can gain force because of their service in producing realistic results in the way of income and career. It is not my intention to cast effectance in the star part in adult motivation. The acquisition of motives is a complicated affair in which simple and sovereign theories grow daily more obsolete. Yet it may be that the satisfaction of effectance contributes significantly to those feelings of interest which often sustain us so well in day-to-day actions, particularly when the things we are doing have continuing elements of novelty.

The Biological Significance of Competence

THE conviction was expressed at the beginning of this paper that some such concept as competence, interpreted motivationally, was essential for any biologically sound view of human nature. This necessity emerges when we consider the nature of living systems, particularly when we take a longitudinal view. What an organism does at a given moment does not always give the right clue as to what it does over a period of time. Discussing this problem, Angyal (1941) has proposed that we should look for the general pattern followed by the total organismic process over the course of time. Obviously this makes it necessary to take account of growth. Angyal defines life as "a process of self-expansion"; the living system "expands at the expense of its surroundings," assimilating parts of the environment and transforming them into functioning parts of itself. Organisms differ from other things in nature in that they are "self-governing entities" which are to some extent "autonomous." Internal processes govern them as well as external "heteronomous" forces. In the course of life there is a relative increase in the preponderance of internal over external forces. The living system expands, assimilates more of the environment, transforms its surroundings so as to bring them under greater control. "We may say," Angyal writes, "that the general dynamic trend of the organism is toward an increase of autonomy. . . . The human being has a characteristic tendency toward self-determination, that is, a tendency to resist external influences and to subordinate the heteronomous forces of the physical and social environment to its own sphere of influence." The trend toward increased autonomy is characteristic so long as growth of any kind is going on, though in the end the living system is bound to succumb to the pressure of heteronomous forces.

Of all living creatures, it is man who takes the longest strides toward autonomy. This is not because of any unusual tendency toward bodily expansion at the expense of the environment. It is rather that man, with his mobile hands and abundantly developed brain, attains an extremely high level of competence in his transactions with his surroundings. The building of houses, roads and bridges, the making of tools and instruments, the domestication of plants and animals, all qualify as planful changes made in the environment so that it comes more or less under control and serves our purposes rather than intruding upon them. We meet the fluctuations of outdoor temperature, for example, not only with our bodily homeostatic mechanisms, which alone would be painfully unequal to the task, but also with clothing, buildings, controlled fires, and such complicated devices as self-regulating central heating and air conditioning. Man as a species has developed a tremendous power of bringing the environment into his service, and each individual member of the species must attain what is really quite an impressive level of competence if he is to take part in the life around him.

We are so accustomed to these human accomplishments that it is hard to realize how long an apprenticeship they require. At the outset the human infant is a slow learner in comparison with other animal forms. Hebb (1949) speaks of "the astonishing inefficiency of man's first learning, as far as immediate results are concerned," an inefficiency which he attributes to the large size of the association areas in the brain and the long time needed to bring them under sensory control. The human lack of precocity in learning shows itself even in comparison with one of the next of kin: as Hebb points out, "the human baby takes six months, the chimpanzee four months, before making a clear distinction between friend and enemy." Later in life the slow start will pay dividends. Once the fundamental perceptual elements, simple associations, and conceptual sequences have been established, later learning can proceed with ever increasing swiftness and complexity. In Hebb's words, "learning at maturity concerns patterns and events whose parts at least are familiar and which already have a number of other associations."

This general principle of cumulative learning, starting from slowly acquired rudiments and proceeding thence with increasing efficiency, can be illustrated by such processes as manipulation and locomotion, which may culminate in the acrobat devising new stunts or the dancer working out a new ballet. It is especially vivid in the case of language, where the early mastery of words and pronunciation seems such a far cry from spontaneous adult speech. A strong argument has been made by Hebb (1949) that the learning of visual forms proceeds over a similar course from slowly learned elements to rapidly combined patterns. Circles and squares, for example, cannot be discriminated at a glance without a slow apprenticeship involving eye movements, successive fixations, and recognition of angles. Hebb proposes that the recognition of visual patterns without eye movement "is possible only as the result of an intensive and prolonged visual training that goes on from the moment of birth, during every moment that the eyes are open, with an increase in skill evident over a perod of 12 to 16 years at least."

On the motor side there is likewise a lot to be cumulatively learned. The playing, investigating child slowly finds out the relationships between what he does and what he experiences. He finds out, for instance, how hard he must push what in order to produce what effect. Here the S-R formula is particularly misleading. It would come nearer the truth to say that the child is busy learning R-S connections—the effects that are likely to follow upon his own behavior. But even in this reversed form the notion of bonds or connections would still misrepresent the situation, for it is only a rare specimen of behavior that can properly be conceived as determined by fixed neural channels and a fixed motor response. As Hebb has pointed out, discussing the phenomenon of "motor equivalence" named by Lashley (1942), a rat which has been trained to press a lever will press it with the left forepaw, the right forepaw, by climbing upon it, or by biting it; a monkey will open the lid of a food box with either hand, with a foot, or even with a stick; and we might add that a good baseball player can catch a fly ball while running in almost any direction and while in almost any posture, including leaping in the air and plunging forward to the ground. All of these feats are possible because of a history of learnings in which the main lesson has been the effects of actions upon the stimulus fields that represent the environment. What has been learned is not a fixed connection but a flexible relationship between stimulus fields and the effects that can be produced in them by various kinds of action.

One additional example, drawn this time from Piaget (1952), is particularly worth mentioning because of its importance in theories of development. Piaget points out that a great deal of mental development depends upon the idea that the world is made up of objects having substance and permanence. Without such an "object concept" it would be impossible to build up the ideas of space and causality and to arrive at the fundamental distinction between self and external world. Observation shows that the object concept, "far from being innate or ready-made in experience, is constructed little by little." Up to 7 and 8 months the Piaget children searched for vanished objects only in the sense of trying to continue the actions, such as sucking or grasping, in which the objects had played a part. When an object was really out of sight or touch, even if only because it was covered by a cloth, the infants undertook no further exploration. Only gradually, after some study of the displacement of objects by moving, swinging, and dropping them, does the child begin to make an active search for a vanished object, and only still more gradually does he learn, at 12 months or more, to make allowance for the object's sequential displacements and thus to seek it where it has gone rather than where it was last in sight. Thus it is only through cumulative learning that the child arrives at the idea of permanent substantial objects.

The infant's play is indeed serious business. If he did not while away his time pulling strings, shaking rattles, examining wooden parrots, dropping pieces of bread and celluloid swans, when would he learn to discriminate visual patterns, to catch and throw, and to build up his concept of the object? When would he acquire the many other foundation stones necessary for cumulative learning? The more closely we analyze the behavior of the human infant, the more clearly do we realize that infancy is not simply a time when the nervous system matures and the muscles grow stronger. It is a time of active and continuous learning, during which the basis is laid for all those processes, cognitive and motor, whereby the child becomes able to establish effective transactions with his environment and move toward a greater degree of autonomy. Helpless as he may seem until he begins to toddle, he has by that time already made substantial gains in the achievement of competence.

Under primitive conditions survival must depend quite heavily upon achieved competence. We should expect to find things so arranged as to favor and maximize this achievement. Particularly in the case of man, where so little is provided innately and so much has to be learned through experience, we should expect to find highly advantageous arrangements for securing a steady cumulative learning about the properties of the environment and the extent of possible transactions. Under these circumstances we might expect to find a very powerful drive operating to insure progress toward competence, just as the vital goals of nutrition and reproduction are secured by powerful drives, and it might therefore seem paradoxical that the interests of competence should be so much entrusted to times of play and leisurely exploration. There is good reason to suppose, however, that a strong drive would be precisely the wrong arrangement to secure a flexible, knowledgeable power of transaction with the environment. Strong drives cause us to learn certain lessons well, but they do not create maximum familiarity with our surroundings.

This point was demonstrated half a century ago in some experiments by Yerkes and Dodson (1908). They showed that maximum motivation did not lead to the most rapid solving of problems, especially if the problems were complex. For each problem there was an optimum level of motivation, neither the highest nor the lowest, and the optimum was lower for more complex tasks. The same problem has been discussed more recently by Tolman (1948) in his paper on cognitive maps. A cognitive map can be narrow or broad, depending upon the range of cues picked up in the course of learning. Tolman suggests that one of the conditions which tend to narrow the range of cues is a high level of motivation. In everyday terms, a man hurrying to an important business conference is likely to perceive only the cues that help him to get there faster, whereas a man taking a stroll after lunch is likely to pick up a substantial amount of casual information about his environment. The latent learning experiments with animals, and experiments such as those of Johnson (1953) in which drive level has been systematically varied in a situation permitting incidental learning, give strong support to this general idea. In a recent contribution, Bruner, Matter, and Papanek (1955) make a strong case for the concept of breadth of learning and provide additional evidence that it is favored by moderate and hampered by strong motivation. The latter "has the effect of speeding up learning at the cost of narrowing it." Attention is concentrated upon the task at hand and little that is extraneous to this task is learned for future use.

These facts enable us to see the biological appropriateness of an arrangement which uses periods of less intense motivation for the development of competence. This is not to say that the narrower but efficient learnings that go with the reduction of strong drives make no contribution to general effectiveness. They are certainly an important element in capacity to deal with the environment, but a much greater effectiveness results from having this capacity fed also from learnings that take place in quieter times. It is then that the infant can attend to matters of lesser urgency, exploring the properties of things he does not fear and does not need to eat, learning to gauge the force of his string-pulling when the only penalty for failure is silence on the part of the attached rattles, and generally accumulating for himself a broad knowledge and a broad skill in dealing with his surroundings.

The concept of competence can be most easily discussed by choosing, as we have done, examples of interaction with the inanimate environment. It applies equally well, however, to transactions with animals and with other human beings, where the child has the same problem of finding out what effects he can have upon the environment and what effects it can have upon him. The earliest interactions with members of the family may involve needs so strong that they obscure the part played by effectance motivation, but perhaps the example of the well fed baby diligently exploring the several features of his mother's face will serve as a reminder that here, too, there are less urgent moments when learning for its own sake can be given free rein.

In this closing section I have brought together several ideas which bear on the evolutionary significance of competence and of its motivation. I have sought in this way to deepen the biological roots of the concept and thus help it to attain the stature in the theory of behavior which has not been reached by similar concepts in the past. To me it seems that the most important proving ground for this concept is the effect it may have on our understanding of the development of personality. Does it assist our grasp of early object relations, the reality principle, and the first steps in the development of the ego? Can it be of service in distinguishing the kinds of defense available at different ages and in providing clues to the replacement of primitive defenses by successful adaptive maneuvers? Can it help fill the yawning gap known as the latency period, a time when the mastery of school subjects and other accomplishments claim so large a share of time and energy? Does it bear upon the self and the vicissitudes of self-esteem, and can it enlighten the origins of psychological disorder? Can it make adult motives and interests more intelligible and enable us to rescue the concept of sublimation from the difficulties which even its best friends have recognized? I believe it can be shown that existing explanations of development are not satisfactory and that the addition of the concept of competence cuts certain knots in personality theory. But this is not the subject of the present communication, where the concept is offered much more on the strength of its logical and biological probability.

Summary

THE main theme of this paper is introduced by showing that there is widespread discontent with theories of motivation built upon primary drives. Signs of this discontent are found in realms as far apart as animal psychology and psychoanalytic ego psychology. In the former, the commonly recognized primary drives have proved to be inadequate in explaining exploratory behavior, manipulation, and general activity. In the latter, the theory of basic instincts has shown serious shortcomings when it is stretched to account for the development of the effective ego. Workers with animals have attempted to meet their problem by invoking secondary reinforcement and anxiety reduction, or by adding exploration and manipulation to the roster of primary drives. In parallel fashion, psychoanalytic workers have relied upon the concept of neutralization of instinctual energies, have seen anxiety reduction as the central motive in ego development, or have hypothesized new instincts such as mastery. It is argued here that these several explanations are not satisfactory and that a better conceptualization is possible, indeed that it has already been all but made.

In trying to form this conceptualization, it is first pointed out that many of the earlier tenets of primary drive theory have been discredited by recent experimental work. There is no longer any compelling reason to identify either pleasure or reinforcement with drive reduction, or to think of motivation as requiring a source of energy external to the nervous system. This opens the way for considering in their own right those aspects of animal and human behavior in which stimulation and contact with the environment seem to be sought and welcomed, in which raised tension and even mild excitement seem to be cherished, and in which novelty and variety seem to be enjoyed for their own sake. Several reports are cited which bear upon interest in the environment and the rewarding effects of environmental feedback. The latest contribution is that of Woodworth (1958), who makes dealing with the environment the most fundamental element in motivation.

The survey indicates a certain unanimity as to the kinds of behavior that cannot be successfully conceptualized in terms of primary drives. This behavior includes visual exploration, grasping, crawling and walking, attention and perception, language and thinking, exploring novel objects and places, manipulating the surroundings, and producing effective changes in the environment. The thesis is then proposed that all of these behaviors have a common biological significance: they all form part of the process whereby the animal or child learns to interact effectively with his environment. The word *competence* is chosen as suitable to indicate this common property. Further, it is maintained that competence cannot be fully acquired simply through behavior instigated by drives. It receives substantial contributions from activities which, though playful and exploratory in character, at the same time show direction, selectivity, and persistence in interacting with the environment. Such activities in the ultimate service of competence must therefore be conceived to be motivated in their own right. It is proposed to designate this motivation by the term effectance, and to characterize the experience produced as a *feeling of efficacy*.

In spite of its sober biological purpose, effectance motivation shows itself most unambiguously in the playful and investigatory behavior of young animals and children. Specimens of such behavior, drawn from Piaget (1952), are analyzed in order to demonstrate their constantly transactional nature. Typically they involve continuous chains of events which include stimulation, cognition, action, effect on the environment, new stimulation, etc. They are carried on with considerable persistence and with selective emphasis on parts of the environment which provide changing and interesting feedback in connection with effort expended. Their significance is destroyed if we try to break into the circle arbitrarily and declare that one part of it, such as cognition alone or active effort alone, is the real point, the goal, or the special seat of satisfaction. Effectance motivation must be conceived to involve satisfaction—a feeling of efficacy—in transactions in which behavior has an exploratory, varying, experimental character and produces changes in the stimulus field. Having this character, the behavior leads the organism to find out how the environment can be changed and what consequences flow from these changes.

In higher animals and especially in man, where so little is innately provided and so much has to be learned about dealing with the environment, effectance motivation independent of primary drives can be seen as an arrangement having high adaptive value. Considering the slow rate of learning in infancy and the vast amount that has to be learned before there can be an effective level of interaction with surroundings, young animals and children would simply not learn enough unless they worked pretty steadily at the task between episodes of homeostatic crisis. The association of interest with this "work," making it play and fun, is thus somewhat comparable to the association of sexual pleasure with the biological goal of reproduction. Effectance motivation need not be conceived as strong in the sense that sex, hunger, and fear are strong when violently aroused. It is moderate but persistent, and in this, too, we can discern a feature that is favorable for adaptation. Strong motivation reinforces learning in a narrow sphere, whereas moderate motivation is more conducive to an exploratory and experimental attitude which leads to competent interactions in general, without reference to an immediate pressing need. Man's huge cortical association areas might have been a suicidal piece of specialization if they had come without a steady, persistent inclination toward interacting with the environment.

REFERENCES

ALLPORT, G. W. *Personality: a psychological interpretation*. New York: Holt, 1937.

ALLPORT, G. W. Effect: a secondary principle of learning. *Psychol. Rev.*, 1946, **53**, 335–347.

ANGYAL, A. *Foundations for a science of personality*. New York: Commonwealth Fund, 1941.

ANSBACHER, H. L., & ANSBACHER, ROWENA R.

(Eds.) *The individual psychology of Alfred Adler.* New York: Basic Books, 1956.

BEACH, F. A. Analysis of factors involved in the arousal, maintenance and manifestation of sexual excitement in male animals. *Psychosom. Med.,* 1942, **4,** 173–198.

BEACH, F. A. Instinctive behavior: reproductive activities. In S. S. Stevens (Ed.), *Handbook of experimental psychology.* New York: Wiley, 1951. Pp. 387–434.

BERLYNE, D. E. Novelty and curiosity as determinants of exploratory behavior. *Brit. J. Psychol.,* 1950, **41,** 68–80.

BERLYNE, D. E. The arousal and satiation of perceptual curiosity in the rat. *J. comp. physiol. Psychol.,* 1955, **48,** 238–246.

BERLYNE, D. E. Attention to change, conditioned inhibition ($S^{I}R$) and stimulus satiation. *Brit. J. Psychol.,* 1957, **48,** 138–140.

BERLYNE, D. E. The present status of research on exploratory and related behavior. *J. indiv. Psychol.,* 1958, **14,** 121–126.

BIBRING, E. The development and problems of the theories of the instincts. *Int. J. Psychoanal.,* 1941, **22,** 102–131.

BRUNER, J. S., MATTER, J., & PAPANEK, M. L. Breadth of learning as a function of drive level and mechanization. *Psychol. Rev.* 1955, **62,** 1–10.

BÜHLER, C. The reality principle. *Amer. J. Psychother.,* 1954, **8,** 626–647.

BÜHLER, K. *Die geistige Entwicklung des Kindes.* (4th ed.) Jena: Gustav Fischer, 1924.

BUTLER, R. A. Discrimination learning by rhesus monkeys to visual-exploration motivation. *J. comp. physiol. Psychol.,* 1953, **46,** 95–98.

BUTLER, R. A. Exploratory and related behavior: a new trend in animal research. *J. indiv. Psychol.,* 1958, **14,** 111–120.

BUTLER, R. A., & HARLOW, H. F. Discrimination learning and learning sets to visual exploration incentives. *J. gen. Psychol.,* 1957, **57,** 257–264.

COFER, C. N. Motivation. *Ann. Rev. Psychol.,* 1959, **10,** 173–202.

COLBY, K. M. *Energy and structure in psychoanalysis.* New York: Ronald, 1955.

DASHIELL, J. F. A quantitative demonstration of animal drive. *J. comp. Psychol.,* 1925, **5,** 205–208.

DIAMOND, S. A neglected aspect of motivation. *Sociometry,* 1939, **2,** 77–85.

DOLLARD, J., & MILLER, N. E. *Personality and psychotherapy.* New York: McGraw-Hill, 1950.

ERIKSON, E. H. *Childhood and society.* New York: Norton, 1950.

ERIKSON, E. H. Growth and crises of the healthy personality. In C. Kluckhohn, & H. A. Murray (Eds.), *Personality in nature, society, and culture.* (2nd ed.) New York: Knopf, 1953. Pp. 185–225.

FENICHEL, O. *The psychoanalytic theory of neurosis.* New York: Norton, 1945.

FRENCH, T. M. *The integration of behavior.* Vol. 1. *Basic postulates.* Chicago: Univer. Chicago Press, 1952.

FREUD, ANNA. The mutual influences in the development of ego and id: introduction to the discussion. In Ruth S. Eissler *et al.* (Eds.), *The psychoanalytic study of the child.* Vol. 7. New York: International Universities Press, 1952. Pp. 42–50.

FREUD, S. *Wit and its relation to the unconscious.* New York: Moffat, Yard, 1961.

FREUD, S. Formulations regarding the two principles in mental functioning. In *Collected papers.* Vol. 4. London: Hogarth and Institute of Psycho-analysis, 1925. Pp. 13–21. (a)

FREUD, S. On narcissism: an introduction. In *Collected papers.* Vol. 4. London: Hogarth and Institute of Psycho-analysis, 1925. Pp. 30–59. (b)

FREUD, S. Instincts and their vicissitudes. In *Collected papers.* Vol. 4. London: Hogarth and Institute of Psycho-analysis, 1925. Pp. 60–83. (c)

FREUD, S. *The ego and the id.* (Trans. by J. Riviere.) London: Hogarth, 1927.

FREUD, S. *Beyond the pleasure principle.* London: Hogarth, 1948.

FREUD, S. *An outline of psychoanalysis.* (Trans. by J. Strachey.) New York: Norton, 1949.

GOLDSTEIN, K. *The organism.* New York: American Book, 1939.

GOLDSTEIN, K. *Human nature in the light of psychopathology.* Cambridge, Mass.: Harvard Univer. Press, 1940.

GROSS, K. *The play of man.* (Trans. by E. L. Baldwin.) New York: Appleton, 1901.

HARLOW, H. F. Mice, monkeys, men, and motives. *Psychol. Rev.,* 1953, **60,** 23–32.

HARLOW, H. F., HARLOW, MARGARET K., & MEYER, D. R. Learning motivated by a manipulation drive. *J. exp. Psychol.,* 1950, **40,** 228–234.

HARTMANN, H. Comments on the psychoanalytic theory of the ego. In Ruth S. Eissler *et al.* (Eds.), *The psychoanalytic study of the child.*

Vol. 5. New York: International Universities Press, 1950. Pp. 74–95.

HARTMANN, H. Notes on the theory of sublimation. In Ruth S. Eissler *et al.* (Eds.), *The psychoanalytic study of the child.* Vol. 10. New York: International Universities Press, 1955. Pp. 9–29.

HARTMANN, H. Notes on the reality principle. In Ruth S. Eissler *et al.* (Eds.), *The psychoanalytic study of the child.* Vol. 11. New York: International Universities Press, 1956. Pp. 31–53.

HARTMANN, H. *Ego psychology and the problem of adaptation.* (Trans. by D. Rapaport.) New York: International Universities Press, 1958.

HARTMANN, H., KRIS, E., & LOEWENSTEIN, R. Notes on the theory of aggression. In Ruth S. Eissler *et al.* (Eds.), *The psychoanalytic study of the child.* Vol. 3/4. New York: International Universities Press, 1949. Pp. 9–36.

HEBB, D. O. *The organization of behavior.* New York: Wiley, 1949.

HEBB, D. O. Drives and the c.n.s. (conceptual nervous system). *Psychol. Rev.,* 1955, **62,** 243–254.

HEBB, D. O. The motivating effects of exteroceptive stimulation. *Amer. Psychologist,* 1958, **13,** 109–113.

HEBB, D. O., & THOMPSON, W. R. The social significance of animal studies. In G. Lindzey (Ed.), *Handbook of social psychology.* Vol. 1. Reading, Mass.: Addison-Wesley, 1954. Pp. 532–561.

HENDRICK, I. Instinct and the ego during infancy. *Psychoanalyt. Quart.,* 1942, **11,** 33–58.

HENDRICK, I. Work and the pleasure principle. *Psychoanalyt. Quart.,* 1943, **12,** 311–329. (a)

HENDRICK, I. The discussion of the instinct to master. *Psychoanalyt. Quart.* 1943, **12,** 561–565. (b)

HILL, W. F. Activity as an autonomous drive. *J. comp. physiol. Psychol.,* 1956, **49,** 15–19.

JOHNSON, E. E. The role of motivational strength in latent learning. *J. comp. physiol. Psychol.,* 1953, **45,** 526–530.

KAGAN, J. Differential reward value of incomplete and complete sexual behavior. *J. comp. physiol. Psychol.,* 1955, **48,** 59–64.

KAGAN, J., & BERKUN, M. The reward value of running activity. *J. comp. physiol. Psychol.,* 1954, **47,** 108.

KARDINER, A., & SPIEGEL, H. War stress and neurotic illness. New York: Hoeber, 1947.

LASHLEY, K. S. Experimental analysis of instinctive behavior. *Psychol. Rev.,* 1938, **45,** 445–471.

LASHLEY, K. S. The problem of cerebral organization in vision. In H. Klüver, *Visual mechanisms.* New York: Jaques Cattell, 1942. Pp. 301–322.

LEUBA, C. Toward some integration of learning theories: the concept of optimal stimulation. *Psychol. Rep.* 1955, **1,** 27–33.

LILLY, J. C. Mental effects of reduction of ordinary levels of physical stimuli on intact, healthy persons. *Psychiat. res. Rep.,* 1956, No. 5.

MASLOW, A. H. *Motivation and personality.* New York: Harper, 1954.

MASLOW, A. H. Deficiency motivation and growth motivation. In M. R. Jones (Ed.), *Nebraska symposium on motivation 1955.* Lincoln, Neb.: Univer. Nebraska Press, 1955. Pp. 1–30.

MCCLELLAND, D. C., ATKINSON, J. W., CLARK, R. A., & LOWELL, E. L. *The achievement motive.* New York: Appleton-Century-Crofts, 1953.

MCDOUGALL, W. *Introduction to social psychology.* (16th ed.) Boston: John Luce, 1923.

MCREYNOLDS, P. A restricted conceptualization of human anxiety and motivation. *Psychol. Rep.,* 1956, **2,** 293–312. (Monogr. Suppl. 6.)

MILLER, N. E. Learnable drives and rewards. In S. S. Stevens (Ed.), *Handbook of experimental psychology.* New York: Wiley, 1951. Pp. 435–472.

MILLER, N. E. Central stimulation and other new approaches to motivation and reward. *Amer. Psychologist,* 1958, **13,** 100–108.

MITTELMANN, B. Motility in infants, children, and adults. In Ruth S. Eissler *et al.* (Eds.), *The psychoanalytic study of the child.* Vol. 9. New York: International Universities Press, 1954. Pp. 142–177.

MONTGOMERY, K. C. The role of the exploratory drive in learning. *J. comp. physiol. Psychol.,* 1954, **47,** 60–64.

MONTGOMERY, K. C., & MONKMAN, J. A. The relation between fear and exploratory behavior. *J. comp. physiol. Psychol.,* 1955, **48,** 132–136.

MORGAN, C. T. *Psysiological psychology.* New York: McGraw-Hill, 1943.

MORGAN, C. T. Physiological mechanisms of motivation. In M. R. Jones (Ed.), *Nebraska symposium on motivation 1957.* Lincoln,

Neb.: Univer. Nebraska Press, 1957. Pp. 1–35.

Mowrer, O. H. *Learning theory and personality dynamics.* New York: Ronald, 1950.

Munroe, R. *Schools of psychoanalytical thought.* New York: Dryden, 1955.

Murphy, G. *Personality: a biosocial approach to origins and structure.* New York: Harper, 1947.

Murray, H. A. *Explorations in personality.* New York and London: Oxford Univer. Press, 1938.

Murray, H. A., & Kluckhohn, C. Outline of a conception of personality. In C. Kluckhohn & H. A. Murray (Eds.), *Personality in nature, society, and culture.* (2nd ed.) New York: Knopf, 1953.

Myers, A. K., & Miller, N. E. Failure to find a learned drive based on hunger; evidence for learning motivated by "exploration." *J. comp. physiol. Psychol.,* 1954, **47,** 428–436.

Nissen, H. W. A study of exploratory behavior in the white rat by means of the obstruction method. *J. genet. Psychol.,* 1930, **37,** 361–376.

Olds, J., & Milner, P. Positive reinforcement produced by electrical stimulation of septal area and other regions of rat brain. *J. comp. physiol. Psychol.,* 1954, **47,** 419–427.

Piaget, J. *The origins of intelligence in children.* (Trans. by M. Cook.) New York: International Universities Press, 1952.

Rapaport, D. *Organization and pathology of thought.* New York: Columbia Univer. Press, 1951.

Rapaport, D. On the psychoanalytic theory of thinking. In R. P. Knight & C. R. Friedman (Eds.), *Psychoanalytic psychiatry and psychology.* New York: International Universities Press, 1954. Pp. 259–273.

Rapaport, D. The theory of ego autonomy: a generalization. *Bull. Menninger Clin.,* 1958, **22,** 13–35.

Rosvold, H. E. Physiological psychology. *Ann. Rev. Psychol.,* 1959, **10,** 415–454.

Schachtel, E. G. The development of focal attention and the emergence of reality. *Psychiatry,* 1954, **17,** 309–324.

Sheffield, F. D., & Roby, T. B. Reward value of a non-nutritive sweet taste. *J. comp. physiol. Psychol.,* 1950, **43,** 471–481.

Sheffield, F. D., Roby, T. B., & Campbell, B. A. Drive reduction vs. consummatory behavior as determinants of reinforcement. *J. comp. physiol. Psychol.,* 1954, **47,** 349–354.

Sheffield, F. D., Wulff, J. J., & Backer, R. Reward value of copulation without sex drive reduction. *J. comp. physiol. Psychol.,* 1951, **44,** 3–8.

Skinner, B. F. *Science and human behavior.* New York: Macmillan, 1953.

Steller, E. The physiology of motivation. *Psychol. Rev.,* 1954, **61,** 5–22.

Tolman, E. C. Cognitive maps in rats and men. *Psychol. Rev.,* 1948, **55,** 189–208.

Welker, W. L. Some determinants of play and exploration in chimpanzees. *J. comp. physiol. Psychol.,* 1956, **49,** 84–89.

Whiting, J. W. M., & Mowrer, O. H. Habit progression and regression—a laboratory study of some factors relevant to human socialization. *J. comp. Psychol.,* 1943, **36,** 229–253.

Wolfe, J. B., & Kaplon, M. D. Effect of amount of reward and consummative activity on learning in chickens. *J. comp. Psychol.,* 1941, **31,** 353–361.

Woodworth, R. S. *Dynamics of behavior.* New York: Holt, 1958.

Yerkes, R. M., & Dodson, J. D. The relation of strength of stimulus to rapidity of habit-formation. *J. comp. Neurol. Psychol.,* 1908, **18,** 459–482.

Young, P. T. Food-seeking drive, affective process, and learning. *Psychol. Rev.,* 1949, **56,** 98–121.

Young, P. T. The role of hedonic processes in motivation. In M. R. Jones (Ed.), *Nebraska symposium on motivation 1955.* Lincoln, Neb.: Univer. Nebraska Press, 1955. Pp. 193–238.

Zimbardo, P. G., & Miller, N. E. Facilitation of exploration by hunger in rats. *J. comp. physiol. Psychol.,* 1958, **51,** 43–46.

ROBERT R. SEARS

*Relation of Early Socialization Experiences to Aggression in Middle Childhood**

THIS report presents one part of a follow-up study of the 5-year-old children whose early socialization experiences were described in *Patterns of Child Rearing* (Sears, Maccoby, & Levin, 1957). It attempts to trace the effects of some of those experiences on the children's aggressive behavior 6 years later.

During the winter of 1951–52, 379 public school kindergarten children in Newton and Watertown, Massachusetts, were selected as subjects for a study of the child rearing antecedents of identification. The design of that research required the measurement of certain aspects of both the children's behavior and the mothers' child rearing practices and attitudes. The measures of identification which seemed appropriate, at that time, related chiefly to the extent of children's adoption of adult role behavior and to the stage of development of guilt feelings and other signs of conscience. Measures of such behavior were obtained from three sessions of doll play, two permissive and one structured (Levin & Sears, 1956; Sears, 1953), and from mother interviews (Sears *et al.*, 1957). These interviews were mainly directed to the measurement of the antecedent (maternal) behavior, however; they were designed to secure information about aspects of the mothers' practices and attitudes that had theoretical relevance to the development of identification. The dimensions measured related to early caretaking, feeding, toileting, the handling of dependent, aggressive, and sexual behavior, and methods of discipline. These interviews were based on a standard series of questions and probes, and permitted entirely free answers. They were secured by trained interviewers in the mothers' own homes, were recorded and transcribed, and then coded on 188 scales. It is the mothers' scores on these scales that provide the antecedent measures in the present longitudinal study of the relation of early child rearing experiences to children's manifestations of aggression at age 12.

FOLLOW-UP STUDY

WHILE the original study was directed to the problem of identification, the theoretical position on which the research was based required measurement of maternal behaviors that were equally relevant to the development of various other aspects of children's personalities. Since the extent and kind of influence of early socialization experiences on later childhood and adult behavior have been studied mainly by clinical techniques, this body of data seemed of considerable potential value both for testing hypotheses concerning developmental relationships and for searching out new ones. What was needed was a set of appropriate measures of the children, at age 12, which could be compared with these earlier obtained reports of their socialization experiences. To these ends, therefore, a follow-up study was planned that would provide measures not only of such presumably identification-induced behavior as adult role choice, resistance to temptation, and sex typing (masculinity-femininity), but of aggression and dependency also.

* REPRINTED with abridgment by permission of the author and the American Psychological Association from *J. abnorm. soc. Psychol.*, 1961, 63, 466–492.

Method

PROCEDURE

THE follow-up measures of the children were obtained in the spring of 1958, when the children were in the sixth grade and were mainly between 11–6 and 12–6 years of age; for communicative convenience they will be called "12-year-olds." This year was chosen because the schools operated on a 6-3-3 division, and the sixth grade was the last occasion on which the children would be together in a single-teacher grade, permitting ratings of school behavior by a teacher who had full time supervision of a given child.

The measures obtained were of four kinds. First, there was a series of self-administering scales, constructed or adapted for the present purpose, for the measurement of masculinity-feminity, self-concept, nurturance, adult versus child role choice, and five aspects of aggressive attitude. Second, standardized teacher interviews were recorded, transcribed, and coded for the measurement of other displays of a few of these same variables. Third, a story completion measure of guilt was obtained. And fourth, a realistic test situation for the measurement of resistance to temptation was administered (Grinder, 1960). The present report describes only those findings relating to aggression which were obtained from the self-administered scales. Although an attempt was made to include measures of the children's aggression in the teacher interviews, the teachers were unable to report on this aspect of behavior with sufficient clarity to provide useful data. This may have resulted, in part, from the institutional nonpermissiveness for child aggression toward either teacher or peers at the sixth grade level. The major difficulty in securing teacher interview measures stemmed from the lack of discriminable differences.

SUBJECTS

OF the original 379 children studied (Sears *et al.*, 1957), approximately 200 had moved out of the school districts in which they had originally lived; to arrange for securing their cooperation and that of the schools and teachers in their new locations promised a very heavy expense. Therefore, the new measures were secured from only those children who were enrolled in the sixth grade classrooms of the schools, in the original towns, in which seven or more of the sample were currently enrolled. The consequence of this selective procedure was that completed aggression attitude scales were obtained from 160 of the original 379 subjects, and also from 377 other sixth graders who had not been in the original study. In the following discussion, the 160 "originals" who had been subjects (Sears *et al.*, 1957) are referred to as the *follow-up sample,* and the others as the 1958 *classmates.* The teachers were interviewed only about members of the sample group—and of course only for that group are the child rearing measures from mother interviews available—so that data analyses involving internal comparisons within the self-administered measures will be presented for the *combined* groups, follow-up sample and classmates, but analyses involving antecedent-consequent comparisons from the 1951–52 mother interviews must be limited to the follow-up sample group.

. . .

Measurement of Aggression

HOW does one measure aggression in 12-year-olds? Clearly, the answer rests on what theory is adopted as to the genesis and dynamics of such behavior. There have been two main views about the matter that have influenced measurement and interpretation in both the clinical and experimental settings. One of these is instinctual and drive oriented; the other rests on a general theory of action and learning. Neither has been spelled out in sufficient detail to permit a purely theoretical derivation of appropriate methods of measurement. However, researchers who lean toward the instinctual view have tended to emphasize the use of projective methods, while those who find action theory more congenial have tended to use social behavioral measures. A brief comment on each will make clear the reasoning that led to the choice of instruments in the present study.

The notion that there is a certain quantum of internal instigation to aggression has been inherent in much of psychological theory for some time. It was expressed most explicitly first by Freud (1922) in his conception of the death instinct. This nativistic position gave little attention to the origins of individual differences in amount or quality of aggressive behavior except by implication; childhood experience and environmental influences could excite or inhibit the expression of the instinctual impulse, and could displace it outward. From the measurement standpoint, such a theory seems to imply that there are various alternative behavioral indices of the underlying motive. The chief aim in choosing one rather than another is to obtain the freest (least inhibited) expression. Thus, a favorite device for the measure of many types of primary or secondary "drive induced" behavior is some projective technique such as the TAT, story completion, or doll play. These methods are assumed to aid in circumventing social inhibitions that would otherwise suppress the full expression of the drive. They represent an effort to sample the "true" uninhibited quantum. However, while there is no question that projective responses do reveal the existence of instigation to aggressive, sexual, achievement, and other socially controlled actions, there is also good evidence that such projections are themselves strongly influenced by momentary conditions of excitation and inhibition (Clark, 1955; R. R. Sears, 1951).

The alternative theory makes no assumption about a quantum of internal instigation that must be uninhibitedly tapped. On the contrary, it presumes that whole classes of aggressive acts are learned as responses to many different stimulus situations. By stimulus generalization, these acts come to be evoked by great ranges of stimuli, both internal and external, including ones that are symbolic or have imaginal qualities only. By response generalization, acts can shift from one action category to another (e.g., from physical to verbal) or from one psychological function to another (e.g., from overt action to imagination or fantasy). Indeed, the lability of expression is so great that even entirely novel stimulational settings and manipulanda seem able to elicit and provide a means of expression of aggressive acts. Each such setting has its own instigative value, deriving from direct reinforcements in the past, as well as from primary or secondary stimulus generalization. This effective instigative value is a cumulation of both excitatory and inhibitory values, of course.[1]

This emphasis on stimulus situations need not exclude internal instigators, including those having essentially the qualities of drives. Indeed, in one respect, *Frustration and Aggression* (Dollard, Doob, Miller, Mowrer, & Sears, 1939), which first formally presented the action and learning theory of aggression, was not at all dissimilar to the earlier instinctual view; it simply relocated the source of impulsion from instincts to a frustration drive created by the cumulated frustrations of motivated behaviors of all kinds. The internal source was changed from a native reservoir of energy to an experience-induced drive state. More importantly, however, this view introduced individual differences into the source of internal instigation, and placed the internal instigator in the same category of operationally definable antecedents as the external ones.

The relevance of these theoretical matters to the problem of measurement lies in the assumptions that must be made about what is being measured. From a drive theory, one seeks to tap that way of behavioral expression of the drive that suffers least interference from either internal controls (e.g., anxiety, conscience) or external threateners (e.g., authority or moral symbols). The acceptability of any index can be evaluated either by a

1 McDougall's (1908) instinct of pugnacity rested somewhere between these two views. It did not assume a pool or reservoir of internal instigation (drive), but neither did it rely explicitly on learning principles to account for individual differences in directions and qualities of aggressive acts; these were instinctually organized action patterns.

priori analysis of the measurement situation with respect to freedom from inhibition, or by appeal to some criterion against which the index can be validated. Projective techniques commonly have received acceptance on a priori grounds—mainly, it is to be feared, as a result of uncritical analysis of the inhibiting potentialities of the test situation—or their validity has been tested against other behavioral measures which are themselves accepted on a priori grounds.

With an action and learning theory, the measurement problem is somewhat different. Measurement in this case means discovering the strength of specifically defined aggressive actions in specifically defined stimulating conditions. It is assumed that the measured "strength" or "amount" is a product of all past direct reinforcements and inhibitions plus all relevant stimulus and response generalizations of both excitation and inhibition. A measure is evaluated by three criteria: agreement by theorists that the measure is relevant to their interests and is not grossly mislabeled, provision of a consistent response value under standard conditions (i.e., adequate reliability), and lawful relationships to independently measured antecedent learning conditions or coincident stimulating conditions. Most measures of aggression, both projective and otherwise, meet the first criterion—if the theorists collected for judging are not too heterogeneous a lot. Reliability is more difficult. Projective methods, particularly those that are susceptible to the influence of permissiveness in their administration, do not usually provide high coefficients on a test-retest basis, though odd-even reliability may be satisfactory. But the most important criterion is the third. If stable and theoretically meaningful relationships can be found between a given measure of aggression and some past experience or concurrent situation, the measure itself must have adequate reliability even though this cannot be demonstrated by formal methods of evaluation. Single acts that cannot be repeated (e.g., a lynching), and acts the potentiality for which suffers modification simply as a result of their own performance (e.g., doll play aggression), provide special difficulty in this respect. Quite a number of them have nevertheless provided useful antecedent-consequent relationships.

To return, now, to the question of how to measure aggressiveness in sixth grade children. There are many types of aggressive actions and many instigating situations that evoke them. The majority of these acts are impossible to measure directly; overt aggression toward mother in the absence of the father, self-aggression when alone, spontaneous fantasy aggression toward symbolic authority figures, etc., do not lend themselves readily to measurement, reliable or otherwise, even though they might be excellent choices from the standpoint of the first and third criteria. What does seem practical, however, is the use of standardized forms of self-report of attitudes, and the securing of reports of overt behavior from outside observers. For the latter, there are three main sources that would be useful to have—parents, teacher, and peers—because of their systematically different stimulus significance to a child. The procedural limitations of the present study led us to seek only the teacher observations, and they proved useless with respect to aggression. For self-reports of attitudes, scales were constructed to measure five aspects of aggression, and they proved useful.

AGGRESSION SCALES

THESE scales were composed of items in the form of declarative sentences with which the subject could express his agreement or disagreement on a five-point scale ranging from "strongly agree" through "not sure" to "strongly disagree." The content of each item was designed to express one type of aggression (or its rejection). The presumption was that the reading of a statement would arouse an imaginal representation of the act or feeling described, and that marking the scale would be, by response generalization, an affirmation or rejection of that representation. A score of 5 was given to the "strongly agree" or "strongly disagree" end of the five-point scale that represented acceptance of the type of aggressive action or feeling portrayed by that item. The next position received a 4, and so on. A total score for each of the five scales was obtained by cumulating these individual item scores for all the items belonging to a given aggression scale. The five scales were as follows:

Aggression anxiety • This scale measured feelings of fear, discomfort, and dislike of aggression. The aggressive stimulus to the arousal of such feelings was placed, in some items, in the person himself ("It upsets me to think some thoughtless word or crack of mine might hurt someone's feelings") and sometimes outside the self ("It makes me uncomfortable to see two of my friends fighting"). These external stimulus conditions ranged from the personal or social, as in the last example, to relatively impersonal or symbolic external events ("If someone gets hurt in an auto accident, I usually try to get a good view of what happened"). The signs of the anxiety in response to aggressive stimulation included references to avoidance behavior, somatic symptoms, guilty feelings, expectations of injury or trouble, and the use of descriptive words indicative of strong negative feelings ("vicious crimes").

Projected aggression • This scale measured the tendency to attribute aggression to sources outside the self. The items included a range of *objects* of hostility, including the self. The *agents* of aggression ranged from specific ("Big dogs are likely to be dangerous") to very general ("Sometimes I feel that there are so many bad people in the world that even my own town is about as dangerous to live in as a real jungle"). The agents to whom aggression was attributed included people, animals, and natural forces. About half the items involved aggression toward the self from other sources, and the other half reflected aggression toward other objects. Of those which reflected aggression toward the self, some involved derogation, and some represented overt aggression.

Self-aggression • All items referred to injury or punishment to the self. Two described impulses toward suicide, two related to self-punishment from other sources than the self, and one referred to accidents to the self.

Prosocial aggression • The dimensions represented by this scale and the next one were first described by Johnson (1951) in her study of doll play aggression in 5- and 8-year-old children. Prosocial aggression is aggression used in a socially approved way for purposes that are acceptable to the moral standards of the group. The items referred to law enforcement, strictness of control, punishment for rule breaking, and insistence on appropriate rules about aggression ("When a person has broken an important rule, he should definitely be punished for it"). A high score on this scale is a positively aggressive score, but the form of aggression is in favor of socially acceptable controls and disciplines. In its extreme form, prosocial aggression probably represents "moral righteousness." However, a low score could be the product of either one of two characteristics in the person: a low level of aggressive reactivity, or a tendency to be aggressive in unacceptable ways, with resistance to authority or the rules of the group. Four of the eight items that composed the scale would be influenced by this rejection of authority, and four would not be. In the absence of other information, then, a low score on this scale cannot be clearly interpreted. A high score does clearly mean a high aggressiveness of this socially accepted sort.

Antisocial aggression • This dimension contrasts with the previous one in the sense that the aggressions referred to here are ones that are normally unacceptable socially in the formal pattern of our culture. Some items included a reference to the positive desirability of powerful aggressive motivation, others to the acceptability of ordinarily disapproved forms of aggression, and still others to the "naturalness" of aggression as a form of social interaction ("Sometimes an actual fight is the only way to settle an argument"). In terms of our contemporary middle class American culture, antisocial aggression represents a much lower level of socialization than does prosocial aggression. A high score may be interpreted as indicating a strongly aggressive person without social control. A low score may describe a person without much aggressive reactivity, or one whose aggression takes other forms, such as the prosocial.[2]

. . .

RELIABILITY

The 1958 Classmates (i.e., the sixth graders who participated in this testing but were *not* members of the follow-up sample) have been used as a group on which to determine the odd-even reliabilities of the five scales. In TABLE 1 are shown the numbers of items remaining in each scale after the second validation series, the number of children on whose papers reliability scores could be calculated, and both the uncorrected and corrected (Spearman-Brown) coefficients of reliability.

TABLE 1. *Odd-even reliabilities of the five aggression scales: 1958 classmates* (Sexes combined)

SCALE	NUMBER OF ITEMS	NUMBER OF CASES	PEARSON r UNCORRECTED	CORRECTED
Aggression anxiety	12	363	.44	.61
Projected aggression	14	361	.44	.61
Self-aggression	5	348	.08	.15
Prosocial aggression	8	364	.46	.63
Antisocial aggression	9	364	.49	.64

The corrected reliability coefficients for aggression anxiety, and projected, prosocial, and antisocial aggression are all .6 or better. That for self-aggression is significant at just the $p = .01$ level, which is scarcely promising for a reliability coefficient! Furthermore, the 10 correlations among the five items, for the 174 classmates boys, range from $-.12$ to $+.31$, with a median of $+.02$; for the 170 girls, the range is $-.14$ to $+.28$, with a median of $+.12$. Nevertheless, as will be seen later, the boys' scores on this scale appear to have certain theoretically predictable relationships with child rearing antecedents, and it may be that, as in the case of certain aptitude tests, the total score has greater stability than is implied by the intercorrelations among its components. Obviously, later results on self-aggression must be interpreted with considerable caution.

2 Technical material describing scale construction, collection of data, and report on reliability follows in the original paper. [Ed.]

Results and Discussion

INTERCORRELATIONS AMONG SCALES

IN TABLE 2 are shown, separately by sex, the intercorrelations among the five scales for the total 1958 group, both follow-up and classmates combined. In TABLE 3 are shown, for the follow-up sample, the intercorrelations among not only the aggression scales but also four measures of child behavior obtained from the mother interviews 7 years earlier. The intercorrelations among the five aggression scales are similar for the follow-up sample and the total population except in one instance; boys' projected and antisocial aggression are correlated .23 in the follow-up sample but only .04 in the total population (which

TABLE 2. *Intercorrelations of aggression scales: total tested population* (Girls: $N = 264$; Boys: $N = 261$)

BOYS \ GIRLS	SCALE	1	2	3	4	5
Aggression anxiety	1		.19	.08	.45	−.44
Projected aggression	2	.35		.44	.18	.17
Self-aggression	3	.24	.39		−.02	.07
Prosocial aggression	4	.50	.13	.12		−.15
Antisocial aggression	5	−.39	.04	.02	−.32	

NOTE.—Girls' figures above the diagonal, boys' below.

TABLE 3. *Intercorrelations of aggression scales and four age 5 measures of child behavior: follow-up sample* (Girls: $N = 84$; Boys: $N = 76$)

BOYS \ GIRLS	SCALE	1	2	3	4	5	6	7	8	9
Aggression anxiety	1		.19	.11	.40	—.48	.18	.04	—.24	.00
Projected aggression	2	.23		.38	.14	.23	—.06	—.03	—.16	—.05
Self-aggression	3	.25	.42		—.01	—.01	.04	.05	—.07	.24
Prosocial aggression	4	.61	.05	.10		—.03	.04	—.08	—.40	.18
Antisocial aggression	5	—.33	.23	.14	—.36		—.08	—.10	—.03	—.12
Aggression: age 5	6	—.21	.05	—.10	—.18	—.03		.14	—.14	.02
Dependency: age 5	7	—.16	.01	.03	.00	.06	.02		.02	.17
Conscience: age 5	8	.30	.08	.00	.04	—.06	—.16	.06		.02
Bed-wetting: age 5	9	—.17	.05	—.18	—.03	.00	.10	.10	—.37	

NOTE.—Girls' figures above the diagonal, boys' below.

includes the sample). The theoretical implications of these matrices will be discussed in connection with results of the antecedent-consequent comparisons.

SEX DIFFERENCES

In TABLE 4 are shown, for the combined groups, the means and *SD*s of the scores on the five aggression scales for each sex, together with the significance of the sex differences. The girls are significantly higher on prosocial aggression and aggression anxiety, while the boys are substantially higher on antisocial aggression. There are no sex differences on the other two scales.

TABLE 4. *Sex differences on the five aggression scales: total tested population* (Girls: $N = 264$; Boys: $N = 261$)

SCALE	GIRLS *M*	GIRLS *SD*	BOYS *M*	BOYS *SD*	SEX DIFFERENCES	*CR*
Aggression anxiety	6.11	1.49	4.82	1.63	1.29	9.46
Projected aggression	4.51	1.87	4.53	1.90	.02	.123
Self-aggression	4.13	1.65	4.27	1.61	.14	.986
Prosocial aggression	5.46	1.48	4.81	1.74	.65	4.61
Antisocial aggression	4.75	1.66	6.09	1.82	1.34	8.80

NOTE.—Figures given here are based on a scale of 1–9 that covered the full range of obtained scores on each test.

As was mentioned earlier, a test of masculinity-femininity was also administered to the children. It was constructed from the 38 items of the Fe scale in Gough's CPI (1957). That scale was revised and revalidated for the present student to make it more suitable for this younger age group. The scale as used had quite satisfactory odd-even reliability, and intrasex validity of the 33 individual items retained from the original form was uniformly acceptable, as was the intersex validity of all but four items.

In the present connection, it is interesting to note that the correlations within each sex between femininity and both prosocial aggression and aggression anxiety are significantly positive, and those between femininity and antisocial aggression are significantly negative. Thus, the directions of differences in means *between* sexes are similarly reflected in directions of correlations *within* each sex.

These findings suggest that high prosocial aggression is a feminine quality, and high antisocial aggression is a masculine one. Coupled with the feminine reluctance to express this latter type of attitude is a higher level of aggression anxiety.

Comment • These sex differences in kinds of aggressive feelings are an objectification of a rather common cultural stereotype. Girls are more fearful, more passive, more conforming to social norms and proprieties; boys are more violent, rougher, and more destructive. It is impossible to tell to what extent our measuring instrument reflects an expression of inner feelings and to what extent it provides opportunity for the acquiescent expression of socially appropriate attitudes. Doubtless both factors influence the responses children make in such a situation. On the one hand, as our theory of measurement suggests, the questionnaire items probably evoke imagery and feelings that are stable and relatively long-enduring; but on the other, one must recognize that the very setting in which the scales are presented contains stimuli appropriate for eliciting stereotyped reactions. The children are seated among their peers of both sexes; they are in the school room; they are faced and instructed by adults. Whatever attitudinal expressions have become attached to these stimulus conditions, whether "stereotypes" or not, are elicited in some degree.

This distinction between feelings and stereotypic attitudes may or may not be important for an understanding of the structure of aggression. But since our present main interest is in the effects of early experience on these behaviors, the issue can be held in abeyance while we discover whether there are, in fact, predictable (or detectable) relations between these measures and the hypothesized antecedents. If so, then the question that needs to be raised—as with any measure—is as to how widely these particular measures may be generalized to other instances of aggressive behavior. The remainder of the present study, however, is devoted to the antecedent-consequent problem.

PERMISSIVENESS AND PUNITIVENESS

THE effect of maternal punitiveness on preschool children's aggressive behavior has been shown in two previous studies. In the earlier (Sears, Whiting, Nowlis, & Sears, 1953), the mothers of 40 3- and 4-year-olds were interviewed with respect to their control of aggression. Ratings of the severity of their customary punishments were made from transcribed interviews. The amount of aggressive behavior shown by the children in a preschool was measured both by teacher ratings and by direct observation. For boys, the relationship between amount of aggression shown and the severity of maternal punitiveness was clearly positive. For girls, however, the relationship was curvilinear, both the most and least severely punished girls being less aggressive than those suffering an intermediate amount of punishment.

An hypothesis was suggested that punishment serves as a form of frustration and hence increases the total instigation to aggression, but that when punishment becomes sufficiently severe, it inhibits the specific actions punished; in such cases, the increased aggressive instigation would be manifested only in forms of aggressive activity different enough from those punished not to suffer from inhibition by means of stimulus or response generalization. To account for the sex difference in the obtained data, it was further hypothesized that although the interviews with boys' and girls' mothers did not reveal any average difference in severity of punishment, the girls, by identification, *felt* more punished than did the presumably less highly identified boys. Support for the initial hypothesis was gained from doll play, in which girls as well as boys showed a direct relationship between frequency of aggressive acts and the severity of their mothers' punishment. The data did not permit a test of the identification hypothesis.

The original study of the present subjects (Sears *et al.*, 1957), made when they were of kindergarten age, likewise found a positive relationship between child aggression and maternal punishment. In this instance, there was no independent measure of the children's aggression; it was rated from the same interview as the measure of severity of punishment for aggression expressed toward the parents, and referred to aggression *in the home* only. However, with these data, there was no evidence of a curvilinear relationship in the girls, and we were forced to conclude either that the previously noted curvilinear relationship was a sampling error, or that the inhibitory influence of severe punishment was evident only in the school and not in the home. Theoretical reasons for the latter interpretation are not immediately obvious.

A second maternal variable shown to be positively related to aggression in the home, in this same study, was permissiveness for expression of aggression toward the parents. Permissiveness was defined as an attitude of acceptance and expectation that a child will want to be aggressive. Although permissiveness and punishment were negatively correlated with one another, both were positively correlated with child's aggression in the home.

Aggression at age 5 • These findings from the total original population are accurately represented in the follow-up sample. In TABLE 5 are shown the correlations, separately by sex of child, between 9 available child measures, including the five aggression scales taken at age 12 and 4 of the measures taken at age 5 (dependency, aggression, conscience, bedwetting), and 12 of the measures of maternal attitude or behavior obtained from the interviews. Attention is called to the *r*'s between the age 5 measure of aggression and the measures of permissiveness and punishment for aggression toward the parents. In the original data on 379 cases, aggression at age 5 (III, 29) correlated with permissiveness for expression of aggression toward parents (III, 30) (boys) .20 and (girls) .24, and with punishment (III, 31) (boys) .14 and (girls) .18. In the follow-up sample, the figures are similar.[3]

These measures of antecedent-consequent relationships are low, but all are in the correct direction to indicate that amount of reported aggression in the home at age 5 was positively related to both *high permissiveness* and *high punishment.* From a theoretical standpoint, this is interpreted to mean that permissiveness represented both cue or signal instigation to aggression, and an implied reinforcement, while punishment produced instigation by frustration, and conflict induced instigation. A third role that can be played by punishment—but for which there was no evidence in the original *Patterns* study comparable to that obtained on girls in the Iowa study (Sears *et al.,* 1953)—is that of inhibitor of the punished response. As will be seen below, this inhibitory influence is clearly detectable by age 12.

Antisocial aggression at age 12 • The five aggression scales provide a more differentiated measure of the children's later aggression than did the single interview rating at age 5. Unfortunately, there is no measure directly comparable to that rating, i.e., a measure of aggression in the home. Probably the one scale most comparable to it, however, is that for antisocial aggression. The early rating attempted to measure the amount of aggression the child showed in the home, mainly that directed at the parents. Since most of the mothers disapproved of such behavior in some degree, it must be considered a major early form of unsocialized—or antisocial—aggression. The items in the antisocial scale did not refer to the same kinds of aggressive acts, nor to the same objects of aggression, but they were meant to be representative of unsocialized and unacceptable forms of aggression at age 12. None of them included a

3 A broader measure of the permissiveness and punitiveness aspects of maternal behavior was constructed by Maccoby and Whiting (unpublished), on the basis of Milton's (1958) factor analysis of the original interview scales, for an analysis of the antecedents of the deviation doll play performed by the children at age 5. The permissiveness measure was constructed by summing four permissiveness scales: aggression toward parents, sex, dependency, and care of house and furniture. The broader punitiveness score was composed of punishment for aggression toward parents, physical punishment, demands for child to be aggressive toward other children, and irritation with dependency. These two constructed measures are called the permissiveness factor and punishment factor scores. Correlations of these scores with the various child measures are given in TABLES 5, 7, and 9, but it must be remembered that they are not independent of the separate scales of which they are composed. In general, they add little beyond what is provided by the individual scales to an interpretation of the mother-child relationships except in connection with aggression anxiety and self-aggression, and they will not be discussed elsewhere.

TABLE 5. *Correlations between the nine child behavior measures* (five aggression scales and four age 5 ratings) *and twelve measures of mothers' child rearing practices or attitudes: follow-up sample*

CHILD BEHAVIOR MEASURES	Permissiveness: Aggression to parents III, 30	Permissiveness factor XVIII, 5	Permissiveness for dependency XV, 5	Punishment: Aggression to parents III, 31	Punishment factor XVIII, 6	Physical punishment III, 46	Deprivation of privileges III, 47	Tangible rewards III, 36	Use of praise III, 37	Withdrawal of love III, 53	Mother warmth III, 15	Severity of toilet training II, 51
	CHILD REARING VARIABLE											
	GIRLS ($N = 84$)											
Aggression anxiety	—.20	—.13	—.02	.24	.23	.07	—.06	.03	.06	—.17	—.04	.10
Projected aggression	—.25	—.22	.05	—.08	—.12	—.09	.04	—.03	—.01	—.03	—.01	.09
Self-aggression	—.09	—.17	—.08	.11	.10	.12	.06	.19	.03	—.40	—.06	.12
Prosocial aggression	—.23	—.12	.08	.18	.21	.22	—.08	—.04	—.02	—.14	—.13	.02
Antisocial aggression	.02	.03	.10	—.13	—.15	—.06	.02	—.02	—.09	—.10	.19	.02
Aggression: age 5	.19	—.04	—.13	.18	.34	.23	.28	.13	.18	—.07	—.33	.03
Dependency: age 5	—.03	—.08	—.14	.09	.03	—.02	—.06	.09	—.11	.33	—.16	.19
Conscience: age 5	.26	.26	.06	—.10	—.23	—.25	.11	—.04	.19	.11	—.09	—.05
Bed-wetting: age 5	—.02	—.07	—.10	.08	.17	.13	—.09	.11	—.02	—.20	—.14	—.01
	BOYS ($N = 76$)											
Aggression anxiety	—.17	—.23	.12	.10	.04	—.03	.13	.04	—.08	.21	.09	.06
Projected aggression	.17	.06	—.12	—.16	—.10	—.12	.18	.08	—.01	.27	.06	.08
Self-aggression	—.06	—.15	—.02	.03	.22	.11	.24	.39	—.14	.48	—.07	.27
Prosocial aggression	—.09	—.20	—.10	.04	—.05	—.04	.06	—.09	—.04	.10	.09	—.03
Antisocial aggression	.18	.23	.04	—.20	—.15	—.08	.10	.04	—.14	—.01	.11	.04
Aggression: age 5	.27	.20	—.11	.11	.11	.22	.00	.04	—.02	.14	—.18	.14
Dependency: age 5	.06	—.04	—.06	.02	.16	.06	—.08	.15	.19	—.10	.06	.19
Conscience: age 5	—.13	—.20	.08	—.03	—.28	—.25	—.14	—.17	.19	.03	.15	—.01
Bed-wetting: age 5	.05	.21	—.02	—.18	—.04	—.02	—.21	—.04	.06	—.22	—.05	.12

NOTE.—Below each named scale is given the code number from Appendix B of *Patterns of Child Rearing* (Sears, Maccoby, & Levin, 1957). Significance levels for girls: when $r = .21$, $p = .05$; when $r = .28$, $p = .01$. Significance levels for boys: when $r = .23$, $p = .05$; when $r = .29$, $p = .01$.

reference to parents or the home, so the similarity is but partial. And, of course, there is the radical difference between mother's report and self-report.

One would expect that antisocial aggression would be negatively correlated with those scales most representative of more highly socialized and acceptable attitudes toward aggression. Among the present dimensions, these would be prosocial aggression and aggression anxiety. In TABLE 2, which shows the intercorrelations obtained from the entire tested population, this expectation can be seen to be fulfilled; for both sexes the *r*'s are negative, although that between antisocial and prosocial in girls is significant at only the .02 level. If we can assume that the total tested population gives the more reliable measure, this low relation is apparently the product of a sampling accident within the smaller follow-up sample, which contributes to the total tested population; in that sample, the relationship in girls disappears altogether, although the other three coefficients are approximately the same as for the larger population (cf. TABLE 3).

A second expectation might be that the rating at age 5 would be positively related to the antisocial score at age 12. This rests on the presumption of a continuity of both the child's habitual reactions and the mother's methods of child rearing. Evidently this reasoning is not sound, for in TABLE 3 it may be seen that for the boys the *r* is −.03 and for the girls, −.08; in other words, effectively zero for both. The implications of this discontinuity from age 5 to age 12 will be considered in a later section.

The relation of permissiveness and punitiveness to all the aggression scales can be seen in TABLE 5. For antisocial, punishment for aggression to parents is negatively related in both sexes, though neither of the coefficients reaches the .05 level of significance. This is the opposite direction from the relations found between these same measures and the rating of aggression at age 5. If it can be presumed that these two child measures are tapping somewhat similar instigation-action sequences, then we may suppose that, during the intervening years, the inhibitory effect of the punishment had an opportunity to be influential; no longer was the punishment for aggression simply a goad to further action —it reduced the tendency to express the punished forms of behavior.

The zero correlations between age 5 ratings and antisocial, however, show that the shift was not a simple unidirectional matter. Some children suffered inhibition—and reduced aggression—while others did not. Likewise some who had been low at age 5 remained low, some became higher at age 12. The reasons for this may involve some constitutional quality in the children, in part, or what is more likely, some unmeasured change in the mother's child rearing behavior. As will be shown below in the section on Change from Age 5 to Age 12, however, there were suggestive differences in the original rearing patterns that are consistently associated with certain of these variations. It may be said at once that the severity of punishment itself played only a limited role.

The contrast, at the two ages, in the relation of severity of punishment for aggression toward parents is presented graphically in FIGURE 1. The abscissa shows three degrees of punishment (III, 31) as measured from the mother interviews taken when the children were age 5. The age 5 measure of aggression was from the same interviews; the age 12 measure is the antisocial aggression scale. As would be expected from the correlations reported in TABLE 5, the age 5 relationship (*t* between low and high groups) in girls is significant at <.01, while in the boys it is nonsignificant. At age 12, the decrease for boys is significant at the .08 level, while the girls show no variations at all. The difference in trend between the two ages is significant for both sexes; the difference between the two *r*'s for each is at the .05 level.

A relation of permissiveness to antisocial aggression is suggested only in the boys, however (+.18). It may be supposed that either the mother's attitude of expecting and tolerating aggression carried over its influence from the early years, or that mothers tended to be somewhat consistent in their levels of permis-

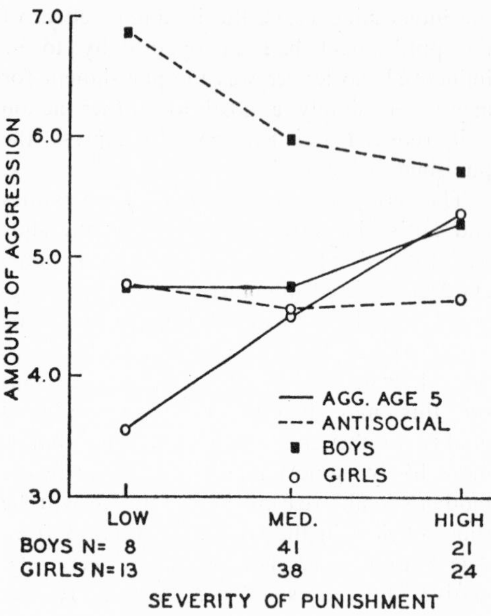

FIGURE 1

Amount of aggression in the home at age 5 and antisocial aggression at age 12 in relation to severity of punishment for aggression toward parents as rated from mother interviews. (The figure is based on only those cases for which measures were available on all three variables.)

siveness as the boys matured. There is no evident relationship between permissiveness and antisocial aggression in girls. The distribution of girls' scores on their mothers' permissiveness for aggression toward parents is severely skewed, however, and the r is probably an inappropriate measure of this relationship. In fact, the seven most permissively treated girls were all above the median on the antisocial aggression scale.

These various relationships may be summarized as follows: for both sexes, high punishment for aggression in the first 5 years of life was associated with a high level of reported aggression in the home, but at age 12 it was associated with a low level of antisocial aggression. In boys, at both ages, high permissiveness was associated with high aggression; in girls, this effect was clearly evident only at the earlier age, with a mere suspicion of it at the later.

In our earlier report (Sears *et al.*, 1957, p. 401), it was shown that mothers of girls were already less permissive of aggression, when the children were but 5 years old, than were the mothers of boys. One cannot but wonder whether the stricter attitude of control toward girls may not have increased even more during the middle childhood years, and produced an essentially homogeneous level of permissiveness—or at least an even more severely truncated distribution. If this were the case, the lack of correlation between the earlier measure of the mothers' attitudes and their daughters' 12-year-old aggressive responses would be quite understandable on purely statistical grounds.

Aggression anxiety and prosocial aggression at age 12 • Three possible effects of punishment have already been mentioned—instigation to aggression by frustration, and by conflict drive, and inhibition of the punished response. A fourth must also be considered —the establishment of anxiety as a response to whatever instigators are present when punishment occurs. In the present context, the anxiety with which we are concerned is elicited by the same stimuli as aggressive responses, plus the response produced cues arising from overt or imaginal or affective aggressive actions. Hence with the present instruments we would expect a positive relationship to develop between punishment for aggression to parents and aggression anxiety. TABLE 5 shows that the expectation is fulfilled in the girls ($p < .05$), but not in the boys. Thus far, then, one can only say that the theoretical prediction is but half-supported.

The relation of punishment to prosocial aggression is the same as to aggression anxiety. High punishment is associated with high prosocial aggression in girls, but is unrelated in boys. This positive effect of punishment is similar to that found in girls for aggression in the home at age 5; at that time, too, this relationship was nonsignificant in boys.

So, what sifts out of these rather complex comparisons is that severe early punishment for aggression tended to reduce antisocial aggression (a little more clearly so in boys) and to increase prosocial aggression (but only in girls). Nevertheless, in both sexes, prosocial aggression is as unrelated to earlier aggression as is antisocial aggression. Since both types of aggression are strongly related to aggression anxiety in both sexes—prosocial positively and antisocial negatively—it comes as a shock to discover that the earlier aggression is *positively* related to aggression anxiety in girls and *negatively* in boys. The implications of this finding are considered below in the section on Aggression Anxiety.

Since the various attitude scale correlations referred to in this discussion of the follow-up sample are approximately replicated in the total tested population (with the single exception of the size of the negative relation between antisocial and prosocial), we are forced to the conclusion that these sex differences surrounding the early measure of aggression and the aggression anxiety measure have something to do with changes that occurred between ages 5 and 12, and with differences in the sources of aggression anxiety for the two sexes.

Mention must be made also of the role of permissiveness in connection with aggression anxiety and prosocial aggression. Both are related negatively to permissiveness, though significantly so only in the girls. Since permissiveness and punishment are rather closely related to one another (see TABLE 9), there is some difficulty in being certain how independent the contributions of the two measures are.

Projected and self-aggression • These two remaining aggression scales are significantly associated with each other and with aggression anxiety and prosocial aggression in boys; the same is true for girls, except that self-aggression seems unrelated to aggression anxiety and prosocial (cf. TABLES 2 and 3).

The relationship to permissiveness and punishment is not entirely clear. In girls, projected aggression acts like part of the anxiety cluster with respect to permissiveness; nonpermissiveness is associated with high projection. In boys, the relation is nonsignificantly opposite. For both, punishment is nonsignificantly negative. The relations for self-aggression can best be considered later; an understanding of their antecedents will require analysis of other variables.

Conclusions • When the children's aggression at home was measured in the original mother interviews, there was evidence that both permissiveness and punishment for aggression served to facilitate such behavior. Permissiveness appeared to serve as both an instigator and a symbolic reinforcer, while punishment had its predominant effect as a further frustration and hence a goad to more aggression. The correlations that displayed these relations in the original group were significant but small; because of the reduced size of the follow-up sample, although the sizes of the correlations are similar, they are no longer statistically significant. However, the directions of the relationships in this smaller group are the same.

The more differentiated measures at age 12 appear to illustrate a rather radical shift in the role of punishment. Formerly an instigator to antisocial aggression, it now seems to have imposed an inhibitory influence on that behavior and to have created aggression anxiety. The interesting thing about the various scales is that the three nonantisocial scales—which are positively related to anxiety —seem, if anything, to enjoy a facilitating effect from punishment. It looks as though the conflict-drive effect of punishment were still operating, producing higher prosocial and self-aggression while the inhibitory influence reduced the antisocial aggression. Projective aggression, which in terms of its correlations with the other scales appears to be a part of both the anxiety cluster and the antisocial, is influenced by permissiveness in the same way as is aggression anxiety, and by punishment in the same way as is antisocial aggression.

Having only two chronological points of measurement—ages 5 and 12—one falls easily into a manner of speaking that implies the operation of one effect of punishment (facilitating) at one age and another effect (inhibiting) at the other. This is improper, of course. One can only suppose that both effects of punishment are always operative. The fact that at the earlier age the two interact in such a way as to allow the facilitative effect to be revealed in group averages, and at a later age the inhibitory effect, probably means that with the particular levels of punishment, permissiveness and other relevant variables occurring in this culture, the facilitating effects are more pronounced in early stages of socialization and the inhibitory ones do not appear so generally until later. Indeed, the concept of conflict-drive itself (Sears *et al.*, 1953) implies the simultaneous influence of both properties.

In summary, the influence of these two child rearing variables may be hypothesized to have been as follows: high punishment for aggression reduced antisocial aggression, but increased aggression anxiety and prosocial aggression, and high permissiveness increased antisocial aggression, but reduced the other two. Only 2 of the 12 correlations on which these statements are based reach the .05 level of significance, but the remaining 10 nonsignificant *r*'s are all in the right direction, and 5 of them are at the .10 level of significance. The evidence overall, in other words, is of just borderline significance, and though these hypotheses are congruent with the theoretical expectations concerning the influence of punishment and permissiveness, the conclusions must be accepted with considerable caution.

ALTERNATIVE RESPONSES: THE CHANGE FROM AGE 5 TO AGE 12

One of the thorniest problems in aggression theory is that of alternative responses (cf. Berkowitz, 1958). It is really two problems, although these are often fused—and confused—into one. The first is catharsis. Both the instinct view and the frustration-drive concept assume a certain quantum of internal instigation that requires expression. If overt aggression is prohibited, then the impulse will be displayed in nonovert or fantasy or some other form of aggression not expected to elicit punishment (or counteraggression). This "discharge" (Freud, 1922), or "goal response" (Dollard *et al.*, 1939), serves to reduce the strength of the residual impulse, thus, decreasing the probability of further aggressive behavior immediately thereafter. The term *catharsis* refers to this letting loose of drive instigated behavior, the lowering of tension, and by analogy to the original use of the term in connection with hysterical symptoms, the reduction of alternative expressions. An instinct theory that made no room for individual differences in the strength of the impulse would predict a negative correlation between the strengths of two temporally adjacent aggressive acts. A behavior theory (Dollard *et al.*, 1939) that did assume individual differences—on the basis of either constitutional factors or stimulus input variation—would make more equivocal predictions, because if the *range* of individual differences were large enough in comparison with the size of the cathartic reduction, a correlational measure could be positive. Obviously correlational methods are inappropriate for this problem. Empirical investigation of this hypothesis has so far led to quite ambiguous results, but they need not concern us here for the present data are irrelevant to the catharsis aspect of alternative responses.

The other aspect has to do with traits, or habitual forms of aggressive action. Regardless of which of the two foregoing views concerning internal instigation is chosen, there is a clear question as to whether the inhibition of one form of aggression is likely to be associated with the stronger development of others. The time interval implied in this question is a long one—months and years—in contrast with that implied in the catharsis hypothesis. Whereas catharsis refers to an action-theory construct of immediate drive reduction and ensuing performance strength, the habitual-form question relates to the learning process and the factors determining choice of expressive form.

With respect to this issue also, there are two possible positions. They are alternative hypotheses concerning the sources of instigation to aggression. One is a drive theory, including both the instinct and the frustration conceptions of the drive's origin. The other is a cue stimulus theory. The drive theory would suggest that observed differences among people in their choice of forms of expression (e.g., antisocial, prosocial, self, etc.) are a function of reinforcement and inhibition, but that one major source of instigation to any given act is a drive. This drive could be constitutional or it could be produced by frustration of any act, including aggression. Given a frustration, then, the drive would be increased in strength and would, thus, strengthen whatever responses did occur. Concretely, it would be predicted that if one form of aggression (e.g., antisocial) were repeatedly punished, and thereby inhibited whenever external or internal stimuli aroused it, alternative forms of aggressive behavior (e.g., prosocial) that did *not* meet with punishment would be stronger than they would be if the first form (antisocial) were not inhibited.

The cue stimulus theory, on the other hand, is based on the assumption that particular forms of aggression are specifically reinforced or inhibited, and that the strength of any one form is causally related to the strength of others only by stimulus and response generalization. Punishing one form would tend to depress other forms, on the average, but positive or negative correlations among different forms would be assumed to result primarily from similar or different schedules of reinforcement the occurrence of which would be a function of consistencies or inconsistencies in the actions of reinforcing agents (e.g., mothers). To be concrete again, we would expect, from this position, that because there [is] a demonstrable consistency of maternal handling of different forms of aggression, the strengths of alternative forms of aggression would tend to be positively correlated regardless of the prolonged inhibition of any one of them.

The data from the present study provide an opportunity to make one useful test of these two hypotheses. All children express *some* aggression toward their parents, and may be presumed to develop a measurable degree of habit strength for such changeworthy behavior (Sears *et al.,* 1957). They also learn to expect gratification because aggression provides a certain control over the parents. Nevertheless, infantile forms of aggression must be relinquished eventually, and hence we may assume that by age 12 all the children, in varying degrees, had suffered inhibition of their changeworthy forms of aggression. That is, since nearly all the mothers had expressed some dislike of aggression when the children were 5, we can assume a continuing pressure against its expression, even though we have no measure of the mothers' behavior during these intervening years.

The drive theory predicts that children who were still highly aggressive at age 5 but who suffered inhibition of this behavior, and relinquished it, should show higher degrees of alternative forms than children who did not relinquish it. The cue stimulus theory predicts the opposite; i.e., the inhibited group should show lower degrees of the alternative forms.

These differential predictions can be tested by comparison of the mean scores on projected, self, and prosocial aggression obtained by two subgroups of children who did and did not, respectively, show the presumed inhibitory effects of punishment. These are children who were all High (H) (upper half of the distribution) on aggression at age 5, and then were found to be either H or Low (L)—same defining basis—on antisocial aggression at age 12.

From a developmental standpoint all these children may be considered as having posed a problem of control to their parents. They had been more severely punished, on average, and also treated more permissively than the other half of the group of children. We do not know how the mothers coped with this problem in the intervening years, but we do know that, at age 12, 29 boys and 23 girls were in the lower half of the distribution on antisocial aggression, while 17 of each sex were in the upper half. One might say that the mothers had coped successfully with the former and unsuccessfully with the latter.

Children at age 5 • There were no differences at all between the means of these two groups' reported dependency, aggression in the home, or conscience. There was one difference in the boys, however, that is relevant to aggression. On the mother rating scale (III, 27) called "extent to which parent has encouraged child to fight back," there was a nonscalar code labeled "Problem hasn't come up; child has always defended self." Of the 17 High-High (HH) boys, 7 were so judged; of the 29 High-Low (HL) boys, only 2 were. The difference by χ^2 is at $p < .01$. Only 1 of the 7 HH boys was treated as nonpermissively as the 2 HL boys with respect to expressing aggression toward other children. The boys who did not reduce their aggression over these years were permitted to—and did—defend themselves against other children by fighting, even at age 5.

Children at age 12 • As is shown in FIGURE 2, the differences in test measures for the boys are much greater than for the girls, although both are in the same direction. They tend to support the drive theory, though not unequivocally. The boys whose aggression

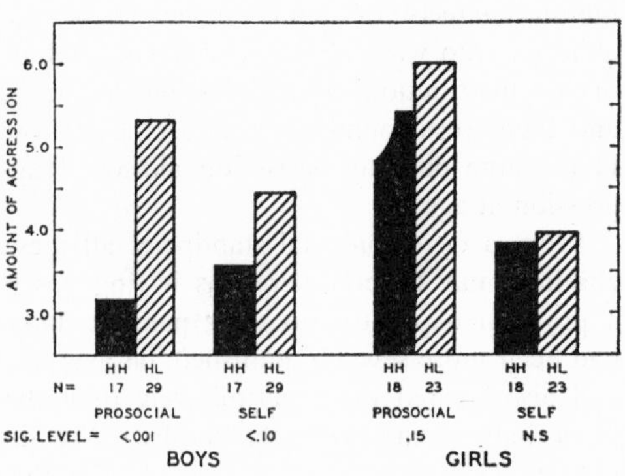

FIGURE 2

Mean frequency of prosocial and self-aggression in two groups equally high on aggression at age 5 but one of which (HH) was high on antisocial aggression at age 12 and the other of which was low (HL).

had decreased (Group HL) were higher, by *t* test, on aggression anxiety ($p = .001$), self-aggression ($p = .10$), and prosocial aggression ($p < .001$). For girls, the equivalent values are $p < .05$, *ns,* and .15. There was no difference on projective aggression in either sex. These differences, particularly those with respect to anxiety and prosocial, are what might be expected from more severe control by both punishment and nonpermissiveness, although the anxiety measure is not one of the alternative forms we are considering here, of course.

Mothers' behavior when children were age 5 • The evidence for any such difference of treatment in the early years is minimal, however. For both sexes, there was slightly less permissiveness for aggression toward parents and toward other children, but none of these four differences reached the .05 level of significance. There was no difference in severity of punishment for aggression toward parents, and only a slight nonsignificant difference on physical punishment, with the HL groups having suffered the more severely. The latter group had also been less strongly encouraged to fight back when attacked by other children.

These nonsignificant differences are all in the right direction to support the inference that the group of originally aggressive children who *did* drop into the lower half of the distribution on antisocial aggression were ones whose mothers were initially more controlling and less inciting of aggression. But the differences in maternal behavior are nowhere near as great as the collateral differences in aggression anxiety and prosocial aggression might lead one to expect.

It is worth adding, perhaps, that none of the following maternal variables showed any differences whatever between these two groups, in either sex: severity of toilet training, warmth, use of the four disciplinary techniques of tangible rewards, praise, deprivation of privileges, or withdrawal of love, not following through on threats of punishment, or who did the disciplining in the family.

These findings suggest that the effective suppression of an aggressive child's early expression of aggression in the home tends to increase the strength of prosocial and self-aggression in the later years. This conclusion is in accord with the drive theory of instigation and in opposition to the cue stimulus theory. What little information can be gained from the mother interview scales suggests, further, that nonpermissiveness rather than punishment was the technique used for controlling the aggressive behavior.

AGGRESSION ANXIETY

In the discussion so far there has been repeated reference to sex differences in the sizes of relationships between the permissiveness-punitiveness antecedents and certain of the aggression scale consequent measures. These differences have been glossed over and treated as if they were possibly no more than variations in sampling. There are certain differences in connection with aggression anxiety that can no longer be ignored, however. The most curious ones are illustrated in TABLE 6, which shows a sharply defined sex difference in direction of correlation between aggression anxiety at age 12 and both aggression and conscience at age 5. Both these correlational differences are significant at $p < .01$.

TABLE 6. *Aggression anxiety and self-aggression: correlations with child behavior variables measured at age five* [a] (Girls: $N = 84$; Boys: $N = 76$)

CHILD BEHAVIOR: AGE 5	CODE NUMBER	AGGRESSION ANXIETY Girls	Boys	SELF-AGGRESSION Girls	Boys
Aggression	III, 29	.18	−.21	.04	−.10
Dependency	III, 10	.04	−.16	.05	.03
Conscience	III, 34	−.24	.30	−.07	.00
Bed-wetting	II, 50	.00	−.17	.24	−.18
Quarreling with sibling	III, 21	.04	−.19	.00	−.08

[a] See also TABLE 3.

What is surprising about this finding is that there is only one significant sex difference among the correlations *within* either of the two sets of child measures made at the respective ages. As can be seen in TABLE 3, the six correlations between (age 5) aggression, dependency, conscience, and bed-wetting are in the same direction and of about the same size for the two sexes except for that between conscience and bed-wetting, and the difference of .12 between the two nonsignificant correlations of aggression with dependency. Likewise, among the five aggression measures taken at age 12, only 1 of the 10 possible comparisons is significant at the .05 level, namely, that between the two correlations of antisocial and prosocial aggression mentioned earlier; for the boys, the r is −.36, and for the girls, −.03. None of the r's relating aggression anxiety to the other four aggression measures is significantly different for the two sexes. Furthermore, aggression anxiety is almost identically related (+.34 and +.37) with the measure of femininity obtained, at age 12, by the self-administered M-F test derived from Gough's CPI Fe scale. Paralleling this intrasex evidence of the "feminine" quality of aggression anxiety is a highly significant sex difference in the means on this scale (see TABLE 4).

Now as to antecedents. The predictable effect of punishment as a determiner of aggression anxiety in girls has already been mentioned. It is to be noted, however, that only punishment for aggression toward parents, and the punishment factor score, are so related (see TABLE 7). Physical punishment and punishment for dependency are not. Neither are the various techniques of discipline: praise, use of tangible rewards, deprivation of privileges, or withdrawal of love. Indeed, the last is somewhat negatively related (−.17).

None of the punishment measures shows a relation to aggression anxiety in boys except withdrawal of love, which surprisingly correlates +.21.

Nonpermissiveness, however, is associated with aggression anxiety in both sexes (TABLE 7), but *only* with respect to aggression toward parents (or as measured by the factor score). Exactly the opposite relation obtains with permissiveness for aggression toward other children (excluding siblings); aggression anx-

TABLE 7. *Aggression anxiety and self-aggression: correlations with child rearing variables* [a]
(Girls: $N = 84$; boys: $N = 76$)

CHILD REARING VARIABLE	CODE NUMBER	AGGRESSION ANXIETY		SELF-AGGRESSION	
		Girls	Boys	Girls	Boys
Permissiveness:					
Aggression to parents	III, 30	—.20	—.17	—.09	—.06
Aggression to other children	III, 28	.27	.14	—.07	—.13
Aggression to siblings	III, 22	.04	—.08	.11	—.19
Dependency to mother	XV, 5	—.02	.12	—.08	—.02
Factor score	XVIII, 5	—.13	—.23	—.17	—.15
Punishment:					
Aggression to parents	III, 31	.24	.10	.11	.03
Dependency to mother	XV, 7	.13	—.13	.10	.23
Physical punishment	III, 46	.07	—.03	.12	.11
Factor score	XVIII, 6	.23	.04	.10	.22
Child encouraged to fight back	III, 27	.23	.07	.01	—.15
Reward for dependency	XV, 6	—.18	.03	—.20	—.15
Withdrawal of love	III, 53	—.17	.21	—.40	.48
Use of praise	III, 37	.06	—.08	.03	—.14
Use of tangible rewards	III, 36	.03	.04	.19	.39
Deprivation of privileges	III, 47	—.06	.13	.06	.24
Severity of toilet training	II, 51	.10	.06	.12	.27
Sex role differentiation	III, 20	—.08	—.06	.15	.10
Mother warmth	III, 15	—.04	.09	—.06	—.07
Father warmth	III, 65	.09	—.15	—.14	—.17
Amount of father care-taking: infancy	II, 18	.11	—.12	.02	.02
Amount of father care-taking: age 5	III, 64	.28	—.04	—.12	—.08
Which parent disciplines (father = 1)	III, 66	—.23	—.06	—.10	—.16

[a] See also TABLE 5.

iety is slightly but nonsignificantly related to this scale in a *positive* direction for boys and significantly at $p < .01$ level in girls. This reversal in the role of permissiveness is the key to a possible explanation of the sex difference.

A glance down the boys' column of TABLE 7 shows but two significant *r*'s (.05 level or better), namely, those with the permissiveness factor score and with withdrawal of love. In the girls' column, however, there are six that reach that level, and three others (including withdrawal of love) close to it. These mother scales are by no means independent of one another, of course, and the actual numbers of significant *r*'s are less important than the kinds of variables that seem to be most connected with aggression anxiety.

The hypothesis is suggested that aggression anxiety has quite different dynamic and genetic qualities for boys and girls. In boys, it is a part of the conformity syndrome, a close relative of conscience, and one of the consequences of relatively high but nonpunitive pressure toward socialization; it is a positive reaction to the same love oriented method of discipline and control that succeeds at an early age in reducing both dependency and aggression toward parents and quarreling among siblings. It is a feminine quality only in the sense that most behavioral representations of rapid and effective socialization in the preschool years are more characteristic of girls and women than of boys and men. It is established by a general aura, in the home, of nonpermissiveness for infantile and destructive impulse expression; the sanctioning power when deviant behavior does occur comes from the threatened loss of the love relationship to the mother. Dynamically, it is one of many responses to stimulation that arouses affiliation desires and conformity behavior.

In girls, aggression anxiety is more complex and has a quite different genesis. Dynamically it is part of the syndrome of forced conformity and subordinated autonomy in which anxiety is evoked by any instigator, internal or external, that serves to arouse incipient aggressive actions or feelings. It is the product of an internalized Type II conflict (Sears & Hovland, 1941) in which the positive response is a forbidden form of aggression, the negative is fear of punishment, and the source of instigation is a frustration induced drive.

This conception is in sharp contrast to that about boys, suggested above. The reasoning that favors some such difference rests on the quantitative reversal of the relationship between aggression and aggression anxiety in the two sexes. Constitutionally, girls are probably less overtly aggressive than boys, and certainly the conditions for their rearing are such as to produce more rapid maturing and relinquishing of earlier changeworthy behavior, aggressive and otherwise. They evidently receive fewer external instigators to aggression and have fewer response produced cues. Girls as a generality, then, should show less aggression anxiety than boys if both sexes have such responses evoked mainly by internal instigations to aggression. On the contrary, girls show much more.

Genetically, the conditions that establish aggression anxiety in girls may be summarized under the label of conditions *antithetical to appropriate sex typing*. With the exception of nonpermissiveness for aggression to parents (which *is* appropriate), all the larger correlations in the girls' column of TABLE 7 are with items of child rearing that either were shown originally (Sears *et al.*, 1957, p. 401) to be different for boys and girls or are related to father involvement and to the punishment of aggression or dependency. The direction of everyone of these *r*'s is opposite to that implied by the sex difference in rearing. Thus, for example, girls are less frequently encouraged to fight back when attacked, but the correlation between this scale and aggression anxiety is positive; likewise, girls are more commonly disciplined by withdrawal of love, but this scale is negatively related to aggression anxiety. The amount of father caretaking at age 5 was not different for the two sexes in the original population, nor is it significantly so in the follow-up sample, but proportion of father discipline was; it seems reasonable to suppose that greater maternal care for girls and paternal participation with boys is appropriate for sex typing in each case. Both these scales show a positive relationship between father participation and aggression anxiety in girls.

Not all of the sex differences in rearing experiences described in the original study are represented in the list of larger correlations with aggression anxiety. Time for completion of weaning, warmth to infant, use of maids and sitters in infancy, kinds of chores required, expectancy of going to college, amount of use of praise and amount of physical punishment, for example, do not show the relation. Neither does sex role differentiation by the mother, the scale measuring the degree to which the mother conceived that there were differences between the sexes that required differences in rearing. One might expect that those mothers who were not aware of sex role differences might treat their daughters less appropriately for feminine sex typing and, thus, produce more aggression anxiety. The *r* of −.08 is of insufficient size to be said to support this expectation, however.

To summarize, this conception of the different dynamics and genetics of aggression anxiety in the two sexes is congruent with the age 5 correlations shown in TABLE 6. There it is seen that, for girls, high aggression anxiety is associated with higher aggression in the home and lower conscience. There is no relation to dependency or quarreling among siblings, as there is among the boys. For the boys, on the other hand, the anxiety is associated with low aggression and high conscience. On the antecedent side (TABLE 7), the different dynamics suggested for the sexes are congruent with the more specifically aggression connected nonpermissiveness in the girls' experience and the more general (factor) nonpermissiveness in the boys', and with the clear influence of punishment in the girls' and its irrelevance in the boys' experience. The other relevant child rearing dimensions that correlate significantly with the anxiety measures in girls are ones which have been shown previously to be relevant to sex-typing, and the direction of correlation in every instance is such as to associate high aggression anxiety with the inappropriate sex-typing practice. The theory also accounts for the greater aggression anxiety of girls than of boys, even though girls are less aggressive in both overt behavior and fantasy (P. S. Sears, 1951); the explanation of this phenomenon is not in terms of a greater frequency of inappropriate sex typing experiences in girls, of course, but is seen as a consequence of the development of internalized Type II conflict.

One further set of differential relationships should also be demonstrable. These have to do with maturity of role choice and nurturance. One would expect that boys would show substantial positive correlations of aggression anxiety with the mature and nurturant forms of behavior, while the girls would show no relationship. TABLE 8 gives evidence for these propositions in the form of correlations between aggression anxiety and four measures reported elsewhere by Maccoby (1961). These measures relate to the positive choice of adult-like roles in connection with *using rule enforcement, accepting rule enforcement, giving nurturance,* and a general series of items having *subordinate-superordinate role choice comparisons.* In the total tested population the girls do have significant *r*'s with respect to all but the giving nurturance scale, though the boys' *r*'s are slightly larger. In the follow-up sample, the sex differences are still larger. On giving nurturance, both sets of figures show a significant positive relation ($p < .01$) in boys and zero relation in girls, as expected. These figures support the expectation so far as nurturance is concerned, but do not with respect to the other forms of mature behavior.

TABLE 8. *Aggression anxiety and adult role: correlations in total tested population and follow-up sample*

ADULT ROLE MEASURES	TOTAL TESTED POPULATION		FOLLOW-UP SAMPLE	
	Girls	Boys	Girls	Boys
Enforcing rules	.17	.18	.15	.25
Accepting rule enforcement	.19	.24	.10	.36
Giving nurturance	.02	.20	−.04	.37
Adult versus child choice	.22	.28	.23	.36
Number of cases	264	261	84	76

Conclusions • It would be an obvious absurdity to suppose that either of these dynamic or genetic conceptions of aggression anxiety is applicable rigidly to one sex only. Undoubtedly many males have had their aggression anxiety somewhat exacerbated by parental punishment for aggression or by too severe demands for aggressive behavior in their relations with other children. The virtually zero correlations between these dimensions and boys' aggression anxiety cannot be interpreted as meaning that those variables have had no influence for *any* boy in the group, but simply that as a cumulative matter within the whole matrix of influences, these are not detectable for the group as a whole. Likewise, in the female, one must assume that the affiliative conforming motivation created in part by nonpermissiveness and by appeal to maturity and conscientiousness is also a determinant of aggression anxiety. The relations with the adult role scales favor this interpretation. Indeed, one cannot but wonder whether both sexes may not about equally derive aggression anxiety in this way, but that girls have overlaid a more severe degree of it by those socializing experiences which, in the exciting of aggressive impulses counter to girls' proper nonaggressive sex role, are inappropriate to the sex-typing process.

In any case, the evidence presented here suggests two quite different dynamic and genetic forms of aggression anxiety. Whatever combinations of them may occur in individual cases, within the limits of our sample, one is predominant in boys and the other in girls at age 12.

SELF-AGGRESSION

Although the internal consistency of the self-aggression scale is virtually nil, the sizes and directions of its relationships with the other child measures are so consistent, both between the follow-up sample and the 1958 classmates and, with one exception, between boys and girls, that its child rearing antecedents seem worth investigation. The one exception is in respect to aggression anxiety; for boys, these two scales are positively related in both groups (follow-up, $r = .25$, and total tested population, $r = .24$), while for girls the slight positive relation is nonsignificant in both groups (respectively, .11 and .08). In view of the different dynamics of aggression anxiety described in the preceding section, this is scarcely surprising, but does warrant an attempt at interpretation. The other relationships of self-aggression are also a little smaller for girls than for boys, but not significantly so. The r with projected aggression is clearly positive in both sexes, while the r's with both prosocial and antisocial aggression are effectively zero.

From a theoretical standpoint (Dollard *et al.*, 1939), self-aggression has been considered a displacement of an aggressive response from the frustrating agent to the self, produced by anticipated punishment for direct aggression toward the agent. Such an expectancy would arise if there had been repeated punishment for being aggressive toward the frustrator. Since aggression toward the self is intrinsically painful, this would be the direction of aggression adopted only if most other objects of displaced aggression were also interdicted.

In the present context, we would expect that high self-aggression would be associated with various child rearing experiences that both heightened frustration and served to prevent the expression of overt aggression toward parents, siblings, and other children. In TABLE 7 are shown the relevant correlations for a test of this hypothesis. It is apparent at once that the boys' self-aggression is significantly related to more socialization variables than the girls'. Indeed, the only significant correlation for the latter is with the nonuse of withdrawal of love as a disciplinary technique.

For the boys, however, there is substantial support for the hypothesis. First, we would expect any early socialization experiences that were strongly frustrating to create high instigation to aggression and, at age 5, high aggression toward the frustrator. In a previous study (Sears *et al.*, 1953), there was some evidence for a positive connection between severe toilet training and aggression in the preschool; in the present follow-up sample of boys there had been a nonsignificant relation ($r = .14$) between severity of toilet training and aggression in the home. Severity of toilet training was correlated .41 with use of physical punishment, which suggests that the hypothetical conditions outlined above were fulfilled—namely, high frustration, with some consequent aggression, and punishment for expressing aggression. As was predicted, there is a significant relation ($r = .27$) between severity of toilet training and self-aggression. None of the other aggression scales is significantly related to this antecedent.

A second source of early frustration was the existence of siblings; we may assume that other children in a family, either older or younger, add not only companionship but also competition for things, space, and people. Here again there is a detectable relationship;

TABLE 9. *Intercorrelations among twelve child rearing measures obtained from the mother interviews: follow-up sample*
(Girls' mothers: $N = 84$; Boys' mothers: $N = 76$)

GIRLS / BOYS CHILD REARING VARIABLE	CODE NUMBER	ITEM	1	2	3	4	5	6	7	8	9	10	11	12
Permissiveness: Aggression to parents	III, 30	1		.70	.24	—.44	—.28	—.30	—.04	—.04	.19	.04	.15	—.29
Permissiveness factor	XVIII, 5	2	.67		.64	—.40	—.35	—.35	—.13	—.07	.16	—.07	.27	—.36
Permissiveness for dependency	XV, 5	3	—.05	.43		—.22	—.35	—.09	—.12	.00	.05	—.14	.35	—.10
Punishment: Aggression to parents	III, 31	4	—.61	—.47	.08		.62	.58	.05	.15	.00	—.02	—.37	.18
Punishment factor	XVIII, 6	5	—.31	—.22	—.04	.61		.70	.10	.18	.00	.07	—.45	.18
Physical punishment	III, 46	6	—.22	—.12	—.04	.34	.68		.08	.22	—.05	—.09	—.34	.21
Deprivation of privileges	III, 47	7	—.07	—.04	.10	.06	.14	.25		.33	.22	—.02	—.11	.20
Tangible rewards	III, 36	8	.01	—.17	—.07	.13	.16	.16	.22		.02	—.08	.07	.21
Use of praise	III, 37	9	.10	—.07	—.13	—.04	—.10	—.12	—.09	—.05		.12	.14	.21
Withdrawal of love	III, 53	10	—.19	—.27	—.16	.36	.34	.41	.34	.32	—.20		—.20	.08
Mother warmth	III, 15	11	.08	.23	.40	—.01	—.24	—.30	—.08	—.06	.15	—.49		—.18
Severity of toilet training	II, 51	12	—.23	—.46	—.26	.31	.34	.41	.03	.21	—.05	.30	—.37	

Note.—Girls' mothers above the diagonal; boys' mothers below.

by *t* test, *only* boys were less self-aggressive than those with siblings ($p = .04$).

A third source of frustration at the earlier age was punishment for aggression and dependency. However, punishment should also have inhibited aggression eventually, so that on two counts a high level of punitiveness would be expected to be positively related to self-aggression. Interestingly enough, punishment for aggression toward parents shows no relation at all ($r = .03$) and physical punishment a nonsignificant amount (.11), while punishment for dependency (.23) and the punishment factor score (.22) are both significantly related. Furthermore, two of the techniques of discipline—which are indirect measures of punishment—are associated in the same way, deprivation of privileges (.24) and withdrawal of love (.48). The use of tangible rewards, which is positively related to deprivation of privileges, is also related positively to self-aggression (.39). (In boys, the four disciplinary techniques have a median intercorrelation of .28, while in girls, the median is .05; see TABLE 9.)

As is the case with nearly all the other antecedent-consequent relations that have been reported in this and similar studies, these correlations are small on an absolute scale. This is to be expected, of course, in view of the multiple antecedents responsible for a given item of behavior; no one variable contributes much of the total variance. The influence of these several types of experience can be displayed more dramatically, however, if comparison is made of a few extreme cases. For example, if the upper and lower halves of the distributions on permissiveness and punishment factor scores are combined as follows:

High permissiveness, low punishment ($N = 17$)

Low permissiveness, high punishment ($N = 23$)

the mean scores on self-aggression for the two subgroups are different at the level, $p = .02$, one-tailed test,[4] with the second subgroup the higher.

Of course, with the relatively low intercorrelations among the child rearing variables (TABLE 9), adding further variables to such a crossbreak rapidly reduces the number of cases. For example, adding severity of toilet training as a third selector to the above crossbreak gives the following:

High permissiveness, low punishment, low severity of toilet training (N = 10)

Low permissiveness, high punishment, high severity of toilet training (N = 17)

The second group has higher mean self-aggression at the level, $p < .01$, one-tailed test. If one uses four variables instead of three for obtaining some cumulative effects on self-aggression, the number of cases becomes very low indeed. However, the second of the following pair of subgroups has higher mean self-aggression at the level, $p < .004$, one-tailed test, even with so few cases; the range of scores for the first group is from 1 to 4 and that for the second group is 4 to 9:

High permissiveness, low punishment, low deprivation of privileges, low use of tangible rewards ($N = 6$)

Low permissiveness, high punishment, high deprivation of privileges, high use of tangible rewards ($N = 8$)

By the time a fifth variable is added, the *N* becomes so small as almost to nullify the advantages of dealing with extreme cases. For instance, if severity of toilet training is now added to the above crossbreak, the *N*s for the first and second groups are only 2 and 6, respectively, and the significance of the difference between means is $p = .02$, one-tailed test.

In the foregoing comparisons, permissiveness has been added to the several punishment measures. As TABLE 7 shows, neither permissiveness for dependency nor for aggression toward parents is at all related to self-aggression, but there are nonsignificant negative correlations with permissiveness for aggression toward siblings (−.19), toward

4 Significance values by one-tailed test refer to hypotheses formulated before the data were collected, and which were derived directly from the more general theory published 19 years earlier (Dollard, Doob, Miller, Mowrer, & Sears, 1939, Ch. 3).

other children (−.15), the permissiveness factor (−.15), and encouragement to fight back when attacked (−.15). In other words, nonpermissiveness in every direction (except towards parents) seems related to self-aggression. If we use the same device for selecting extreme cases of nonpermissiveness alone, as was illustrated above in connection with punishment plus nonpermissiveness, the following tiny subgroups are shown to be significantly different at the level, $p = .05$, one-tailed test; the second group's being the higher, of course:

High permissiveness, low punishment, high permissiveness for aggression to other children, high encouragement to fight back ($N = 3$)

Low permissiveness and high punishment on same scales ($N = 7$)

Restriction on early expression of aggression • According to the theory (Dollard *et al.*, 1939), self-aggression should develop most vigorously when the early expressions of aggression are successfully inhibited. There are three ways of testing this proposition in the present data, and all the appropriate comparisons show correlations or mean differences in the predicted directions, though the levels of significance are not very convincing.

1. The comparison of age 5 aggression with antisocial aggression offers one test. The 29 boys who were judged high at age 5 but low at age 12 expressed more self-aggression than the 17 boys who remained high at age 12 ($p = .05$, one-tailed test). It will be recalled that the permissiveness factor score was significantly lower for the more inhibited of these subgroups; so this present rather tenuous difference can be reasonably interpreted as related to the restriction produced by such nonpermissiveness.

2. A second test involves toilet training and bed-wetting. In the earlier study of these children, it was shown that severe toilet training was positively related to ineffective control of urination. In the present follow-up sample this correlation is only .12, however, and there are an almost exactly equal number of boys who had severe toilet training and who did and did not suffer from enuresis at age 5. If we may interpret the enuresis as a form of disguised aggression, then the 13 boys who showed such behavior may be considered less restricted in early aggression than the 12 boys who did not suffer enuresis. As predicted, the former had lower self-aggression scores than the latter, but the difference does not quite reach the .10 level, one-tailed test. Now, if we add the differential effects of high and low frustration to this comparison, as in the following pair of groups, we find a much larger difference in the predicted direction:

High bed-wetting, low severity of toilet training ($N = 12$)

Low bed-wetting, high severity of toilet training ($N = 12$)

The second group—with restricted early aggression and high level of frustration—was more self-aggressive at age 12, $p < .001$, one-tailed test, than the first group, which had *un*restricted aggression (in the form of bed-wetting at age 5) and a relatively low level of frustration (nonsevere toilet training).

3. A third test takes us back to the most highly controlled subgroup of boys as measured by the factor scores for permissiveness and punishment. These boys were subjected to low permissiveness and high punishment. The restriction hypothesis predicts that those who were already low in their expression of aggression at age 5 ($N = 6$) would show greater self-aggression at age 12 than those who were still high at age 5 ($N = 5$); for this comparison, the 10 boys rated on the middle point of the nine-point aggression scale at age 5 are disregarded. As predicted, the restricted group does show higher self-aggression than the nonrestricted group, but $p = .20$. If we add to this comparison the congruently extreme groups on amount of quarreling with siblings that the mother reported, we get too few cases in the cells to permit further testing. However, it is worth noting that the boy who obtained the highest self-aggression score in the entire follow-up sample was not only in the least aggressive-in-the-home-at-age-5 group but also received the lowest possible rating on amount of quar-

reling with siblings, and was in the earliest toilet trained group although he suffered the third highest severity of toilet training. In other words, he was not only in the least permissive and most punitive home atmosphere, but he suffered very severe frustration very early, responded to it by submission, and was highly restricted (inhibited) in his aggression at age 5.

These various bits of evidence support the proposition that, in boys, restricted expression of aggression in the earliest years is associated with a higher level of self-aggression in middle childhood, but the statistical significance of the differences cited is too low to give great confidence in their replicability. Nevertheless, these findings, coupled with the predicted influences of punishment and nonpermissiveness, do give one an optimistic sense of rightness about the general theory that self-aggression is a displacement of strong aggression from frustrating parental agents to the self as a consequence of anticipation of punishment for expressing aggression directly toward the frustrators or other immediately available objects.

Aggression anxiety • It will be recalled that the correlation between aggression anxiety and self-aggression was the only one among the age 12 scales that was significantly different for the sexes; the boys' r was higher than the girls'. The findings reported above suggest a reason. In boys, nonpermissiveness is prominent among the child rearing antecedents for both responses; hence a positive relation between the two is to be expected. But for girls, what little suggestion there is of meaningful antecedents to self-aggression lies nonsignificantly in this same area (e.g., low permissiveness factor) and in only one narrow aspect of the antifeminine sex-typing area (low reward of dependency and low use of withdrawal of love). The other relevant antecedents to girls' aggression anxiety are unrelated to self-aggression. Thus, it is to be expected that these two scales would themselves be but weakly correlated in girls.

Role of the father • So far we have been concerned mainly with theoretical properties of behavior, such as punishment, permissiveness, and restriction (inhibition) of action. However, the measures of these dimensions, with the exception of the factor scores, have referred to particular substantive dimensions, e.g., permissiveness for aggression toward parents, or toward other children, punishment for dependency, physical punishment, etc. Furthermore, all of these measures imply, even when they do not explicitly state, an agent of the action as well as a substantive quality, e.g., punishment (*by mother*) for dependency (*toward mother*). There are, in other words, three aspects to every child rearing dimension: a property that represents a theoretical variable in the general theory of action and learning (e.g., punishment); a substantive property that describes a dimension within the special theory of human social interaction (e.g., dependency, aggression); an agent, also defined within this latter theory, who is the opposite member of a dyad in which the child is object (e.g., mother, father).

In the discussion of permissiveness and punitiveness as determiners of antisocial aggression, aggression anxiety, and self-aggression, we have been concerned with the first of these three aspects. Evidence concerning the effects of these two antecedents was sought wherever it might be found, regardless of the substantive dimension being measured; sometimes the factor score gave the strongest correlation, sometimes one of the more specific dimensions. When the antecedents of aggression anxiety came under consideration, however, the marked sex differences required more careful consideration of the second and third aspects, the substantive quality of the dimensions involved and the agents; conclusions concerning the sex-different dynamic and genetic characteristics of aggression anxiety were stated in terms of the sex appropriateness of socialization procedures. This kind of principle belongs in the special theory of human social interaction, a theory that in its present degree of development is certainly "special" to human behavior and may be more narrowly limited than that; recent efforts to define transcultural variables are promising, but their success has not yet been fully assessed (Sears, 1961; Whiting & Child, 1953).

Any consideration of the role of specific persons in socialization belongs to the special theory. In connection with girls' aggression anxiety, evidence was presented that high *father* participation in a girl's rearing at age 5 was conducive to high anxiety. There is some indication that fathers also have a special influence on the development of self-aggression in boys. The evidence will be described but briefly, and only for purposes of suggesting an hypothesis in the realm of the special theory (where fruitful hypotheses are harder to come by than in the general theory of action and learning); for while trends within the data are quite consistent, almost none of the crucial antecedent-consequent comparisons reaches a satisfactory level of statistical significance.

It will be noted in TABLE 7 that two scales involving the father show small correlations with self-aggression, his coldness, and his degree of participation in discipline when both parents are present. These two measures are uncorrelated with one another, and hence it is theoretically possible to maximize their combined effects by a crossbreak as follows:

FATHER	N	% HIGH ON SELF-AGGRESSION
Cold		
Father chief disciplinarian	13	46
Parents about equal	12	8
Mother chief disciplinarian	17	35
Warm		
Father chief disciplinarian	14	28
Parents about equal	12	25
Mother chief disciplinarian	7	14

Regardless of whether the father is described as warm or cold, if he is the chief disciplinarian of the 5-year-old boy, the boy is more likely to have a high self-aggression score at age 12 than if his mother is the chief disciplinarian. Likewise, if the father is cold, regardless of which parent does the disciplining, the self-aggression scores are higher. None of the comparisons approaches significance by either t tests between means or by χ^2. The top and bottom groups of the list maximize these joint effects.

A third variable that may be influential is the father's strictness. In general, the parent who is stricter tends to be the chief disciplinarian (by χ^2, $p < .01$), and there is a close positive relationship (by χ^2, $p < .001$) between the father's rated strictness and his adoption of the chief disciplinary role. In order to see the effects of his strictness per se, then, the first and fourth groups above must be used for the next crossbreak.

FATHER	N	% HIGH ON SELF-AGGRESSION
Cold, chief disciplinarian		
High strictness	7	28
Low strictness	6	67
Warm, chief disciplinarian		
High strictness	4	75
Low strictness	10	10

In spite of the large percentage difference in the top pair of groups, the actual means are almost identical; by both t test and χ^2 the difference is not significant. Between the strict and lenient *warm* fathers, however, the percentage difference in high self-aggression scores faithfully represents a large mean difference also; by χ^2, $p < .02$, and by t test, $p < .01$.

In summary, there are minimal indications that high participation of the father as disciplinarian, and his coldness, are both conducive to self-aggression, but only in a warm father does his strictness have a facilitating effect. This latter finding is reminiscent of our earlier discovery (Sears *et al.*, 1957) that a mother's withdrawal of love was influential on the development of conscience only if the mother was warm to start with; she could not affect a child if she tried to withdraw something she had never given! With the fathers, one may suspect that somewhat the same principle holds—his being strict can frustrate his son only if there would be love gained in the absence of strictness.

These hypotheses are presented blind, in one sense. We do not know to what extent the effects of the father's behavior are simply reflections of the operation of the general principles of learning and action involving punishment and nonpermissiveness. It may be that fathers used more of the tactics that produced self-aggression than did mothers, and that the seeming effect of father behavior as such is but a reflection of the more intense use of them. Even if this is so, however, a principle having to do with the influence of fathers, as such, would be a useful addition to the special substantive theory of socialization (in our culture) if it could be substantiated.

PROSOCIAL AGGRESSION

There is little to be added, concerning prosocial aggression, to what was mentioned in the initial discussion of punishment and permissiveness. Like aggression anxiety, with which it is strongly correlated, it is significantly higher in girls than in boys (TABLE 4). Within the boys' group, it correlates significantly with the femininity measure, and within the total tested group of girls, likewise; within the follow-up sample of girls, however, this positive relation is reduced almost to zero. Again we are presumably dealing with sampling error.

So far as antecedents are concerned, the same high permissiveness and high punishment associated with aggression anxiety in girls are found similarly associated with prosocial aggression, though none of the other anti-sex-typing variables appears to be related. For boys, there is some slight evidence of the same nonpermissiveness that was found in aggression anxiety, and a complete lack of any other child rearing correlate.

Summary

A FOLLOW-UP sample of 76 boys and 84 girls from the original population of 202 boys and 177 girls described in *Patterns of Child Rearing* (Sears *et al.*, 1957) was given a set of self-administering aggression scales at age 12. These included measures of antisocial, prosocial, projected, and self-aggression and aggression anxiety. Reliabilities of all but the self-aggression scale were satisfactory.

Intersex comparisons showed significantly higher scores for girls on aggression anxiety and prosocial aggression, and for boys on antisocial aggression. Intrasex correlations with a measure of masculinity-femininity, derived from Gough's (1957) Fe scale, were in directions congruent with these obtained sex differences in mean scores.

Among the aggression measures, antisocial aggression was negatively correlated with both prosocial aggression and aggression anxiety, and had virtually zero relation to projected and self-aggression. These latter, however, were significantly related positively to aggression anxiety. In other words, there appeared to be an anxiety cluster including four of the scales, with *r*'s ranging from 0 to + .50, and antisocial aggression, with *r*'s between it and the members of the anxiety cluster ranging from 0 to —.44.

Antecedents of these age 12 scores were sought among the ratings of the mother interviews that had been obtained when the children were in kindergarten (age 5). Primary attention was given to dimensions involving permissiveness and punitiveness, such as those for control of aggression and dependency and methods of discipline.

Antisocial aggression was found to be positively related to high permissiveness and low punishment. The former of these two effects was the same as that with respect to aggression in the home at age 5 (rated from mother interviews); the latter effect was just the opposite from that found at age 5. At the earlier period punishment incited aggression, preponderantly, while at age 12 the negative correlations are interpreted as exemplifying the inhibitory influence of punishment.

Prosocial aggression and aggression anxiety likewise were found to be associated with high permissiveness, but in these instances *high* punishment was related to the two aggression measures. This was the opposite of the relation with antisocial aggression.

Evidence was presented to support an expectation, based on a theory of frustration induced drive, that the successful inhibition of early forms of aggression in severely punished children would produce heightened amounts of aggression anxiety, prosocial, and self-aggression at a later age.

An important sex difference was found in the antecedents for aggression anxiety, a fact that led to a theoretical interpretation that this phenomenon has different dynamic and genetic characteristics for the two sexes. In boys, this anxiety appears to be a part of a general pattern of rapid socialization and high conformity in a love oriented atmosphere of tight control of aggression. In girls, such anxiety appears to be conflict induced by an internalized Type II conflict derived from socialization experiences that exacerbate their aggressive activities because the preponderant training is antithetical to appropriate feminine sex-typing. This interpretation is supported by a series of antecedent-consequent relationships, as well as by a cluster of intercorrelations between aggression anxiety and earlier forms of behavior, that are almost entirely different for boys and girls.

Self-aggression in boys was found to be strongest in those who had suffered most severe frustrations and the most severe control of outward directed aggression in their early years. Early successful restriction of aggressive behavior, as in severe toilet training with early success and in low expressions of aggression toward parents and siblings, was also conducive to high self-aggression.

REFERENCES

BERKOWITZ, L. The expression and reduction of hostility. *Psychol. Bull.,* 1958, **55,** 257–283.

CLARK, R. A. The effect of sexual motivation on phantasy. In D. C. McClelland (Ed.), *Studies in motivation.* New York: Appleton-Century-Crofts, 1955.

DOLLARD, J., DOOB, L. W., MILLER, N. E., MOWRER, O. H., & SEARS, R. R. *Frustration and aggression.* New Haven: Yale Univer. Press, 1939.

FREUD, S. *Beyond the pleasure principle.* London: International Psycho-Analytical Press, 1922.

GOUGH, H. G. *California Psychological Inventory: Manual.* Palo Alto, Calif.: Consulting Psychologists Press, 1957.

GRINDER, R. E. Parental child rearing practices, guilt, and resistance to temptation of sixth grade children. *Amer. Psychologist,* 1960, **15,** 399. (Abstract.)

HOLLINGSHEAD, A. B., & REDLICH, F. C. *Social class and mental illness.* New York: Wiley, 1958.

JOHNSON, ELIZABETH Z. Attitudes of children toward authority as projected in their doll play at two age levels. Unpublished doctoral dissertation, Harvard Univer., Graduate School of Education, 1951.

LEVIN, H., & SEARS, R. R. Identification with parents as a determinant of doll play aggression. *Child Develpm.,* 1956, **27,** 135–153.

MACCOBY, ELEANOR E. The taking of adult roles in middle childhood. *J. abnorm. soc. Psychol.,* 1961, **63,** 493–503.

MACCOBY, ELEANOR E., & GIBBS, PATRICIA K. Methods of child rearing in two social classes. In W. E. Martin & Celia B. Stendler (Eds.), *Readings in child development.* New York: Harcourt, Brace & World, 1954.

MCDOUGALL, W. *An introduction to social psychology.* London: Methuen, 1908.

MILTON, G. A. A factor analytic study of child rearing behaviors. *Child Develpm.,* 1958, **29,** 381–392.

SEARS, PAULINE S. Doll play aggression in normal young children: influence of sex, age, sibling status, and father's absence. *Psychol. Monogr.,* 1951, **65,** No. 6 (Whole No. 323).

SEARS, PAULINE S. Child rearing factors as related to playing of sex-typed roles. *Amer. Psychologist,* 1953, **8,** 431. (Abstract.)

SEARS, R. R. Effects of frustration and anxiety on fantasy aggression. *Amer. J. Orthopsychiat.,* 1951, **21,** 498–505.

SEARS, R. R. Transcultural variables and conceptual equivalence. In B. Kaplan (Ed.), *Studying personality cross-culturally.* New York: Row, Peterson, 1961.

SEARS, R. R., & HOVLAND, C. I. Experiments on motor conflict: II. Determination of mode of resolution by comparative strengths of conflicting responses. *J. exp. Psychol.,* 1941, **28,** 280–286.

SEARS, R. R., MACCOBY, ELEANOR E., & LEVIN,

H. *Patterns of child rearing.* New York: Row, Peterson, 1957.

SEARS, R. R., WHITING, J. W. M., NOWLIS, V., & SEARS, PAULINE S. Some child rearing antecedents of aggression and dependency in young children. *Genet. psychol. Monogr.*, 1953, **47,** 135–234.

WARNER, W. L., MEEKER, MARCHIA, & EELLS, K. *Social class in America.* Chicago: Science Research Associates, 1949.

WHITING, J. W. M., & CHILD, I. L. *Child training and personality: a cross-cultural study.* New Haven: Yale Univer. Press, 1953.

WILLARD W. HARTUP

*Nurturance and Nurturance-Withdrawal in Relation to the Dependency Behavior of Preschool Children**

THIS investigation is based on the hypothesis that non-nurturance by an adult is more strongly associated with the occurrence of dependency behavior in young children than is nurturance alone. The naturalistic studies of Sears *et al.* (1953), Beller (1955), and Smith (1953) all contain data which show a positive relationship between amount of parental frustrations (non-nurturance) and the frequency of dependency behavior observed in young children. Similar results were obtained in the laboratory studies of Gewirtz (1948, 1954, 1956), although Carl's laboratory findings with respect to this hypothesis were inconclusive (1949).

The present study was designed to explore the relationship between one specific form of non-nurturance—the withdrawal of nurturance—and young children's acquisition of responses which elicit adult approval. This relationship was studied in the laboratory where some manipulation of the relevant antecedent conditions was possible.

The method of this study has been to provide a comparison in the learning of simple responses which elicit adult approval between a group of children consistently nurtured by an experimenter and another group who were nurtured and then rebuffed (nurturance-withdrawal). It was predicted that children in the presence of an adult female experimenter who withdraws her nurturance in this fashion will learn simple tasks eliciting adult approval in fewer trials and with fewer errors than children in the presence of an experimenter who has been consistently nurturant. This prediction is based, in part, on those aspects of psychoanalytic theory which suggest that attempts by the child to institute closeness and seek affection are most strongly related to the anxiety generated at times of separation from the mother or when the child has experienced loss of the mother's love (Freud, 1938). It is believed that the withdrawal of nurturance by a female experimenter is similar to certain aspects of the caretaker-child relationship. If so, such behavior by the experimenter should generate certain amounts of anxiety in young children which, in turn, should motivate dependency behavior.

Certain aspects of behavior theory are also relevant to the present prediction. Miller (1948) and Mowrer (1950) suggest that the capacity of a neutral stimulus to evoke anxiety is strengthened through association with increases in drive or delay in primary reinforcement; presumably it is association such as this which results in children becoming anxious when the mother is absent or nonnurturant. If children in our culture commonly do learn to respond in this way to the non-nurturance of adults, if anxiety does motivate behavior, and if adult nurturance has acquired the capacity to reduce anxiety and thereby reinforce behavior for the young child, the experimental prediction formulated for this investigation can be made.

* REPRINTED by permission of the author and the Society for Research in Child Development from *Child Develpm.*, 1958, 29, 191–201.

Method

SUBJECTS

SUBJECTS used in this investigation were 34 preschool children—15 boys and 19 girls—in attendance at the Harvard University Preschool during the spring of 1954. The subjects ranged in age from three years, ten months, to five years, six months. The mean age of the children in the sample was four years, seven months; the standard deviation was 4.7 months. The preschool population at the time of the experiment was typical of many laboratory nursery schools in that the children were all from academic, professional, or business homes, and were free from severe emotional disturbances and physical handicaps. Two subgroups were drawn from this sample. These subgroups were counterbalanced with respect to sex of child and dependency rating made by the preschool teachers on scales of the type used by Beller (1955). Two young women served as experimenters.[1] Each experimenter worked with a randomly-assigned half of the subjects in each group.

PROCEDURE

Each child was brought individually to the laboratory room for the experimental session. This room was equipped with one-way mirrors for observation and was furnished with a child's table and chairs, an adult-sized table with comfortable chair, and a large bench. The experimental session proceeded as follows:

1. For a period of five minutes, the experimenter interacted nurturantly with the child while the child played with toys. For purposes of this experiment nurturance consisted of adult behavior which rewarded, encouraged, supported, or showed affection to the child; during this five-minute period the experimenter attempted to maximize these qualities in her behavior toward the child. Children in both experimental groups experienced this period of nurturant interaction with the experimenter.

2. Children in the consistent-nurturance group (hereafter called group C) then immediately experienced a second five-minute period like the first.

3. The second five minutes for the nurturance-withdrawal group (group NW) were marked by the experimenter's behaving non-nurturantly toward the child. She ceased to interact with the child, withdrew from his proximity, and did not reward any of the child's supplications beyond telling him that she was "busy." The experience of children in group NW, having first a period of nurturant interaction, then a period of non-nurturance from the experimenter, has been called "nurturance-withdrawal."

4. Children in both experimental groups were then asked by the experimenter to learn two tasks, the reward for which was the verbal approval of the experimenter. Task I consisted of learning a simple *position* concept in an arrangement of two blue and two red one-inch blocks. The task was presented to the child as a guessing game. The experimenter placed the blocks on the floor first in this order (reading from the child's left): red, red, blue, blue. She then said: "I'm thinking of one of the blocks and I want to see if you can guess which one it is. Point with your finger to the one you think is right and I'll tell you if it's the right one." The child's first guess was always unsuccessful, as was his second. The third guess was always successful. This introductory procedure was followed to eliminate chance successes on the first guess. On each succeeding trial the arrangement of the blocks was changed through all the possible order-permutations. The correct block was always the block in the same position in the row as the one which the child chose on his third guess. The performance criterion was three consecutive correct trials. Task II consisted of copying from memory a row of adjacent blue, red, and yellow one-inch cubes which were shown to the child for five seconds per trial. Six blocks were arranged in the following order: red, yellow, blue, blue, yellow, red. The performance

1 The author wishes to thank Mrs. Carla F. Berry and Miss Willa Dinwoodie for their assistance in this regard.

criterion was one perfect reproduction of the arrangement completed by the child from his own supply of blocks. Measures used in the subsequent analysis of the data were: (a) number of errors to criterion on task I; (b) number of trials to criterion on task I; (c) number of errors to criterion on task II; (d) number of trials to criterion on task II. Error- and trial-scores were correlated .93 on task I, .96 on task II.

Measures of the child's tendency to be dependent on adults were from three sources: (a) observation during the period of nurturant interaction in the laboratory; (b) ratings of the child's dependency on adults made by the preschool teachers; and (c) observations of the child's dependency on adults in preschool made by observers.

Behavior categories used for the laboratory observations were as follows:

1. Asks for verbal help and information
2. Asks for material help
3. Seeks reassurance and rewards
4. Seeks positive attention
5. Seeks to be near
6. Seeks physical contact
7. Seeks negative attention
8. Initiates verbal interaction with experimenter

Frequencies in categories 1 through 7 were summed to yield a measure of dependence on the experimenter. Category 8, "verbal interaction," was used independently in the analysis of data.

The following seven-point scales were used for the teacher ratings of the child's dependence on adults in the preschool situation:

1. Seeks recognition
2. Seeks unnecessary help
3. Seeks necessary help
4. Seeks physical contact and proximity
5. Seeks attention

Each child was rated by two of his teachers (reliability coefficients ranged between .73 and .99). The ratings of the two teachers on each scale were pooled; a summary rating score was then obtained by summing the pooled ratings on all five scales. This summary rating score was used to counter-balance the two subgroups as described above and was also used in analyzing the learning scores.

Behavior categories used for the preschool observations of dependency on the teacher were:

1. Seeks recognition and approval
2. Seeks unnecessary help
3. Seeks necessary help
4. Seeks physical contact
5. Seeks to be near
6. Seeks positive attention
7. Seeks negative attention

Frequencies in the seven categories were summed to yield the preschool observation measure of dependence on the teacher which was used in the statistical analysis.

The intercorrelations among the two laboratory scores, the summary teacher rating, and the preschool observation total score are reported in TABLE 1.

The data from the learning tasks were studied by a triple-classification analysis of variance technique for unequal cell-entries (Walker & Lev, 1953). The three independent variables in this analysis were (a) sex of

TABLE 1. *Intercorrelations among four measures of dependency* ($N = 34$)

	1	2	3	4
1. Verbal interaction with experimenter: laboratory	—			
2. Dependence on experimenter: laboratory	.13	—		
3. Dependence on preschool teacher: teacher rating	.03	.40 *	—	
4. Dependence on preschool teacher: observer score	.00	.11	.31	—

* Significant beyond .05 level.

TABLE 2. *F ratios from four analyses of variance based on number of trials on task I according to sex of child, dependence, and experimental condition*

SOURCE	ANALYSIS 1 * ($N = 27$)	ANALYSIS 2 * ($N = 33$)	ANALYSIS 3 * ($N = 32$)	ANALYSIS 4 * ($N = 31$)
Sex of Child	16.153 §	2.618	3.988	2.953
Dependence	7.163 †	.002	.527	6.571 †
Experimental Condition	13.859 ‡	4.574 †	1.759	1.438
Sex × Dependence	3.053	3.630	.028	.015
Sex × Condition	6.744 †	2.098	3.549	6.437
Dependence × Condition	2.224	.792	2.249	1.488
Sex × Dependence × Condition	.215	.570	.005	1.186

* The measures of dependence used were: analysis 1, frequency of verbal interaction initiated by child in the laboratory session; analysis 2, frequency of dependence on adults observed in the laboratory session; analysis 3, teachers' ratings of dependence; analysis 4, dependence on preschool teachers as recorded by observers.
† Significant between .05 and .01.
‡ Significant between .01 and .001.
§ Significant beyond .001.

child; (b) dependency scores as described above and by which the group was separated into two subgroups—high dependency (all cases above the median on the score being used) and low dependency (all cases below the median); (c) experimental treatment, consistent nurturance versus nurturance-withdrawal. Four analyses of variance were completed for each trial- or error-score from the learning tasks: one for each summary dependency score described above. The results of these analyses are summarized in the tables which follow.

Results

TASK I—NUMBER OF TRIALS

TABLE 2 shows that the *F* ratio for the experimental variable was significant beyond the .01 level in analysis 1 and beyond the .05 level in analysis 2. The means for groups C and NW are reported in TABLE 3 along with the *t* ratio for the difference between means. These data show that NW children (who had experienced nurturance-withdrawal) took fewer trials to complete the task than C children (who had experienced consistent nurturance). TABLE 2 also shows that in two analyses there was a significant interaction between experimental condition and the sex of child. This interaction may be interpreted to indicate that the effects of nurturance-withdrawal by a female adult are dependent on the sex of the child. The data reported in TABLE 3 show more clearly the effects of this interaction: nurturance-withdrawal was clearly associated with faster learning of the task for girls, but there was no difference between the means for boys in group C and in group NW.

The *F* ratio for sex of child was significant in one of the analyses reported in TABLE 2, and the direction of mean differences showed that boys as a group learned the task in fewer trials than girls. This difference is believed to

TABLE 3. *Mean number of trials on task I for boys and girls in two experimental groups*

	GROUP C	N	GROUP NW	N	t	p
Boys	15.86	7	16.14	7	..	n.s.
Girls	35.22	9	16.10	10	2.570	$.02 > p > .01$
Boys and Girls	26.77	16	16.11	17	2.041	$.05 > p > .01$

relate to some feature of the task itself rather than the social conditions of the experiment since the same difference was not found in the data for task II; however, the aspect of task I producing the sex difference was not clear from observation of the children in the experiment. The dependency variable was also significant in two analyses; subgroup means showed that the more dependent children (as measured by verbal interaction) learned task I more quickly than the less dependent children, but that more dependent children (as measured by preschool observation) learned task I less quickly than the less dependent children.

TASK I—NUMBER OF ERRORS

Since the error-measure was highly correlated with the trials-measure on task I similar results would be expected and were obtained from the analyses of variance. *F* ratios for the experimental variable were significant in analyses 1 and 2 (TABLE 4). Again, significant interaction between sex of child and experimental condition was found (in analysis 4, TABLE 4). TABLE 5 reports the means for the experimental groups according to sex of child, and once more the results show significant differences between the experimental groups for girls but not for boys.

The *F* ratio for sex of child was significant in one analysis indicating that boys learned the task faster than girls. The dependency variable was significant in two analyses, but mean differences were in the same inconsistent directions as in the analysis of trial-scores on task I.

TASK II—NUMBER OF TRIALS

The distribution of scores on this measure significantly departed from normality; hence the results are not reported here.

TABLE 4. *F ratios from four analyses of variance based on number of errors on task I according to sex of child, dependence, and experimental condition*

SOURCE	ANALYSIS 1 * ($N = 27$)	ANALYSIS 2 * ($N = 33$)	ANALYSIS 3 * ($N = 32$)	ANALYSIS 4 * ($N = 31$)
Sex of Child	9.421 ‡	1.360	2.581	1.385
Dependence	5.060 †	.190	1.050	6.577 †
Experimental Condition	10.519 ‡	4.640 †	1.232	.924
Sex × Dependence	1.943	4.063	.003	.532
Sex × Condition	4.267	1.560	3.262	6.118 †
Dependence × Condition	2.458	1.364	1.610	.772
Sex × Dependence × Condition	.074	1.219	.003	1.414

* The measures of dependence used were: analysis 1, frequency of verbal interaction initiated by child in the laboratory session; analysis 2, frequency of dependence on adults observed in the laboratory session; analysis 3, teachers' ratings of dependence; analysis 4, dependence on preschool teachers as recorded by observers.
† Significant between .05 and .01.
‡ Significant between .01 and .001.

TABLE 5. *Mean number of errors on task I for boys and girls in two experimental groups*

	GROUP C	N	GROUP NW	N	t	p
Boys	18.14	7	18.71	7	..	n.s.
Girls	39.33	9	17.30	10	2.71	$.02 > p > .01$
Boys and Girls	30.06	16	17.88	17	1.90	$.10 > p > .05$

TABLE 6. *F ratios from four analyses of variance based on number of errors on task II according to sex of child, dependence, and experimental condition*

SOURCE	ANALYSIS 1 * ($N = 24$)	ANALYSIS 2 * ($N = 29$)	ANALYSIS 3 * ($N = 28$)	ANALYSIS 4 * ($N = 28$)
Sex of Child	.169	1.567	.170	.056
Dependence	2.146	.493	5.318 †	1.359
Experimental Condition	.501	2.788	4.755 †	.521
Sex × Dependence	2.332	1.691	2.667	.314
Sex × Condition	.003	.014	.373	1.682
Dependence × Condition	1.155	.037	.311	.167
Sex × Dependence × Condition	.263	.048	.376	1.983

* The measures of dependence used were: analysis 1, frequency of verbal interaction initiated by child in the laboratory session; analysis 2, frequency of dependence on adults observed in the laboratory session; analysis 3, teachers' ratings of dependence; analysis 4, dependence on preschool teachers as recorded by observers.

† Significant between .05 and .01.

TASK II—NUMBER OF ERRORS

The results for errors on task II were consistent with respect to experimental condition with those found on task I, although at a lesser level of significance. TABLE 6 shows that one *F* ratio for the conditions variable was significant beyond the .05 level.

The mean number of errors on task II made by the two experimental groups are reported in TABLE 7. These data are consistent with those for task I and suggest that faster learning was produced under the nurturance-withdrawal condition than under a condition of uninterrupted nurturance. No significant interaction effects were discovered in the analyses of variance.

The *F* ratios for sex of child were not significant in these analyses; the dependency variable (when measured by teacher ratings) yielded a significant *F*, and the means suggest that more dependent children learned task II faster than less dependent children.

Discussion

THE findings for girls uniformly support the hypothesis that nurturance-withdrawal is associated with more efficient performance on the learning tasks than consistent nurturance. The results for boys, however, showed that there were no differences between the nurturance-withdrawal and the consistent nurturance groups. Actually, the results for boys were not so clearly negative. When the boys' groups were divided according to the measures of dependence, *highly* dependent boys were found to respond much as the girls while *low* dependent boys responded in the reverse fashion. Thus, highly dependent boys (who may be assumed to be generally anxious concerning their relationships with adults) did learn more efficiently when the experimenter withdrew her nurturance. The boys in the low dependency group who were consistently nurtured learned more efficiently than boys

TABLE 7. *Mean number of errors on task II for boys and girls in two experimental groups*

	GROUP C	*N*	GROUP NW	*N*	*t*	*p*
Boys	12.40	5	6.17	6	1.121	$.30 > p > .20$
Girls	8.33	9	4.44	9	1.420	$.20 > p > .10$
Boys and Girls	9.79	14	5.07	15	1.750	$.10 > p > .05$

in this group who experienced nurturance-withdrawal. Although the number of cases in these subgroups was small, this trend in the data suggests support for the hypothesis concerning the influence of nurturance-withdrawal for highly dependent boys as well as for the girls.

The fact that the findings for boys were so equivocal is an interesting one for further exploration. It may be that boys respond differently from girls to the nurturance-withdrawal of a *female* experimenter. Psychoanalytic theory regarding Oedipal relationships suggests that the punitiveness of a like-sexed adult should be more threatening to a child than the punitiveness of an opposite-sexed adult. It would be comparatively easy to incorporate sex of experimenter as a variable in a study such as this. However, since the results of this study suggest that nurturance-withdrawal fails to motivate only *low* dependent boys, there may be some sort of complex interaction among experimental conditions which this study failed to bring to light. For example, boys of this age who are not overtly dependent on adults may have moved further than highly dependent boys toward identifying with the male sex role, which in our culture contains certain elements of independence and self-reliance. Boys who *are* highly identified with the male role might well respond with greater anxiety to the mothering nurturance of the experimenter than to the condition in which the experimenter ceases to be attentive and leaves the child alone. If this were the case, most efficient learning would then have taken place in the low dependency boys under conditions of consistent nurturance. The experiment contains no measure of identification by which this interpretation can be checked.

The relationships of sex of child and dependence to speed of learning on the experimental tasks are far from being clear-cut in these data. Boys tended to learn task I faster than girls, but not task II. Dependence, as measured either by verbal interaction in the laboratory session or by teacher ratings, was positively associated with speed of learning; however, dependence as rated by observers in the preschool proved to be negatively associated with speed of learning. The sources of these inconsistencies probably lie in the situational and procedural differences involved in the various measures of dependence; the intercorrelations among the dependency measures suggest that the various measures did *not* measure similar behavioral traits. It does not appear possible, therefore, without further study, to suggest the manner in which motivation to be dependent modifies the effects of nurturance-withdrawal on speed of learning in young children.

The general significance of these findings is felt to be clear and in the direction suggested by the hypothesis tested: nurturance-withdrawal stimulates faster learning than nurturance alone on simple cognitive tasks for girls, and probably also for boys. There may be, however, some second- or third-order interaction between nurturance-withdrawal, sex of child, sex of experimenter, and dependence which influences the behavior of boys under conditions like those of this experiment.

Summary

THIRTY-FOUR four-year-old preschool children were divided into two experimental groups equated on the basis of sex and teachers' ratings of dependence on adults in preschool. Individual subjects in one group (C) were consistently nurtured by a female experimenter during a 10-minute period of interaction, after which two simple tasks were learned by the child. The subjects in the second group (NW) experienced nurturant interaction with the experimenter during only five minutes, then experienced five minutes of non-nurturant response from the experimenter, and finally were asked to learn the tasks. The data were treated by an analysis of variance technique in which learning scores were divided according to sex of child, dependency ratings, and experimental condition.

Children in group NW took fewer trials to learn task I than children in group C. Although the group findings were significant, analysis according to sex of child showed that nurturance-withdrawal was most clearly associated with faster learning in girls. Children in group NW made fewer errors in learning both task I and task II, although these findings were most significant for girls.

It is felt that these results support the hypothesis that nurturance-withdrawal supplies greater motivation than consistent nurturance for children's behavior which is designed to gain the reassurance of adults.

REFERENCES

BELLER, E. K. Dependency and independence in young children. *J. genet. Psychol.,* 1955, **87,** 25–35.

CARL, J. An experimental study of the effect of nurturance on preschool children. Unpublished doctoral dissertion, State Univer. of Iowa, 1949.

DOLLARD, J., & MILLER, N. E. *Personality and psychotherapy.* New York: McGraw-Hill, 1950.

FREUD, S. Three contributions to the theory of sex. In *The basic writings of Sigmund Freud.* New York: Random House, 1938.

GEWIRTZ, J. L. Succorance in young children. Unpublished doctoral dissertation, State Univer. of Iowa, 1948.

GEWIRTZ, J. L. Three determinants of attention-seeking in young children. *Monogr. Soc. Res. Child Develpm.,* 1954, **19,** No. 2 (Serial No. 59).

GEWIRTZ, J. L. Does brief social deprivation enhance the effectiveness of a social reinforcer ("approval")? *Amer. Psychologist,* 1956, **11,** 428. (Abstract.)

HARTUP, W. W. Nurturance and nurturance-withdrawal in relation to the dependency behavior of preschool children. Unpublished doctoral dissertation, Harvard Univer., 1955.

MILLER, N. E. Studies of fear as an acquirable drive: I. Fear as motivation and fear-reduction as reinforcement in the learning of new responses. *J. exp. Psychol.,* 1948, **38,** 89–101.

MOWRER, O. H. *Learning theory and personality dynamics.* New York: Ronald, 1950.

SEARS, R. R., *et al.* Some child-rearing antecedents of dependency and aggression in young children. *Genet. Psychol. Monogr.,* 1953, **47,** 135–234.

SMITH, H. T. A comparison of interview and observation measures of mother behavior. Unpublished doctoral dissertation, Harvard Univer., 1953.

WALKER, H. M., & LEV, J. *Statistical inference.* New York: Holt, 1953.

BERNARD C. ROSEN *and* ROY D'ANDRADE

The Psychosocial Origins of Achievement Motivation[*]

THE purpose of this study is to examine the origins of achievement motivation (*n* Achievement) within the context of the individual's membership in two important groups: family and social class. Specifically, this paper explores, through the observation of family interaction, the relationship between achievement motivation and certain child-training practices, and the relationship between these practices and the parents' social class membership.

The importance of group membership for personality development has been demonstrated many times. Perhaps the most important of these groups is the family, whose strategic role in the socialization process has led investigators to study the nexus between child-rearing practices and motivation formation. Thus, Winterbottom (1958) examined the relationship between independence-mastery training and achievement motivation and found that achievement motivation is strongest among boys whose mothers (all of whom were middle class) expected relatively early indications of self-reliance and mastery from them.

Since many socialization practices are known to be dissimilar between social groups (Ericson, 1947; Havighurst & Davis, 1955), it might be expected that independence training practices would also differ. A study by McClelland, Rindlisbacher, and de Charms (1955), later replicated by Rosen (1959), demonstrated this to be the case: middle-class parents place greater stress upon independence training than lower class parents. The deduction from this finding that classes differ in their level of *n* Achievement was shown to be correct by Rosen (1956) who found that, on the average, *n* Achievement scores for middle-class adolescents were significantly higher than those for their lower class counterparts.

Significantly, although these studies flow logically from one another, in none of them were all three variables—group membership, child training practices, and *n* Achievement —studied simultaneously. Furthermore, there were certain gaps in these studies which called for theoretical and methodological modifications and additions. The nature of these gaps, and the contributions which it was the research objective of this study to make, are as follows:

Theoretical • The keystone around which studies of the origins of achievement motivation have been built is the notion that training in independent mastery is an antecedent condition of *n* Achievement (McClelland & Friedman, 1952; Winterbottom, 1958). This approach grew out of McClelland's and his associates' theory of the nature and origins of motivation. They argue that all motives are learned, that "they develop out of repeated affective experiences connected with certain types of situations and types of behavior. In the case of achievement motivation, the situation should involve 'standards of excellence,' presumably imposed on the child by the culture, or more particularly by the parents as representatives of the culture, and the behavior should involve either 'competition' with those standards of excellence or attempts

* REPRINTED with abridgment by permission of Bernard C. Rosen and The American Sociological Association from *Sociometry,* 1959, 22, 185–195; 215–218.

to meet them which, if successful, produce positive affect or, if unsuccessful, negative affect. It follows that those cultures or families which stress competition with standards of excellence or which insist *that the child be able to perform certain tasks well by himself* . . . should produce children with high achievement motivation" (McClelland, Atkinson, Clark, & Lowell, 1953).

Two distinctly different kinds of child-training practices are implicit in this theory. The first is the idea that the child is trained to do things "well"; the second, the notion that he is trained to perform tasks "by himself." The former has been called *achievement training* (Child, Storm, & Veroff, 1958) in that it stresses competition in situations involving standards of excellence; the latter has been called *independence training* in that it involves putting the child on his own. The failure to disentangle these two concepts has resulted in a focus of attention upon independence training largely to the exclusion of achievement training, although the former is primarily concerned with developing self-reliance, often in areas involving self-caretaking (e.g., cleaning, dressing, amusing, or defending oneself). Although both kinds of training practices frequently occur together, they are different in content and consequences and needed to be examined separately. We believe that of the two training practices, achievement training is the more effective in generating *n* Achievement.

There is another component of independence training—one which is explicit in the idea of independence—that needed further exploration: *autonomy*. By autonomy, we mean training and permitting the child to exercise a certain amount of freedom of action in decision making. Although a related aspect of autonomy—*power*—was studied by Strodtbeck (1958), who examined the relationship between power distribution in the family, *n* Achievement, and academic achievement among a group of Jewish and Italian adolescents, no study had examined simultaneously the self-reliance and autonomy components of independence training. The operation of both components, we believed, tends to increase the power of independence training to generate *n* Achievement, since in itself high parental expectations for self-reliance may cause rebellion, feelings of rejection, or of apathy on the part of the child, while autonomy without parental expectations for self-reliance and achievement may be perceived as mere permissiveness or indifference.

In association with parental demands that the child be self-reliant, autonomous, and show evidence of high achievement, there must be sanctions to see that these demands are fulfilled. Winterbottom found that mothers of children with high *n* Achievement gave somewhat more intense rewards than mothers of children with low *n* Achievement. Little was known about the role of negative sanctions, or of the relative impact of sanctions from either parent. Further study was required of the degree and kind of sanctions employed by both parents to see that their demands are met.

Methodological • This study departed from two practices common in studies of the origins of *n* Achievement. The first practice is to derive data exclusively from ethnographic materials; the second, to obtain information through questionnaire-type interviews with mothers. Interviews and ethnographies can be valuable sources of information, but they are often contaminated by interviewer and respondent biases, particularly those of perceptual distortion, inadequate recall, and deliberate inaccuracies. There was a need for data derived from systematic observation of parent-child relations. It is not enough to know what parents *say* their child-rearing practices are; these statements should be checked against more objective data, preferably acquired under controlled experimental conditions, that would permit us to *see* what they do. In this study, experiments were employed which enabled a team of investigators to observe parent-child interaction in problem-solving situations that were standardized for all groups and required no special competence associated with age or sex.

An equally strong objection can be raised against the tendency to ignore the father's role in the development of the child's need to achieve. Apart from an earlier study of father-son power relations, no efforts had been made to determine the father's contribution to achievement and independence training—a surprising omission even granted the mother's importance in socializing the child in American society. Although we were not prepared to take a position on the nature of the role relationships between father, mother, and son with respect to this motive, we deliberately created experimental conditions which would enable us to observe the way in which the three members of the family interacted in a problem-solving situation. Finally, this study incorporated in one design the variables of group membership, child-training practices, and motivation, variables that heretofore had not been studied simultaneously. In so doing we hoped to establish the nexus among class membership, socialization practices, and achievement motivation.

Hypotheses

THIS study was designed to provide data that would permit testing two basic hypotheses.

1. Achievement motivation is a result of the following socialization practices: (a) *achievement training,* in which the parents set high goals for their son to attain, indicate that they have a high evaluation of his competence to do a task well, and impose standards of excellence upon tasks against which he is to compete, even in situations where such standards are not explicit; (b) *independence training,* in which the parents indicate to the child that they expect him to be *self-reliant,* while at the same time permit him relative *autonomy* in situations involving decision making where he is given both freedom of action and responsibility for success or failure; (c) *sanctions,* rewards and punishments employed by parents to ensure that their expectations are met and proper behavior is reinforced. Although each contributes to the development of achievement motivation, achievement training is more important than independence training. Neither [is] effective without supporting sanctions.

2. Differences in the mean level of achievement motivation between social classes is in part a function of the differential class emphases upon independence and achievement training: middle-class parents are more likely than lower class parents to stress self-reliance, autonomy, and achievement in problem-solving situations, particularly those involving standards of excellence. They are more likely to recognize and reward evidences of achievement, as well as to be more sensitive of and punitive toward indications of failure.

Experimental Procedure

THE subjects selected to provide data needed for the testing of these hypotheses about the origins of achievement motivation were 120 persons who made up 40 family groups composed of a father, mother, and their son, aged nine, ten, or eleven. The selection of the family groups began with testing the boy. Seven schools in three northeastern Connecticut towns were visited by the same field worker who administered a Thematic Apperception Test individually and privately to 140 boys, aged nine, ten, or eleven. As is customary in the TAT procedure, the subject was presented with a set of four ambiguous pictures and asked to tell a story about each. His imaginative responses were then scored according to a method developed by McClelland and his associates which involves identifying and counting the frequency with which imagery about evaluated performance in competition with a standard of excellence appears in the thoughts of a person when he tells a brief story under time pressure. Experience has shown that this imagery can be identified objectively and reliably. It is the assumption of this test that the more the individual shows indications of evaluated performance connected with affect in his fantasy, the greater the degree to which achievement motivation is part of his personality (McClelland *et al.,* 1953). The stories were scored by two judges; the Pearsonian coefficient of correlation between scorers was .87, a level of reliability similar to those reported in earlier studies with this measure.

Subjects with scores of plus 2 to minus 4 (approximately the bottom quartile) were labeled as having low *n* Achievement, those with scores of plus 9 to plus 22 (approximately the top quartile) as having high *n* Achievement. Any boy with an I.Q. score below 98, with physical defects, whose parents were separated, or who had been raised during part of his life by persons or relatives other than his parents (e.g., grandparents) was eliminated from the sample.

Forty boys, matched by age, race, I.Q., and social class were chosen for further study. All were white, native born, and between nine and eleven years of age; the average was ten years. Half of the boys had high *n* Achievement scores, half had low scores. In each achievement motivation category, half of the boys were middle class, half were lower class. Their social class position was determined according to a modified version of the Hollingshead Index of Social Position (1953) which uses the occupation and education of the chief wage-earner—usually the father—as the principal criteria of status. The middle-class father (class II or III) held either a professional, managerial, white-collar position or was self-employed as an owner of a small- to medium-size business. Often one or both parents in middle-class families were college graduates; all were high-school graduates. The parents of lower class (IV or V) boys were quasi-skilled or skilled workers in local factories, or owners of very small farms—often the farmers held factory jobs as well. Relatively few of these parents had completed high school, none had gone beyond high school.

It can be seen that the study was designed in such a way that the subjects fell into one of four cells, with the achievement motivation level of the boys and the class position of the parents as the classificatory variables. Within each cell there were ten families. This four-cell factorial design was constructed so as to facilitate the use of the analysis of variance technique in the statistical analysis of the data.

. . . A pair of observers visited each family group, usually at night. There were two teams of observers, each composed of a man and woman. Both teams had been trained together to ensure adequate intra- and interteam reliability.

Once in the home, the observers explained that they were interested in studying the factors related to success in school and eventually to a career, and that the son was one of many boys selected from a cross-section of the community. When rapport had been established, the parents and their son were placed at a table—usually in the kitchen—and it was explained that the boy was going to perform certain tasks.

EXPERIMENTAL TASKS

. . . Tasks were devised which the boy could do and which would involve the parents in their son's task performance. The tasks were constructed so that the subjects were often faced with a choice of giving or refusing help. . . . A category system, similar to the Bales system (1951), was devised to permit scoring interaction between parents and son so that the amount and form of each subject's participation could be examined. The investigators were able to learn from . . . interaction data how self-reliant the parents expected their son to be, how much autonomy they permitted him in decision-making situations, and what kind and amount of affect was generated in a problem-solving situation.

. . .

The five tasks used in this study are as follows:

1. *Block Stacking.* The boys were asked to build towers out of very irregularly shaped blocks. They were blindfolded and told to use only one hand in order to create a situation in which the boy was relatively dependent upon his parents for help. His parents were told that this was a test of their son's ability to build things, and that they could *say* anything to their son but could not touch the blocks. A performance norm was set for the experiment by telling the parents that the average boy could build a tower of eight blocks; they were asked to write down privately their estimate of how high they

thought their son could build his tower. The purposes of this experiment were (a) to see how high were the parents' aspirations for and evaluations of their son, e.g., if they set their estimates at, above, or below the norm; (b) to see how self-reliant they expected or permitted their son to be, e.g., how much help they would give him.

There were three trials for this task. The first provided measures of parental evaluations and aspirations not affected by the boy's performance; the second and third trial estimates provided measures affected by the boy's performance. The procedure for the third trial differed from the first two in that the boy was told that he would be given a nickel for each block he stacked. Each member of the family was asked to estimate privately how high the boy should build his tower. No money would be given for blocks stacked higher than the estimate nor would the subject receive anything if the stack tumbled before he reached the estimate. Conservative estimates, hence, provided security but little opportunity for gain; high estimates involved more opportunity for gain but greater risk. The private estimates were then revealed to all and the family was asked to reach a group decision. In addition to securing objective measures of parental aspiration-evaluation levels, the observers scored the interaction between subjects, thus obtaining data as to the kind and amount of instructions the parents gave their son, the amount of help the son asked for or rejected, and the amount and kind of affect generated during the experiment.

2. *Anagrams.* In this task the boys were asked to make words of three letters or more out of six prescribed letters: G, H, K, N, O, R. The letters, which could be reused after each word was made, were printed on wooden blocks so that they could be manipulated. The parents were given three additional lettered blocks, T, U, and B, and a list of words that could be built with each new letter. They were informed that they could give the boy a new letter (in the sequence T, U, B) whenever they wished and could say anything to him, short of telling him what word to build. There was a ten-minute time limit for this experiment. Since this is a familiar game, no efforts were made to explain the functions of the task.

The purposes of this experiment were: (a) to see how self-reliant the parents expected their son to be, e.g., how soon they would give him a new letter, how much and what kind of direction they would give him, if they would keep him working until he got all or most of the words on the list or "take him off the hook" when he got stuck. And (b) to obtain, by scoring interaction between the subjects, measures of the affect generated by the problem-solving process, e.g., the amount of tension shown by the subjects, the positive and negative remarks directed toward one another.

3. *Patterns.* In this experiment the parents were shown eight patterns, graduated in difficulty, that could be made with Kohs blocks. The subjects were informed that pattern 1 was easier to make than pattern 2, pattern 3 was more difficult than 2 but easier than 4, and so forth. The subjects were told that this was a test of the boy's ability to remember and reproduce patterns quickly and accurately. Each parent and boy was asked to select privately three patterns which the boy would be asked to make from memory after having seen the pattern for five seconds. All three patterns were chosen *before* the boy began the problem solving so that his performance in this task would not affect the choice of the patterns. Where there were differences of choice, as inevitably there were, the subjects were asked to discuss their differences and make a group decision. Insofar as possible the observers took a verbatim account of the decision-making process, scoring for three kinds of variables: (a) the number of acts each subject contributed to the decision-making process, (b) the number of times each individual initiated a decision, and (c) the number of times each subject was successful in having the group accept his decision or in seeing to it that a decision was made.

The purposes of this experiment were: (a) to obtain another measure of the parents' evaluations of and aspirations for the boy, e.g., whether they would pick easy or difficult tasks for him to do; (b) to get a measure of the autonomy permitted the boy, e.g., whether they would let him choose his own patterns or impose their choices upon him; and (c) to see how much help they would give him and what affect would be generated by the experiment.

4. *Ring Toss.* In this experiment each member of the group was asked to choose privately ten positions, from each of which the boy was to throw three rings at a peg. The distance from the peg was delineated by a tape with 1-foot graduations laid on the floor. The subjects were told that this was a test of discrimination and judgment and that after each set of three tosses they would be asked to make a judgment as to the best distance from which to make the next set of tosses. Group decisions were made as to where the boy should stand. The purposes of this experiment were: (a) to see whether the parents imposed standards of excellence upon a task for which no explicit standard had been set, e.g., whether the parents would treat this as a childish game or see it as a task which could and should be done well. Would they choose easy or difficult positions? (b) To determine how much autonomy they permitted their son, e.g., would they let him choose his own position?

5. *Hatrack.* The Maier Hatrack Problem was used in this experiment. The boy was given two sticks and a C-clamp and instructed to build a rack strong enough to hold a coat and hat. His parents were told that this was a test of the boy's ability to build things. In this task no one was given the solution at the beginning of the experiment. For the first time the parents had no advantage over the boy—a most uncomfortable position for many parents, particularly the fathers. This stress situation was created deliberately to maximize the possibility of the problem generating affect, as was often the case, with some hostility being directed at the observers. After seven minutes the parents were given the solution to the problem. The purposes of this experiment were: (a) to see how self-reliant the parents expected their son to be. After receiving the solution what kind of clues would the parents give the boy? How hard would they expect him to work on his own? (b) to obtain measures of the affect created in an unusually frustrating situation. How would the parents handle their frustration? Would they turn it against the boy?

CATEGORY SYSTEM

References have been made to the use of a category system for scoring interaction between subjects. A brief description of this system, shown in TABLE 1, is in order. Most of the subjects' verbal and some of their motor behavior (e.g., laughing, handclapping, scowling) was scored in one of twelve categories. In eight of these categories were placed acts involving relatively strong affect. Four additional categories were used to distinguish between various kinds of statements—either giving, requesting, or rejecting directions—which contained very little or no affect. A distinction was made between negative and positive affective acts. Affective acts associated with explicit or implicit evaluations of the boy's performance which aimed at motivating or changing his behavior were scored differently from affective acts which involved reactions to the boy and only indirectly to his performance.

Directional acts by the parents were remarks designed to help the boy perform his task. A distinction was made between *specific* directions (S) which were acts instructing the subject to do particular things which would facilitate task completion, and *nonspecific* (N) which were acts aimed at giving the subject some information but not specific enough to enable him to rely entirely upon it. It was believed that nonspecific statements were more likely than specific statements to create self-reliance in the child.

The affective acts were schematized in two sets—one positive, the other negative. The first set was comprised of acts involving direct expressions of emotions toward another person, not necessarily in the context of task performance, either of a positive character (+X), such as expressions of love or ap-

TABLE 1. *The system of categories used in scoring parent-child interaction*

+X	Expresses approval, gives love, comfort, affection
+T	Shows positive tension release, jokes, laughs
+E	Gives explicit positive evaluation of performance, indicates job well done
+P	Attempts to push up performance through expression of enthusiasm, urges, cheers on
N	Gives nonspecific directions, gives hints, clues, general suggetions
S	Gives specific directions, gives detailed information about how to do a task
aa	Asks aid, information, or advice
ra	Rejects aid, information, or advice
–P	Attempts to push up performance through expressions of displeasure; urges on, indicating disappointment at speed and level of performance
–E	Gives explicit negative evaluation of performance, indicates job poorly done
–T	Shows negative tension release, shows irritation, coughs
–X	Expresses hostility, denigrates, makes sarcastic remarks

proval, or of a negative character (–X), such as indications of hostility and rejection. Another set was of acts involving release of tension, either associated with positive affect (+T) such as grins, laughter, jokes, or negative affect (–T) such as scowls, coughs, or irritated gestures. Tension-release acts differ from acts of direct emotion (X) in that the former were not focused toward any person but were diffused, undirected reactions to the general situation. The next set of acts involved parental evaluation of the boy's performance. Those acts in which the parents stated that the boy was doing the task well were scored as positive evaluations (+E), while statements that the boy was doing poorly were scored as negative evaluations (–E). The last two categories involved acts aimed at urging or pushing the boy to perform more effectively. These "pushing up the performance level acts" were scored in one of two categories. Those acts in which the parents "cheered" the boy on while at the same time indicating that they expected him to do better were scored as positive pushing acts (+P); negative pushing acts (–P) were statements in which the parents sought to improve the boy's performance by indicating in a threatening way that they thought he could do better.

Only four kinds of acts were scored for the boy: whether he asked for aid (aa), rejected aid (ra), showed positive tension (+T) or negative tension (–T). An act was defined as the smallest segment of verbal or motor behavior which could be recognized as belonging to one of the twelve categories in the system. The actor rather than the target of the acts was used as the observer's frame of reference.

. . .

Discussion and Summary

THE question of how achievement training, independence training, and sanctions are related to achievement motivation may be rephrased by asking, How does the behavior of parents of boys with high *n* Achievement differ from the behavior of parents whose sons have low *n* Achievement?

To begin with, the observers' subjective impressions are that the parents of high *n* Achievement boys tend to be more competitive, show more involvement, and seem to take more pleasure in the problem-solving experiments. They appear to be more interested [in] and concerned with their son's performance; they tend to give him more things to manipulate rather than fewer; on the average they put out more affective acts. More objective data show that the parents of a boy with high *n* Achievement tend to have higher aspirations for him to do well at any given task, and they seem to have a higher regard for his competence at problem solving. They set up standards of excellence for the boy even when none is given, or if a standard is given will expect him to do "better than average." As he progresses they tend to react to his performance with warmth and approval, or, in the case of the mothers especially, with disapproval if he performs poorly.

It seems clear that achievement training contributes more to the development of *n* Achievement than does independence training. Indeed, the role of independence training in generating achievement motivation can only be understood in the context of what appears to be a division of labor between the fathers and mothers of high *n* Achievement boys.

Fathers and mothers both provide achievement training and independence training, but the fathers seem to contribute much more to the latter than do the mothers. Fathers tend to let their sons develop some self-reliance by giving hints (N) rather than always telling "how to do it" (S). They are less likely to push (P) and more likely to give the boy a greater degree of autonomy in making his own decisions. Fathers of high *n* Achievement boys often appear to be competent men who are willing to take a back seat while their sons are performing. They tend to beckon from ahead rather than push from behind.

The mothers of boys with high achievement motivation tend to stress achievement training rather than independence training. In fact, they are likely to be more dominant and to expect less self-reliance than the mothers of boys with low *n* Achievement. But their aspirations for their sons are higher and their concern over success greater. Thus, they expect the boys to build higher towers and place them farther away from the peg in the Ring Toss experiment. As a boy works his mother tends to become emotionally involved. Not only is she more likely to reward him with approval (Warmth) but also to punish him with hostility (Rejection). *In a way, it is this factor of involvement that most clearly sets the mothers of high* n *Achievement boys apart from the mothers of low* n *Achievement boys:* the former score higher on every variable, expect specific directions. And although these mothers are likely to give their sons more option as to exactly (fewer Specifics) what to do, they give them less option about doing something and doing it well. Observers report that the mothers of high *n* Achievement boys tend to be striving, competent persons. Apparently they expect their sons to be the same.

The different emphasis which the fathers and mothers of high *n* Achievement boys place upon achievement and independence training suggests that the training practices of father and mother affect the boy in different ways. Apparently, the boy can take and perhaps needs achievement training from both parents, but the effects of independence training and sanctions, in particular Autonomy and Rejection, are different depending upon whether they come from the father or mother. In order for high *n* Achievement to develop, the boy appears to need more autonomy from his father than from his mother. The father who gives the boy a relatively high degree of autonomy provides him with an opportunity to compete on his own ground, to test his skill, and to gain a sense of confidence in his own competence. The dominating father may crush his son (and in so doing destroys the boy's achievement motive), perhaps because he views the boy as a competitor and is viewed as such by his son. On the other hand, the mother who dominates the decision-making process does not seem to have the same affect on the boy, possibly because she is perceived as *imposing her standards* on the boy, while a dominating father is perceived as *imposing himself* on the son. It may be that the mother-son relations are typically more secure than those between father and son, so that the boy is better able to accept higher levels of dominance and rejection from his mother than his father without adverse affect on his need to achieve. Relatively rejecting, dominating fathers, particularly those with less than average warmth—as tended to be the case with the fathers of low *n* Achievement boys—seem to be a threat to the boy[s] and a deterrent to the development of *n* Achievement. On the other hand, above-average dominance and rejection, coupled with above-average warmth, as tends to be the case with mothers of high *n* Achievement boys, appear to be a spur to achievement motivation. It will be remembered that the fathers of high *n* Achievement boys are on the average less Rejecting, less Pushing, and less Dominant—all of which points to their general hands-off policy.

It is unlikely that these variables operate separately, but the way in which they interact in the development of achievement motivation is not clear. Possibly the variables interact in a manner which produces cyclical effects roughly approximating the interaction that characterized the experimental task situations of this study. The cycle begins with the parents imposing standards of excellence upon a task and setting a high goal for the boy to achieve (e.g., Ring Toss, estimates and choices in Block Stacking and Patterns). As the boy engages in the task, they reinforce acceptable behavior by expressions of warmth (both parents) or by evidences of disapproval (primarily mother). The boy's performance improves, in part because of previous experience and in part because of the greater concern shown by his parents and expressed through affective reaction to his performance and greater attention to his training. With improved performance, the parents grant the boy greater autonomy and interfere less with his performance (primarily father). Goals are then reset at a higher level and the cycle continues.

REFERENCES

BALES, R. F. *Interaction process analysis*. Reading, Mass.: Addison-Wesley, 1951.

CHILD, I. L., STORM, T., & VEROFF, J. Achievement themes in folk tales related to socialization practice. In J. W. Atkinson, *Motives in fantasy, action, and society*. Princeton, N.J.: Van Nostrand, 1958.

ERICSON, MARTHA C. Social status and child-rearing practices. In T. M. Newcomb & E. L. Hartley (Eds.), *Readings in social psychology*. New York: Holt, 1947.

HAVIGHURST, R. J., & DAVIS, A. Social class differences in child-rearing. *Amer. sociol. Rev.* 1955, **20**, 438–442.

HOLLINGSHEAD, A. B. & REDLICH, F. C. Social stratification and psychiatric disorders. *Amer. sociol. Rev.* 1953, **18**, 163–169.

MCCLELLAND, D. C., & FRIEDMAN, G. A. A cross-cultural study of the relationship between child-training practices and achievement motivation, appearing in folk tales. In G. E. Swanson, T. M. Newcomb, & E. L. Hartley (Eds.) *Readings in social psychology*. New York: Holt, 1952.

MCCLELLAND, D. C., ATKINSON, J. W., CLARK, R. A., & LOWELL, E. L. *The achievement motive*. New York: Appleton-Century-Crofts, 1953.

MCCLELLAND, D. C., RINDLISBACHER, A., & DECHARMS, R. Religious and other sources of parental attitudes toward independence training. In D. C. McClelland *et al.* (Eds.), *Studies in motivation*. New York: Appleton-Century-Crofts, 1955.

ROSEN, B. C. The achievement syndrome: a psychocultural dimension of social stratification. *Amer. sociol. Rev.* 1956, **21**, 203–211.

ROSEN, B. C. Race, ethnicity, and the achievement syndrome. *Amer. sociol. Rev.* 1959, **24**, 47–60.

SAKODA, J. M. Directions for a multiple-group method of factor analysis. Univer. of Connecticut, June, 1955. (Mimeographed.)

SEARS, R. R., MACCOBY, ELEANOR E., & LEVIN, H. *Patterns of child rearing*. New York: Row, Peterson, 1957.

STRODTBECK, F. L. Family interaction, values, and achievement. In D. C. McClelland, A. L.

Baldwin, U. Bronfenbrenner, & F. L. Strodtbeck, *Talent and society*. Princeton, N. J.: Van Nostrand, 1958.

TRYON, R. C. *Cluster analysis.* Ann Arbor, Mich.: Edwards Brothers, 1939.

WINTERBOTTOM, M. R. The relation of need for achievement to learning experiences in independence and mastery. In J. W. Atkinson, *Motives in fantasy, action, and society*. Princeton, N.J.: Van Nostrand, 1958.

ERIK H. ERIKSON

Eight Ages of Man*

EDITOR'S INTRODUCTION

ONE OF the criticisms of Freudian theory is that it neglects the culture. Critics point out that Freud was treating patients who had been reared by Victorian standards with an excessive emphasis upon prudery. It was to be expected, then, that Freud would find in his clients neurotic effects of sexual repression, and that his theory would emphasize the central role of sex. That theory, the reader will recall, postulated stages, at each one of which some part of the body was a source of erotic pleasure, and during which the child's libido was directed toward himself, one of his parents, playmates of his own sex, or, eventually, a marriage partner. Thus Freud described the infant during the first year of life as being in the oral stage, with the mouth serving as the chief source of pleasure and with the baby's love-energy in this narcissistic period being directed toward himself.

Erikson's training in cultural anthropology as well as in psychoanalysis makes him view the developmental process differently. He, too, postulates stages, but he sees at each stage a crisis that has its roots in the demands of society. Society requires that certain tasks be mastered at a particular stage of development. There is a crisis when the child is faced with these tasks, a conflict between the demands of the old biological self and the task required. Resolution of the crisis adds a new dimension to the personality. We see the crisis illustrated, during the first year of life, according to Erikson, in the constant conflict between inner needs and outer demands. It takes time for bodily functions to mature, and during that time the infant must endure some suffering—as when he is hungry and must wait for food. It is the way in which a mother ministers to the baby during such inevitable frustrations that creates a sense of trust or of mistrust in the infant. Resolution of each crisis in ensuing life-stages adds a new quality to the ego—either a positive or a negative dimension, depending upon how parents or parent surrogates impose societal demands.

1. Basic Trust vs. Basic Mistrust

THE FIRST demonstration of social trust in the baby is the ease of his feeding, the depth of his sleep, the relaxation of his bowels. The experience of a mutual regulation of his increasingly receptive capacities with the maternal techniques of provision gradually helps him to balance the discomfort caused by the immaturity of homeostasis with which he was born. In his gradually increasing waking hours he finds that more and more adventures of the senses arouse a feeling of familiarity, of having coincided with a feeling of inner goodness. Forms of comfort, and people associated with them, become as familiar as the gnawing discomfort of the bowels. The infant's first social achievement, then, is his willingness to let the mother out of sight without undue anxiety or rage, because she has become an inner certainty as well as an outer predictability. Such con-

* REPRINTED from *Childhood and Society* by Erik H. Erikson. By permission of W. W. Norton & Company, Inc. Pp. 247–274.

sistency, continuity, and sameness of experience provide a rudimentary sense of ego identity which depends, I think, on the recognition that there is an inner population of remembered and anticipated sensations and images which are firmly correlated with the outer population of familiar and predictable things and people.

What we here call trust coincides with what Therese Benedek has called confidence. If I prefer the word "trust," it is because there is more naïveté and more mutuality in it: an infant can be said to be trusting where it would go too far to say that he has confidence. The general state of trust, furthermore, implies not only that one has learned to rely on the sameness and continuity of the outer providers, but also that one may trust oneself and the capacity of one's own organs to cope with urges; and that one is able to consider oneself trustworthy enough so that the providers will not need to be on guard lest they be nipped.

The constant tasting and testing of the relationship between inside and outside meets its crucial test during the rages of the biting stage, when the teeth cause pain from within and when outer friends either prove of no avail or withdraw from the only action which promises relief: biting. Not that teething itself seems to cause all the dire consequences sometimes ascribed to it. As outlined earlier, the infant now is driven to "grasp" more, but he is apt to find desired presences elusive: nipple and breast, and the mother's focused attention and care. Teething seems to have a prototypal significance and may well be the model for the masochistic tendency to assure cruel comfort by enjoying one's hurt whenever one is unable to prevent a significant loss.

In psychopathology the absence of basic trust can best be studied in infantile schizophrenia, while lifelong underlying weakness of such trust is apparent in adult personalities in whom withdrawal into schizoid and depressive states is habitual. The re-establishment of a state of trust has been found to be the basic requirement for therapy in these cases. For no matter what conditions may have caused a psychotic break, the bizarreness and withdrawal in the behavior of many very sick individuals hides an attempt to recover social mutuality by a testing of the borderlines between senses and physical reality, between words and social meanings.

Psychoanalysis assumes the early process of differentiation between inside and outside to be the origin of projection and introjection which remain some of our deepest and most dangerous defense mechanisms. In introjection we feel and act as if an outer goodness had become an inner certainty. In projection, we experience an inner harm as an outer one: we endow significant people with the evil which actually is in us. These two mechanisms, then, projection and introjection, are assumed to be modeled after whatever goes on in infants when they would like to externalize pain and internalize pleasure, an intent which must yield to the testimony of the maturing senses and ultimately of reason. These mechanisms are, more or less normally, reinstated in acute crises of love, trust, and faith in adulthood and can characterize irrational attitudes toward adversaries and enemies in masses of "mature" individuals.

The firm establishment of enduring patterns for the solution of the nuclear conflict of basic trust versus basic mistrust in mere existence is the first task of the ego, and thus first of all a task for maternal care. But let it be said here that the amount of trust derived from earliest infantile experience does not seem to depend on absolute quantities of food or demonstrations of love, but rather on the quality of the maternal relationship. Mothers create a sense of trust in their children by that kind of administration which in its quality combines sensitive care of the baby's individual needs and a firm sense of personal trustworthiness within the trusted framework of their culture's life style. This forms the basis in the child for a sense of identity which will later combine a sense of being "all right," of being oneself, and of becoming what other people trust one will become. There are, therefore (within certain limits previously defined as the "musts" of child care), few frustrations in either this or the following stages which the growing child cannot endure if the frustration leads to the ever-renewed experience of greater sameness and stronger continuity of development, toward a final integration of the individual life cycle with some meaningful wider belongingness. Parents must not only have certain ways of guiding by prohibition and permission; they must also be able to represent to the child a deep, an almost somatic conviction that there is a meaning to what they are doing. Ultimately, children become neurotic not from frustrations, but from the lack or loss of societal meaning in these frustrations.

But even under the most favorable circumstances, this stage seems to introduce into psychic life (and become prototypical for) a sense of inner division and universal nostalgia for a paradise forfeited. It is against this powerful combination of a sense of having been deprived, of having been divided, and of having been abandoned—that basic trust must maintain itself throughout life.

Each successive stage and crisis has a special relation to one of the basic elements of society, and this for the simple reason that the human life cycle and man's institutions have evolved together. In this chapter we can do little more than mention, after the description of each stage, what basic element of social organization is related to it. This relation is twofold: man brings to these institutions the remnants of his infantile mentality and his youthful fervor, and he receives from them—as long as they manage to maintain their actuality—a reinforcement of his infantile gains.

The parental faith which supports the trust emerging in the newborn, has throughout history sought its institutional safeguard (and, on occasion, found its greatest enemy) in organized religion. Trust born of care is, in fact, the touchstone of the *actuality* of a given religion. All religions have in common the periodical childlike surrender to a Provider or providers who dispense earthly fortune as well as spiritual health; some demonstration of man's smallness by way of reduced posture and humble gesture; the admission in prayer and song of misdeeds, of misthoughts, and of evil intentions; fervent appeal for inner unification by divine guidance; and finally, the insight that individual trust must become a common faith, individual mistrust a commonly formulated evil, while the individual's restoration must become part of the ritual practice of many, and must become a sign of trustworthiness in the community.[1] We have illustrated how tribes dealing with one segment of nature develop a collective magic which seems to treat the Supernatural Providers of food and fortune as if they were angry and must be appeased by prayer and self-torture. Primitive religions, the most primitive layer in all religions, and the religious layer in each individual, abound with efforts at atonement which try to make up for vague deeds against a maternal matrix and try to restore faith in the goodness of one's strivings and in the kindness of the powers of the universe.

Each society and each age must find the institutionalized form of reverence which derives vitality from its world-image—from predestination to indeterminacy. The clinician can only observe that many are proud to be without religion whose children cannot afford their being without it. On the other hand, there are many who seem to derive a vital faith from social action or scientific pursuit. And again, there are many who profess faith, yet in practice breathe mistrust both of life and man.

2. Autonomy vs. Shame and Doubt

IN DESCRIBING the growth and the crises of the human person as a series of alternative basic attitudes such as trust vs. mistrust, we take recourse to the term a "sense of," although, like a "sense of health," or a "sense of being unwell," such "senses" pervade surface and depth, consciousness and the unconscious. They are, then, at the same time, ways of *experiencing* accessible to introspection; ways of *behaving*, observable by others; and unconscious *inner states* determinable by test

1 This is the communal and psychosocial side of religion. Its often paradoxical relation to the spirituality of the individual is a matter not to be treated briefly and in passing (see *Young Man Luther*). (E.H.E.)

and analysis. It is important to keep these three dimensions in mind, as we proceed.

Muscular maturation sets the stage for experimentation with two simultaneous sets of social modalities: holding on and letting go. As is the case with all of these modalities, their basic conflicts can lead in the end to either hostile or benign expectations and attitudes. Thus, to hold can become a destructive and cruel retaining or restraining, and it can be become a pattern of care: to have and to hold. To let go, too, can turn into an inimical letting loose of destructive forces, or it can become a relaxed "to let pass" and "to let be."

Outer control at this stage, therefore, must be firmly reassuring. The infant must come to feel that the basic faith in existence, which is the lasting treasure saved from the rages of the oral stage, will not be jeopardized by this about-face of his, this sudden violent wish to have a choice, to appropriate demandingly, and to eliminate stubbornly. Firmness must protect him against the potential anarchy of his as yet untrained sense of discrimination, his inability to hold on and to let go with discretion. As his environment encourages him to "stand on his own feet," it must protect him against meaningless and arbitrary experiences of shame and of early doubt.

The latter danger is the one best known to us. For if denied the gradual and well-guided experience of the autonomy of free choice (or if, indeed, weakened by an initial loss of trust) the child will turn against himself all his urge to discriminate and to manipulate. He will overmanipulate himself, he will develop a precocious conscience. Instead of taking possession of things in order to test them by purposeful repetition, he will become obsessed by his own repetitiveness. By such obsessiveness, of course, he then learns to repossess the environment and to gain power by stubborn and minute control, where he could not find large-scale mutual regulation. Such hollow victory is the infantile model for a compulsion neurosis. It is also the infantile source of later attempts in adult life to govern by the letter, rather than by the spirit.

Shame is an emotion insufficiently studied, because in our civilization it is so early and easily absorbed by guilt. Shame supposes that one is completely exposed and conscious of being looked at: in one word, self-conscious. One is visible and not ready to be visible; which is why we dream of shame as a situation in which we are stared at in a condition of incomplete dress, in night attire, "with one's pants down." Shame is early expressed in an impulse to bury one's face, or to sink, right then and there, into the ground. But this, I think, is essentially rage turned against the self. He who is ashamed would like to force the world not to look at him, not to notice his exposure. He would like to destroy the eyes of the world. Instead he must wish for his own invisibility. This potentiality is abundantly used in the educational method of "shaming" used so exclusively by some primitive peoples. Visual shame precedes auditory guilt, which is a sense of badness to be had all by oneself when nobody watches and when everything is quiet—except the voice of the superego. Such shaming exploits an increasing sense of being small, which can develop only as the child stands up and as his awareness permits him to note the relative measures of size and power.

Too much shaming does not lead to genuine propriety but to a secret determination to try to get away with things, unseen—if, indeed, it does not result in defiant shamelessness. There is an impressive American ballad in which a murderer to be hanged on the gallows before the eyes of the community, instead of feeling duly chastened, begins to berate the onlookers, ending every salvo of defiance with the words, "God damn your eyes." Many a small child, shamed beyond endurance, may be in a chronic mood (although not in possession of either the courage or the words) to express defiance in similar terms. What I mean by this sinister reference is that there is a limit to a child's and an adult's endurance in the face of demands to consider himself, his body, and his wishes as evil and dirty, and to his belief in the infallibility of those who pass such judgment. He may be apt to turn things around, and to consider as evil only the fact that they exist: his chance will come when they are gone, or when he will go from them.

Doubt is the brother of shame. Where shame is dependent on the consciousness of being upright and exposed, doubt, so clinical observation leads me to believe, has much to do with a consciousness of having a front and a back—and especially a "behind." For this reverse area of the body, with its aggressive and libidinal focus in the sphincters and in the buttocks, cannot be seen by the child, and yet it can be dominated by the will of others. The "behind" is the small being's dark continent, an area of the body which can be magically dominated and effectively invaded by those who would attack one's power of autonomy and who would designate as evil those products of the bowels which were felt to be all right when they were being passed. This basic sense of doubt in whatever one has left behind forms a substratum for later and more verbal forms of compulsive doubting; this finds its adult expression in paranoiac fears concerning hidden persecutors and secret persecutions threatening from behind (and from within the behind).

This stage, therefore, becomes decisive for the ratio of love and hate, cooperation and willfulness, freedom of self-expression and its suppression. From a sense of self-control without loss of self-esteem comes a lasting sense of good will and pride; from a sense of loss of self-control and of foreign overcontrol comes a lasting propensity for doubt and shame.

If, to some reader, the "negative" potentialities of our stages seem overstated throughout, we must remind him that this is not only the result of a preoccupation with clinical data. Adults, and seemingly mature and unneurotic ones, display a sensitivity concerning a possible shameful "loss of face" and fear of being attacked "from behind" which is not only highly irrational and in contrast to the knowledge available to them, but can be of fateful import if related sentiments influence, for example, interracial and international policies.

We have related basic trust to the institution of religion. The lasting need of the individual to have his will reaffirmed and delineated within an adult order of things which at the same time reaffirms and delineates the will of others has an institutional safeguard in the *principle of law and order*. In daily life as well as in the high courts of law—domestic and international—this principle apportions to each his privileges and his limitations, his obligations and his rights. A sense of rightful dignity and lawful independence on the part of adults around him gives to the child of good will the confident expectation that the kind of autonomy fostered in childhood will not lead to undue doubt or shame in later life. Thus the sense of autonomy fostered in the child and modified as life progresses, serves (and is served by) the preservation in economic and political life of a sense of justice.

3. Initiative vs. Guilt

THERE is in every child at every stage a new miracle of vigorous unfolding, which constitutes a new hope and a new responsibility for all. Such is the sense and the pervading quality of initiative. The criteria for all these senses and qualities are the same: a crisis, more or less beset with fumbling and fear, is resolved, in that the child suddenly seems to "grow together" both in his person and in his body. He appears "more himself," more loving, relaxed and brighter in his judgment, more activated and activating. He is in free possession of a surplus of energy which permits him to forget failures quickly and to approach what seems desirable (even if it also seems uncertain and even dangerous) with undiminished and more accurate direction. Initiative adds to autonomy the quality of undertaking, planning and "attacking" a task for the sake of being active and on the move, where before self-will, more often than not, inspired acts of defiance or, at any rate, protested independence.

I know that the very word "initiative" to many, has an American, and industrial connotation. Yet, initiative is a necessary part of every act, and man needs a sense of initiative for whatever he learns and does, from fruit-gathering to a system of enterprise.

The ambulatory stage and that of infantile

genitality add to the inventory of basic social modalities that of "making," first in the sense of "being on the make." There is no simpler, stronger word for it; it suggests pleasure in attack and conquest. In the boy, the emphasis remains on phallic-intrusive modes; in the girl it turns to modes of "catching" in more aggressive forms of snatching or in the milder form of making oneself attractive and endearing.

The danger of this stage is a sense of guilt over the goals contemplated and the acts initiated in one's exuberant enjoyment of new locomotor and mental power: acts of aggressive manipulation and coercion which soon go far beyond the executive capacity of organism and mind and therefore call for an energetic halt on one's contemplated initiative. While autonomy concentrates on keeping potential rivals out, and therefore can lead to jealous rage most often directed against encroachments by younger siblings, initiative brings with it anticipatory rivalry with those who have been there first and may, therefore, occupy with their superior equipment the field toward which one's initiative is directed. Infantile jealousy and rivalry, those often embittered and yet essentially futile attempts at demarcating a sphere of unquestioned privilege, now come to a climax in a final contest for a favored position with the mother; the usual failure leads to resignation, guilt, and anxiety. The child indulges in fantasies of being a giant and a tiger, but in his dreams he runs in terror for dear life. This, then, is the stage of the "castration complex"; the fear of having the (now energetically eroticized) genitals harmed as a punishment for the fantasies attached to their excitement becomes intensified.

Infantile sexuality and incest taboo, castration complex and superego all unite here to bring about that specifically human crisis during which the child must turn from an exclusive, pregenital attachment to his parents to the slow process of becoming a parent, a carrier of tradition. Here the most fateful split and transformation in the emotional powerhouse occurs, a split between potential human glory and potential total destruction. For here the child becomes forever divided in himself. The instinct fragments which before had enhanced the growth of his infantile body and mind now become divided into an infantile set which perpetuates the exuberance of growth potentials, and a parental set which supports and increases self-observation, self-guidance, and self-punishment.

The problem, again, is one of mutual regulation. Where the child, now so ready to overmanipulate himself, can gradually develop a sense of moral responsibility, where he can gain some insight into the institutions, functions, and roles which will permit his responsible participation, he will find pleasurable accomplishment in wielding tools and weapons, in manipulating meaningful toys—and in caring for younger children.

Naturally, the parental set is at first infantile in nature: the fact that human conscience remains partially infantile throughout life is the core of human tragedy. For the superego of the child can be primitive, cruel, and uncompromising, as may be observed in instances where children overcontrol and overconstrict themselves to the point of self-obliteration; where they develop an over-obedience more literal than the one the parent has wished to exact; or where they develop deep regressions and lasting resentments because the parents themselves do not seem to live up to the new conscience. One of the deepest conflicts in life is the hate for a parent who served as the model and the executor of the superego, but who (in some form) was found trying to get away with the very transgressions which the child can no longer tolerate in himself. The suspiciousness and evasiveness which is thus mixed in with the all-or-nothing quality of the superego, this organ of moral tradition, makes moral (in the sense of moralistic) man a great potential danger to his own ego—and to that of his fellow men.

In adult pathology, the residual conflict over initiative is expressed either in hysterical denial, which causes the repression of the wish or the abrogation of its executive organ by paralysis, inhibition, or impotence; or in overcompensatory showing off, in which the scared individual, so eager to "duck," instead "sticks his neck out." Then also a plunge into psychosomatic disease is now common. It is as if the culture had made a man over-advertise himself and so identify with his own advertisement that only disease can offer him escape.

But here, again, we must not think only of individual psychopathology, but of the inner powerhouse of rage which must be submerged at this stage, as some the fondest hopes and the wildest phantasies are repressed and inhibited. The resulting self-righteousness—often the principal reward for goodness—can later be most intolerantly turned against others in the form of persistent moralistic surveillance, so that the prohibition rather than the guidance of initiative becomes the dominant endeavor. On the other hand, even moral man's initiative is apt to burst the boundaries of self-restriction, permitting him to do to others, in his or in other lands, what he would neither do nor tolerate being done in his own home.

In view of the dangerous potentials of man's long childhood, it is well to look back at the blueprint of the life-stages and to the possibilities of guiding the young of the race while they are young. And here we note that according to the wisdom of the ground plan the child is at no time more ready to learn quickly and avidly, to become bigger in the sense of sharing obligation and performance than during this period of his development. He is eager and able to make things cooperatively, to combine with other children for the purpose of constructing and planning, and he is willing to profit from teachers and to emulate ideal prototypes. He remains, of course, identified with the parent of the same sex, but for the present he looks for opportunities where work-identification seems to promise a field of initiative without too much infantile conflict or Oedipal guilt and a more realistic identification based on a spirit of equality experienced in doing things together. At any rate, the "Oedipal" stage results not only in the oppressive establishment of a moral sense restricting the horizon of the permissible; it also sets the direction toward the possible and the tangible which permits the dreams of early childhood to be attached to the goals of an active adult life. Social institutions, therefore, offer children of this age an *economic ethos,* in the form of ideal adults recognizable by their uniforms and their functions, and fascinating enough to replace, the heroes of picture book and fairy tale.

4. Industry vs. Inferiority

THUS the inner stage seems all set for "entrance into life," except that life must first be school life, whether school is field or jungle or classroom. The child must forget past hopes and wishes, while his exuberant imagination is tamed and harnessed to the laws of impersonal things—even the three R's. For before the child, psychologically already a rudimentary parent, can become a biological parent, he must begin to be a worker and potential provider. With the oncoming latency period, the normally advanced child forgets, or rather sublimates, the necessity to "make" people by direct attack or to become papa and mama in a hurry: he now learns to win recognition by producing things. He has mastered the ambulatory field and the organ modes. He has experienced a sense of finality regarding the fact that there is no workable future within the womb of his family, and thus becomes ready to apply himself to given skills and tasks, which go far beyond the mere playful expression of his organ modes or the pleasure in the function of his limbs. He develops a sense of industry—i.e., he adjusts himself to the inorganic laws of the tool world. He can become an eager and absorbed unit of a productive situation. To bring a productive situation to completion is an aim which gradually supersedes the whims and wishes of play. His ego boundaries include his tools and skills: the work principle (Ives Hendrick) teaches him the pleasure of work completion by steady attention and persevering diligence. In all cultures, at this stage, children receive some *systematic instruction,* although . . . it is by no means always in the kind of school which literate people must organize around special teachers who have learned how to teach literacy. In preliterate people and in nonliterate pursuits much is learned from adults who become teachers by dint of gift and inclination rather than by appointment, and perhaps the greatest amount is learned from older children. Thus the *fundamentals of technology* are developed, as the child becomes ready to handle the utensils, the tools, and the weapons used by the big people. Literate people, with more specialized careers, must prepare the child by teaching him things which first of all make him literate, the widest possible basic education for the greatest number of possible careers. The more confusing specialization becomes, however, the more indistinct are the eventual goals of initiative; and the more complicated social reality, the vaguer are the father's and mother's role in it. School seems to be a culture all by itself, with its own goals and limits, its achievements and disappointment.

The child's danger, at this stage, lies in a sense of inadequacy and inferiority. If he despairs of his tools and skills or of his status among his tool partners, he may be discouraged from identification with them and with a section of the tool world. To lose the hope of such "industrial" association may pull him back to the more isolated, less tool-conscious familial rivalry of the Oedipal time. The child despairs of his equipment in the tool world and in anatomy, and considers himself doomed to mediocrity or inadequacy. It is at this point that wider society becomes significant in its ways of admitting the child to an understanding of meaningful roles in its technology and economy. Many a child's development is disrupted when family life has failed to prepare him for school life, or when school life fails to sustain the promises of earlier stages.

Regarding the period of a developing sense of industry, I have referred to *outer and inner hindrances* in the use of new capacities but not to aggravations of new human drives, nor to submerged rages resulting from their frustration. This stage differs from the earlier ones in that it is not a swing from an inner upheaval to a new mastery. Freud calls it the latency stage because violent drives are normally dormant. But it is only a lull before the storm of puberty, when all the earlier drives reemerge in a new combination, to be brought under the dominance of genitality.

On the other hand, this is socially a most decisive stage: since industry involves doing things beside and with others, a first sense of division of labor and of differential opportunity, that is, a sense of the *technological ethos* of a culture, develops at this time. We have pointed in the last section to the danger threatening individual and society where the schoolchild begins to feel that the color of his skin, the background of his parents, or the fashion of his clothes rather than his wish and his will to learn will decide his worth as an apprentice, and thus his sense of *identity*—to which we must now turn. But there is another, more fundamental danger, namely man's restriction of himself and constriction of his horizons to include only his work to which, so the Book says, he has been sentenced after his expulsion from paradise. If he accepts work as his only obligation, and "what works" as his own criterion of worthwhileness, he may become the conformist and thoughtless slave of his technology and of those who are in a position to exploit it.

5. Identity vs. Role Confusion

WITH the establishment of a good initial relationship to the world of skills and tools, and with the advent of puberty, childhood proper comes to an end. Youth begins. But in puberty and adolescence all sameness and continuities relied on earlier are more or less questioned again, because of a rapidity of body growth which equals that of early childhood and because of the new addition of genital maturity. The growing and developing youths, faced with this physiological revolution within them, and with tangible adult tasks ahead of them are now primarily concerned with what they appear to be in the eyes of others as compared with what they feel they are, and with the question of how to connect the roles and skills cultivated earlier with the occupational prototypes of the day. In their search for a new sense of continuity and sameness, adolescents have to refight many of the battles of earlier years, even though to do so they must artificially appoint perfectly well-meaning people to play the roles of adversaries; and they are ever ready to install lasting idols and ideals as guardians of a final identity.

The integration now taking place in the form of ego identity is, as pointed out, more than the sum of the childhood identifications. It is the accrued experience of the ego's ability to integrate all identifications with the vicissitudes of the libido, with the aptitudes developed out of endowment, and with the opportunities offered in social roles. The sense of ego identity, then, is the accrued confidence that the inner sameness and continuity prepared in the past are matched by the sameness and continuity of one's meaning for others, as evidenced in the tangible promise of a "career."

The danger of this stage is role confusion. Where this is based on a strong previous doubt as to one's sexual identity, delinquent and outright psychotic episodes are not uncommon. If diagnosed and treated correctly, these incidents do not have the same fatal significance which they have at other ages. In most instances, however, it is the inability to settle on an occupational identity which disturbs individual young people. To keep themselves together they temporarily overidentify, to the point of apparent complete loss of identity, with the heroes of cliques and crowds. This initiates the stage of "falling in love," which is by no means entirely, or even primarily, a sexual matter—except where the mores demand it. To a considerable extent adolescent love is an attempt to arrive at a definition of one's identity by projecting one's diffused ego image on another and by seeing it thus reflected and gradually clarified. This is why so much of young love is conversation.

Young people can also be remarkably clannish, and cruel in their exclusion of all those who are "different," in skin color or cultural background, in tastes and gifts, and often in such petty aspects of dress and gesture as have been temporarily selected as *the* signs of an in-grouper or out-grouper. It is important to understand (which does not mean condone or participate in) such intolerance as a defense against a sense of identity confusion. For adolescents not only help one another temporarily through much discomfort by forming cliques and by stereotyping themselves, their ideals, and their enemies; they also perversely test each other's capacity to pledge fidelity. The readiness for such testing also explains the appeal which simple and cruel totalitarian doctrines have on the minds of the youth of such countries and classes as have lost or are losing their group identities (feudal, agrarian, tribal, national) and face world-wide industrialization, emancipation, and wider communication.

The adolescent mind is essentially a mind of the *moratorium*, a psychosocial stage between childhood and adulthood, and between the morality learned by the child, and the ethics to be developed by the adult. It is an ideological mind—and, indeed, it is the ideological outlook of a society that speaks most clearly to the adolescent who is eager to be affirmed by his peers, and is ready to be confirmed by rituals, creeds, and programs which at the same time define what is evil, uncanny, and inimical. In searching for the social values which guide identity, one therefore confronts the problems of *ideology* and *aristocracy*, both in their widest possible sense which connotes that within a defined world image and a predestined course of history, the best people will come to rule and rule develops the best in people. In order not to become cynically or apathetically lost, young people must somehow be able to convince themselves that those who succeed in their anticipated adult world thereby shoulder the obligation of being the best. We will discuss later the dangers which emanate from human ideals harnessed to the management of super-machines, be they guided by nationalistic or international, communist or capitalist ideologies. In the last part of this book we shall discuss the way in which the revolutions of our day attempt to solve and also to exploit the deep need of youth to redefine its identity in an industrialized world.

6. Intimacy vs. Isolation

THE strength acquired at any stage is tested by the necessity to transcend it in such a way that the individual can take chances in the next stage with what was most vulnerably precious in the previous one. Thus, the young adult, emerging from the search for and the insistence on identity, is eager and willing to fuse his identity with that of others. He is ready for intimacy, that is, the capacity to commit himself to concrete affiliations and partnerships and to develop the ethical strength to abide by such commitments, even though they may call for significant sacrifices and compromises. Body and ego must now be masters of the organ modes and of the nuclear conflicts, in order to be able to face the fear of ego loss in situations which call for self-abandon: in the solidarity of close affiliations, in orgasms and sexual unions, in close friendships and in physical combat, in experiences of inspiration by teachers and of intuition from the recesses of the self. The avoidance of such experiences because of a fear of ego loss may lead to a deep sense of isolation and consequent self-absorption.

The counterpart of intimacy is distantiation: the readiness to isolate and, if necessary, to destroy those forces and people whose essence seems dangerous to one's own, and whose "territory" seems to encroach on the extent of one's intimate relations. Prejudices thus developed (and utilized and exploited in politics and in war) are a more mature outgrowth of the blinder repudiations which during the struggle for identity differentiate sharply and cruelly between the familiar and the foreign. The danger of this stage is that intimate, competitive, and combative relations are experienced with and against the selfsame people. But as the areas of adult duty are delineated, and as the competitive encounter, and the sexual embrace, are differentiated, they eventually become subject to that *ethical sense* which is the mark of the adult.

. . .

The danger of this stage is isolation, that is the avoidance of contacts which commit to intimacy. In psychopathology, this disturbance can lead to severe "character-problems." On the other hand, there are partnerships which amount to an isolation à deux, protecting both partners from the necessity to face the next critical development—that of generativity.

7. Generativity vs. Stagnation

IN THIS book the emphasis is on the childhood stages, otherwise the section on generativity would of necessity be the central one, for this term encompasses the evolutionary development which has made man the teaching and instituting as well as the learning animal. The fashionable insistence on dramatizing the dependence of children on adults often blinds us to the dependence of the older generation on the younger one. Mature man needs to be needed, and maturity needs guidance as well as encouragement from what has been produced and must be taken care of.

Generativity, then, is primarily the concern in establishing and guiding the next generation, although there are individuals who, through misfortune or because of special and genuine gifts in other directions, do not apply this drive to their own offspring. And indeed, the concept generativity is meant to include such more popular synonyms as *productivity* and *creativity,* which, however, cannot replace it.

It has taken psychoanalysis some time to realize that the ability to lose oneself in the meeting of bodies and minds leads to a gradual expansion of ego-interests and to a libidinal investment in that which is being generated. Generativity thus is an essential stage on the psychosexual as well as on the psychosocial schedule. Where such enrichment fails altogether, regression to an obsessive need for pseudo-intimacy takes place, often with a pervading sense of stagnation and personal impoverishment. Individuals, then, often begin to indulge themselves as if they were their own—or one another's—one and only child; and where conditions favor it, early invalidism, physical or psychological, becomes the vehicle of self-concern. The mere fact of having or even wanting children, however, does not "achieve" generativity. In fact, some young parents suffer, it seems, from the retardation of the ability to develop this stage. The reasons are often to be found in early childhood impressions; in excessive self-love based on a too strenuously self-made personality; and finally (and here we return to the beginnings) in the lack of some faith, some "belief in the species," which would make a child appear to be a welcome trust of the community.

As to the institutions which safeguard and reinforce generativity, one can only say that all institutions codify the ethics of generative succession. Even where philosophical and spiritual tradition suggests the renunciation of the right to procreate or to produce, such early turn to "ultimate concerns," wherever instituted in monastic movements, strives to settle at the same time the matter of its relationship to the Care for the creatures of this world and to the Charity which is felt to transcend it.

If this were a book on adulthood, it would be indispensable and profitable at this point to compare economic and psychological theories (beginning with the strange convergencies and divergencies of Marx and Freud) and to proceed to a discussion of man's relationship to his production as well as to his progeny.

8. Ego Integrity vs. Despair

ONLY in him who in some way has taken care of things and people and has adapted himself to the triumphs and disappointments adherent to being, the originator of others or the generator of products and ideas—only in him may gradually ripen the fruit of these seven stages. I know no better word for it than ego integrity. Lacking a clear definition, I shall point to a few constituents of this state of mind. It is the ego's accrued assurance of its proclivity for order and meaning. It is a post-narcissistic love of the human ego—not of the self—as an experience which conveys some world order and spiritual sense, no matter how dearly paid for. It is the acceptance of one's one and only life cycle as something that had to be and that, by necessity, permitted of no substitutions: it thus means a new, a different love of one's parents. It is a comradeship with the ordering ways of distant times and different pursuits, as expressed in the simple products and saying of such times and pursuits. Although aware of the relativity of all the various life styles which have given meaning to human striving, the possessor of integrity is ready to defend the dignity of his own life style against all physical and economic threats. For he knows that an individual life is the accidental coincidence of but one life cycle with but one segment of history; and that for him all human integrity stands or falls with the one style of integrity of which he partakes. The style of integrity developed by his culture or civilization thus becomes the "patrimony of his soul," the seal of his moral paternity of himself (". . . pero el honor/Es patrimonio del alma": Calderón). In such final consolidation, death loses its sting.

The lack or loss of this accrued ego integration is signified by fear of death: the one and only life cycle is not accepted as the ultimate of life. Despair expresses the feeling that the time is now short, too short for the attempt to start another life and to try out alternate roads to integrity. Disgust hides despair, if often only in the form of "a thousand little disgusts" which do not add up to one big remorse: *mille petits dégôuts de soi, dont le total ne fait pas un remords, mais un gêne obscure."* (Rostand)

Each individual, to become a mature adult, must to a sufficient degree develop all the ego qualities mentioned, so that a wise Indian, a true gentleman, and a mature peasant share and recognize in one another the final stage of integrity. But each cultural entity, to develop the particular style of integrity suggested by its historical place, utilizes a particular combination of these conflicts, along with specific provocations and prohibitions of infantile sexuality. Infantile conflicts become creative only if sustained by the firm support of cultural institutions and of the special leader classes representing them. In order to approach or experience integrity, the individual must know how to be a follower of image bearers in religion and in politics, in the economic order and in technology, in aristocratic living and in the arts and sciences. Ego integrity, therefore, implies an emotional integration which permits participation by followership as well as acceptance of the responsibility of leadership.

Webster's Dictionary is kind enough to help us complete this outline in a circular fashion. Trust (the first of our ego values) is here defined as "the assured reliance on another's integrity," the last of our values. I suspect that Webster had business in mind rather than babies, credit rather than faith. But the formulation stands. And it seems possible to further paraphrase the relation of adult integrity and infantile trust by saying that healthy children will not fear life if their elders have integrity enough not to fear death.

9. An Epigenetic Chart

IN THIS book the emphasis is on the childhood stages. The foregoing conception of the life cycle, however, awaits systematic treatment. To prepare this, I shall conclude this chapter with a diagram. In this, as in the diagram of pregenital zones and modes, the diagonal represents the normative sequence of psychosocial gains made as at each stage one more nuclear conflict adds a new ego quality, a new criterion of accruing human strength. Below the diagonal there is space for the precursors of each of these solutions, all of which begin with the beginning; above the diagonal there is space for the designation of the derivatives of these gains and their transformations in the maturing and the mature personality.

The underlying assumptions for such charting are (1) that the human personality in principle develops according to steps predetermined in the growing person's readiness to be driven toward, to be aware of, and to interact with, a widening social radius; and (2) that society, in principle, tends to be so constituted as to meet and invite this succession of potentialities for interaction and attempts to safeguard and to encourage the proper rate and the proper sequence of their enfolding. This is the "maintenance of the human world."

But a chart is only a tool to think with, and cannot aspire to be a prescription to abide by, whether in the practice of child-training, in psychotherapy, or in the methodology of child study. In the presentation of the psychosocial stages in the form of an *epigenetic chart* analogous to the one employed . . . for an analysis of Freud's psychosexual stages, we have definite and delimited methodological steps in mind. It is one purpose of this work to facilitate the comparison of the stages first discerned by Freud as sexual to other schedules of development (physical, cognitive). But any one chart delimits one schedule only, and it must not be imputed that our outline of the psychosocial schedule is intended to imply obscure generalities concerning other aspects of development—or, indeed, of existence. If the chart, for example, lists a series of conflicts or crises, we do not consider all development a series of crises: we claim only that psychosocial development proceeds by critical steps —"critical" being a characteristic of turning points, of moments of decision between progress and regression, integration and retardation.

It may be useful at this point to spell out the methodological implications of an epigenetic matrix. The more heavily-lined squares of the diagonal signify both a sequence of stages and a gradual development of component parts: in other words, the chart formalizes a progression through time of a differentiation of parts. This indicates (1) that each critical item of psychosocial strength discussed here is systematically related to all others, and that they all depend on the proper development in the proper sequence of each item; and (2) that each item exists in some form before its critical time normally arrives.

If I say, for example, that a favorable ratio of basic trust over basic mistrust is the first step in psychosocial adaptation, a favorable ratio of autonomous will over shame and doubt, the second, the corresponding diagrammatic statement expresses a number of fundamental relations that exist between the two steps, as well as some facts fundamental to each. Each comes to its ascendance, meets its crisis, and finds its lasting solution during the stage indicated. But they all must exist from

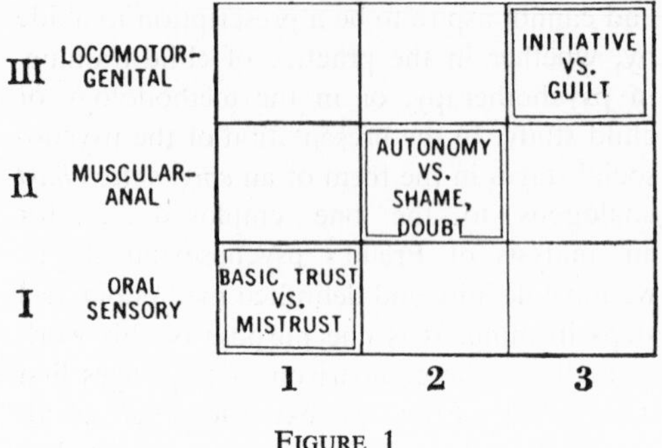

FIGURE 1

the beginning in some form, for every act calls for an integration of all. Also, an infant may show something like "autonomy" from the beginning in the particular way in which he angrily tries to wriggle himself free when tightly held. However, under normal conditions, it is not until the second year that he begins to experience the whole *critical opposition of being an autonomous creature and being a dependent one;* and it is not until then that he is ready for a decisive encounter with his environment, an environment which, in turn, feels called upon to convey to him its particular ideas and concepts of autonomy and coercion in ways decisively contributing to the character and the health of his personality in his culture. It is this encounter, together with the resulting crisis, that we have tentatively described for each stage. As to the progression from one stage to the next, the diagonal indicates the sequence to be followed. However, it also makes room for variations in tempo and intensity. An individual, or a culture, may linger excessively over trust and proceed from I 1 over I 2 to II 2, or an accelerated progression may move from I 1 over II 1 to II 2. Each such acceleration or (relative) retardation, however, is assumed to have a modifying influence on all later stages.

An epigenetic diagram thus lists a system of stages dependent on each other; and while individual stages may have been explored more or less thoroughly or named more or less fittingly, the diagram suggests that their study be pursued always with the total configuration of stages in mind. The diagram invites, then, a thinking through of all its empty boxes: if we have entered Basic Trust in I 1 and Integrity in VIII 8, we leave the question open, as to what trust might have become in

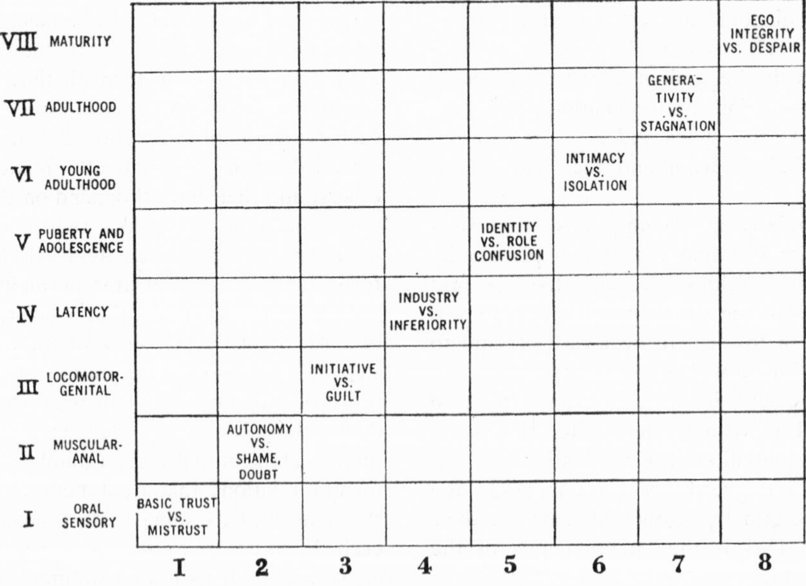

FIGURE 2

a stage dominated by the need for integrity even as we have left open what it may look like and, indeed, be called in the stage dominated by a striving for autonomy (II 1). All we mean to emphasize is that trust must have developed in its own right, before it becomes something more in the critical encounter in which autonomy develops—and so on, up the vertical. If, in the last stage (VIII 1), we would expect trust to have developed into the most mature *faith* that an aging person can muster in his cultural setting and historical period, the chart permits the consideration not only of what old age can be, but also what its preparatory stages must have been. All of this should make it clear that a chart of epigenesis suggests a global form of thinking and rethinking which leaves details of methodology and terminology to further study.[2]

2 To leave this matter truly open, certain misuses of the whole conception would have to be avoided. Among them is the assumption that the sense of trust (and all the other "positive" senses postulated) is an *achievement,* secured once and for all at a given state. In fact, some writers are so intent on making an *achievement scale* out of these stages that they blithely omit all the "negative" senses (basic mistrust, etc.) which are and remain the dynamic counterpart of the "positive" ones throughout life. The assumption that on each stage a goodness is achieved which is impervious to new inner conflicts and to changing conditions is, I believe, a projection on child development of that success ideology which can so dangerously pervade our private and public daydreams and can make us inept in a heightened struggle for a meaningful existence in a new, industrial era of history. The personality is engaged with the hazards of existence continuously, even as the body's metabolism copes with decay. As we come to diagnose a state of relative strength and the symptoms of an impaired one, we face only more clearly the paradoxes and tragic potentials of human life.

PART IV

Socialization Processes in Family and School

EVERY individual from Alaska to Zanzibar is involved in a process of acculturation, beginning at birth, that differs from society to society. What and how he is fed, how and when he is toilet-trained, with whom and in what he sleeps, what language he will speak, and how he will use the language—all such questions are decided in one way in culture A and in quite a different way in culture B. For years accounts of how the Navaho and the Zuni, the Papuans and the Samoans rear their young have been available in the literature and have helped students of child development appreciate the relativism of even our most cherished mores.

But the differences in cultural mores are significant for reasons other than the fact of relativism. As cultural anthropologists have pointed out, the importance of mores lies in the relationship between socialization practices and adult personality and character. Societies differ with respect to who will be the chief agent of socialization; how weaning, toilet-training, and masturbation are dealt with; how socializing agents control the young; and what children are rewarded and punished for. These differences are reflected in the personality of the growing child.

Some of the relationships between child training and personality are direct and easy to trace. When we know what attitudes and ideals are held dear in a society, we can find instances of the encouragement of those attitudes by a system of rewards and punishments. American middle-class parents, for example, are known to cherish initiative and independence in the economic sphere; they facilitate the development of these traits in the young by encouraging male offspring in particular to deliver newspapers, mow lawns, and do other odd jobs. The boy who fails to show enough initiative in this respect may be labeled as lazy by his parents.

But some of the relationships between socialization practices and later development are not so obvious to the observer and only become tentatively established through careful research. Whiting and Child (1953) analyzed data for over fifty different cultures in which child-rearing practices have been studied. Among other findings, they discovered a relationship between the age at which weaning, modesty training, sex training, and independence training were initiated and the prevalence of feelings of guilt among adults. Very early socialization of these behaviors was correlated with strong guilt feelings, with the strength of guilt feelings declining as age of onset of socialization increased.

The first paper in this section illustrates how character and personality are molded in a modern society quite different from our own. Bronfenbrenner discusses his observations of character education in the U.S.S.R., where the goal of the state is to train the young in socialist morality. Although the family retains a primary responsibility for the child's correct upbringing, the state is so vitally interested in how the child turns out that *it* is the final authority on how the child should be reared. In contrast to societies where the jurisdiction of the parents is almost limitless, the Soviet family only has authority as the state delegates it. To ensure correct socialist upbringing, both family and school (as the chief agents of socialization) must utilize such approved techniques as group criticism, self-criticism, and group-oriented punishments. It is in the reliance upon these techniques that Bronfenbrenner finds the greatest difference between Soviet socialization and our own.

In some of the collective settlements of Israel we find a unique system of socialization, where the child is reared from infancy outside the home. Soon after birth the infant is placed in a communal nursery, to be cared for by a trained worker and her aides. Later he moves to a communal toddlers' and then to a kindergarten house. Visits with his parents evenings and holidays are part of the routine. On the one hand we note that under such a system, children are raised by experts trained in the most modern of child-rearing techniques—a training that most parents lack. We also note that children have the opportunity to establish a tension-free relationship with a parent who is *not* the disciplinary agent and hence not a frustrator to the child. On the other hand, children must always share the group leader and are inevitably subject to strong pressures from the peer group. How children raised in a kibbutz (as the communal settlement is called) fare under such a system of group upbringing has been an intriguing question for research. The answers found have not always agreed; a paper by Rapaport (1958) surveys the present state of knowledge and defines the questions still to be answered.

Studies of cultural differences in child-rearing practices have interested many an investigator, but so have studies of subcultural differences. In our own society, methods of child-rearing among lower- and middle-class parents have been studied intensively for the past two decades, with conflicting results. In 1947 Davis and Havighurst published their *Father of the Man,* reporting (on the basis of their study of parents in the Chicago area) that middle-class parents tended to be stricter than lower-class parents in such matters as the weaning, toilet-training, scheduling, and general freedom of movement of their children. The lower-class child was pictured as having an easier, more permissive, less frustrating upbringing than his middle-class peer. The Maccoby and Gibbs paper included here, first published in 1954, presents an altogether different picture; these investigators found in their study of families in the Boston area that middle-class parents were more permissive.

How to resolve such contradictory findings? One explanation offered by Sears, Maccoby, and Levin (1957) is that lower-class permissiveness with respect to freedom of movement may actually reflect rejection; the child is permitted greater freedom of movement, but it is because his parents want him out of the way. With respect to feeding, weaning, and toilet-training, the explanation may lie in the time interval between the two studies (Bronfenbrenner, 1958). Middle-class mothers during the nineteen thirties and early forties were being urged to schedule rigorously and to train early, and the mothers in the Chicago study apparently followed this advice. In the late nineteen forties and fifties, however, there was considerable agitation for permissive child rearing, and the middle-class mother, always susceptible to "expert" advice, made an abrupt about-face so that her child's personality would not be "warped" by the more restrictive practices. The Boston mothers, queried almost a decade after the Chicago mothers, might have been reflecting a cultural change (Bronfenbrenner, 1958).

But why did the lower-class mother change from more permissive to more restrictive practices during this same period? The explanation may lie in a cultural lag. Changes in mores often start at the top of the social-class hierarchy and work themselves down. While scholarly journals of the early forties were criticizing restrictive practices, lower-class mothers in prenatal clinics were being urged by nurses to abandon their foolishly permissive ways for the more "scientific" method of bringing up baby. The Maccoby and Gibbs paper apparently mirrors the greater permissiveness of middle-class parents, at least as it existed in the fifties.

Cultures and subcultures, then, influence the developing personality and make for uniformity of personality within a culture, but it is to the family that we turn to find antecedents of individual differences in adult personalities. Certain variables in parent behavior have been and continue to be investigated to discover their impact upon the developing personality. Such factors as warmth versus hostility, democratic versus authoritarian methods of control, and restrictiveness versus permissiveness appear to have predictable though complex effects—complex, that is, because a parent can be warm and permissive, or warm and restrictive; permissive and hostile, or permissive and accepting; or any of a number of combinations of factors.

Among the earliest large-scale attempts to weigh the effects of parent behavior were the studies conducted at the Fels Institute in the nineteen forties. The Fels Parent Behavior Scales, thirty in number, were developed to rate such items as "general babying," "coerciveness of suggestion," and "severity of actual penalties." By means of factor analysis three important variables in home climate were identified: democracy, acceptance of the child (or warmth), and indulgence. Correlates of these parent behaviors in child behavior were sought in the nursery school. Children from homes rated as high in democracy were found to be more socially outgoing, though the outgoingness might be of the aggressive as well as the friendly kind. They were more likely to enjoy high status in their group and were also rated as showing more curiosity and constructiveness. Indulged children, on the other hand, had a lower social status with their peers and were apprehensive about participating in physical activities. Baldwin concludes that democratic parents stimulate the child so that he engages in more peer activities, is more successful with these activities, and is better able to contribute original, creative ideas to the group.

Since the Fels studies, continued efforts have been made to pinpoint the factors in parent behavior that might significantly alter child behavior. Space does not permit a full review here, but the interested reader ought to become acquainted with some of the major investigations in the field. The Sears, Maccoby, and Levin (1957) investigation reported on a number of parental behavior variables and their correlation with child problems. A highly significant variable was the use of love-oriented techniques of discipline (praise as reward and withdrawal of love as punishment), or object-oriented techniques (tangible rewards and physical punishment). Love-oriented techniques appeared to produce fewer behavior problems.

Schaefer (1961), himself a major investigator, has reviewed the findings on parent behavior and has suggested that such behaviors can be described by two variables—warmth-hostility and control-autonomy. His circumplex model shows how differing degrees of each variable can be combined.

Becker also reviews the consequences of parental behaviors, including such factors as psychological and physical discipline, restrictiveness, permissiveness, inconsistency, and sex of parent and child. Becker's words of caution in conclusion are well taken—that the majority of parents do not carry on the "pure" practices which research focuses on, but use a variety of mixed procedures; also, that there are probably many routes that can be taken in becoming a good parent.

The Becker *et al.* paper included here is illustrative of the factor analytic approach used by many investigators working in this field. The study is particularly important because it includes the influence of the father as well as the mother in the production of child behavior problems.

When the effects of parent behavior are measured over time, some interesting findings emerge. Kagan and Moss (1962) found in the Fels longitudinal studies that parent behaviors affect children differently at different ages and that effects differ according to the sex of the child. The authors speak of a "sleeper effect" in maternal interactions; they found that early interactions were more prognostic of future behaviors than contemporaneous behaviors. Thus, protection and hostility toward girls during their first three years of life were better correlates of adult withdrawal in anxiety-arousing situations than any type of maternal behaviors during later periods of the child's life.

While the impact of the father upon the socialization process has had less attention in the literature than that of the mother, there have, however, been some studies of father absence. When children from father-absent homes are compared with those from homes in which father is present, it is possible to assess the effects of the father on the development of the child. Using the technique of doll play, Bach studied the effects of the father's temporary absence from home during World War II. His discussion of the theoretical, practical, and therapeutic implications of his findings reveals the significance of the study.

A Harris, Gough, and Martin (1959) study is a rather special case of socialization influences. These investigators were trying to find out if there is a relationship between authoritarian child-training practices and ethnic bias in children. At the time of the study, there was considerable research interest in the "authoritarian personality," a personality characterized by intolerance, suspiciousness, ethnic prejudice, and rightist political attitudes. Recently there has been some interest in authoritarianism of the left—that is, in the concept that dogmatic, rigid, and intolerant attitudes exist in the extreme left as well as in the extreme right. While there are speculations about how a parent of the authoritarian left might influence a child's development, no studies have been forthcoming as yet.

Perhaps this brief review is enough to substantiate the statement that there are some consistent consequences of parental behaviors, although many variables must be considered, and must be considered in interaction with each other.

The last paper in this section has to do with the school and the group as agents in the socialization process. The early experimental work of Lewin, Lippitt, and White (1939) showed that the kind of leadership exerted by the person in charge of a group affected the quality of work and the interpersonal relationships of group members. Under democratic leadership boys were more friendly toward one another and work morale continued to be good even when the leader was not present. Both of these positive conditions were lacking under autocratic leadership. The Spaulding study included here is part of a large-scale investigation of classroom climate that attempted to assess how teacher behavior might affect pupil self-concept and learning. Because of the size of his sample and the design of his study, it was possible for this investigator to resolve some of the contradictions in earlier studies.

Finally, the reader is referred to a paper by Polansky, Lippitt, and Redl (1950), which helps to explain in part the conditions under which antisocial behavior is likely to spread in a group. The authors reject the easy explanation of the bad apple in the barrel and search for the answer in the social structure of the group.

REFERENCES

Baldwin, A. The effect of home environment on nursery school behavior. *Child Develpm.*, 1949, **20**, 49–61.

Becker, W. Consequences of different kinds of parental disciplines. *Annu. Rev. Child Develpm.*, in press.

Bronfenbrenner, U. Socialization and social class through time and space. In Eleanor E. Maccoby, T. M. Newcomb, & E. L. Hartley (Eds.), *Readings in social psychology*. New York: Holt, 1958.

Davis, A., & Havighurst, R. J. *Father of the man.* Boston: Houghton Mifflin, 1947.

Harris, D. B., Gough, H. G., & Martin, W. E. Children's ethnic attitudes: II. Relationship to parental beliefs concerning child training. *Child Develpm.*, 1950, **21**, 169–181.

Kagan, J., & Moss, H. A. *Birth to maturity: a study in psychological development.* New York: Wiley, 1962.

Lewin, K., Lippitt, R., & White, R. K. Patterns of aggressive behavior in experimentally created "social climbers." *J. soc. Psychol.*, 1939, **10**, 271–299.

Polansky, N., Lippitt, R., & Redl, F. An investigation of behavioral contagion in groups. *Hum. Relat.*, 1950, **3**, 319–348.

Rapaport, D. Behavior research in collective settlements in Israel. *Amer. J. Orthopsychiat.*, 1958, **28**, 587–597.

Schaefer, E. S. Converging conceptual models for maternal behavior and for child behavior. In J. C. Glidewell (Ed.), *Parental attitudes and child behavior.* Springfield, Ill.: Charles C Thomas, 1961.

Sears, R. R., Maccoby, Eleanor E., & Levin, H. *Patterns of child rearing.* New York: Row, Peterson, 1957.

Whiting, J. W. M., & Child, I. L. *Child training and personality.* New Haven: Yale Univer. Press, 1953.

URIE BRONFENBRENNER

*Soviet Methods of Character Education: Some Implications for Research**

EVERY society faces the problem of the moral training of its youth. This is no less true of Communist society than of our own. Indeed, Communist authorities view as the primary objective of education not the learning of subject matter but the development of what they call "socialist morality." It is instructive for us in the West to examine the nature of this "socialist morality" and the manner in which it is inculcated, for to do so brings to light important differences in the ends and means of character education in the two cultures. For research workers in the field of personality development, such an examination is especially valuable, since it lays bare unrecognized assumptions and variations in approach. Accordingly, it is the purpose of this paper to provide a much-condensed account of Soviet methods of character education and to examine some of the provocative research questions that emerge from the contrast between the Soviet approach and our own.

The Work and Ideas of A. S. Makarenko

TO EXAMINE Soviet methods of character training is to become acquainted with the thinking and technology developed primarily by one man—Anton Semyonovich Makarenko. Makarenko's name is virtually a household word in the Soviet Union. His popularity and influence are roughly comparable to those of Dr. Spock in the United States, but his primary concern is not with the child's physical health but with his moral upbringing. Makarenko's influence extends far beyond his own voluminous writings since there is scarcely a manual for the guidance of Communist parents, teachers, or youth workers that does not draw heavily on his methods and ideas. His works have been translated into many languages and are apparently widely read not only in the Soviet Union but throughout the Communist bloc countries, notably East Germany and Communist China. Excellent English translations of a number of his works have been published in Moscow (1949, 1953, 1959) but they are not readily available in this country.

Makarenko developed his ideas and methods over the course of a lifetime of practical work with young people. In the early 1920's, as a young school teacher and devout Communist, Makarenko was handed the assignment of setting up a rehabilitation program for some of the hundreds of homeless children who were roaming the Soviet Union after the civil wars. The first group of such children assigned to Makarenko's school, a ramshackle building far out of town, turned out to be a group of boys about 18 years of age with extensive court records of housebreaking, armed robbery, and manslaughter. For the first few months, Makarenko's school served simply as the headquarters for the band of highwaymen who were his legal wards. But gradually, through the development of his group-orientated discipline techniques, and through what can only be called the compelling power of his own moral convictions, Makarenko was able to develop a sense of group responsibility and commitment

* REPRINTED with abridgment by permission of the author and The Religious Education Association of the United States and Canada from *Relig. Educ.*, 1962, 57 (4, Res. Suppl.), S45–S61.

to the work program and code of conduct that he had laid out for the collective. In the end, the Gorky Commune became known throughout the Soviet Union for its high morale, discipline, and for the productivity of its fields, farms, and shops. Indeed, Makarenko's methods proved so successful that he was selected to head a new commune set up by the ministry of Internal Affairs (then the Cheka, later to become the GPU and NKVD). In the years which followed, Makarenko's theories and techniques became widely adopted throughout the USSR and now constitute the central core of Soviet educational practice.

To turn to the ideas themselves, we may begin with an excerpt from what is possibly the most widely read of Makarenko's works, *A Book for Parents* (1959).

> But our [Soviet] family is not an accidental combination of members of society. The family is a natural collective body and, like everything natural, healthy, and normal, it can only blossom forth in socialist society, freed of those very curses from which both mankind as a whole and the individual are freeing themselves.
>
> The family becomes the natural primary cell of society, the place where the delight of human life is realized, where the triumphant forces of man are refreshed, where children—the chief joy of life—live and grow.
>
> Our parents are not without authority either, but this authority is only the reflection of societal authority. The duty of a father in our country towards his children is a particular form of his duty towards society. It is as if our society says to parents:
>
> You have joined together in good will and love, rejoice in your children and expect to go on rejoicing in them. That is your personal affair and concerns your own personal happiness. Within the course of this happy process you have given birth to new human beings. A time will come when these beings will cease to be solely the instruments of your happiness, and will step forth as independent members of society. For society, it is by no means a matter of indifference what kind of people they will become. In delegating to you a certain measure of societal authority the Soviet State demands from you the correct upbringing of its future citizens. Particularly it relies on you to provide certain conditions arising naturally out of your union; namely, your parental love.
>
> If you wish to give birth to a citizen while dispensing with parental love, then be so kind as to warn society that you intend to do such a rotten thing. Human beings who are brought up without parental love are often deformed human beings [Makarenko, 1959, p. 29].

Characteristic of Makarenko's thought is the view that the parent's authority over the child is delegated to him by the state and that duty to one's children is merely a particular instance of one's broader duty towards society. A little later in his book for parents, the author makes this point even more emphatically. After telling the story of a boy who ran away from home after some differences with his mother, he concludes by affirming: "I am a great admirer of optimism and I like very much young lads who have so much faith in Soviet State that they are carried away and will not trust even their own mothers" (Makarenko, 1959, p. 37–38). In other words, when the needs and values of the family conflict with those of society, there is no question about who gets priority. And society receives its concrete manifestation and embodiment in the *collective,* which is an organized group engaged in some socially useful enterprise.

This brings us to Makarenko's basic thesis that optimal personality development can occur only through productive activity in a social collective. The first collective is the family, but this must be supplemented early in life by other collectives specially organized in schools, neighborhoods, and other community settings. The primary function of the collective is to develop socialist morality. This aim is accomplished through an explicit regimen of activity mediated by group criticism, self-criticism, and group-oriented punishments and rewards.

Makarenko's ideas are elaborated at length in his semibiographical, semifictional accounts of life in the collective (1949, 1953). It is in these works that he describes the principles and procedures to be employed for building the collective and using it as an instrument of character education. More relevant to our purposes, however, is the manner in which these methods are applied in school settings, for it is in this form that they have become most systematized and widely used.

Socialization in the School Collective

THE account which follows is taken from a manual (Novikova, 1959) for the training and guidance of "school directors, supervisors, teachers, and Young Pioneer leaders." The manual was written by staff members of the Institute on the Theory and History of Pedagogy at the Academy of Pedagogical Sciences and is typical of several others prepared under the same auspices and widely distributed throughout the USSR.

This particular volume carries the instructive title: *Socialist Competition in the School.* The same theme is echoed in the titles of individual chapters: "Competition in the Classroom," "Competition between Classrooms," "Competition between Schools," and so on. It is not difficult to see how Russians arrive at the notion, with which they have made us so familiar, of competition between nations and between social systems. Moreover, in the chapter titles we see already reflected the influence of dialectical materialism: Conflict at one level is resolved through synthesis at the next higher level, always in the service of the Communist collective.

Let us examine the process of collective socialization as it is initiated in the very first grade. Conveniently enough, the manual starts us off on the first day of school with the teacher standing before the newly assembled class. What should her first words be? Our text tells us:

> It is not difficult to see that a direct approach to the class with the command "All sit straight" often doesn't bring the desired effect since a demand in this form does not reach the sensibilities of the pupils and does not activate them.

How does one "reach the sensibilities of the pupils" and "activate them"? According to the manual, here is what the teacher should say: "Let's see which row can sit the straightest." This approach, we are told, has certain important psychological advantages. In response,

> The children not only try to do everything as well as possible themselves, but also take an evaluative attitude toward those who are undermining the achievement of the row. If similar measures arousing the spirit of competition in the children are systematically applied by experienced teachers in the primary classes, then gradually the children themselves begin to monitor the behavior of their comrades and remind those of them who forget about the rules set by the teacher, who forget what needs to be done and what should not be done. The teacher soon has helpers.

The manual then goes on to describe how records are kept for each row from day to day for different types of tasks so that the young children can develop a concept of group excellence over time and over a variety of activities, including personal cleanliness, condition of notebooks, conduct in passing from one room to the other, quality of recitations in each subject matter, and so on. In these activities considerable emphasis is placed on the externals of behavior in dress, manner, and speech. There must be no spots on shirt or collar, shoes must be shined, pupils must never pass by a teacher without stopping to give greeting, there must be no talking without permission, and the like. Great charts are kept in all the schools showing the performance of each row unit in every type of activity together with their total overall standing. "Who is best?" the charts ask, but the entries are not individuals but social units—rows, and later the "cells" of the Communist youth organization which reaches down to the primary grades.

At first it is the teacher who sets the standards. But soon, still in the first grade, a new wrinkle is introduced: Responsible monitors are designated in each row for each activity. In the beginning their job is only to keep track of the merits and demerits assigned each row by the teacher. Different children act as monitors for different activities and, if one is to believe what the manual says, the monitors become very involved in the progress of their row. Then, too, group achievement is not without its rewards. From time to time the winning row gets to be photographed "in parade uniforms" (all Soviet children must wear uniforms in school), and this photograph is published in that pervasive Soviet institution, the wall newspaper. The significance of the achievements is still further enhanced, however, by the introduction of competition between *classes* so that the winning class and the winning row are visited by delegates from other classrooms in order to learn how to attain the same standard of excellence.

Now let us look more closely at this teacher-mediated monitoring process. In the beginning, we are told, the teacher attempts to focus the attention of children on the achievements of the group; that is, in our familiar phrase, she accentuates the positive. But gradually, "it becomes necessary to take account of negative facts which interfere with the activity of the class." As an example we are given the instance of a child who despite warnings continues to enter the classroom a few minutes after the bell has rung. The teacher decides that the time has come to evoke the group process in correcting such behavior. Accordingly, the next time that Serezha is late, the teacher stops him at the door and turns to the class with this question: "Children, is it helpful or not helpful to us to have Serezha come in late?" The answers are quick in coming. "It interferes, one shouldn't be late, he ought to come on time." "Well," says the teacher, "How can we help Serezha with this problem?" There are many suggestions: get together to buy him a watch, exile him from the classroom, send him to the director's office, or even to exile him from the school. But apparently these suggestions are either not appropriate or too extreme. The teacher, our text tells us, "helps the children find the right answer." She asks for a volunteer to stop by and pick Serezha up on the way to school. Many children offer to help in this mission.

But tragedy stalks. The next day it turns out that not only Serezha is late, but also the boy who promised to pick him up. Since they are both from the same group, their unit receives two sets of demerits and falls to lowest place. Group members are keenly disappointed. "Serezha especially suffered much and felt himself responsible, but equal blame was felt by his companion who had forgotten to stop in for him."

In this way, both through concrete action and explanation, the teacher seeks to forge a spirit of group unity and responsibility. From time to time, she explains to the children the significance of what they are doing, the fact "that they have to learn to live together as one friendly family, since they will have to be learning together for all of the next ten years, and that for this reason one must learn how to help one's companions and to treat them decently."

By the time the children are in the second grade, the responsibilities expected of them are increased in complexity. For example, instead of simply recording the evaluations made by the teacher, the monitors are taught how to make the evaluations themselves. Since this is rather difficult, especially in judging homework assignments, in the beginning two monitors are assigned to every task. In this way, our text tells us, they can help each other in doing a good job of evaluation.

Here is a third grade classroom:

> Class 3-B is just an ordinary class; it's not especially well disciplined nor is it outstandingly industrious. It has its lazy members and its responsible ones, quiet ones and active ones, daring, shy, and immodest ones.
>
> The teacher has led this class now for three years, and she has earned the affection, respect, and acceptance as an authority from her pupils. Her word is law for them.
>
> The bell has rung, but the teacher has not yet arrived. She has delayed deliberately in order to check how the class will conduct itself.
>
> In the class all is quiet. After the noisy class break, it isn't so easy to mobilize yourself and to quell the restlessness within you! Two monitors at the desk silently observe the class. On their faces is reflected the full importance and seriousness of the job they are performing. But there is no need for them to make any reprimands: the youngsters with pleasure and pride maintain scrupulous discipline; they are proud of the fact that

their class conducts itself in a manner that merits the confidence of the teacher. And when the teacher enters and quietly says be seated, all understand that she deliberately refrains from praising them for the quiet and order, since in their class it could not be otherwise.

During the lesson, the teacher gives an exceptional amount of attention to collective competition between "links." (The links are the smallest unit of the Communist youth organization at this age level.) Throughout the entire lesson the youngsters are constantly hearing which link has best prepared its lesson, which link has done the best at numbers, which is the most disciplined, which has turned in the best work.

The best link not only gets a verbal positive evaluation but receives the right to leave the classroom first during the break and to have its notebooks checked before the others. As a result the links receive the benefit of collective education, common responsibility, and mutual aid.

"What are you fooling around for? You're holding up the whole link," whispers Kolya to his neighbor during the preparation period for the lesson. And during the break he teaches her how better to organize her books and pads in her knapsack.

"Count more carefully," says Olya to her girl friend. "See, on account of you our link got behind today. You come to me and we'll count together at home."

In the third grade still another innovation is introduced. The monitors are taught not only to evaluate but to state their criticisms publicly.

Here is a typical picture. It is the beginning of the lesson. In the first row the link leader reports basing his comments on information submitted by the sanitarian and other responsible monitors: "Today Valadya did the wrong problem. Masha didn't write neatly and forgot to underline the right words in her lesson. Alyoshi had a dirty shirt collar."

The other link leaders make similar reports (the Pioneers are sitting by rows).

The youngsters are not offended by this procedure: they understand that the link leaders are not just tattle-telling but simply fulfilling their duty. It doesn't even occur to the monitors and sanitarians to conceal the shortcomings of their comrades. They feel that they are doing their job well precisely when they notice one or another defect.

Also in the third grade, the teacher introduces still another procedure. She now proposes that the children enter into competition with the monitors, and see if they can beat the monitor at his own game by criticizing themselves. "The results were spectacular: if the monitor was able to talk only about four or five members of the row, there would be supplementary reports about their own shortcomings from as many as eight or ten pupils."

To what extent is this picture overdrawn? Although I have no direct evidence, the accounts I heard from participants in the process lend credence to the descriptions in the manual. For example, I recall a conversation with three elementary school teachers, all men, whom I had met by chance in a restaurant. They were curious about discipline techniques used in American schools. After I had given several examples, I was interrupted: "But how do you use the collective?" When I replied that we really did not use the classroom group in any systematic way, my three companions were puzzled. "But how do you keep discipline?"

Now it was my turn to ask for examples. "All right," came the answer. "Let us suppose that 10-year-old Vanya is pulling Anya's curls. If he doesn't stop the first time I speak to him, all I need do is mention it again in the group's presence; then I can be reasonably sure that before the class meets again the boy will be talked to by the officers of his Pioneer link. They will remind him that his behavior reflects on the reputation of the link."

"And what if he persists?"

"Then he may have to appear before his link—or even the entire collective—who will explain his misbehavior to him and determine his punishment."

"What punishment?"

"Various measures. He may just be censured, or if his conduct is regarded as serious, he may be expelled from membership. Very often he himself will acknowledge his faults before the group."

Nor does the process of social criticism and control stop with the school. Our manual tells us, for example, that parents submit periodic reports to the school collective on the behavior of the child at home. One may wonder how parents can be depended on to turn in truthful accounts. Part of the answer was supplied to me in a conversation with a Soviet agricultural expert. In response to my questions, he explained that, no matter what a person's job, the collective at his place of work always took an active interest in his family life. Thus a representative would come to the worker's home to observe and talk with his wife and children. And if any undesirable features were noted, these would be reported back to the collective.

I asked for an example.

"Well, suppose the representative were to notice that my wife and I quarreled in front of the children [my companion shook his head]. That would be bad. They would speak to me about it and remind me of my responsibilities for training my children to be good citizens."

I pointed out how different the situation was in America where a man's home was considered a private sanctuary so that, for example, psychologists like myself often had a great deal of difficulty in getting into homes to talk with parents or to observe children.

"Yes," my companion responded. "That's one of the strange things about your system in the West. The family is separated from the rest of society. That's not good. It's bad for the family and bad for society." He paused for a moment, lost in thought. "I suppose," he went on, "if my wife didn't want to let the representative in, she could ask him to leave. But then at work, I should feel ashamed." (He hung his head to emphasize the point.) "Ivanov," they would say, "has an uncultured wife."

But it would be a mistake to conclude that Soviet methods of character education and social control are based primarily on negative criticism. On the contrary, in their approach there is as much of the carrot as the stick. But the carrot is given not merely as a reward for individual performance but explicitly for the child's contribution to group achievement. The great charts emblazoned "Who IS Best?" which bedeck the halls and walls of every classroom have as entries the names not of individual pupils but of rows and links (the link is the smallest unit of Communist youth organization, which of course reaches into every classroom, from the first grade on). It is the winning unit that gets rewarded by a pennant, a special privilege, or by having their picture taken in "parade uniforms." And when praise is given, as it frequently is, to an individual child, the group referent is always there: "Today Peter helped Kate and as a result his unit did not get behind the rest."

Helping other members of one's collective and appreciating their contributions—themes that are much stressed in Soviet character training—become matters of enlightened self-interest, since the grade that each person receives depends on the overall performance of his unit. Thus the good student finds it to his advantage to help the poor one. The same principle is carried over to the group level with champion rows and classes being made responsible for the performance of poorer ones.

Here, then, are the procedures employed in Soviet character education. As a result of Khrushchev's educational reforms, they may be expected to receive even wider application in the years to come, for, in connection with these reforms, several new types of educational institutions are to be developed on a massive scale. The most important of these is the "internat," or boarding school, in which youngsters are to be entered as early as three months of age with parents visiting only on weekends. The internat is described in the theses announcing the reforms as the kind of school which "creates the most favorable conditions for the education and communist upbringing of the rising generation" (Communist Party of Soviet Russia, 1958). The number of boarding schools in the USSR is to be increased during the current seven-year plan from a 1958 level of 180,000 to 250,000 in 1965 (figures cited in *Pravda,* November 18, 1958), and according to I. A. Kairov, head of the Academy of Pedagogical Sciences, "No one can doubt that, as material conditions are created, the usual general educational school will be supplanted by the boarding school" (Kairov, 1960).

If this prophecy is fulfilled, we may expect that in the years to come the great majority of Soviet children (and children in some other countries of the Communist bloc as well) will from the first year of life onward be spending their formative period in collective settings and will be exposed daily to the techniques of collective socialization we have been describing. It is therefore a matter of considerable practical and scientific interest to identify the salient features of these techniques and subject them to research study, in so far as this becomes possible within the framework of our own society.

Guiding Principles of the Soviet Approach to Character Training

As a first approximation, we may list the following as distinguishing characteristics or guiding principles of communist methods of character education.

1. The peer collective (under adult leadership) rivals and early surpasses the family as the principal agent of socialization.
2. Competition between groups is utilized as the principal mechanism for motivating achievement of behavior norms.
3. The behavior of the individual is evaluated primarily in terms of its relevance to the goals and achievements of the collective.
4. Rewards and punishments are frequently given on a group basis; that is to say, the entire group benefits or suffers as a consequence of the conduct of individual members.
5. As soon as possible, the tasks of evaluating the behavior of individuals and of dispensing rewards and sanctions is delegated to the members of the collective.
6. The principal methods of social control are public recognition and public criticism, with explicit training and practice being given in these activities. Specifically, each member of the collective is encouraged to observe deviant behavior by his fellows and is given opportunity to report his observations to the group. Reporting on one's peers is esteemed and rewarded as a civic duty.
7. Group criticism becomes the vehicle for training in self-criticism in the presence of one's peers. Such public self-criticism is regarded as a powerful mechanism for maintaining and enhancing commitment to approved standards of behavior, as well as the method of choice for bringing deviants back into line.

There are of course many other important features of the Soviet approach to socialization, but the seven listed above are those which present the greatest contrast to the patterns we employ in the West. It is for this reason that they are selected for special consideration here. We shall now proceed to examine each feature in greater detail with particular attention to the research ideas which it may generate.[1]

. . .

Group Criticism and Self-Criticism

THE feature of Soviet socialization practices which clashes most sharply with the American pattern is the Russians' widespread resort to the procedure of criticizing others and one's self in public. The practice is common throughout all levels of Soviet society from school, farm, and factory to the highest echelons of the party. Thus by being taught these techniques in early childhood, Soviet youths are being prepared in patterns of response that will be expected and even required of them throughout their life span. Since such practices are uncommon in American society, it is not surprising that they have not been subjected to research study in any direct way. As already noted, however, the work of Asch and others (Asch, 1956; Berenda, 1950) testifies to the power of an overwhelming majority forcing the deviant member of the group to conform to majority opinion. In these experiments members of the majority do not engage in criticism but simply give responses which conflict with

1 Sections in the original report, "The Family Versus the Collective" and "Group Incentives," have been deleted here, together with references therein. [Ed.]

the reality perceptions of the experimental subject. The effect on the subject is to lead him, in an appreciable number of instances, to change his own response in the direction of the majority. In a sense, such alteration represents a confession of his own previous "error." Obviously, the experiments cannot be said to reproduce explicit features of Soviet group criticism and self-criticism, but the fit could be made much closer by instructing confederates to engage in criticism and by asking the subject to admit that his previous responses had not been correct. Such variations would of course make even more salient questions of scientific ethics that invariably arise when experiments of this kind are viewed from the perspective of the Western Judeo-Christian moral tradition. (It is doubtful, incidentally, that such questions would ever be raised in a Communist society.) Still ways can probably be found to conduct experiments on the processes of group criticism and self-criticism without doing serious violence to our own ethical traditions.

The fact remains, however, that such socialization procedures as group criticism and self-criticism have moral implications and hence may be expected to have moral consequences; that is to say, they are likely to influence the moral attitudes, actions, and character structure of the individuals on whom they are employed. Moreover, it is doubtful whether such consequences are fully or even adequately reflected by the measures of conscience and guilt currently employed in research on moral development. Certainly it would be important to know about the nature of conscience and guilt in the "new Soviet men" who have been exposed to a lifetime of experience in group criticism and self-criticism. But in building "socialist morality" Soviet educators are less concerned with such questions as whether the individual tends to blame others or himself than with his sense of commitment to the collective, especially in the face of competing individualistic values and preferences.

Accordingly, perhaps the most important research implication to be drawn from our examination of Soviet methods of character education is the necessity of expanding the spectrum of what we conceive as moral development beyond the characteristically Judeo-Christian concern with personal responsibility and guilt to a consideration of the broader moral issues inherent in the relation of man to man and of the individual to his society.

We have tried to take some beginning steps in this direction in the research on character development being conducted at Cornell by Bronfenbrenner, Devereux, and Suci. Specifically, as a point of departure we have distinguished five hypothetical extreme types of character structure representing the presumed products of five divergent patterns of socialization and moral development in children and adolescents. These five are tentatively designated as self-oriented, adult-oriented, peer-oriented, collective-oriented, and objectively-principled character structures.[2]

The self-oriented child is motivated primarily by impulses of self-gratification without regard to the desires or expectations of others or to internalized standards. Such an asocial and amoral orientation is presumed to arise when the child's parents are so permissive, indifferent, inconsistent, or indulgent that immediate self-indulgence becomes the practicable and, in the long run, most rewarding course of action for the child. The development of this personality type is further facilitated by participation in peer groups which encourage self-indulgence and exact neither loyalty nor discipline from their members.

The adult-oriented child is one who accepts parental strictures and values as final and immutable. He is completely submissive to parental authority and the moral standards imposed by the parent. This orientation generalizes to adult authority outside the home in school and community. In other words, here is the oversocialized "good child," already a little adult, who causes no trouble but is

2 A similar typology, but unlinked to particular patterns and agents of socialization, has recently been proposed by Peck and Havighurst (1960).

relatively incapable of initiative and leadership. He is presumed to be the product of intensive socialization within the nuclear family but with minimal experience outside the home.

In contrast, the peer-oriented child is an adaptive conformist who goes along with the group and readily accepts every shift in group opinion or conduct. This is the "outer-directed" character type of Riesman's (1950) typology or the future "organization man" described by Whyte (1956). His values and preferences reflect the momentary sentiments of his social set. The optimal circumstances for the development of this personality type involve a combination of parents who are either permissive or actively encourage conformity to group norms, accompanied by early and extensive participation in peer groups requiring such conformity as the price of acceptance. The norms of such groups, however, are ephemeral in character and imply no consistent standards or goals.

The prototype of the collective-oriented personality is of course the "new Soviet man"—a person committed to a firm and enduring set of values centering around the achievement of enduring group standards and goals. These group values take precedence over individual desires or obligations of particular interpersonal relationships. Such an orientation presumably springs from a developmental history in which from the very outset the parents place the needs and demands of the collective above those of the child or of particular family members. Affection and discipline are bestowed in the name and interests of the social group and the child spends most of his formative years in collective settings under the guidance of adults and leaders who train him in the skills and values of collective living.

Finally, the behavior of the objectively-principled child is guided by values which, although learned through experience in the family and in peer groups, do not bind him to undeviating conformity to the standards of the one or the other. This is the "inner-directed" personality of Riesman's (1950) typology. On one occasion he may act in accordance with the standards of his parents, on another with the mores of the peer group, or in still a third instance he may take a path which deviates from the preferences of both parents and peers. There is, however, a consistency in pattern of response from one situation to the next which reflects the child's own now autonomous standards of conduct. The developmental history posited for this type of character structure assumes a strong, differentiated family organization with high levels of affection and discipline but at the same time considerable opportunity granted to the child to participate in selected but varied peer-group experiences both with and without adult supervision. These peer groups, in turn, are also characterized by high levels of affectional involvement and their own particular disciplinary codes. The hypothesis implicit in this developmental sequence is that an autonomous set of moral standards is developed from having to cope with different types of discipline in a variety of basically accepting social contexts, so that the child is forced to compare and come to terms with different codes of behavior imposed by different persons or groups each of whom is supportive and wins his liking and respect. This hypothesis, though highly speculative, derives in part from some of our research results (Bronfenbrenner, 1961a, 1961b, 1961c) which suggested that children who are rated by teachers and peers as high in social responsibility and initiative tend to come from families where parental affection and discipline are relatively strong, parental roles are moderately differentiated (e.g., one parent tends to exercise authority slightly more than the other), but the child also participates in many group activities outside the home. Unfortunately, in these initial studies very little information was obtained about the child's experiences in peer-group settings.

We are currently in the process of devising instruments for measuring the five types of character structure outlined above as these are manifested both in attitudes and behavior. Several of our instruments have yielded promising results in pilot studies but have also brought to light shortcomings in theory and method. The principal value of the approach in its present stage of development is its capacity to generate fruitful hypotheses and research designs for the investigation of character development as a social process.

The last consideration brings us back to the main objective of this paper. Its primary purpose is not to argue for a particular theoretical orientation or methodology; the sole and central aim is to encourage and assist behavioral scientists and educators to give careful attention to the problems and processes implicit in collective methods of character education such as those employed in the Soviet Union and elsewhere in the Communist bloc. We have tried to show that these problems and processes have considerable social relevance and theoretical importance far beyond their immediate social context. We have also attempted to demonstrate that they can be made amenable to empirical investigation. This paper will have served its purpose if it contributes to a renewal of research interest in the study of extrafamilial groups as socializing agents, for such scientific study should do much to enhance our understanding of intriguing social processes through which human character is formed.

REFERENCES

ASCH, S. E. Studies of independence and conformity: a minority of one against a unanimous majority. *Psychol. Monogr.,* **1956, 70,** No. 9 (Whole No. 416).

BERENDA, R. W. *The influence of the group on the judgments of children.* New York: King's Crown Press, 1950.

BRONFENBRENNER, U. The changing American child. In E. Ginsberg (Ed.), *Values and ideals of American youth.* New York: Columbia Univer. Press, 1961. Pp. 71–84. (Also in *Merrill-Palmer Quart.,* 1961, **7,** 73–84.) (a)

BRONFENBRENNER, U. Some familial antecedents of responsibility and leadership in adolescents. In L. Petrullo & B. M. Bass (Eds.), *Leadership and interpersonal behavior.* New York: Holt, Rinehart & Winston, 1961. Pp. 239–272. (b)

BRONFENBRENNER, U. Toward a theoretical model for the analysis of parent-child relationships in a social context. In J. C. Glidewell (Ed.), *Parental attitudes and child behavior.* Springfield, Ill.: Charles C Thomas, 1961. Pp. 90–109. (c)

COMMUNIST PARTY OF THE SOVIET UNION. *Ob ukreplenii svyazi shkoli s zhiznyu i o dalneishem razvitii sistemi naraodnogo obrazovaniya b strane* [On the strengthening of ties between school and life and the further development of the system of public education in the country]. (Theses of the Central Committee of the Communist Party of the Soviet Union.) Moscow: Gospolitizdat, 1958.

KAIROV, I. A. [Long range plans for the development of pedagogical sciences and coordination of the work of the Academy and Chairs of Pedagogy of Pedagogical Institutes, U.S.S.R.] (Translation of an article in *Sovetsk. Pedag.,* 1960, **24,** 16–44.) New York: United States Joint Publications Research Service, 1960.

MAKARENKO, A. S. *Pedagogicheskaya poema* [A pedagogical poem]. (Available in English under the title *The road to life,* translated by Ivy and Tatiana Litvinov. Moscow: Foreign Languages Publishing House, 1951.) Leningrad: Leningradskoye gazetno-zhurnalnoye i knizhnoye izdatelstvo [Leningrad Newspaper-Periodical and Book Publishing House], 1949.

MAKARENKO, A. S. *Learning to live.* Moscow: Foreign Languages Publishing House, 1953.

MAKARENKO, A. S. *Knigda dlya roditelei* [A book for parents]. (Available in English. Moscow: Foreign Languages Publishing House, undated.) Petrozavodsk: Gosudarstvennoye Izadatelstov Karel'skoi A.S.S.R. [State Publishing House of the Karelian Autonomous Soviet Socialist Republic], 1959.

MILLER, D. R., & SWANSON, G. E. *Inner conflict and defense.* New York: Holt, Rinehart & Winston, 1960.

NOVIKOVA, L. E. (Ed.) *Sotsialisticheskoye sorevnovaniye b shkole* [Socialist competition in the school]. Moscow: Uchpedgiz, 1950.

PECK, R. F., & HAVIGHURST, R. J. *The psychology of character development.* New York: Wiley, 1960.

RIESMAN, D. (with N. Glazer & R. Denney). *The lonely crowd: a study of the changing American character.* New Haven: Yale Univer. Press, 1950.

WHYTE, W. H. *The organization man.* New York: Doubleday, 1956.

ELEANOR E. MACCOBY, PATRICIA K. GIBBS, *and the* STAFF OF THE LABORATORY OF HUMAN DEVELOPMENT, HARVARD UNIVERSITY

Methods of Child-Rearing in Two Social Classes[1,*]

Introduction

WE KNOW that in the United States there are identifiable class groups which differ in many of their values, beliefs and practices. The ways in which these classes bring up their children are especially interesting. For, if we assume that many of the foundations of adult personality are laid in the experiences of early childhood, greater understanding of the differences in behavior of adults from different classes should come from knowing something about the differences and similarities in their early childhood training.

For the present study, 372 mothers were interviewed concerning their methods of raising their children. The interview, which employed a standard list of open-ended questions, took about two hours, on the average, and was mechanically recorded. The families were selected from two areas in the Greater Boston metropolitan area: one section was largely suburban-residential, the other was a working-class residential area adjoining a large industrial plant. As the first step in selecting a sample, public schools were chosen in neighborhoods which appeared to offer a wide range of social class groups. The kindergarten children (aged five to six) in these schools and their parents were taken as the original population for study. Families were then excluded from the target group if either of the child's parents was foreign born, if the child was not living with both natural parents, or if the child was a twin or suffered from some physical handicap. Interviews were obtained with 80% of the mothers in the families finally designated for study.

Each family in the sample was given a score on a scale of socioeconomic status (henceforth called SES). The scores were computed as follows: the occupation of the husband was rated on the Warner scale of occupational status (Warner, Meeker, & Eells, 1949), and this rating was given a weight of two; then a score for income (with a weight of one) was added, and the resulting scores were grouped into nine class intervals. The distribution of cases on this nine-point scale is as follows:

Socioeconomic Status	*Number of Cases*
1 (high)	39
2	59
3	49
4	51
5	43
6	25
7	57
8	26
9 (low)	23

1 This article reports a selected set of findings, drawn from a larger study of "Identification in Young Children," conducted in 1951–1952 by the Laboratory of Human Development at Harvard University. Primary responsibility for planning and conducting the study rested with Professor Robert R. Sears, Director of the Laboratory, and Dr. Harry Levin, Dr. Eleanor E. Maccoby, Dr. John W. M. Whiting, and Dr. Pauline S. Sears. The study was made possible by a grant from the National Institute of Mental Health (M-461).

* REPRINTED by permission of Eleanor E. Maccoby from W. E. Martin & Celia B. Stendler (Eds.), *Readings in Child Development*. New York: Harcourt, Brace & World, 1954. Pp. 380–396.

For the analysis which follows, the cases have been divided into two main groups: "upper-middle," which includes groups 1 through 4 on the SES scale (198 cases), and "upper-lower" which includes families with a score of 5 through 9 on the SES scale (174 cases). Our upper-middle group represents those occupational groups which are classed 1, 2, and 3 on the Warner scale of occupational status, and which Warner labels as upper-middle. Predominant in the group are professional and business families. The upper-lower group includes the occupational groups which would be classed 4 through 7 on the Warner occupational status scale, and are primarily blue-collar people (skilled and semi-skilled, with relatively few unskilled or service).

A problem in labeling the class groups concerns our group with an SES score of 5 (comparable to Warner's occupational group 4), whom he labels lower-middle. In our sample, this group includes such occupations as dance-band musician, low-income salesman, construction foreman, self-employed painter and decorator, manager of a small restaurant who helps with the cooking, etc. For the analysis which follows, this group has been classed with the upper-lower group, and makes up about one-fourth of the group. The upper-lower group, then, while it includes primarily blue-collar people whom Warner would class as upper-lower, also includes a group of lower-middle families. The entire group could reasonably be labeled a "common man" group (Kahl, 1953), or a "working class" group.

Infant Feeding

THERE are few differences between the classes in infant feeding practices: upper-middle mothers breast feed slightly more often (not significantly so); they begin weaning slightly later, but complete weaning earlier; and they schedule slightly more rigidly (not significantly so). Characteristically, both groups had only general time-schedules of feeding, which they would modify according to the demands of the infant, seldom waking the infant for a feeding or allowing him to cry very long from hunger. Neither group was characterised by abrupt weaning: both made the transition from sucking to drinking gradually, and applied only very moderate pressure on the child to give up sucking (TABLE 1).

Toilet Training

TOILET training is somewhat more severe among the lower group. There is somewhat

TABLE 1. *Infant feeding, by social class*

	UPPER MIDDLE	UPPER LOWER	t	p
Per cent who breast-fed child	43%	37%	—	
Average length of breast-feeding (for those breast-fed)	2.8 mo.	2.6 mo.	—	
Age of beginning weaning *	10 mo.	9½ mo.	1.42	
Age at completion of weaning	12½ mo.	13½ mo.	2.48	<.02
Severity of weaning 1 = mild 9 = severe	4.9	4.9	—	
Scheduling of feeding 1 = complete self-demand 9 = rigid schedule	5.1	4.6	1.62	

* Weaning is defined as a change from the sucking mode of taking food to the drinking and chewing modes. Thus, transition from the breast or bottle to the cup is considered weaning; transition from the breast to the bottle is not.

TABLE 2. *Toilet training, by social class*

	UPPER MIDDLE	UPPER LOWER	*t*	*p*
Age of beginning bowel training	11¼ mo.	10¾ mo.	.88	
Age of completing bowel training	19¼ mo.	18 mo.	1.85	
Severity of toilet training *	3.8	4.6	4.05	<.01
1 = mild				
9 = severe				

* This scale takes into account training for both bowel and bladder control.

more punishment and scolding for accidents, more "shaming," more worry on the part of the mother when the child is slow in learning sphincter control. Two mothers in the lower group rubbed their children's faces in their soiled diapers in an effort to teach them how "disgusting" accidents were. However, most commonly, the upper-lower mother was only moderately severe: that is, she would spank occasionally for toilet accidents, or lose her temper if the child soiled himself after she had thought he was completely trained, but would be fairly gentle in the early stages of training (TABLE 2).

Sex Training

CLEARLY, sex training is much more severe in the lower group (TABLE 3). Following are excerpts from two interviews, illustrating the kind of material on which the above ratings were based.

The wife of a research chemist who has a college degree and earns $7000 a year, said:

Interviewer: How do you feel about allowing Sue to run about without her clothes on?

Respondent: She has always been very free

TABLE 3. *Sex training, by social class*

	UPPER MIDDLE	UPPER LOWER	*t*	*p*
Nudity permissiveness	5.5	3.3	7.57	>.01
1 = not at all permissive				
9 = completely permissive				
Amount of pressure for modesty	2.8	4.0	5.4	>.01
1 = no pressure				
8 = a great deal of pressure				
Age of beginning modesty training	3 yrs.	2½ yrs.	2.58	>.01
Masturbation permissiveness	4.6	3.1	6.6	>.01
1 = not at all permissive				
9 = completely permissive				
Severity of pressure against masturbation	3.8	4.6	4.16	>.01
1 = no pressure				
8 = a great deal of pressure				
Permissiveness: sex play among children	4.3	2.9	6.74	>.01
1 = not at all permissive				
9 = completely permissive				
Severity of pressure against sex play with other children	3.6	4.7	4.27	>.01
1 = no pressure				
8 = severe pressure				

to run about with or without her clothes. As a tiny child she much preferred not wearing clothes, and I think that most small children feel that way and have no self-consciousness about it. As far as training about clothes are concerned, as far as our own feelings about it, we feel that children are children, and that they should be perfectly free.

I. What have you done about it when you have noticed her playing with herself?

R. Nothing has been done about that at all when we have noticed anything of that kind, but with her there hasn't been very much obvious play.

I. How important do you feel it is to prevent this in a child?

R. Well, I think that it isn't important. It's natural, and they'll get over it if you don't make an issue of it.

I. How about sex play with other children —has this come up yet?

R. No.

I. What about children wanting to look at each other, or go to the toilet together, or giggling together—how do you feel about it when you notice this sort of thing going on among the children?

R. Well, the children go to the toilet together quite freely. When she has visitors or whatever, they go to the toilet together and that's just treated naturally.

In contrast are the remarks of the wife of a policeman (the family income is $3500 a year):

R. I don't think it is a good policy to bring things to their minds, to enlighten them on things until they first bring the subject up themselves. I have taught her that she shouldn't undress in front of her brother. She does have a habit at night of putting on her pajama top and then she will wait and go into the bathroom with just her panties. I, of course, in turn corrected her and told her it would be polite to put on her bottom to the pajamas before she went to the bathroom. She did say to me that she was covered up, but then she put on her pajamas fully and then went out.

I. When did you start teaching her this?

R. When she was old enough to know, I would say. She knows that she can't ever take any clothing off outdoors or anything like that. Even her shoes.

I. What have you done about it when you have noticed her playing with herself?

R. I never have.

I. How important do you feel it is to prevent this in a child?

R. I think it is very important to prevent it. I really do. Actually, as to how I would cope with it, I really don't know. I ran into difficulty with my niece here, who is the same age. I just took her aside and talked to her. I explained to her that it wasn't nice to do, and if Aunt Janet ever saw her doing it again, she would have to punish her. As far as my little girl, I haven't seen it.

I. How about sex play with other children —has this come up yet?

R. No. Never. It has happened in the neighborhood, I know, but not as far as I am concerned. And I hope it never does. My heart would be broke.

I. What about children wanting to look at each other, or go to the toilet together, or giggling together—how do you feel about it when you notice this sort of thing going on among the children?

R. I never have noticed it.

I. Would you allow this, or do you think you would step in?

R. I would stop it immediately. I don't think it is good at all.

A fairly large number of incidents of sex play among neighborhood children were reported and described by the mothers; among the upper-lower mothers, the reaction was generally one of shock and shame, and the children were punished. Upper-middle mothers discouraged the more active forms of sex behavior, but more often by separating the children or admonishing them than by punishment, and they seemed to react with less emotional intensity.

In the interview, the mothers were not asked how frequently their children masturbated, but a conjecture based on the mothers' free comments would be that the lower mothers would be less likely to report that their children masturbated, because their higher level of sex anxiety would prevent their seeing (or believing) this behavior in their children.

Aggression Control

THE upper-middle mothers allow (and even encourage) at least as much aggression among neighborhood children as do the upper-lower mothers. Aggression toward parents is fairly strictly controlled in both groups, but upper-middle mothers overlook it somewhat more often than the upper-lower mothers (TABLE 4).

The wife of a day laborer (income $2500) expresses the following attitude toward aggressive behavior in her small son:

I. How about when Jim is playing with one of the other children in the neighborhood and there's a quarrel or a fight. How do you handle this?

R. Well I generally go out and ask them what happened. As a rule he will tell me the truth, and if he started it, he will tell me, and then I'll say, "Well, you hit him first, he should hit you back. If you don't hit him, he won't hit you." We'll talk it out, I will sit down and talk to him but then if I find he's keeping it up, then he comes in the house here until he cools down, until he can act like himself again, behave like himself, like he should.

I. Some people feel it is very important for a child to learn not to fight with other children, and other people feel there are times when a child has to learn to fight. How do you feel about this?

R. Well, I don't want him to run from anybody. Course it's always the two big ones around here that pick on the small ones, and it's hard for a small one to go fight with a big one. With the kids his age, and I know he can't hurt them too badly, no, I'll send him out, I'll tell him, "You've got to learn," and he'll go out.

TABLE 4. *Training for aggression control, by social class*

	UPPER MIDDLE	UPPER LOWER	t	p
Permissiveness: aggression toward other children 1 = not at all permissive 9 = completely permissive	5.1	4.6	2.46	>.02
How much parent encouraged child to fight back if attacked 1 = never 8 = strongly encouraged	4.2	4.3	—	
Permissiveness: aggression toward siblings 1 = not at all permissive 9 = completely permissive	4.7	4.5	—	
Permissiveness: aggression toward parents 1 = not at all permissive 9 = completely permissive	3.6	2.8	3.84	> .01
Severity of punishment for aggression toward parents 1 = no punishment 8 = severe punishment	5.3	5.8	3.47	>.01

I. So you encourage him to fight back?

R. To a certain extent. If they keep it clean —when it comes to kicking and biting, I don't like it.

I. What do you tell him?

R. He knows he's not supposed to fight, and kicking, he knows it can hurt—they can hurt themselves if they kick sometimes in the wrong place where they don't mean to but it happens. And his father has taught him that he has two good hands, use them, and you don't have to bite. That's the only thing that gets me mad, when he comes home with teeth marks on him and their mothers don't think nothing of it—their children are angels. I don't mind them fighting if they play clean.

I. Sometimes a child will get angry at his parents and hit them or kick them or shout angry things at them. How much of this sort of thing do you think parents ought to allow in a child of Jimmy's age?

R. They shouldn't allow it. The first time they strike back they should be told right then and there, because sometimes no matter how young a child is if he's old enough to raise his hand he's old enough to be taught right.

I. How do you handle it if Jim acts like this —could you give me an example?

R. Jimmy has never kicked me—he's offered to hit me, but I just told him, I said: look, now, I'm a little bit bigger than you are and my hands are a little bit larger, and you can get a worse bruise out of it than I could, I can hurt more than you can, and if you don't want to get hurt, don't you hurt me. He'll try it, he'll take a little step closer, but then he looks at my hand and he looks at his hand, he just don't see no use in it. You can reason with him, he's an easy kid to reason with. I guess you call it judgment because he can judge from his hand to my hand that he would get a worse beating out of it than I would.

A doctor's wife on the other hand, expressed a somewhat more permissive attitude about aggression toward parents:

R. Well he does that—since going to school, he's learned that also. I pay no attention to it unless he really kicked me in the shin or something I would, but if he says things to me, I just pretend I don't hear them, I don't pay any attention to him. That's just what I tell my little girl, because she answers him back. I say, "Pay no attention to him" —just ignore it, unless he actually starts hitting you or something.

I. Has he ever hit at you or kicked at you?

R. Oh, yes, he's hit me.

I. What have you done about it?

R. I just try to push him away and tell him that it hurts and I don't like it—that's all.

Restrictions and Achievement Demands

THE upper-middle mothers seem to impose fewer restrictions and demands upon their five-year-olds than do the upper-lower mothers. Messiness at the table is somewhat less often permitted for the upper-lower children, and these children are subject to more stringent requirements about such things as hanging up their clothes, keeping their feet off the furniture, and being quiet around the house. Few mothers in either group give their children regular jobs to do around the house—they do not, in general, require the children to help with dishes, make beds, set the table, or take care of younger children. The most common type of task assigned is that of keeping the child's own toys and clothes picked up, and of helping to empty waste baskets or ash trays, but these tasks are not assigned on a regular basis or enforced strictly for either class group.

The upper-middle children are allowed somewhat more freedom to cross streets or go several houses away to visit other children, and the mother is less likely to check constantly on their whereabouts.

The findings in connection with demands for school achievement are complex: although the upper-middle families take it for granted that their children will go to college, they do not seem to be so concerned about current school achievement as the lower families are. Possibly, the upper-middle children adjust to school more easily; for the lower families, current school performance may be more of a problem, and more parental pressure may be required to keep the child performing up to even an average standard. In any case, our data do not show any tendency for the lower parents to de-value school achievement—on the contrary, they seem emphatically interested in having their children do well in school (TABLE 5).

TABLE 5. *Restrictions and achievement demands, by social class*

	UPPER MIDDLE	UPPER LOWER	*t*	*p*
Must child stay at table throughout meal? (restriction) 1 = no restrictions 8 = high restrictions	3.4	3.5	—	
Amount of restriction of use of fingers at table 1 = no restrictions 9 = high restrictions	4.6	5.1	3.11	<.01
Amount of restriction: interrupting adult conversation 1 = no restrictions 9 = high restrictions	4.4	4.6	—	
Pressure for conformity with table standards and restrictions 1 = no pressure 9 = high pressure	4.7	5.2	3.23	<.01
Restrictions: care of house and furniture 1 = few restrictions 9 = many restrictions	6.3	6.6	2.16	<.05
Pressure: neatness and orderliness 1 = no pressure 9 = high pressure	5.5	5.9	2.93	<.01
Strictness about bedtime 1 = not at all strict 9 = very strict	5.4	5.5	—	
Strictness about noise 1 = not at all strict 9 = very strict	4.5	4.9	2.29	<.05
Sex role differentiation: (mother's expectation for child to be "masculine" or "feminine") 1 = no differentiation 9 = high differentiation	5.0	5.4	1.66	
Restrictions: physical mobility (How far away from the house may the child go alone?) 1 = no restrictions 9 = high restrictions	4.5	4.8	1.88	
Giving child regular jobs 1 = no jobs given 9 = many regular jobs given	3.9	3.8	—	

TABLE 5 (*Continued*)

	UPPER MIDDLE	UPPER LOWER	*t*	*p*
Keeping track of child	4.3	4.8	2.37	<.05
1 = rarely checks				
9 = constantly checks				
Extent of demand for instant obedience	5.0	5.0	—	
1 = no demands for obedience				
9 = child must obey instantly				
How far is child expected to go in school	6.4 *	4.3 *	11.4	>.01
1 = grade school				
9 = graduate school				
How important is it for child to do well in school	5.1	5.9	3.4	>.01
1 = unimportant				
9 = very important				

* A score of 6.4 on this scale means that the mother says she expects the child to go through college, and states no reservations about it. A score of 4.3 means that she feels he certainly should finish high school, and may go to college if he wants to badly or if he shows unusual abilities.

Techniques of Discipline

IT IS evident that the upper-lower mothers more often use the "negative" techniques of discipline: physical punishment, ridicule, deprivation of privileges. They are slightly (but not significantly) less likely to use praise and reasoning. The comparison between classes on the use of withdrawal of love is unclear. The raters made an over-all rating from each interview on the frequency of use of this technique, but in almost half the cases, there was insufficient information in the interview to permit making a rating. Where the rating could be made, it was based upon such remarks as, "I tell my children they have to call me Mrs. Jackson when they are naughty: only good children can call me mother," or "When he does that, I just look at him coldly," or "I was disgusted with her, and I just locked her out of the house and told her she couldn't come in and whine around me." A low score on withdrawal of love would be based upon such remarks as, "Even when he's naughty and I have to punish him, I try to show him that I still love him." In the cases where the rating could be made, there was a tendency (not significant) for the upper-lower mothers to use withdrawal of love more often (TABLE 6).

On the other hand, the checklist score on withdrawal of love (see footnote, TABLE 6) revealed that the upper-middle mothers more often used remarks in their scolding which could be interpreted as withdrawal of love. Possibly, the interview rating took cognizance of more extreme and less subtle forms of the technique. In any case, our data do not permit us to say which class uses this technique more frequently or more severely.

Agents of Child Care and Discipline

AS might be expected, there are few differences between the classes in the identity of the person who has main responsibility for child care: in both classes it is the mother. When the child is a baby, the father gives occasional help, and the upper-middle child is occasionally left with a sitter or a part-time maid, but all the caretaking done by agents other than the mother adds up to a very small amount in the average home. Of course, there are a few instances in which the child is regularly left with someone else while the mother

TABLE 6. *Techniques of discipline, by social class*

	UPPER MIDDLE	UPPER LOWER	*t*	*p*
If no trouble at table, what does mother do?	3.9	4.4	2.04	<.05
1 = always praise				
8 = never praise				
If children play well together, what does mother do?	4.0	4.3	1.33	
1 = always praise				
8 = never praise				
Frequency of use of isolation	5.7	5.5	—	
1 = never used				
9 = very often used				
Extent of use of withdrawal of love (rating)	4.1	4.5	1.64	
1 = never used				
9 = very often used				
Proportion of scolding statements involving withdrawal of love *	6.4	6.0	4.5	<.01
1 = low proportion				
9 = high proportion				
Extent of use of reasoning	5.0	4.8	1.22	
1 = never used				
9 = very often used				
Extent of use of reward	4.6	4.9	.89	
1 = never used				
9 = regularly used				
Can child earn money?	3.8	3.8	—	
1 = yes, regular earning system				
9 = money not used as reward				
Extent of use of praise	4.8	4.8	—	
1 = never used				
9 = very often used				
Extent of use of ridicule	3.6	.4.0	2.28	<.05
1 = never used				
9 = very often used				
Extent of use of deprivation of privileges	4.6	5.1	2.02	<.05
1 = never used				
9 = very often used				
Extent of use of physical punishment	3.9	4.8	4.84	<.01
1 = never used				
9 = very often used				

* The mother was asked to fill out a checklist of possible remarks which could be made in scolding a child, indicating which of the remarks she made often, occasionally, or never. Some of the statements were considered indicative of withdrawal of love, such as "Go away—I don't want to look at you until you can smile." Others were not so relevant to withdrawal of love, such as "That wasn't a very smart thing to do." Total scores were based on the number of withdrawal of love statements the mother used, minus the number of other types of statements she used.

works, but this is rare in our sample. When both parents are at home, there are some families where the father takes over the discipline of the children, others where he leaves it entirely to the mother, and still others where they share discipline (whichever one is involved or nearer the child handles any incidents which require discipline), but there is no difference between the classes in the tendency for one parent instead of the other to take over the disciplinary function. The policy decisions about child-rearing (such as whether the child is sick enough to be kept home from school, whether the child shall take music lessons, whether the child shall have chores to do, how far away from the house the child may go alone, etc.) are left mostly to the mother in both classes, although the husband is consulted on most major and some minor decisions. In both classes, the father is slightly stricter than the mother in terms of severity of discipline and his demands for obedience and self-restraint (TABLE 7).

TABLE 7. *Agents of child care, by social class*

	UPPER MIDDLE	UPPER LOWER	*t*	*p*
Amount of caretaking of infant by mother (proportional)	5.2	5.5	1.66	
1 = practically none				
9 = all				
Amount of caretaking of infant by father	3.2	3.1	—	
1 = none				
8 = more than mother				
Amount of caretaking of infant by other agent	3.2	2.4	3.53	<.01
1 = none				
8 = more than half				
What other agents were there?				
a) older sibling	2%	7%		
b) maid, sitter	58%	12%		
c) grandmother	35%	61%		
d) other relative	5%	20%		
	100% *	100% *		
How much care does father give now?	3.7	4.0	1.67	
1 = none				
9 = quite a bit				
Who is disciplinarian? (When both parents are present)	5.1	5.2	—	
1 = husband				
9 = wife				
Responsibility for policy regarding children	4.2	4.1	—	
1 = mother entirely responsible				
9 = father almost entirely				
Who is stricter with child?	4.6	4.3	1.51	
1 = father				
9 = mother				

* These percentages are based upon the cases where some other agent was involved in infant caretaking.

Affective Atmosphere in the Home

THE upper-middle mothers are slightly more demonstrative toward their five-year-olds and seem to have a somewhat warmer relationship with them than the upper-lower mothers, although the majority of mothers in both classes are warm toward their children and display only minor elements of hostility toward them. There were a few cases in the sample where a clear pattern of rejection emerged and those which did occur were found primarily among the upper-lower families. Mothers in both classes seemed to accept the role of mother easily, and there was relatively little conflict between outside interests (including career interests) and the demands of the mother role—in both classes, other roles were subordinated to the mother role. Mothers in the upper-middle group were somewhat more pleased about the advent of a new child—possibly because, on the average, they waited longer to begin their families.

The relationships between the mother and father differ somewhat along class lines: the upper-lower mothers are more critical of their husbands, and there is more open quarreling between the two parents in this group over child-rearing practices than among the upper-middle families. In both classes, the husbands are inclined to believe that their wives are not strict enough with the children, while the wives tend to believe that their husbands are too strict (TABLE 8).

TABLE 8. *Affective atmosphere, by social class*

	UPPER MIDDLE	UPPER LOWER	t	p
Warmth of affectional bond (mother to infant) 1 = mother very cold 9 = mother very warm	5.8	5.8	—	
Amount of affectional demonstrativeness (mother to child) 1 = none 9 = a great deal	5.8	5.3	3.29	<.01
How often mother finds time to play with child for mother's pleasure 1 = very often 9 = practically never	4.8	4.9	—	
Nature of affectional relationship (mother to five-year-old child) 1 = extremely warm 9 = predominantly hostile	4.5	5.1	2.73	<.01
Nature of affectional relationship (father to child) 1 = extremely warm 9 = predominantly hostile	4.0	4.5	2.02	<.05
Rejection by mother 1 = no rejection 9 = complete rejection	1.7	2.1	2.23	<.05
Mother's attitude toward mother role 1 = values it highly 9 = subordinate to other roles	4.4	4.3	—	
Mother's child-rearing anxiety 1 = no anxiety 9 = extreme anxiety	3.4	3.2	1.05	

TABLE 8 (*Continued*)

	UPPER MIDDLE	UPPER LOWER	*t*	*p*
How mother felt when found she was pregnant 1 = delighted 9 = displeased	2.9	3.4	1.87	
How father felt when found mother was pregnant 1 = delighted 9 = displeased	2.5	2.7	—	
Mother's evaluation of father 1 = critical 9 = admiring	6.5	5.7	3.56	<.01
Family authority 1 = mother complete authority 9 = father complete authority	4.4	4.8	2.33	<.05
Wife thinks husband too strict or not strict enough? 1 = too strict 5 = not strict enough	2.9	2.8	—	
Husband thinks wife too strict or not strict enough? 1 = too strict 5 = not strict enough	3.3	3.5	1.37	
Extent of mother-father disagreement re child-rearing 1 = perfect agreement 9 = complete disagreement	4.6	5.4	3.45	<.01

Education, Ethnic Origin and Social Class

THE above findings reveal, in sum, a picture of greater warmth and permissiveness, and less severity in socialization, among the upper-middle families, with the more severe child training occurring among the lower group.

A legitimate reservation to accepting these findings at their face value might be the possibility that the upper-middle mothers were telling the interviewers not what they actually do but what they believe would be the "right" thing to say to the interviewer. The upper-lower mothers, one might argue, having had less exposure to modern child-rearing doctrine, would not know so well what was the "proper" answer to the questions, and would therefore be more frank.

Unfortunately, we did not ask mothers about how much modern child-rearing literature they had read. One indirect method for checking the above possibility is available, however: we may assume that the better-educated mothers have more access to modern doctrine, via reading and direct college training. If we compare upper-middle mothers at a given education level with upper-lower mothers at the same education level, then any differences between them ought to reflect more clearly the actual differences in class-rearing practices, rather than their knowledge about what they *ought* to be doing, since knowledge has been held constant insofar as it is correlated with education.

Comparisons within and between education groups show that education makes very little difference in the severity of toilet training: at every education level, the upper-lower mothers are more severe in their training methods than the upper-middle mothers. Similarly, the amount of disagreement between mothers and fathers on child-rearing policy appears to be a function of class rather than education. And as might be expected, the amount of use of people outside the immediate family for infant caretaking is also a function of class rather than education: presumably, at any education level, it is only the upper-middle SES group who can afford maids and sitters.

Sex permissiveness is related independently to both class and education. Regardless of class level, the better educated the mother is the more permissive she is of sex behavior in her children. At the same time, at each education level, the upper-middle mothers are more permissive than the upper-lower mothers in this sphere, and significantly so. The same situation prevails with respect to the extent of use of physical punishment: education seems to reduce the use of this technique of discipline, but when mothers of similar education are compared, it appears that the upper-lower mothers use physical punishment more.

As far as permissiveness for aggression toward the parents is concerned, education and SES level interact in an interesting fashion: when a mother is in the upper-middle SES bracket, the better educated she is the more she is likely to allow her child some freedom to express aggression toward her. In the lower SES group, however, very little such aggression is permitted, regardless of the mother's education. We find therefore that if we compare upper-middle mothers who are well educated with upper-lower mothers who also have a relatively high level of education, the upper-middle mothers are more permissive of aggression; but at the lower education levels, there is no difference between the classes in this respect. A similar situation prevails with respect to the amount of affectional demonstrativeness: among the well-educated mothers, the upper-middle group is more demonstrative, but at the lower education levels, there is no difference between upper-middle and upper-lower mothers.

Among the well-educated mothers, the amount of affection and respect felt for the husband seems to depend quite clearly upon class level: if a woman is well educated but her husband's occupation is low on the status scale, she does not think so well of him as when his occupation places him in the higher brackets; when the wife is not so well educated, her esteem for her husband does not seem to depend so clearly on how "successful" he is occupationally.

To sum up the findings with respect to class and education: when education is held constant, significant differences between classes are still found on the major scales for which sizeable differences were reported earlier. This fact provides some grounds for confidence that the class differences which have been discovered are not simply a result of the mothers' telling us what they believe we would like to hear.

Another problem in interpretation of the findings arises because of differences in the ethnic background of the families in the study. While our sample did not include any cases in which the parents of the five-year-olds being studied were foreign born, there was a large group in which one or more of the child's grandparents were foreign born. As might be expected, the ethnic origins of the families in the sample were related to their social class: the upper-lower group included most of the families of South European origin (Italian) and many of those from the British Empire. The upper-middle class, on the other hand, included most of the families of Eastern European (Jewish) origin, as well as the bulk of the group with no foreign-born grandparent. It is possible, therefore, that the class differences reported earlier simply reflect greater permissiveness in the East European cultural tradition, and stricter child-rearing among the Italian and British culture groups.

In order to test this possibility, differences in child training methods among the groups of different ethnic origin were examined. In most instances, there were no differences between ethnic groups in a direction which would produce the class differences which have been reported. And when differences between ethnic groups were found, the social class differences were still found *within* the ethnic groups studied. It appears, then, that the differences in child-rearing practices between social classes which were reported earlier cannot be traced to differences in the ethnic origins of the two classes.

Relationship Between These and Previous Findings

THERE are relatively few studies on child-rearing practices among different social classes. The major findings of a few such studies are summarized below.

1. Davis and Havighurst (1946). This study reports interviews with 48 "middle class" and 52 "lower class" mothers. They report that middle class mothers wean and toilet-train their children earlier than lower class mothers, schedule infant feedings more rigidly, assign children household tasks (such as cooking and sewing) earlier, and control the children more closely (by not allowing them to go to the movies alone, for example). In general, Davis and Havighurst felt that their findings showed the lower class to be more permissive in their child-rearing practices than the middle class. See also Ericson (1947) for a report and discussion of these findings.
2. E. M. Duvall (1946). Duvall asked mothers in a wide range of social classes in Chicago to write down the "things that a good mother does" and the "things that a good child does." The lower class mothers more often revealed a "traditional" concept of child-rearing: that is, they believed that a good child is one who respects and obeys his parents, and that a good parent is one who keeps house well and takes care of the physical needs of the child. The middle class mothers, on the other hand, believed that a good mother is one who loves the child and guides him with understanding, while the good child is one who is happy and eager to learn, and who loves and confides in his parents.
3. E. H. Klatskin (1952). In connection with the Rooming-In Project at Yale, 223 families filled in questionnaires about their child training methods. Klatskin found that the lower class were in general less permissive in their child-rearing than the middle class, and he found no differences between classes in the age of weaning or the scheduling of feeding, with the middle class beginning toilet training somewhat later than the lower class.

The findings of Kinsey *et al* (1948), while not specifically directed at child training, provide some relevant information on social class differences: they find the lower class groups to be stricter in their insistence on modesty, and more opposed to masturbation, than upper-middle groups. Presumably, these mores would be reflected in child training.

As noted earlier, the present study shows the upper-middle class to be more permissive, and less severe in child training than the upper-lower class. These findings are consistent with all the findings listed above except those of Davis and Havighurst. Since the present study was done at least ten years later than the Davis and Havighurst study, it is possible that the differences in the two sets of findings reflect changes during this time: that the upper-middle class have become more permissive, while the upper-lower group have been undergoing little change in their child-rearing or have actually become more strict. This explanation does not seem very plausible, however, for several reasons. The mothers in the present study were asked whether they were more or less strict with their children than their own mothers had been with them. The upper-lower mothers reported the greatest difference between themselves and their own mothers: that is, they more often said they were more lenient than their own mothers had been, while the upper-middle mothers more often felt that they were following the child-rearing practices of their mothers, or were being even more strict. Furthermore, when we compare the older mothers in the sample with the younger ones, we do not find any tendency for the older mothers among the upper-middle class to be more strict, which should be the case if there has been a significant increase in permissiveness during the last ten years.

It is possible that Davis and Havighurst were dealing with a "lower" group who were farther down the economic scale than the "upper-lower" group described in the present study, and that severity of child-rearing characterizes the upper-lower and lower-middle segment of the class hierarchy, but not the truly "lower" segment. However, when we examine child-rearing practices at each step of our SES scale, we find that the relationships of class to child-rearing are in general linear, and that on scales which show the upper-lower group to be more severe, the very lowest groups in our sample (SES 8 and 9) are the most severe of all. This suggests that if our sample of "lower" families had been confined to the lowest end of the SES scale, the differences between this group and the upper-middle group in child-rearing would have been even greater, in the direction of greater severity in the lower class.

The most plausible explanation for at least some of the differences between this study and that of Davis and Havighurst seems to be that somewhat different items were chosen for study, and that the findings have been interpreted differently. For example, Davis and Havighurst report that middle class children masturbate more often than lower class children, and they attribute this to the child's higher anxiety level which results from his more severe socialization. In the light of the current study, it would appear that an equally plausible explanation is that the middle class child feels more free to masturbate openly, since he is less severely punished for it, or that the mother is emotionally more able to see and report this behavior in her child. Similarly, the fact that lower class children were allowed to stay out later at night and go to the movies alone at an earlier age was cited by Davis and Havighurst as an example of the less restricted, less frustrating childhood of lower class children. Yet the current study finds that the lower class mother is less willing to be "bothered" by the child (expects that the child be quiet in the house, pick up his toys and clothes, be careful about damaging furniture, eat quietly and neatly, etc.), and it is possible that her willingness to have the child stay away from the house in the evening reflects a certain relief on the mother's part when the child is not present to interfere with housekeeping and other adult activities.

Summary and Conclusions

INTERVIEWS were conducted with 198 upper-middle class, and 174 upper-lower class mothers of kindergarten children. They were asked about their methods of bringing up their children: feeding, toilet training, sex training, and aggression training were discussed, as were the techniques of discipline the mother employed, the number and identity of the people involved in the child's early training, and the kinds of achievements the mother expected of the child and the nature of the restrictions imposed upon him. The major findings are as follows:

1. The classes do not differ significantly in their infant feeding practices: they are similar in age and severity of weaning, and in the proportion of mothers who breast-feed. The upper-middle class schedule infant feedings slightly more rigidly, but not significantly so.

2. The upper-lower mothers are more severe in their toilet training. The two classes are similar in the age at which they toilet-train their children, but the upper-lower mothers employ more punishment and scolding in connection with toilet accidents.

3. Upper-lower mothers are much more severe in sex training. They begin modesty training at an earlier age, and insist upon higher standards of modesty. The upper-middle mothers are likely to ignore masturbation and certain forms of sex play among the children, or seek to distract the child without making an issue; the upper-lower mothers tend to react with considerable emotion, and punish the child for such behavior.

4. Upper-middle parents allow their children more freedom to show aggression toward the parents than do the upper-lower parents.

5. Upper-lower parents employ physical punishment, deprivation of privileges, and ridicule as techniques of controlling their children more commonly than do upper-middle parents. It appears likely that the upper-middle parents use reasoning and praise more often, and possibly some forms of withdrawal of love, although these findings are not consistent.

6. Mothers in the upper-middle class are somewhat warmer and more demonstrative toward their young children than are upper-lower mothers.

7. The relationship between the husband and wife is characterized by more mutual respect and affection in the upper-middle class. Among the upper-lower mothers, there is more criticism of the husband, and the two parents disagree more about methods of bringing up their children.

8. There is no difference between the classes in the extent of involvement of the father in the rearing of children.

9. The tendency for the upper-middle mothers to be more permissive and less severe in their child training than the upper-lower mothers holds up when the mothers' education, age, or ethnic origin are held constant.

Taken together, the findings imply that the upper-middle class are more "permissive" than the upper-lower class in child-rearing. Both classes bring pressure to bear on the child to give up the direct expression of some of his "natural" impulses and to substitute more mature behavior for infantile behavior, but the upper-middle group appear to be more tolerant of infantile behavior and to employ less severe punishment in the process of training.

REFERENCES

DAVIS, A., & HAVIGHURST, R. J. Social class and color differences in child-rearing. *Amer. sociol. Rev.*, 1946, **11,** 698–710.

DUVALL, EVELYN M. Conceptions of parenthood. *Amer. J. Sociol.*, 1946, **52,** 193–203.

ERICSON, MARTHA C. Child-rearing and social status. In T. M. Newcomb, & E. L. Hartley (Eds.), *Readings in social psychology*. New York: Holt, 1947. Pp. 494–501.

KAHL, J. A. Educational and occupational aspirations of "common man" boys. *Harvard educ. Rev.*, 1953, **23,** 186–203.

KINSEY, A. C., POMEROY, W. B., & MARTIN, C. E. *Sexual behavior in the human male*. Philadelphia: Saunders, 1948.

KLATSKIN, E. H. Shifts in child care practices in three social classes under an infant care program of flexible methodology. *Amer. J. Orthopsychiat.*, 1952, **22,** 52–61.

WARNER, W. L., MEEKER, MARCHIA, & EELLS, K. *Social class in America*. Chicago: Science Research Associates, 1949.

WESLEY C. BECKER, DONALD R. PETERSON, LEO A. HELLMER, DONALD J. SHOEMAKER, *and* HERBERT C. QUAY

Factors in Parental Behavior and Personality as Related to Problem Behavior in Children[*]

DURING the past decade there has been an increasing interest in developing a conceptual system for the analysis of parental behavior. In seeking this goal, a few have turned to factor analysis as a means of organizing observations around a relatively small number of dimensional concepts. The hope is for the development of a measurable set of dimensions which will permit more refined studies of the relationships between parent and child behavior. The work of Baldwin, Kalhorn, and Breese (1945) at the Fels Institute, Roff's (1949) subsequent factor analysis of the Fels data, and the recent work by Sears, Maccoby, and Levin (1957) have been among the more important contributions toward achievement of this end.

The goals of the present study are three: (*a*) to examine the factor organization of the Fels Parent Behavior scales as independently applied to mothers and fathers, (*b*) to investigate possible relationships between questionnaire personality factors and parental behavior, and (*c*) to find out which aspects of parental behavior are most closely related to behavior disorders in children. The concern with the first goal arises from the need for a scheme to assess maternal and paternal behavior independently in testing many hypotheses about child development. The second goal arises out of an interest in more parsimonious means of gathering information for the assessment of parental behavior. The step taken in this study is considered only a beginning. The third goal is a kind of jumping the gun in our search for important relationships between parent and child behavior.

Procedure

SUBJECTS

THE *S*s consisted of two groups of families, one with a child not in need of clinical services ($N = 25$) and the other with a child in need of clinical services ($N = 32$).[1] The following criteria for selection were used for both groups: age of child between 6 and 12 years, parents living together, Caucasian extraction, and willingness to cooperate. Since all but two families who were asked to participate agreed to do so, cooperativeness did not act as a selective factor. Families were admitted to the clinic group if they met the above criteria and if they were seeking help for a problem with their child other than one associated with brain damage or intellectual deficit. Families were admitted to the nonclinic group on the recommendation of teachers who were instructed to select children who did not need special psychological services.[2]

TABLE 1 presents the means and standard

1. Complete data were available for only 30 fathers of the clinic group. Therefore the *N* is two less than for mothers. This accounts for minor discrepancies in *r*'s between the same variables in the mother and father matrices.

2 The aim was to maximize child adjustment variance. Since separate criteria of adjustment are present in the study, accuracy of teacher judgment is not at issue.

* REPRINTED by permission of Wesley C. Becker and the American Psychological Association from *J. consult. Psychol.*, 1959, 23, 107–118.

TABLE 1. *Sample characteristics*

VARIABLE	CLINIC GROUP		NONCLINIC GROUP	
	Mean	*Sigma*	*Mean*	*Sigma*
Age of child	8.7	2.1	9.1	2.1
Child IQ	107.0	15.5	113.2	14.3
Socioeconomic status (Warner)	34.7	10.4	35.1	9.6
Age of mother	35.5	6.0	38.6	5.9
Mother IQ	117.7	15.2	115.2	15.3
Mother education	13.3	2.2	13.8	2.0
Age of father	37.2	5.2	39.9	5.8
Father IQ	124.3	15.0	124.0	15.8
Father education	14.7	2.9	15.4	3.0

deviations for several sample characteristics. As one might expect in a university town, the average education and intelligence of these groups are above national norms. The only important sampling imbalance to arise was on sex of child. In the clinic group there were 24 boys and 8 girls. In the nonclinic group there were 13 boys and 12 girls.

COLLECTION OF DATA

The present analysis covers ratings made from interviews with parents, scores on the Guilford-Martin personality inventories, IQ and socioeconomic status estimates, and other background variables. All data but the interview ratings were gathered in accordance with standard procedures, as will be clear from the description of variables given below. The ratings were obtained as follows:

Two rating schedules were completed from the interview. The first consisted of 17 of the 30 Fels Parent Behavior scales. These 17 scales were selected on the basis of Roff's (1949) factor analysis in such a way that each factor had at least two rating scales loading highly (all but one over .50) on the factor. A detailed description of these scales can be found in Baldwin *et al.* (1945). The only modification of the scales involved changing the word *home* to mother or father on a few of the scales. For example, if the scale read "adjustment of home" it was changed to "adjustment of mother," or to "adjustment of father." The second rating schedule was derived from Himmelweit's (1952) analysis of Ackerson's (1942) case records on 3,000 problem children. This schedule required three-point ratings on eight behavior characteristics loading on a *personality problem* factor (sensitivity, absent-mindedness, seclusiveness, day-dreaming, inefficiency in work, inferiority feelings, changeability of moods, and nervousness) and 11 behavior characteristics loading on a *conduct* problem factor (truancy from home, truancy from school, stealing, fighting, lying, destructiveness, swearing, disobedience, rudeness, selfishness, temper tantrums). Only the summed scores for personality problem and conduct problem were used in the analysis. Two additional child behavior variables were also rated from the mother interviews, namely: child school progress (retarded, average, advanced) and child social development (problem in peer relations, average peer relations, exceptionally good peer relations).

Since many of the parents had entered a clinic to deal with their problem children, interviews were not completely structured. Instead, a list of topics to be covered was drawn up, and the interviewer was left free to cover the topics in the most convenient order. This procedure is not unlike that used at the Fels Institute, except that repeated interviews were not possible. Four staff psychologists and one advanced clinical psychology student served as interviewers. Ratings were made immediately following the interviews. In no case did the same interviewer see both parents or have outside knowledge of the child's behavior.

RATING RELIABILITIES

The design of this study did not permit a check of two-rater reliability. However, Baldwin has present detailed evidence that the Fels scales are sufficiently well defined to produce two-rater reliabilities in the .50 to .75 range. The writers' use of the Fels scales differed in two ways from their use at the Fels Institute. First, ratings in this study were based on an interview in the clinic rather than on a home interview and observation period. Second, mothers and fathers were rated separately rather than as a composite. It is not known how these changes affect reliabilities.

The training of raters was accomplished by having all raters evaluate the same recorded interviews during the preliminary phase of the study. Through discussion, the structure of the interview and problems in rating were clarified. About midway through the study, a case was selected at random to check rater agreement. Using five- to seven-point scales, the percentage of agreement scores between raters showed 60% perfect agreement, 24% with a deviation of one, and 16% with a deviation greater than one.

Because the final data (correlations) are based on scores from five different raters, it seems unlikely that individual rater biases have systematically affected the findings. A possible source of systematic bias, however, comes from the inability to prevent interviewers from knowing whether or not they were dealing with a clinic or nonclinic parent. The parents had to talk about their children, and this made it impossible to hide their group affiliation. While all raters made a conscious attempt to avoid such a bias, this must remain an unresolved problem.

Separate estimates of the degree of child personality problem and child conduct problem were obtained from mother and father. Interparental agreement was .71 for the former and .85 for the latter.

METHOD OF ANALYSIS

Two parallel matrices were formed, one for mothers and one for fathers. Pearson *r*'s were computed and 12 centroid factors extracted using unit communalities (fixed). Ten factors from each analysis were rotated by an electronic computer to orthogonal simple structure using the quartimax routine (Neuhaus & Wrigley, 1954).[3] *The factors are presented as rotated by this mathematical procedure.*

DESCRIPTION OF VARIABLES

The 46 variables entering each factor analysis are described below. The direction of a high score on each variable is indicated following the titles.

1. Age of parent: older
2. Age of child: older
3. Sex of child: male
4. Number of children in family: more
5. Marital change on part of parent (previous marriage): none
6. Parent IQ estimate (WAIS: Information, Comprehension, Vocabulary): high
7. Child IQ estimate (WISC: Information, Comprehension, Vocabulary): high
8. Socioeconomic status (Warner scale): low
9. Education of parent: high
10. Guilford S: shy
11. Guilford T: introspective
12. Guilford D: depressed
13. Guilford C: emotionally unstable
14. Guilford R: rhathymic
15. Guilford G: active
16. Guilford A: socially ascendent
17. Guilford M: masculine attitudes and interests
18. Guilford I: lack of inferiority feelings (self confident)
19. Guilford N: not nervous
20. Guilford O: objective
21. Guilford Ag: agreeable
22. Guilford Co: cooperative
23. Clinic-nonclinic group: nonclinic
24. Fels, adjustment of parent: maladjusted
25. Fels, activeness of parent: inactive

3 An orthogonal solution was employed in order to show the relationships between child behavior and parent behavior in the clearest fashion. If the goal were only one of defining factors in parent behavior, an oblique solution might have been preferred. A real possibility in an oblique solution, however, is that child behavior would come out as separate factors and parent behavior as separate factors, and their interrelations would be hidden in higher-order factors. Thus a complete higher-order solution would have been required to bring out the essential relationships which are just as easily (and more economically) demonstrated with an orthogonal solution.

Inspection of factor plots indicates that the obtained solution would not be appreciably modified by an oblique solution. Hyperplane counts could be improved, but the same factors would probably remain with the same relative order of importance of variables loading on them. The fact that the obtained results parallel closely many of Roff's oblique factors adds confidence to the above conclusion.

The reader may legitimately ask why simple correlational analysis would not suffice to deal with parent-child interrelations. The answer is that the factor analysis allows one to see constellations of relationships which aid in interpretation of the correlations and at the same time allows for the control of the effects of other factors in the analysis (suppressors and inflators) in interpreting relationships.

26. Fels, sociability of parent: unsociable
27. Fels, coordination of parent: uncoordinated
28. Fels, emotionality toward child: nonemotional (objective)
29. Fels, readiness of enforcement: lax
30. Fels, severity of penalties: mild
31. Fels, justification of disciplinary policy: arbitrary
32. Fels, quantity of suggestion: nonsuggesting
33. Fels, coerciveness of suggestion: noncoercive (optional)
34. Fels, duration of contact with child: brief
35. Fels, democracy of policy: dictatorial
36. Fels, readiness of explanation: thwarts curiosity
37. Fels, general protectiveness: nonprotective (exposing)
38. Fels, solicitous for child's welfare: nonsolicitous
39. Fels, effectiveness of disciplinary policy: ineffective
40. Fels, disciplinary friction: nonfriction (concordant)
41. Child conduct problem, mother informant: problem
42. Child conduct problem, father informant: problem
43. Child personality problem, mother informant: problem
44. Child personality problem, father informant: problem
45. Child school progress: advanced
46. Child social development: advanced

Results

THE results of the quartimax solutions for mothers and for fathers are presented in TABLE 2.[4] The factors have been ordered so that similar factors from the mother and father solutions have the same factor number. Very close matches are apparent for Factors I to VII. The reader should note that this has been achieved by "blind," analytic rotation methods. Part of the reason for successful matches derives from the fact that 11 of the 46 variables are based on the same data in each analysis (Variables 2, 3, 4, 7, 8, and 40–46). This overlap particularly affects the first two pairs of factors, though similar factors would likely have emerged even without overlap.

As a partial check on linearity of relationships, r's were computed separately for clinic and nonclinic groups. Nonlinearity of regression should be indicated by a positive r in one group and a negative r in the other (providing that the groups differ in means on one or both variables). By and large, within group r's showed consistent patterns. The main area of deviation was in the relationship of permissiveness variables (see TABLE 8) to parent-child harmony variables (see TABLE 3). For example, in the mother analysis mildness of penalties correlates −.47 with conduct problem in the nonclinic group and +.41 in the clinic group. The reader should keep in mind that only consistent linear relationships are revealed in a factor analysis. Other important relationships may be obscured.

[4] The correlation matrices have been deposited with the American Documentation Institute. Order Document No. 5781 from ADI Auxiliary Publications Project, Photoduplication Service, Library of Congress, Washington 25, D.C., remitting $1.25 for microfilm or $1.25 for photocopies.

Discussion

THE results will be discussed with respect to the three questions posed earlier, but in a modified order. To aid the reader in following the discussion, the more important factor pairs will be presented in separate tables. Variables loading over .30 will be described so that a *positive factor loading coincides with the description given.*

RELATIONSHIPS BETWEEN PARENT AND CHILD BEHAVIOR

Relationships between parent and child behavior appear primarily on Factor Pairs I and II. Factor Pair I is presented in TABLE 3 along with Roff's parent-child harmony factor and Meyer's (1947) correlations of "parent behavior" with the degree of aggressive behavior shown by children in nursery school. A good match is apparent between mother and father Factor I, collectively described as general family maladjustment. The results indicate that Roff's parent-child harmony factor coincides with Himmelweit's child conduct problem factor and repeat Meyer's findings

TABLE 2. *Quartimax factor loadings*

VARIABLE	MOTHER FACTORS									
	I	II	III	IV	V	VI	VII	VIII	IX	X
1	−.30	.24	−.12	.17	.16	.39	.02	.17	−.27	.23
2	−.45	−.05	.13	.55	.04	.16	−.06	.02	.06	.11
3	.24	−.17	.15	−.45	.00	−.01	.04	.10	−.05	.50
4	−.12	.15	−.09	.31	.17	−.17	−.44	.12	−.18	−.12
5	.22	.28	.21	−.18	.04	.15	.22	−.26	.06	−.23
6	.07	.02	−.18	.04	−.20	.78	.12	−.05	−.11	.12
7	−.20	.21	.07	.34	−.51	.46	.09	−.05	−.14	.20
8	−.11	−.01	.16	−.04	−.10	−.73	−.08	.14	.12	.27
9	−.04	.11	−.28	.01	−.10	.73	−.08	−.14	−.10	−.12
10	.08	−.04	.44	.02	−.03	−.06	−.06	.82	−.06	−.16
11	.06	−.26	.42	−.04	−.13	.23	−.08	.56	.29	−.18
12	.26	−.12	.72	.09	.03	−.06	.05	.49	−.06	−.23
13	.20	−.18	.77	.18	.05	.09	.02	.23	.01	−.14
14	−.10	.00	−.13	.08	.12	.00	.00	−.83	−.07	.09
15	.01	−.29	.19	−.08	.42	.10	−.04	−.57	.11	−.10
16	.03	−.14	−.34	.00	−.14	.26	−.23	−.63	.13	.00
17	−.10	−.25	−.46	.23	−.43	.22	.12	.08	.13	−.25
18	−.22	.02	−.73	.12	.08	.16	−.06	−.34	.17	.12
19	−.26	.09	−.83	.11	−.15	.17	−.11	.08	.06	.04
20	−.14	.12	−.81	−.02	−.10	.12	.27	−.17	.02	−.01
21	−.30	−.06	−.44	.02	.07	.07	.38	.17	−.20	−.11
22	−.13	−.18	−.46	.06	−.05	.30	.57	−.07	−.19	−.03
23	−.51	.74	−.21	.03	−.05	−.08	−.08	−.11	−.05	−.08
24	.56	−.22	.34	−.02	−.11	−.19	.24	.14	.32	−.08
25	−.44	.06	−.09	−.12	.14	−.14	−.22	.20	−.32	.28
26	.20	−.10	.11	−.30	.17	−.19	−.19	.62	−.15	.09
27	.33	.11	.19	.49	−.04	−.01	.16	.19	−.17	.01
28	−.54	.02	−.37	−.07	−.30	.05	−.30	.08	−.37	−.01
29	−.04	−.01	.17	.16	−.10	.09	.12	.00	−.79	.11
30	.04	.09	.11	−.17	.02	.15	−.02	−.16	−.77	−.14
31	.35	−.21	.18	.29	.43	−.15	.22	−.18	.42	−.04
32	−.39	.14	−.05	.20	−.38	−.10	−.16	.06	−.57	−.11
33	−.02	.18	.01	.10	−.25	.15	.07	.24	−.75	.03
34	−.03	−.02	.08	.03	.86	−.05	−.08	.04	.10	−.05
35	.36	−.19	.16	.04	.71	−.05	.06	−.19	.24	−.11
36	.41	−.16	.32	.25	.43	−.38	.12	−.05	.26	−.04
37	.09	−.03	−.23	.49	.14	.19	−.08	−.20	−.32	.11
38	−.33	−.14	−.06	.64	−.06	.07	−.02	−.32	−.12	.01
39	.83	−.27	.23	.00	.14	−.05	−.02	.03	−.03	.06
40	−.82	.08	−.07	.02	−.06	.03	−.06	−.12	−.10	−.18
41	.89	.00	.14	−.03	.06	.08	−.15	.05	−.07	.00
42	.81	.00	.20	−.10	−.08	.13	−.17	.12	−.05	−.08
43	.16	−.82	.10	.08	.13	−.05	−.02	−.04	.13	.14
44	.11	−.82	.12	.04	.01	−.10	.01	.00	.15	.16
45	−.06	.54	−.09	.23	−.33	.23	−.07	.07	.11	−.27
46	−.45	.37	−.11	.17	−.02	.02	−.24	−.02	.07	.35

TABLE 2 (*Continued*)

FATHER FACTORS										
I	II	III	IV	V	VI	VII	VIII	IX	X	VARIABLE
—.36	.20	.37	.39	.03	.10	.25	—.19	—.26	—.11	1
—.35	.05	.14	.54	.16	.16	.18	—.31	—.08	—.15	2
.13	—.18	—.17	—.02	—.26	—.29	.17	—.06	.15	.54	3
—.10	.12	—.07	.16	.05	—.05	.24	.12	—.01	—.60	4
.28	.23	—.08	.06	—.09	.21	—.16	—.30	—.08	.35	5
.02	.02	.10	—.07	—.19	.70	.28	—.02	.03	—.10	6
—.16	.36	—.07	.42	.10	.26	.07	—.16	.06	.29	7
—.20	.01	.26	—.12	—.07	—.70	.07	.11	.20	—.01	8
—.04	.10	—.21	.02	—.10	.81	.06	.09	—.09	.00	9
—.03	—.02	.71	—.02	—.01	.15	.08	.15	.37	.28	10
.10	.11	.64	—.08	—.10	.19	.03	.05	.25	—.28	11
—.06	—.13	.87	.19	—.03	—.10	.21	.07	.04	.03	12
—.07	—.09	.81	.29	—.05	—.24	.10	—.06	—.04	.00	13
—.04	—.06	—.34	.24	.00	—.44	—.23	—.31	—.38	.10	14
.32	—.08	.09	.27	.13	—.26	—.22	—.54	—.22	—.06	15
.18	—.01	—.62	.15	—.03	—.32	—.08	—.32	—.07	—.17	16
.31	—.13	—.47	.37	—.05	—.02	.16	.05	.22	—.01	17
.23	.20	—.77	.13	—.11	—.12	.05	—.16	.10	—.02	18
—.22	.08	—.78	—.03	.00	.07	.05	.26	.11	—.02	19
—.01	—.01	—.83	.24	.00	.18	.12	.04	.01	.16	20
—.16	—.05	—.54	.13	—.11	.16	.54	.07	.12	.60	21
—.04	—.06	—.45	.26	—.11	.39	.53	.13	.16	.08	22
—.47	.74	—.12	.05	—.19	—.06	—.07	.05	.02	—.04	23
.40	—.60	.11	.09	.27	.18	—.13	.05	.29	.13	24
.10	.16	.07	.01	—.14	—.03	—.09	.69	.13	—.18	25
.18	—.01	.33	.01	.04	—.08	.09	.25	.59	—.05	26
.41	—.21	.19	.07	.06	.08	—.01	.55	.07	.11	27
—.51	.23	—.06	—.28	—.36	.10	—.25	—.23	—.07	—.19	28
.48	.00	.07	.15	—.48	—.04	—.10	.38	—.37	—.09	29
—.06	.15	.07	.07	—.29	.22	—.11	—.09	—.71	—.04	30
.34	—.17	.17	.01	.65	—.19	—.03	.09	—.24	—.01	31
—.11	.36	—.10	.16	—.50	.04	—.34	.10	—.08	—.02	32
.06	.28	.15	—.02	—.71	—.02	.14	.21	—.28	—.03	33
.12	—.10	—.31	.14	.54	.23	.00	—.08	.07	—.40	34
.20	—.24	.09	.10	.78	—.16	—.10	.02	.06	—.08	35
.13	—.60	.03	.08	.40	—.18	.04	.22	—.07	.00	36
—.22	—.04	—.21	.64	.08	—.01	—.30	.07	—.07	—.07	37
—.12	.06	—.16	.42	.21	—.12	—.50	.24	—.14	—.24	38
.79	—.30	.10	.07	.26	.04	.20	.09	.11	—.06	39
—.79	.14	.08	.12	.04	—.17	.14	—.05	—.09	—.02	40
.84	—.08	—.13	—.06	.02	—.06	.25	—.08	—.04	.01	41
.84	—.04	—.10	—.16	.04	—.01	.16	—.06	—.03	.00	42
.10	—.84	.09	—.02	.20	.04	—.02	—.18	—.02	.01	43
.11	—.84	.05	.09	—.01	—.10	—.02	.05	.13	—.02	44
.05	.62	—.08	.25	—.03	.31	—.16	—.10	.24	.02	45
—.39	.44	.01	.14	.21	—.09	.22	.26	—.02	—.08	46

TABLE 3. *Factor Pair I—general family maladjustment*

VARIABLE	MOTHER LOADINGS	FATHER LOADINGS	ROFF [a]	MEYER [a]
41. Child conduct problem, mother informant	.89	.84		
42. Child conduct problem, father informant	.81	.84		
39. Fels, ineffective disciplinary policy	.83	.79	.61	.65
40. Fels, much disciplinary friction	.82	.79	.63	.57
28. Fels, emotional toward child	.54	.51	.33	
24. Fels, maladjusted	.56	.40		
23. Clinic family	.51	.47		
2. Younger child	.45	.35		
46. Retarded social development	.45	.39		
27. Fels, uncoordinated parent	.33	.41		
31. Fels, arbitrary disciplinary policy	.35	.34		
1. Younger parent	.30	.36		
25. Fels, active parent	.44	(.10)		
36. Fels, nonreadiness of explanation (thwarting)	.41	(.13)		.49
32. Fels, much suggesting	.39	(.11)		
35. Fels, dictatorial policy	.36	(.20)		.52
38. Fels, solicitous for child's welfare	.33	(.12)		
21. Guilford Ag, hostile	.30	(.16)		
29. Fels, lax enforcement	(−.04)	.48		
15. Guilford G, active	(.01)	.32		
17. Guilford M, masculine	(−.06)	.31		

[a] The values from Roff are loadings on his parent-child harmony factor. The values from Meyer are *correlations* with aggressiveness of children in nursery school.

concerning child aggressiveness and parent behavior.

There are a number of interesting hypotheses which may be deduced concerning family relationships fostering conduct problems in children. Diagramatically, the following relationships are suggested:

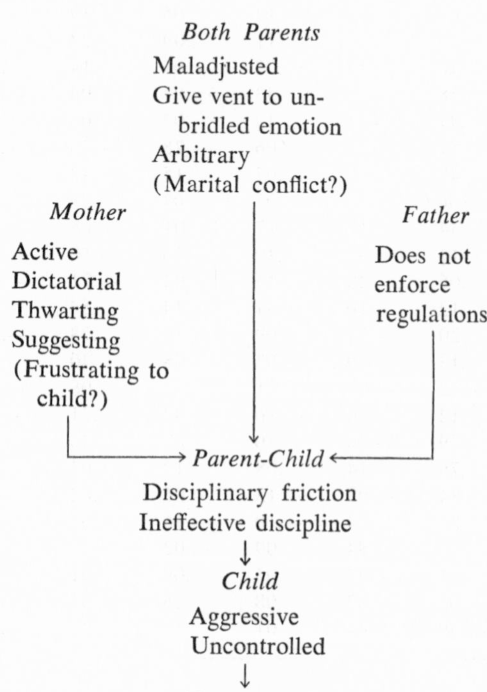

In his recent book, Sears *et al.* (1957) points out that mothers who were very permissive with regard to aggressive acts, but also very punitive and frustrating, would tend to have the most aggressive children. The relationships indicated above suggest another possibility. Where one parent is punitive and frustrating toward the child (instigating aggression) and the other parent is lax about discipline, conditions are right for the development of an aggressive child. A number of other possibilities are suggested. Both parents give vent to emotions easily, providing a *model* of uncontrolled behavior. Parental conflict seems an inescapable deduction. Displaced expressions of this conflict in interaction with the child are possible. Conflicting reinforcement of child behavior by each parent is very likely.

The most interesting finding to emerge from this analysis is presented in TABLE 4

TABLE 4. *Factor Pair II—child personality problem*

VARIABLE	MOTHER LOADINGS	FATHER LOADINGS
43. Child personality problem, mother informant	.82	.84
44. Child personality problem, father informant	.82	.84
23. Clinic family	.74	.74
45. Retarded school progress	.54	.62
46. Retarded social development	.37	.44
36. Fels, nonreadiness of explanation (Thwarts curiosity)	(.16)	.60
24. Fels, maladjusted	(.22)	.60
32. Fels, much suggesting	(.14)	.36
7. Child IQ low	(.21)	.36
39. Fels, ineffective disciplinary policy	(.27)	.30

which summarizes the loadings in Factor Pair II. The loadings of the first five variables indicate that the same factor has been extracted from each matrix, a factor centering on personality problem in the child. However, when a comparison is made of parental behavior variables loading on the factor, four associations above .30 are found with father behavior and *none* with mother behavior. The most marked parental differences are seen on the maladjustment rating and the nonreadiness of explanation (thwarting) rating. At face value, these findings suggest the hypothesis that the adjustment of father is more critical in determining personality problems in children than is the adjustment of mother. However, even though sex of child does not load on this factor, the high weighting of boys over girls in the clinic sample may be important in evaluating this finding. The mother results cannot be attributed to attenuated ranges for mothers on these variables. Note the failure of protectiveness variables to load on this factor.

Standard practice in psychiatry and clinical psychology for years has been to see mother and child in therapy in problem-child cases. Usually this practice has been defended on the assumption the mother relationship is more important in child development. The above findings suggest a need to re-evaluate this assumption and to explore in more detail the role of the father in child development.[5]

There are two other factor pairs where both parent and child behavior loadings are found. The loadings on Factor Pair IV (see TABLE 5) suggest that both parents are more

TABLE 5. *Factor Pair IV—protectiveness (concern for child)*

VARIABLES	MOTHER LOADINGS	FATHER LOADINGS	ROFF
37. Fels, protective	.49	.64	.69
38. Fels, solicitous for child's welfare	.64	.42	.53
2. Younger child	.55	.54	
7. Child IQ low	.34	.42	
1. Younger parent	(.17)	.39	
17. Guilford M, feminine interests	(.23)	.37	
27. Fels, uncoordinated parent	.49	(.07)	
3. Child sex female	.45	(.02)	
4. Few children in family	.31	(.16)	
26. Fels, unsociable	.30	(−.01)	.37
34. Fels, extensive contact with child	(.03)	(.14)	.69

protective of younger children and of children with lower IQs, while the loadings on Factor Pair V (see TABLE 6) indicate that higher intelligence in the child and advanced school progress are related to democratic attitudes on the part of the mother. This latter finding is of considerable interest, but of course does not indicate a causal relationship. A best guess would be that causality is operating in

[5] It is of interest to note that the father groups also show more significant differences in means on the Fels scales than do the mother groups. In addition, a preliminary analysis of items from a parental attitude inventory developed by Peterson indicated greater differences between fathers than mothers when clinic and nonclinic groups are compared.

TABLE 6. *Factor Pair V—democracy of policy*

VARIABLE	MOTHER LOADINGS	FATHER LOADINGS	ROFF
35. Fels, democratic policy	.71	.78	.62
34. Fels, extensive contact with child	.86	.54	
31. Fels, rational disciplinary policy	.43	.65	.64
32. Fels, little suggesting	.38	.50	
36. Fels, readiness of explanation (satisfies curiosity)	.43	.40	.62
28. Fels, nonemotional toward child	.30	.36	.33
7. Child IQ high	.51	(−.10)	
17. Guilford M, masculinity of interests	.43	(.05)	
15. Guilford G, inactive	.42	(.13)	
45. Child school progress advanced	.33	(.03)	
33. Fels, noncoercive use of suggestion	(.25)	.71	.61
29. Fels, lax enforcement	(.10)	.48	

both directions. A mother can be more democratic with a bright child, and having a democratic mother is a positive stimulus for the growth of intelligence. In Roff's analysis, parental encouragement of intellectual skills, "accelerational attempt," loaded on the democracy factor. Elsewhere Baldwin *et al.* (1945) demonstrated significant increases in IQ over a three-year period by children of high democratic mothers in comparison with children of low democratic mothers.

COMPARISON OF MOTHER AND FATHER BEHAVIOR PATTERNS

One of the important methodological questions this study sought to answer was the degree of applicability of Roff's factor analysis of the Fels scales when mother and father behavior was independently assessed. Five of the nine interpretable factor pairs can be related in some way to the seven factors derived by Roff. Factor Pair I, corresponding to Roff's parent-child harmony factor, has already been presented in TABLE 3. A good match was found in this case between mother and father behavior patterns. Also it has been indicated that this factor ties in with conduct problems in the child and maladjustment in the parents.

Of the remaining four factor pairs, two show a good match between mothers and fathers, and two do not. Each of these four factor pairs will be discussed in turn.

Factor Pair IV (TABLE 5) represents a general protectiveness factor called *concern for the child* by Roff. There is a close repetition of Roff's patterns for both mothers and fathers. The major deviation from Roff's loadings is on the duration of contact variable. A possible explanation for this difference lies in the fact that Roff's analysis was on parents of preschool children, while the current study involves parents of grammar school children. Perhaps the amount of contact with child is only associated with protectiveness before society places many demands on a child's time. Baldwin (1955) has previously indicated several important relationships between protectiveness and child behavior.

Mother and Father Factors V (Table 6) show a close match to Roff's democracy factor. While there is considerable agreement between mother and father factor loadings, there are also important differences. A democratic approach to child rearing in the mother shows relationships with inactivity and masculinity of interests.[6] Democracy in the father takes on more of a permissiveness flavor than in the mother. For most purposes, it would appear feasible to use the same procedures in evaluating this factor for mothers and fathers.

A very poor match is found between Mother and Father Factor VIII (TABLE 7). Mother Factor VIII contains the typical extraversion components (R, S, G, A) and seems to be particularly characterized by *sociability* on the Fels scales. Father Factor VIII is primarily described by *general activity*.

It is quite possible that the same factor is being assessed in each case, namely, extraversion, but that in our culture male extraversion

6 Item analysis indicates that this association is mainly due to such items as "Do odors of perspiration disgust you?" or "Are you disgusted at the sight of ragged or soiled fingernails?" High democratic mothers more frequently answer these questions "no."

TABLE 7. *Mother Factor VIII—Guilford extraversion*

VARIABLES	MOTHER LOADINGS	ROFF (*Soc-Adj*)
14. Guilford R, rhathymic	.83	
10. Guilford S, sociable	.82	
16. Guilford A, socially ascendant	.63	
26. Fels, sociable	.62	.70
15. Guilford G, active	.57	
11. Guilford T, not introspective	.56	
12. Guilford D, free from depression	.49	
18. Guilford I, lack of inferiority feelings	.34	
38. Fels, nonsolicitous for child's welfare	.32	.36
24. Fels, adjusted	(.14)	.55
28. Fels, nonemotional toward child	(—.08)	.33

Father Factor VIII—general activity

VARIABLES	FATHER LOADINGS	ROFF
25. Fels, active parent	.69	.76
27. Fels, coordinated parent	.55	.53
15. Guilford G, active	.54	
29. Fels, strict enforcement	.38	
16. Guilford A, socially ascendant	.32	
14. Guilford R, rhathymic	.31	
2. Younger child	.31	
5. Previous marriage by father	.30	

is revealed behaviorally by activity (task orientation) and female extraversion by sociability. In Roff's analysis of the Fels scales, a sociability-adjustment factor and an activity factor were found. However, Roff rated activeness of *home,* sociability of *family,* adjustment of *home,* and coordination of *household.* There was no attempt to separate the behavior of mother and father. Roff's activeness factor appears to tie in with Father Factor VIII, and the sociability component of Roff's sociability-adjustment factor with Mother Factor VIII. These findings clearly indicate a need for separate scaling procedures for evaluating maternal and paternal behavior in the extraversion area.

The final factor pair defined mainly by the Fels scales is presented in TABLE 8. Here again the mother-father match is poor. Mother

TABLE 8. *Mother Factor IX—permissiveness*

VARIABLES	MOTHER LOADINGS	ROFF
29. Fels, lax enforcement	.79	.51
30. Fels, mild penalties	.77	.61
33. Fels, noncoercive use of suggestions	.75	
32. Fels, low quantity of suggestion	.57	
31. Fels, rational disciplinary policy	.42	
28. Fels, nonemotional toward child	.37	
37. Fels, nonprotective	.32	
25. Fels, inactive	.32	
24. Fels, adjusted	.32	

Father Factor IX—warm, extraversion-hostile, withdrawal

VARIABLES	FATHER LOADINGS
30. Fels, mild penalties	.71
26. Fels, sociable	.59
14. Guilford R, rhathymic	.38
10. Guilford S, sociable	.37
29. Fels, lax enforcement	.37

Factor IX is clearly a permissiveness factor similar to that reported by Roff except that the suggestion scales are included in the present factor and were not in Roff's.[7] It is apparent that Father Factor IX also leans toward the permissiveness realm but has an essentially different composition. If one looks at the op-

7 The instructions for the quantity of suggestion scale indicate that the rater should disregard the amount of control exercised in disciplinary situations. This is less easily done in a clinic interview than in a home observation session. This shift in rating conditions is a possible basis for the difference in factor composition.

posite poles from those given in TABLE 8, a certain familiar ring is detected. The negative pattern involves severe penalties (hostility), reclusiveness, inhibited disposition, and vigilance, in the sense of looking for trouble. This is suggestive of the schizoid personality.

The importance of the need to *demonstrate* (not assume) that factor patterns derived from the analysis of mother behavior or "parent behavior" are applicable to father behavior is made especially clear in the following example. Assume, as the writers had for part of their analysis, that Roff's analysis (see TABLE 8) had been used to define a permissiveness factor for fathers. The best estimate of this factor would be a weighted combination of readiness of enforcement (Variable 29) and severity of penalties (Variable 30). For clinic fathers permissiveness, so defined, is found to correlate +.37 with disciplinary friction, and for the nonclinic fathers the correlation is −.48. If the components of permissiveness are examined separately, it is found that the source of the association for clinic fathers is an r of +.47 between *nonenforcement* and disciplinary friction, while the source of the association for the nonclinic fathers is an r of −.55 between *mild penalties* and disciplinary friction. An assumption was made that a factor found with mothers would hold for fathers and it did not. For similar reasons the reader is cautioned not to assume generalizability of the factor patterns reported herein to non-middle-class families.

QUESTIONNAIRE FACTORS AND PARENT BEHAVIOR

The final question to be evaluated is the relationship of questionnaire personality factors to parent behavior factors. In general the relationships are not high. Mother Factors I, IV, and V show a few low to moderate loadings of Guilford factors, and Mother Factor II, comprising primarily Guilford scores, shows a few loadings of parent behavior variables. Father Factors I, VII, and IX also show low to moderate loadings of Guilford factors. At present one might recommend the substitution of Guilford G for ratings of activity of fathers and Guilford R and S for ratings of sociability of mother. Other components of parental behavior will require special efforts at questionnaire development.

As TABLE 9 illustrates, there is a high cohesiveness of the Guilford factor *scores*.

TABLE 9. *Factor Pair III—Guilford adjustment*

VARIABLES	MOTHER LOADINGS	FATHER LOADINGS
20. Guilford O, objective	.81	.83
19. Guilford N, not nervous	.83	.78
13. Guilford C, emotionally stable	.77	.81
12. Guilford D, free from depression	.72	.87
18. Guilford I, lack of inferiority feelings	.73	.77
10. Guilford S, sociable	.44	.71
11. Guilford T, not introspective	.42	.64
16. Guilford A, socially ascendant	.34	.62
17. Guilford M, masculine interests	.46	.47
21. Guilford Ag, agreeable	.44	.54
22. Guilford Co, cooperative	.46	.45
28. Fels, nonemotional toward child	.37	(.06)
24. Fels, adjusted	.34	(.11)
36. Fels, readiness of explanation (satisfies curiosity)	.32	(.03)
1. Younger parent	(−.12)	.37
14. Guilford R, rhathymic	(.13)	.34
26. Fels, sociable	(.11)	.33
34. Fels, brief contact with child	(−.08)	.31

Eleven of the 13 Guilford factor scores show appreciable loadings on what appears to be a *self-perception-of-adjustment* factor, or simply Guilford adjustment. This factor parallels the second-order emotional stability or neuroticism factor discussed by Eysenck (1953). On the basis of an unpublished study by Becker, this factor should also correlate highly with Cattell's second-order factor called anxiety—dynamic integration. Studies by Farber, Spence, and Bechtoldt (1957) suggest that the Taylor Manifest Anxiety Scale would also load highly on this factor. Considering the current interest in, and claims for anxiety scales, it is important to note the lack of association of this factor with problems in children and the relatively small associations with parent behavior ratings. From the present findings one must conclude that the domain of personality being tapped by the Guilford inventories is quite limited.

THE REMAINING FACTORS

The three factor pairs which have not yet entered the discussion deserve brief mention. No attempt has been made to interpret the last factor in each analysis. Factor Pair VII is of minor importance, loading mainly on the Guilford agreeableness and cooperativeness scales. Factor Pair VI repeats closely in both mother and father analyses and is defined by parental education, IQ, and socioeconomic status. It is interesting that the only child variable to load on this factor, besides child IQ, is school progress. This result suggests that while a minimum parental intelligence is necessary to do a good job as parents, more intelligence does not necessarily lead to better family adjustment. The generally accepted principle of the prepotency of feeling over reasoning is consistent with this result.

Summary

THIS study sought to examine the factor organization of the Fels Parent Behavior scales independently for mothers and fathers, to investigate relationships between questionnaire personality factors and parental behavior, and to find out which aspects of parental behavior are most closely related to behavior disorders in children.

Two groups of families, one with a child not in need of clinical services ($N = 25$) and the other with a child in need of clinical services ($N = 32$), were examined. Parents were individually given the Guilford-Martin personality inventories, an IQ measure, and an interview which permitted rating of 17 Fels Parent Behavior scales and of the kinds of problem behavior displayed by their children. Two independent factor analyses were carried out to orthogonal simple structure, one with 46 mother-and-child variables and one with 46 father-and-child variables. Nine factors in each analysis were interpreted.

Child behavior problems loaded primarily on two factors. Conduct problems (aggressive, uncontrollable) in the child coincided with Roff's parent-child harmony factor in both the mother and the father analyses. The pattern of loadings indicated that in families with conduct problem children, both parents are maladjusted, give vent to unbridled emotions, and tend to be arbitrary with the child. In addition, the mother tended to be active (tense), dictatorial, thwarting, and suggesting, whereas the father tended not to enforce regulations. On the other hand, a factor defined mainly by personality problems in the child (shy, sensitive, inferior) showed associations *only* with father behavior ratings. The father was rated as maladjusted and thwarting of the child. The many important associations between father and child behavior lead to the conclusion that future research, and perhaps therapeutic practice, should *give more consideration to the role of the father in child development.*

The mother analysis repeated five of Roff's seven parent behavior factors, namely: parent-child harmony, protectiveness (concern), democracy, permissiveness, and sociability (Roff's sociability-adjustment). Roff's activeness *of home* appeared only as activeness of the father. The father analysis showed parallel factors for parent-child harmony, protectiveness, and democracy, but a factor designated general activity and a factor designated warm-extraversion versus hostile-withdrawal appeared in place of sociability and permissiveness. These findings suggest differences in the organization of maternal and paternal behavior which measurement procedure must take into account.

In general, the Guilford questionnaire factors showed little association with parent behavior ratings, the major exceptions being on factors called sociability and activeness. A number of suggestive correlations are present, however, which might help in devising questionnaires for assessing parent behavior.

REFERENCES

ACKERSON, L. *Children's behavior problems.* Chicago: Univer. Chicago Press, 1942.

BALDWIN, A. L. *Behavior and development in childhood.* New York: Dryden, 1955.

BALDWIN, A. L., KALHORN, J., & BREESE, E. H. Patterns of parent behavior. *Psychol. Monogr.,* 1945, **58,** 1–75.

EYSENCK, H. J. *The structure of human personality.* New York: Wiley, 1953.

FARBER, I. E., SPENCE, K. W., & BECHTOLDT, H. P. Emotionality, introversion-extraversion, and conditioning. Paper read at Midwest Psychol. Ass., Chicago, May, 1957.

HIMMELWEIT, H. T. A factorial study of "children's behavior problems." (Unpublished manuscript, 1952.) Cited by H. J. Eysenck in *The structure of human personality.* New York: Wiley, 1953, 88–90.

MEYER, CHARLENE T. The assertive behavior of children as related to parent behavior. *J. Home Econ.,* 1947, **39,** 77–80.

NEUHAUS, J. O., & WRIGLEY, C. F. The quartimax method: an approach to orthogonal simple structure. *Brit. J. statist. Psychol.,* 1954, **7,** 81–91.

ROFF, M. A factorial study of the Fels parent behavior scales. *Child Develpm.,* 1949, **20,** 29–45.

SEARS, R. R., MACCOBY, ELEANOR E., & LEVIN, H. *Patterns of child rearing.* New York: Row, Peterson, 1957.

GEORGE R. BACH

Father-Fantasies and Father-Typing in Father-Separated Children*

THE average American father differs considerably from the classical streotype of a punishment-threatening, tyrant-giant as depicted in European psychoanalytic theory. Still the local U.S. culture is largely patriarchal and paternal opinions are still decisive in the settling of most major family issues. Although the frequently absent father may relegate to the more often present mother the majority of actual punishment executions, and coming home from work, he may be "seldom in a mood to institute disciplinary measures" (Murray & Morgan, 1945, p. 259), his children (above the age of three and one-half years) are, nevertheless, accurately aware of the preferential power position that the father has in the family.

The psychological nature of a child's relationship to his father is, therefore, of great consequence to the child's present security and later outlook. It is not surprising that complications in this relationship are found in the history of many individuals with adjustment difficulties and that clinical studies of young adults have shown that respect and affection for the father is more characteristic for satisfactory home adjustment than the presence of sentiments of respect and affection for the mother (Murray & Morgan, 1945).

These impressions gained in clinical practice warrant our research interests in theories and facts concerning father-child relationships.

The kind of emotional experiences that a son or daughter has within the dynamics of the father-child relationship are given much emphasis in practical mental hygiene (English & Pearson, 1945), and in systematic clinical theories (Fenichel, 1945). Nevertheless, non-speculative, empirical studies of this relationship have been primarily sociological in nature, relating, for example, the intelligence or attitude test scores of children to the occupational, educational or political status of their fathers (cf. Jones, 1946).

The present research trend seems to be away from such "ecological" studies (Lewin, 1944) as more analytical approaches to the parent-child relationship become popular. Several investigators have attempted to investigate the emotional aspects of this relationship (e.g., Murray & Morgan, 1945). However, most of these concentrate on maternal influences (Levy, 1943; Symonds, 1939), or the father and mother are considered as one "parental unit" (Baldwin, Kalhorn, & Breese, 1945). Much useful information concerning the father has come incidentally out of these studies, but more specific investigations of the intimate, emotional aspects of father-child contact are needed. The present paper reports a research effort in this direction.

Methodology

SUBJECTS

THE conditions of war, generally so destructive to systematic research, provided in this case an opportunity for an investigation of the emotional reactions of children to prolonged separation from the father. The enlist-

* REPRINTED with abridgment by permission of the author and the Society for Research in Child Development from *Child Develpm.*, 1946, 17, 63–80.

ment of mature men with families made it possible to locate in Cleveland, Ohio, an experimental group of twenty normally adjusted school children, equally divided as to sex, ages six to ten, of average intelligence, and lower middle-class, urban background, whose fathers had been with the Armed Forces abroad from one to three years, and who were still away at the time of the investigation in the Spring of 1945.

A control group of children matched for age, sex, intelligence, school and home background, was also available. The fathers of the control children were deferred from military service and were living with their families. School and home background and overt manifestations of the parent-child relationship were ascertained by intensive interviews of mothers and teachers. These interviews followed the methodology of the Fels Research Group (Baldwin *et al.,* 1945; Champney, 1939, 1941).

THE DOLL PLAY TECHNIQUE

The children's emotional reactions to separation from the father were studied by means of a standardized projective doll play technique which was developed by the author from recent experiments conducted by Sears and his associates at Iowa (Bach, 1945; Phillips, 1945; Pintler, 1945; Pintler, Phillips, & Sears, 1946).

The doll play experiments took place in a special room in each of the two elementary schools attended by the subjects.

Each child subject was introduced to the experimenter by the teacher. On three occasions, separated by two to four days, the experimenter took the child from the classroom to the experimental room for a twenty-minute play session. The entire experimental routine, including the experimenter-child relationship before, during and after the three play sessions, was standardized according to a detailed Manual of Instructions. This manual was prepared by the writer in cooperation with Gloria Bremer, who acted as co-experimenter. The essential features of this procedure are summarized below.

Play Materials

The child was presented with a semi-realistic roofless doll house having the dimensions of 22″ x 28″. This doll house simulated in stream-lined form a five-room, middle-class family home. There was a living room, dining room, kitchen, bathroom, two bedrooms, a hall and a large closet. Most of the stream-lined furniture was glued to the floor to inhibit manipulative construction play and to encourage play with the dolls proper, thus stimulating social fantasies.

Four dolls, a father, a mother, and two children, a boy and a girl, were available to the child. All subjects were given the same family constellation. The parent dolls were 5″ and the child dolls 3″ tall. The dolls had a realistic appearance and could easily be made to assume any desired posture.

Initial Instigation of Fantasy

After a brief explanation of the physical facilities of the doll house, the experimenter invited the child to make up a story or play. The experimenter made it clear that it could be any kind of a story; that the child could make the four "people in this home" act in any way he wanted them to.

After the experimenter gave these instructions, he began the recording of the fantasy responses. After twenty minutes the recording was discontinued and the play session terminated.

All of the children in this study entered the task with interest, and while activating the dolls, they verbally reported what the dolls did, how they felt, etc.

The Subject-Experimenter Relationship

Once the experimenter felt that the subject had understood and accepted the task, his role was that of a very friendly, sympathetic, interested, but non-interfering, non-suggesting, listener, onlooker and recorder of the child's story. The experimenter unobtrusively recorded without loss of rapport-contact with the child. No attempt was made to conceal from the subject the scoring work or to deny its connection with his play. The experimenter, upon being questioned, would explain to the child, "I like to collect stories; I like your story."

The experimenter never suggested any theme or fantasy actions to the child even when the child did attempt to get play suggestions from him. Such questions for fantasy support were turned back to the subject by such comments as, "It is your story; it is your play; it is up to you what to make it; it can be anything you want it to; you know how to do it"; etc.

The experimenter made a few standardized comments designed to reduce anxiety or inhibition, or to stimulate expressiveness, and to terminate the session in a way meaningful to the child. For example, whenever for purposes of more reliable recordings, the meaning of a doll play fantasy could be clarified by a fuller degree of expression of the child's fantasy, the child was encouraged to be more expressive either verbally or manipulatively with such comments as, "Show me what they do," or "Make them act it out," or "Tell me what they are doing." This stimulation of expression was used only on the rare occasions when it became necessary for the understanding of the meaning or direction of the doll actions. But in any cases of any type of stimulation, suggestions of fantasy content were avoided.

In this way the requirement of assuring the same instigating condition for the projective father fantasies of both the experimental and the control groups was thought to be fulfilled. Yet the standardization of the S-E relationship did not interfere with maintenance of a rapport which made the child feel: "Here is a sympathetic, friendly, non-teacher-like, non-authoritative adult with whom I can be free and spontaneous and who likes me and my stories."

Record Taking

The experimenter took a running account of the play fantasies during the three sessions as the subject produced them. He classified the fantasy content into a few pre-defined categories by means of symbols which were entered on a record sheet. After some experience and practice, it was possible to record doll actions and experiences separately for each of the four characters of the doll drama. These doll actions and experiences were the child's fantasies and constituted the recording units. A scoring symbol stood for a single unit of thematic action for a doll character during a fifteen-second interval as indicated by an electric timer (buzzer).

When two or more doll characters were active in any doll-doll interaction, as many symbols denoting the nature of the action were recorded as dolls were involved and the direction of the social interaction between the dolls was indicated by means of arrows. In this way every doll action was recorded under one of the fantasy categories previously defined in the manual.

This system of recording had a degree of reliability of 89.81 per cent average agreement for all categories between the two experimenters who shared in the collection of these data. This estimate of reliability was obtained on twelve pre-experimental doll play sessions with one of the experimenters taking turns scoring the same subjects from behind a one-way vision screen, while the other experimenter recorded while working with the child.

Major Doll Play Fantasies

All doll play fantasies were immediately classified by the experimenter into various categories. The fantasy categories of particular relevance to the present study are given below.

Stereotype Fantasies: Dramatizations of dolls which in content simulate habitual routine actions and experiences that could ordinarily be expected (on the basis of stereotypes of "home" and family life) to be performed by real persons in an analogous actual setting. Stereotyped doll actions and experiences are like photographic reproductions of commonly appropriate, "proper," non-individualistic, social behavior (e.g., polite greetings, sitting down to eat dinner, to listen to the radio, going to bed, using the toilet properly, etc.).

Fantasy Aggression: The child made the doll act or described the doll as acting or intending to act injurious, punishing, disparaging, or depreciative towards another doll, or the child described the doll character as being in an aggressive attitude, nature, manner, or mood, etc.

Aggressive fantasies were subdivided according to the social direction of these aggressions, and their severity, e.g., killing was a sub-category of fantasy aggression. Other subdivisions include justification of hostile aggressions, defensive rationalization, aggression in response to commands in the nature of a retort or insubordination.

Fantasy Affection: The doll's actions denoted praise, reward, affection, friendliness, helpfulness towards other characters or enjoyment of another character's company.

Authoritative Fantasies: Included doll-doll interactions of an imperative, directive, ordering, or commanding nature.

Submissive Fantasies: Obliging and submissive doll actions in response to aggressive and/or directive instigation on the part of the other doll characters.

Other categories included such fantasies as *Escaping, Chasing, Depressed,* and *Elated Moods, Sexual Investigation,* and *Repetitiveness.*

Non-Thematic Behavior Categories

In addition to the subject's thematic productions, the experimenters paid close attention to and recorded the idiosyncrasies of the subject's behavior in the experimental situation other than his fantasies proper. Various types of non-thematic behavior were defined, tallied, and ratings of the emotional involvement and degree of inhibitions were made.

The reliability of some of these non-thematic data was found to be too low to be usable here. Individual differences between the investigators with respect to judgments and insights were apparently involved in some of these clinically important observations.

ANALYSIS

The records obtained by the procedure briefly outlined above furnished detailed information of the quality of projective fantasies concerned with inter-personal family relationships. They permitted tabulation and statistical analyses without any post-experimental ratings or classifications.

In so far as the hypothesis that fantasy responses are projective is justified (Rapaport, 1942), the data present in effect an inventory of the child's actual emotional adjustment to his own family.

Since it was the purpose of this study to see whether this adjustment was influenced by prolonged separation from the father, the data were analyzed to yield a comparison between the father-fantasies of the experimental (father-separated) group with the father-fantasies of the control (father-home) group. It was thought that knowing in detail the way father-separated children elaborated about the father in their fantasies would yield some clues as to the psychogenetic importance of the father in the personality development of the child. Consequently, the statistical comparison between the two groups was limited to those fantasies in which the father character was involved.

Results: Father-Fantasies

THE first group of the results of this comparison is given in TABLE 1. As can be seen, the experimental (father-separated) and the control (father-home) group produced about the same total amount of projective doll play fantasies concerned with family life (TABLE 1, line 1). There was a slight, but nevertheless significant, preponderance of total number of fantasies involving the father character in the control group (lines 2 and 3). This difference was due to the fact that some of the father-separated children tended to leave the father out of the family scene more often, thus simulating the actual state of affairs in their own homes. This was to be expected on the basis of previous results reported on younger children by Bach (1945, pp. 25–26), who estimated that 75 per cent of the normal pre-school child's doll play fantasies are rather faithful reproductions of reality conditions.

It would, however, seem misleading to interpret this statistical difference to mean that on the whole the father-separated children left the father out of their fantasies of family life. On the contrary, as TABLE 1, line 3 shows, one should stress the fact that in spite of actual prolonged absence of the father from the home, the experimental group did include the father in 22 per cent of their fantasies as compared with 25 per cent, the usual chance elaboration of one out of the set of four dolls. The control group indeed showed this 25 per cent. *Thus, when strong emotionally conditioned drives find their expression in fantasy, the percentage of reproductive, reality-simulating fantasies is lowered.* This was found to be the case also in the school fantasies of the strongly frustrated group of children studied by Bach (1945).

However, the fact that the difference between the experimental and the control groups with respect to total amount of father-fantasies was significant would have made it statistically misleading to compare absolute amounts of the father-fantasy categories between the two groups, and necessitated the translation of the raw figures into per cents using the total number of father-fantasies as the base line. In other words, the results were analyzed for differences in the *relative* distribution of the specific types of father-fantasies, since one group (the control) had a greater total of all father-fantasies regardless of specific type. The results of this analysis are shown in FIGURE 1.

. . .

Among the sixteen comparisons that were made, eleven statistically significant differences between the father-fantasies of the two groups were found. The bars in FIGURE 1 show the eleven categories of father-fantasy that significantly differentiated the father-separated from the father-home children. The experimental (father-separated) group is represented in the figure by the solid black bars.

TABLE 1. *Mean frequencies of projective fantasies during three twenty-minute sessions of doll play*

FANTASY CATEGORIES	EXPERIMENTAL: FATHER ABSENT *Av.* $N = 20$	*S.D.*	CONTROL: FATHER HOME *Av.* $N = 20$	*S.D.*	*Diff.*	*t*	*l.o.c.*
1. Total number of doll actions of any kind	433.85	104.41	461.57	84.78	−27.72	0.797	N.S.
2. Total number of doll actions involving father	92.80	27.30	113.01	25.17	−20.21	2.129	<5%
3. Per cent of doll actions involving father	22.49	5.52	25.27	3.37	−2.78	3.501	<1%

The experimental group has a preponderance of *stereotyped fantasies* about family life. More specifically, the father-separated children elaborated more intensively the leisure time living room recreational activities of the family. In these fantasies the father was shown to enjoy sitting with the children and listening to the mother play the piano, or just sitting and reading the paper while the children amused themselves in the living room, etc.

Very significant were the differences found in *fantasy aggression*. The proportion of the father's aggressive behavior toward both the family as a whole and the children in particular is less in the fantasies of the father-separated children. The father is also less often the recipient of the mother's hostility and no child in the experimental group

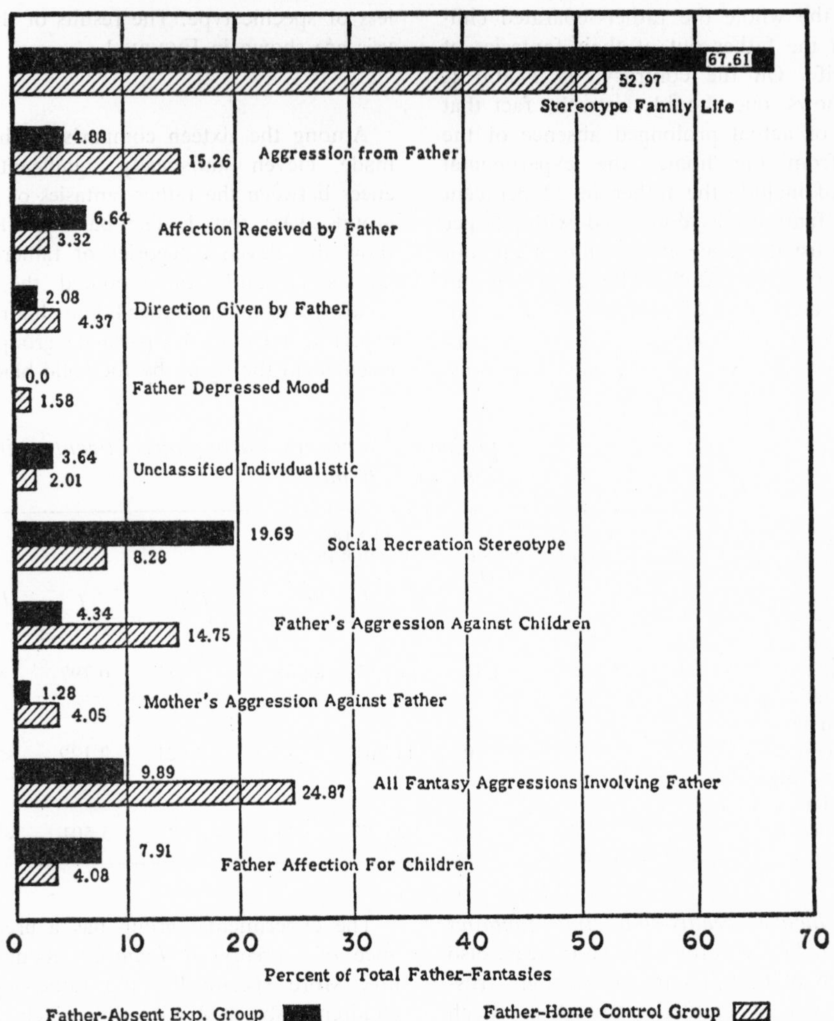

FIGURE 1

Significant differences in father-fantasies of children.

represented the father as being in a depressive or angry mood at any time. In general, the father-separated children had relatively fewer aggressive fantasies that involved the father than did the control children.

The results on the fantasy aggressions of the school age child are similar to Sears' recent finding of reduced fantasy aggression in preschool boys who were separated from their fathers during the war (Sears, Pintler, & Sears, 1946).

With respect to *affectionate fantasies,* it was found that the father-separated group pictured the father as giving more affection to his children, as well as receiving more affection from his family.

The experimental group also produced fewer *authoritative fantasies* that showed the father in a demanding and authoritarian role.

In summary, *father-separated children produce an idealistic fantasy picture of the father, who has a good time with his family and who is enjoyed by them. He gives and receives much affection and has little marital discord. This fantasy-father shows very little hostility and does not exert his authority.* The children of the control group, however, living as they do in daily contact with their fathers, elaborate significantly more upon the punitive function of the father and his contribution to intrafamily hostility.

In so far as these differences are the result of prolonged separation, they seem to indicate the existence of strong drives for paternal affection, and for a harmoniously functioning father-mother relationship. Why would the child, whose doll play fantasies tend to be simulations of reality, otherwise include the actually absent father in such a large proportion of his thematic production? And since Bach (1945) has previously shown that stereotyped-idealistic and repetitive doll play fantasies tend to be diagnostic (projective) of strong positive wishes, the existence of a strong drive for the possession of a loving and generous father is evident from the present data. However, since the fantasies of the experimental children are very similar to the stereotyped, non-aggressive fantasies found in girls living under ordinary family conditions (Bach, 1945; Pintler *et al.*, 1946), the pronounced differences between the experimental and the control groups may reflect to some extent the increase in amount and extent of maternal-feminine social stimulation. The theoretical implications of these results are discussed in more detail later, but there is no question about the fact that the projective doll play technique is a rather sensitive indicator of psychological changes brought about by changes in the social environment of the child (Bach, 1945).

Further Results: Sex Differences

THE reader will have noticed that the major results of this study were reported for the two groups as a whole without reference to sex differences. This was made possible by the initial equalization of the number and the psycho-sociological characteristics of the boys and girls in the two groups studied. Although the major interest of the writer is in the question of the effect of father-separation on children in general, it is interesting to ask the question whether boys and girls differ in their reaction to this separation factor.

. . .

As was expected on the basis of previous studies (Bach, 1945; Pintler *et al.*, 1946), appreciable sex differences were observed. The nature of these differences is consistent with the previously reported results on younger children: the boys showed a significantly greater amount of aggressive fantasies and the girls exceeded in affectionate fantasies and in stereotype.

Since it seems that these sex differences are general and apparently a rather stable personality factor related to cultural sex-typing (Bach, 1945; Pintler *et al.*, 1946), it would be misleading to emphasize that the father-separated girl makes the father in her fantasy even less aggressive and more affectionate than does the boy, because one would expect this without the separation factor on the basis of the known sex differences in projective doll play fantasies. Rather, it is possible that school-age children of either sex are about equally affected by father-separation. This is an interesting conjecture, however, which fortunately is receiving further experimental attention (cf. Sears *et al.*, 1946).

Further Results: Father-Typing

IN ORDER to determine whether stimulus variables in the immediate social environment of the child during the separation period influenced the pronounced idealistic fantasies found in these children, some follow-up analyses within the experimental group were made.

The data gathered in the home interviews included information about maternal *"father-typing."* Father-typing is a dispositional concept that denotes the general personality characterizations of the father that mothers (or other persons close to the child) give to the child, e.g., "Your father is strong"; "Your father is strict"; "Your father is a hard and mean man"; "Your father is a kind and generous man"; etc.

As was mentioned previously, the mothers of all the children were interviewed. At least two two-hour home visits were made to each of the families, and the instructions for home interviews that H. Champney devised (1939, 1941) were followed in a modified form. Among the modifications used was an original interview schedule, part of which was designed to record data concerning father-typing. A copy of one of the data sheets on father-typing that was used in these interviews is shown on page 309.

In addition to this direct type of evidence of father-typing, the interviewers rated the fathers' pre-war behavior on the Fels-Scales on the basis of mothers' reports. This somewhat unorthodox procedure provided an additional opportunity to assess maternal attitudes towards the absent father. The interviewer's and the teacher's descriptions of how the children's mothers talked about their absent husbands also gave valuable clues on father-typing, e.g., a typical correlate of unambiguously unfavorable father-typing was a mother's open expression of her contempt of her husband by warning her child "not to be like your father." All these data were used to select the cases in which by all indications the father-typing was unambiguously unfavorable.

Four cases, two boys and two girls, were located where the mothers described the absent father in only depreciative or critical terms, without any positive or favorable comments. In these cases it was felt safe to assume that the children heard only "bad things" about their absent father. There were more cases with some negative father-typing but only in these four was the father-typing devoid of any positive, compensatory features whatsoever.

In our search for a contrasting group, we again found only two boys and two girls where it was safe to infer from the various interview data that their mothers provided the children with unambiguously favorable, perhaps idealistic father-typing, i.e., these children heard the absent father spoken of in affectionate, appreciative value terms only, and the child was praised whenever his behavior reminded the mother of her husband.

This procedure of selection was somewhat subjective, but since this is a first empirical investigation of father-typing, we had to be content with the poor degree of refinement achieved in this pilot study. The clinical and systematic importance of the possibility that mere verbal symbolization may have social substitute value, warranted the relatively extensive labor considering the few cases.

FIGURE 2 shows the three statistically significant differences that were found when the two subgroups (father-typing-unfavorable versus father-typing-favorable) were compared along the eleven fantasy categories which had significantly differentiated the experimental group as a whole from the control group. The discovery of these differences is evidence that the nature of the father-fantasies that characterized the father-separated children was, in fact, influenced in certain respects by the father-typing variable.

The fantasies of the children with unfavorable father-typing (striped bars in FIGURE 2) picture the father to be relatively more aggressive, particularly against his children. At the same time he receives more affection from them.

Further inspection and study of our father-typing data corroborated the statistically significant *finding of curiously ambivalent aggressive-affectionate father-fantasies in cases where the maternal father-typing tended to be depreciative.*

These results force our attention to the further study of verbal father-typing and mother-typing as a stimulus-variable which in itself can modify the child's emotional relationship to his parents, even though the "typing" may be merely a more or less truthful expression of the degree of marital harmony or discord that exists in the family.

Furthermore, since father-typing is relatively easily controllable, full knowledge of

SAMPLE-PAGE OF ORIGINAL INTERVIEW SCHEDULE

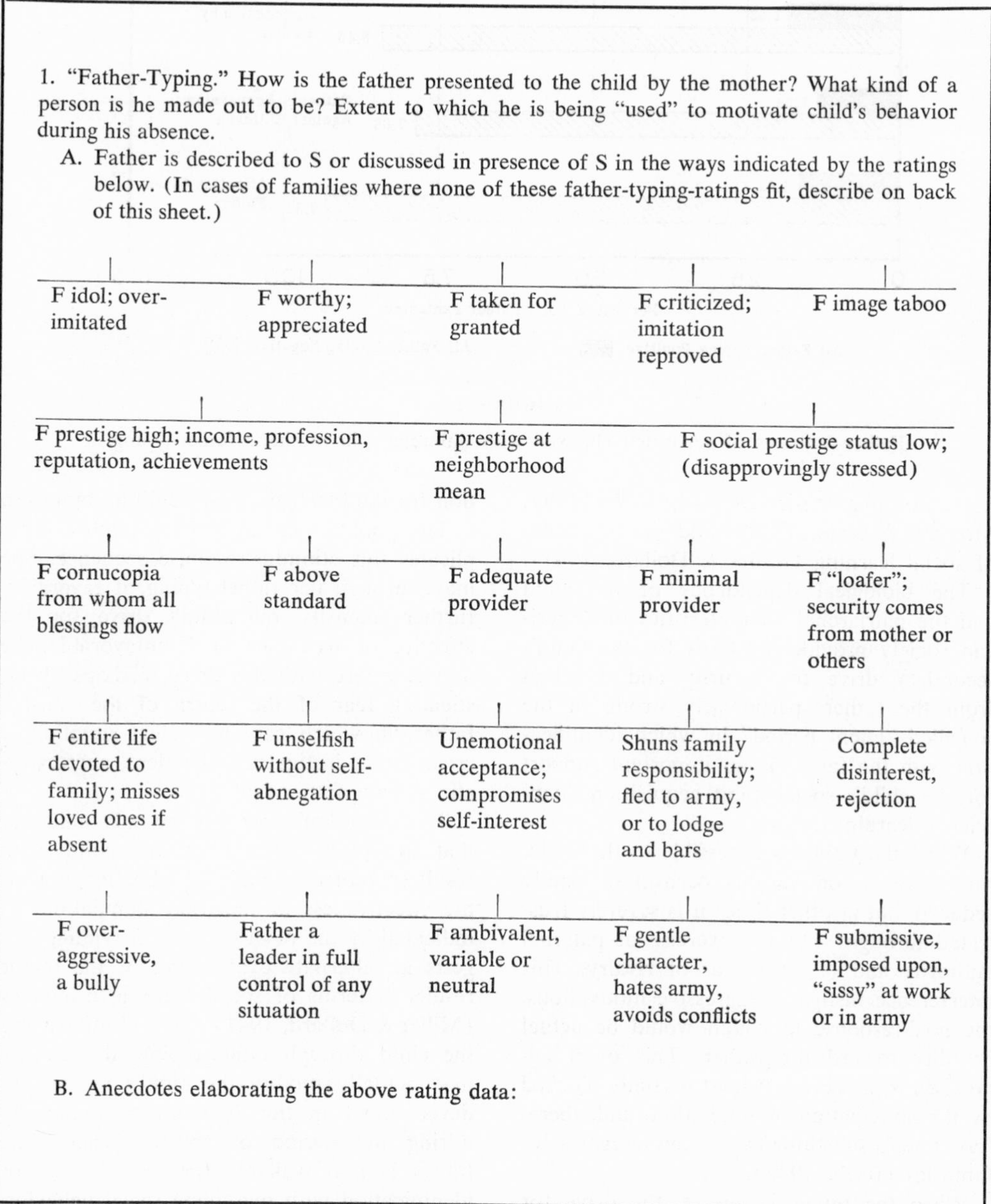

1. "Father-Typing." How is the father presented to the child by the mother? What kind of a person is he made out to be? Extent to which he is being "used" to motivate child's behavior during his absence.

A. Father is described to S or discussed in presence of S in the ways indicated by the ratings below. (In cases of families where none of these father-typing-ratings fit, describe on back of this sheet.)

F idol; over-imitated	F worthy; appreciated	F taken for granted	F criticized; imitation reproved	F image taboo

F prestige high; income, profession, reputation, achievements	F prestige at neighborhood mean	F social prestige status low; (disapprovingly stressed)

F cornucopia from whom all blessings flow	F above standard	F adequate provider	F minimal provider	F "loafer"; security comes from mother or others

F entire life devoted to family; misses loved ones if absent	F unselfish without self-abnegation	Unemotional acceptance; compromises self-interest	Shuns family responsibility; fled to army, or to lodge and bars	Complete disinterest, rejection

F over-aggressive, a bully	Father a leader in full control of any situation	F ambivalent, variable or neutral	F gentle character, hates army, avoids conflicts	F submissive, imposed upon, "sissy" at work or in army

B. Anecdotes elaborating the above rating data:

this variable may be of practical value in prophylactic parent-education, in psychotherapy, and in the control of the personality development of children who have lost one or both parents.

Theoretical Considerations

Of systematic interest is the fact that the obtained data make theoretical sense when interpreted in the light of the frustration-

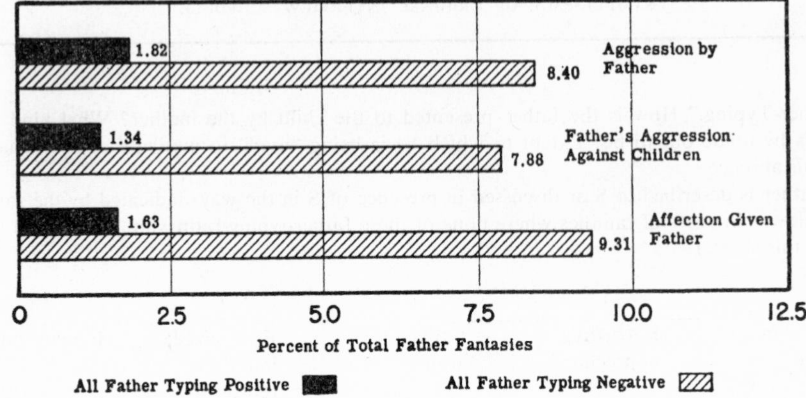

FIGURE 2

Father-fantasies of separated children with differences in mother's father-typing.

aggression hypothesis (Dollard, Doob, Miller, Mowrer, & Sears, 1939), and the principles of social learning (Miller & Dollard, 1941).

The biological dependency of the child and the patriarchal characteristics of American society provide the basis for the child's secondary drive for security and affection from the father, particularly strong in the so-called "latent period" in which identification with the father is an important support for the child's social habit acquisition (conscience learning).

While the father is accessible to the child, this drive is, on various occasions, readily reduced, but at other times it is severely frustrated through: (1) the exercise of paternal authority and (2) the fear of rivalry. This interference instigates aggressive motivations, the goal-response to which would be actual hostility toward the father. This overt aggression is, however, at least partially blocked by the anticipation of retaliation, and, therefore, finds a substitute expression in aggressive fantasies (Bach, 1945).

When the father is absent, the drive for affection, security, and companionship has no opportunity to be reduced, and the absence of the father prevents father-instigated interference and the occasion for rivalry. Consequently, there is less instigation for aggressive fantasies, and the severely deprivated drive for paternal affection provides strong instigation for the idealistic, wish-fulfilling fantasies.

The mother as a social stimulus complicates this stimulus-response sequence. She may, through her father-typing, if favorable, further intensify the child's drive for the affection of his father, or, if unfavorable, she may interfere with this drive, perhaps by instigating fear of the return of the "nasty" father, in which case a conflict situation is created that instigates ambivalent, aggressive-affectionate father-fantasies.

This is undoubtedly not the only influence that the mother exerts on the child as a result of father-absence. As a matter of fact, the effectiveness of maternal stimulation, as indicated by the results on father-typing, suggests an alternate explanation of the major results in terms of social learning principles (Miller & Dollard, 1941). Beyond influencing the child through father-typing, the mother may actually modify the child's personality development in the direction of femininity during the period of father-absence. The father is not available for imitation of or identification with masculine social behavior, and there is now more opportunity to imitate the feminine attitudes, manners, and values of the mother (cf. Seward, 1946, pp. 153–154). The idealistic father-fantasies of *both* the separated boys and the separated girls with their stereotyped, affectionate and non-aggressive themes are very similar to the doll play fantasies *characteristically produced by girls* (in contrast to boys) under ordinary family conditions (Bach, 1945; Pintler *et al.*, 1946). This "feminization" of the father-separated child's fantasy may then be a reflection of the increased potency of the mother as a social stimulus. The idealistic father-fantasies may, therefore, not only be an expression of the child's wish for an affectionate father but may actually also be symptomatic of a personality reorganization produced by exclusive maternal domination. If this interpretation is a valid one, the results of this study assume some significance with respect to the dynamics of cultural "sex-typing." However, further research into these relationships is required before an empirical evaluation can be made of the differential effects on personality development of the various stimulus variables that come into play because of father-separation.

Practical Implications

AT THE time of this writing, problems of family readjustment after war experiences are of acute interest (Hill, 1945). The results of the present investigation suggest some insights of practical value pertaining to these problems.

The stereotyped, idealistic fantasy picture that the child has of the absent father may initially be a handicap in the re-establishment of a realistic father-child relationship. The child may experience a certain degree of disappointment over the wished for reunion. The father's resumption of domination and authority would certainly come in conflict with the child's idealistic expectations. Consequently, the instigation of feelings of paternal rejection is a strong possibility. The father can be expected to be puzzled by this and may develop the impression that his child has become estranged from him. This may lead to some disturbance of the morale of the family group.

But these unfortunate consequences of the child's way of having previously adjusted to separation will most likely be a temporary episode in the readjustment to reality, and the possibility of a seriously ineffective adjustment to the situation can be avoided by explaining to the returning father and to the mother the nature of the psychological forces at work in their child's mind.

Therapeutic Implications

THE fundamental question of the effect of fantasy experiences on the development of overt behavior characteristics deserves a brief comment. It is a reasonable hypothesis based on observed effects of play therapy (Rogerson, 1939) that fantasy expressions have behavior modification potentialities similar to gratifying and painful reality experiences.

This can be so by virtue of the cathartic and/or anxiety characteristics of the fantasy response. These characteristics, together with the imitations and identifications noticeable in children engaged in doll play fantasies, should provide sufficient conditions for at least vicarious social learning.

To be sure, these behavior processes still need patient and careful empirical clarification, but such research effort seems justified by the indication that many of the factors that influence a child's fantasy also influence his actual personality development. Consequently, *fantasy control* can become one of our most practical tools in our efforts to control personality development. The technical complications involved in the study and instigation of children's fantasies should not deter from this all-important possibility.

Summary

THE father-fantasies of twenty father-separated children six to ten years of age and those of twenty control, father-home children, are compared by means of a standardized doll play technique. The father-separated children produced an idealistic and feminine fantasy picture of the father when compared with the control children, who elaborated the father's aggressive tendencies. The nature of the maternal father-typing seemed to influence this difference. Practical, clinical and theoretical implications of these results are discussed.

REFERENCES

BACH, G. R. Young children's play fantasies. *Psychol. Monogr.*, 1945, **59**.

BALDWIN, A. L., KALHORN, J., & BREESE, F. H. Patterns of parent behavior. *Psychol. Monogr.*, 1945, **58**, 1–75.

CHAMPNEY, H. *The Fels Parent-Behavior Rating Scales.* Yellow Springs, Ohio: Antioch Press, 1939.

CHAMPNEY, H. The measurement of parent behavior. *Child Develpm.*, 1941, **12**, 131–166.

DOLLARD, J., DOOB, L. W., MILLER, N. E., MOWRER, O. H., & SEARS, R. R. *Frustration and aggression.* New Haven: Yale Univer. Press, 1939.

ENGLISH, O. P., & PEARSON, G. H. J. *Emotional problems of living.* New York: Norton, 1945.

FENICHEL, O. *The psychoanalytic theory of neurosis.* New York: Norton, 1945.

HILL, R. The returning father and his family. *Marriage Fam. Living*, 1945, **7**, 31–34.

JONES, H. E. Environmental influences on mental development. In L. Carmichael (Ed.), *Manual of child psychology.* New York: Wiley, 1946. Pp. 592–599.

LEVY, D. M. *Maternal overprotection.* New York: Columbia Univer. Press, 1943.

LEWIN, K. Constructs in psychology and psychological ecology. Authority and frustration. *Univer. Iowa Stud. Child Welf.*, 1944, **20**, 3–29.

MILLER, N. E., & DOLLARD, J. *Social learning and imitation.* New Haven: Yale Univer. Press, 1941.

MURRAY, H. A., & MORGAN, C. A clinical study of sentiments: II. Sentiments towards parents. *Genet. Psychol. Monogr.*, 1945, **32**.

PHILLIPS, R. Doll play as a function of the realism of the materials and the length of the experimental session. *Child Develpm.*, 1945, **16**, 123–143.

PINTLER, M. H. Doll play as a function of experimenter-child interaction and the initial organization of the materials. *Child Develpm.*, 1945, **16**, 145–166.

PINTLER, M. H., PHILLIPS, R., & SEARS, R. R. Sex differences in the projective doll play of preschool children. *J. Psychol.*, 1946, **21**, 73–80.

RAPAPORT, D. Principles underlying projective techniques. *Charact. & Pers.*, 1942, **10**, 213–219.

ROGERSON, C. H. *Play therapy in childhood.* New York: Oxford Univer. Press, 1939.

SEARS, R. R., PINTLER, M. H., & SEARS, PAULINE S. Effect of father separation on preschool children's doll play aggression. *Child Develpm.*, 1946, **17**, 219–243.

SEWARD, G. H. *Sex and the social order.* New York: McGraw-Hill, 1946.

SYMONDS, P. M. *The psychology of parent-child relationships.* New York: Appleton-Century, 1939.

ROBERT LYTTON SPAULDING

Achievement, Creativity, and Self-Concept Correlates of Teacher-Pupil Transactions in Elementary Schools*

STUDIES of classroom climate have emphasized the importance of learner supportive relationships in elementary education. Several of these studies (among them Lewin, Lippitt, & White, 1939; Anderson & Brewer, 1946; and Flanders, 1951) have shown positive attitude changes regarding self and others among pupils after experiencing "democratic," "socially integrative," or "learner-centered" group processes. Stern (1963), however, in summarizing the literature on effects of teaching method, concluded that "the amount of cognitive gain is largely unaffected by the autocratic or democratic tendencies of the instructor [p. 426]."

The present study was concerned with attitudinal and cognitive correlates of teacher-pupil affective transactions in a sample of fourth and sixth grade classrooms in a modern, suburban California school system. An attempt was made to replicate the findings of previous investigators regarding attitudes toward the self and then to identify specific dimensions of teacher-pupil transactions which were significantly related to academic achievement and creative thinking.

Objectives

THE main objectives of the study were to provide data regarding the following hypotheses:

Hypothesis 1: There are significant main effects of the condition of placement within one or another of the twenty-one classrooms in the sample with respect to pupil height of self-concept, cognitive flexibility, problem-solving, cognitive synthesis, originality, reading achievement, and mathematics achievement.

Hypothesis 2: A teacher-pupil transactional pattern representing the "integrative" teacher behavior syndrome, identified by Anderson and Brewer (1946), is associated with superior pupil originality, cognitive flexibility, and higher over-all self-concept.

Hypothesis 3: A teacher-pupil transactional pattern representing the "learner-supportive" behavior syndrome, identified by Withall (1948), is associated with superior pupil originality, cognitive flexibility, and higher over-all self-concept.

Hypothesis 4: A teacher-pupil transactional pattern representing the behavior of the academically oriented teacher, identified by Bush (1954), is associated with superior reading and mathematics achievement.

Hypothesis 5: A teacher-pupil transactional pattern representing the counseling type of teacher behavior, identified by Bush (1954), is associated with higher pupil over-all self-concept.

Hypothesis 6: A teacher-pupil transactional pattern representing the behavior of teachers oriented toward fostering creativity in pupils, as identified by Bush (1954), is associated with superior pupil originality and cognitive flexibility.

Hypothesis 7: Teacher classroom behavior

* This paper, which is a summary statement of the author's research on teacher-pupil transactions, is reproduced here with his permission.

characterized by a relatively *high degree* of private or semi-private communication with children, of overt facilitation of task oriented behavior, of concern for divergent responses in children, of attentiveness to pupil needs, of the use of control techniques involving humor—and a relatively *low degree* of negative evaluation, of domination through threat, of firmness in tone, of teacher-supportive control, of harsh "taskmaster" behavior, and of grim domination—is predicted to be associated with superior pupil reading achievement, mathematics achievement, originality, cognitive flexibility, and higher over-all self-concept.

Hypothesis 8: A teacher-pupil transactional pattern representing "democratic" leader behavior, as identified by Lewin, Lippitt, and White (1939), is associated with superior pupil reading and mathematics achievement, cognitive flexibility, originality, and higher over-all self-concept.

Procedure

AN antecedent-consequent design was used covering one academic year. The data were gathered in an upper middle-class, suburban California city of about 50,000 population. Ten of the larger elementary schools in the city were selected to represent a cross section of the school population. All teachers in these schools who were teaching in self-contained classrooms at the fourth or sixth grade levels were asked to participate. The twenty-one classrooms obtained in this manner were located in nine different elementary school buildings and included a sample of 507 boys and girls who were registered in school from October through June of the academic year 1960–61.

Pupil mental ability, socioeconomic status, and chronological age were measured in the fall. Data were subsequently obtained regarding class size, the proportion of boys in each class, the sex of the teacher, the presence or absence of experimental mathematics materials (School Mathematics Study Group), and grade level. At mid-year teacher-pupil transactions and the classroom physical activity level of the children were recorded. The target variables—pupil reading and mathematics achievement, self-concept, and creative thinking—were measured in May and June.

By means of a small transmitting microphone which each teacher wore, a remote radio receiver and tape recorder, and the use of a trained observer seated at the rear of the classroom, continuous, 15-second time samples of teacher-pupil transactions on three full mornings of normal school activity were obtained. Data from the third morning were used in subsequent statistical analyses.

The recorded data were first coded according to eight molar categories of teacher behavior using as much of the 15-second period immediately preceding each sampling signal as necessary to provide background for interpretation. These molar categories were: approval, disapproval, instruction (managing, structuring), listening, observation, personal activity, communication with adults, and temporary absence from the classroom. Approval and disapproval were given priority over other categories and double scoring was reduced to a minimum.

Each unit of transaction which had been classified into one of the first four molar categories—approval, disapproval, instruction (managing, structuring), or listening—was further coded for sex of pupil (or, if it involved a group, the size of the group), publicity of communication, specific technique used in communicating or listening, and the objective nature of the communication. Teacher approval, disapproval, and instruction (managing, structuring) units were also coded for tone or mood and the source of authority appealed to in the transaction. Instructing (managing, structuring) and listening units were further encoded with respect to covert sequential reinforcement or non-reinforcement.[1]

Satisfactory levels of observer reliability were obtained after a series of simultaneous observations in trial classrooms. Tape analysis

1 Sequential reinforcement or non-reinforcement as used in this study referred to the covert maneuvering of the teacher as she kept the class discussion on the chosen topic without overtly approving or disapproving any particular response of the pupils.

reliability was obtained by means of several independent analyses of audio tapes by two trained persons.

The stability of the data obtained during the third day of observation and recording was examined using a split-half technique. Halves were set up using the units of every other consecutive decade of sampling, with each decade representing a period of 2½ minutes of transaction. Percentage scores were computed for each half in the twenty-one classrooms and the resulting pairs correlated. A total of 113 out of 144 categories were found to have stability coefficients of .50 or better over episodes within the third morning using the Spearman-Brown prophecy formula. Scores for each classroom in each of these 113 categories of teacher-pupil transaction were intercorrelated. The resulting matrix was factored and rotated to obtain seventeen interpretable factors. Teacher component scores were then computed for each of the seventeen factors, representing the degree to which each teacher transacted with pupils in a manner identified by the loadings on each factor.

An index of pupil performance for each of the target variables was obtained by a multiple regression technique. Each pupil was assigned a score (one or zero) to indicate his presence or absence in each of the twenty-one classroom "conditions." A separate regression equation was computed for each target variable, employing pupil mental ability, socioeconomic status, chronological age, and sex, in addition to the classroom "variables" as predictors. The several sets of regression weights for the classroom "variables" (B weights, in this case) entering into the regression equations (one equation for each target variable) formed a set of indices of pupil performance.

Using these sets of B weights as "scores" on the target variables and the teacher behavior component scores as antecedent variables, an intercorrelation matrix was prepared. Tests of the hypotheses regarding patterns of behavior were made by matching loadings on the teacher-pupil transaction factors, which were derived empirically in this study, with protocol or descriptive statements of specific teacher behavior patterns published in the literature.

A test of the first hypothesis—the significance of classroom placement considered globally—was made by computing two multiple regression equations. The first employed pupil mental ability, socioeconomic status, chronological age, and sex as predictors. In the second equation, classroom placement, considered generally, was added as a predictor.

Results

1. The factor of placement of children within one or another of the twenty-one research classrooms was found to be significantly related to all the target pupil variables—height of self-concept, differentiation of self-concept, reading achievement, mathematics achievement, cognitive flexibility, problem solving, cognitive synthesis, and originality.

2. Height of self-concept was found to be significantly related positively with one component of the "socially integrative" teacher behavior identified by Anderson and Brewer (1946)—"calm, acceptant transactions in general with private, individualized instruction and a concern for divergency, attention to task, and the use of task appropriate procedures and resources."

3. The "learner-supportive" category described by Withall (1948) was found to contain some of the same components as the "socially integrative" pattern. Pupil self-concepts were found to be significantly higher in classrooms in which teachers were more "learner supportive" on the basis of the same transactional component mentioned in paragraph *2* above—"calm, acceptant transactions in general with private, individualized instruction and a concern for divergency, attention to task, and the use of task appropriate procedures and resources."

4. Predictions of superior reading and mathematics achievement in classrooms taught by "academically oriented" teachers as described by Bush (1954) were unsup-

ported by the results of this study. Reading and mathematics gains were not found to be significantly related to the transactional component most closely resembling the "academic" type of teacher.

5. Predictions of significantly higher overall self-concepts in classrooms taught by teachers oriented toward counseling (as described by Bush, 1954) were not substantiated.

6. No support was given for the hypothesis that superior pupil originality and cognitive flexibility would be present in classrooms taught by "creative" teachers (as identified by Bush, 1954). On the contrary, some evidence was present that the reverse was true —that teacher-pupil transactions representing the "creative" type of teacher behavior are negatively correlated with cognitive flexibility and originality.

7. Strong support was found (nine out of twelve correlations in the predicted direction and significant at or beyond the .05 level of probability) for positive relationships between pupil self-concepts and teacher behavior characterized by a *high degree* of private or semi-private communication with children, of overt facilitation of task oriented behavior, of concern for divergent responses in children, of attentiveness to pupil needs, of the use of control techniques involving humor—and a relatively *low degree* of negative evaluation, of domination through threat, of firmness in tone, of teacher-supportive control, of harsh "taskmaster" behavior, and of grim domination. Moderate support was given (nine out of twelve correlations in the predicted direction with two reaching significance and one significant correlation contrary to prediction) for positive relationships between this same pattern of teacher behavior and pupil gains in reading. Slight support (a consistent pattern in the predicted directions with one predicted correlation reaching statistical significance) was provided with respect to cognitive flexibility and originality. Gains in mathematics were not found to be related in any consistent or statistically significant way.

8. Conflicting results were obtained with respect to "democratic" leader behavior as identified by Lewin, Lippitt, and White (1939). Of the three components bearing closest resemblance to the "democratic" pattern as derived from the White and Lippitt (1960) protocols, two were found to be generally negatively correlated and one positively correlated. For example, "good natured, personalized control with concern for sources of error, character, self-control, and proper social relations" was found to be significantly negatively correlated with cognitive flexibility and originality, contrary to prediction, and "acceptant transactions, controlling through standards, with appeal to convention as the source of authority, and avoiding negative evaluation" was found significantly positively correlated with height of self-concept (and correlated positively at the .06 level with originality).

9. The classrooms of two teachers in the sample were observed to have conditions which were related positively with almost all the criteria of pupil growth and development employed in this study. These two teachers had differential behavior patterns which were related to differences in pupil performance. The more directive of the two—though generally a very warm and friendly person—had a classroom in which pupils performed exceptionally well on measures of reading, mathematics, cognitive flexibility, and problem-solving. The more acceptant, receptive, responsive, and observant teacher—though a highly controlling but nondirective person —had a classroom in which pupils enjoyed exceptionally high self-esteem and were outstanding in originality—while performing almost as well in reading, mathematics, cognitive flexibility, and problem-solving as the pupils of the more directive teacher.

Conclusions and Implications

1. Results obtained in this study support in general the findings of previous investigators regarding positive relationships between a "socially integrative," "learner-supportive,"

or "learner-centered" group atmosphere and positive attitudes toward the self. Significant positive correlations were found between height of self-concept and the degree to which the teachers in the study were calm, acceptant, supportive, and facilitative. Significant negative correlations with pupil height of self-concept were found with dominative, threatening, grim, and sarcastic teacher behavior.

2. The findings reported by Heil, Powell, and Feifer (1960) that consistency, structure, routine, and orderliness in classroom teacher behavior are correlated positively with pupil achievement gains are supported by results obtained in this study. The teacher component "businesslike lecture method with insistence upon attention to task and conformity to rules of procedure" was found to be correlated significantly with pupil achievement gains in reading and mathematics and with problem-solving performance. This component of teacher behavior was found also to be significantly related positively with pupil self-esteem.

3. The findings of this study support also the contention of White and Lippitt (1960) that democratic classroom procedures are efficient only when an element of structure and control is present. Of the three components of "democratic" teacher classroom behavior which were identified in this study on basis of comparisons with protocols published by White and Lippitt, only one was found to be significantly related positively with the criteria used. Thus, "acceptant transactions, with control through standards, and an appeal to convention as the source of authority, avoiding negative evaluation" was found to be significantly related positively with height of self-concept and related at the .06 level of probability with originality in thinking. The critical element of control in the democratic pattern of leader behavior is emphasized by White and Lippitt (1960) in the following way:

> The most efficient procedure does appear to be, as a rule democracy—*if* democracy is sharply differentiated from laissez-faire, with clear acceptance not only of active leadership but also of the firm use of authority when firmness is called for, and explicit delegation of authority to certain individuals when such delegation is appropriate [p. 292].

The "democratic" teachers in this study who showed this element of control avoided evaluating pupil behavior negatively in public and obtained pupil cooperation through an emphasis upon standards set by society—a society in which the children were expected to participate as responsible members. They appealed primarily to convention and broad social needs as sources of authority rather than to peer authority or to the vested authority of the teacher.

4. Cognition appears to be disturbed primarily by negative or autocratic dimensions of classroom climate. Negative relationships with cognitive performance were found with dominating-threatening teacher behavior. Pupils made significantly fewer gains in reading and performed less well in tests of cognitive flexibility and originality in classrooms where teachers were relatively more dominating or threatening and where they used shame, ridicule, or public admonition more frequently as a means of control.

The results also suggest that cognitive gains are related to the number and level of complexity of cognitive encounters in the classroom when they take place in an orderly, businesslike fashion in the absence of domination, threat, or ridicule. The necessity for cognitive encounter is suggested by significant negative correlations which were obtained in this study with academic achievement and creative thinking and teacher behavior which was overly good natured and personal, centering upon existing pupil interests, social problems, and past experiences rather than the development of new concepts and generalizations.

5. Differential effects of teacher classroom behavior on pupil performance were noted incidentally in the study. Children who were striving to please the teacher behaved differently in class and subsequently varied in their performances on the spring measures. The

work of Heil, Powell, and Feifer (1960) emphasizes the importance of further studies of the effects of patterns of teacher behavior with respect to different types of children. The impact of affective dimensions of classroom transactions can be expected to be much greater with children who are generally anxious or disoriented. The amount of structure provided; the degree of order present; the clarity of goals; the degree of flexibility in the use of time, materials, and space; and the level of cognitive encounter encouraged and permitted are variables which need to be considered more extensively in subsequent studies of the behavior of types of children in the classroom setting.

REFERENCES

ANDERSON, H. H., & BREWER, J. E. Studies of teachers' classroom personalities: II. Effects of teachers' dominative integrative contacts on children's classroom behavior. *Appl. Psychol. Monogr.*, 1946, **8.**

BUSH, R. N. *The teacher-pupil relationship.* Englewood Cliffs, N.J.: Prentice-Hall, 1954.

FLANDERS, N. A. Personal-social anxiety as a factor in experimental learning situations. *J. educ. Res.*, 1951, **45,** 100–110.

HEIL, L. M., POWELL, MARION, & FEIFER, I. Characteristics of teacher behavior related to the achievement of children in several elementary grades. Brooklyn: Brooklyn College, 1960. (Cooperative Research Project No. 352, Mimeographed.)

LEWIN, K., LIPPITT, R., & WHITE, R. K. Patterns of aggressive behavior in experimentally created "social climates." *J. soc. Psychol.*, 1939, **10,** 271–299.

STERN, G. G. Measuring noncognitive variables in research on teaching. In N. L. Gage (Ed.), *Handbook of research on teaching.* Chicago: Rand McNally, 1963. Pp. 398–447.

WHITE, R. K., & LIPPITT, R. *Autocracy and democracy.* New York: Harper, 1960.

WITHALL, J. The development of a technique for the measurement of social-emotional climate in classrooms. Unpublished doctoral dissertation, Univer. of Chicago, 1948.

PART V

Intellective Processes in Children

The years since Sputnik have seen a tremendous surge of research interest on the part of American psychologists in the intellective development of children. Studies in increasing number are appearing in the literature on various phases of the genetic process in perception, cognition, and language. The genetic study of epistemology in particular has received considerable attention, largely because of the work of one man—Jean Piaget. From years of painstaking research with colleagues in Geneva, he has evolved a well-developed theoretical model of how children acquire knowledge. His work has been rather slow to be recognized in America, in part because of a time lag in the appearance of translations, in part because his work is difficult to understand, and in part because of criticisms of his methods.

A major target of the critics has been the seemingly casual research techniques of Piaget and his fellow-workers. In his earliest publications he reported his theory of how intelligence developed, supported chiefly by evidence derived from informal, nonstandardized interviews with children. Then, however, Piaget was developing theory; in the past decade or more, there have been a large number of controlled studies done at Geneva and a respectable body of statistical data accumulated. These studies are reported in *Archives Psychologiques* and *Études d'Épistémologie Génétique.* In addition, some thirty-eight of the tests of logical intelligence have been standardized and are being readied for publication.

Fortunately more and more American psychologists are coming to discard the notion that if a study doesn't exist in English, it doesn't exist at all, and they are discovering the literature that exists in French. Fortunately, also, for the monolingual, some excellent works on Piaget are appearing in English. For the reader who may be having his first introduction to this body of theory in these readings and wants to go further, Flavell's *The Developmental Psychology of Jean Piaget* is a comprehensive and understandable volume, an invaluable contribution to the literature. Hunt's excellent *Intelligence and Experience* cannot be neglected by students who want a solid grounding in theory, and who want to see Piagetian theory in its relationship to the American stream.

A Genetic Conception of Intelligence

A brief explanation of Piaget's genetic conception of intelligence may help to establish the significance of the selections. Intelligence develops, according to Piaget, not by virtue of maturation alone, nor by learning alone, but as a result of the interaction of the child and his environment. As the child performs upon objects or events in the environment, he develops notions of time, space, matter, and causality. For example, the actions of an infant in his playpen lead him to the discovery that he cannot pull a long narrow toy through the bars when it is in a horizontal position, but that the toy will go through when it is in a vertical position. Such actions help eventually to organize space concepts in the mind of the child. Inevitably, early ideas about space, time, matter, and causality contain errors. However, since there is order in the physical world, when in the course of development he observes the discrepancy between what he has always believed and what actually exists, the child gives up his earlier, erroneous notions.

Occasionally this process happens right under the eyes of an experimenter who is administering one of the tests of logical intelligence. A nine-year-old who has recognized the equality of two round balls of clay will affirm, when one of them is made into a sausage, that equality no longer exists, that the sausage now weighs less than the ball that has not been transformed. He does not see that weight is conserved, even though shape is changed. Next, he voices doubts—perhaps he has been wrong?—and he may contradict his first statement. Then suddenly his whole mien changes; he becomes quite alert and excited. "Oh, it is the same," he now avers. "You didn't add anything and you didn't take anything away, so it's got to be the same. Being longer just makes up for it's not being so fat. You could squash in the ends and it would be the same." The child is identifying two variables—length and thickness—and seeing that an increase in one dimension must be compensated for by a decrease in the other, if weight is to be conserved. Equilibrium has been disturbed, and equilibrium has been restored—but at a higher cognitive level.

Equilibrium refers to that state of stability where sensory inputs are in harmony with previously acquired knowledge. Note, in the example above, that new elements of perception have entered the child's system to cause a disturbance, which in this case has been resolved by the acquisition of a new concept—that of conservation of weight; that is, that weight remains the same regardless of change in shape. The child achieves this higher equilibrium because he can now reverse a process; he can mentally cancel out the change that has been made on the ball of clay and restore the clay to its original state.

The transition in thinking that occasionally happens in the testing room occurs in real life, although probably not with such dramatic suddenness. In acquiring the concept of conservation, the child first centers on one dimension and so is mistaken in his thinking; then he progresses to the step where he hesitates and waivers back and forth between conservation and non-conservation, particularly when the new variant of the task is perceptually very different from the old (as, for example, when one of the balls of clay is made into a flat pancake); finally he perceives two variables in their relationship to each other and so has achieved a higher equilibrium.

Two processes are essential in the attainment of a higher equilibrium: assimilation and accommodation. At any stage in development there exists an already present meaning-structure for a particular object or event. Assimilation is the process of incorporating new elements into this existing structure, or *schema,* to use the Piagetian term, just as food is assimilated in the digestive process. Accommodation is the adjustment of the schema itself to new elements; the term refers to the changes that take place in the existing meaning-structure to adapt it to the new inputs. For example, by four or five months of age, the infant begins to coordinate vision and grasping. Suppose a cradle-gym were suspended across the middle of his cradle, within reach of the infant. Suppose also a cord were dangling from the same support as the cradle-gym. The infant grasps the cord without any realization of the causal relationship involved, that pulling the cord will make bells on the cradle-gym jingle. Surprised by the result, he seeks the cord again and repeats the performance. The infant already had a meaning-structure for grasping; now he accommodates the notion of a dangling string to the grasping schema: a cord is to grasp. In addition, there has been assimilated the new element of cord-grasping as making an interesting event happen. The two processes, assimilation and accommodation, are complementary, occurring as part of each behavioral sequence as the child adapts to the environment.

Piaget's main concern has been, Under what laws does knowledge develop and change? In answering the question, Piaget has described stages of development. The inclusion of the concept of stage in his theory has netted Piaget considerable criticism. There are some who interpret "stage" in the Gesell sense of the term as a biological imperative applying to all children of a certain age; these people are critical since such an interpretation minimizes individual life experiences. Piaget, however, uses "stage" in a statistical sense, to denote the probability that a certain percentage of children at a particular age will be functioning intellectually in a certain way. Thus, when he describes an operational stage in logical thinking as occurring between seven and twelve years of age, he means that one can predict with some statistical certainty that children during these years will be growing in their use of logical operations.

To other critics, stage implies a discontinuity in development, rather than a continuous process, and they reject the notion of discontinuity. However, Piaget does not view the process as discontinuous; in fact, in analyzing protocols of test responses provision is made for a transition from one stage to another. Thus, in the conservation of weight test involving the balls of clay, one can find at one of the substages a transition point; the child may, for example, indicate his belief in the equality of sausage and ball, but when one ball is flattened out into a pancake so that its appearance is even more completely changed, he may abandon conservation once more. He has moved from the stage where any perceptual change is misleading to a stage where only gross perceptual differences will influence him.

THE SENSORIMOTOR STAGE

THE first stage that Piaget describes in the development of intelligence is the sensorimotor. During the first eighteen months of life, the infant is growing in his notions of space, time, matter, and causality. The selection by Piaget in Part III (pp. 146–154) is an illustration of the growth of the concept of causality—that the infant through his own actions finds that he can prolong and even bring about interesting events. Related to causality is the concept of probability; Piaget points out that the infant comes to recognize the likelihood that the footsteps he hears approaching are those of his mother. It is more difficult to trace the beginnings of the concept of time back to the cradle, although Piaget offers some illustrations of how the toddler is able to retain a series of events in his mind. If asked where his mother is, for example, the child can point in the direction his mother has gone.

With respect to the organization of space and matter, the big concept to develop during this period is that of permanence of object. The infant, as Piaget shows, at first believes that an object no longer exists when it disappears from sight. Show an infant a toy and take it away, and he shows no signs of looking for it; it is a case of out of sight, out of mind. But sometime during the first year, the infant realizes that an object can be hidden but can exist in hiding, thus he develops the notion of permanence of object. The delight of the baby in the game peekaboo probably indicates the dawning realization of the permanence of an object.

In the next phase of the development of perception, the object can be moved from one spot to another while the child looks on. Now he will search for the object, but he begins at the spot where he first found it. A watch is placed under cushion A and then is moved to cushion B. The child will look for it, but will begin the search under cushion A, before looking under cushion B. If the watch is then moved to cushion C, he'll begin at A, go to B and then to C to find it. We cannot explain what is happening in terms of sensory experience alone. The infant has *seen* the watch being placed under C, but he still begins to search at A. On the basis of his earlier experience he has stored away information as to where to expect the watch, and he needs additional interactions to learn differently. A bit later he may start at A but move directly to C and locate the missing object.

According to Piaget, the infant's actions are facilitating the organization of space in the mind and providing the foundation for the development of four different operations possible to any system of displacements. The first operation is that of combining factors: the infant discovers that the action $(A \rightarrow) + (B \rightarrow)$ takes him to cushion C (the basis for understanding that $2 + 3 = 5$). A reversible operation is also possible: he can go from cushion B to A and be back at the starting place again (the basis for knowing that if $2 + 3 = 5$, then $5 - 3 = 2$). The operation of associativity is also illustrated: the infant can jump from A to C and then go to D, or go from A to B and then jump to D, which is the same as saying $(2 + 3) + 4 = 2 + (3 + 4)$, or that he can reach the same goal by different routes. And finally Piaget finds illustrated the operation of identity, which is a null operation and is performed when any object is combined with its opposite.

Note that these operations are performed as sensorimotor acts; not for many years will they be internalized as logical operations of thought.

THE PREOPERATIONAL STAGE [1]

THE next stage in the development of logical intelligence is the preoperational, extending roughly to six or seven years of age. The child's thinking during this stage is distinguished by what it lacks, namely, logical operations and particularly reversibility. The child cannot reverse a thought process and so he is at the mercy of his perceptions, which often mislead him. In one of the Geneva tests, "Cows in the Field," the child is presented with two pieces of green cardboard to represent fields of grass. A cow is placed on each field, and the child is asked if each cow will have the same amount to eat as the other. Then a barn (a small block) is placed on one field, and the child now asserts inequality of grass area. When a barn is added to the other field, he recognizes equality once more. The six-year-old may say, "The barn takes up some room and each side has a barn so the grass is the same." Then barns are added one at a time to each field, but in one field the barns are lined up in a horizontal row with their sides touching, whereas in the other field the barns are scattered. The child continues to assert equality while the barns are equal in number, but only up to a certain point. Beyond that point (which may be as many as ten barns), unoccupied space in the fields begins to *look* different; one field *looks* to the eye as if there were indeed a great deal more grass. At this point the child in the preoperational stage falters; he is judging in terms of his perceptions, and so he now says that one cow has more to eat than the other. He'll aver that they were equal before but not now. To his way of thinking, nothing could be the same that looked so different; in fact, he may explain the lack of conservation by saying that they look different and by pointing to the free area on one side. Or he may give an answer indicating that the one cow can eat all around the edges of the barns, while the other cow cannot, and so the areas are not the same. Because he cannot perform certain mental operations upon the data before him, he is misled by his perceptions.

During the preoperational stage, the child also lacks the ability to think in terms of more than one variable. We have seen an example of this in the ball of clay problem, where the young child centers on only one dimension of the sausage, either thickness or length, and is unable to coordinate the two. He lacks the logical operations that would enable him to see that an increase in length is compensated for by a decrease in thickness.

Lacking is the ability, also, to combine classes and thus establish a hierarchy in classification. Thus, in giving responses to one test problem, he will tell the examiner that the rose is, indeed, a flower, and will identify certain other flowers by name. However when one asks, "If all the roses in the world were to die, would there be any flowers?", one is likely to get a negative answer. A rose is a rose and comprises at the same time the complete class, "flowers." The child is neither capable of understanding the ascending nature of a hierarchy (that is,

1 Some descriptions of stages include the preoperational as part of the stage of concrete operations which follows here as a separate stage.

combining subclasses into a supraclass), nor its descending nature (taking away from the supraclass one of the subclasses and still having something left).

In fact, the child at this stage finds it hard to attribute several characteristics to one thing. This writer is reminded of a five-year-old American girl in Geneva, asking her mother why it rained. The mother explained the phenomenon in terms of the evaporation-condensation cycle. The child listened quietly, but then said, "But that's not what Françoise said. She said God made it rain." The mother replied, "Françoise is a Catholic and she is offering a religious explanation. She would think that rain happened as I explained it to you, but that there is something behind all the natural causes, and that the something is God." "Françoise is a Catholic?", the child questioned doubtfully, "Isn't it funny that she's a Catholic, and she speaks French, too!" The child in the preoperational stage assigns to the person only one variable at a time; a supraclass of French-Catholics is as difficult to cope with as the problem of being a resident simultaneously of Dayton, Ohio, and the United States.

THE STAGE OF CONCRETE OPERATIONS

THE child's thinking processes change, however, as he continues to interact with the physical world. After about six or seven years of age, we begin to see the emergence of logical operations. The child becomes able to reverse a process; mentally he can restore the sausage of clay to its original shape and thus see that the amount of clay is conserved. (Later he will recognize conservation of weight.) He can combine subclasses into a supraclass and take the supraclass apart, so he knows that if all the birds in the world died, there would be no ducks left, but that if all the ducks died, there would still be some birds. Or, he may use an identity operation to arrive at a logical conclusion; he may say of the barns that are scattered on one field of grass, "Just line these up like the ones on that side, and you'll see they're the same." And, finally, there is the operation of associativity; we can combine $3 + (4 + 2)$ to make 9, or we can combine $(3 + 4) + 2$ and get the same result. The same goal can be reached by different paths.

The model that Piaget believes mirrors the thought of the child is a group-like structure, or *groupement*. Piaget uses the term *groupement* in the Poincaré sense of the word *groupe* to refer to a system of displacements. The child can shift the data around mentally in the four different ways, described above, as he tests reality. Note that at this stage the child is using concrete data to make the displacements; he is not able to think abstractly about a problem. Adults often do the same thing. If we forget a formula which is an abstraction, we may mentally reconstruct a specific situation, work out the relationship of one variable to another, and arrive at the solution to the problem at the level of a concrete operation.

THE STAGE OF FORMAL THINKING

ROUGHLY at about eleven or twelve years of age, Piaget again finds changes commencing in the child's thought processes. Now thought is decreasingly tied to the concrete; the adolescent becomes more and more capable of abstract reasoning. He reasons in terms of propositions, and he can make logical combinations of these propositions. He can compare by conjunction as when he says, "Both A and B make a difference." He can combine by disjunction, as when he says, "It's got to be this or that." He can combine by implication, "If it's this, then that happens." Or he can combine by incompatibility, "When this happens, then that doesn't." His thinking is in terms of possible combinations and not with objects or events directly.

Each of these combinations can then be transformed by identity, negation, reciprocation, and correlation. For example, one can start with a conjunctive statement, "Both p and q make a difference," and perform an identity transformation by substituting equivalent factors for either p or q, or both. Or one might negate both factors by hypothesizing that neither one will make a difference. Or one might transform the conjunction by reciprocation, that is, by hypothesizing that either p is what it seems to be and q has no effect, or that p has an effect and q is not what it seems to be. And lastly, a transformation by correlation can be made, as when the subject states a positive correspondence between p and q.

The reader with some knowledge of symbolic logic will understand more fully the Piaget model of adolescent thinking, for Piaget uses the language and symbols of logic. For such a reader, Inhelder and Piaget (1958) describe the formal structure of thought and offer an example of the sixteen binary operations (pp. 103–104). If one exhausts all possible combinations and transformations, one will have stated sixteen different hypotheses to explain a phenomenon where there are two propositions.

Some Tests of Logical Intelligence • One of the best ways for the student to build an understanding of Piaget into his nervous system is to try out on children some of the tests developed in Geneva. Trying "Cows in the Field" with a five-year-old and a seven-year-old, and "Classification of Animals" with a seven- and a ten-year-old should, if the children are roughly equivalent in rate of development, give the reader a concrete illustration of how children's thinking changes. Directions for administration and analysis of these tests are included below.[2]

COWS IN THE FIELD

Materials:

2 sheets of green construction paper (12″ x 18″)
2 small toy cows
28 cubes (1″ x 1″)

Procedure:

"Let's imagine that these two sheets of paper are two fields of grass. We'll put a cow in each field. Now, does each cow have as much to eat as the other?" (Have the child measure the sheets, if he expresses a doubt, and establish the equality of the two fields.)

2 Directions and analysis are adapted from J. Piaget and Bärbel Inhelder, *La Genèse des Structures Logiques Élémentaires*. Neuchâtel: Delachaux & Niestlé. 1959.

"Suppose we put a barn on this field. Now, will each cow have the same amount to eat?"

"Suppose we put one in the other. Now, will each cow have the same?"

"Now we'll add another barn to this field like this [placing the cube so that it touches the first cube] and another barn to this field like this [placing the cube far away from first cube]. Now will each cow have the same? Tell me why."

"Now we add three barns to each field like this." (In field A, the barns are next to each other; in field B the barns are scattered.) "Now will each cow have the same? Tell me why."

"Now we'll add five more barns on each side [placed as before]. Will each cow have the same now? Tell me why."

"And if we add four more to each side?" (Do it.) "Tell me why."

Analysis:

STAGE 1:

The experimenter finds it difficult to pursue the inquiry, for the child cannot understand the problem.

STAGE 2:

(A) The child's judgments are based upon perception, without operational addition and subtraction. The child recognizes the grass areas as equal so long as the arrangement of barns is identical, but as n increases, the child ceases to recognize equality.

The child is dependent upon inspection for his judgments; he cannot combine equal parts to make invariant wholes

There is no evidence of elementary operations (reversibility, identity, etc.).

(B) Intermediate—there is a conflict between intuition and operation. The child will admit equality for, say, three barns ("It's the same. You've got the same number of barns on each side. You just put them a different way."), but still has to reason out the answer for more barns. There is no generalization.

STAGE 3: *Immediate Operational Composition.*

The child sees equality as a logical necessity: "If the barns are the same size, and there are just as many of them, then there's got to be the same amount of grass left; you started with the same and you took away the same, so the remainder has to be the same."

CLASSIFICATION OF ANIMALS

Materials:

3 ducks (class A)
4 birds—not ducks (class B)
5 animals—not birds (class C)
2 inanimate objects (class D)
Labels: "ducks," "birds," "animals"
3 plastic packets

Procedure:

"Here are some cards with pictures on them. You see, here we have a ______, and here is a ______." (Let child supply names.) "Can you make some piles with animals that are like each other? Find the cards with the same kind of animal two or more times and put them together."

"Here are some labels that say 'ducks,' 'birds,' and 'animals.' Suppose we put each label in an envelope."

"This envelope says 'birds.' Can we put these [the ducks] in here and still keep the same label? Why?"

"This label says 'animals.' Can we put these [the birds] in here and still keep the same label? Why?

"This label says 'ducks.' Can we put these [birds] in here and still keep the same label? Why?"

"This label says 'birds.' Can we put these [animals] in here and still keep the same label? Why?" (Examiner spreads out all the cards.)

"Are there more ducks than birds? Why?"

"Are there more animals than ducks? Why?"

"Are there more animals than birds? Why?"

"If all the ducks in the world were killed, would there be any birds left? Why? If all the birds in the world were killed, would there be any ducks left? Why? If all the animals in the world were killed, would there be any birds left? Why? If all the birds were killed, would there be any animals left?"

Analysis:

STAGE 1: *Spontaneous Classification.*

The subject can make spontaneous but not logical classifications. He can separate out animals that walk from animals that fly, or domestic animals from wild animals, but he does not have the notion of hierarchy.

The notion of inclusion of classes is missing; the child will say that ducks are animals, but he is unwilling to place the pictures of ducks in the pile labeled "animals."

STAGE 2: *Partial Success.*

The beginnings of the quantification of inclusion—that $A < B$; the child will recognize that if all the birds were dead, there would still be animals left, for example, the dog.

His answers may be correct with certain classes of animals but not with all.

STAGE 3: *Immediate Success.*

The subject gives an indication of the concept of inclusion of classes—$A < B < C < D$.

The subject can reverse a process: $A + A' = B$; therefore $A = B - A'$.

Many students when they first read the test protocols find it hard to believe that a child (and especially an American child) would ever give the response to the sausage of clay, "It's lighter now because it's skinnier." Hearing children give predicted responses can be an eye-opener for such students, whether the responses are piped in English or in French. And, lest we become smug about the superior level of adult knowledge, this writer might repeat one of Piaget's stories about a woman who was going on an airplane trip and who asked the clerk in a luggage shop for a long narrow bag that would hold as much clothing as a square-shaped one, but, of course (she said) wouldn't weigh as much! Conservation in all areas is not achieved even by many adults. In fact, graduate students in Geneva, training to give the tests, were often chagrined to find that their husbands or wives, mothers and fathers, or other adult guinea pigs (including themselves) were functioning on some of the tests at an operational or even a preoperational level!

Validation and Training Experiments • Piaget's work has generated a tremendous amount of research on both sides of the Atlantic. Flavell's book includes an excellent summary and evaluation of this research. Much of the work has consisted of validation studies to see whether the picture of logical development is really as Piaget describes it. In general, the answer is that it is; an individual investigator may quarrel over a minor point, but it appears that children in America, England, Norway, and even some Middle Eastern countries grow in logical intelligence as Piaget has described.

Americans, however, are rarely satisfied with the status quo; tell an American that children don't as a rule acquire conservation of weight until their ninth year, and the American immediately sets about to accomplish the feat in the eighth year. We find, then, a second group of studies in the literature devoted to attempts to speed up the process of development through training. Many of the studies have selected the concept of conservation for training, perhaps because this is conspicuous in Piagetian theory.

By and large, the attempts to train for the acquisition of conservation have been unsuccessful, perhaps because the investigators have not concentrated on the logical operations involved. Training has consisted of practice tasks, perhaps with a two-pan balance. The child masters the task, but not the concept, for there is no transfer to other situations. In real life, however, conservation is achieved as the child grows in his ability to perform logical operations, to reverse a process or combine elements to make a whole, or to deal with two variables at the same time. These operations develop as the child performs actions upon events or objects in his environment, in a wide variety of situations. As he plays with sand and mud, divides up candy bars, counts objects forward and backward, assimilates and accommodates, the child arrives at the stage where he recognizes first that *substance* is conserved, later that *weight* is conserved, and finally that *volume* remains the same even though the shape is changed. It would be possible to teach this or any other concept at the verbal level, but true understanding (as tested by transfer) is only built into the nervous system as the child operates upon the environment and internalizes the operations. Training on specific tasks has not facilitated the development of conservation, but no one to date has attempted to give children a *variety* of tasks with training emphasis upon *operations.*

To see how the actions of the individual lead to operations that are eventually internalized, we turn to another of the Geneva tests. The following is one involving arrangements of numbers, or permutations, to see whether the child can discover the rule predicting how many two-digit numbers can be made by combining a given number of digits. Here are the directions and the test analysis:

ARRANGEMENTS OF NUMBERS

Materials:

30 cards bearing the digit, 1, in a pile
30 cards bearing the digit, 2, in a pile
30 cards bearing the digit, 3, in a pile

30 cards bearing the digit, 4, in a pile
1 card bearing the digit, 5, in a pile

Procedure:

Explain that the word "digit" means any of the figures 0–9.

Present the child with the first two piles and ask, "How many different two-digit numbers could you make using these two figures only?" (Let the child predict.) "Put them in a column, in an order that will help you decide if you've got them all." (11, 12, 21, 22.)

"Now here is a third pile with the digit 3. We'll leave the numbers you've just made here. Now next to that column, make another one. This time use digits from all three piles, but you must make numbers of two digits only. How many numbers do you think you could make? Which ones will they be? Now do it. Remember you can use the same combinations that you did the first time." (Let the child work at it.)

"Is that all? Are you sure there are no more you could make? Would there be a quick way of telling ahead of time how many two-digit numbers you could make? "Now arrange the numbers in order in the column, to make sure that you haven't missed any. How can you be sure?"

Repeat the procedure, using four piles of figures. Have the child predict, and then add the new numbers to the last column he has made. "And if we added a fifth pile? How many numbers could you make? With two piles you made four numbers. With three piles you made nine. With four, you made sixteen. With five, you could make? How many new ones would you add to this last column? Which ones would you add?"

"And with twelve figures how many could you make? Is there a law or rule that would help you decide how many numbers, without having to make them? Explain why it works that way."

Analysis:

STAGE 1: *Empirical arrangements only.*

There is trial-and-error only; no system is employed. Each time the child is asked, "Is that all?" he searches for another combination in response to the implication of the question, until he finally quits.

STAGE 2: *Search for a system and debut of the idea of chance.*

The child begins haphazardly but when asked, "How can you arrange them so as to be sure that's all?" he will arrange them systematically.

He counts and adds to find the total but cannot predict.

STAGE 3: *Comprehension of the system of arrangements; discovery of the law that holds even for large numbers.*

(A) The child discovers that for a number having a certain number of elements ($n = 3$ or 4) there exists the law of the square (association of an element with itself), but he does not understand the reason.

He can generalize but only at the empirical level.

(B) The reason is understood. The child will respond, "There are two different numbers, first repeated and then reversed, to give you four: 11, 22, 12, 21."

The child may be confused at first with three elements but discovers his error: "There are three different members and you can invert them, so that makes three twice, or six: 12, 13, 23; 21, 31, 32. Oh yes, then you've got each number repeated once: 11, 22, 33. Altogether there are nine." Once the error of thinking is

> discovered, the child grasps the law and applies it: "Multiply 4 × 4. There are four numbers and you can arrange them in four ways"; or, "With one numeral and three others, you can make four combinations and then do the same thing with the digit 2, etc., for sixteen in all"; or, "Each number can go with four other numbers: 1 with 1, 1 with 2, 1 with 3, 1 with 4. You can do this four times."

It is not at all unusual for eight-year olds to arrive at the *law* of the square. With the examiner prompting by saying, "With two digits you made four numbers, with three you made nine, with four you made sixteen; how many numbers can you make with five digits?" many children can give the right answer, but they cannot explain their answer satisfactorily. They recognize that the digit is multiplied by itself, but *why* this should be so they do not know. Graduate students who observe the test being given will pick up the "law of the square" and remember it for a time, but without being able to explain why the law applies. It is only as the child combines elements and arranges them in some kind of order (seriating, in the above problem) to make sure that he has the maximum, that one can eventually explain, "Each digit can go with itself once and with every other digit once." One knows this to be true because one has performed this action.

Permutation problems occur in a natural setting as well as in the laboratory. A little girl who has three blouses and three skirts that can be worn each with the other may figure out that she has available nine different outfits. A little boy playing with a toy train may be curious to see how many different combinations he can make with four different kinds of freight cars and four different kinds of passenger cars. Through such actions, the operations of combining and seriating become internalized. Eventually the child can bring into an abstract and verbal form certain methods of reasoning which were already present in his behavior at an earlier stage. Without actions, only verbalism results.

Piaget's intensive observations of his own children during the early years of their lives have given us insight into the interaction process out of which intelligent thought develops. We must not overlook in his descriptions the role played by Piaget in furthering that development. In doing the experiments, he set the stage by providing materials and stimulating interest in them. Conceivably, many (if not most) parents engage in play with their infants to the same end, thus explaining in part similarities in the genetic process among all children. But the impact of instruction upon that development has not been a concern of Piaget's; he leaves the province of pedagogy to others and stays within the already extensive domain of inquiry he has mapped out for himself.

The first papers in this section have been selected to give the student exposure to many facets of Piagetian theory. At the outset there is the paper by Piaget himself, which provides a nice introduction to his methods and to the insights they provide into children's thinking. (Inhelder, 1962, who is Piaget's chief co-worker, can be read for an overview of the genetic process according to the Genevan school.) Next, papers by Wohlwill and Lowe and Smedslund inquire into the psychological processes in the transition from non-conservation to conservation. Beilin and Franklin (1962) are also interested in conservation. They have devised an ingenious test of age and training effects but, because of space limitations, their paper could not be reprinted here. Lovell's follow-up study of the Inhelder and Piaget (1958) work on adolescent thinking is the fourth selection included. This paper will have more meaning for the student who has read the original work, but it will also be helpful to the student who has had difficulty in reading the original, for Lovell does not use the language of algebra in his report.

Other Investigations of Intellective Processes

WHETHER instruction can be separated out from development is the point raised by Vygotsky, the Russian psychologist, from whose book a chapter is included here. Russians, even more than Americans, are confident that training methods can be found to speed up developmental processes, and they are doing considerable work in the psychology of learning. Vygotsky sees instruction as playing a major role in the development of knowledge; in his study he contrasts the impact of classroom instruction upon concept development with development as it originates in the child's personal experience. Instruction, according to Vygotsky, can activate large areas of consciousness and so influence cognitive development. The paper is a very stimulating one, with fresh insights into intellective processes on every page.

Developmental processes have not been the only concern of cognitive psychologists. Some investigators have examined individual differences in cognitive functioning and have hypothesized that individuals may be characterized by a cognitive style which will affect how they approach cognitive tasks. Kagan, Moss, and Sigel (1963) have done work in this vein. Their study of longitudinal data on Fels children reveals a consistent pattern of relationships among cognitive measures for a given individual. It appears that the child develops a preferred strategy in the cognitive area. Some have a tendency to analyze and differentiate the stimulus environment, while others are "lumpers" and think in terms of categories of undifferentiated stimuli. This preferred strategy is implicated in a wide variety of behaviors.

The last two papers in this section deal with linguistic problems. Interest in the science of language is a relatively new one for child psychologists. For many years investigators concentrated on the developmental process. As a result of the work of such people as McCarthy (1954), we have some notion of how children learn to talk, the stages of language development, the vocabulary size and the forms of grammar children may be expected to have at different levels, and the influence of socioeconomic and family variables upon language development.

But there is another way in which language can be studied. We can look at the structure of a language and investigate its impact upon the child. The reader may be familiar with the work of Whorf (1956), whose thesis was that the language used in a particular culture is a shaper of ideas. We perceive the physical world in a particular way because of the linguistic system that prevails in our culture. Furthermore, we are not conscious of the phenomena of language, and so we do not realize the extent to which our ideas are shaped by it. The Hopi

Indians have one word that covers everything that flies, except birds. Thus insect, airplane, and flier are all designated by one word. We would have difficulty with such a classification system; similarly, the Eskimo would be bothered with our one word "snow" that includes falling snow, slushy snow, and hard-packed snow. Even such sacred concepts as space, time, and matter are not essential to a consistent picture of the universe. In fact, it is only by loosening the shackles of linguistic habits that the great thinkers of all times have been able to help us to see the world differently.

To the linguist, language is a code of signals, culturally derived, to transmit meanings and thus to regulate behavior. In the young child, verbal regulation of behavior is not yet operating. Verbal instruction may *initiate* behavior, but because of other conflicting factors, it does not control behavior. Luria's psychophysiological experiments in this area are particularly rewarding.

When language development is studied from the standpoint of linguistics, we get some interesting insights into how the child acquires a language *system.* Brown's work is invaluable here; in the paper co-authored with Berko, they described their attempts to find out how the child acquires parts of speech. The young child defines a hole as "to dig," while the adult gives a definition in the same part of speech as the word to be defined. *Grammatical* meaning apparently develops as the child matures, with or without the study of grammar.

REFERENCES

BEILIN, H., & FRANKLIN, IRENE C. Logical operations in area and length measurement: age and training effects. *Child Develpm.*, 1962, **33**, 607–618.

FLAVELL, J. H. *The developmental psychology of Jean Piaget*. Princeton, N.J.: Van Nostrand, 1963.

HUNT, J. McV. *Intelligence and experience.* New York: Ronald, 1961.

INHELDER, BÄRBEL. Some aspects of Piaget's genetic approach to cognition. In W. Kessen & C. Kuhlman (Eds.), Thought in the young child. *Monogr. Soc. Res. Child Develpm.*, 1962, **27**, No. 2 (Serial No. 83), 19–34.

INHELDER, BÄRBEL, & PIAGET, J. *The growth of logical thinking from childhood to adolescence.* New York: Basic Books, 1958.

KAGAN, J., MOSS, H. A., & SIGEL, I. E. Psychological significance of styles of conceptualization. In J. C. Wright & J. Kagan (Eds.), Basic cognitive processes in children. *Monogr. Soc. Res. Child Develpm.*, 1963, **28**, No. 2 (Serial No. 86), 73–112.

MCCARTHY, DOROTHEA. Language development in children. In L. Carmichael (Ed.), *Manual of child psychology.* New York: Wiley, 1954. Pp. 492–630.

PIAGET, J. *The language and thought of the child.* New York: Harcourt, Brace & World, 1926.

WHORF, B. *Language, thought and reality: selected writings.* (John B. Carroll, Ed.) Cambridge, Mass.: Technology Press (M.I.T.) and New York: Wiley, 1956.

JEAN PIAGET

How Children Form Mathematical Concepts[*]

It is a great mistake to suppose that a child acquires the notion of number and other mathematical concepts just from teaching. On the contrary, to a remarkable degree he develops them himself, independently and spontaneously. When adults try to impose mathematical concepts on a child prematurely, his learning is merely verbal; true understanding of them comes only with his mental growth.

This can easily be shown by a simple experiment. A child of five or six may readily be taught by his parents to name the numbers from 1 to 10. If 10 stones are laid in a row, he can count them correctly. But if the stones are rearranged in a more complex pattern or piled up, he no longer can count them with consistent accuracy. Although the child knows the names of the numbers, he has not yet grasped the essential idea of number: namely, that the number of objects in a group remains the same, is "conserved," no matter how they are shuffled or arranged.

On the other hand, a child of six and a half or seven often shows that he has spontaneously formed the concept of number even though he may not yet have been taught to count. Given eight red chips and eight blue chips, he will discover by one-to-one matching that the number of red is the same as the number of blue, and he will realize that the two groups remain equal in number regardless of the shape they take.

The experiment with one-to-one correspondence is very useful for investigating children's development of the number concept. Let us lay down a row of eight red chips, equally spaced about an inch apart, and ask our small subjects to take from a box of blue chips as many chips as there are on the table. Their reactions will depend on age, and we can distinguish three stages of development. A child of five or younger, on the average, will lay out blue chips to make a row exactly as long as the red row, but he will put the blue chips close together instead of spacing them. He believes the number is the same if the length of the row is the same. At the age of six, on the average, children arrive at the second stage; these children will lay a blue chip opposite each red chip and obtain the correct number. But they have not necessarily acquired the concept of number itself. If we spread the red chips, spacing out the row more loosely, the six-year-olds will think that the longer row now has more chips, though we have not changed the number. At the age of six and a half to seven, on the average, children achieve the third stage: they know that, though we close up or space out one row of chips, the number is still the same as in the other.

In a similar experiment a child is given two receptacles of identical shape and size and is asked to put beads, one at a time, into both receptacles with both hands simultaneously—a blue bead into one box with his right hand and a red bead into the other with his left hand. When he has more or less filled the two receptacles, he is asked how they compare. He is sure that both have the same number of beads. Then he is requested to pour the blue beads into a receptacle of a different size and shape. Here again we see differences in understanding according to age. The smallest children think that the number has changed: if, for instance, the beads fill the new receptacle to a higher level, they

 From *Scient. Amer.*, 1953, **189**, 74–79.

think there are more beads in it than in the original one: if to a lower level, they think there are fewer. But children near the age of seven know that the transfer has not changed the number of beads.

In short, children must grasp the principle of conservation of quantity before they can develop the concept of number. Now conservation of quantity of course is not in itself a numerical notion; rather, it is a logical concept. Thus these experiments in child psychology throw some light on the epistemology of the number concept—a subject which has been examined by many mathematicians and logicians.

The mathematicians Henri Poincaré and L. E. J. Brouwer have held that the number concept is a product of primitive intuition, preceding logical notions. The experiments just described deny this thesis, in our opinion. Bertrand Russell, on the other hand, has supported the view that number is a purely logical concept: that the idea of cardinal number derives from the logical notion of category (a number would be a category made up of equivalent categories) while the notion of ordinal number derives from the logical relationships of order. But Russell's theory does not quite fit the psychological processes as we have observed them in small children. Children at the start make no distinction between cardinal and ordinal number, and besides, the concept of cardinal number itself presupposes an order relationship. For instance, a child can build a one-to-one correspondence only if he neither forgets any of the elements nor uses the same one twice. The only way of distinguishing one unit from another is to consider it either before or after the other in time or in space, that is, in the order of enumeration.

Study of the child's discovery of spatial relationships—what may be called the child's spontaneous geometry—is no less rewarding than the investigation of his number concepts. A child's order of development in geometry seems to reverse the order of historical discovery. Scientific geometry began with the Euclidean system (concerned with figures, angles and so on), developed in the 17th century the so-called projective geometry (dealing with problems of perspective) and finally came in the 19th century to topology (describing spatial relationships in a general qualitative way—for instance, the distinction between open and closed structures, interiority and exteriority, proximity and separation). A child begins with the last: his first geometrical discoveries are topological. At the age of three he readily distinguishes between open and closed figures: if you ask him to copy a square or a triangle, he draws a closed circle; he draws a cross with two separate lines. If you show him a drawing of a large circle with a small circle inside, he is quite capable of reproducing this relationship, and he can also draw a small circle outside or attached to the edge of the large one. All this he can do before he can draw a rectangle or express the Euclidean characteristics (number of sides, angles, etc.) of a figure. Not until a considerable time after he has mastered topological relationships does he begin to develop his notions of Euclidean and projective geometry. Then he builds those simultaneously.

Curiously enough, this psychological order is much closer to modern geometry's order of deductive or axiomatic construction than the historical order of discovery was. It offers another example of the kinship between psychological construction and the logical construction of science itself.

Let us test our young subjects on projective constructions. First we set up two "fence posts" (little sticks stuck in bases of modeling clay) some 15 inches apart and ask the child to place other posts in a straight line between them. The youngest children (under the age of four) proceed to plant one post next to another, forming a more or less wavy line. Their approach is topological: the elements are joined by the simple relationship of proximity rather than by projection of a line as such. At the next stage, beyond the age of four, the child may form a straight fence if the two end posts parallel the edge of the table, or if there is some other straight line to guide him. If the end posts are diagonally across the table, he may start building the line parallel to the table's edge and then change direction and form a curve to reach the second post. Occasionally a youngster may make a straight line, but he does so only by trial-and-error and not by system.

At the age of seven years, on the average, a child can build a straight fence consistently in any direction across the table, and he will check the straightness of the line by shutting one eye and sighting along it, as a gardener lines up bean poles. Here we have the essence of the projective concept; the line is still a topological line, but the child has grasped that the projective relationship depends on the angle of vision, or point of view.

One can proceed to study this with other experiments. For instance, you stand a doll on a table and place before it an object oriented in a certain direction: a pencil lying crosswise, diagonally or lengthwise with respect to the doll's line of vision, or a watch lying flat on the table or standing up. Then you ask the child to draw the doll's view of the object, or, better still, ask him to choose from two or three drawings the one that represents the doll's point of view. Not until the age of about seven or eight can a child deduce correctly the doll's angle of vision.

A similar experiment testing the same point yields the same conclusions. Objects of different shapes are placed in various positions between a light and a screen, and the child is asked to predict the shape of the shadow the object will cast on the screen.

Ability to coordinate different perspectives does not come until the age of 9 or 10. This is illustrated by an experiment I suggested some time ago to my collaborator Dr. Edith Meyer. The experimenter sits at a table opposite the child, and between the child and herself she places a cardboard range of mountains. The two see the range from opposite perspectives. The child is then asked to select from several drawings the ones that picture both his own and the opposite person's views of the mountain range. Naturally the youngest children can pick out only the picture that corresponds to their own view; they imagine that all the points of view are like their own. What is more interesting, if the child changes places with the experimenter and sees the mountains from the other side, he now thinks that his new view is the only correct one; he cannot reconstruct the point of view that was his own just a little while before. This is a clear example of the egocentricity so characteristic of children—the primitive reasoning which prevents them from understanding that there may be more than one point of view.

It takes a considerable evolution for children to come, at around the age of 9 or 10, to the ability to distinguish between and coordinate the different possible perspectives. At this stage they can grasp projective space in its concrete or practical form, but naturally not in its theoretical aspects.

At the same time the child forms the concept of projective space, he also constructs Euclidean space; the two kinds of construction are based upon one another. For example, in lining up a straight row of fence posts he may not only use the sighting method but may line up his hands parallel to each other to give him the direction. That is, he is applying the concept of conservation of direction, which is a Euclidean principle. Here is another illustration of the fact that children form mathematical notions on a qualitative or logical basis.

The conservation principle arises in various forms. There is first the conservation of length. If you place a block on another of the same length and then push one block so that its end projects beyond the other, a child under six will suppose that the two blocks are no longer of equal length. Not until near the age of seven, on the average, does the child understand that what is gained at one end of the block is lost at the other. He arrives at this concept of the conservation of length, be it noted, by a process of logic.

Experiments on a child's discovery of the conservation of distance are especially illuminating. Between two small toy trees standing apart from each other on a table you place a wall formed of a block or a thick piece of cardboard, and you ask the child (in his own language, of course) whether the trees are still the same distance apart. The smallest children think the distance has changed; they are simply unable to add up two parts of a distance to a total distance. Children of five or six believe the distance has been reduced, claiming that the width of the wall does not count as distance; in other words, a filled-up space does not have the same value as an empty space. Only near the age of seven do children come to the realization that intervening objects do not change the distance.

However you test them, you find the same thing true: children do not appreciate the principle of conservation of length or surface until, somewhere around the age of seven, they discover the reversibility that shows the original quantity has remained the same (*e.g.*, the realignment of equal-length blocks, the removal of the wall, and so on). Thus the discovery of logical relationships is a prerequisite to the construction of geometrical concepts, as it is in the formation of the concept of number.

This applies to measurement itself, which is only a derived concept. It is interesting to study how children spontaneously learn to measure. One of my collaborators, Dr. Inhelder, and I have made the following experiment: We show the child a tower of blocks on a table and ask him to build a second tower of the same height on another table (lower or higher than the first) with blocks of a different size. Naturally we provide the child with all the necessary measuring tools. Children's attempts to deal with this problem go through a fascinating evolution. The youngest children build up the second tower to the same visual level as the first, without worrying about the difference in height of the tables. They compare the towers by stepping back and sighting them. At a slightly more advanced stage a child lays a long rod across the tops of the two towers to make sure that they are level. Somewhat later he notices that the base of his tower is not at the same level as the model's. He then wants to place his tower next to the model on the same table to compare them. Reminded that the rules of the game forbid him to move his tower, he begins to look around for a measuring standard. Interestingly enough, the first that comes to his mind is his own body. He puts one hand on top of his tower and the other at its base, and then, trying to keep his hands the same distance apart, he moves over to the other tower to compare it. Children of about the age of six often carry out this work in a most assured manner, as if their hands could not change position on the way! Soon they discover that the method is not reliable, and then they resort to reference points on the body. The child will line up his shoulder with the top of his tower, mark the spot opposite the base on his thigh with his hand and walk over to the model to see whether the distance is the same.

Eventually the idea of an independent measuring tool occurs to the child. His first attempt in this direction is likely to be the building of a third tower next to and the same height as the one he has already erected. Having built it, he moves it over to the first table and matches it against the model; this is allowed by the rules. The child's arrival at this stage presupposes a process of logical reasoning. If we call the model tower A, the second tower C and the movable tower B, the child has reasoned that $B = C$ and $B = A$, therefore $A = C$.

Later the child replaces the third tower with a rod, but at first the rod must be just the same length as the height of the tower to be measured. He then conceives the idea of using a longer rod and marking the tower height on it with his finger. Finally, and this is the beginning of true measurement, he realizes that he can use a shorter rod and measure the height of the tower by applying the rod a certain number of times up the side.

The last discovery involves two new operations of logic. The first is the process of division which permits the child to conceive that the whole is composed of a number of parts added together. The second is the displacement, or substitution, which enables him to apply one part upon others and thus to build a system of units. One may therefore say that measurement is a synthesis of division into parts and of substitution, just as number is a synthesis of the inclusion of categories and of serial order. But measurement develops later than the number concept, because it is more difficult to divide a continuous whole into interchangeable units than to enumerate elements which are already separate.

To study measurement in two dimensions, we give the child a large sheet of paper with a pencil dot on it and ask him to put a dot in the same position on another sheet of the same size. He may use rods, strips of paper, strings, rulers or any other measuring tools he needs. The youngest subjects are satisfied to make a visual approximation, using no tools. Later a child applies a measuring tool, but he measures only the distance of the point from the side or bottom edge of the paper and is surprised that this single measurement does not give him the correct position. Then he measures the distance of the point from a corner of the paper, trying to keep the same slant (angle) when he applies the ruler to his own sheet. Finally, at about the age of eight or nine, he discovers that he must break up the measurement into two operations: the horizontal distance from a side edge and the perpendicular distance from the bottom or top edge. Similar experiments with a bead in a box show that a child discovers how to make three-dimensional measurements at about the same age.

Measurement in two or three dimensions brings us to the central idea of Euclidean space, namely the axes of coordinates—a system founded on the horizontality or verticality of physical objects. It may seem that even a baby should grasp these concepts, for after all it can distinguish between the upright and lying-down positions. But actually the representation of vertical and horizontal lines brings up quite another problem from this subjective awareness of postural space. Dr. Inhelder and I have studied it with the following experiments: Using a jar half-filled with colored water, we ask our young subjects to predict what level the water will take when the jar is tipped one way or another. Not until the age of nine, on the average, does a child grasp the idea of horizontality and predict correctly. Similar experiments with a plumb line or a toy sailboat with a tall mast demonstrate that comprehension of verticality comes at about the same time. The child's tardiness in acquiring these concepts is not really surprising, for they require not only a grasp of the internal relationships of an object but also reference to external elements (*e.g.*, a table or the floor or walls of the room).

When a child has discovered how to construct these coordinated axes by reference to natural objects, which he does at about the same time that he conceives the coordination of perspectives, he has completed his conception of how to represent space. By that time he has developed his fundamental mathematical concepts, which spring spontaneously from his own logical operations.

The experiments I have described, simple as they are, have been surprisingly fruitful and have brought to light many unexpected facts. These facts are illuminating from the psychological and pedagogical points of view; more than that, they teach us a number of lessons about human knowledge in general.

JOACHIM F. WOHLWILL *and* ROLAND C. LOWE

*Experimental Analysis of the Development of the Conservation of Number**

IN PIAGET's theory of intellectual development (1950), a central role is assigned to the child's conceptualization of the principle of "conservation," i.e., his realization of the principle that a particular dimension of an object may remain invariant under changes in other, irrelevant aspects of the situation. For instance, children who lack conservation will assert that the relative weight of two objects has changed when the shape of one of them is altered or that numerical equality between two collections of objects no longer holds following a change in the length over which they extend. This phenomenon, which has been demonstrated for a variety of other dimensions, including those of volume, area and length, represents, according to Piaget, a manifestation of the immature level of functioning of the child's mental processes and of their failure to conform to the operational structures of logical thought.

Although Piaget has described some of the precursors of this notion of conservation in children who have not yet attained this level, little is known thus far about the specific ways in which the transition from lack of conservation to the presence of conservation takes place. It is apparent, however, that an adequate explanation of this problem ultimately requires a clearer understanding of the psychological processes at work in this transition phase.

One approach to this goal is to expose children presumed to be slightly below the age of onset of conservation to selected, systematically manipulated learning experiences, designed to call into play different factors believed to be important in the development of conservation. Any differential changes in the children's tendency to give conservation responses should then reflect the role played by the particular factors manipulated. At the same time, a more detailed examination of the interrelationship among different tasks involving conservation and closely related concepts should likewise extend our understanding of the nature of this problem.

The domain of number lends itself particularly well to the investigation of the development of conservation, for several reasons. First of all, recent empirical work (Dodwell, 1960; Elkind, 1961; Wohlwill, 1960) has given strong support to the notion that the attainment of the level of conservation marks a clearly defined stage in the formation of the number concept. Secondly, in this domain the problem of conservation can be readily related to development in other aspects of the number concept (e.g., counting, arithmetical skills, etc.), rather than constituting the somewhat isolated, *sui generis* problem which conservation appears to represent for such dimensions as weight or volume. Thirdly, and most important, the number dimension occupies a unique position in regard to the question of conservation, insofar as the number of elements contained in a particular collection is exactly identifiable by the corresponding integer; by the same token, the *fact* of conservation—i.e., that the number of a collection remains invariant under changes in the spatial arrangement of its elements—is readily verifiable, through the operation of counting. This feature creates an opportunity for

* REPRINTED by permission of the authors and the Society for Research in Child Development from *Child Develpm.*, 1962, 33, 153–167.

assessing the role of symbolic, mediational processes, as well as of reinforcement, in the development of conservation.

This very uniqueness of the number dimension represents of course a potential limitation, as regards the applicability of the results to the problem of conservation in general. It is of considerable interest, therefore, that a rather similar investigation of the acquisition of the conservation of weight has simultaneously been carried out by Smedslund (1961); its results will thus provide us with a valuable basis for comparison, as we will note in the discussion section.

THREE ALTERNATIVE THEORETICAL VIEWS OF NUMBER CONSERVATION

If one looks closely at the problem confronting the child in the conservation situation, several different interpretations of the acquisition of this principle suggest themselves. We may label these alternatives the reinforcement hypothesis, the differentiation hypothesis, and the inference hypothesis.

The *reinforcement hypothesis* would propose that, as a child obtains increasing experience in counting numerical collections of different types and in different arrangements, he gradually learns that alterations in the perceptual dimensions of a set do not change its number, i.e., that the same number is obtained from counting the set after as before such a change. Accordingly, systematic reinforced practice in counting rows of elements prior and subsequent to changes in the length of the rows should promote conservation.

The *differentiation* hypothesis would interpret lack of conservation in the young child as a response to an irrelevant but highly visible cue (length) which typically shows substantial correlation with that of number. The child thus has to learn to differentiate the dimension of number from this irrelevant cue. Repeated experience designed to neutralize the cue of length, and thus to weaken the association between it and the dimension of number in the child's thinking, should be expected, then, to facilitate conservation responses.

The *inference* hypothesis, finally, is based in part on Piaget's own analysis of the role of learning in the development of logical operations (1959). Piaget maintains that experiential factors can only become effective, in this realm of development, to the extent that [they build] on the child's previously developed structures of thought, as through the activation of a reasoning process prior to, but logically related to the one to be developed. In the case of conservation, one possible implication might be that by dint of cumulative exposure to the effects of adding an element to a collection, or subtracting one from it, the child may be led to *infer* conservation as the result of a change involving neither addition nor subtraction. This implication is supported, incidentally, by the explanations frequently voiced by children who admit conservation, e.g., "it's still the same, because you haven't taken any away."

Prior work by the senior author also bears on this last alternative. First, in the course of a sequential analysis of the development of the number concept (Wohlwill, 1960), it was found that success on tasks involving simple addition and subtraction not only regularly preceded success on a task embodying the principle of conservation, but appeared, in a certain number of subjects, to lead to the emergence of conservation responses. In a subsequent pilot study (Wohlwill, 1959), it was found, furthermore, that subjects given a limited set of trials involving addition and subtraction subsequently made more conservation responses than subjects given equivalent training on conservation, though the difference did not reach significance.

The results of this pilot study suggested the possibility of a more extended investigation of the development of the conservation of number, by bringing to bear each of the abovementioned theoretical interpretations in the context of a small-scale learning experiment and determining the effectiveness of the various conditions of learning in bringing about conservation, both in a limited and a generalized sense. This is the main aim of the study to be reported, a subsidiary purpose being to provide information regarding the cross-situational generality of number conservation and its relationship to other types of number skills.

Method

THE experiment was conducted in two sessions over two successive days (except for two *S*s, for whom the interval between sessions was two and six days, respectively). The general design called for (a) a predominantly verbal pretest, partly of a diagnostic character, to reveal *S*'s ability to deal with number concepts, and partly dealing specifically with conservation; (b) a "nonverbal" test of conservation given in the form of a series of multiple-choice trials; (c) a training series on tasks presumed to be related to number conservation; and finally (d) a repetition of both the nonverbal and verbal tests of conservation to provide a measure of learning or change with respect to the understanding of this notion. This design is summarized in TABLE 1.

TABLE 1. *Design of the study*

ORDER	FIRST DAY	ORDER	SECOND DAY
1.	Diagnostic Questions	1.	Training Series (trials 10 to 18)
2.	Verbal Conservation Pretest	2.	Nonverbal Conservation Posttest
3.	Pretraining in Number Matching	3.	Verbal Conservation Posttest
4.	Nonverbal Conservation Pretest		
5.	Training Series (trials 1 to 9)		

PROCEDURE

Diagnostic Questions

1. *Number Production.* *S* was shown a pile of red poker chips and was told, "Give me six of them."

2. *Number Equivalence.* *E* laid out a row of seven red chips. *S* was told, "Put down just as many of your chips over here (indicating an imaginary row paralleling *E*'s row), as I have here."

3. *Number vs. Length.* *E* laid out a row of six blue chips extending beyond the limits of his own row of seven red chips (*S*'s row being longer than *E*'s). *S* was asked, "Who has more chips, you or I?" If he answered that he had more, but without having counted the chips, he was asked, "How do you know?"

These three questions concerned, respectively, the child's ability to (a) reproduce a particular cardinal number, (b) establish a relationship of numerical equivalence between two collections, and (c) respond to the dimension of number independent of irrelevant perceptual cues (e.g., length).

Verbal Conservation Pretest

4. Two rows of seven chips each, one blue and the other red, were placed parallel to each other so that both rows were of the same length, and the chips in one row were directly opposite those in the other. *S* was asked, "Who has more chips, you or I?" This question, hereafter referred to as Q, was repeated for all the items in this part.

5a. *E* then extended the red row in both directions to a length about twice that of the blue row. (Q)

5b. The red row was subdivided into two rows of four and three chips placed parallel to *S*'s blue row. (Q)

5c. The red chips were placed in a vertical pile in front of the blue row. (Q)

5d. The red chips were inserted into an opaque tube. (Q)

Question 4 served chiefly a preparatory function, i.e., to set up the following questions of conservation. Question 5a represented the main criterion of number conservation, while 5b to 5d indicate the generalizability of conservation. Accordingly, questions 5a to 5d were cumulative: if a *S* did not assert equality at any point, the remaining questions were omitted.

6. Questions 4 and 5a were repeated with 12 chips in each row instead of seven.

The suggestive nature of the questions (Q) used above ("Who has more chips, you or I?") requires comment. It should be noted that its initial use (in question 4) is in a situation where perceptual cues mitigate against the child's following the suggestion of inequality implicit in the question: the matched rows of chips afford a strong cue for direct perception of equivalence.[1] Second, the suggestion applied both in the pre- and the posttests and thus may be presumed to have played a constant role on both occasions.

Pretraining in Number Matching • The apparatus used here, shown in FIGURE 1, consisted of an upright panel containing three windows which had the numerals 6, 7, 8 inscribed on them from left to right. The *Ss* were told they were going to play a game,

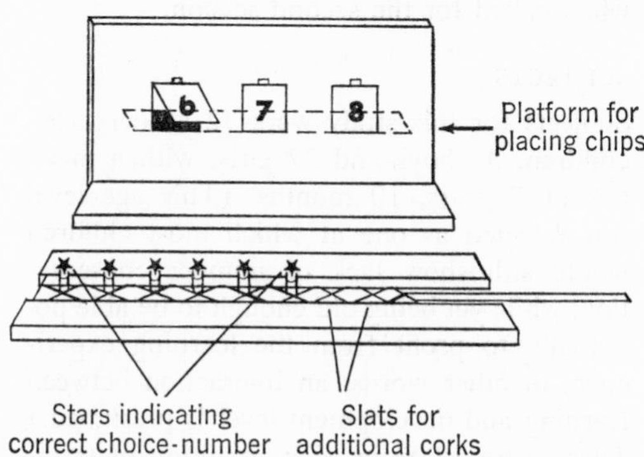

FIGURE 1

Apparatus for nonverbal conservation and training trials, showing device for presenting variable-length rows of sample numbers and display-board for choice numbers.

1 All but 14 of the *Ss* did in fact resist *E*'s suggestion, usually through some such answer as "we both do" or "you and me." The 14 *Ss* who failed to do so were made to count the two rows, whereupon the question was again put to them. If *S* persisted in following the suggestion of inequality, *E* confronted them with the results of their counting and, if necessary, told him outright "So we both have the same, don't we?" This procedure was necessary in order to proceed to the following part, where *S*'s prior knowledge of the equivalence of the two rows had to be presupposed.

in which they would find a chip hidden behind one of the windows, and that the object of the game was to get as many chips as they could. For the pretraining phase, the procedure consisted in presenting singly a series of six 5 by 5 in. cards showing six, seven, or eight colored stars arranged in simple configurations. On each trial a colored chip was hidden behind the corresponding window. *S* was informed that the number of stars on the card would tell him behind which window the chip was hidden and urged to count the stars. When *S* opened the correct window, he was instructed to remove the chip and place it onto a board at his side. He was told to fill up the board with chips; if he found "a lot" of them, he would on the following day receive a toy. The purpose of this series was to create a set in the child to respond to number, as well as to familiarize *Ss* with the specific numbers shown. A correction procedure was used which involved having *Ss* correct any mistakes made in counting the stars and guiding *S* to the correct window when, as occasionally happened, a *S* counted correctly but made an incorrect choice.

Nonverbal Conservation Pretest • This series consisted of three two-phase trials. *Ss* were presented with a row of colored stars, either six, seven, or eight in number, mounted on a set of corks which rested on a series of connected scissors-like slats. This apparatus, depicted in FIGURE 1, permitted lengthening or shortening the row while preserving the straight-line arrangement. *E* told *S* that he was to count the stars in order to find the chip behind the correct window. Following *S*'s initial response, he was made to return the chip to *E*, who replaced it behind the same window, and then, depending on the trial, either extended or shortened the row of stars. *S* was allowed to count only on the first phase; he thus had to find the correct window on the second phase on the basis of the knowledge gained in the first and in the face of the perceptual changes in the row of stars.

Training • There were four conditions of training: Reinforced Practice, Addition and

Subtraction, Dissociation, and Control. The three experimental conditions were designed to relate, respectively, to the reinforcement, inference, and differentiation hypotheses presented in the introduction. Each training series consisted of 18 trials, broken up into two sets of nine which were administered on successive days. The apparatus used was the same as in the conservation pretest trials.

a. *Reinforced Practice* (RP). The procedure here was the same as for the preceding conservation trials, with this modification: if *S* made an incorrect response on the second phase of the trial, he was told to count the stars, so as to find out which window he should have chosen. *E* then exposed the chip behind that window but did not allow *S* to remove the chip.

b. *Addition and Subtraction* (A&S). These trials were similar to the conservation trials, except that on two-thirds of the trials, following the *S*'s initial response after counting, *E* either added or subtracted a star at the end of the row before changing its length. The remaining third of the series consisted of straight conservation trials which were interspersed with the A&S trials.

c. *Dissociation* (Diss.). Unlike the above, these were single-phase trials, with the length of the row varying from one trial to the next over a range of four times the smallest length. *S* was urged to count the stars and open the corresponding window; if correct, he received the chip. Over the series of trials each number of stars appeared equally often at each of the different settings of length.

d. *Control.* This series of trials consisted likewise of single-phase trials as in the Dissociation condition, but the length of the row remained fixed throughout at its minimum spread.

Posttests • The nonverbal conservation posttest, consisting of three conservation trials as in the pretest, followed immediately upon the completion of the training trials. (For *S*s in groups Diss. and Control, *E* prefaced these trials with a remark to the effect that they would again have to find the chips twice in a row, the second time without counting.) Any *S* responding correctly on the last trial of this posttest was asked: "How did you know where to look for the chip that time?"

The *verbal* conservation posttest, consisting of a repetition of questions 4 through 6 as given in the pretest, concluded the experimental session.

At the end of the second session, each child was shown a variety of dime-store toys from which he picked one to take back with him as his "prize." Altogether, each of the sessions lasted about 20 to 25 minutes per child. The children's level of attention and motivation appeared to have remained high throughout these sessions, the "game" aspect of the situation apparently having proved effective in capturing their interest. This was reflected in their universal eagerness to return to it when called for the second session.

SUBJECTS

Subjects for this study were 72 kindergarten children, 35 boys and 37 girls, with a mean CA of 5 years, 10 months. (This age level was selected as one at which most children would still show lack of number conservation, while yet being old enough to be able potentially to profit from the learning experience; in other words, an interaction between learning and development level is presumed.) There were 18 *S*s in each condition of training, *S*s being assigned to their group according to a predetermined order. The four subgroups were closely matched as to their mean CA. (The range of the means was one month.)

The children were enrolled in the kindergarten classes of three public schools in Worcester, Massachusetts, located in predominantly lower-middle-class neighborhoods. They thus had been and were being exposed to a variety of activities in the area of number skills, consisting mainly of counting, number-matching, and identifying simple numerals.[2]

2 The authors are greatly indebted to the principals and teachers of the Freeland, Columbus Park and Woodland Elementary Schools in Worcester, Massachusetts, for their splendid cooperation in providing subjects and facilities for this investigation. We also wish to acknowledge the assistance of the Worcester Country Day School in connection with a pilot study from which this investigation evolved.

Results

THE presentation of the results of the experiment is divided into three sections: the verbal pretest, including the diagnostic and verbal conservation questions; the learning of nonverbal conservation; and the transfer of training to the verbal posttest.

Verbal Pretest • Considering first the diagnostic questions, only one of the 72 *S*s failed question 1, while four failed question 2. On question 3, however, only 20 *S*s gave a correct response (i.e., based on counting the chips either before or in justification of their judgments). These results show that the *S*s had adequate facility in counting and dealing with numbers symbolically in simple situations, such as producing a required number of elements and in matching two groups for number. Their success on these two tasks, however, contrasted sharply with their performance on question 3 where the task required the abstraction of number as independent from certain irrelevant perceptual cues. It should be noted that, since this question followed question 2 without a break, some *S*s may have seen *E* take a chip from his row in setting up question 3. Thus, some of the correct responses may have been facilitated by this circumstance. In fact, nine *S*s explicitly based their answers on this cue. (Control over this factor in a subsequent study did indeed result in lowering still further the number of *S*s succeeding on this question, so as to equate it in difficulty with the conservation question, 5a.)

On the verbal conservation items, only nine of the 72 *S*s answered correctly on question 5a. A breakdown of the incorrect responses shows that 41 *S*s responded to the length of the rows, while 22 responded to the density of the elements. This tendency to regard the longer row as more numerous was also found on question 3 of the diagnostic questions.

As for the generality of the *S*s' concept of number conservation, of the nine *S*s who succeeded on question 5a, six extended their conservation to 5b, five to 5c, and four to 5d. On question 6, on the other hand, involving conservation for 12 elements, seven of these *S*s showed conservation, in addition to one who had not responded correctly on question 5a. Thus, when conditions were qualitatively different, generalization was somewhat lower than it was when the new situation differed only in a quantitative way.

Nonverbal Conservation Learning • TABLE 2 summarizes the performance of each group on the verbal and nonverbal tests of conservation, before and after the learning series.

An analysis of variance revealed no significant differences among training groups with respect to learning of nonverbal conservation ($F = 1.73$; $p > .05$ for 3 and 68 *df*). However, the mean over-all difference scores differed significantly from 0 ($t = 3.95$; $p < .01$), showing that for the total group as a whole conservation did increase from pre- to posttest.

A comparison between the responses of the A&S and RP groups on the conservation trials of their respective training series shows that the former *S*s were correct on 48 per cent of their trials, while the latter were correct on 47 per cent. It will be recalled that only six conservation trials were given in the A&S

TABLE 2. *Performance on conservation before and after training*

Condition of Training	VERBAL CONSERVATION *			NONVERBAL CONSERVATION †		
	Pretest	*Posttest*	*Net Change*	*Pretest*	*Posttest*	*Net Change*
A&S	1	3	+2	1.05	1.77	+.72
RP	2	3	+1	1.22	1.50	+.28
Diss.	4	2	−2	1.05	1.16	+.11
Control	2	4	+2	1.44	1.96	+.52

* Number of Ss giving correct responses on question 5a.
† Mean correct responses out of three trials.

series, while the RP series consisted wholly of 18 conservation trials for which, in addition, a correction procedure was used. Hence, direct training on conservation was no more effective than the more intermittent practice afforded on the A&S trials.

It was also found that the A&S group had greater success on the A&S trials than on the straight conservation trials: for the former, 59 per cent of the responses were correct, as compared to the 48 per cent for the conservation trials. This finding, which is consistent with the results of previous research (Wohlwill, 1960), represents of course a prerequisite for the use of the A&S trials as a training experience.

The training trials under the control and dissociation condition, which involved only rote counting, were quite easy for these *S*s: a near perfect performance was the norm.

Transfer of Training to Verbal Posttest • With respect to verbal conservation, there were very few changes in any group. The number of *S*s showing conservation of number on the pretest was nine, while 12 *S*s showed it on the posttest. Two *S*s changed to conservation from the A&S group, two from the Control group, and one from the RP group. Two *S*s, in the Diss. group, who had shown conservation on the pretest, failed to do so on the posttest (cf. TABLE 2).

It is interesting to note that, whereas on the pretest of verbal conservation only four of the nine *S*s having conservation showed perfect extension of this concept on items 5b through 5d, on the posttest nine of the 12 *S*s showing conservation did show this extension, the remaining three *S*s belonging to the group of five who had not shown conservation on the pretest. This seems to indicate the unstable nature of the *S*s' conservation, as acquired in this situation.

Of the 12 *S*s showing conservation on question 5a of the posttest, 11 again showed conservation for 12 elements (question 6).

Discussion

IN THIS section we will consider some of the more specific implications of the results for the nonverbal conservation learning and for the transfer to the verbal test, leaving until a later section certain more general conclusions suggested by this investigation.

Nonverbal conservation learning. As regards the "learning" of conservation within the limited context of the training trials, a significant amount of improvement from pre- to posttest did take place for the group as a whole, but the lack of significant differential effects due to the conditions of training and the fact that the Control group gained more than either the Reinforced Practice or the Dissociation groups clearly prevents us from attributing beneficial effects to any specific learning condition.

The failure of the RP group to outperform the others nevertheless deserves comment. It had actually been anticipated that this group, which received essentially one continuous series of conservation trials, would as a result of this extended practice show the greatest amount of learning from pre- to posttest, although such learning might not necessarily transfer to the verbal posttest. The contrary results bear out the ineffectiveness of continued reinforced practice in bringing about conservation responses, even of a purely empirical sort (i.e., "pick the window where the chip was before"), which the above-mentioned pilot study (Wohlwill, 1959) had already hinted at in a much shorter training series. Whether a still more extended series than that used in the present study might have yielded a greater amount of learning remains an open question, of course.

The greatest amount of improvement from the pre- to the posttest trials, on the other hand, took place in the A&S group, exposed to 12 addition and subtraction trials, set off against six conservation trials; these results are thus at least consistent with the possible role of a process of inference (i.e., conservation as the end-product of changes involving neither addition nor subtraction) to which the previous studies (Wohlwill, 1959, 1960) had pointed.[3]

3 It is worth noting that in a subsequent study, modeled closely after the present one, training with addition and subtraction again resulted in the greatest amount of improvement in (nonverbal) conservation,

Finally, as regards the virtual absence of learning in the Dissociation group, it might be suggested, in retrospect, that the very act of counting the stars interfered with directing the child's attention to the cue of length, which the condition was designed to neutralize. If so, no improvement on the conservation trials, based on explicit disregard of the biasing cue of length, would result.

Transfer to verbal conservation questions. Perhaps the major finding of the study is that none of the above procedures proved in any way effective in leading to an understanding of the principle of number conservation, such as the verbal posttest demanded. For instance, over the four training groups combined, a total of 10 *S*s shifted from zero or one conservation responses on the nonverbal pretest to three on the posttest, yet these shifts did not bring with them a single change to conservation on the verbal posttest.

In explanation for this failure of the nonverbal conservation learning to transfer to the verbal posttest, one might suggest that the nonverbal learning situation favored the development of an essentially empirical rule, i.e., "the correct number remains the same as before after *E* shortens or lengthens the row," or simply "look for the chip behind the window where the chip was just previously." If this were the case, little if any transfer to the very different situation confronting the child in the verbal conservation questions would be expected. The verbalizations elicited from those *S*s who made a correct response on the last posttest conservation trial lend some support to this argument: many of the *S*s actually gave no meaningful explanation for their choice at all (e.g., "I just knew," or "I thought hard about the stars"), while most of the rest responded in such terms as "It was there before."

Interestingly enough, Smedslund (1961), on the basis of his work on the learning of the conservation of weight, similarly argues for the very limited, nonconceptual nature of such learning. In his study, *S*s were exposed to an extended series of judgments of the relative weight of two masses of plasticine, before and after one of these was deformed in shape; each judgment was reinforced by weighing the two objects on a balance. While *S*s did learn to anticipate correctly the conservation of weight of the deformed object, the author feels that this learning was mainly that of an empirical fact, rather than of a logical principle, as shown both in the kind of explanations offered by the children, and in the lack of transfer of the learning to problems embodying logically equivalent principles (e.g., transitivity relationships).[4] Parenthetically, it is worth noting that in Smedslund's study a training procedure embodying addition and subtraction of matter, in a manner somewhat analogous to that of our A&S condition, yielded nearly as much learning as continued practice on conservation problems.

There remains, however, an alternative interpretation of our results. It is based on a major difference between the nonverbal and verbal tests of conservation, which might itself have accounted for the lack of transfer observed: while the nonverbal test involved a match between a given collection of elements and the corresponding, symbolically indicated number, the verbal test entailed rather the equivalence of the numerosity of two collections of elements. Thus, it is conceivable that the children did in fact learn, in their

though the superiority over the control group still failed to be significant. In other respects, too, this study, in which the learning series was increased to 24 trials and the pre- and posttests of conservation to six trials each, yielded results which were closely comparable to those reported here.

4 Perhaps more convincing evidence on this point comes from an ingenious "extinction" procedure which Smedslund (personal communication) has most recently utilized. This consisted in confronting *S*s with apparent nonconservation, the weight of the deformed object being altered by surreptitiously adding or removing a small amount of plasticine. Under these circumstances *S*s who had acquired conservation through their learning experience readily acceded to the lack of conservation which they seemed to be witnessing, i.e., abandoned their recently "learned" conservation. In contrast, *S*s who had developed conservation spontaneously tended to invent explanations in order to reconcile this apparent contradiction, such as "we must have lost something on the floor."

Since the preparation of this paper portions of Smedslund's work (including the material of the personal communication referred to in the previous paragraph) have appeared in print (1961). (Additional papers in this series, to be published in the same journal, are in press as of this writing.)

nonverbal training, that the *absolute* number of elements remained unchanged, without transferring this principle to the *relative* number of elements in two collections, in the verbal test. Implausible as this possibility may seem to a sophisticated adult, it is borne out by the total inefficacy of asking the children to count the two collections after a nonconservation response on the verbal posttest: of 23 *S*s who were asked to do so, 19 persevered in their nonconservation responses when the question was repeated, immediately after ascertaining that there were seven chips in each row. Most recently, furthermore, Gréco (1962) has obtained clear evidence that children may show conservation in the first or absolute sense, without showing it in the second or relative sense.

Finally, the use of nonverbal methods in the investigation of children's thinking deserves brief comment. While the ineffectiveness of the nonverbal training procedures in our study may seem to cast doubt on the fruitlessness of such methods, they have been used to good advantage in several other recent studies (Braine, 1959; Wohlwill, 1960); moreover, the pitfalls of the verbal interrogation approach, at least as used by Piaget, have been persuasively analyzed (Berko & Brown, 1960, pp. 536f; Braine, 1959).[5] Perhaps the central point is that it is incumbent on those applying nonverbal methods to determine, by varied and appropriate transfer tests, the breadth and depth of the child's understanding of the principles or concepts in question —a point which appears of special relevance to the application of automatic teaching methods to instruction in this and similar areas.

Conclusions

ALTHOUGH the predominantly negative outcome of this investigation does not allow us to give any definitive answer to the question posed at the outset, concerning the mechanisms involved in the child's acquisition of the concept of the conservation of number, a few general conclusions regarding this problem may be permissible.

First, the strong tendency of the children in this investigation to respond on the basis of differences in length in making numerical comparisons between two collections, even without the element of perceptual *change* introduced in the conservation situation (cf. question 3), lends some weight to the interpretation of lack of conservation as a failure to differentiate number from irrelevant perceptual cues, pointing to an aspect of the problem which appears to have received insufficient attention in Piaget's theoretical account of conservation.

Second, the consistent tendency across several studies for the A&S conditions to yield the most improvement in nonverbal conservation suggests that a process of inference may be operative in the development of number-conservation, even if this inference may be too limited in scope to lead to a generalized understanding of the principle. In view of the fact that children typically receive considerable experience in simple addition and subtraction in the very time period in which conservation generally appears (i.e., in late kindergarten and early first grade), this factor merits further attention.

Third, our investigation highlights the considerable gap separating the ability to *enumerate* collections by counting from a true understanding of the number concept, as it is reflected in the principle of conservation. In this respect the present results are entirely in agreement with those obtained in previous work on the development of the number concept (Dodwell, 1960; Wohlwill, 1960). Furthermore, even repeated identification of a collection with a particular number symbol, independent of length, appears to be relatively ineffective in bringing about conservation, thus raising the question of the adequacy of a mediation-theory approach to this particular aspect of concept formation.

In a more positive vein, two suggestions for

5 Relevant in this connection is a study most recently reported by Yost, Siegel, and McMichael (1961), demonstrating considerable positive transfer from a nonverbal presentation of a probability-relationship problem to the corresponding verbal version of this problem as used by Piaget. These authors likewise found that by their nonverbal procedures the problem could be dealt with successfully at a much earlier age than Piaget had found, thus confirming the similar findings of Braine (1959).

future attacks on this problem might be offered. The first is to construct a set of learning experiences which would not only be more extended but, more important, cover a wider variety of situations (i.e., stimulus materials, configurations, specific numbers involved, etc.). This would be in line with Harlow's (1951) emphasis on *generalized* experience as a prerequisite for the learning of broad concepts and principles in primates as well as in man. It is plausible to suppose, in fact, that it is precisely such generalized experience—in the classroom, at play, and in other everyday activities of children of this age level—which represents the basis for the seemingly spontaneous appearance of conservation in the child.

The second suggestion is to undertake a thorough, intensive analysis of the ontogenesis of conservation in a selected number of children followed longitudinally. Special attention might be paid to the types of explanations given by the child at various stages, as well as to the stability and generalizability of conservation responses once they appear. Inhelder and Noelting, at the University of Geneva, have in fact already launched such a longitudinal project, with preliminary results that appear promising (cf. 1957).

Summary

THIS study represents an attempt to determine more specifically the nature of the processes at work in the development of the notion of the conservation of number (invariance of number under changes in length or configuration of a collection), as studied by Piaget. The investigation was in the form of a nonverbal matching-from-sample type learning experiment, preceded and followed by verbal questions to measure the child's understanding of the conservation principle. There were four conditions of training, involving respectively the role of reinforced practice on conservation, of dissociation of biasing perceptual cues, and of inferential mechanisms based on the recognition of the effects of addition and subtraction of elements; a control group was also included. Subjects were 72 kindergarten-age children.

The results indicate an over-all increase in nonverbal conservation responses from a pre- to a posttest, within the limited context of the learning task, but they show no significant differences attributable to the conditions of training. Transfer of conservation learning to the verbal posttest was negligible under all conditions, indicating that whatever learning may have taken place was of a rather restricted type, representing perhaps more the formation of an empirical rule than the understanding of a general principle.

These results, together with additional findings pertaining to the relationship of certain number skills to conservation, are discussed in terms of their implications for the problem of the development of conservation.

REFERENCES

BERKO, JEAN, & BROWN, R. Psycholinguistic research methods. In P. H. Mussen (Ed.), *Handbook of research methods in child development.* New York: Wiley, 1960, Pp. 517–557.

BRAINE, M. D. S. The ontogeny of certain logical operations: Piaget's formulation examined by nonverbal methods. *Psychol. Monogr.,* 1959, **73,** No. 4 (Whole No. 475).

DODWELL, P. C. Children's understanding of number and related concepts. *Canad. J. Psychol.,* 1960, **14,** 191–203.

ELKIND, D. The development of quantitative thinking: a systematic replication of Piaget's studies. *J. genet. Psychol.,* 1961, **98,** 37–46.

GRÉCO, P. Quotité et quantité. In J. Piaget (Ed.), Structures numériques élémentaires. *Études d'Épistemol. génét.,* 1962, **13.**

HARLOW, H. F. Thinking. In H. Helson (Ed.), *Theoretical foundations of psychology.* Princeton, N.J.: Van Nostrand, 1951. Pp. 452–505.

INHELDER, BÄRBEL, & NOELTING, G. Le passage d'un stade au suivant dans le développement des fonctions cognitives. *Proc. 15th Int. Congr. Psychol.,* Brussels, 1957, 435–438.

PIAGET, J. *The psychology of intelligence.* London: Routledge & Kegan Paul, 1950.

PIAGET, J. Apprentissage et connaissance. In J. Piaget (Ed.), La logique des apprentissages.

Études d'Épistemol. génét., 1959, **10**, 159–188.

Smedslund, J. The acquisition of conservation of substance and weight in children. II and III. *Scand. J. Psychol.*, 1961, **2**, 71–87.

Wohlwill, J. F. Un essai d'apprentissage dans le domaine de la conservation du nombre. In J. Piaget (Ed.), L'apprentissage des structures logiques. *Études d'Épistemol. génét.*, 1959, **9**, 125–135.

Wohlwill, J. F. A study of the development of the number concept by scalogram analysis. *J. genet. Psychol.*, 1960, **97**, 345–377.

Yost, P. A., Siegel, A. E., & McMichael, J. E. Nonverbal probability judgments by young children. Paper read at Soc. Res. Child Develpm., University Park, Pa., March, 1961.

JAN SMEDSLUND

*The Acquisition of Conservation of Substance and Weight in Children: I. Introduction**

THIS series of articles will be concerned with the following specific problem: What processes are involved in children's acquisition of conservation of substance and weight? These phenomena are defined as follows. A subject has conservation of substance when he thinks the amount of substance in an object must necessarily remain unchanged during changes in its form, as long as nothing is added or taken away. Similarly, a subject has conservation of weight when he thinks the weight of an object must necessarily remain unchanged during changes in its form, as long as nothing is added or taken away.

The classical test for the study of conservation of substance and weight employs pieces of plasticine. The child is presented with two equal balls of plasticine and is told that they are equally heavy. Then one of the balls is changed into a sausage or something else, and in the test of conservation of substance the following standard question is asked: "Do you think there is more plasticine in the ball, or the same amount in both, or more in the sausage?" The corresponding question in the test of conservation of weight is: "Which is heavier, the ball or the sausage, or do they weigh the same?" After the child has answered the question he is asked: "Why do you think so?"

Children with conservation of substance answer that the objects contain the same amount of plasticine because they contained the same amount in the beginning; because only the shape is changed; or because nothing has been added or taken away. Children with conservation of weight answer that the objects weigh the same, and use the same arguments as in the case of conservation of substance. Children who do not have a principle of conservation usually rely on perceptual features of the objects: The sausage contains more because it is longer; the ball weighs more because it is thicker and rounder, because it looks a little bigger, etc.

Transition Ages

SEVERAL earlier studies have established the generality of the developmental transition from non-conservation to conservation in the domains of substance and weight. The classical study of Piaget & Inhelder (1941) first drew attention to these phenomena. These writers did not report the exact number and ages of their subjects, but stated that conservation of substance is reached on the average around 7–8 years, and conservation of weight around 9–10 years. Furthermore, their data seemed to indicate that conservation of substance and weight are invariably acquired in this order, i.e. subjects with conservation of weight always have conservation of substance but not vice versa.

The generality of this sequence seemed to be confirmed in parallel studies of children's interpretations of the melting of sugar in water and of the swelling of popcorn on a hot plate. In each situation they observed

* REPRINTED by permission of the author and the publisher from *Scand. J. Psychol.*, 1961, 2, 11–20; 85–87.

some children who asserted conservation of substance and denied conservation of weight, but they observed no children who asserted conservation of weight but denied conservation of substance. This early study was conducted by means of Piaget's *méthode clinique,* which consists of flexible and intuitively directed conversation and play. This method has proved very fruitful in the initial steps of research, but has the drawback that it cannot be exactly replicated, and it allows for unknown degrees of subjectivity in the procedure and interpretations.

A study by Inhelder (1944) verified the substance–weight sequence and indicated that these tests, together with those of conservation of volume and transitivity of weight, may have considerable diagnostic utility in practical application. The general developmental level of feeble-minded children and adults was reported as being clearly reflected in the test-responses.

A large scale standardization by Vinh-Bang (in preparation) has provided reliable and exact information on the transition ages in the population of Geneva. Nearly 1500 children between 4 and 12 years of age were given a battery of some thirty objective tests, including conservation of substance and conservation of weight. The 50 per cent level for the acquisition of conservation of substance is at 7½ years, and the corresponding level for conservation of weight is at 8 years. See also Vinh-Bang (1959). The study of Lovell (1960) in England gave approximately the same results. On the other hand, Smedslund (1959) found somewhat earlier transition ages in a group of children (sons and daughters of delegates to the international committees and organizations) from a socio-economically superior milieu in Geneva.

The studies of conservation of number by Slater (1958) in England and by Hyde (1959) with European and non-European subjects in Aden further support the hypothesis that the rate of development of concepts of conservation is influenced by environment.

Possible Interpretations

HISTORICALLY, the diverging interpretations of the phenomena of cognitive development may be traced to the conflict between the classical philosophical schools of *empiricism* and *rationalism.* Briefly stated, the former assumes that everything that is in the mind comes from experience. The latter asserts that there are certain structures and categories which impose themselves by necessity upon the human mind and which exist independently of any experience. In contemporary psychology one may discern at least four major interpretations of the type of developmental phenomena to be studied here (and combinations of them).

NATIVISM

According to this point of view, the human nervous system is organized in such a way that the intrinsic validity of the inference of conservation is immediately recognized at the moment when the child has acquired a knowledge of the empirical elements involved. This line of thought assumes that even very small children are always logical *within those limited areas where they have sufficient knowledge.* Development is seen as a process where appropriate inferential behavior is immediately applied to every new domain of experience.

LEARNING THEORY

This continues the old empiricist tradition and assumes that the child acquires the concepts of conservation as a function of repeated external reinforcements. According to this point of view, the subjective validity and necessity of the inference of conservation derives from an *empirical law.* The children discover empirically that as long as nothing is added or taken away, objects maintain the same amount of substance and the same weight, irrespective of changes of shape.

Alternatively, learning theorists may interpret the development transition as resulting from *social* reinforcements. The sanctions from adults and older children may gradually lead to the "correct" behavior relative to physical substance and weight. The training in the rules of language may contribute in various ways to the same outcome.

MATURATION THEORY

This theory asserts that logical structure may not be present from the beginning in children's behavior, but that it develops as a function of nervous maturation and independently of experience. No amount of experience can bring about a given type of inferential behavior in a child who is not mature enough, and once he has reached a sufficient degree of nervous maturation his experiences are immediately integrated into a logical framework. Small children may be "illogical," but there is nothing one can do about it, just wait for nature to take its course.

EQUILIBRATION THEORY

This is the position of Piaget and his co-workers (Piaget, 1950; 1957), who assert that logical structure is not originally present in the child's thinking, but that it develops as a function of an internal process, equilibration, which is heavily dependent on *activity* and *experience*. This point of view differs radically from that of learning theory, since practice is not assumed to act through external reinforcements, but by a process of mutual influence of the child's activities on each other. Logical inferences are not derived from any properties of the external world, but from the placing into relationship (*mise-en-relation*) of the subject's own activities. The process of equilibration is not identical with maturation, since it is highly influenced by practice which brings out latent contradictions and gaps in mental structure, and thereby initiates a process of inner reorganization. The theory is somewhat similar to Festinger's theory of cognitive dissonance (1957) and Heider's theory of balance (1958), but is more general.

These are, briefly, the four main theories of the mechanisms of cognitive development. Needless to say, many psychologists may choose intermediate positions, e.g. by postulating some kind of *interaction* of learning and maturation.

Nativism and learning theory represent opposite positions with respect to the role of experience, but they share the idea that children's thinking is essentially similar to that of adults. Both theories assume that in situations with insufficient knowledge adults will behave like children, and that in situations with sufficient knowledge children will behave like adults.

Critical Discussion

THE well-established findings of Piaget and his collaborators in a variety of fields seem to have excluded *nativism* as a serious possibility. (For a summary of many of these findings see Piaget, 1950, pp. 129–147.) Children below a certain age do not, for example, have notions of conservation, and they seem to acquire these notions at a relatively late stage of their development. Young children show amazingly "illogical" behavior even in situations where they seem to be in possession of all the relevant knowledge necessary for a correct conclusion. A child may know that nothing has been added to or taken away from a piece of clay, and still assert that the amount of clay and the weight has increased or diminished when the form is changed from ball to sausage. Even when every possible precaution is taken to ensure that the child has grasped the essential elements of the situation, one may observe the same type of perception-bound, "irrational" behavior.

We must conclude that the available evidence is clearly against the theory that logical structure follows automatically when the elements of a situation have been understood.

It is most tempting to apply some variant of *learning theory* to the developmental process. However, this application encounters a number of obstacles, some of which stem from the fact that it is so difficult to imagine how conservation can be established by external reinforcements in the normal life of children.

Let us begin with conservation of substance. According to Piaget and Inhelder (1941) this notion is established before conservation of weight and volume, i.e. before there exists any unequivocal empirical criterion of conservation. The subject cannot *observe* the conservation of substance during changes in form. On the contrary, his perceptual schemata lead him to suppose that the amount changes, and he has to fight to overcome the impact of how things "look." "It *looks* as if there were more in the ball, but I *know* it can't be." Thus, the child acquires conservation of substance by learning to *ignore* the appearance of things and his own direct experience.

In the experiment of melting sugar in water (Piaget & Inhelder, 1941), some children with conservation of substance asserted that the melted sugar was still there, even though they thought that the glass with the sugar would weigh exactly the same as the other glass with pure water, and that the water level would be the same in the two glasses. In this case, the child ignores the visual disappearance of substance, and asserts conservation without relying on a single empirical support. Even the taste is supposed to disappear after some time. It is difficult to imagine by what means children in normal conditions could be led by their observations to assume exact conservation of substance.

There are at least three possible auxiliary hypotheses, which depart more or less from a strict learning theory interpretation, but which nevertheless attribute a crucial role to external reinforcement.

1. The subject may have learned empirically that objects become larger when something is added to them and smaller when something is taken away. This may be generalized in some complex way to the class of situations where nothing is added or taken away and where consequently no change is assumed.

The difficulty with this explanation is that even very young children understand that nothing has been taken away or added in the conservation test, and still think that the amount of substance has increased or decreased. They do not appear to regard the absence of adding and taking away as a relevant argument for conservation, and this is really the crucial problem. Why does this argument suddenly become relevant and lead to the idea that conservation is logically necessary?

2. It may be thought that the discovery of *empirical reversibility,* i.e. the fact that one may return to the point of departure after a deformation, would be sufficient to induce conservation. More generally, the set of expectancies associated with other possible deformations remain unchanged by any given deformation, and by some complex mechanism this might lead to the notion of conservation.

A large amount of evidence shows that empirical reversibility cannot explain the acquisition of conservation. Even very young children know practically always that one may return to the starting point; the sausage can be remade into a ball that contains exactly as much plasticine as the unchanged standard. Even so, the sausage is seen as containing *more* or *less* plasticine than the standard! Finally, it should be noted that in the experiment with the melting of sugar, children assert conservation of substance even though the melting process is not empirically reversible in their field of experience.

3. One may assume that the lack of conservation of substance stems from a *difficulty of recall,* and that this can be improved upon by a process of "learning to learn." Perhaps the small child is unable to recall the initial state of equality, after just one presentation? This hypothesis is clearly contradicted by the available evidence, since the children, with few exceptions, do remember the initial state. However, they do not feel that the initial state of equality is relevant for the judgment of the state after the deformation, and learning theory probably cannot easily provide an explanation of how this is changed.

The preceding considerations are equally valid for conservation of weight. In this case, however, learning theory might seem to be in a somewhat better position, since weight is a directly observable factor. Perhaps children learn directly that weight does not change with changes in form? Again the answer seems to be negative. It is well known that the direct kinesthetic–tactile impression of weight is highly unreliable and extremely sensitive to irrelevant visual stimuli. We have repeatedly observed how children *confirm* their idea of non-conservation by weighing the objects in their hands. "Yes, I can feel that the sausage is heavier than the ball"; "the ball is much heavier now," etc. Again, we must conclude that the children acquire conservation *against* the perceptual appearance of things.

It has been suggested that children learn conservation of weight by means of scales. The answer to this is that children relatively seldom play with scales. Furthermore, the scales designed for children and available in the nurseries are technically rather primitive and do not easily lend themselves to any test of the principle of conservation.

A direct learning interpretation of the acquisition of conservation of weight also fails to explain why conservation of substance seems regularly to precede it genetically, although conservation of substance has no unambiguous observable referent.

Learning theorists may also try to explain the transition from non-conservation to conservation as a result of accumulated direct and indirect *social reinforcements*. We are aware of no evidence pointing to any direct training in these matters in the homes, and the sequential development of the various notions does not have any obvious connection with the teaching program in nurseries and schools. On the other hand, as mentioned above, several recent studies have shown an effect of children's socio-economic and cultural background on the speed of acquisition of the various concepts of conservation. This is in accordance both with a learning theory interpretation and an equilibration theory interpretation. The former would attribute the acceleration to a higher frequency of direct and/or indirect reinforcements, whereas the latter would assume that certain environments more frequently than others confront the child with complex intellectual problems, thus forcing him to organize his thinking.

Altogether, we may conclude that, despite apparent difficulties, one cannot discard the possibility of a learning theory interpretation of the acquisition of notions of conservation. Among recent authors on this subject, Apostel (1959) apparently believes in this possibility, whereas Berlyne (1960) introduces so many new assumptions into the Hullian framework that it becomes almost indistinguishable from the equilibration theory.

The *maturation theory* is in some ways a relatively plausible one. It takes account of the general observations of pre-logical behavior and of the absence of evidence for direct learning. The great difficulty from this point of view is (*a*) to explain the *time lag* between the occurrence of the various notions of conservation (Piaget, 1950; Vinh-Bang, 1959), and (*b*) to explain the accelerating *v.* retarding effects of the various environments. These two types of observations show that the maturation hypothesis is invalid as a general explanation, and that maturation can at most be a necessary condition for certain other processes to occur. The main problem is to discover the nature of these other processes.

Most of the arguments so far presented are not only *against* the three other interpretations, but also *for* the equilibration theory. The following tentative conclusions may be drawn from the preceding discussion: that the existing evidence seems to exclude nativism as a possible interpretation, and that maturation can at most be a contributing factor in providing the necessary neurological conditions for the acquisition of the successively more complex cognitive levels. The respective validities of learning theory and equilibration theory remain undetermined, although many findings seem to point against the former. In what follows, we will focus on the problem of how experience influences cognitive development, and on the question of learning *v.* equilibration. A brief review of some relevant earlier studies will conclude this introductory paper.

Relevant Previous Studies

THE direct predecessor of the present investigations was a study by Smedslund (1959). It was designed to show the effects of direct external reinforcement on the acquisition of conservation and transitivity of weight.

The experiment on conservation learning included three groups of subjects between 5;10 and 7;1, who consistently asserted nonconservation. Group A ($N = 8$) went through a series of 30 empirical controls on a pair of scales, permitting direct observation that objects do not change weight during deformation. Group B ($N = 8$) likewise had 30 controls on the scales, but 11 of the items of deformation were exchanged for items of addition and subtraction.

It was thought that if the learning theory interpretation were true, group A should learn more and faster than group B, since A had only direct reinforcements of the response category to be learned. On the other hand, equilibration theory would lead one to expect more improvement in group B, since this involved practice on the operations of addition and subtraction, whose combination is assumed to lie beneath the concept of conservation. ("Nothing is added and nothing is taken away.") Finally, there was a group C ($N = 5$) which did not take part in any practice sessions, and which functioned as a control.

There was a considerable amount of learning in both the experimental groups and no significant difference between them, although group A had slightly better results. Taken at their face value these results seemed to indicate that a concept of conservation of weight may be acquired as a function of external reinforcements. Furthermore, the slight advantage of group A over group B was in the direction of confirming the learning theory interpretation and went against the equilibration theory.

However, there are at least two alternative interpretations of the findings which, if true, would radically change the conclusions.

1. It is quite possible that what occurred was a simple response learning leading to a *pseudoconcept* without the quality of insight and necessity that accompanies the genuine concept. The genuine concept of conservation is inaccessible to experimental extinction, whereas the outcome of simple response learning would presumably be easy to extinguish. In article III of this series the outcome of an experimental test of this possibility will be reported.

2. The possibility of an easy response learning in group B (the majority of the items involved simple deformations which were identical to those in group A), may have inhibited any tendency to active cognitive reorganization induced by the small number of addition/subtraction items; cf. the discussion of Gréco's experiments below. A more crucial test would be to compare a condition with only addition/subtraction items with a condition with only deformation items. The outcome of such an experiment is described in article II of this series.

The experiment of Wohlwill (1959) on the acquisition of conservation of number is highly relevant for our purpose. A subject has conservation of number when he thinks that the number of objects in a collection must necessarily remain unchanged during changes in the spatial arrangement of the collection, as long as nothing is added or taken away.

Wohlwill posed the problem of whether conservation of number develops from the operations of adding and subtracting by means of some inferential process, or whether it results from direct reinforcement. He decided to check this by comparing the outcome of direct external reinforcement of conservation with the outcome of reinforcement of the operations of adding and subtracting.

The results show a not quite significant but highly suggestive superiority of the group trained on additions and subtractions as compared with the group trained directly on conservation over deformations. Since ordinary S-R learning principles would lead one to expect more learning in the latter group, this experiment represents a very suggestive strengthening of the equilibration theory. Wohlwill's data are at variance with our own, reported above, and this provided further encouragement to repeat our experiment with a more clearcut design involving only addition/subtraction items *v.* only deformation items.

The study of Gréco (1959*a*) concerns the learning to understand successive spatial rotations. The materials were a cardboard tube and a wooden rod to which were fastened a black, a white, and a red bead, in that order. The rod with the beads is moved into the tube until it is completely hidden and the child is asked: "Which color comes out first at the other end?" This simple question is answered correctly by most children at the age of 5–6 years. The tube with the rod inside is then rotated slowly and horizontally 180 degrees, once or twice, and the question of which color comes out is again asked. Gréco was interested in whether young children could learn to understand the meaning of the successive rotations of the tube. To the adult the rotations form a kind of logical grouping. The rotations may be combined with each other to deduce the effect, and the outcome is considered as *logically necessary*. If red is expected to come out in the direct order, then black must come out after one rotation and red again after two rotations.

Gréco's design involved two main experimental groups, D and S. The subjects in group D learned one rotation and two rotations separately to perfection, before they were presented with a mixed set of items containing both one and two rotations. The subjects in group S were mainly trained on the mixed set of items. The subjects in both groups learned to anticipate correctly the outcome of both one and two rotations. After a period of between one and three months a post-test was given to test the stability of the achievements. Furthermore, the *generalization* to *n* rotations was studied and the *transfer* to an analogous situation (a rotating disk with red and black placed in diametrically opposite positions). The data show a striking difference between the two groups. The children in group D had forgotten practically everything they had learned, whereas the children in group S had retained almost everything. The children in S also showed a considerable, but not complete generalization to *n* rotations and some transfer to an analogous situation.

Gréco's conclusion is as follows: In this situation it is possible for most pre-school children to learn behavior that is seemingly equivalent to the performance of older children. However, this learning seems to proceed in two ways which lead to quite different results. The subjects in group D seemed to have learned the outcome of one and two rotations separately as empirical laws and with no understanding of their "necessary" character. The subjects in group S never had a possibility to learn in this way; directly confronted with the more complex mixed set of items, they were probably forced into an intense "structuring activity." Apparently this led them to understand that two rotations represent the outcome of one rotation and another rotation.

These findings seem to strengthen the hypothesis that situations which permit simple response learning are detrimental to the occurrence of more profound cognitive reorganizations. Unfortunately, the two experimental conditions differed in several other respects, such as standardized *v.* clinical procedure and massed *v.* distributed practice. This makes the interpretation very uncertain.

The experiment of Morf (1959) concerned the acquisition of certain operations of class-inclusion. In a typical test the subject is presented with a collection of wooden beads, most of which are brown and a few are white. The subject is led to acknowledge explicitly that all the beads are made of wood and that most of them are brown and only a few are white. Finally, the following question is asked: "Can you tell me whether there are more brown beads or more beads made of wood?" The typical answer of the 5–6 year old is: "There are more brown beads because there are only two or three white ones."

No amount of reformulation or rearrangement of the materials seems to bring these children to understand the correct answer. Morf wanted to find out whether it was possible for children to acquire the operations of class-inclusion as a function of some kind of training or practice.

Very briefly, the findings were as follows: With a method of various empirical controls and with several concrete materials the outcome was completely negative as far as the correct answer was concerned. The outcome of a method of free play was likewise negative. A third technique tried to make the relations between the total class and the subclasses directly visible, but again there was no real learning. Finally, some success was obtained with a technique involving exercise of the operations of *logical multiplication.*

The children were trained in seeing objects as being simultaneously members of two or more classes, and this induced learning in 7 of 30 subjects. These results, as far they go, are more in accordance with equilibration theory than with ordinary learning theories.

Churchill (1958) in a study of the acquisition of conservation of number, apparently succeeded in inducing conservation to a considerable extent, but the exact procedure is not given in the summary that has been available.

Tentative Generalizations

THE preceding experiments are mostly very complex and exploratory and have served to raise questions rather than answer them. Nevertheless, they permit us to formulate certain tentative generalizations, which may act as a frame of reference for further research.

1. The possibility of inducing a cognitive reorganization depends on the subject's already available schemata. If he has a structure which already approaches the given notion, the probability of the desired reorganization is high, whereas if he is still far from the notion, the chances are small that he will change sufficiently during a limited series of experimental sessions. Gréco (1959*b*) was able to show that children of the same age as those in the experiment with the rotating tube were unable to learn an exactly analogous but purely empirical and arbitrary problem. The probable reason was that the subjects in the former experiment already had a beginning "intuition" about the rotations, whereas the subjects in the latter experiment had to start from scratch. The studies of children's learning at different age levels by Gréco (1959*b*), Goustard (1959), and Matalon (1959) all demonstrate directly how the ability to profit from experience depends on the initial developmental level.

2. Situations which permit immediate and simple response learning with empirical control are unlikely to lead to any profound cognitive reorganization. This is exemplified by Gréco's group D and by our own groups A and B. For evidence supporting this interpretation see article III of this series.

3. Situations stressing empirical control, which do not permit simple response learning, may or may not induce a cognitive reorganization, which probably depends on the conditions mentioned under 1. Morf's groups with empirical control and our own experiment on learning of transitivity of weight (Smedslund, 1959) gave completely negative results. Correct inferences of transitivity and class-inclusion involve different stimuli and different responses in each new situation, and thus would be expected to yield little learning on the basis of current learning theories. These situations would also be expected to yield little improvement on the basis of equilibration theory, since they emphasize the empirical outcomes instead of the activities of the subject. Positive results were found in Gréco's group S.

4. Direct exercise of the relevant operations is likely to induce cognitive change to the extent that the conditions mentioned under 1 are favorable. This is exemplified by Morf's group, trained on the multiplication of classes, and by Wohlwill's addition/subtraction group.

These are only vague statements with little predictive value. In the subsequent articles attempts will be made to determine the exact conditions for the acquisition of conservation of substance and weight and to construct a more specific theory.

REFERENCES

APOSTEL, L. Logique et apprentissage. *Études d'Épistémol. génét.*, 1959, **8,** 1–138.

BERLYNE, D. E. Les équivalences psychologiques et les notions quantitatives. *Études d'Épistémol. génét.*, 1960, **12,** 1–76.

CHURCHILL, E. M. The number concepts of the young child. Leeds: *Leeds Univer. Res. Stud.*, 1958, **17,** 34–49; **18,** 28–46.

FESTINGER, L. *A theory of cognitive dissonance.* New York: Row, Peterson, 1957.

GOUSTARD, M. Étude psychogénétique de la résolution d'un problème (Labyrinthe en T). *Études d'Épistémol. génét.*, 1959, **10,** 83–112.

GRÉCO, P. L'apprentissage dans une situation à structure opératoire concrète: les inversions successives de l'ordre lineaire par des rotations de 180°. *Études d'Épistémol. génét.*, 1959, **7,** 68–182. (a)

GRÉCO, P. Induction, déduction et apprentissage. *Études d'Épistémol. génét.*, 1959, **10,** 3–59. (b)

HEIDER, F. *The psychology of interpersonal relations.* New York: Wiley, 1958.

HYDE, D. M. An investigation of Piaget's theories of the development of the concept of number. Unpublished doctoral thesis, Univer. of London, 1959.

INHELDER, BÄRBEL. *Le diagnostic du raisonnement chez les débiles mentaux.* Neuchâtel: Delachaux & Niestlé, 1944.

LOVELL, K., & OGILVIE, E. A study of the conservation of substance in the Junior School child. *Brit. J. educ. Psychol.*, 1960, **30,** 109–118.

MATALON, B. Apprentissages en situations aléatoires et systematiques. *Études d'Épistémol. génét.*, 1959, **10,** 61–91.

MORF, A. Apprentissage d'une structure logique concrète (inclusion). Effets et limites. *Études d'Épistémol. génét.*, 1959, **9,** 15–83.

PIAGET, J. *The psychology of intelligence.* London: Routledge & Kegan Paul, 1950.

PIAGET, J. Logique et équilibre dans les comportements du sujet. *Études d'Épistémol. génét.*, 1957, **2,** 27–117.

PIAGET, J., & INHELDER, BÄRBEL. *Le développement des quantités chez l'enfant.* Neuchâtel and Paris: Delachaux & Niestlé, 1941.

SLATER, G. W. A study of the influence which environment plays in determining the rate at which a child attains Piaget's 'operational' level in his early number concepts. Unpublished dissertation, Birmingham Univer., 1958.

SMEDSLUND, J. Apprentissage des notions de la conservation et de la transitivité du poids. *Études d'Épistémol. génét.*, 1959, **9,** 85–124.

VINH-BANG. Évolution des conduites et apprentissage. *Études d'Épistémol. génét.*, 1959, **9,** 3–13.

VINH-BANG. Elaboration d'une échelle de développement du raisonnement. Genève: Institut des Sciences de l'Éducation. (In preparation.)

WOHLWILL, J. Un essai d'apprentissage dans le domaine de la conservation du nombre. *Études d'Épistémol. génét.*, 1959, **9,** 125–135.

JAN SMEDSLUND

The Acquisition of Conservation of Substance and Weight in Children: III. Extinction of Conservation of Weight Acquired "Normally" and by Means of Empirical Controls on a Balance

IN THE first article (Smedslund, 1961*a*) [1] two main theories of the origin of principles of conservation were described. The first maintains that such principles ultimately derive from some kind of reinforcement mediated by external stimuli ("Learning theory"). The second assumes that the principles of conservation derive primarily from the inner organization and mutual coordination of the subject's schemata. Before children acquire conservation of substance and weight, they already have the conception that adding means increment in amount and that subtracting means decrement. By coordinating these two operations into an organized whole, the absence of adding and subtracting is eventually seen as meaning no change in amount, i.e., conservation ("Equilibration theory").

In two earlier studies (Smedslund, 1959, 1961*b*) it was shown that 5- to 7-year-old children may acquire a notion of conservation of weight by means of controls on a balance. When the invariance of the weight of an object over deformations was empirically demonstrated, a number of children began to assert conservation of weight even in situations where the balance was not present. This fact would seem to support the learning theory interpretation. On the other hand, it may be that such acquisition involves a pseudoconcept of conservation only, without the functional properties of a "normally" acquired concept.

This paper reports an experiment testing two predictions about the extinction of conservation. On the basis of learning theory one may expect that a notion of conservation can always be extinguished, regardless of whether it has been established in the laboratory or in normal life. This follows from the assumption that notions of conservation are dependent on external reinforcement. On the other hand, it follows from equilibration theory that a genuine principle of conservation should be practically impossible to extinguish, since it reflects an inner "logical" necessity. The experiment is not decisive since the interpretation of the outcome will have to rest on many uncertain assumptions. However, it will serve to reveal some of the functional properties of artificially and normally acquired notions.

Procedure

A NUMBER of 5- to 7-year-old children were given the pretest of conservation of weight described by Smedslund (1961*b*). The sub-

1 This is the third in a series of papers, the second of which (Smedslund, 1961b) has been omitted here, but is discussed by Smedslund in this selection. The omitted paper is directed chiefly to an examination of two alternative interpretations of the acquisition of conservation of weight, by external reinforcement and internal equilibration. Evidence that a few subjects *did* show acquisition of the concept after experiences with the balance led Smedslund to conduct this follow-up investigation. [Ed.]

jects who showed no traces of conservation were given two training sessions with empirical controls of conservation of weight on a balance. The training sessions were identical to those described in the earlier paper.

In the posttest, 11 subjects gave only correct answers and explanations referring to the initial state (they weigh the same because they weighed the same in the beginning). These 11 subjects and 13 subjects of the same age who already showed complete conservation of weight in the pretest, participated in the extinction trials. The extinction of the principle of conservation of weight was attempted by cheating the subjects. Three items were prepared for the extinction procedure, but sometimes only the first or the first two were employed (notably when extinction occurred after the first or second item). All the objects were made of plasticine. In presenting each item the subject was told that the two objects weighed the same.

1. *Two brown balls.* One of them is changed into a *sausage* and a piece is taken away from it, inconspicuously. The child is asked to predict whether the two objects will now weigh the same or whether one of them will weigh more, and if so, which one. The objects are placed on the balance and lack of conservation is observed. Finally, the subject is asked to explain why the ball is heavier than the sausage.

2. *Two red bricks.* One is changed to a *cake* and a piece is taken away, inconspicuously. Prediction, control and explanation.

3. *Two green sausages.* One is changed into a *ball* and a piece is taken away, inconspicuously. Prediction, control and explanation.

Results

THE main outcome of the experiment is shown in TABLE 1.

None of the subjects who had acquired the principle during the experiment showed any resistance to extinction, whereas about half of the subjects who had acquired the concept in a "normal" way maintained it in the face of apparent non-conservation. The typical be-

TABLE 1. *Number of subjects who showed resistance v. non-resistance to extinction in groups having acquired conservation of weight by means of controls on a balance scale (E) and in normal life (N)*

	GROUP E	GROUP N
Resistance	0	6
Non-resistance	11	7

havior of those who did not resist was to show little surprise and to switch rapidly back to non-conservation with explanations referring to the perceptual appearance of the objects: "The ball weighs more, because it is rounder and fatter," "The brick will weigh more, because it is bigger," etc. The subjects who resisted said: "We must have taken a little away from that one (the lighter object)," "I think you have taken away some of the clay!" "We must have lost some clay on the floor," etc.

Discussion

THE results seem to show that the subjects who acquired a notion of conservation by means of controls on the balance had learned only a relatively arbitrary empirical law. They were not very shocked or surprised when the law was falsified, and rapidly modified their predictions and explanations. On the other hand, several subjects in the group who had acquired the notion of conservation in a "normal" way, did not give up their conception, and thought that some material had been taken away.

The occurrence of resistance to extinction in group N is consistent with the equilibration theory. From the learning theory point of view it may be argued that the significance of the resistance is unclear; after all, there were only three extinction trials, and the concepts may have been overlearned by the subjects in group N. With more extinction trials all the subjects might have given up the idea of conservation. This argument is not very cogent in view of the explanations given by the subjects who resisted. They seemed to regard the change in relative weight as a sign that something had been taken away (or added to the other object), and this mechanism should make them fairly independent of the empirical outcomes.

It should be noted that it was impossible to predict extinction from the subject's initial explanations. The subjects in the two groups generally gave the same types of explanations before the extinction trials. The most frequent was: "They will weigh the same because they weighed the same in the beginning." Obviously, this explanation may be given by subjects with highly different concepts of conservation; and, consequently, one should not rely too much on the verbal behavior in making inferences about the functional properties of a concept of conservation.

REFERENCES

SMEDSLUND, J. Apprentissage des notions de la conservation et de la transitivité du poids. *Études d'Épistemol. génét.*, 1959, **9,** 85–124.

SMEDSLUND, J. The acquisition of conservation of substance and weight in children. I. Introduction. *Scand. J. Psychol.*, 1961, **2,** 11–20. (a)

SMEDSLUND, J. The acquisition of conservation of substance and weight in children. II. External reinforcement of conservation of weight and of the operations of addition and subtraction. *Scand. J. Psychol.*, 1961, **2,** 71–84. (b)

K. LOVELL

A Follow-Up Study of Inhelder and Piaget's The Growth of Logical Thinking*

I. Introduction

INHELDER and Piaget's book, *The Growth of Logical Thinking,* first appeared in English in 1958, and it has been reviewed in this journal by Bruner (1959) and Parsons (1960). This paper describes a follow-up study using some of the experiments described in this important book under rather more controlled conditions, in the sense that we can specify the population from which our subjects were drawn, and at the same time give more exact details of our apparatus and procedures. The need to limit the length of this paper permits us to give a bare outline only of our work, and it will be assumed that readers have access to the book.

II. Procedure

MATERIALS

INHELDER and Piaget describe some fifteen experiments, of which we have repeated ten. Unfortunately, exact details of the design of their apparatus are not given, and we had to make up the apparatus as best we could and adapt it somewhat. Furthermore, it was necessary to overcome considerable technical problems before some of the experiments would work. Nevertheless, we managed to construct apparatus that eventually functioned fairly satisfactorily, and exact details may be obtained from the writer; the experiments we carried out are listed below, and a few notes are given when the apparatus differed somewhat in detail from that inferred from the description provided in the book.

(1) Flexibility of Rods. Five rods, three of steel, two of phosphor bronze. The three steel rods were all of different diameters, the phosphor bronze rods having the same diameters as the two thicker steel rods. Weights could be screwed on the ends of the rods, and the tips of the rods were made to touch the table top.

(2) Oscillation of Pendulum.

(3) Falling Bodies on an Inclined Plane. Help had to be obtained from Professor Inhelder before this experiment would work satisfactorily. Even so the procedure used has to be structured more than we had wished.

(4) Effects of Invisible Magnetization.

(5) Combinations of Colourless Chemical Bodies.

(6) The Conservation of Motion on a Horizontal Plane.

(7) Equilibrium in the Hydraulic Press. An all-glass 50 c.c. hypodermic syringe, the piston of which could be loaded with different weights, was connected to a length of narrow glass tubing. Alongside was an exact duplicate of the apparatus so the subject could work with two liquids of different densities at the same time. One liquid was tap water tinged very slightly red, and the other was concentrated salt solution tinged very slightly blue.

(8) Equilibrium in the Balance. The balance arm (and the associated supporting framework) was made from Meccano strips. By this means the distance of the weights from the fulcrum could be quickly obtained. The weights were cut so that the weight plus attached hook weighed 2, 5, 10 or 20 g.

(9) Projection of Shadows.

* REPRINTED by permission of the author and the British Psychological Society from *Brit. J. Psychol.*, 1961, 52, 143–153.

(10) Correlations. Each of forty postcards had the head of a girl drawn on it. The shape of the face, hair style and colouring differed for each girl, but the hair and eyes were coloured as indicated in the book. Inhelder and Piaget give no stages earlier than IIIA, but the writer laid down criteria for I, IIA and IIB stages.

SUBJECTS

Our population consisted of 34 average and bright primary school pupils; 14 average and bright preparatory school pupils (aged 8–11 years); 39 grammar school pupils; 50 secondary modern school pupils; 50 comprehensive school pupils; 10 training college students; 3 able adults whose ages ranged from 25 to 32 years of age; thus making 200 subjects in all. In the comprehensive and secondary modern schools approximately equal numbers were drawn from the top and bottom streams of each year group.

GENERAL TECHNIQUE

Each subject was examined, individually, on four experiments, with everyone taking the experiment involving the combinations of colourless chemical liquids (no. 5). After the subject had been introduced to the materials, and after some general discussions and sometimes free experimentation, he was asked to perform certain standard tasks and asked certain standard questions. The subject's actions were noted and his replies recorded verbatim. Details of the exact procedure used in each experiment may be obtained from the writer. It must be stressed, however, that the experimenter was quite free to vary the procedure by asking supplementary questions, or by prompting, or by experimenting slightly differently, if he thought it would be helpful. In brief our procedure was semi-structured and this is the best that one can do if the clinical approach is to be combined with some degree of standardization of procedure. The subjects were asked "to think aloud" as much as possible.

Usually Inhelder and Piaget give details of three stages of thinking; stages II and III usually being subdivided further into "A" and "B" stages. After examining our protocols it was thought better to subdivide the Inhelder and Piaget stages still further, and we usually used nine stages, viz:

I; I–IIA; IIA; IIA–IIB; IIB; IIB–IIIA;
IIIA; IIIA–IIIB; IIIB.

In this way we were, in our opinion, able to classify our protocols within the framework provided by the authors. Each protocol was studied by the writer and by the experimenter independently, and given a rating on the scale of stages. The results were compared and after discussion a final rating was given to each protocol. The assessment of some of the protocols was not an easy matter, and we cannot be sure that the more difficult ones were always rated correctly, although the ratings of these are not likely to be more than one stage out in the nine-stage scale that was usually used. In the experiment involving invisible magnetization the authors give a stage III only, not stages IIIA and IIIB, and we have kept to this.

III. Results

A NUMBER of tables are now given showing how the different groups performed on the various experiments. All our results are included.

It is important to know to what extent the level of thinking of our subjects remained the same throughout the four experiments that each one undertook. To determine this we used Kendall's coefficient of concordance W, which specifies the degree of association between a number of sets of rankings. First, the rank of each subject was calculated, separately for each of the four experiments. W was then calculated from formula 9.16 given by Siegel (1956, p. 234); this allows for tied observations. Furthermore, if the total number of cases concerned is N, and $N > 7$, we may find the probability of any value as large as an observed W, by calculating $\chi^2 = k(N - 1)\ W$, with d.f. $= N - 1$, where k is the number of sets of rankings (Siegel, 1956, p. 236, formula 9.18). Accordingly χ^2 was calculated for each W and the probability associated with so large

TABLE 1. *Number of subjects at the various stages of thinking on the test of Colourless Chemical Liquids*

TYPE OF SUBJECT	STAGE									TOTAL
	I	*I–IIA*	*IIA*	*IIA–IIB*	*IIB*	*IIB–IIIA*	*IIIA*	*IIIA–IIIB*	*IIIB*	
Primary	2	6	20	4	1	1	.	.	.	34
Preparatory	2	2	8	2	.	.	.	.	.	14
Least able, sec. modern	3	7	7	2	3	1	1	.	.	24
Least able, comprehensive	.	14	6	4	.	.	.	.	.	24
Ablest sec. modern	1	2	6	3	2	2	7	2	1	26
Ablest comprehensive	.	3	.	5	7	4	7	.	.	26
Grammar, training college and adults	1	.	4	2	8	6	11	8	12	52
									Total	200

TABLE 2. *Number of subjects at the various stages of thinking on the test of Flexibility of Rods*

TYPE OF SUBJECT	STAGE									TOTAL
	I	*I–IIA*	*IIA*	*IIA–IIB*	*IIB*	*IIB–IIIA*	*IIIA*	*IIIA–IIIB*	*IIIB*	
Least able, sec. modern	5	6	5	3	2	2	1	.	.	24
Ablest sec. modern	.	1	2	2	9	6	3	.	3	26
									Total	50

TABLE 3. *Number of subjects at the various stages of thinking on the test of Oscillation of a Pendulum*

TYPE OF SUBJECT	STAGE									TOTAL
	I	*I–IIA*	*IIA*	*IIA–IIB*	*IIB*	*IIB–IIIA*	*IIIA*	*IIIA–IIIB*	*IIIB*	
Primary	3	3	5	2	1	2	.	.	.	16
Preparatory	.	5	3	2	3	1	.	.	.	14
Least able, comprehensive	2	6	7	8	.	1	.	.	.	24
Ablest comprehensive	.	2	6	.	3	3	8	4	.	26
Grammar, training college and adults	.	.	3	5	1	6	15	3	19	52
									Total	132

TABLE 4. *Number of subjects at the various stages of thinking on the test of Falling Bodies on an Inclined Plane*

	STAGE									
TYPE OF SUBJECT	*I*	*I–IIA*	*IIA*	*IIA–IIB*	*IIB*	*IIB–IIIA*	*IIIA*	*IIIA–IIIB*	*IIIB*	TOTAL
Primary	2	4	4	4	3	1	.	.	.	18
Preparatory	.	.	12	1	1	.	.	.	.	14
Grammar	.	.	.	.	4	4	2	.	4	14
									Total	46

TABLE 5. *Number of subjects at the various stages of thinking on the test of Invisible Magnetization*

	STAGE							
TYPE OF SUBJECT	*I*	*I–IIA*	*IIA*	*IIA–IIB*	*IIB*	*IIB–III*	*III*	TOTAL
Primary	5	.	4	1	4	1	1	16
Grammar, training college and adults	.	1	.	2	14	10	11	38
							Total	54

TABLE 6. *Number of subjects at the various stages of thinking on the test of the Conservation of Motion on a Horizontal Plane*

	STAGE									
TYPE OF SUBJECT	*I*	*I–IIA*	*IIA*	*IIA–IIB*	*IIB*	*IIB–IIIA*	*IIIA*	*IIIA–IIIB*	*IIIB*	TOTAL
Primary	5	1	3	2	3	1	1	.	.	16
Least able, sec. modern	.	5	2	8	4	2	3	.	.	24
Ablest sec. modern	.	3	3	8	5	1	4	1	1	26
Grammar and adults	.	.	3	1	9	.	6	.	9	28
									Total	94

TABLE 7. *Number of subjects at the various stages of thinking in the test of Equilibrium in the Hydraulic Press*

	STAGE									
TYPE OF SUBJECT	*I*	*I–IIA*	*IIA*	*IIA–IIB*	*IIB*	*IIB–IIIA*	*IIIA*	*IIIA–IIIB*	*IIIB*	TOTAL
Primary	.	1	10	5	2	.	.	.	.	18
Preparatory	.	3	6	1	4	.	.	.	.	14
Grammar	.	.	.	.	3	3	2	3	3	14
									Total	46

TABLE 8. *Number of subjects at the various stages of thinking in the test of Equilibrium in the Balance*

TYPE OF SUBJECT	STAGE									TOTAL
	I	*I–IIA*	*IIA*	*IIA–IIB*	*IIB*	*IIB–IIIA*	*IIIA*	*IIIA–IIIB*	*IIIB*	
Least able, comprehensive	.	.	.	.	.	.	.	.	.	24
Ablest comprehensive	.	.	3	5	13	1	4	.	.	26
Training college	.	.	.	.	4	6	.	.	.	10
									Total	60

TABLE 9. *Number of subjects at the various stages of thinking in the test of the Projection of Shadows*

TYPE OF SUBJECT	STAGE									TOTAL
	I	*I–IIA*	*IIA*	*IIA–IIB*	*IIB*	*IIB–IIIA*	*IIIA*	*IIIA–IIIB*	*IIIB*	
Least able, comprehensive	.	1	6	6	11	.	.	.	.	24
Ablest comprehensive	.	.	.	.	18	5	1	1	1	26
									Total	50

TABLE 10. *Number of subjects at the various stages of thinking in the test of Correlations*

TYPE OF SUBJECT	STAGE									TOTAL
	I	*I–IIA*	*IIA*	*IIA–IIB*	*IIB*	*IIB–IIIA*	*IIIA*	*IIIA–IIIB*	*IIIB*	
Primary	.	5	6	4	2	1	.	.	.	18
Least able, sec. modern	4	8	3	2	.	2	1	3	1	24
Ablest sec. modern	.	1	.	.	.	5	8	5	7	26
									Total	68

a value of χ^2 was found by referring to Siegel (1956, Table C, p. 249). TABLE 11 shows the values of W, and the probability of finding an associated χ^2 as large, P_{χ^2}, for the differing groups of experiments and subjects.

Even if there is a substantial degree of association between the level of thinking displayed by our subjects on each of four experiments, it is necessary to determine if the experiments (coupled with the manner in which the protocols were assigned to stages by Inhelder and Piaget) were in fact drawn from the same population of experiments. For example, it could be that a particular experiment was rather easier or more difficult for one reason or another. Accordingly the Kruskal–Wallis one-way analysis of variance by ranks was used, as this test will decide if a number of different samples are drawn from the same population. The test assumes only that the variables studied have an underlying continuous distribution, and that ordinal

TABLE 11. *Values of W, and the probability of finding a χ^2 as large associated with W and H in differing groups of experiments and subjects*

	GROUP OF EXPERIMENTS	NO. AND TYPE OF SUBJECTS	TOTAL N	W	$P\chi^2$	P_H
1	Chemical Combinations Pendulum Hydraulic Press Falling bodies	14 preparatory 14 grammar	28	0.89	<0.01	>0.05
2	Chemical Combinations Invisible Magnetization Pendulum Conservation of Motion	16 primary 25 grammar 3 adults	44	0.81	<0.01	>0.05
3	Chemical Combinations Pendulum Balance Shadows	50 comprehensive	50	0.73	<0.01	<0.01
4	Chemical Combinations Flexibility of Rods Conservation of Motion Correlations	50 sec. modern	50	0.59	<0.01	<0.01
5	Chemical Combinations Hydraulic Press Falling Bodies Correlations	18 primary	18	0.52	<0.01	>0.01
		Total	190			

measurement is possible for each variable. These conditions are fulfilled in the case of our data. First, the total number of subjects at each stage on each of the four tests was calculated, and the rank of each subject found from the single series that resulted. Thus H, the statistic used in the Kruskal–Wallis test, was calculated from formula 8.3 given by Siegel (1956, p. 192), as this allows for tied observations. Since in our case there were four samples, and the number of subjects in each sample is greater than five, H is distributed approximately as χ^2 with d.f. $= k - 1$, where k is the number of samples. Once again the probability of finding a χ^2 as large as H was found by referring to Siegel (1956, Table C, p. 249). Hence TABLE 11 shows also the probability of finding a χ^2 as large as H, P_H, for the differing groups of experiments and subjects.

The results of the remaining ten training college students were not analysed in this manner on account of the smallness and homogeneity of the sample. The four experiments which they undertook were: Chemical Combinations, Pendulum, Invisible Magnetization, and Equilibrium in the Balance.

Reference to the values of P_H in TABLE 11 shows that the experiments in the first, second and fifth groups may be regarded as random samples drawn from the same population of experiments. In the third and fourth groups, however, $P_H < 0.01$ indicating that one or more experiments in each group cannot be so regarded. Experience gained in examining the subjects indicated that the Projection of Shadows, and Correlations experiments found in the third and fourth groups, respectively, were likely to be responsible for this. Consequently the remaining three experiments in each of these groups were subjected to the Kruskal–Wallis test; and for each of the two groups of three experiments the value of H so obtained was such that $P_H > 0.05$.

IV. Discussion

THE following discussion deals principally with the educational implications of the study, and in order to be succinct the findings are grouped under a number of points.

(1) The main stages in the development of logical thinking proposed by Inhelder and Piaget have been confirmed. It seems that the authors are correct in suggesting that it is only rarely that average to bright junior school children reach the stage of formal thinking. The ablest of the secondary modern and comprehensive school pupils certainly attain the stage of formal thought, but not all the older grammar school pupils always do so. There is a suggestion that ill-digested snippets of knowledge, mental set, and expectancy, are affecting thinking more in the students than among the school pupils. The student with the poorest performance was aged 19 years, and on the four experiments her replies were classified at the IIA–IIB, IIB and IIB–IIIA stages. She had obtained a pass in Art at G.C.E. "A" level. However, the least able of the secondary modern and comprehensive school pupils certainly remain at a low level of logical thought even at 15 years of age, and many of these do not seem to pass beyond the IIA–IIB stage of thinking. This is a finding the authors do not mention, and it leads one to suspect that the school population in Geneva which they examined consisted of able children.

(2) By getting each subject to undergo four experiments and analysing the results by means of a non-parametric statistical technique, it has been possible to show that there is a considerable agreement between the levels of thinking that the subjects display in the four experiments. Moreover, the value of the coefficient of concordance W declines as the population becomes more homogeneous with respect to mental age. Naturally there is no exact correspondence since the experiments and "intelligence" tests do not measure exactly the same thinking skills. Among the preparatory and grammar school pupils $W = 0.89$, and among the primary and grammar school pupils $W = 0.81$ (TABLE 11). In these groups the Mental Ages of the pupils ranged from 8 years to well above 15 years (the M.A. usually accepted for average adults), whereas in the primary school group alone, for which $W = 0.52$, the mental ages would range from 8 to 13 or 15 years. The authors give no evidence on this issue, but one would certainly expect some such stability of thinking skills if their general theory is correct. Again the Kruskal–Wallis test gave reasonable grounds for assuming that eight of the ten experiments may be regarded as samples drawn from the same population of experiments. The Correlations experiment is too easy for secondary, but not for primary pupils, compared with the other eight experiments; while the Projection of Shadows test placed too many subjects at stage IIB.

(3) The majority of our protocols show much the same kind of reasoning as those of Inhelder and Piaget, and support many of their statements. For example, the authors maintain that, at the level of formal thought, the child comes to the Projection of Shadows experiment assuming proportionality from the start. Below is a copy of part of the protocol of a boy aged 13 years 3 months.

> "What happens to the shadow as you move the ring up and down the scale?" *"Nearer the wall smaller, further away bigger."* "Use two rings of different size, and move them until their shadows are exactly the same size, that is, they cover each other exactly." Places the 5 cm. diameter ring at 20 cm. from light, and 10 cm. diameter ring at 40 cm. "Why do the rings have to go in these positions?" *"Well 10 is twice 5, and 40 is twice 20."* After placing three rings of different diameter[s] correctly in position he is asked to place four rings of different diameters in position so that their shadows coincide. He places 5

cm. ring at 10 cm. from light, 10 cm. ring at 20 cm., 15 cm. ring at 30 cm., and 20 cm. ring at 40 cm. from light. "Tell me exactly what you have done about the position of the rings." *"Well 5 is 10 cm. from torch, 10 is twice as big so it goes at 20 cm., 15 is half as big again so it goes at 30, and 20 is twice 10 so it goes here at 40."* "What is the rule for placing the rings so that their shadows are the same size?" *"Well—twice the diameter means twice the distance from the torch, three times the diameter three times the distance and so on."*

This subject started with the idea of proportion and systematically continued with that in mind.

On the other hand there were occasions when the actions and replies did not follow the pattern of the Geneva children. Some of the more important of these instances are now briefly listed.

CHEMICAL COMBINATIONS

(*a*) According to the authors, the child at stage II should add each liquid in turn to *g* before attempting to combine two liquids with *g* in combinatorial fashion. This was not always the case. Some of our subjects combined two liquids with *g* combinatorially before trying each one in turn with *g*.

(*b*) At stage IIIB the child is supposed to try, quite spontaneously, to ascertain the functions of liquids 2 and 4, and to search for combinations, other than $1 + 3 + g$, that would give the yellow coloration. We found that only a few of the grammar school pupils, and very few of the other secondary school pupils, showed this spontaneity. But on prompting a subject he would often readily experiment to determine the effects of liquids 2 and 4; and on asking him what combinations he would have used had the combination $1 + 3 + g$ not worked, he often replied with unused combinations, showing that he had anticipatory schemata available to him. In this case he was assessed as at the IIIA stage.

PENDULUM

(*a*) Our subjects seemed to need more prompting than was necessary for the Geneva subjects; in the sense that they did not readily switch from the serialization of one variable to the serialization of another.

(*b*) We found children who could serially order particular variables but drew the wrong conclusions. Perception seemed to be at fault in these instances.

EQUILIBRIUM IN THE BALANCE

Among the fifty children in a comprehensive school and ten training college students, we did not find anyone who replied like the authors' SAM, p. 174/175, who said, "If you want to calculate, it's best to consider it (distance) horizontally, if you want to understand it, vertically is better." In other words, we did not find anyone who understood that force and height compensate one another, so that the work done is the same in both instances as did the authors' subjects at stage IIIB. Perhaps the principle of "work done" comes only from direct teaching as such. The whole problem of the effectiveness of teaching will be raised later.

PROJECTION OF SHADOWS

Inhelder and Piaget suggest that before stage IIIA, although subjects know how to construct inverse correspondences, they prefer direct ones. Consequently they tend to calculate distances by starting from the screen rather than the light source. We found only five subjects out of fifty who made any attempt to measure from the screen.

FLEXIBILITY OF RODS

Our subjects appeared to have much greater difficulty than the Geneva subjects in recognizing similarities of thickness.

CONSERVATION OF MOTION

The authors maintain that there is an orderly development in reasoning about the obstacles that prevent the movement of the balls, culminating at stage IIIB in understanding the principle of inertia. In the present study there were some children who were reasoning at the stage II level, yet on being asked the final key question as to what would happen if there were no obstacles tending to prevent the motion, replied that the balls would "go on for ever" or words to that effect.

CORRELATIONS

At the very beginning of the experiment (but not later on in the procedure) we had to prompt some of our subjects rather more than it appears the authors did.

INVISIBLE MAGNETIZATION

Exclusions were frequently used, but disjunctions far less frequently used than Inhelder and Piaget would have us believe. Indeed, disjunctions were rarely found at all. It was not possible to get this apparatus to work as satisfactorily as we would have liked.

Overall it would seem that the authors have somewhat forced the development of the child's thinking into a theoretical framework. A similar view has been expressed by the writer elsewhere (Lovell, 1959; Lovell & Ogilvie, 1960) in connexion with other Piagetian studies carried out at Leeds University. This statement in no way detracts from the value of the insights which the Geneva school has given the world; for if Piaget's works were stripped of their logic of algebra, they would, in our view, still be of great importance.

(4) Teaching, in the sense of instruction, does not seem to have affected the results as much as had been expected. There are, of course, problems such as that of "work done" where direct teaching is necessary; but instruction generally seems to be of greatest value when the thinking skills are almost, or are actually available to the subject. If the power to think at the requisite level is not present, knowledge gained by instruction is either forgotten, or it may remain rote knowledge and be regurgitated when required. The evidence for the general viewpoint just expressed is twofold.

(*a*) Only four of the experiments used in this study are ever taught, as such, in secondary school science. These are: Pendulum, Hydraulic Press, Equilibrium in Balance (Principle of Moments) and possibly Falling Bodies on an Inclined Plane. Yet the level of thinking skills attained by the pupils on all the experiments they undertook showed a good degree of association whether such experiments had been encountered in school or not.

(*b*) We have protocols indicating that a particular experiment had been "taught" in science lessons and yet the subjects were quite unable to reach the stage of formal thinking when they were given the experiment in this study. Below is part of the protocol of John C. aged 12 years 8 months obtained in the Balance experiment. It will be remembered that the authors used this experiment to prove whether or not the notion of proportion comes earlier than the IIIA stage of thinking.

"Place the 10 g. weight at hole 10, and the 5 g. weight at hole 18 on the other side. Now make the arm level so it will stay by itself." Places the 10 g. at hole 10, and the 5 g. at hole 18. Adds 1 g. at hole 6 on side of 5 g. Then places the 1 g. at hole 7, then at hole 4, and finally at hole 8. *"That's about as good as I can get it. There's a way to do this because we did it in science. It's a certain distance from the fulcrum but I've forgotten."* After having been asked to do the next task he comments before he acts. *"From the previous experiment (question) I've noticed the further out you put them the heavier they are."* Three questions later he is asked to "place the 20 g. weight on one side, and two weights 10 g. and 5 g. on the other so that the arm is level." Places 20 g. at hole 7 on left-hand arm. After much trial and error he finishes up with 10 g. at hole 19, and 5 g. at hole 10 on the right-hand side. There is nowhere near a balance and he comments: *"It would probably balance better if there was a hole between holes 9 and 10."* "Can you give me any law that takes into account weight and distance from the centre?" *"Ah yes, there is a law but I can't remember properly. But if 20 g. was placed on 5 holes and 10 g. was on*

> *10 holes it would balance.*" "Why?" *"10 goes into 20 twice so it goes twice as far out on here (the arm) and it balances."* "If you place a 20 g. weight on one side at hole 10, and a 10 g. weight at hole 18 on the other side, what about the angles the arms make with the horizontal?" *"I know they should be the same. I'm trying to remember what the science teacher told us but I've no memory for weight and things. We were told they were equal, and we did work it out and he did show us the reason."*

The notion of proportionality was not available to this boy in the Shadows experiment either. Thus we would tend to agree with the authors that when operational schemata are available to the subject, he can work out his problem spontaneously, or understand when academic teaching deals with the relevant concept.

(5) It is our opinion that the cultural milieu, climate of opinion, or the general experience to which the person is subjected, is of the greatest importance in developing thinking skills. It is in effect the *Zeitgeist* that appears to be of such great consequence. Part of the Zeitgeist is, of course, the atmosphere of the classroom; in the way the teacher poses and discusses problems; but not instruction, as such. The child at the primary stage who did best in all four experiments was a girl aged 10 years 9 months, of I.Q. 127 as assessed by the N.F.E.R. Primary Verbal Intelligence Test No. 1. Her teacher made these comments about her: "She always seems so much more mature than her friends. She mixes a great deal with intelligent adults and has travelled widely in this country and abroad."

(6) It seems unlikely that the thinking skills displayed in working these experiments are relevant only to scientific or technical problems. Tables 1–10 show that the experiments separate, in varying degrees, the fast from the slow learners in the secondary modern and comprehensive schools. Since children are not "streamed" on their ability to solve such problems, it is reasonable to suppose that the thinking skills have relevance when solving problems in history, geography, etc. . . .

(7) Many of the experiments which have been used by Piaget are in themselves learning situations; cf. Lovell & Ogilvie (1960). The experiments used in this study are no exception.

(8) If the suggestions outlined under points 4 and 5 are correct, then it seems that in teaching more needs to be done in the way of posing problems to children and in getting them to suggest possibilities and possible solutions. At junior school level, for example, it might be helpful to try to get children to arrive at conclusions by means of the inductive method. Naturally the number of variables involved would have to be kept small. How successful this would be, and how much transfer of training there should be is not known. Many junior school teachers are of the opinion, resulting from experience, that work should remain at the descriptive and observational level regardless of subject. It is certain, of course, that maturation is likely to fix a lower age limit, different for each child, below which certain thinking skills are not available to him.

(9) This type of experiment might provide another opportunity to study, in young able persons, the effects of strong emotion on logical thinking. Such experiments might also provide a method of studying intellectual deterioration due to age, brain lesions, or certain of the psychoses, in persons who had formerly given evidence of formal thinking.

REFERENCES

Bruner, J. S. Inhelder and Piaget's *The Growth of Logical Thinking:* I. A psychologist's viewpoint. *Brit. J. Psychol.*, 1959, **50,** 363–370.

Lovell, K. A follow-up study of some aspects of the work of Piaget and Inhelder on the child's conception of space. *Brit. J. educ. Psychol.*, 1959, **29**, 104–117.

Lovell, K., & Ogilvie, E. A study of the conservation of substance in the Junior School child. *Brit. J. educ. Psychol.,* 1960, **30,** 109–118.

PARSONS, G. Inhelder and Piaget's *The Growth of Logical Thinking:* II. A logician's viewpoint. *Brit. J. Psychol.,* 1960, **51,** 75–84.

SIEGEL, S. *Nonparametric statistics for the behavioural sciences.* London: McGraw-Hill, 1956.

L. VYGOTSKY

The Development of Scientific Concepts in Childhood[*]

I

To devise successful methods of instructing the schoolchild in systematic knowledge, it is necessary to understand the development of scientific concepts in the child's mind. No less important than this practical aspect of the problem is its theoretical significance for psychological science. Yet our knowledge of the entire subject is surprisingly scanty.

What happens in the mind of the child to the scientific concepts he is taught at school? What is the relationship between the assimilating of information and the internal development of a scientific concept in the child's consciousness?

Contemporary child psychology has two answers to these questions. One school of thought believes that scientific concepts have no inward history, i.e., do not undergo development but are absorbed ready-made through a process of understanding and assimilation. Most educational theories and methods are still based on this view. It is nevertheless a view that fails to stand up under scrutiny, either theoretically or in its practical applications. As we know from investigations of the process of concept formation, a concept is more than the sum of certain associative bonds formed by memory, more than a mere mental habit; it is a complex and genuine act of thought that cannot be taught by drilling but can be accomplished only when the child's mental development itself has reached the requisite level. At any age, a concept embodied in a word represents an act of generalization. But word meanings evolve. When a new word has been learned by the child, its development is barely starting; the word at first is a generalization of the most primitive type; as the child's intellect develops, it is replaced by generalizations of a higher and higher type—a process that leads in the end to the formation of true concepts. The development of concepts, or word meanings, presupposes the development of many intellectual functions: deliberate attention, logical memory, abstraction, the ability to compare and to differentiate. These complex psychological processes cannot be mastered through the initial learning alone.

Practical experience also shows that direct teaching of concepts is impossible and fruitless. A teacher who tries to do this usually accomplishes nothing but empty verbalism, a parrotlike repetition of words by the child, simulating a knowledge of the corresponding concepts but actually covering up a vacuum.

Leo Tolstoy, with his profound understanding of the nature of word and meaning, realized more clearly than most other educators the impossibility of simply relaying a concept from teacher to pupil. He tells of his attempts to teach literary language to peasant children by first "translating" their own vocabulary into the language of folk tales, then translating the language of tales into literary Russian. He found that one could not teach children literary language by artificial explanations, compulsive memorizing, and repetition, as one teaches a foreign language. Tolstoy writes:

* Reprinted by permission of the publisher from L. Vygotsky, *Thought and Language*. New York: John Wiley & Sons, Inc., 1962. Pp. 82–118.

> We have to admit that we attempted several times . . . to do this, and always met with an invincible distaste on the part of the children, which shows that we were on the wrong track. These experiments have left me with the certainty that it is quite impossible to explain the meaning of a word. . . . When you explain any word, the word "impression," for instance, you put in its place another equally incomprehensible word, or a whole series of words, with the connection between them as incomprehensible as the word itself.

What the child needs, says Tolstoy, is a chance to acquire new concepts and words from the general linguistic context.

> When he has heard or read an unknown word in an otherwise comprehensible sentence, and another time in another sentence, he begins to have a hazy idea of the new concept; sooner or later he will . . . feel the need to use that word—and once he has used it, the word and the concept are his. . . . But to give the pupil new concepts deliberately . . . is, I am convinced, as impossible and futile as teaching a child to walk by the laws of equilibrium [Tolstoy, 1903, p. 143].

The second conception of the evolution of scientific concepts does not deny the existence of a developmental process in the schoolchild's mind; it holds, however, that this process does not differ in any essential from the development of the concepts formed by the child in his everyday experience and that it is pointless to consider the two processes separately. What is the basis for this view?

The literature in this field shows that in studying concept formation in childhood most investigators have used everyday concepts formed by children without systematic instruction. The laws based on these data are assumed to apply also to the child's scientific concepts, and no checking of this assumption is deemed necessary. Only a few of the more perspicacious modern students of child thought question the legitimacy of such an extension. Piaget draws a sharp line between the child's ideas of reality developed mainly through his own mental efforts and those that were decisively influenced by adults; he designates the first group as *spontaneous,* the second as *nonspontaneous,* and admits that the latter may deserve independent investigation. In this respect, he goes farther and deeper than any of the other students of children's concepts.

At the same time, there are errors in Piaget's reasoning that detract from the value of his views. Although he holds that the child in forming a concept stamps it with the characteristics of his own mentality, Piaget tends to apply this thesis only to spontaneous concepts and assumes that they alone can truly enlighten us on the special qualities of child thought; he fails to see the interaction between the two kinds of concepts and the bonds that unite them into a total system of concepts in the course of the child's intellectual development. These errors lead to yet another. It is one of the basic tenets of Piaget's theory that progressive socialization of thinking is the very essence of the child's mental development. But if his views on the nature of nonspontaneous concepts were correct, it would follow that such an important factor in the socialization of thought as school learning is unrelated to the inner developmental processes. This inconsistency is the weak spot of Piaget's theory, both theoretically and practically.

Theoretically, socialization of thought is seen by Piaget as a mechanical abolition of the characteristics of the child's own thought, their gradual withering away. All that is new in development comes from without, replacing the child's own modes of thought. Throughout childhood, there is a ceaseless conflict between the two mutually antagonistic forms of thinking, with a series of compromises at each successive developmental level, until adult thought wins out. The child's own nature plays no constructive part in his intellectual progress. When Piaget says that nothing is more important for effective teaching than a thorough knowledge of spontaneous child thought (Piaget, 1933), he is apparently prompted by the idea that child thought must be known as any enemy must be known in order to be fought successfully.

We shall counter these erroneous premises

with the premise that the development of nonspontaneous concepts must possess all the traits peculiar to child thought at each developmental level because these concepts are not simply acquired by rote but evolve with the aid of strenuous mental activity on the part of the child himself. We believe that the two processes—the development of spontaneous and of nonspontaneous concepts—are related and constantly influence each other. They are parts of a single process: the development of concept formation, which is affected by varying external and internal conditions but is essentially a unitary process, not a conflict of antagonistic, mutually exclusive forms of mentation. Instruction is one of the principal sources of the schoolchild's concepts and is also a powerful force in directing their evolution; it determines the fate of his total mental development. If so, the results of the psychological study of children's concepts can be applied to the problems of teaching in a manner very different from that envisioned by Piaget.

Before discussing these premises in detail, we want to set forth our own reasons for differentiating between spontaneous and nonspontaneous—in particular scientific—concepts and for subjecting the latter to special study.

First, we know from simple observation that concepts form and develop under entirely different inner and outer conditions, depending on whether they originate in classroom instruction or in the child's personal experience. Even the motives prompting the child to form the two kinds of concepts are not the same. The mind faces different problems when assimilating concepts at school and when left to its own devices. When we impart systematic knowledge to the child, we teach him many things that he cannot directly see or experience. Since scientific and spontaneous concepts differ in their relation to the child's experience, and in the child's attitude toward their objects, they may be expected to follow differing developmental paths from their inception to their final form.

The singling-out of scientific concepts as an object of study also has a heuristic value. At present, psychology has only two ways of studying concept formation. One deals with the child's real concepts but uses methods—such as verbal definition—that do not penetrate below the surface; the other permits incomparably deeper psychological analysis, but only through studying the formation of artificially devised experimental concepts. An urgent methodological problem confronting us is to find ways of studying *real* concepts in *depth*—to find a method that could utilize the results already obtained by the two methods used so far. The most promising approach to the problem would seem to be the study of scientific concepts, which are real concepts yet are formed under our eyes almost in the fashion of artificial concepts.

Finally, the study of scientific concepts as such has important implications for education and instruction. Even though these concepts are not absorbed ready-made, instruction and learning play a leading role in their acquisition. To uncover the complex relationship between instruction and the development of scientific concepts is an important practical task.

These were the considerations that guided us in separating scientific from everyday concepts and subjecting them to comparative study. To illustrate the kind of question we tried to answer, let us take the concept "brother"—a typical everyday concept, which Piaget used so skillfully to establish a whole series of peculiarities of child thought—and compare it with the concept "exploitation," to which the child is introduced in his social science classes. Is their development the same, or is it different? Does "exploitation" merely repeat the developmental course of "brother," or is it, psychologically, a concept of a different type? We submit that the two concepts must differ in their development as well as in their functioning and that these two variants of the process of concept formation must influence each other's evolution.

II

TO STUDY the relationship between the development of scientific and that of everyday concepts, we need a yardstick for comparing them. To construct a measuring device, we must know the typical characteristics of everyday concepts at school age and the direction of their development during that period.

Piaget demonstrated that the schoolchild's concepts are marked primarily by his lack of conscious awareness of relationships, though he handles relationships correctly in a spontaneous, unreflective way. Piaget asked seven- to eight-year-olds the meaning of the word *because* in the sentence, "I won't go to school tomorrow because I am sick." Most of the children answered, "It means that he is sick"; others said, "It means that he won't go to school." A child is unable to realize that the question does not refer to the separate facts of sickness and of school absence but to their connection. Yet he certainly grasps the meaning of the sentence. Spontaneously, he uses *because* correctly, but he does not know how to use it deliberately. Thus, he cannot supply a correct ending to the sentence, "The man fell off his bicycle because. . . ." Often he will substitute a consequence ("because he broke his arm") for the cause. Child thought is nondeliberate and unconscious of itself. How, then, does the child eventually reach awareness and mastery of his own thoughts? To explain the process, Piaget cites two psychological laws.

One is the law of awareness, formulated by Claparède, who proved by very interesting experiments that awareness of difference precedes awareness of likeness. The child quite naturally responds in similar ways to objects that are alike and has no need to become aware of his mode of response, while dissimilarity creates a state of maladaptation which leads to awareness. Claparède's law states that the more smoothly we use a relationship in action, the less conscious we are of it; we become aware of what we are doing in proportion to the difficulty we experience in adapting to a situation.

Piaget uses Claparède's law to explain the development of thinking that takes place between the seventh and the twelfth year. During that period the child's mental operations repeatedly come in conflict with adult thinking. He suffers failures and defeats because of the deficiencies of his logic, and these painful experiences create the need to become aware of his concepts.

Realizing that need is not a sufficient explanation for any developmental change, Piaget supplements Claparède's law by the law of shift, or displacement. To become conscious of a mental operation means to transfer it from the plane of action to that of language, i.e., to re-create it in the imagination so that it can be expressed in words. This change is neither quick nor smooth. The law states that mastering an operation on the higher plane of verbal thought presents the same difficulties as the earlier mastering of that operation on the plane of action. This accounts for the slow progress.

These interpretations do not appear adequate. Claparède's findings may have a different explanation. Our own experimental studies suggest that the child becomes aware of differences earlier than of likenesses, not because differences lead to malfunctioning, but because awareness of similarity requires a more advanced structure of generalization and conceptualization than awareness of dissimilarity. In analyzing the development of concepts of difference and likeness, we found that consciousness of likeness presupposes the formation of a generalization, or of a concept, embracing the objects that are alike; consciousness of difference requires no such generalization—it may come about in other ways. The fact that the developmental sequence of these two concepts reverses the sequence of the earlier behavioral handling of similarity and difference is not unique. Our experiments established, for instance, that the child responds to pictorially represented action earlier than to the representation of an object, but becomes fully conscious of the object earlier than of action.[1]

The law of shift is an example of the wide-

[1] Identical pictures were shown two groups of preschool children of similar age and developmental level. One group was asked to act out the picture—which would indicate the degree of their immediate grasp of its content; the other group was asked to tell about it in words, a task requiring a measure of conceptually medi-

spread genetic theory according to which certain events or patterns observed in the early stages of a developmental process will recur in its advanced stages. The traits that do recur often blind the observer to significant differences caused by the fact that the later processes take place on a higher developmental level. We can dispense with discussing the principle of repetition as such, since we are concerned merely with its explanatory value in respect to the growth of awareness. The law of shift, like the law of awareness, may at best answer the question of why the schoolchild is not conscious of his concepts; it cannot explain how consciousness is achieved. We must look for another hypothesis to account for that decisive event in the child's mental development.

According to Piaget, the schoolchild's lack of awareness is a residue of his waning egocentrism, which still retains its influence in the sphere of verbal thought just beginning to form at that time. Consciousness is achieved when mature socialized thinking crowds out the residual egocentrism from the level of verbal thought.

Such an explanation of the nature of the schoolchild's concepts, based essentially on his general inability to become fully conscious of his acts, does not stand up in the face of facts. Various studies have shown that it is precisely during early school age that the higher intellectual functions, whose main features are reflective awareness and deliberate control, come to the fore in the developmental process. Attention, previously involuntary, becomes voluntary and increasingly dependent on the child's own thinking; mechanical memory changes to logical memory guided by meaning, and can now be deliberately used by the child. One might say that both attention and memory become "logical" and voluntary, since control of a function is the counterpart of one's consciousness of it. Nevertheless, the fact established by Piaget cannot be denied: The schoolchild, though growing steadily in awareness and mastery, is not aware of his conceptual operations. All the basic mental functions become conscious and deliberate during school age, *except* intellect itself.

To resolve this seeming paradox, we must turn to the basic laws governing psychological development. One of them is that consciousness and control appear only at a late stage in the development of a function, after it has been used and practiced unconsciously and spontaneously. In order to subject a function to intellectual and volitional control, we must first possess it.

The stage of undifferentiated functions in infancy is followed by the differentiation and development of perception in early childhood and the development of memory in the preschooler, to mention only the outstanding aspects of mental development at each age. Attention, which is a correlate of the structuring of what is perceived and remembered, participates in this development. Consequently, the child about to enter school possesses, in a fairly mature form, the functions he must next learn to subject to conscious control. But concepts—or rather preconcepts, as they should be called at that stage—are barely beginning to evolve from complexes at that time, and it would indeed be a miracle if the child were able to become conscious of them and to govern them, during the same period. For this to be possible, consciousness would not merely have to take possession of its single functions but to create them.

Before continuing, we want to clarify the term *consciousness* as we use it in speaking of nonconscious functions "becoming conscious." (We use the term *nonconscious* to distinguish what is not yet conscious from the Freudian "unconscious" resulting from repression, which is a late development, an effect of a relatively high differentiation of consciousness.) The activity of consciousness can take different directions; it may illumine only a few aspects of a thought or an act. I have just tied a knot—I have done so consciously, yet I cannot explain how I did it, because my awareness was centered on the knot rather than on my own motions, the *how* of my action. When the latter becomes

ated understanding. It was found that the "actors" rendered the sense of the represented action situation, while the narrators enumerated separate objects.

the object of my awareness, I shall have become fully conscious. We use *consciousness* to denote awareness of the activity of the mind—the consciousness of being conscious. A preschool child who, in response to the question, "Do you know your name?" tells his name lacks this self-reflective awareness: He knows his name but is not conscious of knowing it.

Piaget's studies showed that introspection begins to develop only during the school years. This process has a good deal in common with the development of external perception and observation in the transition from infancy to early childhood, when the child passes from primitive wordless perception to perception of objects guided by and expressed in words—perception in terms of meaning. Similarly, the schoolchild passes from unformulated to verbalized introspection; he perceives his own psychic processes as meaningful. But perception in terms of meaning always implies a degree of generalization. Consequently, the transition to verbalized self-observation denotes a beginning process of generalization of the inner forms of activity. The shift to a new type of inner perception means also a shift to a higher type of inner activity, since a new way of seeing things opens up new possibilities for handling them. A chessplayer's moves are determined by what he sees on the board; when his perception of the game changes, his strategy will also change. In perceiving some of our own acts in a generalizing fashion, we isolate them from our total mental activity and are thus enabled to focus on this process as such and to enter into a new relationship to it. In this way, becoming conscious of our operations and viewing each as a process of a certain *kind*—such as remembering or imagining—leads to their mastery.

School instruction induces the generalizing kind of perception and thus plays a decisive role in making the child conscious of his own mental processes. Scientific concepts, with their hierarchical system of interrelationships, seem to be the medium within which awareness and mastery first develop, to be transferred later to other concepts and other areas of thought. Reflective consciousness comes to the child through the portals of scientific concepts.

Piaget's characterization of the child's spontaneous concepts as nonconscious and nonsystematic tends to confirm our thesis. The implication that *spontaneous,* when applied to concepts, is a synonym of *nonconscious* is obvious throughout his writings, and the basis for this is easily seen. In operating with spontaneous concepts, the child is not conscious of them because his attention is always centered on the object to which the concept refers, never on the act of thought itself. Piaget's view that spontaneous concepts exist for the child outside any systematic context is equally clear. According to him, if we wish to discover and explore the child's own spontaneous idea hidden behind the nonspontaneous concept he voices, we must begin by freeing it from all ties to a system. This approach resulted in the kind of answers expressing the child's nonmediated attitude toward objects that fill all the books of Piaget.

To us it seems obvious that a concept can become subject to consciousness and deliberate control only when it is a part of a system. If consciousness means generalization, generalization in turn means the formation of a superordinate concept that includes the given concept as a particular case. A superordinate concept implies the existence of a series of subordinate concepts, and it also presupposes a hierarchy of concepts of different levels of generality. Thus the given concept is placed within a system of relationships of generality. The following example may illustrate the function of varying degrees of generality in the emergence of a system: A child learns the word *flower,* and shortly afterwards the word *rose;* for a long time the concept "flower," though more widely applicable than "rose," cannot be said to be more general for the child. It does not include and subordinate "rose"—the two are interchangeable and juxtaposed. When "flower" becomes generalized, the relationship of "flower" and "rose," as well as of "flower" and other subordinate concepts, also changes in the child's mind. A system is taking shape.

In the scientific concepts that the child acquires in school, the relationship to an object is mediated from the start by some other concept. Thus the very notion of scientific concept implies a certain position in relation to other concepts, i.e., a place within a system of concepts. It is our contention that the rudiments of systematization first enter the child's mind by way of his contact with scientific concepts and are then transferred to everyday concepts, changing their psychological structure from the top down.

III

THE interrelation of scientific and spontaneous concepts is a special case within a much broader subject: the relation of school instruction to the mental development of the child. Several theories concerning this relationship have been advanced in the past, and the question remains one of the major preoccupations of Soviet psychology. We shall review three attempts to answer it, in order to place our own study within the broader context.

The first and still most widely held theory considers instruction and development to be mutually independent. Development is seen as a process of maturation subject to natural laws, and instruction as the utilization of the opportunities created by development. Typical of this school of thought are its attempts to separate with great care the products of development from those of instruction, supposedly to find them in their pure form. No investigator has yet been able to achieve this. The blame is usually laid on inadequate methods, and the failures are compensated for by redoubled speculative analyses. These efforts to divide the child's intellectual equipment into two categories may go hand in hand with the notion that development can run its normal course and reach a high level without any assistance from instruction—that even children who never attend school can develop the highest forms of thinking accessible to human beings. More often, however, this theory is modified to take into account a relationship that obviously exists between development and instruction: The former creates the potentialities; the latter realizes them. Education is seen as a kind of superstructure erected over maturation; or, to change the metaphor, education is related to development as consumption to production. A one-sided relationship is thus conceded: Learning depends on development, but the course of development is not affected by learning.

This theory rests on the simple observation that any instruction demands a certain degree of maturity of certain functions: One cannot teach a one-year-old to read, or a three-year-old to write. The analysis of learning is thus reduced to determining the developmental level that various functions must reach for instruction to become feasible. When the child's memory has progressed enough to enable him to memorize the alphabet, when his attention can be held by a boring task, when his thinking has matured to the point where he can grasp the connection between sign and sound—then instruction in writing may begin. According to this variant of the first theory, instruction hobbles behind development. Development must complete certain cycles before instruction can begin.

The truth of this last statement is obvious; a necessary minimum level does exist. Nevertheless, this one-sided view results in a series of misconceptions. Suppose the child's memory, attention, and thinking have developed to the point where he can be taught writing and arithmetic; does the study of writing and arithmetic do anything to his memory, attention, and thinking, or does it not? Traditional psychology answers: Yes, in so far as they exercise these functions; but the process of development as such does not change; nothing new happens in the mental growth of the child; he has learned to write —that is all. This view, characteristic of old-fashioned educational theory, also colors the writings of Piaget, who believes that the child's thinking goes through certain phases and stages regardless of any instruction he may receive; instruction remains an extraneous factor. The gauge of the child's level of development is not what he has learned through instruction but the manner in which he thinks on subjects about which he has been taught nothing. Here the separation—indeed, the opposition—of instruction and development is carried to its extreme.

The second theory concerning development and instruction identifies the two processes. Originally expounded by James, it bases both processes on association and habit formation, thus rendering instruction synonymous with development. This view enjoys a certain revival at present, with Thorndike as its chief protagonist. Reflexology, which has translated associationism into the language of physiology, sees the intellectual development of the child as a gradual accumulation of conditioned reflexes; and learning is viewed in exactly the same way. Since instruction and development are identical, no question of any concrete relationship between them can arise.

The third school of thought, represented by Gestalt psychology, tries to reconcile the two foregoing theories while avoiding their pitfalls. Although this eclecticism results in a somewhat inconsistent approach, a certain synthesis of the two opposite views is achieved. Koffka states that all development has two aspects, maturation and learning. Although this means accepting in a less extreme form both of the older points of view, the new theory represents an improvement on the two others, in three ways.

First, Koffka admits some interdependence between the two aspects of development. On the basis of a number of facts, he demonstrates that maturation of an organ is contingent on its functioning, which improves through learning and practice. Maturation, in turn, provides new opportunities for learning. But Koffka merely postulates mutual influence without examining its nature in detail. Second, this theory introduces a new conception of the educational process itself as the formation of new structures and the perfecting of old ones. Instruction is thus accorded a meaningful structural role. A basic characteristic of any structure is its independence from its original substance—it can be transferred to other media. Once a child has formed a certain structure, or learned a certain operation, he will be able to apply it in other areas. We have given him a pennyworth of instruction, and he has gained a small fortune in development. The third point in which this theory compares favorably with the older ones is its view of the temporal relation between instruction and development. Since instruction given in one area can transform and reorganize other areas of child thought, it may not only follow maturing or keep in step with it but also precede it and further its progress. The admission that different temporal sequences are equally possible and important is a contribution by the eclectic theory that should not be underestimated.

This theory brings us face to face with an old issue reappearing in a new guise: the almost forgotten theory of formal discipline, usually associated with Herbart. It maintained that instruction in certain subjects develops the mental faculties in general, besides imparting the knowledge of the subject and specific skills. In practice, this led to the most reactionary forms of schooling, such as the Russian and the German "classical gymnasiums," which inordinately stressed Greek and Latin as sources of "formal discipline." The system was eventually discarded because it did not meet the practical aims of modern bourgeois education. Within psychology itself, Thorndike, in a series of investigations, did his best to discredit formal discipline as a myth and to prove that instruction had no far-reaching effects on development. His criticism is convincing in so far as it applies to the ludicrous exaggerations of the doctrine of formal discipline, but it does not touch its valuable kernel.

In his effort to disprove Herbart's conception, Thorndike experimented with the narrowest, most specialized, and most elementary functions. From the point of view of a theory that reduces all learning to the formation of associative bonds, the choice of activity would make little difference. In some experiments he gave his subjects practice in distinguishing between the relative lengths of lines and then tried to establish whether this practice increased their ability to distinguish between sizes of angles. Naturally, he found that it did not. The influence of instruction on development has been postulated by the theory of formal discipline only in relation to such subjects as mathematics or languages, which involve vast complexes of psychic functions. The ability to gauge the length of lines may not affect the ability to distinguish between angles, but the study of the native language—with its attendant sharpening of concepts—may still have some bearing on the study of arithmetic. Thorndike's work merely makes it appear likely that there are two kinds of instruction: the narrowly specialized training in some skill, such as typing, involving habit formation and exercise and more often found in trade schools for adults, and the kind of instruction given schoolchildren, which activates large areas of consciousness. The idea of formal discipline may have little to do with the first kind but may well prove to be valid for the second. It stands to reason that in the higher processes emerging during the cultural development of the child, formal discipline must play a role that it does not play in the more elementary processes: All the higher functions have in common awareness, abstraction, and control. In line with Thorndike's theoretical conceptions, the qualitative differences between the lower and the higher functions are ignored in his studies of the transfer of training.

In formulating our own tentative theory of the relationship between instruction and development, we take our departure from four series of investigations (Assen'eva *et al.*). Their common purpose was to uncover these complex interrelations in certain definite areas of school instruction: reading and writing, grammar, arithmetic, natural science, and social science. The specific inquiries concerned such topics as the mastering of the decimal system in relation to the development of the concept of number; the child's awareness of his operations in solving mathematical problems; the processes of constructing and solving problems by first-graders. Much interesting material came to light on the development of oral and written language during school age, the consecutive levels of understanding of figurative meaning, the influence of mastering grammatical structures on the course of mental development, the understanding of relationships in the study of social science and natural science. The investigations focused on the level of maturity of psychic functions at the beginning of schooling, and the influence of schooling on their development; on the temporal sequence of instruction and development; on the "formal discipline" function of the various subjects of instruction. We shall discuss these issues in succession.

1. In our first series of studies, we examined the level of development of the psychic functions requisite for learning the basic school subjects—reading and writing, arithmetic, natural science. We found that at the beginning of instruction these functions could not be considered mature, even in the children who proved able to master the curriculum very successfully. Written language is a good illustration. Why does writing come so hard to the schoolchild that at certain periods there is a lag of as much as six or eight years between his "linguistic age" in speaking and in writing? This used to be explained by the novelty of writing: As a new function, it must repeat the developmental stages of speech; therefore the writing of an eight-year-old must resemble the speech of a two-year-old. This explanation is patently insufficient. A two-year-old uses few words and a simple syntax because his vocabulary is small and his knowledge of more complex sentence structures nonexistent; but the schoolchild possesses the vocabulary and the grammatical forms for writing, since they are the same as for oral speech. Nor can the difficulties of mastering the mechanics of writing account for the tremendous lag between the schoolchild's oral and written language.

Our investigation has shown that the development of writing does not repeat the developmental history of speaking. Written speech is a separate linguistic function, differing from oral speech in both structure and mode of functioning. Even its minimal development requires a high level of abstraction.

It is speech in thought and image only, lacking the musical, expressive, intonational qualities of oral speech. In learning to write, the child must disengage himself from the sensory aspect of speech and replace words by images of words. Speech that is merely imagined and that requires symbolization of the sound image in written signs (i.e., a second degree of symbolization) naturally must be as much harder than oral speech for the child as algebra is harder than arithmetic. Our studies show that it is the abstract quality of written language that is the main stumbling block, not the underdevelopment of small muscles or any other mechanical obstacles.

Writing is also speech without an interlocutor, addressed to an absent or an imaginary person or to no one in particular—a situation new and strange to the child. Our studies show that he has little motivation to learn writing when we begin to teach it. He feels no need for it and has only a vague idea of its usefulness. In conversation, every sentence is prompted by a motive. Desire or need lead to request, question to answer, bewilderment to explanation. The changing motives of the interlocutors determine at every moment the turn oral speech will take. It does not have to be consciously directed—the dynamic situation takes care of that. The motives for writing are more abstract, more intellectualized, further removed from immediate needs. In written speech, we are obliged to create the situation, to represent it to ourselves. This demands detachment from the actual situation.

Writing also requires deliberate analytical action on the part of the child. In speaking, he is hardly conscious of the sounds he pronounces and quite unconscious of the mental operations he performs. In writing, he must take cognizance of the sound structure of each word, dissect it, and reproduce it in alphabetical symbols, which he must have studied and memorized before. In the same deliberate way, he must put words in a certain sequence to form a sentence. Written language demands conscious work because its relationship to inner speech is different from that of oral speech: The latter precedes inner speech in the course of development, while written speech follows inner speech and presupposes its existence (the act of writing implying a translation from inner speech). But the grammar of thought is not the same in the two cases. One might even say that the syntax of inner speech is the exact opposite of the syntax of written speech, with oral speech standing in the middle.

Inner speech is condensed, abbreviated speech. Written speech is deployed to its fullest extent, more complete than oral speech. Inner speech is almost entirely predicative because the situation, the subject of thought, is always known to the thinker. Written speech, on the contrary, must explain the situation fully in order to be intelligible. The change from maximally compact inner speech to maximally detailed written speech requires what might be called deliberate semantics—deliberate structuring of the web of meaning.

All these traits of written speech explain why its development in the schoolchild falls far behind that of oral speech. The discrepancy is caused by the child's proficiency in spontaneous, unconscious activity and his lack of skill in abstract, deliberate activity. As our studies showed, the psychological functions on which written speech is based have not even begun to develop in the proper sense when instruction in writing starts. It must build on barely emerging, rudimentary processes.

Similar results were obtained in the fields of arithmetic, grammar, and natural science. In every case, the requisite functions are immature when instruction begins. We shall briefly discuss the case of grammar, which presents some special features.

Grammar is a subject which seems to be of little practical use. Unlike other school subjects, it does not give the child new skills. He conjugates and declines before he enters school. The opinion has even been voiced that school instruction in grammar could be dispensed with. We can only reply that our analysis clearly showed the study of grammar to be of paramount importance for the mental development of the child.

The child does have a command of the

grammar of his native tongue long before he enters school, but it is unconscious, acquired in a purely structural way, like the phonetic composition of words. If you ask a young child to produce a combination of sounds, for example *sk,* you will find that its deliberate articulation is too hard for him; yet within a structure, as in the word *Moscow,* he pronounces the same sounds with ease. The same is true of grammar. The child will use the correct case or tense within a sentence but cannot decline or conjugate a word on request. He may not acquire new grammatical or syntactic forms in school but, thanks to instruction in grammar and writing, he does become aware of what he is doing and learns to use his skills consciously. Just as the child realizes for the first time in learning to write that the word *Moscow* consists of the sounds *m-o-s-k-ow* and learns to pronounce each one separately, he also learns to construct sentences, to do consciously what he has been doing unconsciously in speaking. Grammar and writing help the child to rise to a higher level of speech development.

Thus our investigation shows that the development of the psychological foundations for instruction in basic subjects does not precede instruction but unfolds in a continuous interaction with the contributions of instruction.

2. Our second series of investigations centered on the temporal relation between the processes of instruction and the development of the corresponding psychological functions. We found that instruction usually precedes development. The child acquires certain habits and skills in a given area before he learns to apply them consciously and deliberately. There is never complete parallelism between the course of instruction and the development of the corresponding functions.

Instruction has its own sequences and organization, it follows a curriculum and a timetable, and its rules cannot be expected to coincide with the inner laws of the developmental processes it calls to life. On the basis of our studies, we tried to plot curves of the progress of instruction and of the participating psychological functions; far from coinciding, these curves showed an exceedingly complex relationship.

For example, the different steps in learning arithmetic may be of unequal value for mental development. It often happens that three or four steps in instruction add little to the child's understanding of arithmetic, and then, with the fifth step, something clicks; the child has grasped a general principle, and his developmental curve rises markedly. For this particular child, the fifth operation was decisive, but this cannot be a general rule. The turning points at which a general principle becomes clear to the child cannot be set in advance by the curriculum. The child is not taught the decimal system as such; he is taught to write figures, to add and to multiply, to solve problems, and out of all this some general concept of the decimal system eventually emerges.

When the child learns some arithmetical operation or some scientific concept, the development of that operation or concept has only begun. Our study shows that the curve of development does not coincide with the curve of school instruction; by and large, instruction precedes development.

3. Our third series of investigations resembles Thorndike's studies of the transfer of training, except that we experimented with subjects of school instruction and with the higher rather than the elementary functions, i.e., with subjects and functions which could be expected to be meaningfully related.

We found that intellectual development, far from following Thorndike's atomistic model, is not compartmentalized according to topics of instruction. Its course is much more unitary, and the different school subjects interact in contributing to it. While the processes of instruction follow their own logical order, they awaken and direct a system of processes in the child's mind which is hidden from direct observation and subject to its own developmental laws. To uncover these developmental processes stimulated by instruction is one of the basic tasks of the psychological study of learning.

Specifically, our experiments brought out the following interrelated facts: The psychological prerequisites for instruction in different school subjects are to a large extent the same; instruction in a given subject influences the development of the higher functions far beyond the confines of that particular subject; the main psychic functions involved in studying various subjects are interdependent—their common bases are consciousness and deliberate mastery, the principal contributions of the school years. It follows from these findings that all the basic school subjects act as formal discipline, each facilitating the learning of the other; the psychological functions stimulated by them develop in one complex process.

4. In the fourth series of studies, we attacked a problem which has not received sufficient attention in the past but which we consider of focal importance for the study of learning and development.

Most of the psychological investigations concerned with school learning measured the level of mental development of the child by making him solve certain standardized problems. The problems he was able to solve by himself were supposed to indicate the level of his mental development at the particular time. But in this way only the completed part of the child's development can be measured, which is far from the whole story. We tried a different approach. Having found that the mental age of two children was, let us say, eight, we gave each of them harder problems than he could manage on his own and provided some slight assistance: the first step in a solution, a leading question, or some other form of help. We discovered that one child could, in co-operation, solve problems designed for twelve-year-olds, while the other could not go beyond problems intended for nine-year-olds. The discrepancy between a child's actual mental age and the level he reaches in solving problems with assistance indicates the zone of his proximal development; in our example, this zone is four for the first child and one for the second. Can we truly say that their mental development is the same? Experience has shown that the child with the larger zone of proximal development will do much better in school. This measure gives a more helpful clue than mental age does to the dynamics of intellectual progress.

Psychologists today cannot share the layman's belief that imitation is a mechanical activity and that anyone can imitate almost anything if shown how. To imitate, it is necessary to possess the means of stepping from something one knows to something new. With assistance, every child can do more than he can by himself—though only within the limits set by the state of his development. Koehler found that a chimpanzee can imitate only those intelligent acts of other apes that he could have performed on his own. Persistent training, it is true, can induce him to perform much more complicated actions, but these are carried out mechanically and have all the earmarks of meaningless habits rather than of insightful solutions. The cleverest animal is incapable of intellectual development through imitation. It can be drilled to perform specific acts, but the new habits do not result in new general abilities. In this sense, it can be said that animals are unteachable.

In the child's development, on the contrary, imitation and instruction play a major role. They bring out the specifically human qualities of the mind and lead the child to new developmental levels. In learning to speak, as in learning school subjects, imitation is indispensable. What the child can do in co-operation today he can do alone tomorrow. Therefore the only good kind of instruction is that which marches ahead of development and leads it; it must be aimed not so much at the ripe as at the ripening functions. It remains necessary to determine the lowest threshold at which instruction in, say, arithmetic may begin since a certain minimal ripeness of functions is required. But we must consider the upper threshold as well; instruction must be oriented toward the future, not the past.

For a time, our schools favored the "complex" system of instruction, which was believed to be adapted to the child's ways of thinking. In offering the child problems he was able to handle without help, this method failed to utilize the zone of proximal development and to lead the child to what he could not yet do. Instruction was oriented to the child's weakness rather than his strength, thus encouraging him to remain at the preschool stage of development.

For each subject of instruction there is a period when its influence is most fruitful because the child is most receptive to it. It has been called the *sensitive period* by Montessori and other educators. The term is used also in biology, for the periods in ontogenetic development when the organism is particularly responsive to influences of certain kinds. During that period an influence that has little effect earlier or later may radically affect the course of development. But the existence of an optimum time for instruction in a given subject cannot be explained in purely biological terms, at least not for such complex processes as written speech. Our investigation demonstrated the social and cultural nature of the development of the higher functions during these periods, i.e., its dependence on co-operation with adults and on instruction. Montessori's data, however, retain their significance. She found, for instance, that if a child is taught to write early, at four and a half or five years of age, he responds by "explosive writing," an abundant and imaginative use of written speech that is never duplicated by children a few years older. This is a striking example of the strong influence that instruction can have when the corresponding functions have not yet fully matured. The existence of sensitive periods for all subjects of instruction is fully supported by the data of our studies. The school years as a whole are the optimum period for instruction in operations that require awareness and deliberate control; instruction in these operations maximally furthers the development of the higher psychological functions while they are maturing. This applies also to the development of the scientific concepts to which school instruction introduces the child.

IV

ZH. I. SHIF, under our guidance, conducted an investigation of the development of scientific and everyday concepts during school age (Shif, 1935). Its chief purpose was to test experimentally our working hypothesis of the development of scientific concepts compared with everyday concepts. The child was given structurally similar problems dealing with either scientific or "ordinary" material, and his solutions were compared. The experiments included making up stories from series of pictures that showed the beginning of an action, its continuation, and its end, and completing fragments of sentences ending in *because* or *although;* these tests were complemented by clinical discussion. The material for one series of tests was taken from social science courses of the second and fourth grades. The second series used simple situations of everyday life, such as: "The boy went to the movies because . . . ," "The girl cannot yet read, although . . . ," "He fell off his bicycle because. . . ." Supplementary methods of study included testing the extent of the child's knowledge and observation during lessons specially organized for the purpose. The children we studied were primary school pupils.

Analysis of the data compared separately for each age group in the table below showed that as long as the curriculum supplies the necessary material *the development of scientific concepts runs ahead of the development of spontaneous concepts.*

CORRECT COMPLETIONS OF SENTENCE FRAGMENTS

	Second Grade (*per cent*)	*Fourth Grade* [2] (*per cent*)
Fragments ending in *because*		
Scientific concepts	79.7	81.8
Spontaneous concepts	59.0	81.3
Fragments ending in *although*		
Scientific concepts	21.3	79.5
Spontaneous concepts	16.2	65.5

2 In the Russian school system, children in the second and fourth grades would be, on the average, eight and ten years old.

How are we to explain the fact that problems involving scientific concepts are solved correctly more often than similar problems involving everyday concepts? We can at once dismiss the notion that the child is helped by factual information acquired at school and lacks experience in everyday matters. Our tests, like Piaget's, dealt entirely with things and relations familiar to the child and often spontaneously mentioned by him in conversation. No one would assume that a child knows less about bicycles, children, or school than about the class struggle, exploitation, or the Paris Commune. The advantage of familiarity is all on the side of the everyday concepts.

The child must find it hard to solve problems involving life situations because he lacks awareness of his concepts and therefore cannot operate with them at will as the task demands. A child of eight or nine uses *because* correctly in spontaneous conversation; he would never say that a boy fell and broke his leg *because* he was taken to the hospital. Yet that is the sort of thing he comes up with in experiments until the concept "because" becomes fully conscious. On the other hand, he correctly finishes sentences on social science subjects: "Planned economy is possible in the U.S.S.R. because there is no private property—all land, factories, and plants belong to the workers and peasants." Why is he capable of performing the operation in this case? Because the teacher, working with the pupil, has explained, supplied information, questioned, corrected, and made the pupil explain. The child's concepts have been formed in the process of instruction, in collaboration with an adult. In finishing the sentence, he makes use of the fruits of that collaboration, this time independently. The adult's help, invisibly present, enables the child to solve such problems earlier than everyday problems.

At the same age level (second grade), *although* sentences present a different picture: Scientific concepts are not ahead of everyday ones. We know that adversative relations appear later than causal relations in the child's spontaneous thinking. A child of that age can learn to use *because* consciously because by then he has already mastered its spontaneous use. Not having mastered *although* in the same way, he naturally cannot use it deliberately in his "scientific" thinking; hence, the percentage of successes is equally low in both test series.

Our data show quick progress in the solution of problems involving everyday concepts: In the fourth grade *because* fragments are completed correctly with equal frequency for everyday and for scientific material. This bears out our assumption that mastering a higher level in the realm of scientific concepts also raises the level of spontaneous concepts. Once the child has achieved consciousness and control in one kind of concepts, all of the previously formed concepts are reconstructed accordingly.

The relationship between scientific and spontaneous concepts in the adversative category presents in the fourth grade a picture very similar to that of the causal category in the second grade. The percentage of correct solutions for tasks involving scientific concepts surpasses the percentage for those involving everyday concepts. If the dynamics are the same for both categories, everyday concepts may be expected to rise sharply in the next stage of development and finally to catch up with scientific concepts. Starting two years later, the whole process of the development of "although" would duplicate that of "because."

We believe that our data warrant the assumption that from the very beginning the child's scientific and his spontaneous concepts—for instance, "exploitation" and "brother"—*develop in reverse directions:* Starting far apart, they move to meet each other. This is the key point of our hypothesis.

The child becomes conscious of his spontaneous concepts relatively late; the ability to define them in words, to operate with them at will, appears long after he has acquired the concepts. He has the concept (i.e., knows the object to which the concept refers), but is not conscious of his own act of thought. The development of a scientific concept, on the other hand, usually *begins* with its verbal definition and its use in non-spontaneous operations—with working on the concept itself. It starts its life in the child's mind at the level that his spontaneous concepts reach only later.

A child's everyday concept, such as "brother," is saturated with experience. Yet, when he is asked to solve an abstract problem about a brother's brother, as in Piaget's experiments, he becomes confused. On the other hand, though he can correctly answer questions about "slavery," "exploitation," or "civil war," these concepts are schematic and lack the rich content derived from personal experience. They are filled in gradually, in the course of further schoolwork and reading. One might say that *the development of the child's spontaneous concepts proceeds upward, and the development of his scientific concepts downward,* to a more elementary and concrete level. This is a consequence of the different ways in which the two kinds of concepts emerge. The inception of a spontaneous concept can usually be traced to a face-to-face meeting with a concrete situation, while a scientific concept involves from the first a "mediated" attitude toward its object.

Though scientific and spontaneous concepts develop in reverse directions, the two processes are closely connected. The development of a spontaneous concept must have reached a certain level for the child to be able to absorb a related scientific concept. For example, historical concepts can begin to develop only when the child's everyday concept of the past is sufficiently differentiated—when his own life and the life of those around him can be fitted into the elementary generalization "in the past and now"; his geographic and sociological concepts must grow out of the simple schema "here and elsewhere." In working its slow way upward, an everyday concept clears a path for the scientific concept and its downward development. It creates a series of structures necessary for the evolution of a concept's more primitive, elementary aspects, which give it body and vitality. Scientific concepts in turn supply structures for the upward development of the child's spontaneous concepts toward consciousness and deliberate use. Scientific concepts grow down through spontaneous concepts; spontaneous concepts grow upward through scientific concepts.

The influence of scientific concepts on the mental development of the child is analogous to the effect of learning a foreign language, a process which is conscious and deliberate from the start. In one's native language, the primitive aspects of speech are acquired before the more complex ones. The latter presuppose some awareness of phonetic, grammatical, and syntactic forms. With a foreign language, the higher forms develop before spontaneous, fluent speech. The intellectualistic theories of language, such as Stern's, which place a full grasp of the relationship between sign and meaning at the very beginning of linguistic development, contain a measure of truth in the case of a foreign language. The child's strong points in a foreign language are his weak points in his native language, and vice versa. In his own language, the child conjugates and declines correctly, but without realizing it. He cannot tell the gender, the case, or the tense of the word he is using. In a foreign language, he distinguishes between masculine and feminine gender and is conscious of grammatical forms from the beginning.

Of phonetics, the same is true. Faultlessly articulating his native speech, the child is unconscious of the sounds he pronounces, and in learning to spell he has great difficulty in dividing a word into its constituent sounds. In a foreign language, he does this easily, and his writing does not lag behind his speech. It is the pronunciation, the "spontaneous phonetics," that he finds hard to master. Easy, spontaneous speech with a quick and sure command of grammatical structures comes to him only as the crowning achievement of long, arduous study.

Success in learning a foreign language is contingent on a certain degree of maturity in the native language. The child can transfer to the new language the system of meanings he already possesses in his own. The reverse is also true—a foreign language facilitates mastering the higher forms of the native language.

The child learns to see his language as one particular system among many, to view its phenomena under more general categories, and this leads to awareness of his linguistic operations. Goethe said with truth that "he who knows no foreign language does not truly know his own."

It is not surprising that an analogy should exist between the interaction of the native and the foreign language and the interaction of scientific and spontaneous concepts, since both processes belong in the sphere of developing verbal thought. However, there are also essential differences between them. In foreign language study, attention centers on the exterior, sonal, physical aspects of verbal thought; in the development of scientific concepts, on its semantic aspect. The two developmental processes follow separate, though similar, paths.

Nevertheless, both suggest a single answer to the question of how new systems are formed that are structurally analogous to earlier ones: *written* speech, *foreign* language, *verbal* thought in general. The experimental evidence yielded by our studies disproves the theory of shift, or displacement, which states that the later stage repeats the course of the earlier one, including the recurrence of difficulties already overcome on the lower plane. All our evidence supports the hypothesis that analogous systems develop in reverse directions at the higher and at the lower levels, each system influencing the other and benefiting from the strong points of the other.

We can now turn to the interrelation of concepts in a system—the focal problem of our analysis.

Concepts do not lie in the child's mind like peas in a bag, without any bonds between them. If that were the case, no intellectual operation requiring co-ordination of thoughts would be possible, nor any general conception of the world. Not even separate concepts as such could exist; their very nature presupposes a system.

The study of the child's concepts at each age level shows that the degree of generality (plant, flower, rose) is the basic psychological variable according to which they can be meaningfully ordered. If every concept is a generalization, then the relationship between concepts is a relationship of generality. The logical aspect of that relationship has been studied much more fully than its genetic and psychological aspects. Our study attempts to fill this gap.

We compared the degree of generality of the child's real concepts with the phases and stages reached by the child in experimental concept formation: syncretism, complex, preconcept, and concept. Our aim was to find out whether a definite relationship existed between the structure of generalization typified by these phases and the degree of generality of concepts.

Concepts of differing degrees of generality may occur in one and the same generalizational structure. For instance, the ideas "flower" and "rose" may both be present at the stage of complex thinking. Correspondingly, concepts of equal generality may appear within different structures of generalization, e.g., "flower" may apply to any and all flowers at the complex stage as well as in conceptual thinking. We found, however, that in spite of this lack of complete correspondence each phase, or generalizational structure, has as its counterpart a specific level of generality, a specific relationship of superordinate and subordinate concepts, a typical combination of the concrete and the abstract. The term *flower,* it is true, may be equally general at the level of complex and of concept, but only in relation to the objects to which it refers. Equal generality here does not imply identity of all the psychological processes involved in the use of this term. Thus, in complex thinking the relationship of "flower" to "rose" is not superordination; the wider and the narrower concepts coexist on the same plane.

In our experiments a mute child learned without much difficulty the words *table, chair, bureau, couch, shelves,* and so on. The term *furniture,* however, proved too hard to grasp. The same child, having successfully learned *shirt, hat, coat, pants,* etc., could not rise above the level of this series and master *clothes.* We found that at a certain level of development the child is incapable of moving "vertically" from one word meaning to another, i.e., of understanding their relationships of generality. All his concepts are on one level, refer directly to objects, and are delimited from one another in the same way that the objects themselves are delimited: Verbal thought is no more than a dependent component of perceptual, object-determined thought. Hence, this stage must be considered an early, presyncretic stage in the development of word meaning. The appearance of the first generalized concept, such as "furniture" or "clothes," is as significant a symptom of progress as the first meaningful word.

The higher levels in the development of word meanings are governed by the law of equivalence of concepts, according to which any concept can be formulated in terms of other concepts in a countless number of ways. We shall illustrate the schema underlying this law by an analogy not ideally accurate but close enough to serve the purpose.

If we imagine the totality of concepts as distributed over the surface of a globe, the location of every concept may be defined by means of a system of co-ordinates, corresponding to longitude and latitude in geography. One of these co-ordinates will indicate the location of a concept between the extremes of maximally generalized abstract conceptualization and the immediate sensory grasp of an object—i.e., its degree of concreteness and abstraction. The second co-ordinate will represent the objective reference of the concept, the locus within reality to which it applies. Two concepts applying to different areas of reality but comparable in degree of abstractness—e.g., plants and animals—could be conceived of as varying in latitude but having the same longitude. The geographical analogy breaks down in several details: The more generalized concept, for instance, applies to a broader area of content, which should be represented by a line, not a point. But it serves to convey the idea that to be adequately characterized each concept must be placed within two continua—one that represents objective content and another that represents acts of thought apprehending the content. Their intersection determines all the relationships of the given concept to others—its co-ordinate, superordinate, and subordinate concepts. This position of a concept within the total system of concepts may be called its measure of generality.

The manifold mutual relations of concepts on which the law of equivalence is based are determined by their respective measures of generality. Let us take two extreme examples: the child's early (presyncretic) words lacking any variation in degree of generality and the concepts of numbers developed through the study of arithmetic. In the first case, obviously, every concept can be expressed only through itself, never through other concepts. In the second case, any number may be expressed in countless ways, because of the infinity of numbers and because the concept of any number contains also all of its relationships to all other numbers. "One," for instance, may be expressed as "1000 minus 999" or, in general, as the difference between any two consecutive numbers, or as any number divided by itself, and in a myriad of other ways. This is a pure example of equivalence of concepts. In so far as equivalence depends on the relationships of generality between concepts, and these are specific for every generalizational structure, the latter determines the equivalence of concepts possible within its sphere.

The measure of generality determines not only the equivalence of concepts but also all of the intellectual operations possible with a given concept. All intellectual operations—comparisons, judgments, conclusions—require some movement within the net of co-ordinates we have outlined. Developmental changes in the structure of generalization cause changes also in these operations. For example, as higher levels of generality and equivalence of concepts are reached, it becomes easier for a child to remember thoughts independently of words. A young child must reproduce the exact words in which a meaning was conveyed to him. A schoolchild can already render a relatively complex meaning in his own words; thus his intellectual freedom increases. In pathological disturbances of conceptual thinking, the measure of generality of concepts is distorted, the balance between the abstract and the concrete is upset, and the relationship to other concepts becomes unstable. The mental act through which both the object and the object's relation to the concept are grasped loses its unity, and thought begins to run along broken, capricious, illogical lines.

One goal of our study of the child's real concepts was to find reliable indices of their structure of generalization. Only with their help could the genetic schema yielded by our experimental studies of artificial concepts be profitably applied to the child's developing real concepts. Such an index was finally discovered in the concept's measure of generality, which varies on the different levels of development, from syncretic formations to concepts proper. Analysis of the child's real concepts also helped us to determine how concepts differ at the various levels in their relationship to the object and to word meaning, and in the intellectual operations they make possible.

Furthermore, the investigation of real concepts complemented the experimental study by making it clear that every new stage in the development of generalization is built on generalizations of the preceding level; the products of the intellectual activity of the earlier phases are not lost. The inner bond between the consecutive phases could not be uncovered in our experiments because the subject had to discard, after each wrong solution, the generalizations he had formed, and start all over again. Also, the nature of the experimental objects did not permit their conceptualization in hierarchical terms.

The investigation of real concepts filled these gaps. The preschooler's ideas (which have the structure of complexes) were found to result, not from grouping images of individual objects, but from elaboration of generalizations predominant during an earlier phase. At a higher level, we found an analogous relationship between old and new formations in the development of arithmetical and algebraic concepts. The rise from preconcepts (which the schoolchild's arithmetical concepts usually are) to true concepts, such as the algebraic concepts of adolescents, is achieved by generalizing the generalizations of the earlier level. At the earlier stage certain aspects of objects had been abstracted and generalized into ideas of numbers. Algebraic concepts represent abstractions and generalizations of certain aspects of numbers, not objects, and thus signify a new departure—a new, higher plane of thought.

The new, higher concepts in turn transform the meaning of the lower. The adolescent who has mastered algebraic concepts has gained a vantage point from which he sees arithmetical concepts in a broader perspective. We saw this especially clearly in experimenting with shifts from the decimal to other numerical systems. As long as the child operates with the decimal system without having become conscious of it as such, he has not mastered the system but is, on the contrary, bound by it. When he becomes able to view it as a particular instance of the wider concept of a scale of notation, he can operate deliberately with this or any other numerical system. The ability to shift at will from one system to another (e.g., to "translate" from the decimal system into one that is based on five) is the criterion of this new level of consciousness, since it indicates the existence of a general concept of a system of numeration. In this as in other instances of passing from one level of meaning to the next, the child does not have to restructure separately all of his earlier concepts, which indeed would be a Sisyphean labor. Once a new structure has been incorporated into his thinking—usually through concepts recently acquired in school—it gradually spreads to the older concepts as they are drawn into the intellectual operations of the higher type.

Our investigation of children's real concepts throws a new light on another important issue in the theory of thought. The Wuerzburg school demonstrated that the course of directed thought is not governed by associative connections, but it did little to clarify the specific factors that actually determine this course. Gestalt psychology substituted the principle of structure for that of association but failed to distinguish thought proper from perception, memory, and all the other functions subject to structural laws; it repeated the pattern of the association theory in reducing all the functions to one level. Our investigations help to transcend this pattern by showing that thought of a higher level is governed by the relations of generality between concepts—a system of relations absent from perception and memory. Wertheimer has demonstrated that productive thinking is contingent on transferring the problem from the structure within which it was first apprehended to an entirely different context or structure. But to transfer an object of thought from structure A to structure B, one must transcend the given structural bonds, and this, as our studies show, requires shifting to a plane of greater generality, to a concept subsuming and governing both A and B.

We can now reaffirm on a sound basis of data that the *absence of a system* is the cardinal psychological difference distinguishing spontaneous from scientific concepts. It could be shown that all the peculiarities of child thought described by Piaget (such as syncretism, juxtaposition, insensitivity to contradiction) stem from the absence of a system in the child's spontaneous concepts—a consequence of undeveloped relations of generality. For example, to be disturbed by a contradiction, the child would have to view the contradictory statements in the light of some general principle, i.e., within a system. But when a child in Piaget's experiments says of one object that it dissolved in water because it was small, and of another that it dissolved because it was big, he merely makes empirical statements of facts which follow the logic of perceptions. No generalization of the kind "Smallness leads to dissolution" is present in his mind, and hence the two statements are not felt to be contradictory. It is this lack of distance from the immediate experience—and not syncretism viewed as a compromise between the logic of dreams and reality—that accounts for the peculiarities of child thought. Therefore these peculiarities do not appear in the child's scientific concepts, which from their very inception carry within them relationships of generality, i.e., some rudiments of a system. The formal discipline of scientific concepts gradually transforms the structure of the child's spontaneous concepts and helps organize them into a system; this furthers the child's ascent to higher developmental levels.

Our disagreement with Piaget centers on one point only, but an important point. He assumes that development and instruction are entirely separate, incommensurate processes, that the function of instruction is merely to introduce adult ways of thinking, which conflict with the child's own and eventually supplant them. Studying child thought apart from the influence of instruction, as Piaget did, excludes a very important source of change and bars the researcher from posing the question of the interaction of development and instruction peculiar to each age level. Our own approach focuses on this interaction. Having found many complex inner ties between spontaneous and scientific concepts, we hope that future comparative investigations will further clarify their interdependence, and we anticipate an extension of the study of development and instruction to lower age levels. Instruction, after all, does not begin in school. A future investigator may well find that the child's spontaneous concepts are a product of preschool instruction, just as scientific concepts are a product of school instruction.

V

APART from theoretical conclusions, our comparative study of scientific and everyday concepts yielded some important methodological results. The methods we worked out for use in this study permit us to bridge the gap between the investigations of experimental and of real concepts. The information gathered on the mental processes of the schoolchild studying social science, schematic and rudimentary as it is, has suggested some possible improvements in the teaching of that subject.

In retrospect, we are aware of some omissions and of some methodological defects, perhaps inevitable in a first approach to a new field. We did not study experimentally and in detail the nature of the schoolchild's everyday concepts. This leaves us without the data needed to describe the total course of psychological development during school age; hence, our criticism of Piaget's basic theses is insufficiently buttressed by reliable, systematically obtained facts.

The study of scientific concepts was conducted in one category only—social science concepts—and the particular concepts selected for study do not form or suggest a system inherent in the logic of the subject. While we learned a good deal about the development of scientific compared with spontaneous concepts, we learned little about the regularities specific to the development of sociological concepts as such. Future studies should include concepts from various fields of school instruction, each set matched against a set of everyday concepts drawn from a similar area of experience.

Last but not least, the conceptual structures that we studied were not sufficiently differentiated. For example, in using sentence fragments ending in *because,* we did not separate the various types of causal relations (empirical, psychological, logical) as Piaget did in his studies. Had we done that, we might have been able to make a finer differentiation between the test performance of schoolchildren of different ages.

These very flaws, however, help in mapping the course of future investigations. The present study is merely a first, very modest step in exploring a new and highly promising area in the psychology of child thought.

REFERENCES

ASSEN'EVA, ZABOLOTNOVA, KANUSHINA, CHANTURIJA, EFES, NEJFEC, *et al.* Unpublished theses of students of the Herzen Pedagogical Institute, Leningrad.

PIAGET, J. Psychologie de l'enfant et l'enseignement de l'histoire. *Bulletin trimestriel de la conference internationale pour l'enseignement de l'histoire,* 1933, No. 2.

SHIF, ZH. *Razvitie zhitejskikh i nauchnykh ponjatij.* Moscow: Uchpedges, 1935.

TOLSTOY, L. *Pedagogicheskie stat'i.* Kushnerev, 1903.

ALEXANDER R. LURIA

Verbal Regulation of Behavior[*]

EDITOR'S INTRODUCTION

The following is a presentation by Professor Luria to a Josiah Macy, Jr., Foundation conference. Invited participants were permitted to break into the presentation with questions. These questions and Luria's answers are included here for their help in clearing up certain points.

I CHOSE the topic "Verbal Regulation of Behavior" for two reasons: first, because I have spent several years working on this problem, and second, and more important, because I believe that verbal regulation of behavior can play a decisive role in the evolution of brain function in man. We know that man is a social animal, and verbalization is a mode of behavior specific to man.

A great psychologist in our country, Vygotsky (1956), taught that the verbal relation with the mother plays a decisive part in the further development of the child. For example, the mother says to the child, "You must take a spoon," and in this way she regulates his behavior. This verbal behavior then becomes interiorized. At the next stage, the child says to himself, "I will take a spoon." This is now autoregulation of behavior. What is at first a function shared between two persons, the mother and the child, later becomes the inner mode of the mental organization by the child himself. Therefore development as a whole is a kind of interiorization of social conduct, creating new levels of behavior. That is why verbal regulation of behavior plays such a decisive role in development.

I hold that the most important way to study this important process is by a precise psychophysiological method, a neurodynamic approach to the analysis of how verbal regulation of behavior is developed. The success of a research depends on the selection, for analysis, of a unit of function and of the indicator by which to analyze it. If these are both well and appropriately chosen, the work will be successful. Let us begin with two experiments. A child of 1 year and 2 months knows what a fish is. I say to the child, "Please bring me the fish." The child grasps the toy fish and gives it to me. Does this mean that verbal regulation has already developed? No, for let us now come to the second experiment in which a toy cat is placed between the child and the fish. I say to the child, "Please bring me the fish." The cat is more interesting than the fish and my verbal instruction comes into conflict with the child's orienting reflex toward the cat. The child hears "fish," but although his eyes are on the fish, his hand goes out to the cat. I can tell, therefore, that at this stage verbal regulation is not yet dominant. It works only if it does not come into conflict with an immediate perception, with an immediate orienting reflex to some other more intense stimulus or one that has the quality of novelty.

Another experiment, also showing that verbal regulation of behavior is not yet operating, demonstrates a different factor. If I say to this child aged 1 year and 2 months, "Please

* REPRINTED by permission of the Josiah Macy, Jr., Foundation from Mary A. B. Brazier (Ed.), *The Central Nervous System and Behavior*. New York: Josiah Macy, Jr., Foundation, 1960. Pp. 359–379.

bring me the cat" (which is on his left), he brings it to me. The same thing happens a second and a third time. But the fourth time, without changing my tone, I say, "Bring me the fish" (which is on his right), and he brings me the cat, repeating his former reactions.

Why does verbal regulation fail in this case? Because another factor, quite different from the orienting reflex, is involved. This is the factor of *inertia* of nervous activity. If two or three times my verbal instruction directed a child's movement toward the *left* side, the child needs to have a great mobility of the nervous system to be able to change this action to the *right* in accord with my verbal instruction.

From a number of experiments of this kind, it can be concluded that, in this early stage of the child's life, about 1 year and 2 months and even up to 1½ years, verbal instruction can only *initiate* behavior. It cannot yet either *stop* or *reverse* behavior. It fails when it comes into conflict with an orienting reflex or the factor of *inertia* working in a different direction.

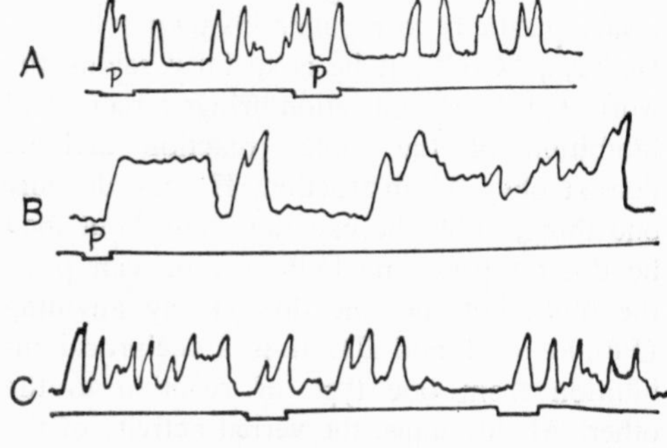

FIGURE 1

Disorganized motor reactions in very young children. The upper traces of (*A*), (*B*), and (*C*) each record the motor reaction of a child (pressing a balloon). In (*C*) only, and in FIGURES 2 to 6, the notches in the lower line indicate the presentation of a light stimulus. (*A*) and (*B*) record simple reactions of V. R. (2 yr. and 4 mo.) and S. M. (2 yr. and 5 mo.) to the instruction, "Press" (P). The reactions are not yet organized, for the children pressed whether or not instructed to do so. (*C*) records conditional motor reactions of V. R. (2 yr. and 4 mo.) to the instruction, "Press when you see a light." The reactions are not coordinated with the signals, for the child pressed even before any signal was presented.

The problem is: How can verbal instruction overcome these difficulties? How is verbal control of behavior developed to a stage at which we can, at least to a certain extent, regulate our behavior?

Passing from these demonstrations of the phenomena, let us now go to special psychophysiological experiments on its analysis. In the experiment shown in FIGURE 1, a child of 2 years and 4 months has a rubber balloon in his hand, and when told to press, he presses. But he does not stop his reaction, for he presses a second, a third, and a fourth time. I gave only *one* instruction, but the excitation this initiated became irradiated, and superfluous movements resulted.

My verbal instruction can start the behavior of the child at this age, but it cannot arrest his behavior. There is a similar result when I make my instruction a little more complicated. I tell the child, "Press when you see a light." This time, the instruction is not as simple as it was in the first experiment. It is now a "conditional instruction." The child has to synthesize both components of the instruction before acting, and the light signal has to become a conditioning signal.

FIGURE 2 shows inhibition of motor reactions. When the child hears the instruction, "Press," he presses immediately without waiting for the light and then, when the light appears, he gives an immediate orienting reflex to the light. He doesn't press any more; he stops.

Doty: Would that hold even with a change of tone of voice, such as a severe command?

Luria: If I tell the child, "You must press once only, and please don't press after that," the additional arresting instruction from the adult doesn't help in this case, and the child presses again and again, because he reacts, not to the semantics of my instructions, but to the intensity of my voice (FIGURE 3). Then if I say, in different voice, "You must not press when there is no light," he does not press, but he also doesn't press even when

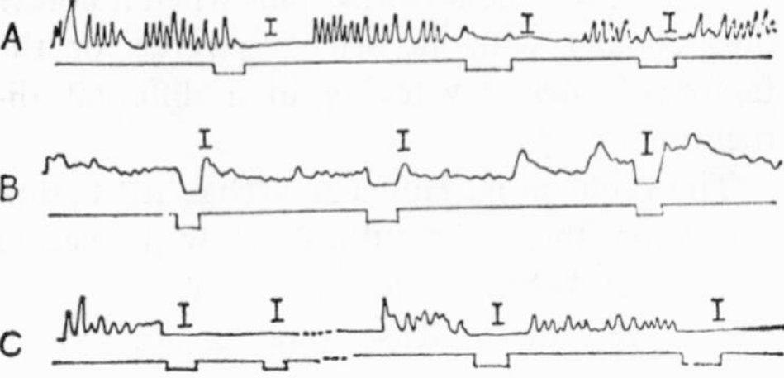

FIGURE 2

Inhibition of motor reactions as a result of an immediate orienting reflex to the signal. I = inhibition of reaction. (*A*) The child (L. L., 1 yr. and 8 mo.) responded to the verbal instruction, "Press," but the moment a light signal was presented the reaction was inhibited. (*B*) The same in another child (S. P., 2 yr. and 6 mo.). (*C*) In the imbecile child (T. G., 7 yr.), instructions resulted in an immediate motor reaction, which was inhibited by the light signal.

the light appears. This is an irradiation of the inhibitory influence of my instruction. I can only conclude that my verbal control of the child's behavior is not yet complete at this stage of development.

FIGURE 4 illustrates another method by which we try to regulate the activity of the child. If my verbal instruction does not help the child, perhaps it may be possible for him to use *his own* verbal activity. I tell him, "You are simultaneously both a soldier and an officer. You give the order, 'Go, go,' and

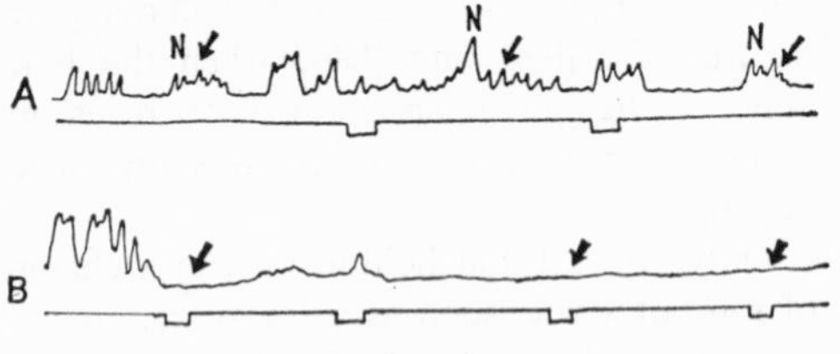

FIGURE 3

Diffuse excitatory and inhibitory reactions to verbal instructions, in very young children. N = "Do not press when there is no light." Arrows indicate errors. (*A*) Prohibitive instructions resulted in a generalized excitation. The child (K. K., 2 yr. and 7 mo.) pressed even though there were no signals. (*B*) Prohibitive instructions resulted in a generalized, irradiated inhibition and the child (S. M., 2 yr. and 1 mo.) ceased to press even though signals were given.

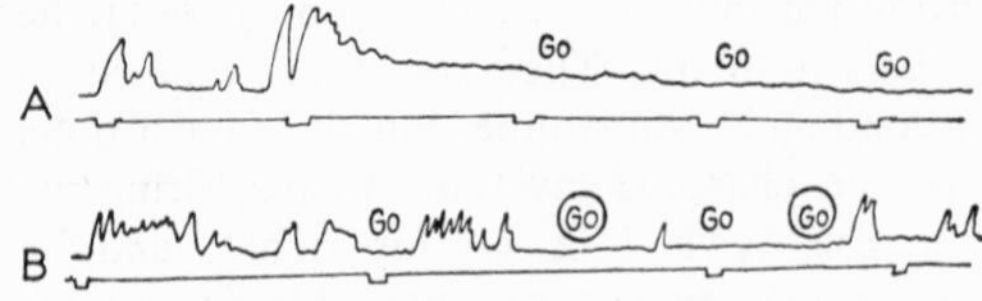

FIGURE 4

Negative interference between the child's verbal and motor reactions. (*A*) On the first two signals shown, there was a motor reaction alone, but when the child (O. O., 2 yr. and 3 mo.) verbalized on the next three signals, his motor reaction was inhibited. (*B*) On the second signal shown, the child (T. S., 2 yr. and 10 mo.) said, "Go" and made a delayed motor reaction. He later gave two verbal responses (circled) in the absence of any signal.

every time you say, 'Go,' you must also press. You have only to obey your own command." With a child of 2 or 3, this advice does not help. The neural mechanisms of the verbal reactions of the child do not yet have the necessary systemic organization or the necessary plasticity to regulate his own behavior. He says, "Go," but he is so busy saying the word that the verbalization brings a reciprocal inhibition of the motor reaction and he doesn't obey his instruction. He can do only one thing, either he can say, "Go," but then he doesn't press the bulb, or, he can press the bulb, but then he doesn't say anything (FIGURE 4 *A* and *B*). It is a reciprocal inhibition from one type of reaction to the other. At this stage, the verbal activity of the child himself cannot help him in the organization of his own behavior. In other words, the directive, controlling function of the child's own speech is not yet developed.

How can I arrange my experiment so that the child will be able to suppress superfluous movements? This is not easy. Since I cannot succeed by the use of the higher function of speech, I now try to train his motor reactions directly. As has been shown, in the first stage when I gave the instruction, "If you see a light, press," a lot of superfluous nonarresting movements were made. In the second stage of the experiment, I give the instruction, "When you see the light, press the balloon and put your hand on the table. Press, and put your hand on the table." Instead of

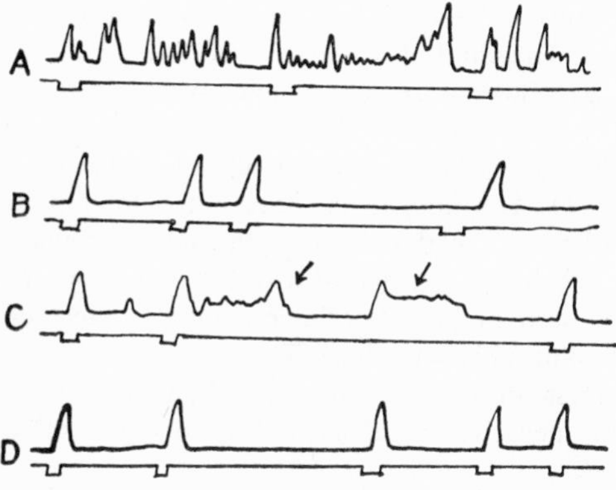

FIGURE 5

Elaboration of the inhibition of a motor reaction in a child (P. A.) of 2 years and 4 months. (*A*) The child gave an immediate motor reaction to the signal. He was allowed to hold the balloon in his hand all the time. (*B*) The child had to put the balloon on the table after every signal and remove his hand. (*C*) With the balloon in his hand, the child began to make errors. (Arrows indicate errors.) (*D*) Continuation of same experiment. Gradual organization of the movements is shown, and coordination of the movements with the signals.

having one instruction, he now has two, and the second inhibits the first, for the child puts his hand on the table and has to put the balloon aside. But that is only a starting point of the experiment. I can gradually proceed to *shorten* the child's activity. First I ask the child to press and put his hand on the table, then to press and put his hand near the balloon, and then to press only (FIGURE 5). I thus gradually reorganize his behavior in several steps: first, replacing the reaction at A with direction B withdrawing the hand, then putting the hand on the balloon and developing an inhibition by reduction of this second external action. That is the mechanism of training an inhibitory process. After such training, I can obtain good control in a child of 2 years and 4 months, without using his own verbalization.

Next, I come to the question: Is it possible to arrest the superfluous movements of the child by a different technique? Let us analyze the factors which made the immediate voluntary inhibition of the child's superfluous movements impossible. Why is the child unable to organize his own movements and arrest his own activity? I believe it is not only because his speech has not yet acquired a regulatory role, but also because the afferent feedback from his own movement is not yet ready at this age. I don't think the child, at this stage, gets good proprioceptive signals from his own movements, signals which should arrest the action at the right time. What will happen if I replace the missing proprioceptive feedback signals for arresting the movement by an exteroceptive signal, if I endow this exteroceptive signal with an arresting function?

The experiment is as follows: I instruct the child, "Press the balloon, and when you press it, you will hear a sound. This sound will be a signal for you to stop pressing." This is a concrete exteroceptive signal which arrests the movement, and the missing regulatory role of verbal instruction and of kinesthetic signals is replaced by a strong and concrete exteroceptive signal with a feedback action. S. V. Yakovleva, in my laboratory, has proved that, in many children, such direction by concrete exteroceptive feedback can result in an organization of motor reaction in cases where the direct method fails. FIGURE 6 gives an illustration of that experiment.

If it is possible to do this in cases when

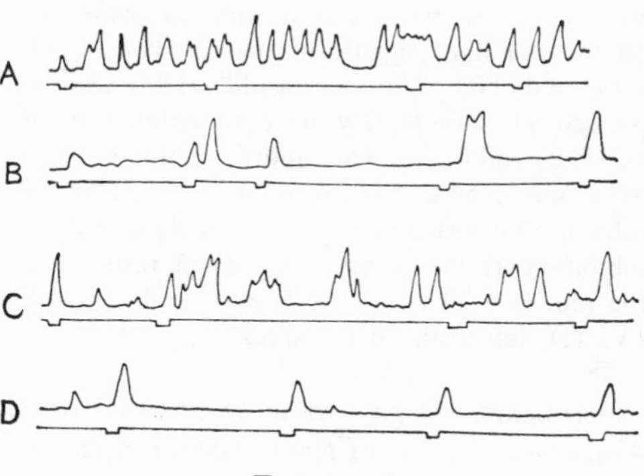

FIGURE 6

Reinforcement by exteroceptive feedback from the ringing of a bell. (*A*) Responses to signal without feedback from bell. (S. M., 2 yr.). (*B*) The same child pressed when he saw the signal and heard the bell. (*C*) and (*D*) Same experiment in another child. (Z. L., 2 yr. and 4 mo.)

the child is only 2½ years of age, perhaps things will be different at the next stage of development. First, let us show how a system of voluntary reaction to a verbal instruction—a positive to one signal and a negative to a second signal—can be obtained in children of different levels of the pre-school age. This is shown in the records of FIGURE 7. In these

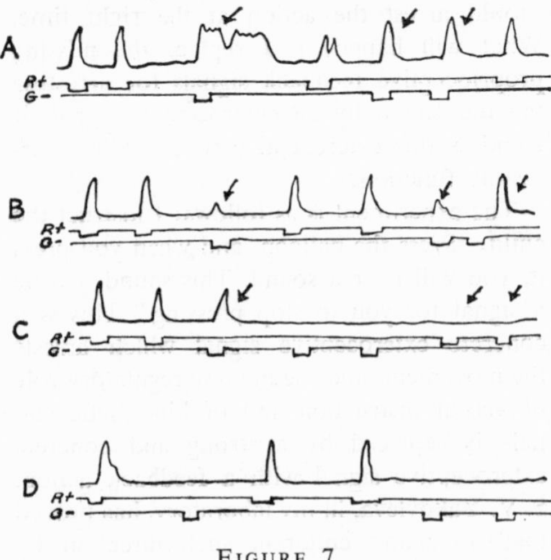

FIGURE 7

Motor reactions to differential signals in children of pre-school age. The upper traces of (*A*), (*B*), (*C*), and (*D*) record the motor reaction of each child (pressing a balloon); the center line is the signal for a red light (R+); and the lowest line is the signal for a green light (G−). Instructions to the children were to press only on the red light signal. Arrows indicate errors. (*A*) and (*B*) The 3-year-old child (S. B.) pressed indiscriminately to both colored lights. (*C*) The child of 4 years and 6 months (R. K.), after one error to the red light (R+), correctly inhibited his reaction to the green light, but this inhibition irradiated and suppressed response to the red. (*D*) The child of 5 years and 6 months (V. T.) differentiated the signals correctly.

experiments, we give to these children of 3, 4½, and 5½ years of age a more complicated task. The child must discriminate between two signals, a red (R+) and a green (G−) one, each with its special signaling function, positive to the red and negative to the green. Instructions are, "If you see a red light, press. If you see a green light, do not press." The results obtained in all three cases are different. The child of 3 years preserves the instruction and can repeat it quite well. He says: "If I see the green, I shall not press." But all the same, he presses to all lights (FIGURE 7 *A*). His knowledge does not help him to follow the verbal instruction and to regulate his behavior. A partial arrest of behavior can be seen in this experiment, but the effect of inhibition is very short. Then, even this partial arrest disappears and the child presses to the negative signal as well as to the positive one.

Also in FIGURE 7, typical results are shown for a child of 4½ years (FIGURE 7 *C*). These are different from these of the 3-year-old. The negative part of the verbal instruction is very short too; but if I reinforce the negative meaning of one of the signals by repeating, "When you see a green light, don't press at all," the child doesn't give any reactions to the negative signal, but now he does not react to the positive stimulus either. This is an irradiation of the inhibitory role of the speech instruction; so the child is still not yet ready for full organization of his behavior by control of the preliminary verbal instruction.

At 5½ years of age, this form of organization of motor behavior is completed (FIGURE 7 *D*). The plasticity of the nervous system is now well developed, and the child's motor reactions can obey the command of the second signaling system; a good system of positive reaction to the red and a negative reaction to the green signals is ready. All these data show that only in the fifth or even sixth year of the life can a verbal instruction provide a stable system of positive and negative motor reaction for a long period of experiment.

Is it possible to obtain the same results in a young child of 3 years of age? What methods of organization can provide a stable control of motor reactions at the stage when a preliminary verbal instruction is not yet able to produce a controlling effect? The experiments show that such a controlling function can be taken over by a system of permanent sanctioning reinforcements from the adult.

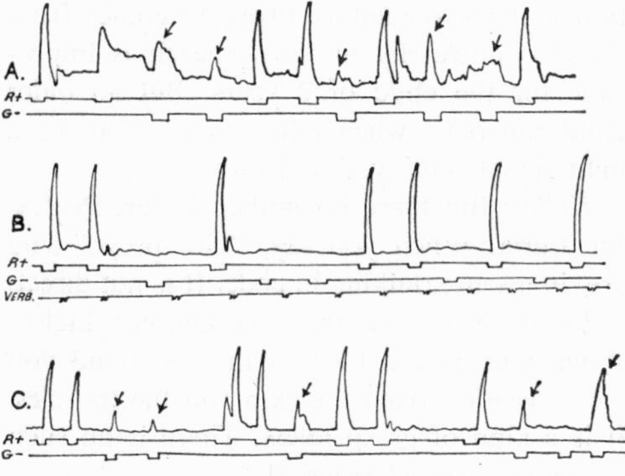

FIGURE 8

Elaboration of differentiating reactions in a child (K. B., 3 yr. and 6 mo.). (From the work of N. P. Paramonova.) Arrows indicate errors. (*A*) Differential motor reactions in response to verbal instructions: "Press when you see the red" (R+). "Do not press on green signal" (G−). Partial inhibition resulted. (*B*) The upper three lines signify the same as in FIGURE 7, (motor reaction, red light, and green light) and the fourth line indicates verbal reinforcement (VERB.) by the experimenter, who said, "Right," when the child responded correctly. (*C*) The same experiment but without verbal reinforcement by the experimenter. The child made errors.

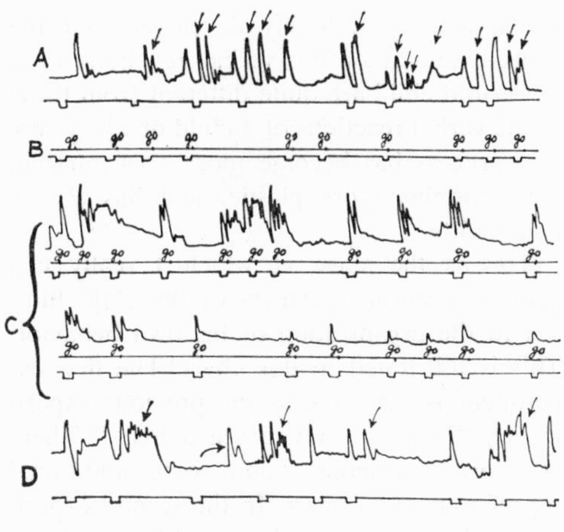

FIGURE 9

Gradual elaboration of motor reaction by the help of the child's own speech. (*A*) Motor reactions after instructions without reinforcement from experimenter. Note errors (arrows). (*B*) Child saying, "Go" on seeing signal. No errors. (*C*) Traces bracketed are continuous and show combined verbal and motor reactions. Above: motor; center: verbal; and below: signal. Note arrest of superfluous motor reactions and development of coordinated responses. (*D*) Motor reactions without verbal accompaniment. Note errors.

FIGURE 8 illustrates such a case. A child of 3 years of age is unable to give a stable system of positive and negative reactions to red (R+) and green (G−) signals if every reaction is not reinforced. But if we reinforce every reaction of the child by saying, "Yes, right," after correct reactions, and, "No, no!" after he makes errors, a system of correct reactions is formed in a short time. At this stage, in a 3-year-old child, a controlling function of the preliminary instruction is not yet ready; reinforcement can come only from outside, from the adult's evaluation of every separate reaction. That is the stage when the voluntary action can be provided only from an interaction of two persons, the adult and the child (Vygotsky, 1956). That is why merely leaving out these permanent reinforcements causes the stable system of positive and negative reaction to disappear. As indicated by arrows, in FIGURE 9 *D,* many disinhibited motor reactions can be observed after the permanent external reinforcement is left out.

Pribram: May I point out something here that is very important from the theoretical standpoint? We are using the word, "reinforcement," synonymously with "instruction." This is hardly new, except to those who have been thinking of reinforcement exclusively in terms of drive and need reduction.

Luria: No! Reinforcement here has a different meaning. It is my indication to the child as to whether the result is correct or incorrect. It is an evaluation of a coincidence of the reaction with the expected results that have been created by the verbal instruction.

Reynolds: Is the child's reaction to its mistake important, for example, whether it is amused or angered?

Luria: It is very important, but one should remember that this is a child of only 3 years.

FIGURE 9 brings us to the decisive point of what I want to report. At the 3-year-old stage, verbal activity is highly developed, but the neurodynamics of the verbal reactions of a 3-year-old child are quite different from those of the verbal reactions of a child of 2½ years. The process has become more concentrated, more mobile, more plastic, and has a new potentiality.

This is the stage at which I really can apply the verbal reactions of the child himself to the organization of his own behavior. This is illustrated in this chart. The first experiment is the same as the previous experiments, "Press when you see a light." There are correct responses and some additional superfluous movements. In the second experiment, the motor reactions of the child are replaced by his verbal reactions. I say, "Don't press the balloon. Simply answer, 'Yes,' when you see the light." The child, when he sees the light, has to give only the verbal answer, "Yes." The result is quite different. He doesn't say many, many times, "Yes, yes, yes, yes." He answers, "yes" every time he has a signal. The mobility of the verbal reaction is higher than the mobility or plasticity of the motor reaction.

Fremont-Smith: What do you mean by "mobility" or "plasticity" in this case?

Luria: The Pavlovian term is "Podviznost." Its translation is mobility, plasticity, flexibility. The motor response of the child at this stage irradiates too much, but the neural processes underlying verbal reaction have more plasticity than the nervous processes underlying the motor reaction of the hand.

Fremont-Smith: But there is a motor component in the verbal response, so you are saying that the motor response of speech has more plasticity than the motor response of the hand.

Luria: Yes, but these motor responses are at different levels. The motor response used in verbalizing has, at this stage, a better neurodynamic organization than the motor response of the hand.

Livingston: Professor Luria, is this a process of individuation as it proceeds from the cephalic end downward, and would foot control come still later?

Luria: Yes, those are the levels of organization, but the regulatory property comes from above. Control by his own speech is impossible for the child of 2 years. But an older child can obey when told, "When you see a light signal, say, 'yes' and press."

Keller: But there is another factor, Professor Luria. When you say, "Go, press," you are, in a sense, talking in code. It is not direct.

Luria: Yes, and there is another factor. When you have a balloon in your hand you get a reaction from the skin and the muscles. It is a kind of grasp reflex. There is no such factor in a verbal reaction.

Keller: That's right; so it might not be a level of integration. It is a code.

Luria: Yes, therefore the verbal reactions are at a better stage of development than the hand reactions. But this still does not mean that a child of 2½ years can use his verbal reaction, for this is still too unorganized.

Purpura: The problem concerning the relative development of different cortical areas subserving motor activities in the newborn animal was investigated by Langworthy (1927a, 1927b). The latter found that in the cat the area presiding over foreleg movements was more fully developed at birth than the hindlimb and face areas. Langworthy's conclusions were based on the effect observed after electrical stimulation of pericruciate cortex. He also noted differences in the histological development of different regions in the motor cortex which, presumably, correlated with the physiological observation. Forelimb movements were apparently obtained before movements of other parts of the body.

Bridger: Perhaps I can explain some Pavlovian terms. In respect to strength, Pavlov meant the size of the conditioned response as related to the strength of the conditioning stimulus. Balance refers to the balance between inhibition and excitation, which is measured by how many trials are required to obtain conditioning as compared with how many trials are required to extinguish or get differentiation. By mobility, Pavlov meant the ability to switch from positive to negative stimuli and back again.

Brazier: Professor Luria, while we are discussing the use of terms, would you explain for me how you are using the word, "irradiated"?

Luria: I mean by this that it is impossible to stop the reaction that was provoked by my stimulus. It continues.

Brazier: You are not thinking in neurological or neurophysiological terms?

Luria: In this experiment, I do not have the grounds for doing so.

Fremont-Smith: And is "irradiation" analogous to "perseveration?"

Luria: Yes, "perseveration" is a very common term among clinicians, and a very good one. In the experiments I am describing, I start from two facts: there is poor voluntary inhibition in the hand and good verbal reaction even without additional external reinforcement. We combine both and tell the child to dictate to himself and to obey himself. This is not easy for a child of 3 years and 9 months, but he can be trained to do it.

The result is illustrated in FIGURE 9 *C*. The child says, "yes," and presses many times. This is a very complicated process, but after a series of training sessions, quite good reactions are developed. He says, "yes" and there are no superfluous movements; so he is now reaching a very important stage. After some combinations of verbal and hand reactions, the verbal reaction of the child begins to play a controlling role over the hand movement. We have created an artificial functional system with the leading control being the verbal command from the child himself.

Fremont-Smith: Isn't the verbal command in each case producing an orienting reflex which inhibits the other?

Luria: Perhaps. The next stage, which I have not yet done but in which I think we shall collaborate with Professor Sokolov, is to combine this method of registering motor reaction with his method of analysis of the orienting reflex. This would be a step further in the investigation of the mechanism behind the result we have produced.

If we leave out speech reaction and once again tell the child not to speak, he returns to his previous behavior. He makes many superfluous movements, as can be seen in FIGURE 9. There are sometimes some appropriate reactions, but only sometimes. This is the stage when verbal reaction is necessary for the child in organizing his own hand movements.

Kelly: What impresses me in FIGURE 9 is that the child's verbal reaction seems to come after his motor reaction rather than before. Instead of giving himself the verbal command and then pressing, he is pressing and then giving himself the verbal command.

Luria: Yes, at this stage, the coordination of verbal and motor reactions is not yet well developed. That is why the child sometimes presses and then speaks, and sometimes the reverse. Imbecile children have the same difficulty.

Bodian: May I just suggest the possibility that, instead of the hand activity, one might try opening of the mouth, without verbalization?

Luria: I have not tested for that. It is a good idea.

Reynolds: I have something relevant to that. At one time, I was trying to count heartbeats of microcrustacea. These are very difficult to count because they are so fast, and as I had no method of counting this electrically, I found it impossible. I was not trying to verbalize; in other words, I wasn't trying to voice "1, 2, 3," but I was trying to say, "1, 2, 3," mentally. I discovered that I could synchronize the clicking of my teeth, that is, a jaw movement. I could move my jaws rapidly enough to keep up with the heart beat of this crustacean and, by doing that, I was able to keep count. In other words, with this jaw movement, I was able to keep track of the numbers, which I could not do without the jaw movement.

Luria: Yes, because at your developmental level, the muscles of your mouth, which are part of the speech system, have more "mobility" (in the sense in which we have been using this term) than have the muscles of other systems. The word "mentality" lies in another realm of discourse. You have changed the semantics. Let us continue with the experimental findings.

FIGURE 10 shows a typical effect in a child of $3\frac{1}{2}$ years of age, not the process of gradual

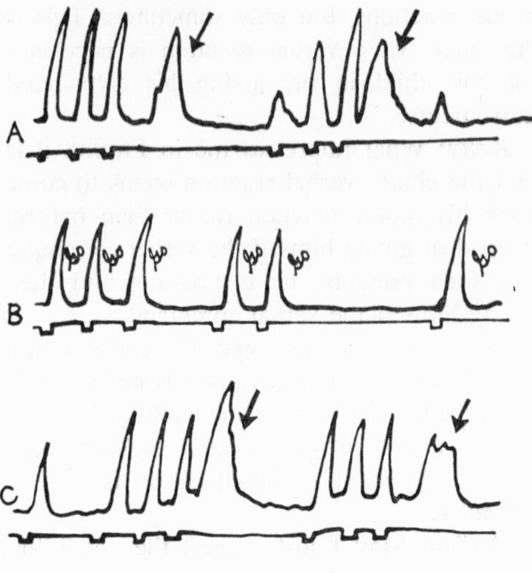

FIGURE 10

The regulating influence of the child's own speech on his motor reactions (L. P., 3 yr. and 6 mo.). The notched lines indicate the presentation of a light signal. Arrows indicate errors. (*A*) Without verbal accompaniment, the child responded to each signal but failed to inhibit response on omission of signal (disinhibition). (*B*) With each motor reaction, the child said, "Go," and responded correctly throughout. (*C*) Once again the verbal reaction was omitted and the disinhibited motor reaction returned.

learning of verbal organization, but the result. In the absence of any verbal instruction, there are superfluous movements. The organization of the movement fails because there are no external regulating verbal components. With the verbal instruction, "Go, Go, Go," the performance is all right.

FIGURE 11 is the record of a child of 3 years. If I make the signal long, he responds with a long movement, very long signals and very long movements. It is an echopraxic reaction. The movement reflects the length of the signal, of the excitation. It is a mirror phenomenon which we often see in clinics.

The child is, to a degree, a slave of the signal, of the physical properties of the stimulus. A long signal evokes a long movement; a short signal, a short movement. But if I introduce the speech of the child, something quite different happens. To a short stimulus, he says, "Go," and to a long stimulus, he says,

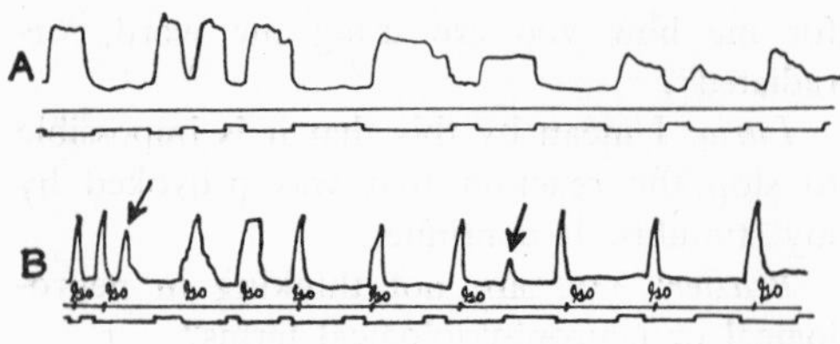

FIGURE 11

The regulating influence of a 3-year-old child's (V. S.) own verbal reaction on his motor response. In both (*A*) and (*B*), the upper traces record the motor reaction, the middle traces the verbal reactions, and the lowest (notched) lines indicate the presentation of light signals. Arrows indicate errors. (*A*) The motor reaction to the signal without speech. (*B*) The same, with the child saying, "Go," every time he responded by pressing a balloon.

"Go," but the movement is not a mirror movement. It no longer reflects the length of the signal. He coordinates his hand movement, not with the stimulus, but with his own verbal reaction. That is very significant, because it shows the mediating role of the verbal reaction in organization of the movement.

It is evident that in this child the verbal system is not yet ready for this. He says, "Press," and he presses. He says "No," but he presses. Why? Because—and this is a very important point—the speech reaction has two properties, a semantic one and an excitatory one activating the motor response. In positive reactions, both activities are excitatory and therefore of the same class. The reaction (of saying "press") is positive semantically and positive in the excitation of a movement. There is a motor excitation both of the hand and of the speech apparatus. But in the negative reaction, both reactions are not of the same class. The child gives a semantically negative reaction, but an excitatory positive motor reaction. At this stage of development of language, the child obeys, not the semantic content of the verbal reaction, but its excitatory property. The child says, "No," but he presses.

FIGURE 12 is the evidence in this experiment. The experiment is designed so that the child has to answer with a "yes" and press to the positive signal; on the negative signal,

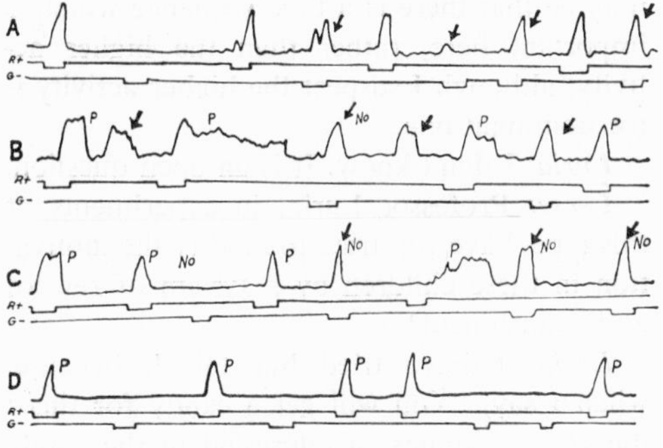

FIGURE 12

Role of the child's own verbal reaction in elaboration of positive and negative responses. Instructions were to press on red (R+) and to refrain on green (G−). Arrows indicate errors. (*A*) Without the child's speech. (*B*) Same, but child now said, "Press" (P) with response and "No" when he refrained. Note at arrows extra motor reactions in absence of signal. (*C*) The same child after training. There were two errors (arrows) where there was disinhibition in spite of child's saying, "No." (*D*) Instructions were, "Press and say 'Go' when you see red; be silent and do not press on green." No errors.

he must withhold both motor and verbal reaction. Both the motor and the verbal responses now have to act in the same direction and he succeeds on the red light (R+). He says "Yes" and he presses. On the green light (G−), he says nothing and does nothing. There are no failures. At this stage, the regulating influence of speech can be utilized only if there is no conflict between the semantic direction of the word and the innervatory excitation of the movement.

If there is a conflict, the child, on getting the negative signal, reacts, not to the semantic, but to the excitatory aspect of the signal.

Brazier: Professor Luria, how do you capture the interest and attention of so young a child to do this?

Luria: That is one of our most difficult tasks, and we have to make many tests before we can start the real experiment. At the first testing, the child does not have sufficient incentive so we can't really start.

Fremont-Smith: Can you get such a child to cooperate consistently with you, or is it only every now and then that you get enough attention from him to get a reliable experiment?

Luria: The experiment has to be short, and there has to be some incentive. If we design the experiment as play for the child, he does better than when it appears to be work.

FIGURE 13 illustrates a different experiment. I instruct the child to press twice to every signal. The child gives two, three, four, even five or six reactions, but he cannot reach a real control of pressing only twice to each signal.

However, when I tell the child to add his verbal comment to this instruction, he can perform correctly. I ask him to say, "Toot, toot." That has no meaning. It is only a verbalization but he obeys, and there are almost no failures. But if I say, "Give your

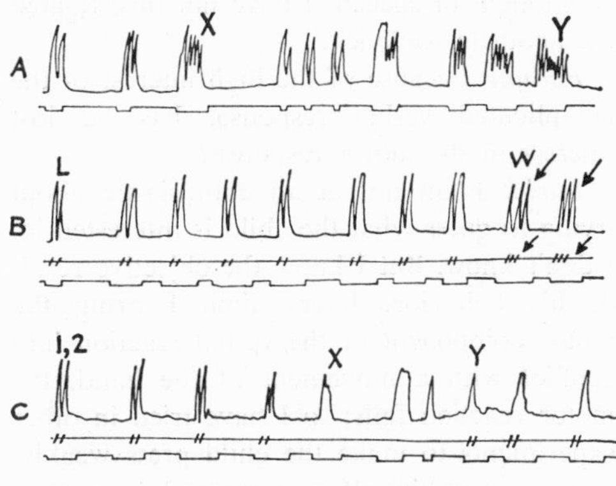

FIGURE 13

The regulating role of the child's speech on complex motor reactions. The hatched lines indicate the child's verbal responses and the notched lines the presentation of a light signal. (*A*) Child was instructed to press twice on seeing a light. Asked how many times he had pressed: at "X" he answered, "Twice," and at "Y" he answered, "Three times." (B) Same, but child told to speak when pressing. Left, instructed to speak loudly (L). Right, instructed to whisper (W). Note correct responses when he spoke loudly but perseveration when he whispered (arrows). (*C*) Child instructed to press twice on each signal and to say, "1, 2." At "X," asked how many times he had pressed, he answered, "Twice." At "Y" after being told to press twice, he said, "Twice."

answers in a whisper," the regulating role of speech is diminished. Failures occur. Instead of saying, "Toot," only twice, he begins to say, "Toot, toot, toot; toot, toot." This is a perseveration in speech and it brings on a perseveration of the motor reaction as well.

In the next part of the experiment, I say to the child, "On every signal, don't say, 'Toot, toot,' but say 'I press twice.' " He says, "I press twice," "I press twice," but he presses only once. Why? Because the dominating influence is not the semantic meaning but the motor component of the speech reaction.

Lilly: I was trying to separate out the motor component of the speech from the acoustic feedback to himself, and wondering which one is the limiting factor.

Luria: In this experiment, I am separating the semantic component from the motor component of speech. I have not investigated the acoustic feedback.

Bodian: Because of the high interest of the complicated verbal response, has he lost interest in the motor response?

Luria: I am not at all enthusiastic about trying to guess what the child is interested in. I don't know. But I know the objective result of his behavior. Every time I bring the motor component of the verbal reaction into conflict with a movement of the hand, the motor reaction fails; so I have tried in other experiments to make the child press weakly, and to give himself a command in a loud voice. In all cases, the decisive role was played, not by the semantic side of the speech, but by the muscular characteristics. That is why I think this is a real stage in the development of speech, one in which the motor component of speech can organize the child's behavior but the semantic side cannot yet do this.

Fremont-Smith: Suppose you reversed the order; suppose you gave the child a command to say, "Toot, toot," and he was then to reinforce this by pressing the bulb. Would you get the same results? It seems to me that this would be interesting because it would make a differentiation between the higher level of the speech activity and the motor level. It may be that there is a time sequence which is important here, rather than the higher activity, although I suspect the higher activity is the dominant one.

Luria: I don't know. It is an open question.

Leese: Professor Luria, in experiments of this type, have you tried to modify the motivation in these children by a system of reward and punishment?

Luria: I have tried but failed, because, when I say, "You will get a candy for this," the child becomes so interested in the candy that he fails in his work. It is not a simple matter to increase the motivation of the young child in this experiment.

Kelly: In this type of model that you have given us here, is the speech serving as the orienting reflex?

Luria: Yes. I think that is the mechanism. The use of speech enhances the orienting reflex.

Leese: But an orienting reflex, if I understand it correctly, and I suspect I don't, does not ever serve an inhibitory function, is that right? Does it ever serve as an inhibitor?

Luria: The preliminary orienting reflex is a factor essential to every conditional reflex. When a conditional reflex is inhibitory in function, the orienting reflex will be conditioned to arrest movement. You can't arrest movement without attention, without orienting.

Leese: So it can serve, then, in that capacity.

Luria: Yes, I think so.

Sokolov: I believe it is well known that external stimulation produces the so-called external inhibition of a conditional reflex. This is the influence of the orienting reflex, produced by external stimulation, upon the conditional reflex. Therefore, the orienting reflex, although being at the same time a kind of excitatory response, can influence the conditional reflex in an inhibitory manner.

Luria: I would like to summarize the material I have presented. After a series of experiments, of which I have shown only a few, we have reached a theory about the development of the regulatory function of speech in the child. This sequence of steps of verbal development in the child proves to be much more complicated than we had originally thought. The first stage is when the child's verbal activity cannot yet play a decisive role in the organization of his own behavior. The second step is when the child's verbal activity begins to play a regulating influence on his behavior, but is not yet complete. At this second stage, the semantic side of speech does not yet have a decisive influence. For the semantic side of speech, if it comes into conflict with the external motor function of speech, fails.

Only at the third stage does the semantic side of speech begin to play a really decisive role. For at this third stage, it is not obligatory for the child to apply externally vocalized speech, because at the moment when semantic control is developed, the child can use his internal subvocal speech. As a result of this interiorized process, the child can obey instructions without speaking loudly and without using the reinforcement of his own externally heard speech.

I should point out that speech has different roles—a nominative role, a generalizing or semantic role, a communicatory role, and a regulating role. The regulating or controlling influence of speech had not been as well investigated as the others, and that is why we focused attention on it, for it is very important in the problem of the mutual relationship of the two signaling systems. I have presented examples from a series of experiments on the organizing regulatory role of the second signal system in motor reactions. . . .

REFERENCES

LANGWORTHY, O. R. Correlated physiological and morphological studies of the development of the electrically responsive areas in the cerebral cortex of the opossum. *Contrib. Embryol.* (Carnegie Inst.) 1927, **19,** 149–176. (a)

LANGWORTHY, O. R. Histological development of cerebral motor areas in young kittens correlated with their physiological reaction to electrical stimulation. *Contrib. Embryol.* (Carnegie Inst.) 1927, **19,** 177–208. (b)

VYGOTSKY, L. S. *Selected psychological papers.* Moscow: Academy of Pedagogical Sciences Press, 1956. (In Russian.)

ROGER BROWN *and* JEAN BERKO

*Word Association and the Acquisition of Grammar**

EVERY natural language is a system. From knowledge of one part it is possible to anticipate correctly many other parts. The linguistic scientist studies some finite set of utterances (his linguistic "corpus") in search of the recurrent elementary units and patterns of combination that will generate the infinite set of utterances belonging to the language. Every child, in learning his first language, does much the same thing with the difference that he does not explicitly formulate most of the rules that govern his language behavior. A child is not, in his first few years, exposed to all possible utterances belonging to the community language but only to that small sample brought to him by his family, his friends, and television. Exposure to this sample, however, teaches him to understand and to produce utterances not actually experienced but implied by what has been experienced. The child may begin as a parrot imitating what others say, but he will end as a poet able to say things that have not been said before but which will be grammatical and meaningful in his community. This is the terminal achievement which a theory of language acquisition must explain.

The linguistic scientist describes language systems at several levels: the *phonological* level of distinctive sound elements and their permissible combinations; the *morphological* level of elementary meaningful forms (*morphemes*) and their combination to make words; the *syntactic* level of sentence creation from words. We have described elsewhere (1960) these three levels and have reported two studies (Berko, 1958; Brown, 1957) concerning the acquisition by children of morphology and syntax. The present study is concerned with syntax and, more particularly, with the child's utilization of the English parts-of-speech.

The linguistic scientist defines the parts-of-speech in purely syntactic or formal terms. He has shown that the English teacher's semantic definitions (e.g., "a noun is the name of a person, place, or thing") are imprecise approximations to the underlying but less obvious syntactic facts. The noun, in descriptive linguistics, is a class of words having similar "privileges of occurrence." Nouns are words that can follow articles and can occur in subject and object positions and, in this respect, are distinct from such other classes of words as the verb, adjective, and adverb. The fact that the words of any language fall into classes of approximate syntactic equivalents is of great interest to the student of language acquisition because it suggests one of the ways in which the lawful flexibility of speech is developed. A new word is ordinarily introduced to a child in a sentence, and this sentence will often serve to identify the part-of-speech to which the new word belongs. If the parts-of-speech have been internalized, this would mean that one vast array of sentence positions is available for the new word and other arrays are not. From the fact that X is a noun one can anticipate all of the grammatically acceptable uses of X and set aside all of the unacceptable uses. Is there evidence that children learn to operate with the parts-of-speech? We suspect that such evidence is to be found in certain well-

* REPRINTED by permission of Roger Brown and the Society for Research in Child Development from *Child Develpm.*, 1960, 31, 1–14.

established facts concerning word association.

Since the experiment of Woodrow and Lowell (1916), it has been known that the word associations of children show consistent differences from the associations of adults. Woodworth (1938) offers as examples of these differences the words appearing in TABLE 1. Woodrow and Lowell and others after them have conceptualized these differences in terms that are primarily semantic. Children are said to give more "contiguity" responses and more "whole-part" responses while adults are said to give more "coordinate," "contrast," and "similarity" responses. In several cases Woodrow and Lowell desert their semantic concepts and speak of "adjective-noun" associations and "verb-object" associations (both of which are more common in children's than in adults' responses). These classifications by parts-of-speech suggest a very general formal principle which contrasts the word associations of children and adults, a principle which so far as we know was first suggested by Ervin (1957). The associative responses of adults belong to the same part-of-speech as the stimulus word more often than do the associative responses of children. We shall speak of the adult type of association as homogeneous-by-part-of-speech (abbreviated Hmg.) and the child's type as heterogeneous-by-part-of-speech (Htg.).

Looking again at the examples of TABLE 1, we see that the response favored by adults is almost invariably Hmg. while that favored by children is Htg. Many of the largest differences found in the Woodrow and Lowell study conform to this syntactic principle though they were not so classified by the authors. In addition to these data from the past there are recent findings of Ervin (1957) who used a list of common words belonging to various parts-of-speech with groups of children in kindergarten and the first, third, and sixth grades. She found large increases with age in Hmg. responses to nouns, verbs, prepositions, adjectives, and adverbs. What is the significance of this apparently reliable developmental trend in word association?

There are, of course, many kinds of association that can link one word with another;

TABLE 1. *Word associations from adults and children*

STIMULUS	RESPONSE	1000 CHILDREN	1000 MEN AND WOMEN
Table	Eat	358	63
	Chair	24	274
Dark	Night	421	221
	Light	38	427
Man	Work	168	17
	Woman	8	394
Deep	Hole	257	32
	Shallow	6	180
Soft	Pillow	138	53
	Hard	27	365
Mountain	High	390	246
	Hill	91	184

similarity or contrast of referents, spatiotemporal contiguity of referents, and high transition probabilities between words are obvious possibilities. Similarity and contrast and contiguity between referents would sometimes lead to Hmg. responses (e.g., *table-chair*) and sometimes to Htg. responses (e.g., *table-eat*). Immediate transitions of high probability will very seldom exist between two words of the same part-of-speech, and so such pairs as *dark-night, deep-hole,* and *soft-pillow* are Htg. Elaborating a suggestion of Ervin's (Berko & Brown, 1960), we propose that the word associations of very young children are governed by such principles as we have cited but that, with increasing age, another principle of association begins to operate which has the effect of increasing the number of Hmg. responses.

From the time that a child begins to use phrases his speech repertoire will manifest the morphological structure that is a universal characteristic of adult speech in any language. The same meaningful forms (morphemes and words) occur in a variety of contexts; not all forms can occur in all contexts but some forms can occur in some of the same contexts. From these morphological universals it follows that words resemble one another in the degree to which they have similar privileges of occurrence. This syntactic similarity is always objectively present in speech involving phrases but probably it takes considerable time and maturity to analyze out syntactic similarity. The appreciation of syntactic similarity is, however, prerequisite to the ability to form meaningful and grammatical sentences that are not imitated from someone else. Suppose a child has learned that such words as *house, barn, table,* and *fence* can all occur in such positions as: "See the ______"; "I own a ______"; "The ______ is new"; and "This ______ is mine." If now he hears for the first time such a sentence as "See the *car*" in which *car* is a new word, he can be prepared to say "I own a *car*"; "The *car* is new"; and "This *car* is mine." Of course, the particular sentence uttered on a given occasion depends on semantic and motivational factors but the universe of sentences from which the particular can be drawn is established by the syntactic kinship linking *car* with *house, barn, table,* and *fence.*

Modern methods of teaching second or foreign languages begin, as does first language learning, with the repetition of phrases which recombine a limited set of meaningful elements. In second language learning, as in first, there comes a time when the student "creates" a phrase by realizing the syntactic implications of the material practiced. This is often accomplished nowadays by implicit induction without any explicit tuition in syntactic rules, and that is exactly the way it is accomplished by all children who become full participants in a first language.

Syntactic similarity is a matter of degree. The parts-of-speech are simply very large and very useful classes of approximate combinational equivalents. Animate nouns are more closely equivalent than nouns in general, and transitive verbs are more closely equivalent than verbs in general. Such popular adult word associations as *bright-dark* are not only semantic antonyms; they are also adjectives having highly similar privileges of occurrence. *Bright* has more sentence contexts in common with *dark* than with such another adjective as *virtuous.* It is our general hypothesis that, as utilization of syntax develops in children, syntactic similarity in words becomes an increasingly important determinant of word association and that the developmental trend from Htg. responses toward Hmg. responses is a manifestation of this great step forward into syntactic operations. We have undertaken to test this hypothesis by relating the child's tendency to give Hmg. word associations to his ability to make correct grammatical use of new words after hearing them in a couple of sentences.

Method

WE WORKED with four groups of 20 subjects each. In each group there were equal numbers of male and female subjects. Groups I, II, and III were students from, respectively, the first, second, and third grades of the Michael Driscoll School in Brookline, Massachusetts. The Driscoll School is a public school in a middle-income residence area. Children in a given group were all taken from the same classroom and simply drawn in the order of the seating arrangement until 20 had served. The fourth group (Group Ad.) consisted of 20 adults, students or staff at M.I.T., who responded to an advertisement asking for subjects.

WORD ASSOCIATION TEST

This test consisted of 36 stimulus words such that there were six words representing each of six parts-of-speech. The words were selected because all have high frequency in the speech of American elementary-school children (Rinsland, 1945) and because in earlier studies they yielded large differences between the associations of children and adults. The words were presented in a constant order to all subjects.

Verbs in English may be subdivided into transitives and intransitives. Intransitive verbs can appear without an object (e.g., "We *laugh*") while transitives almost always occur with some sort of object (e.g., "We *sent* something"). For the present experiment the transitives and intransitives were treated as two parts-of-speech, and there were six words representing each of them.

Nouns in English can be separated into "count nouns" and "mass nouns." The names are suggested from a distinction of reference; count nouns usually name bounded objects (e.g., *table, house*) while mass nouns name extended substances (e.g., *milk, sand*). However, there is also a clear syntactic distinction; count nouns in the singular can be preceded by *a* while mass nouns cannot (e.g., *a table* but not *a sand*) and, in addition, count nouns, when preceded by *some,* appear in the plural whereas mass nouns appear in the singular (e.g., *some tables* but *some milk*). On the present list of stimulus words there were six mass nouns and six count nouns.

In addition to the two varieties of noun and two varieties of verb, there were six adjectives and six adverbs on the list. The complete list is as follows:

Count Nouns (C.N.): table, house, foot, needle, apple, doctor.
Mass Nouns (M.N.): milk, water, sand, sugar, air, cheese.
Adjectives (Adj.): dark, soft, cold, white, sweet, hard.
Transitive Verbs (T.V.): to send, to bring, to find, to take, to hit, to invite.
Intransitive Verbs (I.V.): to skate, to come, to live, to laugh, to stand, to walk.
Adverbs (Adv.): quickly, slowly, sadly, now, softly, gently.

Many English words belong to more than one part-of-speech. It is possible in English to *table* a motion and to *foot* a bill but *table* and *foot,* in the vast majority of their occurrences, function as nouns and, when presented in isolation as stimulus words, are apprehended as nouns by most English-speaking adults. The words on the present list belong primarily to one part-of-speech though they may have secondary membership in others. The verbs were presented as infinitives with preceding *to* so that their verbal character would be clear.

USAGE TEST

The general plan of this test was to introduce to *S* a new word (actually a pronounceable nonsense syllable) by using it in two sentences. The two sentences were adequate to place the word in one of six parts-of-speech: the count noun, mass noun, transitive verb, intransitive verb, adjective, or adverb. After this introduction to the word, *S* was asked to use it in sentences of his own creation, and these were scored as correct if the new word was used as it ought to be in view of the part-of-speech implied by the introductory sentences.

As "new words" 12 nonsense syllables were used: *wug, boff, latt, roog, stog, huft, nass, sib, bik, rik, nare,* and *pilk.* There were 12 problems in all with two syllables assigned to each of the six parts-of-speech. The syllables were rotated through all 12 problems so that there was no regular association between any syllable and any particular problem. The syllable *wug* will be used here to indicate the general character of the presentations.

For each problem, *S* was shown a colorful picture of either a girl, a boy, a man, a woman, a cat, or a dog, and *E* read text of the following kind: "Do you know what a *wug* is? This is a picture of a little girl thinking about a *wug.* Can you make up what that might mean?" This was the presentation identifying *wug* as a count noun. Where *wug* was to be identified as an intransitive verb, *E* would say: "Do you know what it means to *wug?* This is a picture of a little boy who wants to *wug.*" With *wug* as mass noun there would be such sentences as: "This is a cat thinking about some *wug.*" With wug as transitive verb such a sentence as this was used: "This is a woman who wants to *wug* something." Where *wug* was to be identified as an adverb, *E* spoke of a dog thinking of doing something *wuggily.*

There were two problems for each part-of-speech and a different syllable for each problem. There were two identifying sentences for each problem and, in the case of the adjectives and adverbs, the appended suffixes *-y* and *-ly.*

The pictures gave no clue to the meaning of the new word and were only included to interest the child and keep his attention. The figures in the pictures were always simply thinking about the new word, not demonstrating its meaning.

PROCEDURE

E was introduced to the children in a class by the teacher, and the class was told that each member would have a chance to look at some pictures and play some games. The children were interviewed individually either in the corridor outside the classroom or in an unused classroom. The Word Association Test was presented first with the remarks: "This is a game called 'say a word.' Have you ever played 'say a word'? Well, this is the way it works. I'm going to say a word and I want you to listen to my word and then say another word, not my word but a different word. Any word is all right so long as it's the first word that comes into your head when you hear my word. Are you ready?"

When the word associations had been recorded, *E* brought out the picture cards and said: "Now we're going to play a making-up game. How are you at making things up? Pretty good? Well, let's see." The problems were presented so as to go through all parts-of-speech once before repeating any of them.

The procedure with adults was the same except that *S* knew he was participating in an experiment on language and *E* did not call either part a game. In explanation of the brightly colored pictures and rather childish text, the adults were told that the tests had been designed for use with children as well as with adults.

SCORING

Scoring on the Word Association Test involves assigning response words to a part-of-speech; scoring on the Usage Test involves determining from *S*'s use of a new word the part-of-speech to which *S* has implicitly assigned the new word. Because English words can belong to more than one part-of-speech and because single sentences employing a new word do not always unequivocally indicate the part-of-speech membership of the new word, there were sometimes problems in scoring.

On the Free Association Test those response words that were marked with characteristic suffixes (adjectives and adverbs) or with the *to* of the verbal infinitive could be confidently classified. With most potentially doubtful responses membership in one part-of-speech is so much more common than membership in another that it was safe to assign the word this primary membership. Where there was some doubt, however, *E* asked *S* to use the response word in a sentence and, in doing so, *S* revealed the part-of-speech he had in mind. It was necessary for *E* mentally to score the responses as they were elicited so that he could resolve scoring problems where necessary.

On the Usage Test *S* sometimes translated the new word into a conventional English word. When told that a man was thinking about some *wug* and asked to "tell what that might mean," *S* sometimes provided a familiar word as a translation, saying for instance, "He is thinking about some *milk*." In such a case the part-of-speech membership of the familiar equivalent was scored and would be correct, in the present instance, as *milk* is a mass noun and that is the part-of-speech implied for *wug*. Where the translation word was not clearly of one part-of-speech, *E* encouraged *S* to "say some more about it."

In other cases *S* interpreted the Usage Test as calling for use of the new word in a sentence and so might provide: "The man has some *wugs* for breakfast every day." In such a case the part-of-speech was inferred from the sentence and, in the present instance, would be scored incorrect as *wug* has been used as a count noun. Not every sentence is unequivocal in this regard, and so it was sometimes necessary to urge *S* to say a little more.

Results

THERE were 36 stimulus words on the Free Association Test, six words for each of six parts-of-speech. Each of the 36 response words (or phrases) was scored as Hmg. or Htg. with reference to its stimulus word, and so for every subject there was a possible maximal score of six Hmg. responses for each of six parts-of-speech. There were 12 new words on the Usage Test, two words for each of six parts-of-speech. Each of the new words was scored Hmg. or Htg. according to the agreement between the part-of-speech implied by the introductory sentences and the part-of-speech implied by *S*'s use or translation of the new word. For each *S*, therefore, there was a possible maximal score of two Hmg. responses on each of six parts-of-speech. After the rules of scoring had been developed by one judge, another judge independently scored 10 complete protocols (360 response words on word association and 120 new words on usage) from the rules. The two scorings agreed perfectly except for three instances where more information should have been elicited, and so it appears that this is essentially an objective scoring problem with no difficulties in the reliability sphere. The mean Hmg. scores for each part-of-speech and each age group appear in TABLE 2.

A two-way analysis of variance with 20 cases in each cell was carried out for the Free Association means and another for the Usage means. The results are summarized in TABLES 3 and 4. Both age and part-of-speech account for large amounts of variance. In addition, there is a significant interaction between the two variables, and it can be seen in both the Free Association and Usage means that the increase with age of Hmg. responses is far less for count nouns than for the other parts-of-speech.

We are not primarily interested in the effects of age and of part-of-speech and so will not compare the 24 individual means for each test. It is, however, worth noting the extraordinary uniformities in TABLE 2. The individual means have been arranged in the order of the grand means of the rows (age groups) and columns (parts-of-speech). When this is done for Free Association, there are only three reversals of one position each in the age order, only four reversals of one position, and a single reversal of two positions in the part-of-speech data. The same sort of ordering of the Usage means results in only three reversals of one position each in the age order, only one reversal of three positions, and one reversal of two positions in the part-of-speech order. There is clear confirmation

TABLE 2. *Mean HMG. scores on free association and usage for each part-of-speech and each age group*

	FREE ASSOCIATION						
Group	*C.N.*	*Adj.*	*I.V.*	*T.V.*	*Adv.*	*M.N.*	*Total*
Ad.	5.10	5.00	4.80	4.45	4.95	2.35	4.44
3rd	4.65	3.65	3.40	2.95	1.95	2.40	3.17
2nd	4.55	3.90	2.75	2.40	2.25	1.90	2.96
1st	3.95	1.25	1.60	1.40	.80	1.20	1.70
Total	4.56	3.45	3.14	2.80	2.49	1.96	3.07

	USAGE						
Group	*C.N.*	*Adj.*	*I.V.*	*T.V.*	*M.N.*	*Adv.*	*Total*
Ad.	1.85	1.75	1.70	1.60	.95	1.20	1.51
3rd	1.45	1.65	1.65	1.75	.55	.55	1.27
2nd	1.55	1.50	1.20	1.10	.70	.45	1.08
1st	1.20	.75	.90	.90	.45	.10	.72
Total	1.51	1.41	1.36	1.34	.66	.58	1.15

TABLE 3. *Analysis of variance for free association means*

SOURCE	SUM OF SQUARES	*df*	VARIANCE ESTIMATE
Age (rows)	453.6167	3	151.2056
Parts-of-Speech (columns)	321.2167	5	64.2433
Interaction	84.6833	15	5.6456
Individual differences (within cells)	1345.3500	456	2.9503
Total	2204.8667	479	

Interaction $F = 1.91$; $p < .05$.
Age $F = 26.78$; $p < .001$.
Parts-of-Speech $F = 11.38$; $p < .001$.

TABLE 4. *Analysis of variance for usage means*

SOURCE	SUM OF SQUARES	*df*	VARIANCE ESTIMATE
Age (rows)	40.0896	3	13.3632
Parts-of-Speech (columns)	67.2688	5	13.4538
Interaction	11.1673	15	.7445
Individual differences (within cells)	208.5556	456	.4574
Total	327.0813	479	

Interaction $F = 1.63$; p about .05.
Age $F = 17.95$; $p < .001$.
Parts-of-Speech $F = 18.07$; $p < .001$.

in this table of the increase with age of Hmg. responses found by Ervin (1957) and also clear evidence that the count noun and adjective function in child speech in advance of other parts-of-speech. Finally, ordering the Free Association and Usage cell means in the order of their grand means results in identical age and part-of-speech orders (except for a reversal of the Adv. and M.N. columns) in the two sets of data. This is a good first indication of the covariation in free association and usage which is the effect predicted by our hypothesis. We proceed to a more detailed presentation of the evidence for this effect.

It would have been possible to compute correlations between the individual scores on usage and the individual scores on free association for each part-of-speech and each age group. We examined these scores and saw that the correlations would be very small, probably because the usage scores can only range from zero to two and because this small sample of usage from each *S* is not a very reliable measure of *S*'s grammatical skills. We decided to work instead with the means of TABLE 2 which yield a greater range of scores and a more reliable estimate of grammatical skill in a kind of *S*. The rank-order correlation between the 24 means from the Free Association Test and the 24 means from the Usage Test is .84, and this is a relationship significant at far better than the .001 level.

Contributing to the rank-order correlation of all 24 means is the tendency for usage and free association scores to increase with age as well as the tendency for scores on the six parts-of-speech to covary for usage and free association. Insofar as the correlation is generated by the former factor, it is possible that we have nothing more here than a tendency for all sorts of language performance scores to move together with increasing age towards adult values. We are interested in something more particular than this. We want to know whether the increasing tendency to give Hmg.

responses in free association can be interpreted as evidence of the developing organization of vocabulary into parts-of-speech which define correct grammatical usage for new words. We shall have better ground for this interpretation if correlations exist with the age variation taken out. One way of accomplishing this effect is to correlate the grand means (across all age groups) for the six part-of-speech columns for free association and usage. This rank order *rho* is .94 and even with only six cases that value is significant at about .01. Another way of testing for this relationship is to correlate the six paired means for each of the four age groups. The results appear in TABLE 5 (together with the previously mentioned *rhos*); three are significant and one is not. The p values for these four samples can be combined to yield a single p value for the relationship of free association to usage. Mosteller and Bush (1954) suggest transforming the individual p values into normal deviates, summing them, and dividing the sum by the square root of the number of observations. The resultant value is itself a normal deviate with a p of about .0002. It seems very certain, therefore, that Hmg. scores for free association are related to Hmg. scores for usage.

TABLE 5. *Rank order correlations between free association and usage HMG. scores*

Rho for all paired means, $N = 24$	.84	$p < .001$
Rho for grand means of the parts-of-speech, $N = 6$	.94	$p = .01$
Rho for adults, $N = 6$	.83	$p = .05$
Rho for 3rd grade, $N = 6$	.46	$p = .40$
Rho for 2nd grade, $N = 6$	.94	$p = .01$
Rho for 1st grade, $N = 6$	.83	$p = .05$
Combined p value for adults, 3rd grade, 2nd grade, 1st grade		$p = .0002$

Discussion

THE change with age in both free association and usage is very striking when one examines individual protocols. For free association, consider the stimulus words *to send*. One first grade child responds *away*, another *letter*, another *a card*, another *mail*, etc. In response to this same word adults give: *to receive, to get, to deliver, to bring, to mail, to fetch*. Both the child responses and the adult responses are semantically related to the stimulus word, and the one set does not seem to be any more so than the other. The difference lies with the fact that the child responses are phrase completions (words that commonly follow the stimulus) while the adult words would almost never follow *to send* in an English sentence but are very closely matched with it in that they are transitive verbs. More specifically, the adult responses are transitive verbs naming human actions which ordinarily have some small inanimate thing as object. This further similarity is semantic but, in addition, involves a closer syntactic match than would be true for transitive verbs in general.

Consider now the sort of thing that happens on the Usage Test with a nonsense syllable intended to be a transitive verb. One first grade child was told: "This is a cat who wants to *niss* something. Can you make up what that might mean?" The child replied: "The cat wants a fish. A *niss* is a fish." To this same problem an adult responded: "The cat wants to catch something. To *niss* is to catch." The child seems to have put together knowledge about cats and the sound of *niss* to come up with a count noun—*fish*. He was not troubled by the fact that this translation violates the part-of-speech membership of *niss*. When *E* says to "*niss* something," that should exclude the possibility of saying "A *niss* is a fish," but, for this child, it does not. Apparently the first grade children paid little attention to the formal marks of the syntactic potentialities of *niss*. The adult, on the other hand, principally attended to these marks. In many cases the translations provided by adults seem to have been suggested by the sound of the new word even as *niss* suggested *fish* to the first grader. However, when this happened with adults, it was almost always within the limits of the class of words suggested by the syntactic cues. In general, then, both the free association results and the usage results seem to be manifestations of the developing organization of vocabulary into syntactic classes.

As the analyses of variance have demonstrated, both age and part-of-speech are highly significant determinants of the number of Hmg. responses on both the Free Association and Usage tests. These two variables may perhaps be conceptualized as a single determinant—the amount of experience with words belonging to a part-of-speech. Experience of words in all six parts-of-speech is bound to increase with age, and Hmg. responses on all parts-of-speech clearly do increase with age. In addition, however, we note in TABLE 2 that the count noun and the adjective produce more Hmg. responses across all age levels than do the other parts-of-speech. While we do not know of any exact tests of the frequency of occurrence in English of words belonging to the various parts-of-speech, it seems to us that no test is needed to persuade the native speaker that count nouns and adjectives are more common than intransitive verbs or transitive verbs or adverbs or mass nouns. This is to say that at any given age a speaker of English is likely to have had more experience of count nouns and adjectives than of the other parts-of-speech we have studied.

The count noun has always the highest number of Hmg. responses and, indeed, does not change greatly in this respect from the first grade to adulthood because it is already at a near peak level in first graders. The count noun is, of course, the kind of word adults regularly undertake to teach children, for these are the names of denotable things: a *man,* a *dog,* a *car,* a *bike.* Surely speakers of English have greater experience of words in this class than of words in any other class.

The low number of Hmg. responses generally obtained for mass nouns requires a special comment. The Htg. responses given to mass nouns were usually count nouns, i.e., members of the same major part-of-speech. There is a good reason why these two varieties of noun were not usually distinguished even by adults. Mass nouns in English can always be used as count nouns. Ordinarily one says *some sand, some water, some marble* but one can say *some sands, some marbles,* and even *some waters.* The difference is that in the former cases a quantity of a uniform substance is suggested while in the latter case varieties or subspecies of some category of substances are suggested. This syntactic overlap seems to result in an overlap on the word association and usage tasks.

We have suggested that degree of experience of words in a part-of-speech is the basic determinant of the degree to which that part-of-speech functions in free association and usage. The significant sort of experience might be the number of words belonging to the part-of-speech or the variety of sentences for each word or the number of occurrences for each sentence. Probably all of these kinds of experience are close correlates in the natural situation. There are many different count nouns in English; there are many different sentences for most count nouns; and there are many sentences involving count nouns that occur very frequently. Without deliberate experimental manipulation of experience it probably will not be possible to determine the relative importance of these factors.

Summary

IT IS a reliable finding that the response words provided by adults in a word association test usually belong to the same parts-of-speech as the respective stimulus words. There are fewer of these homogeneous-by-part-of-speech responses with young children; the tendency to associate words within a part-of-speech increases with age. The present paper suggests that this change in word associations is a consequence of the child's gradual organization of his vocabulary into the syntactic classes called parts-of-speech. To test the degree to which *S* has accomplished this latter grammatical task, a Usage Test was designed. In this test a new word was used in a couple of sentences which sufficed to indicate the part-of-speech to which the new word belonged. After hearing these sentences, *S* was asked to create some sentences of his own using the new word, and his performance was scored correct if it employed the word in ways permitted by its part-of-speech membership. Four groups of *S*s (adults and first, second, and third grade children) were given a Word Association Test (consisting of stimulus words belonging to six different parts-of-speech) and also a Usage Test (consisting of new words assigned to the same six parts-of-speech). The Word Association Test was scored for homogeneous responses within each part-of-speech and the Usage Test for correct usage in accordance with each part-of-speech. It was found that scores on both tests regularly increased with age and that scores on the two tests were closely related to one another. It was concluded that the formal change in word association and the ability to make correct grammatical use of new words are two manifestations of the child's developing appreciation of English syntax.

REFERENCES

BERKO, JEAN. The child's learning of English morphology. *Word,* 1958, **14,** 150–177.

BERKO, JEAN, & BROWN, R. Psycholinguistic research methods. In P. H. Mussen (Ed.), *Handbook of research methods in child development.* New York: Wiley, 1960.

BROWN, R. Linguistic determinism and the part of speech. *J. abnorm. soc. Psychol.,* 1957, **55,** 1–5.

ERVIN, SUSAN M. Grammar and classification. Paper read at Amer. Psychol. Ass., New York, September, 1957.

MOSTELLER, F., & BUSH, R. R. Selected quantitative techniques. In G. Lindzey (Ed.), *Handbook of social psychology.* Vol. 1. Reading, Mass.: Addison-Wesley, 1954. Pp. 289–334.

RINSLAND, H. D. *A basic vocabulary of elementary school children.* New York: Macmillan, 1945.

WOODROW, H., & LOWELL, F. Children's association frequency tables. *Psychol. Monogr.,* 1916, **22,** No. 97.

WOODWORTH, R. S. *Experimental psychology.* New York: Holt, 1938.

PART VI

Stability of Individual Personality and Behavior Through Time

IT IS fitting that this book of readings should close with a section on the stability of individual personality and behavior over time. In a sense the preceding sections have established the case for stability. The papers in Part I dealt with genetic and constitutional factors determining infant behavior, and obviously the influence of such factors does not stop as the child leaves infancy; individual differences in body chemistry, which remain basically the same, continue to contribute to individual differences in behavior during childhood and adult life.

In the area of constitutional determinants, one of the factors that has been researched beyond the period of human infancy is the rate of maturation, which is stable. Rate of maturation is determined by comparing skeletal age with chronological age. Skeletal age is measured by X-raying the hand and wrist and by comparing the state of development of the bony structure with that of established age norms. In this manner, development of the skeleton as a whole can be assessed for research purposes as fast- or slow-maturing, or as early- or late-maturing (the latter being the terminology usually employed).

Does the rate of maturation influence behavior and, if so, how? Data from the Berkeley Growth Study reported in the Mussen and Jones paper give a positive answer to the first part of the question, and the data reveal differences in feelings of adequacy and anxiety between physically accelerated and physically retarded boys. As the authors point out, such feelings may not be due to physical status per se so much as to interpersonal relationships within the family. Cultural differences in attitudes toward boys in each group undoubtedly make a difference also. The six-foot sixteen-year-old who looks like a man is more likely to be treated in an adult fashion in our society than is his physically underdeveloped peer who still looks like a child. The differing behaviors of each boy may be, in part, a response to the behaviors of others toward him.

Studies of the impact of early experiences also support the case for stability. Experiences of emotional or perceptual deprivation can affect later development, as we have seen in Part II. The effects of such deprivation tend to persist, since the foundation for later learnings is faulty. The child whose concept development is inadequate, as was true for the children in the Goldfarb study, is likely to be a school-learning problem. Without the basic foundation, concept learning, it is difficult for the school to build. And while some deficiencies can be made up, there *are* learnings acquirable only during a brief and critical period in infancy. Such traits as basic trust, as the Erikson paper pointed out, are apparently learned early in life when the helpless condition of the human mammal facilitates learning.

Interpersonal relationships within the family group probably operate to maintain stability of personality also. The concept of perceptual constancy has been offered as an explanation of why this should be so. Parents learn to perceive their offspring in a particular way and tend to look for those behaviors that confirm their expectations. Thus the four-year-old who is "all boy" will find his mother regaling his father with tales of the day's devilment; from their amused conversation the child learns that such behaviors *really* please his parents. Out of such reinforcement, the child's perception of himself is built up, and a pattern of response to parental expectations emerges.

One of the early investigators of stability of personality was Neilon, whose paper is included here. Neilon was able to locate a sizable group of young adults for whom descriptions had been written by Mary Shirley (1933) fifteen years earlier. Neilon's finding, that adolescent sketches of personality could be matched with descriptions written when the subjects were babies, served as an impetus for other investigations of persistence of behavioral characteristics.

Most of the later studies of stability of behavior have relied upon already existing data from longitudinal research. In fact, the existence of such data makes possible the testing of developmental hypotheses that emerge with new insights into human behavior. But a clearer, sharper focus on stability is possible when longitudinal projects are designed with such a hypothesis in mind. The Purdue longitudinal studies constitute such a project; in these studies children have been followed in early childhood and will be followed again at the age of nine years, to investigate the persistence of individuality. The Purdue investigators are finding, as the paper by Martin reveals, that it is the individuality of the individual that persists through time. When repeated measures of drive systems such as dependency, nurturance, and aggression are taken through the nursery-school years, the profile of the social behavior of an individual tends to be strikingly unique and stable. That is, a given child will manifest the same relative amount of a certain behavior over the years from age two to five, and the importance of this behavior in his total behavior pattern will be unique.

Will the profile change during middle childhood? In general, the literature supports the concept of stability, but there are qualifications, as the Kagan and Moss paper shows. Where the culture tends to support a trait, as, for example, dependency in girls, the trait persists. Where the trait is frowned upon, as, for example, dependency in boys, the trait tends to lose its strength. Kagan and Moss (1962) also found that for some children behavioral tendencies crystallize between ages six and ten, while for others the school and peer group during those years bring pressures for change.

Is foresight as good as hindsight? Can one predict on the basis of early behaviors which children are likely to change but little and which ones a great deal? Prediction and outcome have been the subject of a very interesting book by Escalona and Heider (1959); Escalona's case descriptions will help the reader who wants to examine this question further. These descriptions show that prediction can, indeed, be made quite accurately in some cases. It fails when the influence of a particular behavior pattern on development could not be accurately assessed. Sometimes one out of many false anticipations was the cause of a major mistake in prediction. In one case, it had been predicted that Karen, a "good" little girl who knew right from wrong at an early age, would grow into a child who would accept *with resignation* the standards imposed upon her. Instead, Karen was found at the age of five to be taking by force what she couldn't hope to get otherwise. Apparently what had happened during the nursery school years was that Karen came to see herself as a child who could not hope to be good by the standards she herself set, and so she had had to seek other means of getting from the environment what she wanted.

Erikson's paper in Part III is helpful here. The child during the preschool years is developing the essential tools for ego integration, but he is in a state of disequilibrium. For some children the prediction of outcome is easy; either they have no serious problems or their problems are quite serious. With others, the predictor can analyze present behaviors and problems, but may predict their resolution inaccurately because the child over the next few years will try various ways to obtain important need gratification, and it is not possible to know which ones the environment will let work. But, as the Martin paper shows, what means a child will try and what need gratification is important are unique to him.

Other dimensions of the child have been explored to test the stability hypothesis. The Honzik *et al.* paper investigates the constancy of mental test scores, using subjects for whom eighteen years of scores were available. While their finding of fluctuation for most subjects might seem to defeat the case for constancy, it should be noted that their over-all finding was that mental test scores increasingly coincide with the socioeconomic level of the family. Ups-and-downs in the life history of an individual were tied to ups-and-downs in test performance, but in the end the children developed a level in test performance comparable with their family level. In other words, the influence of the family milieu is steadying.

For the final paper we return once more to the biological sphere and to Tanner's fascinating account of the inexorableness of growth regulators. In the years to come, the marriage of chemistry and cybernetics will undoubtedly make it possible to answer the questions raised in this paper. Perhaps, too, such a marriage will reveal regulators to explain some facets of human behavior heretofore a mystery to man.

REFERENCES

Escalona, Sibylle K., & Heider, Grace. *Prediction and outcome: a study in child development.* New York: Basic Books, 1959.

Kagan, J., & Moss, H. A. *Birth to maturity: a study in psychological development.* New York: Wiley, 1962.

Shirley, Mary M. *The first two years: a study of twenty-five babies.* Vol. 3. Minneapolis: Univer. Minnesota Press, 1933.

PAUL HENRY MUSSEN *and* MARY COVER JONES

*Self-Conceptions, Motivations, and Interpersonal Attitudes of Late- and Early-Maturing Boys**

WHILE many intensive case studies show that personal and social adjustment during adolescence may be profoundly influenced by rate of physical maturation, there is a scarcity of systematic data on the relationship between the adolescent's physical status and his underlying motivations, self-conceptions and interpersonal attitudes. There is, however, a small body of evidence which demonstrates that greater physical maturity is associated with greater maturity of interest among girls (Stone & Barker, 1939) and that early-maturing boys differ from their late-maturing peers in both overt behavior and reputational status. In one study (Jones & Bayley, 1950) in which a staff of trained observers assessed a large group of adolescents on a number of personality variables, boys who were consistently retarded in physical development were rated lower than those who were consistently accelerated, in physical attractiveness, grooming, and matter-of-factness; and higher in sociability, social initiative (often of a childish, attention-getting sort), and eagerness. Reputation Test (Tryon, 1939) data indicated that classmates regarded the late-maturing boys as more attention-getting, more restless, more bossy, less grown-up and less good-looking than those who were physically accelerated.

On the basis of these findings, it may be inferred that adult and peer attitudes toward the adolescent, as well as their treatment and acceptance of him, are related to his physical status. This means that the sociopsychological environment to which late-maturers are subjected—and consequently the social learning situations they encounter—may be significantly different from that of their early-maturing peers. As a consequence, according to the ratings summarized above, they acquire different patterns of overt social behavior. It seems reasonable to hypothesize that groups differing in physical status will also differ in more covert aspects of behavior and personality.

Indirect evidence relevant to this hypothesis comes from an investigation of the long-term consequences of physical acceleration or retardation during adolescence. [M.C.] Jones (1957) found that group differences in physique had practically disappeared by the time her early- and late-maturing subjects reached their early thirties. Nevertheless, young adults who had been physically retarded adolescents differed from those who had been accelerated in several important psychological characteristics. In general, it appeared that the adult subjects could be described much as they had been during adolescence. Thus, those who had been early-maturers scored higher on the good impression, socialization, dominance, self-control (low score on impulsivity), and responsibility scales of the California Personality Inventory, while those who had been slow in maturing scored higher on the flexibility scale. On the Edwards Personal Preference Schedule, early-maturers scored significantly higher on the dominance scale, while the late-maturing were high in succorance. Jones concludes that the early-maturing "present a consistently favorable personality picture with regard to . . . important social variables" (1957). Moreover, there was some evidence

* REPRINTED by permission of the authors and the Society for Research in Child Development from *Child Develpm.*, 1957, 28, 243–256.

that these men had attained more stable vocational adjustments than those who had been late in maturing. These group differences in later adjustment suggest that the sociopsychological atmosphere in which the adolescent lives may have profound immediate and enduring effects on his personality structure as well as on his overt behavior.

The present study was designed to investigate the relationship between maturational status and certain important, covert aspects of personality during late adolescence. Personality structure was assessed by means of the Thematic Apperception Test (TAT) which seems to be the most appropriate and sensitive instrument for this purpose. More specifically, on the basis of the literature reviewed above and other general works on the psychology of adolescence (Farnham, 1951; H. E. Jones, 1943, 1949), we formulated and tested a series of propositions relating to differences between the physically retarded and the accelerated in self-conceptions, underlying motivations, and basic interpersonal attitudes. These variables were translated into TAT categories—needs (*n*), press (*p*), and descriptions (defined briefly in Table 1)—and the scores of early- and late-maturers in each of these categories were compared. The propositions and the rationale underlying them, together with the TAT variables involved, follow.

1. In view of their obvious physical retardation, relatively unfavorable reputations and disadvantageous competitive position in many activities, the late-maturing boys are more likely to have feelings of inadequacy. Hence, more boys in this group than in the early-maturing group are likely to have negative self-conceptions (TAT category: *negative characteristics*).

2. The adolescent in our culture generally desires some independence and adult status. This may be the source of a major problem for the late-maturer, however, since he is often regarded and treated as a small boy by adults and peers and is not likely to be granted independence as early as physically accelerated boys. Therefore, it may be anticipated that more late- than early-maturers regard adults, particularly their parents, as dominating, forcing them to do things they don't want to or preventing them from doing things they want to do (high scores in *p Dominance*). Moreover, the parental treatment these boys experience and parental refusal to grant them independent status may be interpreted as personal rejection. Hence, we predicted that more late-maturing boys would score high in *p Rejection*.

3. These feelings of being dominated and rejected may result in attitudes of rebellion against the family and in feelings of hostility. We therefore expected that more of the late-maturing group would reveal strong aggressive needs (high scores in *n Aggression*) and desires to escape from (*n Autonomy—leaving parents*), or to defy, the family (*n Autonomy —defying parents*).

4. On the basis of the data indicating that slow-maturers showed a great deal of social interest (although often of an immature kind), we hypothesized that more members of this, than of the early-maturing group would reveal strong interests in friendly, intimate interpersonal relationships (high scores in *n Affiliation*).

5. Assuming that, as Jones and Bayley (1950) suggest, the social initiative and attention-getting devices of the late-maturers are of a compensatory nature, we would expect this group to be basically dependent and to have strong needs for support from others. These should be manifest by higher scores in TAT *n Succorance* and *p Nurturance*. The latter may be considered a more indirect measure of dependence, a kind of wish-fulfilling view of the world as helpful and friendly.

6. The early-maturer, being regarded and treated as more adult, is more likely to become self-confident, and to acquire high status goals. For these reasons, we predicted that more of the physically accelerated would give evidence of high achievement goals (high scores in *n Achievement*) and concern with personal recognition (high scores in *n Recognition*).

7. Late-maturing boys in our culture probably face more problems of personal adjust-

ment than do their early-maturing peers. As a result of this, they may become more aware of their problems, and, as the high degree of flexibility of young adults who had been retarded in maturing suggests, more insightful. Hence we predicted that they would be more willing and able than early-maturers to face their own feelings and emotions (low scores in the TAT variable *denial of feeling*).

In summary, we attempted to test seven propositions related to differences in the personalities of early- and late-maturing boys. It was hypothesized that more late-maturers would score high in variables relating to negative self-conceptions, dependence, aggression, affiliation, rebelliousness, and feelings of being dominated and rejected. More early-maturers, on the other hand, were expected to reveal strong achievement and recognition needs, feelings of personal success, and tendencies toward denial of feelings.

Procedure

THE 33 seventeen-year-old male subjects of this investigation were members of the Adolescent Growth Study which included a normal sample of boys in an urban public school system (H. E. Jones, 1940). The subjects of the present investigation represented two contrasting groups, selected on the basis of their physical maturity status: 16 of them had been among the most consistently accelerated throughout the adolescent period; the other 17 had been among the most consistently retarded.[1] All of them took the Thematic Apperception Test, which provides the basic data of this study, at age 17.

The TAT consisted of 18 pictures: nine from the Murray set which is now standard (cards 1, 5, 6, 7BM, 10, 11, 14, 15, 17); five pictures from the set generally used in 1938 when these data were collected (a man and woman seated on a park bench; a bearded old man writing in an open book; a thin, sullen, young man standing behind a well-dressed older man; a tea table and two chairs; an abstract drawing of two bearded men); and four designed especially for this investigation (the nave of a large church; a madonna and child; a dramatic view of mountains; a boy gazing at a cross which is wreathed in clouds).

The tests were administered individually. Each card was projected on a screen while the subject told a story which was recorded verbatim. Standard instructions were given for the Murray cards, and subjects were asked to describe the feelings elicited by the other four pictures. Most of the stories were brief, consisting of only one or two sentences.

As we noted earlier, each of the personality variables involved in the seven propositions was translated into a TAT scoring category. The scoring scheme involved counting the relevant needs, press, and descriptions of the heroes of the stories, the assumption being that the storyteller has identified with the hero: the hero's needs are the same as the boy's; the press that impinge upon the hero are the ones that affect the boy telling the story. A total of 20 needs, press, and descriptive categories, each defined as specifically as possible, was developed in the analysis of the protocols. A score for each subject for each TAT category was derived by counting the number of stories in which it appeared. A list of the categories used, together with brief descriptions of them, is found in TABLE 1.

To test the reliability of this analysis, one of the authors (PM) and another psychologist[2] independently scored 15 complete protocols (300 stories). The percentage of interrater agreement was 90, computed by the usual formula (number of agreements divided by number of agreements plus number of disagreements).

In order to eliminate bias, the scoring used in the present study was done "blind," that is, independently of knowledge of the subject's maturational status.

1 The present sample includes 27 of Jones and Bayley's (1950) 32 subjects (the 16 most consistently retarded and 16 most consistently accelerated boys in the study). The other five boys had not taken the TAT at age 17. The six subjects who were in the present study but not in Jones and Bayley's study are the three "runners-up" from each end of the physical maturity distribution, i.e., the three who were closest to the 16 most accelerated cases and the three cases next to the 16 most retarded.

2 We are indebted to Dr. Virginia B. Ware for her participation in this aspect of the study.

TABLE 1. *Number of early- and late-maturers scoring high in TAT variables*

TAT VARIABLE	DEFINITION OF VARIABLE	HIGH EARLY-MATURERS	HIGH LATE-MATURERS	CHI SQUARE VALUE	*p*
Proposition 1					
Negative Characteristics	H is described in negative terms (e.g., imbecile, weakling, fanatic)	5	13	6.80	<.01
Proposition 2					
p Dominance 1 ...	H forced by parents to do something he doesn't want to	4	8	1.73	.09
p Dominance 2 ...	H prevented by parents from doing something he wants to	6	8	.31	>.30
p Dominance 3 ...	Total instances of H's being forced by parents to do something and/or prevented from doing something	7	11	1.46	.11
p Rejection	H rejected, scorned, or disapproved of by parents or authorities	5	11	3.69	.03
Proposition 3					
n Aggression 1	H is aggressive in physical, asocial way	8	3	3.88	.02
n Aggression 2	H is mad at someone, argues	7	4	1.52	.10
n Aggression 3	Total of all H's aggressive actions	11	8	1.26	.10
n Autonomy 1	H leaves home	7	10	.75	.20
n Autonomy 2	H disobeys or defies parents	7	11	1.46	.11
n Autonomy 3	Total of instances in which hero leaves and/or defies his parents	3	9	4.16	.02
Proposition 4					
n Affiliation 1	H establishes good relations with his parents	8	8	.00	>.50
n Affiliation 2	H falls in love, has a romance, marries	9	14	2.66	.05
n Affiliation 3	Total instances in which H establishes and/or maintains friendly relations	8	12	1.46	.11
Proposition 5					
n Succorance	H feels helpless, seeks aid or sympathy	7	12	2.43	.06
p Nurturance 1 ...	H is helped, encouraged, or given something by parents	5	8	.93	.18
p Nurturance 2 ...	H is helped, encouraged, or given something by someone else (not parents)	8	14	3.88	.02

TABLE 1. (*Continued*)

TAT VARIABLE	DEFINITION OF VARIABLE	HIGH EARLY-MATURERS	HIGH LATE-MATURERS	CHI SQUARE VALUE	*p*
Proposition 6					
n Achievement	H attempts to attain a high goal or to do something creditable	9	10	.02	>.50
n Recognition	H seeks fame and/or high prestige status	9	8	.28	>.30
Proposition 7					
Denial of Feeling ..	S states that picture elicits no thoughts or feelings	9	5	2.43	.06

Results

FREQUENCY distributions of the scores of all subjects were made for all the TAT variables. Each distribution was then dichotomized at the point which most nearly enabled the placing of half of the 33 subjects above, and half of them below, the dividing point. Subjects having scores above this point were considered high in this particular variable; those with scores below this point were considered low in this variable. Chi square tests were used to test the seven propositions, i.e., to ascertain whether or not high scores in certain TAT variables were in fact more characteristic of one group (late- or early-maturers) than of the other.

TABLE 1 lists the TAT variables, the number of late- and early-maturers with high scores in the variable, the chi square value obtained and the level of significance. It should be noted that the hypotheses tested were one-sided hypotheses, while the chi square value is in terms of a two-sided hypothesis. When chi square has only one degree of freedom, the square root of chi square has a distribution which is the right hand half of a normal distribution. In order to test a one-sided hypothesis, the chi square test must be converted into the equivalent value in terms of a unit normal deviate (Fisher, 1938). The levels of significance reported in TABLE 1 were evaluated in these terms.

TABLE 1 shows that, as had been predicted, more late-maturing than early-maturing boys revealed feelings of inadequacy and negative self-concepts, i.e., scored high in the TAT variable *negative characteristics.* Hence proposition 1 was confirmed. This finding is consistent with the frequently made clinical observation that retardation in physical maturation may be an important source of personal maladjustments and attitudes of inferiority.

Proposition 2 stated that more late-maturers regard their parents as highly dominating and rejecting. The evidence summarized in TABLE 1 substantially supported this proposition. While the difference was not statistically significant, more late- than early-maturers scored high in *p Dominance by parents* (total). There was a marked difference between the groups in the variable which involves parental domination by forcing the child to do something he does not want to do (*p Dominance by parents, forcing*). However, examination of the data with respect to the variable *p Dominance by parents* (*prevention*) makes it necessary to reject that part of the proposition which maintains that late-maturers are more likely to view their parents as highly restrictive of their activities.

That aspect of proposition 2 which deals with feelings of rejection was confirmed by our data. Compared with the early-maturing group, a significantly greater proportion of the late-maturers told stories in which the hero was rejected by parents or authority figures. These feelings of rejection may stem from different sources. In some cases, the parents' behavior may make it clear that they are disappointed in their physically retarded son whom they regard as immature. The boy, perceiving this attitude, may interpret it as rejection. In other cases, parental reluctance to allow the late-maturing boy to establish his independence may lead to considerable tension in the family and the boy's feelings of rejection may simply reflect the ongoing parent-child conflict.

It is possible that earlier in their teens, soon after the physical changes of adolescence became apparent, many of the early-maturing boys also experienced conflicts with their parents, arising from difficulties in establishing their independence or in handling emerging heterosexual interests. At that time they too may have felt dominated or rejected. However, by the age of 17, when these data were collected, these boys were ordinarily treated as adults and granted more freedom. Hence, they were more likely to have resolved many of their conflicts with their parents and to feel accepted and independent.

The hypothesis (part of proposition 3) that more late-maturers would be highly aggressive was rejected on the basis of the evidence given in Table 1. In fact, the differences between the two groups on all the TAT aggression variables were in the opposite direction from the prediction. High scores in the variables relating to aggression of the most overt and violent type were significantly more frequent among the early-maturers, and more members of this group also scored high in measures of milder (verbal) aggression and of total aggression. While late-maturers may experience more problems of adjustment and greater frustrations than their early-maturing peers, they apparently do not manifest greater aggressive motivation. It may be that their own feelings of inadequacy or fears of retaliation and punishment for aggression inhibit their expression of hostile feelings, even in fantasy. On the other hand, the early-maturers who feel more secure personally, and recognize their own relatively advantageous physical and social status, may feel freer to express their aggressive needs. Since aggression is a culturally stereotyped masculine trait, it seems possible that the physically accelerated, being accepted as mature and identifying readily with adult males, are more likely to acquire this characteristic. In any case, the finding that early-maturers express higher aggressive motivation during late adolescence seems consistent with Jones' finding that, as young adults, they score high on the dominance scale of the Edwards Personal Preference test (M. C. Jones, 1957). Perhaps the relatively strong aggressive motivation of the early-maturer, or the mature sex-role identification it may imply, serves as a basis for the development of later qualities of leadership and persuasiveness.

As Table 1 indicates, the other aspect of proposition 3 was confirmed: a significantly greater proportion of late- than of early-maturers displayed strong motivations to escape from, or defy, their parents. These may be essentially aggressive reactions, stemming from feelings of parental domination and rejection, or they may reflect the late-maturers' awareness of their strife with their parents whom they perceive as blocking their drives for independence. These strong needs for escape and defiance may also be considered evidence of a generally immature way of handling parent-child conflicts. Perhaps, by the age of 17, the early-maturers have already resolved many of their conflicts with their families and/or have learned to handle these in less rebellious and in more direct and mature ways.

Proposition 4 stated that, compared with their early-maturing peers, more late-maturers would manifest strong needs for establishing close social contacts with others. While there was some confirmatory evidence, the results were not clear-cut. When all affiliative needs were considered together (score for *n Affiliation—total*), the group differences were in the predicted direction, but not statistically significant. Examination of the protocols revealed that almost all instances of affiliation concerned either parents or the opposite sex; there were very few stories involving close, friendly associations between like-sexed peers. The two major types of affiliation were scored separately. As Table 1 shows, late-maturers did not differ from early-maturers with respect to need for affiliation with parents, but a significantly greater proportion of the former group displayed strong motivation for heterosexual affiliation.

In view of the late-maturers' strong feelings of inadequacy and dependent needs (see below), it is surprising that a greater proportion of this group did not exhibit strong needs to establish and maintain close bonds with their parents. This may be due to the late-maturers' more intense conflicts with their parents at this age (17 years), their fears of being rejected and dominated by them, and their generally defiant attitudes which prevent them from admitting, even in fantasy, their strong underlying needs to form close contacts with them.

The significant difference between the groups in *n Affiliation* (*love, romance, marriage*) is subject to several possible interpretations. For one thing, this category may refer to general needs to establish close relations with others (with peers or adults other than parents) and not merely to desire for contact with the opposite sex. The set of stimulus cards may not have been adequate to elicit responses indicative of more general affiliative needs; hence, these were expressed through responses in the heterosexual affiliation category. If this is true, proposition 4 was confirmed, and the late-maturers' high scores in this variable indicate their greater general interest in establishing and maintaining friendly relationships.

It is also possible that the late-maturers' strong affiliative needs are actually directed only toward members of the opposite sex, i.e., that *n Affiliation* (*love, romance, marriage*) measures specifically heterosexual interests. Assuming that this is true, there is another plausible explanation for the discovered difference. As we saw earlier, the late-maturer may be afraid to admit that he desires close associations with his parents. He may also feel that his immaturity and poor reputational status prevent him from establishing successful social relationships with like-sexed peers. Hence, he may "displace" his affiliative needs to members of the opposite sex, who, in his fantasies, may seem more responsive.

A third possible explanation of the difference is based on Jones and Bayley's findings that the late-maturers show less overt interest in girls and are regarded as less good-looking (1950). From these data, it may be inferred that the physically retarded probably do not have successful and rewarding experiences with girls. Hence their heightened need for affiliation with the opposite sex, expressed in the TAT, may reflect their attempts to satisfy in fantasy needs which they cannot satisfy adequately in reality.

The data were generally supportive of proposition 5 which stated that late-maturers are likely to have strong underlying dependent needs. A higher proportion of this group than of their early-maturing peers scored high in *n Succorance,* the difference between the two groups approaching statistical significance ($p = .06$). Furthermore, high scores in the category involving receiving help and support from others (not including parents) (*p Nurturance—non-parents*)—an indirect measure of dependent needs—were significantly more characteristic of the physically retarded than of the physically accelerated. In view of the late-maturers' attitudes toward their parents, discussed above, it is not surprising to find that perceptions of parents as kindly and supportive (high scores in *p Nurturance-parents*) were not significantly more common in this group than in the early-maturing group.

On the basis of the data involving the TAT variables *n Achievement* and *n Recognition,* we rejected proposition 6 which stated that more early-maturers would be self-confident and have high needs for achievement and personal recognition. In our culture there is strong pressure to develop needs for achievement and personal recognition, and, according to our results, these needs and feelings may become intense regardless of—or perhaps in spite of—the child's maturational status, feelings of personal adequacy, dependency, and adjustment to parents.

Two interesting incidental findings from the TAT data seem to be consistent with the proposition that more early- than late-maturers are likely to be self-confident. Seven boys in this sample of 33 adolescents told stories in which the hero was helpful or kind to someone else (*n Nurturance*). Of this group, six were early-maturers, while only one was a late maturer ($\chi^2 = 2.09$, $p = .07$). Insofar as *n Nurturance* may be a measure of the storyteller's own feelings that he can accept an active, mature role, more of the accelerated group feel self-assured with respect to having attained mature status.

The other incidental finding which seems to support proposition 6 is based on responses only to card 1 of the Murray series which depicts a young boy contemplating a violin which rests on a table in front of him. Eight of the subjects spoke of the boy (the hero) as a prodigy or a genius. Of these, seven were early-maturers; only one was physically retarded ($\chi^2 = 5.25$, $p = .01$). If the attribution of this prestige status and accomplishment to the hero reflects the subject's own feeling that he has been an achiever, it follows that more of the physically accelerated have positive self-concepts. In view of the small number of cases involved, both of these findings must be considered tentative, but they do offer some evidence in support of proposition 6.

Proposition 7, which stated that relatively few of the physically retarded boys are unwilling or unable to face their own feelings and emotions, received some support from the TAT data summarized in TABLE 1. A smaller proportion of the members of this group than of the physically accelerated group specifically denied that the pictures evoked any feelings or emotions (e.g. "It doesn't make me think of anything"). While this variable may not adequately measure *denial of feeling* as a major defense mechanism, this result seems to indicate that late-maturers are more sensitive to their own feelings and more ready to admit and face them openly. Since these qualities are basic to the development of psychological insight, it may be inferred that late-maturers, as a group, are more likely to become insightful individuals.

Discussion

THE results of the study support the general hypothesis that, in our culture, the boy whose physical development is retarded is exposed to a sociopsychological environment which may have adverse effects on his personality development. Apparently, being in a disadvantageous competitive position in athletic activities, as well as being regarded and treated as immature by others, may lead to negative self-conceptions, heightened feelings of rejection by others, prolonged dependent needs, and rebellious attitudes toward parents. Hence, the physically retarded boy is more likely than his early-maturing peer to be personally and socially maladjusted during late adolescence. Moreover, some of his attitudes are likely to interfere with the process of identification with his parents, which is generally based on perceptions of them as warm and accepting (Payne & Mussen, 1956). This, in turn, may inhibit or delay the acquisition of mature characteristics and attitudes which are ordinarily established through identification with parents. Fortunately for the late-maturers' subsequent adjustments, they seem more willing and able to face their feelings and emotions. This may be a result of their awareness of others' attitudes toward their immaturity or their feelings of personal inadequacy and dependency.

The physically accelerated boys, on the other hand, are likely to experience environmental circumstances which are much more conducive to good psychological adjustment. Hence, their psychological picture, as reflected in their TAT stories, is much more favorable. By the time they were 17, relatively few early-maturers harbored strong feelings of inadequacy, perceived themselves as rejected or dominated by parents or authorities, or felt rebellious toward their families. As a group, they appeared to have acquired more self-confidence and had probably made stronger identifications with mature adults. Hence, they perceived themselves as more mature individuals, less dependent and in need of help, and more capable of playing an adult male role in interpersonal relationships.

These findings assume additional, probably greater, importance when they are considered in the light of [M.C.] Jones' findings on the early adult (age 33) adjustments of boys who had been retarded or accelerated in physical maturing (1957). It should be recalled that by this age physical differences between the two groups had practically disappeared. Certain important psychological differences were noted, however, and these were consistent with the differences at age 17, reported in the present study. For example, the responses of the early-maturing group to two paper-and-pencil tests revealed that, as young adults, they were more dominant, more able to make a good impression and more likely to be turned to for advice and reassurance; more self-controlled; and more willing and able to carry social responsibility. In short, they present a general picture of psychological maturity. Moreover, more of the early-maturers seemed to have made successful vocational adjustments. In contrast to this, when the late-maturers became adults, they tended to be highly dependent individuals who could be described, on the basis of their test responses, as tending to be rebellious, touchy, impulsive, self-indulgent, and insightful. Most of these characteristics are indicative of poor adjustment and psychological immaturity. Fewer members of this group had made good vocational adjustment.

The striking correspondence between the two descriptions of the groups, derived from different kinds of tests and collected at widely separated periods of time, lends further support to Jones' conclusion that "the adolescent handicaps and advantages associated with late- or early-maturing appear to carry over into adulthood to some extent" (1957). It seems clear that many attributes of adolescent personality (patterns of motivation, self-conceptions, and attitudes toward others) characteristic of late- and early-maturing boys are relatively stable and durable rather than situational and transitory. This may be attributable to the fact that in our culture adolescence is generally a critical and difficult period of adjustment. Within a relatively brief interval of time, the child must work out numerous complex and vitally important personal problems —e.g., adaptation to his changed biological and social status, establishment of independence, vocational adjustment. In dealing with these problems, he may acquire new behaviors and personality attributes which have broad ramifications, not only on his current adjustment, but also on his subsequent development. If the adolescent can cope with his problems without too much inner stress and turmoil, his self-esteem, feelings of adequacy, and consequently his subsequent adjustment, are likely to be enhanced. On the other hand, if his problems induce great tension and anxiety, he is likely to feel frustrated and inadequate, and, if these feelings are maintained, to adjust less satisfactorily as an adult.

Obviously, the adolescent's success or failure, as well as ease or tension, in handling his problems will be determined to a large degree by the sociopsychological forces to which he is subjected during this time, and these, as we have seen, may be significantly related to his rate of maturation. Thus, physical status during adolescence—mediated through the sociopsychological environment—may exert profound and lasting influences on personality. For this reason, many aspects of the adult's behavior and personality seem consistent with his adolescent adjustments, attitudes and motivations.

Insofar as our results permit generalization, they suggest that some important aspects of motivation, such as needs for achievement and personal recognition, are not significantly affected by maturational status. It may be that among subjects whose achievements are strongly encouraged and rewarded from very early childhood, the need to achieve becomes powerful and resistant to change even in the face of feelings of helplessness and inadequacy. The latter may inhibit the achievement-oriented overt behavior of some late-maturers, but the underlying motivation to achieve seems as strong in this group as it is among the physically accelerated.

In conclusion, it should be noted that, although rate of maturing and associated factors may affect personality development, the relationship between physical status and psychological characteristics is by no means simple. A vast number of complex, interacting factors, including rate of maturation, determine each adolescent's unique personality structure. Hence, in any specific instance, the *group* findings of the present study may not be directly applicable, for other physical, psychological, or social factors may attenuate the effects of late- or early-maturing. For example, an adolescent boy who is fundamentally secure and has warm, accepting parents and generally rewarding social relationships may not develop strong feelings of inadequacy even if he matures slowly. Analogously, the early-maturing boy who has deep feelings of insecurity, for whatever reasons, will probably not gain self-confidence simply because he matures early. In summary, in understanding any individual case, generalizations based on the data of the present study must be particularized in the light of the individual's past history and present circumstances.

Summary

THE present investigation was designed to test seven propositions concerning the relationship between rate of physical maturation and important aspects of personality structure, specifically, self-conceptions, underlying motivations, and basic interpersonal attitudes. The TAT protocols of 33 seventeen-year-old boys —16 who had been consistently physically accelerated throughout adolescence and 17 who had been consistently retarded—were analyzed according to a scoring schema involving 20 needs, press, and descriptive categories. The scores of early- and late-maturers in each of the categories were compared.

An earlier study (Jones & Bayley, 1950) demonstrated that late-maturing boys are more likely than their early-maturing peers to encounter a generally unfavorable sociopsychological environment. Analysis of the data of the present study indicates that this situation may have adverse effects on the personalities of the physically retarded. These boys are more likely to have negative self-conceptions, feelings of inadequacy, strong feelings of being rejected and dominated, prolonged dependency needs, and rebellious attitudes toward parents. In contrast, the early-maturing boys present a much more favorable psychological picture during adolescence. Relatively few of them felt inadequate, rejected, dominated, or rebellious toward their families. More of them appeared to be self-confident, independent, and capable of playing an adult role in interpersonal relationships. Early- and late-maturing groups did not differ significantly from each other in needs for achievement or personal recognition.

These findings make it clear that rate of physical maturing may affect personality development in crucially important ways. However, it is important to note that in any particular case the effects of early- or late-maturing may be significantly modified by the individual's psychological history and present circumstances.

REFERENCES

FARNHAM, M. L. *The adolescent.* New York: Harper, 1951.

FISHER, R. A. *Statistical methods for research workers.* (7th ed.) Edinburgh: Oliver & Boyd, 1938.

JONES, H. E. Observational methods in the study of individual development. *J. consult. Psychol.,* 1940, **4,** 234–238.

JONES, H. E. *Development in adolescence.* New York: Appleton-Century, 1943.

JONES, H. E. Adolescence in our society. In *The family in a democratic society: anniversary papers of The Community Service Society of New York.* New York: Columbia Univer. Press, 1949. Pp. 70–82.

JONES, MARY C. The later careers of boys who were early- or late-maturing. *Child Develpm.,* 1957, **28,** 113–128.

JONES, MARY C., & BAYLEY, NANCY. Physical maturing among boys as related to behavior. *J. educ. Psychol.,* 1950, **41,** 129–148.

PAYNE, D. E., & MUSSEN, P. H. Parent-child relations and father identification among adolescent boys. *J. abnorm. soc. Psychol.,* 1956, **52,** 358–362.

STONE, C. P., & BAKER, R. G. The attitudes and interests of premenarcheal and postmenarcheal girls. *J. genet. Psychol.,* 1939, **54,** 27–71.

TRYON, CAROLINE M. Evaluation of adolescent personality by adolescents. *Monogr. Soc. Res. Child Develpm.,* 1939, **4,** No. 4.

PATRICIA NEILON

Shirley's Babies After Fifteen Years: A Personality Study[*]

ALTHOUGH mothers, nurses, and other observers of children have often been convinced that there is some continuity of "characteristicness," or general personality pattern in developing individuals, this continuity has been elusive of objective psychological measurement. That individuality exists in early infancy has been demonstrated by several investigators. That it also exists in adulthood is, of course, accepted, and differences are measured. That the pattern of personality shown in infancy continues through life, or that it changes its form of expression as growth and development proceed has, however, never been established. Just as manifestations of brightness change with age, manifestations of individuality might change with development, while leaving the child in the same relative place in his group at successive measurements. Even assuming continuity of personality patterns, the individual who cries a great deal as an infant would not necessarily be expected to cry a great deal as an adult. The personality characteristic which caused the excessive crying in infancy might persist though, and be expressed in a different manner in adulthood. We do not know merely from the infant's crying, however, what form of expression this characteristic might take later. The infant who cries a great deal might babble a great deal as a toddler, and be talkative as an adult. Or, the same infant who cries a great deal might be subject to severe temper tantrums at preschool age, and have an inclination to impulsiveness or emotionality in adulthood. The entire personality pattern, including emphases and details, might continue from infancy with changes in expression to adulthood. Or, perhaps, some elements of individuality might be retained while others disappeared with development and experience. Or, there is a third possibility that differences which existed in infancy, perhaps due to differences in age at birth, physical and physiological conditions [continue to influence development throughout early and later childhood]. Although these and other more complex possibilities unquestionably exist, they have not been investigated. In part this is due to the difficulties of measurement in the field of personality, and in part to the lack of attempts at measurement of the same individuals after long intervals of time have elapsed. Moreover, measurements which are suitable for infants or children are inapplicable to adults and vice versa, so that continuity of measurements is impossible. As a result, most students of child personality have used the cross-sectional approach to investigate age and sex differences in a certain trait, or to produce experimental modifications. Rarely have they attempted to measure continuity in the natural environment.

Early biographers seem to have believed in the emergence of individuality in infancy. Shinn (1900, p. 55), for example, says: "Our baby showed temperament and luckily of the easy-going and cheerful kind from her first day (though we could hardly see this except by looking back afterward)." Hogan (1900, p. 15) refers to the child's "early inclination to know what was going on about him," which continued, as did his seeming "happiest when he was let alone." In 1925, Wooley described the development of "Agnes, a Domi-

* REPRINTED by permission of Patricia Neilon Naka and The Journal Press from *J. genet. Psychol.*, 1948, 73, 175–186.

nant Personality in the Making," on the basis of teachers' reports of the child while attending the Merrill Palmer School. This little girl, a sample case, remained the same in her basic personality pattern of aggressive dominant behavior from ages two to five.

In the more recent literature, evidence concerning continuity of individuality is given firstly in studies of certain personality traits, secondly in studies using personality tests and rating scales, and thirdly in studies which aim at total personality investigation, usually by use of a descriptive technique. The individual's characteristic modes of response have tended to persist in the areas of perseveration, which was investigated by Cushing (1929), smiling, which was investigated by Washburn (1929), laughter, which was investigated by Brackett (1933), and crying, which was investigated by Bayley (1932). After studying "problem" behavior in a large and representative sample, however, Macfarlane (1939) concluded that "transitoriness" tended to be the rule rather than "persistence." Using time sampling techniques in studying preschool children, individual consistency has been found by Green (1933) in "frequency of group play," by Loomis (Jones & Burks, 1936) in the ratio of number of contacts initiated to those received," and by Jersild (1942) in conflict behavior in two observation periods separated by a year's time interval. Because they demonstrate some degree of stability in personality, reports of continuity of such traits or behavior items are valuable. The question of the continuity of total personality pattern, however, is far more complex. While the above reports are objective, they are, for our purposes, limited in scope. Attempts to investigate "total personality," on the other hand, often sacrifice objectivity to completeness.

Halfway between studies of single traits and studies using descriptive methods to investigate total personality are studies of the continuity of individuality which use standard personality tests and rating scales as measuring devices. Test-retest techniques used by Jones and Burks (1936) and Tryon (1934) have shown that children tend to say the same sorts of things about themselves on two tests separated in time. While personality tests are the most objective of the measures available, such studies cannot adequately demonstrate the continuity or lack of continuity of individuality. In the first place, test-retest reliability, deliberately made a part of the test, might insure measured continuity. To many, in the second place, a person's impression of himself is not so important an aspect of personality as is the impression of him gained by others, which is not measured by a personality test. Finally, a test is also limiting, and totality is again sacrificed to objectivity. The rating scale, which is a semi-objective measure, has also been applied to this problem. Bonham and Sargent (Murphy, Murphy, & Newcomb, 1937) used the method on 38 children from birth to two and one-half years finding no consistently positive relationships in ratings except for good looks. Using the same method on 140 preschool children for three consecutive years, Stutsman (1935) found constancy in ratings and in profile patterns based on ratings suggesting personality types. Besides evidence from studies of separate personality traits and studies using personality tests and rating scales, the third type of evidence concerning continuity of individuality is from studies of total personality. In *Biographies of Child Development,* for instance, Gesell *et al.* (1939) conclude:

> Our data [from ten years of study at the Yale clinic] do not lend support to the concept of a relatively standard pattern of infancy. Nor are the findings of embryology in harmony with such a concept. From the standpoint of embryology the infant is already far advanced in the cycle of life. He is already stamped with individuality rather than with a standard pattern. . . . This perpetuation of characteristicness is not incompatible with morphogenesis and maturing. It is, however, inconsistent with the idea that individual differences at birth are slight and increase with age, or that the period of infancy is in any sense neutral or generic when compared with later periods of the life cycle [p. 304].

There seemed to have been persistent temperamental differences in twins *T* and *C*

(Gesell & Thompson, 1941), and Johnny and Jimmy (McGraw, 1939). After a series of studies of the same group of children for five years at Columbia University (Jersild, 1933; McKinnon, 1942), "consistency," it was concluded, "rather than inconsistency is characteristic of development." Also using a descriptive technique, Allport (1937) studied his own son. Here personality predictions made by the parents when the boy was four months old were compared with records of parents at two later ages and with records of four different teachers at succeeding age levels. "The prognosis at the age of four months," Allport declares, "is borne out in most respects . . . two of the initially dominant characteristics have shifted their emphasis. . . . But on the whole the schedule is consistent throughout." From this material, Allport advances the hypothesis that "from early infancy there is a consistency in the development of personality." Roberts and Fleming (1943), with data from 25 women at precollege, college, and post-college levels found that the ratio of persisting to fluctuating traits was 3:2.

Elimination of the experimenter's bias, which is a factor in all biographical studies, is achieved by Gesell *et al.* (1939). Movies of five children at ages one and five were used. From the movies, a trained observer who was unacquainted with the children ranked them on 15 behavior traits including energy, demeanor, dependence, social responsiveness, and the like. Out of 75 rankings, 48 coincided, 21 were displaced by one rank order, five were displaced by two rank orders, and one was displaced by three rank orders. "Our periodic cinema records," Gesell writes, "clearly show prophetic characters in behavior traits in the first year."

In the investigation of continuity of individuality, in summary, positive findings are more conclusive than negative ones. An impression of continuity was reported by early biographers. Continuity is likewise found in certain separate traits and behavior items. Investigators of "total personality" have been unable to retain both completeness and objectivity, between which a balance must be struck. Since a breaking down of "totality" has usually given negative results, it would seem that strict quantitative measurement of behavior must be discarded in this area. The method of the Gesell *et al.* study (1939) provides another sort of objectivity. The matching method advocated by Vernon (1935, 1936a, 1936b) allows the use of total personality, but eliminates the strong effect which the bias of the single experimenter exerts upon the results in the case study or descriptive method. In one study reported by Vernon (1935), character sketches of 25 subjects were written by each of three experimenters on the basis of the behavior of the subects during performance tests. Each experimenter then tried to identify the sketches of the other two. This method applied to growing children should provide evidence about the continuity of individuality.

This is essentially the method adopted in this study. Extensive personality data on infants were presented by Dr. Mary Shirley in her *The First Two Years: a Study of Twenty-Five Babies* (1933). After two years of standardized observations of the children as well as two years acquaintance with them and their families, Dr. Shirley wrote personality sketches. These sketches and later sketches of the same children prepared by the writer were used in a matching procedure to investigate the continuity of individuality.

The plan for the personality follow-up of the 25 babies, which was begun 15 years after the original study, included the objective measurements of the subjects who would be available for study, and the writing of new personality sketches which were to be matched with the original sketches written by Dr. Shirley. The writer did not consult the Shirley sketches after the study was begun, and did not know the pseudonyms used by Shirley until the follow-up sketches were completed. Two formal personality tests were used in the follow-up, the Goodenough *Speed of Association Test* (1942) and the Rundquist-Sletto *Minnesota Survey of Opinions* (1936). In addition to these formally developed scales of personality measurement, a five-point rating scale of 23 traits, and a scale of six special abilities were also used. The *Speed of Association Test, the Minnesota Survey of Opinions,* and the scale for self-rating were administered to the subject in this order. Following this was a more or less standardized interview concerning the subject's interests, in which a general impression of his personality picture could be gained. An interview was also held with each of the mothers. During this interview, the mother rated her child on the 23 traits and six special abilities. She was also encouraged to talk about the child, and to state why she placed him in each of the rating categories. Many anecdotes illustrating the various characteristics of the child were related, and his place in the family group was estimated. Each mother was also asked whether or not she believed the child to have changed in such respects as were referred to on the rating scale or in his general behavior pattern. Rating scales and special ability scales were mailed to the fathers. All of the objective data were interpreted in the light of the short interviews with the subjects and mothers, and personality sketches were written of the children as they seemed to be at the age of 17.

The original group of 25 babies was above average in socio-economic status, education, and intelligence. Such a superior sample was originally chosen by Dr. Shirley because it was felt that better coöperation of parents could be obtained than would have been the case if a sample more representative of the population at large had been chosen. At the end of two years, Shirley had 19 of her original 25 subjects. Fifteen years later, it was possible to gather partial data on all of these, and full data on 16.

The finished adolescent sketches were two to four typewritten pages in length. To the Shirley infant sketches proper, material was added from her sections of "Incidental Reactions" and "Personality as Revealed in Speech." This made the infant sketches comparable in length to the adolescent sketches. Since sex was readily determined in all sketches, the sexes were separated for the matching procedure. There were five sketches of adolescent girls to be matched with six infant sketches, and 10 sketches of adolescent boys to be matched with 13 infant sketches. One of the adolescent boy sketches had to be thrown out because there was no comparable infant sketch. Keeping the extra infant sketches made matching more difficult by eliminating the possibility of automatically matching the last sketch in either series. Because of the length of the sketches, the matching task was a difficult one. It was performed by graduate students and staff members at the Institute of Child Welfare, University of Minnesota, who carefully read and reread the material, weighed and re-evaluated the evidence. Ten judges matched the sketches of girls (five versus six cases), and five judges matched the sketches of boys (10 versus 13 cases). Although statistically the chances for success are approximately equal for both tasks, the matching of 10 versus 13 cases is psychologically far more difficult. The greater number of cases necessitated more than twice the amount of reading, and made an almost impossible demand upon the memories of the judges. With 10 personality sketches and 10 pictures Vernon (1936b) found matching "almost impossible" for judges, even though this would involve less reading than the matching of two sets of sketches.

Chances of successful choice are both reduced and increased by the limitations of the matching process. Taking the simpler five versus six matching as an example, the chances that the first adolescent girl's sketch would be correctly matched would be one in six. Assuming this first match to be correct, the chances that the second sketch would be correctly matched would be reduced to one in five. And assuming the first two to be correctly matched, there would be one chance in four that a third would also be successfully matched, and so on, the task being made easier by process of elimination after every successful matching. The chances of matching all sketches successfully, therefore, would be 1/6! When there are incorrect matches, however, the problem becomes more complex. If the first adolescent girl's sketch were incorrectly matched, it might be matched with either the sixth infant sketch, which has no mate, or with any of the four others. In the latter case, two incorrect matches would automatically come about. If the first two adolescent girls' sketches were incorrectly matched, there would automatically be at least three, and quite possibly four errors.

Chapman (1935, 1936) has given formulae for the solution of this rather complex problem which are based on the possible permutations of the cases. In matching five versus six sketches, a total of 720 (6!) permutations are possible, but only one of these arrangements allows for the correct matching of all sketches. When there are four correct matches, and one error, there are five possible permutations, that is the sixth or extra infant sketch might be matched with any one of the five adolescent sketches. The chances of making one error, then, would be 5/720. Other probabilities can be worked out by Chapman's formula. TABLE 1 shows the probabilities of

TABLE 1. *Probabilities of the chance success of one judge in matching personality sketches*

NUMBER OF SUCCESSES	PROBABLE CHANCES IN 100 5 vs. 6 cases	10 vs. 13 cases
0	43	46
1	37	36
2	15	14
3	4	3
4	0.07	0.06
5	0.01	0.008

the chance success of one judge in matching five versus six and 10 versus 13 cases worked out by this formula. It must be emphasized that these figures apply only to the chances of successful matching by one judge. The highest number of successful matchings obtained by any judge for the five versus six cases was four, and for the 10 versus 13 cases, five.

The results of 10 judges in matching the five adolescent sketches and six infant sketches of girls are shown in TABLE 2. The majority of the judges succeeded at the 4 per cent level of probability, three succeeded

TABLE 2. *Successes of ten judges in matching personality sketches of girls* (5 vs. 6 cases)

NUMBER OF CORRECT JUDGMENTS	PROBABILITY LEVEL	NUMBER OF JUDGES
0	43%	0
1	37	0
2	15	1
3	4	6
4	0.07	3
5	0.01	0
		10 Total

at the .07 per cent level, and one at the 15 per cent level. The mean number of successes for all of the judges is 3.2. The significance of this figure can be calculated by another special method. According to Chapman (1935), the mean of random matchings is, by sampling theory, t/u, ($t =$ the smaller number of items to be matched; $u =$ the larger number of items to be matched). This agrees with Zubin's (1933) discussion of the problem of matching equal numbers of items, in which the mean of random matchings is one, and the standard deviation is also one. For the more general case, which can apply with either equal or unequal numbers, Chapman gives the formula for the standard deviation. He gives also a formula for calculating the skewness of the distribution of random matchings which becomes more leptokurtic and more skewed as the difference between the numbers to be matched increases. The distribution takes the shape of Pearson's Type III Curve. Tables, which are correct to six places, have been worked out by Salvosa (1930) for this function. Area under the Type III curve above the obtained mean value in terms of the standard deviation can be determined from these tables. Using this procedure, it was found that there is less than one chance in 1,000,000 that the mean of 10 judges in matching five versus six cases would equal or exceed 3.2.

The results of five judges in matching the 10 adolescent sketches of boys with 13 infant sketches, which are less clear cut, are shown

TABLE 3. *Successes of five judges in matching personality sketches of boys* (10 vs. 13 cases)

NUMBER OF CORRECT JUDGMENTS	PROBABILITY LEVEL	NUMBER OF JUDGES
0	46%	0
1	36	1
2	14	2
3	3	1
4	0.06	0
5	0.008	1
		5 Total

in TABLE 3. These results are less clear cut probably because of the difficulty of the task, and the difficulty of obtaining judges for the task. One judge did succeed, however, at the .008 per cent level. The mean number of successes for all of the judges in this case is 2.6. Applying Chapman's formula to this figure, there are only 25 chances in 100,000 that the mean of five judges in matching 10 versus 13 cases would equal or exceed 2.6.

The successes of individual judges as well as the high mean numbers of successes for both tasks as compared to chance demonstrate some common element in the sketches at both levels. Since the writer was not familiar with the earlier sketches nor with the pseudonyms used for the children at the time of preparing the later sketches, and since similarity existed in the sketches of the two-year-olds which were based on subjective thorough acquaintance, and the sketches of the same children at 17 which were based on objective tests and rating material, we conclude that personality similarities exist.

Taking the subject rather than the judge as the unit may shed more light on the results. TABLE 4 shows that one of the girls, Winnie, was always matched correctly by the 10 judges, while Judy was never matched correctly. It seems possible, in other words, to rank the subjects according to ease of matching: Winnie, whom 10 out of 10 judges matched correctly; Virginia Ruth, matched correctly by nine judges; Sibyl by seven; Patty by six; and Judy who was never matched correctly. In considering the problem of the probability of repeated successes in matching the same adolescent sketch, the only method of attack seems to be in considering the matching of each adolescent sketch as a separate task independent of other matching. This, of course, is not the case. As stated above, the chances of matching the first case are one in six, while after one sketch is correctly matched, the probability that a second will be correctly matched is one in five and so on. Considering each matching as a simple choice of one of six sketches also ignores the fact that the correct match for any given sketch may already be incorrectly matched elsewhere. For calculating the probability of repeated successes, nevertheless, the simplest method is one in which each adolescent sketch is considered separately, or as if it were the first to be matched. The probability that one sketch would be matched correctly by all judges, using this line af reasoning, is $1/6^n$ while other probabilities are worked out through use of the

TABLE 4. *Distribution of ten matchings of infant and adolescent personality sketches of girls*

ADOLESCENT SKETCH	TIMES OUT OF 10 MATCHED WITH FOLLOWING INFANT SKETCH					
	Winnie	*Va. Ruth*	*Sibyl*	*Judy*	*Patty*	*Carol*
Winnie	10 *					
Va. Ruth		9 *				1
Sibyl			7 *	3		
Judy			2	*	3	5
Patty				3	6 *	

binominal expansion. This trend of difference between subjects in matchability was less definite for the boys on account of the small number of judges used. Fred and Harvey seemed to be most frequently matched, however. It is possible to interpret the trend in three ways. Ease of matching could be attributable, firstly, to the greater degree of similarity in personality in some cases. Perhaps, secondly, it might be due to more adequate description of some cases, at one or both levels. Allied with this is the third possibility that some individuals are more outstanding, and therefore can be matched more successfully than the generality even though the degree of similarity or dissimilarity between early and later status is similar for all.

. . .

Summary

PERSONALITY sketches of 19 children written by Shirley (1933) on the basis of observations during the first two years of life were matched with personality sketches of 15 of the same children prepared by the writer on the basis of test and rating material. Later sketches were prepared without acquaintance with the earlier ones. Five judges matched 10 sketches of adolescent boys, and 10 judges matched five sketches of adolescent girls. Both the results of the individual judges and the mean scores of all judges in matching were significant as compared to chance. Following are the conclusions of the investigation.

1. Personality similarities in an individual persist over a period of time.

2. Some individuals are more readily identifiable after a period of time, presumably due to greater uniqueness of personality pattern.

3. The matching technique, utilizing total impression, allows for the demonstration of similarities in personality pattern in the same individual over a period of time.

REFERENCES

ALLPORT, G. W. *Personality: a psychological interpretation.* New York: Holt, 1937.

BAYLEY, NANCY. A study of the crying of infants during mental and physical tests. *J. genet. Psychol.,* 1932, **40,** 306–329.

BRACKETT, C. W. Laughing and crying of preschool children. *J. exp. Educ.,* 1933, **2,** 119–126.

CHAPMAN, D. W. The generalized problem of correct matchings. *Ann. math. Statist.,* 1935, **6,** 85–95.

CHAPMAN, D. W. The significance of matching with unequal series. *Amer. J. Psychol.,* 1936, **48,** 167–169.

CUSHING, H. M. A perseverative tendency in preschool children: a study of personality differences. *Arch. of Psychol.,* 1929, No. 108.

GESELL, A., *et al. Biographies of child development.* New York: Harper, 1939.

GESELL, A., & THOMPSON, H. Twins *T* and *C* from infancy to adolescence. *Genet. Psychol. Monogr.,* 1941, **25,** 3–121.

GOODENOUGH, F. L. The use of free association in the objective measurement of personality. In Q. McNemar & Maude A. Merrill (Eds.), *Studies in personality.* New York: McGraw-Hill, 1942. Pp. 87–103.

GREEN, E. H. Friendships and quarrels among preschool children. *Child Develpm.,* 1933, **4,** 237–252.

HOGAN, L. *A study of a child.* New York: Harper, 1900.

JERSILD, A. T. The constancy of certain behavior patterns in young children. *Amer. J. Psychol.,* 1933, **45,** 125–129.

JERSILD, A. T. *Child psychology.* (Rev. ed.) Englewood Cliffs, N.J.: Prentice-Hall, 1942.

JONES, MARY C., & BURKS, B. S. Personality development in childhood: a survey of problems, methods, and experimental findings. *Monogr. Soc. Res. Child Develpm.,* 1936, **1,** No. 4.

MACFARLANE, JEAN W. The guidance study. *Sociometry,* 1939, **2,** 1–23.

MCGRAW, M. B. Later development of children specially trained. *Child Develpm.,* 1939, **10,** 1–19.

MCKINNON, K. M. Consistency and change in behavior manifestations. *Child Develpm. Monogr.,* 1942, **30.**

MURPHY, G., MURPHY, LOIS B., & NEWCOMB.

T. M. *Experimental social psychology*. New York: Harper, 1937.

Roberts, K. E., & Fleming, V. V. Persistence and change in personality patterns. *Monogr. Soc. Res. Child Develpm.*, 1943, **8,** No. 3.

Rundquist, E. A., & Sletto, R. E. *Personality in the depression: a study in the measurement of attitudes*. Minneapolis: Univer. Minnesota Press, 1936.

Salvosa, L. R. Tables of Pearson's type III function. *Ann. math. Statist.*, 1930, **1,** 191–198.

Shinn, M. *The biography of a baby*. Boston: Houghton Mifflin, 1900.

Shirley, Mary M. *The first two years: a study of twenty-five babies*. Vol. 1. Minneapolis: Univer. Minnesota Press, 1931.

Shirley, Mary M. *The first two years: a study of twenty-five babies*. Vol. 3. Minneapolis: Univer. Minnesota Press, 1933.

Stutsman, R. Constancy in personality trends. *Psychol. Bull.*, 1935, **32,** 701–702. (Abstract.)

Tryon, Caroline M. Constancy and generality of emotional adjustment in adolescents as measured by a questionnaire. *Psychol. Bull.*, 1934, **31,** 585–586. (Abstract.)

Vernon, P. E. Can the "total personality" be studied objectively? *Charact. & Pers.*, 1935, **4,** 1–10.

Vernon, P. E. The evaluation of matching method. *J. educ. Psychol.*, 1936, **27,** 1–17. (a)

Vernon, P. E. The matching method applied to investigations of personality. *Psychol. Bull.*, 1936, **33,** 149–177. (b)

Washburn, R. W. A study of the smiling and laughing of infants in the first year of life. *Genet. Psychol. Monogr.*, 1929, **6,** 403–537.

Wile, I. S., Neary, L., Mace, L., & Davies, R. The continuity of the neurotic processes. *Amer. J. Orthopsychiat.*, 1934, **4,** 49–72.

Wooley, H. T. Agnes: a dominant personality in the making. *J. Genet. Psychol.*, 1925, **32,** 569–598.

Zubin, J. The chance element in matching. *J. educ. Psychol.*, 1933, **24,** 674–681.

JEROME KAGAN *and* HOWARD A. MOSS

*The Stability of Passive and Dependent Behavior from Childhood Through Adulthood**

A BASIC assumption of developmental theory is that adult behaviors are often established in early childhood. Although retrospective reports obtained from the verbal protocols of adults support this assumption, it has been difficult to produce a more objective demonstration of the long term stability of childhood behavior patterns. This unhappy state of affairs is a consequence of the expense and difficulty associated with collecting long term longitudinal information on a large sample of children. Only extensive, longitudinal research programs, as exemplified by the Berkeley Growth Study or the Fels Research Institute, can furnish the answers to this developmental problem.

This paper presents one set of results which have emerged from a recent study of a group of "normal" adults from the Fels longitudinal research population for whom extensive information was available from birth through adolescence. The findings deal specifically with the long term stability of passive and dependent behavior in the face of situations which are frustrating and/or demand problem solving activity. This particular behavioral variable was chosen for initial analysis because theoretical essays on personality development emphasize that the early dependence of the child on the parent is of the utmost importance in shaping his future personality. That is, the development of a variety of adult motives and behaviors [is] based on the quality and intensity of the dependent relationship with the mother and mother-substitute figures. Further, psychological symptoms are theoretically attributed to inconsistency in the gratification of the child's dependent overtures and/or to denial or inhibition of dependent motives or behavior.

In addition to the longitudinal material, each subject was recently assessed during early adulthood by means of both interview and test procedures. The adult assessment was focused on the behavioral variables of dependency, aggression, achievement, and sexuality and on the degree of conflict and type of defensive responses associated with behavioral strivings in these areas. It was anticipated that there might be important sex differences with respect to occurrence of these behaviors, and the assessment procedures were designed to detect these potential sex differences.

Method

THE SAMPLE

THE subjects (*S*s) in this analysis were 27 male and 27 female Caucasian adults born between 1930 and 1939 who had recently been through a comprehensive assessment program which included an average of five hours of tape recorded interview and a variety of test procedures. The *S*s were between 20 and 29 years of age at the time of the assessment. In addition, these *S*s had fairly complete longitudinal records from 3 to 10 years of age. The *S*s were predominantly middle class but came from a variety of vocational backgrounds including agricultural, skilled labor, tradesmen, and professional groups. The religious affiliations of the group included 43 Protestants, 10 Catholics and 1

* REPRINTED by permission of the authors and the Society for Research in Child Development from *Child Develpm.*, 1960, 31, 577–591.

Jewish subject. The mean Wechsler-Bellevue IQ of the group was 120 with an IQ range of 97 to 142.

INTERVIEW VARIABLES: ADULT ASSESSMENT

Each *S* was interviewed by the senior author for approximately five hours over two to three sessions. *The interviewer had absolutely no knowledge of any of the longitudinal information on the* Ss. Since these *S*s had been studied by psychologists for over 20 years, rapport was usually excellent, and defensive and evasive answers were infrequent. Following the interviews, each *S* was rated (7-point scale) on 59 variables. Six of these adult interview variables dealt specifically with passive and dependent behavior; abridged definitions of these variables follow:

Degree to which dependent gratifications were sought in choice of vocation. This variable assessed the degree to which security was an important aspect of job choice, the degree to which the subject looked to his employer for gratification of his dependent needs, reluctance to shift jobs because of temporary loss of security. For nonworking women, emphasis was placed on her attitudes about the importance of security in her husband's job.

Degree of dependent behavior toward a love object. This variable assessed the degree to which the subject sought advice and emotional support from a love object (sweetheart, husband, wife), degree to which the subject looked for stability and wisdom in a love object, degree to which responsibility for decision making was given to love object.

Degree of dependent behavior with parents. This variable assessed the degree to which the subject looked for advice, support, emotional encouragement, and nurturance from one or both parents.

Degree of dependent behavior toward nonparental figures. This variable assessed the degree to which the subject sought advice, emotional support, and nurturance from nonparental figures who were not love objects, e.g., friends, relatives, and teachers.

Tendency to display behavioral withdrawal in the face of anticipated failure. This variable assessed the frequency and consistency with which *S* tended to withdraw from tasks and situations which he thought were difficult to master and in which failure was anticipated.

Degree of conflict over dependent behavior. This variable assessed the degree to which the subject avoided placing himself in dependent positions, his derogation of dependent behavior in self and others, and his emphasis on the value and importance of independent behavior.

A random sample of 32 taped interviews were independently studied and rated. The interrater reliabilities for the six dependency variables ranged from .63 to .82 with an average coefficient of .74.

PROCEDURE FOR EVALUATION OF CHILDHOOD BEHAVIOR

The junior author, who had no knowledge of the adult psychological status of the *S*s, evaluated narrative reports based on direct observation of the child in a variety of situations. Summaries of interviews with the child and the mother were also available. The observation reports were based on (a) semiannual visits to the home in which a staff member observed the child interact with mother and siblings for a two to four hour period, (b) semiannual or annual observations of the child in the Fels experimental nursery school and day camp settings, (c) interviews with the child, and (d) observations of the child in the classroom. After studying this material, the psychologist rated each child for a comprehensive set of variables (7-point scale). The rater studied the material for each *S* for ages 3 to 6 and made his ratings. Following a period of interpolated work, he then studied all the material for each *S* for ages 6 to 10 and again made the ratings. A period of approximately six months intervened between the evaluation of the material for any one child for ages 3 to 6 and 6 to 10. The rater felt that retroactive inhibition was sufficiently intense to mask any halo effect of the preschool ratings upon the later ratings made for 6 to 10 years of age. That is, the amount of material studied and the large number of variables rated militated against the recall of specific ratings over such a long period of time. In addition, the high degree of interrater reliability for these ratings supports the above statement. Independent ratings of the four childhood dependency variables by a second psychologist produced satisfactory interrater reliabilities. The product-moment correlations for each variable were all in the .80's with an average reliability of .86. The four childhood variables which involved passive and dependent behavior were defined as follows:

Tendency to behave in a passive manner when faced with environmental obstacles or stress (rated for ages 3 to 6 and 6 to 10). This variable assessed the degree to which the child was behaviorally passive in the face of external frustrations and failed to make any active mastery attempts to obtain desired goal objects following frustration. The rating of a passive behavioral reaction emphasized withdrawal from the frustration but included whining, crying, and soliciting help.

Tendency to seek support, nurturance, and assistance from female adults when under stress: general dependence (rated for age 3 to 6). This variable assessed the *S*'s behavioral tendency to obtain assistance, nurturance, or affection from mother and other female adults when confronted with a threat to his well-being, a problem, or loss of a desired goal object. Dependent behavior included seeking out adults when faced with a problem or personal injury, reluctance to start a task without help or encouragement, seeking assistance of others, seeking affection from and close contact with female adults.

Tendency to seek affection and emotional support from female adults (rated for ages 6 to 10). This variable assessed the degree to which the child sought affection or emotional encouragement from mother or mother substitute figures. Evidence included kissing, holding hands, clinging, seeking encouragement or proximity to female adults.

Tendency to seek instrumental assistance from female adults (rated for ages 6 to 10). This variable assessed the degree to which the child sought instrumental help with specific problems from mother, teachers, or other female authority figures. Instrumental dependent acts included seeking help with tasks, seeking help when physically threatened.

As mentioned above the average interrater reliability for these four variables was +.86. The distributions for both the childhood and interview variables were normal. Product-moment correlations were computed between each of the childhood variables and the six interview based dependency variables obtained in adulthood with separate analyses for males and females.

TACHISTOSCOPIC PERCEPTION

After the interviews and interview ratings were completed, each adult *S* was seen for a variety of test procedures, one of which was a tachistoscopic perception task. A series of 14 scenes were drawn to suggest action in the areas of dependency, aggression, sexuality, and physical danger. Three motivationally neutral, control pictures were also included.[1] For nine of the 14 pictures, separate pairs of illustrations were made for males and females so that the sex of the central figure was the same as the sex of the subject. The pictures were black and white line drawings with minimal background details. A brief description of the three dependency pictures follows:

1. A young adult in the foreground (male for male *S*s and female for female *S*s) is on his knees clutching to the waist of a figure of the same age but of opposite sex who is standing and looking forward. The figure on the floor is looking up at the face of the standing figure.
2. A young adult in the foreground (male for male *S*s and female for female *S*s) has his arms extended in an imploring gesture toward an adult of the same sex who is standing in the background with his back to the figure in the foreground.
3. A young adult (male for male *S*s and female for female *S*s) is seated on a chair with head buried in the abdomen of an adult of the opposite sex who is standing and comforting the seated figure.

The 14 pictures were presented seven times at seven different exposure speeds and in six different orders. The seven speeds ranged from .01 to 1.0 seconds. The pictures were shown initially at the fastest exposure (.01 second), and each succeeding series was presented at a slower exposure speed. All exposures were above threshold and all *S*s reported seeing something at each exposure.

1 Photostats of the 14 stimuli are available upon request.

The *S* sat in a light proof room, 22 in. from a flash-opal milk glass screen. The image was projected from the back of the screen, and the field was constantly illuminated by a 35 mm. projector (30 ft.-candles at the screen). The subject was told to state for each picture (a) the sex of each figure, (b) the approximate ages of each figure, and (c) what each figure on the picture was doing. The *S* was given three practice pictures to adapt him to the task and its requirements, and the entire protocol was electrically recorded and transcribed verbatim.

The protocols were scored for recognition threshold for each picture. Recognition threshold was defined as the first series at which the picture was described accurately and all succeeding trials were accurately described. The distribution of recognition thresholds differed among the 14 pictures and were markedly skewed either to the low or high end of the scale. Thus, the distribution of recognition thresholds for each picture was divided at the median into early and late recognition groups for statistical operations.

Results

STABILITY OF DEPENDENT BEHAVIOR

TABLE 1 presents the product-moment correlations between the childhood and adult ratings of passive and dependent behavior.

The major result is that passive and dependent behaviors were fairly stable for females but not for males. For girls the ratings of passivity during ages 6 to 10 correlated significantly with the adult ratings of a dependent orientation in vocational choice, dependency on love object, dependency on parents, and withdrawal to failure. Childhood passivity was inversely correlated with adult conflict over dependent behavior. That is, females who were passive as children were apt to accept their dependent behavior in adulthood and show minimal anxiety over their dependent motives. Only dependent behavior toward nonparental figures failed to show a significant, positive correlation with the childhood ratings of passivity. Similarly, the childhood ratings of both instrumental and emotional dependency on female adults, for girls aged 6-10, predicted adult ratings of dependency on love object, dependency on parents, and withdrawal to anticipated failure situations.

For the men there were only two significant correlations between the childhood dependency ratings and those based on the adult interview. Boys who were high on instrumental dependency for ages 6 to 10 were high on dependent behavior towards nonparental figures in adulthood. Second, emotional dependence during ages 6 to 10 was positively correlated with adult withdrawal to failure.

Of the 18 correlations between each of

TABLE 1. *Correlations between passive-dependent behavior in childhood and adulthood*

	ADULT DEPENDENCY VARIABLES											
Childhood Variables	*Dependency in Vocation* M	*Dependency in Vocation* F	*Dependency on Love Object* M	*Dependency on Love Object* F	*Dependency on Parents* M	*Dependency on Parents* F	*Dependency on Others* M	*Dependency on Others* F	*Withdrawal to Failure* M	*Withdrawal to Failure* F	*Dependency Conflict* M	*Dependency Conflict* F
Passivity (Ages 3 to 6)	—.07	.24	.10	.23	—.28	.25	.04	.19	.06	.26	.03	.01
Passivity (Ages 6 to 10)	.11	.73 **	.25	.36 *	—.20	.54 **	.04	.06	.21	.52 **	—.26	—.63
General Dependence (Ages 3 to 6)	—.06	.21	.13	.20	—.07	.07	.11	—.06	.12	.00	.05	.26
Emotional Dependence (Ages 6 to 10)	.21	.08	.18	.37 *	.02	.51 **	—.02	.06	.35 *	.37 *	—.12	—.31
Instrumental Dependence (Ages 6 to 10)	.19	.39 *	.06	.58 **	.14	.32	.37 *	.01	.09	.39 *	—.04	—.17

* $p < .05$, one tail.
** $p < .01$, one tail.

TABLE 2. *Intercorrelations among childhood dependency variables*

	PASSIVITY (6 to 10)		GEN. DEP. (3 to 6)		EMOT. DEP. (6 to 10)		INSTR. DEP. (6 to 10)	
	M	*F*	*M*	*F*	*M*	*F*	*M*	*F*
Passivity (3 to 6)	.82 **	.76 **	.74 **	.83 **	.26	.80 **	.38	.79 **
Passivity (6 to 10)	..	..	.40 *	.63 **	.43 *	.65 **	.53 **	.61 **
General Dependence (3 to 6)	..	..	..	..	.37	.61 **	.38 *	.63 **
Emotional Dependence (6 to 10)	..	..	..	..	..	..	.60 **	.79 **
Instrumental Dependence (6 to 10)	..	..	..	..	..	..	..	..

* $p < .05$, two tails.
** $p < .01$, two tails.

the three childhood variables for ages 6 to 10 and the six adult variables, 60 per cent were significant in the expected direction for females, while only 9 per cent were significant for the men.

TABLES 2 and 3 present the intercorrelations among the childhood and adult interview variables respectively.

The correlations among the passive and dependency variables between ages 3 to 6 and 6 to 10 were generally more consistent for girls than for boys. That is, for girls the correlations among passivity and general dependence for ages 3 to 6 and the three variables for ages 6 to 10 were all consistently high. For boys the stability of the passivity rating for ages 3 to 6 and 6 to 10 was quite high. However, the relationships between passivity for 3 to 6 and the two dependency behaviors for 6 to 10 were not as high as they were for girls. This finding suggests that overt seeking of affection and/or instrumental aid in school age boys begins to be dissociated from a passive withdrawal reaction to problem situations.

The intercorrelations among the adult dependency variables were generally positive for both sexes. Dependency on parents and dependency on love objects were each associated with withdrawal to failure and negatively related to conflict over dependency. It is interesting to note that women who are dependent on their parents tended to be dependent on their love object but not on friends or authority figures. Men, on the other hand, who were dependent on their parents tended to be dependent on friends and authority figures rather than on a love object. Dependency on parents and friends usually involves instrumental aid with problems, while dependency on a love object more often included the soliciting of emotional support and affection. It will be recalled that one of the two significant correlations for males

TABLE 3. *Intercorrelations among adult dependency variables*

	DEPENDENCE LOVE OBJECT		DEPENDENCE PARENTS		DEPENDENCE OTHERS		WITHDRAWAL		DEPENDENCE CONFLICT	
	M	*F*	*M*	*F*	*M*	*F*	*M*	*F*	*M*	*F*
Dep. Vocation	.61 **	.42 *	.53 **	.49 **	.12	−.10	.41 *	.50 **	−.61 **	−.56 **
Dep. Love Object	..	..	.24	.54 **	.48 **	.16	.49 **	.54 **	−.66 **	−.50 **
Dep. Parents	..	..	..	..	.39 *	.03	.44 **	.57 **	−.59 **	−.71 **
Dep. Others	..	..	..	..	..	..	.38 *	−.15	−.46 **	.15
Withdrawal	..	..	..	..	..	..	..	..	−.57 **	−.70 **
Dep. Conflict	..	..	..	..	..	..	..	..	..	..

* $p < .05$, two tails.
** $p < .01$, two tails.

between childhood and adult dependency involved instrumental dependency for ages 6 to 10 with adult dependency on nonparental authority figures. Emotional dependency for boys age 6 to 10 showed no correlations with the adult dependency variables. Thus, male dependent behavior is apt to emphasize the seeking of instrumental assistance with problems, while females are likely to seek affection and emotional support in addition to instrumental aid.

It is important to note that passive and dependent behavior for ages 6 to 10 showed a better relation to adult dependent behavior than the ratings for 3 to 6 years of age. This finding indicates that important age changes occur between ages 3 and 10 and that behavior displayed during the first few years of school is a better index of adult functioning than the earlier preschool behavior patterns.

TACHISTOSCOPIC PERCEPTION OF DEPENDENT PICTURES

There were significant sex differences in recognition threshold for the three dependency pictures with the females recognizing all three pictures earlier than the males. The scene that depicted a person imploring a same sexed adult (picture 2) yielded the most significant sex difference ($p < .001$, two tails). The picture of the adult on his knees clutching on to an opposite sexed adult (picture 1) and that of the seated adult holding on to an opposite sexed adult (picture 3) yielded sex differences significant at the .005 and .08 levels, respectively, for two tails. The aggressive pictures, on the other hand, produced opposite results, for the females recognized two of the four aggression pictures significantly later than the men ($p < .01$, two tails). There were no significant sex differences for the sex, physical danger, or three neutral scenes.

There was not a highly consistent relationship between recognition threshold for the dependent scenes and the interview ratings of dependency conflict. Only recognition of the scene that illustrated a man on his knees in front of a woman (picture 1) showed a relation to dependency conflict, and this held only for males. The males who were above the median in recognition threshold for this scene (late recognition) were rated as more conflicted over dependent behavior than males who recognized this picture early ($p = .07$, two tails). For the females, recognition threshold for the dependency pictures showed no significant relation to ratings of dependency conflict.

Discussion

THE results support a basic hypothesis of developmental theory which states that the acquisition of certain adult response patterns begins in early childhood. The differential stability of passive-dependent behavior for men and women is probably the result of several factors. However, one set of processes which may contribute to this phenomenon is derived from the commonly accepted hypothesis that passive and dependent behavior is less punished in females than in males. Further, females are often encouraged to be passive while men are expected to be independent and autonomous in the face of frustration. Parental and peer group punishment for passive and dependent behavior should result in some inhibition of this behavior in males. Thus, we would not expect this class of behavior to be as stable for men as for women. Studies of both overt behavior and fantasy (Hattwick, 1937; Kagan, 1959; Sanford, Adkins, Miller, & Cobb, 1943; Watson, 1959; Whitehouse 1949) all indicate that dependent responses are more frequent for girls than for boys. Further, the sex stereotypes presented by communication media fit this description. The analysis of children's books by Child, Potter, and Levine (1946) indicated that girls are portrayed as passive while boys are presented as independent and heroic. Finally, a study of the likes and dislikes of 10-year-old children (Tyler, 1955) confirms the belief that girls accept passive behavior as more appropriate for their sex role than do boys.

The present tachistoscopic threshold data support the notion that men are more conflicted over dependent behavior than women. It will be recalled that the women recognized all three scenes depicting dependent behavior much earlier than the men. This finding suggests that the tendency to perceive dependent behavior in adults is much weaker in men than it is in women. One possible cause of this "weaker perceptual hypothesis" is that dependent action is less acceptable to men, i.e., that men are more conflicted over dependent behavior. This conclusion finds support in the correlation, for men, between late recognition of dependency (picture 1) and the interview rating of dependency conflict.

Detailed analysis of the 54 cases indicates that there was a greater proportion of men, than women, who shifted from high dependency during childhood to independent behavior as adults. The women tended to be either dependent or independent for both childhood and adulthood. For example, in comparing emotional dependence for ages 6 to 10 with adult dependency on parents, not one female showed a major shift from high dependency in childhood to low dependency in adulthood. For the men, however, 20 per cent were rated very dependent during the ages 6 to 10 and very independent in adulthood.

The authors do not suggest that passive and dependent behavior in girls is rigidly fixed at school age and that change is a rare or unusual phenomenon. It must be kept in mind that the social milieu of these particular subjects remained rather constant throughout their lives. Their familial and extrafamilial environments were not disrupted to any marked degree. The parents and peers of these *S*s retained their same values, their reference groups remained constant, and, in most cases, their geographical travel was limited. Thus, the degree of behavioral stability obtained for these females might not hold for populations that are more mobile or transient, for different ethnic or class samples, or for people subjected to major traumata during adolescence and early adulthood.

Implicit in these results is a strategy for certain research problems in developmental psychology. It would appear that a select group of theoretically relevant behaviors become clearly established as preferential response tendencies as early as 6 to 10 years of age. This means that one can study the child longitudinally without having to wait 15 to 20 years before asking important questions of the data. Since the current philosophy of financial support for research allows an investigator to chart a 5 to 10 year program, it is now feasible for one investigator to see the products of a longitudinally oriented project in a reasonable length of time.

Although case history material can never prove an hypothesis, it often facilitates scientific communication by placing some flesh on the skeleton of a correlation matrix. The following case material is presented to give the reader a clearer picture of the material upon which our childhood evaluations were based and to illustrate dramatically the degree of constancy of behavioral passivity for two specific individuals.

Case A • Miss A is a 21-year-old, unmarried woman, who was in her senior year in an Eastern college. She was one of the most independent women in our sample and one who showed a strong reaction against dependent behavior in a wide variety of situations. As an adult she was described as a woman with a very strong need for recognition by others combined with a striving for achievement related goals. She had a strong desire to nurture others and often sought out situations in which she could give advice, support, and encouragement to peers. Miss A stated during the interview that she liked to keep her personal problems to herself. She did not like to discuss her personal problems because she felt that this behavior made her appear "helpless and weak." Statements like this indicate very strong conflict and anxiety over being in a passive-dependent position with other people. She was trying to sever any semblance of a dependent relation with her mother and derogated the latter because the mother seemed to be dependent upon her for companionship. Miss A sometimes felt lonely but said that she fights these feelings and tries to be able to live with them, for she does not like to admit that she needs friends or companionship. Her relationship with men seems to be consistent with the above pattern, for she tends to withdraw from heterosexual relationships that become too intense. Miss A said that she does not like men [who] make demands upon her, and she avoids men who attempt to place her in a passive role or position.

The following material represents selected verbatim excerpts from the longitudinal material on this subject.

Age 3 years, 4 months: Summary of Fels Nursery School Observations. S seems to be able to control and channel her behavior so that she got done just what she wanted to get done. In this activity she was very independent and capable. She was very social but also had a streak of aloof self-sufficiency, and she always made her individuality felt. She was what might be called a strong personality, often very intense, quite stubborn. . . . Her most outstanding characteristic was her consistent independence and integrity. In spite of the fact that she imitated and followed certain boys, she seemed to do this very much from her own choice, and she never lost the flavor of her individuality. She was capable of being social and seemed to enjoy contacts but at all times she was her own master. She would often withdraw from play and go on in her own direction at any time that she wished. . . . She was independent with adults and at times negativistic just to be devilish. She seemed somewhat self-conscious and had some cute little tricks. . . . In all, she could be characterized best by being called "tough minded." She shows determination and will, originality and spark, curiosity and interest in factual detail. She likes to quibble and argue, to verbalize, to construct, to accomplish. She is an individualist, independent and stubborn.

Age 5 years, 4 months: Fels Nursery School Observation. S seems to be vigorous, ruthless, competitive, highly sensual young woman, but one felt quite often that antagonism toward others was simply a direct response to their behavior. . . . She has grown far more social and also popular with an increasingly large crowd of special friends in a gang. She could be, when she chose, quite a successful leader, forging ahead and organizing a group on a hike, directing them and arranging things, and particularly keeping order in a fair sharing of the tools in the carpentry shop. . . . Many of *S*'s conflicts with the adult world seemed a direct imitation of a certain boy. She needed a chance to grumble, would scornfully refuse any adult suggestions or orders, would usually go officially ahead to carry them out. She was quite demanding, often shouting an order to an assistant. . . . With her other work the same drive for strong achievement was also evident, sticking to anything until it was finished, whatever the group stimuli. *S* still had real trouble in fine motor coordination, would growl as she worked, "I'm doing this as well as I can steer my pencil." For all her teeth gritted effort, the final results would still be relatively crude. She was very skilled in the use of puzzles and interested in the problems of designs and the way things fit together. She scorned any of the ready-made designs for the Christmas tree decorations.

Age 7 years: Observation in Fels Day Camp. S came accompanied by one friend. *S* did not seem overwhelmed by the large proportion of adults around, but in her sturdy self-sufficient manner went ahead with her own activities. Her friend was at first rather shy and withdrawn and *S,* with her usual confident bullying and bossing of the adults, tended to take the girl under her wing and make sure she had a good time. *S* remains an exceptionally eager, imperturbable young woman. On a number of small issues she did insist on her own way, on just how long she would stay in the gym and play before lunch, but was quite reasonable about making compromises. She chose a rather difficult necklace to make and got quite mad when it didn't work out well. She kept doggedly with it, very self-sufficient, and continuing all on her own after getting some initial advice. . . . Her major effort was put on self-appointed tasks, to be able to master jumping over the horse at the gym where she took numerous tumbles until she succeeded. In spite of her distractability and preference for the apparatus she did set herself to learning the new skills required there.

Age 9 years: Report from Teacher. S is one of the most responsible children in the group. . . . She is self-reliant, independent, and knows how to plan her time well. She enters all games with enthusiasm, is very well coordinated, is full of personality and "joie de vivre."

Case B • Miss B is a 23-year-old, unmarried woman, who is working and living with her parents. She was one of the most overtly dependent women in the sample. During the interview she was very dependent on the interviewer for structure and was rather mild and meek. Her most typical reaction to failure or stressful situations is to deny or withdraw and she says quite blithely, "I'm not a worrier." She is very sensitive to the opinions of other people and usually conforms with their expectations for her. She accepts her passive-dependent role with authority people and with love objects. *S* tends to be very dependent on peers for advice, likes being close to the family, and tends to see herself as inadequate in the face of problem situations.

Following are selected excerpts from her longitudinal records:

Age 2 years, 6 months: Fels Nursery School Observation. At the first day of nursery school, *S* seemed rather frightened and very reluctant to leave her mother this morning. The mother had to carry her and hold her in the car until the door was shut. For the first few miles she cried and then suddenly stopped and began to take an interest in the various animals and objects. She cried when she reached the nursery school but stopped as soon as she left the other children. On the second day of nursery school she cried again but seemed much less frightened and more angry. During the nursery school she stood watching the other children and at one point ran to another girl and stood beside her. The other little girl paid no attention, and *S* trailed after her. *S* wandered around and, when the teacher went to the house, *S* rushed to follow her and stood around the teacher. S tagged after another little girl all morning. During the nursery school two-week period she was timid and tense.

Age 3 years: Fels Nursery School Summary. At first, *S* was timid and tense and was gathered under the wing of another peer and her cohorts. From then on she was "at home" with the group. She followed another girl's lead and joined in the activities the other girl organized. On days when this girl was absent she was at loose-ends and tended to return to her original dependence on an adult. Several weeks after her nursery school stay she visited the school one morning for several hours. She was a little apprehensive at first but made no real protest. She stood around not joining in the play until an adult suggested an activity.

Age 4 years: Fels Nursery School Summary. *S* cried the first day of nursery school after she saw another girl cry. She stayed close to the teacher the first few days and watched the other children with a worried expression on her face. Indoors she chose small blocks or color cubes to play with. In the yard *S* was very cautious about trying out the apparatus, particularly when there was any balancing involved. She has a high, whining nasal voice, and several letter substitutions made her speech rather difficult to understand. She was quite complying with adult requests. Frequently, she appealed to adults for help in conflicts, such as getting a turn to slide, which is a situation she could have handled for herself.

Age 6 years: Visit to the School. *S* is retiring, quiet, and shy. She doesn't show the enthusiasm that most of the children in the class do. She seems content. . . . She goes to the teacher for suggestions and skips to her seat jubilantly with a word of approval from the teacher. *S* recites a bit timidly in front of the whole class but accepts the teacher's support and gets through successfully. Her voice is a little soft and her enunciation is not clear. *S* volunteers information a bit tentatively and without enthusiasm. The teacher reports that *S* is about the brightest of the average group. *S* is not a leader but she is very sweet and cooperative and is never any trouble.

Age 6 years, 6 months: Summary of Fels Day Camp Observations. *S* was outclassed in almost every respect in this group but fluttered happily about after the others doing the best she could. She occasionally withdrew or grew silent but, when encouraged by an adult, she soon recovered. She was not insensitive and did not seem to have her security disturbed more than momentarily. She seems to feel a great confidence and trust in adults and could always be bought off or led along. She lacked initiative in almost every way. She could not go ahead on any craft project nor could she assert herself socially. She needed help and encouragement, hung about the adults, not exposing herself to the center of the group. She is essentially a conformist and wanted only to do what was right. She got into no mischief and had little sense of fun. She was happiest when settled into a situation that was approved and guided by an adult, and at these times she would proddle along very happily. Her main interests lay in conforming to any plans laid by adults and working on simple handcrafts. She was rather unsure in her accomplishments. She was often physically apprehensive.

Age 7 years, 6 months: Summary of Fels Day Camp Observations. The most characteristic aspect of *S*'s day camp behavior was her ability, high conformity, and social reticence. She did not participate in social activities to any extent and was generally ignored by the other children. She clung to adults, wanted to assist them when possible, and wanted their approval and comforting in all her activities. She seemed to be somewhat apprehensive of physical contacts, especially if they became at all rough. She was apprehensive about almost any physical danger. Her actual physical ability was not particularly poor, and, when she was put into athletic situations, she did surprisingly well. Her general lack of physical participation seems not to be due to poor ability as much as to lack of motivation and apprehension.

Age 8 years: Visit to the School. S is always anxious to do what is right all of the time. She is not a discipline problem. *S* shows no interest in physical activities. Initially, she is lost at school work and takes some time to adjust to new work. *S* was pretty tentative in her first attempt to get the teacher's attention and held up her paper hesitantly. She was very pleased when the teacher came to her. She was uncertain about the problems although they had similar ones before.

Age 8 years, 8 months: Fels Day Camp Summary. S is a small, dark looking girl, bent over, with thick dark hair and a tired face. Her voice is high but with no force; her hands [hang] limp at the wrists. Much of this lack of force seemed related to her personality, and at the races she surprised us by doing remarkably well. *S* obeyed adults implicitly and wanted to have their sanction for even small acts which the group had already been given permission for. She has a rather cringing, servile manner. This clinging around adults was particularly marked the first day when she ate her lunch with them.

Age 9 years, 8 months: Fels Day Camp Summary. S is a rather pathetic looking little girl. Rather thin, droopy eyed, clammy handed, somehow reminiscent of an orphan in an old melodrama. She seems nearer to seven or eight than her actual age and with a kind of naivete and unsureness about all she did. She was an exceedingly compliant child in taking the tests, even the reading tests which she obviously disliked, without a murmur.

Summary

THIS paper summarized some results from a larger investigation of the stability of behavior in a group of subjects who were part of the Fels Research Institute's longitudinal population. This report dealt specifically with the long term stability of passive and dependent behavior from childhood through adulthood.

The *S*s were 27 males and 27 females for whom extensive longitudinal information was available from birth through adolescence. One psychologist studied narrative reports based on observations of the child in various settings and rated each child on four variables describing types of passive and dependent behavior for ages 3 to 6 and ages 6 to 10. A second psychologist, who had no knowledge of the childhood data, interviewed each *S* in adulthood and rated each *S* on six variables related to aspects of adult passive and dependent behavior. In addition, each adult *S* was administered a tachistoscopic perception task in which scenes illustrating dependent activity were presented at seven different exposure speeds.

The results revealed that passive and dependent behaviors were quite stable for women, but minimally stable for men. Over 60 per cent of the correlations between the childhood (ages 6 to 10) and adult ratings of dependency were statistically significant for females, while only 9 per cent were significant for men. For example, the correlation between passive withdrawal from problem situations for ages 6 to 10 and adulthood was .52 ($p < .01$) for women and .21 for men. Similarly, the correlation between emotional dependence for ages 6 to 10 and adult dependency on parents was .51 ($p < .01$) for women and .02 for men. The correlations between the ratings for ages 3 to 6 and adulthood were considerably lower and not statistically significant.

It was suggested that environmental disapproval and punishment of dependent behavior in young males led to inhibition of and conflict over dependency in the growing boy. The social acceptance of passive and dependent behavior in females would be expected to result in greater stability for this class of responses for women than for men. The fact that females recognized the tachistoscopically presented dependency scenes earlier than the men was interpreted as support for this explanation.

Case history material for two female subjects was presented to illustrate the type of information utilized in this study.

REFERENCES

CHILD, I. L., POTTER, E. H., & LEVINE, ESTELLE M. Children's textbooks and personality development: an exploration in the social psychology of education. *Psychol. Monogr.*, 1946, **60,** No. 279.

HATTWICK, BERTHA. Sex differences in behavior of nursery school children. *Child Develpm.*, 1937, **8,** 323–355.

KAGAN, J. The stability of TAT fantasy and stimulus ambiguity. *J. consult. Psychol.*, 1959, **23,** 266–271.

SANFORD, R. N., ADKINS, M. M., MILLER, R. B., & COBB, E. N. Physique, personality and scholarship: a comprehensive study of school children. *Monogr. Soc. Res. Child Develpm.*, 1943, **8,** No. 1.

TYLER, LEONA E. The development of vocational interests: I. The organization of likes and dislikes in ten year old children. *J. genet. Psychol.*, 1955, **86,** 33–44.

WATSON, R. I. *Psychology of the child.* New York: Wiley, 1959.

WHITEHOUSE, ELIZABETH. Norms for certain aspects of the Thematic Apperception Test on a group of nine and ten year old children. *J. Pers.*, 1949, **1,** 12–15.

WILLIAM E. MARTIN

Singularity and Stability of Profiles of Social Behavior[1, 2, *]

This paper concerns itself with two attributes of development in the young child, individuality (or singularity) and stability, neither of which has received much attention in research into psychological development. There are several reasons for this neglect. In the first place, we are committed to a nomothetic rather than an idiographic science, despite the repeated *cri de cœur* for the latter from Gordon Allport. Sears has stated the position sharply: "The role of the experimentalist . . . requires a study of variables rather than persons. The clinician is person-oriented; the experimentalist is variable-oriented" (1953, p. 142). Second, our measures are normative rather than ipsative: "i.e., the behavior of a given individual is but a point or mark on a normative scale" (Broverman, 1962, p. 295). Normative data permit us to determine the stability of an individual's behavior in space and time but only relative to the behavior of other individuals within a group, as in Kagan and Moss (1962). Also to be considered are the hazards and lack of support for longitudinal investigation. Without repeated measures of the same variables on the same subjects over time, we cannot delineate individual patterns of development. From normative, cross-sectional data we can conclude something about the relation between two or more variables, but only within the group, not within an individual. Baldwin's series of observations of individual children (1946) demonstrated that two characteristics can be positively correlated within an individual, but negatively correlated within a group and, in so doing, differentiated between *common* and *individual* attributes (*see* McClelland, 1951, pp. 208–213). Finally, there is the contemporary emphasis on modifiability of behavior and personality. Parents, teachers, therapists, experimentalists—all seek change. The Zeitgeist hardly encourages an investigation of stability and continuity.

The consequence has been a discrepancy between abstractions from fact and our articles of faith. For the latter attest to the uniqueness and integrity of the individual and his development and lead to the expectation of singularity and stability or, at least, continuity. We recognize Susan as an individual whose behavior and development are predictable, from situation to situation, from one time to another. Thus, we say at times of Susan, "How characteristic of her"; at others, "How unlike her," or "She isn't herself today" (Allport, 1961, p. 14). Common sense supports such observations; unfortunately, except in the case of physical growth, there is little in the mass of empirical data we have gathered to confirm this belief in the uniqueness of the individual through time.

1 An earlier report of these findings was presented as part of a symposium, "Development and Structure of Social Motives in Young Children: A Longitudinal Study," Society for Research in Child Development, Berkeley, California, April 12, 1963.

2 The data reported here were collected during the initial phase of an ongoing longitudinal investigation of the influences of family experiences on the behavioral development of children. Major financial support was provided by the Indiana Agricultural Experiment Station. For invaluable assistance and counsel in the analysis of the data, we are indebted to Dr. James Norton.

* This article is based upon a paper delivered to the biennial meeting of the Society for Research in Child Development in Berkeley, California, April, 1963. It is reprinted here with the permission of the author.

To provide evidence for individuality, stability, and continuity of psychological development, and—incidentally—to establish the utility and feasibility of short-term longitudinal investigation (Merminod, 1962, p. 16), we embarked in 1956 on a program of repeated and multiple measures of a number of variables in young children, together with the collection of information about their mothers, fathers, and siblings. We selected seven major variables, all generally accepted to be acquired motivational characteristics, present to some degree in all children and adults, and inferable from observation: Dependency, Nurturance, Aggression, Control-Dominance, Autonomous Achievement, Avoidance-Withdrawal, and Friendship-Affiliation.

The datum of the present report (the first of a series) is the frequency with which each of these goal-directed behaviors was manifested by young children in repeated time-sampling observation of behavior in free play in a nursery school setting.

Method

SUBJECTS

THE nature of the investigation required the selection of families who were likely to be available over a long period of time. For several reasons, the Purdue University Nursery School provided a source of such families: (a) it was the most firmly established and oldest of the programs of the Child Development Laboratories; (b) with its not inconsiderable tuition, its patrons tended to represent the more residentially stable element of the community, the heads of the families being either members of the University faculty with tenure or professional and business men, more or less permanently settled in the town. The price of such stability was, of course, a high degree of selectivity in the subjects with respect to socioeconomic status and such related variables as age of parents and size of family, not to mention those factors which are associated with fixity of residence.

For each of four successive academic years, from 1956–1957 through 1959–1960, the staff of the Purdue Nursery School selected 16 of the 18 or 19 children to be enrolled in the younger group from the long waiting list in accordance with the following criteria: (a) age range (as of time of entrance) from 2 years, 7 months, through 3 years, 6 months; (b) two boys and two girls from each three-month span within the age range.

Of the 16 families in each of the four groups, only those whose children remained in the nursery school for at least two years were included in the longitudinal "sample." TABLE 1 gives the summary statistics by group and sex within group for number and age of child and parent subjects, IQ and ordinal position of child subjects, and paternal occupation.

BEHAVIOR VARIABLES

THE variables to be observed were behavior systems, with "system" referring to "a set of responses and response tendencies which seem to share a common drive or goal" (Child, 1954, p. 661). For group I subjects, 30 goal responses were defined, in the manner of Gewirtz (1948), and classified into six systems or categories (TABLE 2). On the basis of a semester's experience with this schedule, the description of goal responses was simplified, some subcategories were added, others combined, and the Achievement-Control category was subdivided into Control-Dominance and Autonomous Achievement. This revised schedule of 34 goal responses in seven categories (TABLE 2) was utilized for the observation of subjects in groups II, III, and IV. The original schedule was retained for group I.

TIME-SAMPLING OBSERVATION [3]

Each child was observed, with some excep-

3 During the five-year period, the following students and staff members of the Department of Child Delevopment and Family Life served, at one time or another, as observers: Judith Flannigan Barany, G. R. Collins, Janet Cordes, Reba M. Gillman, Gerald Groden, Lois Harrison, Marilyn Kelsey Hepworth, Martha H. Herrick, Bess-Gene Holt, Martha Carlson Lowe, Ivan E. Pangrac, Constance Cisco Rupel, Roma Crawford Rupp, Jeraldine Withycombe, and Sylvia Wittkower. Dr. Abraham Blum bore major responsibility for the time-sampling observation in the first two years of the investigation.

TABLE 1. *Description of subjects*

PERIOD OF STUDY	GROUPS I 1956–1958	II 1957–1959	III 1958–1960	IV 1959–1960
Children				
Number				
Boys	7	6	8	8
Girls	8	6	5	5
Both	15	12	13	13
Mean Age [a]				
Boys	3.0	3.2	3.0	2.9
Girls	3.0	3.1	3.1	3.1
Both	3.0	3.2	3.1	3.0
Mean IQ [b]				
Boys	115.3	118.7	111.5	123.8
Girls	121.1	116.8	126.2	120.0
Both	118.4	117.8	117.2	122.3
Ordinal Position				
Only	1	2	2	2
Younger	10	3	6	4
Medial	3	2	3	6
Older	1	5	2	1
Mothers				
Mean Age [a]				
Boys	38.8	29.2	34.1	34.4
Girls	35.1	34.2	30.3	34.4
Both	36.8	31.7	32.7	34.4
Fathers				
Mean Age [a]				
Boys	40.6	31.7	37.6	39.6
Girls	38.9	36.1	34.5	35.3
Both	39.7	33.9	36.4	37.9
Occupation				
Professional				
University	9	6	8	8
Non-University	0	2	1	1
Business	6	4	4	3
Student	0	0	0	1

[a] As of September 30 of year of entrance of S child into nursery school.
[b] Stanford-Binet (1937 Revision).

tions,[4] for 12 five-minute periods during the middle eight weeks of each of the four semesters he attended nursery school. A child was observed only when engaged in "free

4 The most notable of these exceptions is that children in group I were observed only in the second, third, and fourth semesters.

TABLE 2. *Time-sampling observation categories with index of agreement (P) between observers by category and subcategory*

ORIGINAL SCHEDULE (GROUP I, SEMESTER 2)	P [a]
DEPENDENCY (DEP)	.80
1. Securing Touching or Holding	.54
2. Securing Being Near	.49
3. Securing Positive Attention	.72
4. Securing Reassurance	.12
5. Securing Attention by Negative Means	.23
NURTURANCE (NUR)	.37
6. Offering Touching or Holding	.00
7. Offering Positive Attention	.38
8. Offering Reassurance	.17
AGGRESSION (AGG)	.55
9. Perceiving Injury to Another	.45
10. Perceiving Discomfort in Another	.22
11. Perceiving Destruction to Inanimate Objects or Constructions	.43
12. Having Object in Own Possession (Control or Retaliation)	.50
13. Having Object Back in Own Possession (Control or Retaliation)	.56
ACHIEVEMENT-CONTROL (CON)	.54
14. Seeking Control of Ongoing Activity by Positive Means	.21
15. Seeking Control of Ongoing Activity by Negative Means	.32
16. Seeking Control of Ongoing Activity by Direct Means	.43
17. Seeking to Facilitate Ongoing Activity	.23
18. Seeking Control by Initiation of New Activity	.20
19. Securing Help in Achieving Goal in Ongoing Activity	.39
20. Perceiving Removal of a Persisting Frustration or Barrier to Reaching of a Goal	.20
21. Seeking to Maintain and Enhance Own Status	.22
AVOIDANCE-WITHDRAWAL (AW)	.68
22. Seeking to Avoid Active Participation by Nonrecognition of Situation	.43
23. Seeking to Avoid Active Participation by Psychological Withdrawal	.40
24. Seeking to Avoid Active Participation by Physical Withdrawal	.44
25. Seeking to Avoid Active Participation by Refusal	.60

26. Seeking to Avoid Active Participation by Criticism or Derogation of Ongoing or Suggested Activity	.33
AFFILIATION-AFFECTION-FRIENDSHIP (FA)	.60
27. Sharing Activity	.62
28. Sharing Affection	.27
29. Establishment, Maintenance, and Expression of Affiliation with a Person	.25
30. Seeking Membership in Established Group	.20

REVISED SCHEDULE (GROUP II, SEMESTER 1)	P [a]
DEPENDENCY (DEP)	.86
1. Securing Touching or Holding	.65
2. Securing Being Near	.64
3. Securing Positive Attention	.78
3a. Securing Aid for Self	.82
4. Securing Reassurance	.23
5. Securing Negative Attention	.34
NURTURANCE (NUR)	.65
6. Offering Touching or Holding	.40
7. Offering Positive Attention	.60
8. Offering Reassurance	. . .
AGGRESSION (AGG)	.73
9. Perceiving Injury to Another	.64
10. Perceiving Discomfort in Another	.44
11. Perceiving Punishment or Derogation of Another	.57
12. Perceiving Destruction to Inanimate Objects or Constructions	.50
13. Having Object in Own Possession	.54
14. Having Object Back in Own Possession	.60
CONTROL-DOMINANCE (CON)	.70
15. Securing Constructive Control	.34
16. Securing Negative Control	.19
17. Securing Authoritarian Control	.51
AUTONOMOUS ACHIEVEMENT (ACH)	.66
18. Seeking to be Independent of Approval of Activity by Others	.78
19. Seeking to Carry Out Task by Self	1.00
20. Seeking to Persist at or Complete Tasks	.75
21. Seeking to Assume Initiative in Carrying Out Activity	.67
22. Seeking to Facilitate Activity	.68
23. Securing Help in Achieving Goal in Ongoing Activity	. . .
24. Securing Removal of Frustration or Barrier to a Goal	1.00
25. Seeking to Maintain and Enhance Own Status	.36
AVOIDANCE-WITHDRAWAL (AW)	.76
26. Seeking Psychological Withdrawal from Situation	.70
27. Seeking Physical Withdrawal from Situation	.33
28. Refusing Involvement in Activity	.67
29. Seeking to Undermine Situation	. . .
FRIENDSHIP-AFFILIATION (FA)	.77
30. Seeking Mutuality through Activity	.76
31. Sharing Affection	.40
32. Seeking Affiliation	.55
33. Seeking Membership in Established Group	.67

[a] P = number of agreements divided by difference between total number of tallies for that category or subcategory and number of agreements.

play," comparatively free of teacher direction and free to interact with other children.

The task of an observer was twofold: First, he had to identify a goal response, utilizing as cues the setting in which the response occurred, the instigation, the instrumental behavior which antedated it, and its object, physical or social. Having done so, he then had to determine whether or not the goal response might properly be classified as one of the 30 (or 33) such responses selected for this investigation and, if so, which one. The problem of obtaining accurate measures was aggravated by the fact that both the number and identity of the observers varied from semester to semester and from group to group. Only one individual was available for observation of the children in group I in their fourth semester; in contrast, six observers shared the responsibility for group IV subjects in the third semester. No single individual observed all subjects in all time periods.

A total of 48⅓ hours, or 580 five-minute samples, of simultaneous observation of two persons was accumulated: (a) eight of 10 possible pairs of observers made 213 five-minute observations of the 18 children constituting group I in the second semester; (b) the two individuals assigned to the same group in the third semester made three simultaneous observations of each of the 16 subjects then present; (c) all possible pairs of four observers were used to obtain a determination of reliability of observation of group II children in their first semester; and (d), finally, one pair made 113 simultaneous observations of these same children in their second semester.

This procedure for simultaneous and independent observation was followed: Each member of a pair had a scoring sheet on which was to be designated the code number for the child, the name of the observer and that of his partner, and the date and the time. The several categories, each with its constituent goal responses, were listed by number and code letters at the left. Numbered columns to the right of this list provided space for the tallying of as many as 15 goal responses during the five-minute period. For any five-minute observation, one individual served as timekeeper, signaling the beginning and end of the observation and also the first goal response that might be tallied in one of the categories; the other member of the pair signaled the second scorable behavior; and so on.

Several levels of accord were possible: the two observers could agree on category *and* subcategory; they could agree on category but not on subcategory; they could disagree on both subcategory and category, but agree that the behavior was scorable; they could disagree on whether the goal response was scorable. Percentage of agreement on category *and* subcategory ranged from 67 to 84 in the four samples of paired observations. The comparable figure from Gewirtz (1948), based on 74 15-minute observations of 43 children by two observers, using 14 goal responses classified into the three categories of Succorance (Dependency), Nurturance, and Aggression, was 88. This discrepancy in observer reliability is not as great as might be anticipated in view of the greater number of observers and behaviors in the present study. If disagreements within categories are ignored, percentage of agreement is substantially increased, ranging from 79 to 90.

The data suggested that accuracy of observation might vary significantly with the rater and with the subject being rated; moreover, there was the possibility of significant subcategory variation. A further analysis of the simultaneous observation data was therefore undertaken to assess the importance of children, observers, and goal responses.

For the purpose of determining subcategory variability, a somewhat different index of agreement was devised: the proportion (P) of all times that a given goal response was seen by either observer [to number of times] that it was seen simultaneously as the same goal response by both observers. The P values, by category and subcategory, are given in TABLE 2 for subjects in group I for the second semester and for subjects in group II for the first semester. For 30 items, the value must be greater than .0167 to exceed chance; the critical value for 33 items is .0147. Except for a few goal responses with very low frequencies, the values exceed, by substantial amounts, these chance probability levels. Revision of the observation schedule presumably accounts for the greater accuracy of the observations of group II children.

The P values for each of the 30 items for each of the 18 children in group I in the second semester were then subjected to angular transformation (Walker and Lev, 1953). Because of missing entries in this table, children were ignored and a single classification of variance between goal responses (with unequal *N*s) was performed and disclosed that the amount of agreement between observers varied significantly from subcategory to subcategory. A substantial portion of this variability is attributable to differences in frequency of appearance of the 30 goal responses: the rank difference correlation coefficient between P and frequency for semester 2 was .495, which is significant beyond the .01 level. However, in the data for group II, there was no association between P and frequency; the coefficient for semester 1 was .029. With the refinement of the observation schedule, the infrequently appearing goal responses seemed to have been as accurately identified as the more common ones; an analysis of variance of these data showed the degree of observer agreement no longer to vary significantly with subcategory.

A series of two-way analyses of variance disclosed no evidence that either children or observer pairs contributed significantly to variability in agreement. These findings permit the conclusion that the time-sampling observation method, as utilized in this investigation, yielded reasonably accurate frequency counts of the goal responses specified.

Circumstances did not allow the making of simultaneous observations on the subjects in groups I and II in later semesters nor on the subjects in groups III and IV at any time. In view of the question of whether the task of delineating these several goal responses becomes easier or more difficult with advance in age of the child, this absence of information is particularly unfortunate. However, in the hope of maintaining a satisfactory level of reliability, each observer, whether experienced or not, was required to participate in a training period at the beginning of each semester and demonstrate, with at least one other observer, an over-all percentage of agreement of 80 for category *and* subcategory before the initiation of systematic observation.

Results [5]

CONSTANCY AND CHANGE IN FREQUENCY OF BEHAVIOR

THE behavior frequencies for the subjects in group I in semester 2 and for the subjects in group II in semester 1 were the sums of the tallies of two observers from simultaneous but independent observations; these were divided by two. Three of the observations for each subject in group I in semester 3 were paired; only the number of agreements by category in these observations were included in the semester totals. Also, in semester 2 for group II subjects, there were some double observations; because these constituted a substantial proportion of the five-minute samples, the frequencies for the single observations were doubled and added to those for the paired observations; these sums were then divided by two. In all other cases, the datum was simply the total of the tallies by category, child, and semester. Finally, in order to correct the totals for some slight variation among children (in groups I and II) in number of five-minute observation periods, the frequency for each behavior category for each child for each semester was divided by the number of minutes of observation and multiplied by 60. The data so summarized were subjected to statistical analysis in order to determine to what extent and with what consistency among groups or replicas (a) the mean frequency for any category of behavior or for all categories changed over time, (b) individual differences within groups in frequency of behavior varied with time, and (c) the rank order of children by frequency of behavior remained invariant over time.

Time Variations in Behavior Frequency • For each group, for each category, and for all categories, an analysis of variance was computed. Of the 31 analyses thus performed, 23 yielded significant between-semesters effects as shown in TABLE 3. The sources of variation in each case were identified by applying Tukey's nonsequential studentized

TABLE 3. *Variations over time in mean frequency of observed behavior by category and by group*
(F tests [a])

GROUP:	I	II	III	IV
DEP				14.14 †
NUR	8.11 †	6.85 †	4.52 †	
AGG	3.52 *	4.17 *	3.61 *	7.60 †
CON	12.37 †	11.45 †		11.76 †
ACH		23.43 †	49.35 †	52.32 †
AW			5.54 †	12.71 †
FA	14.40 †	18.34 †		28.35 †
All	15.21 †	51.84 †	23.34 †	127.16 †

[a] F = MS for semesters/MS for semesters X children with *df:* group I, 2 and 28; group II, 3 and 33; groups III and IV, 3 and 36.
* Significant at less than .05 level.
† Significant at less than .01 level.

5 This report is devoted exclusively to the frequency data for the several categories; an analysis of the subcategory frequencies may be found in Emmerich (1964). Comparable data on singularity and stability of doll play behavior are presented in Smock (1964).

TABLE 4. *Semester differences in mean frequency of observed behavior by category and by group*
(studentized range tests)

SEMESTER	GROUP	DEP	NUR	AGG	CON	ACH	AW	FA	All
1 to 2	II				+ †				+ †
	III					+ *			+ *
	IV	+ *		+ *				+ *	+ †
1 to 3	II			+ †	+ †	+ †		+ †	+ †
	III			− *		+ †			
	IV	+ †		+ †	+ *	+ †		+ †	+ †
1 to 4	II		+ †		+ †	+ †		+ †	+ †
	III					+ †	+ *		+ †
	IV	+ †		+ †	+ †	+ †	+ †	+ †	+ †
2 to 3	I				+ *			+ †	+ *
	II					+ †			+ †
	III		− †	− *		+ *			
	IV	+ *				+ †		+ †	+ †
2 to 4	I		+ †	+ *	+ †			+ †	+ †
	II		+ †			+ †		+ †	+ †
	III		− *			+ †	+ *		+ †
	IV				+ †	+ †	+ †	+ †	+ †
3 to 4	I		+ †						
	II							+ *	+ *
	III					+ †	+ †		+ †
	IV						+ †		

* Significant at less than .05 level.
† Significant at less than .01 level.

range test (Scheffé, 1953) with the extended and corrected tables of the studentized range q provided by May (1952). The results are given in TABLE 4.

In all groups, frequency of behavior tended to increase with time. Only four significant decreases were registered, all in group III: two in Nurturance and two in Aggression. In general, the increases were the more apparent, the longer the lapse of time. Change was least evident within the second year of observation, semesters 3 to 4. The fact of increase in frequency with time was most clearly established in all categories combined (FIGURE 1), in Autonomous Achievement (FIGURE 2), and in Friendship-Affiliation.

Time Variations in Individual Differences in Behavior Frequency • For each group, for each category, and for all categories, the differences between the variances for all possible pairs of semesters were tested, using the formula appropriate for related measures (Walker and Lev, 1953, p. 190). No pervasive or marked tendency for either expansion or restriction of the range of individual differences with time was apparent. Of the 165 differences tested, only 36 proved to be significant, 29 representing an increase, seven a decrease. The data for group IV provided half of these significant changes. There was some slight positive association between the incidence of differences between variances and the length of time elapsed. Across categories, there was some diversity: individual differences in Aggression were most variable (with nine of 21 possible comparisons significant); in contrast, none of the tests for Dependency was significant.

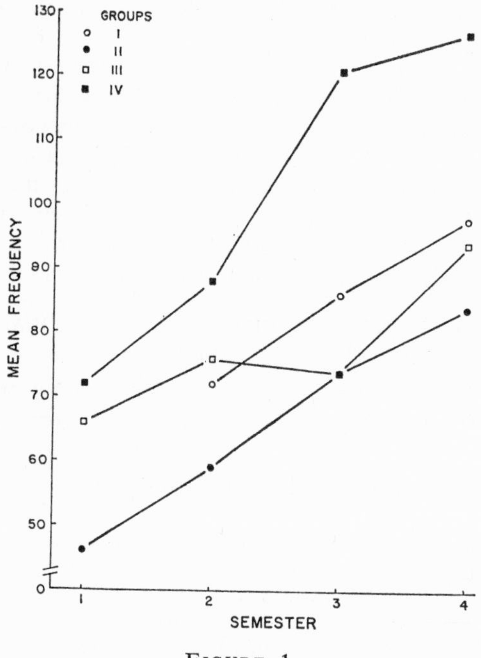

FIGURE 1

Mean frequency of all behaviors observed in successive semesters in four groups of children (60 minutes per child per semester).

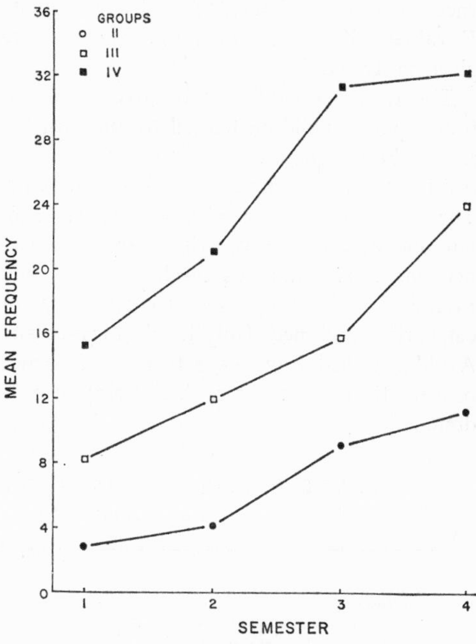

FIGURE 2

Mean frequency of Autonomous Achievement behavior observed in successive semesters in three groups of children (60 minutes per child per semester).

Time Variations in Rank Ordering of Children by Behavior Frequency • Within each group, for each category, and for all categories, the frequencies for subjects were ranked for each semester. For each of the 31 tables of ranks, an analysis of variance was performed and Kendall's coefficient of concordance was computed. The results, together with the associated average rank-differ-

TABLE 5. *Stability over time in rank ordering of children within groups by frequency of observed behavior*

GROUP:	I			II			III			IV		
	W	$\bar{r}'$	*F*	*W*	$\bar{r}'$	*F*	*W*	$\bar{r}'$	*F*	*W*	$\bar{r}'$	*F*
DEP	.46	.19	1.71	.58	.44	4.16 †	.57	.42	3.94 †	.55	.40	3.64 †
NUR	.36	.05	1.15	.19	−.08	<1	.35	.13	1.62	.35	.13	1.59
AGG	.67	.50	4.00 †	.65	.54	5.67 †	.66	.54	5.74 †	.63	.51	5.20 †
CON	.63	.44	3.36 †	.45	.27	2.50 *	.59	.45	4.33 †	.64	.52	5.33 †
ACH				.60	.46	4.45 †	.52	.36	3.26 †	.37	.16	1.76
AW	.17	−.24	<1	.18	−.09	<1	.33	.11	1.48	.34	.12	1.54
FA	.63	.44	3.34 †	.51	.34	3.07 †	.38	.17	1.83	.42	.22	2.14 *
All	.68	.52	4.19 †	.36	.15	1.69	.67	.56	6.15 †	.74	.65	8.55 †

Note.—W = Kendall's coefficient of concordance. $\bar{r}'$ = average rank-difference correlation coefficient. F = MS for children/MS for children X semesters, an approximate test with *df:* group I, 13.3 and 26.6; group II, 10.5 and 31.5; groups III and IV, 11.5 and 34.5.

* Significant at less than .05 level.

† Significant at less than .01 level.

ence correlation coefficients and approximate *F* values (Kendall, 1948, pp. 81–84), are given in TABLE 5.

The degree of stability is striking. In all four replicas, children tended to manifest the same relative amount of Aggression and Control-Dominance over the period of two years. The same can be said of the subjects, in all but one of the groups, with respect to Dependency, Autonomous Achievement, and Friendship-Affiliation; and to all behavior categories combined. Only in Nurturance and Avoidance-Withdrawal was there no evidence of a relatively enduring rank ordering of children.

Summary • This analysis of behavior frequencies disclosed a rather provocative conjunction of constancy and change: Frequency of behavior increased with age but in such a way that a child tended to maintain his position in the group with respect to the frequency of behavior exhibited. To examine further this phenomenon of stability in the context of change, a somewhat different form of analysis of the same data was undertaken.

CONSTANCY AND CHANGE AND INDIVIDUAL DIFFERENCES IN BEHAVIOR PROFILE

For this analysis, the frequency of behavior in any category was expressed as a propor-

TABLE 6. *Sums of arcsin transforms of proportional frequency data by behavior category, semester, and group*

		SEMESTERS				
GROUP		1	2	3	4	All
I	DEP		52.50	46.98	42.13	141.60
	NUR		8.07	7.93	12.79	28.79
	AGG		13.74	15.58	16.34	45.66
	CON		26.02	29.06	30.59	85.67
	ACH					
	AW		12.08	11.32	13.45	36.85
	FA		18.34	22.74	21.19	62.27
II	DEP	37.96	34.88	30.99	29.31	133.14
	NUR	10.42	9.19	10.08	12.52	42.20
	AGG	11.71	12.44	13.81	11.56	49.52
	CON	20.62	25.41	23.24	23.68	92.96
	ACH	11.38	12.42	16.38	17.81	57.98
	AW	8.24	6.41	8.02	7.04	29.71
	FA	12.18	13.70	15.09	17.49	58.46
III	DEP	38.16	36.54	37.91	34.41	147.01
	NUR	10.94	11.62	7.82	7.97	38.35
	AGG	14.61	15.54	9.80	11.26	51.21
	CON	19.08	17.54	20.45	18.27	75.33
	ACH	18.57	21.24	24.90	27.74	92.44
	AW	9.42	10.01	8.11	11.98	39.53
	FA	15.01	16.32	13.72	14.92	59.97
IV	DEP	41.25	38.18	35.97	34.13	149.52
	NUR	6.22	7.10	6.28	5.91	25.50
	AGG	10.30	13.18	12.47	11.64	47.59
	CON	14.48	14.86	15.56	17.85	62.76
	ACH	27.37	27.02	27.87	27.72	109.97
	AW	10.64	10.18	9.78	13.87	44.47
	FA	11.13	13.50	16.93	15.60	57.15

tion of the total frequency in all categories, providing an *ipsative* measure. On the assumption that the only source of random variation in these data was "error" in sampling the behavior of a given child within a given semester, two sets of five-minute observations (each totaling 30 minutes in most cases) were selected at random for each child for each semester. Within each set, the category frequency proportions were computed and then subjected to angular transformation to provide a variable more suited to the assumptions of analysis of variance. The sums of these arcsin transforms are given in TABLE 6 by category, semester, and group. These data were treated in an essentially nomothetic manner to answer the following questions: (a) Was there a well-differentiated pattern or profile for each group? (b) If so, did the profile change with time? (c) Were there individual differences? TABLE 7 summarizes the analyses of variance.

Behavior Profile • In each of the replicas, the relative frequency varied significantly from one category of behavior to another. Application of Tukey's nonsequential studentized range test revealed the following: In group I, differences between all possible pairs of sums of arcsin transforms were significant beyond the .01 level. All differences were similarly significant in group II with a few exceptions: Aggression differed from Friendship-Affiliation only beyond the .05 level; there were no differences between Autonomous Achievement and Friendship-Affiliation, between Aggression and Autonomous Achievement, or between Nurturance and Aggression. In group III, Nurturance was not significantly different from Avoidance-Withdrawal, and Aggression differed from Friendship-Affiliation at or beyond the .05 level; all other contrasts met the .01 criterion. For the last of the groups, all except two of the differences were significant beyond the .01 level;

TABLE 7. *Summary of analysis of variance of arcsin transforms of proportional frequency data by group*

GROUP	SOURCE	*df*	MEAN SQUARE	*F*
I	Behaviors (B)	5	19.4687	593.00 †
	B × Semesters (S)	10	.3101	9.45 †
	B × Children (C)	70	.1271	3.88 †
	B × S × C	140	.0446	1.36 *
	error (B × Sets within S × C)	225	.0328	
II	Behaviors (B)	6	13.0388	286.95 †
	B × Semesters (S)	18	.2507	5.52 †
	B × Children (C)	66	.1450	3.19 †
	B × S × C	198	.0483	1.06
	error (B × Sets within S × C)	288	.0454	
III	Behaviors (B)	6	14.1329	340.35 †
	B × Semesters (S)	18	.2236	5.38 †
	B × Children (C)	72	.1657	3.99 †
	B × S × C	216	.0499	1.20
	error (B × Sets within S × C)	312	.0415	
IV	Behaviors (B)	6	18.0545	525.10 †
	B × Semesters (S)	18	.1461	4.25 †
	B × Children (C)	72	.1161	3.38 †
	B × S × C	216	.0297	<1
	error (B × Sets within S × C)	312	.0344	

* Significant at less than .05 level.
† Significant at less than .0005 level.

no difference existed between Friendship-Affiliation and Control-Dominance or between Avoidance-Withdrawal and Aggression. Clearly, each group had a well-delineated behavior profile. Moreover, that profile was palpably consistent from replica to replica; only Autonomous Achievement—in groups II, III, and IV—varied noticeably in relative importance. FIGURE 3 presents the profiles for three of the four groups with each of the arcsin sums expressed as the number of studentized range values (5 per cent level) to make the patterns comparable across replicas.

Time Variations in Behavior Profile • Although the interaction between behaviors and semesters was highly significant in all groups, changes in behavior profile were not substantial. TABLE 8 presents the results of studentized range tests of the differences. There was a tendency for a decrease in the relative amount of Dependency and for increases in Autonomous Achievement and Friendship-Affiliation. Of the 144 multiple range tests, 34 were significant: 10 of 21 for Dependency, all decreases; seven of 18 for Autonomous Achievement, all increases; and six of 21 for Friendship-Affiliation, all increases.

Individual Differences • The behavior profile varied from child to child, as indicated by the significant interaction between behavior categories and children in all four groups. Again applying the studentized range test, these individual differences were found to be attributable to Dependency and Aggression in all groups; to Nurturance only in group I; to Control-Dominance in groups I, II, and IV; to Achievement in groups II, III, and IV; to Avoidance-Withdrawal in group

TABLE 8. *Changes in behavior profile over time*
(studentized range tests)

SEMESTER	GROUP	DEP	NUR	AGG	CON	ACH	AW	FA
1 to 2	II				+ †			
	III							
	IV							
1 to 3	II	− †				+ †		
	III			− †		+ †		
	IV	− †						+ †
1 to 4	II	− †				+ †		+ †
	III					+ †		
	IV	− †						+ †
2 to 3	I	− †						+ †
	II	− *				+ *		
	III		− *	− †				
	IV							+ *
2 to 4	I	− †	+ †		+ †			
	II	− †				+ †		+ *
	III			− *		+ †		
	IV	− *					+ *	
3 to 4	I	− †	+ †					
	II							
	III						+ *	
	IV						+ *	

* Significant at less than .05 level.
† Significant at less than .01 level.

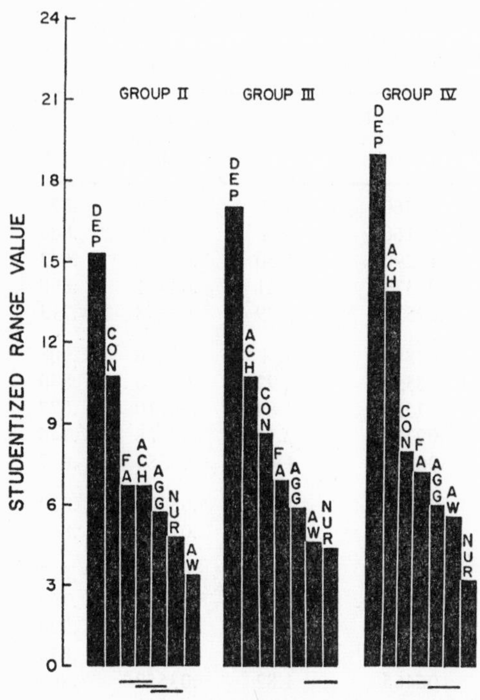

FIGURE 3

Behavior profiles in three groups of children. Common underlining indicates no significant differences between categories.

IV; and to Friendship-Affiliation in groups I and II.

Summary • This series of analyses served to describe a profile of behavior which was characteristic to a significant extent of all four groups of children; which changed significantly with time in all groups, but substantively only in Dependency, Autonomous Achievement, and Friendship-Affiliation; and which varied significantly from child to child, in all groups in Dependency and Aggression and, in all but one of the groups, in Control-Dominance and Autonomous Achievement.

CONSTANCY AND CHANGE IN INDIVIDUAL BEHAVIOR PROFILES

With repeated samples of behavior of the same subjects, it was possible to determine whether there could be identified for each child a profile and, if so, whether that profile changed with age. TABLE 9 summarizes the results of the analyses of variance.

Individual Behavior Profiles • For every subject, the F value for behaviors was highly significant, denoting well-articulated, individual behavior profiles. In TABLE 10 are

TABLE 9. *Summary of analyses of variance of arcsin transforms of proportional frequency data for individual children*

GROUP	S	MEAN SQUARE BEHAVIORS	F [a]	MEAN SQUARE BEHAVIORS × SEMESTERS	F [b]	MEAN SQUARE ERROR	r [c]
I	1	1.4805	51.69	.05890	2.06	.02864	.924
	2	1.6907	25.77	.04821	<1	.06560	.919
	3	1.7264	37.02	.09925	2.13	.04663	.845
	4	.7906	20.70	.07290	1.91	.03820	.766
	5	1.0338	37.33	.06937	2.51	.02769	.823
	7	1.5269	48.14	.08248	2.60 *	.03172	.854
	8	1.3906	73.88	.03850	2.05	.01882	.921
	9	1.5267	77.69	.05324	2.71 *	0.1965	.902
	10	1.5539	35.33	.07928	1.80	.04398	.861
	12	1.7348	63.90	.05773	2.13	.02715	.906
	13	1.2020	47.72	.03733	1.48	.02519	.912
	15	1.1940	43.34	.13209	4.80 †	.02755	.728
	16	1.5761	41.84	.01511	<1	.03767	.972
	17	1.2574	27.69	.02648	<1	.04541	.939
	18	1.5635	104.60	.06439	4.31 †	.01494	.886

TABLE 9. (*Continued*)

GROUP	*S*	MEAN SQUARE BEHAVIORS	*F* [a]	MEAN SQUARE BEHAVIORS × SEMESTERS	*F* [b]	MEAN SQUARE ERROR	*r* [c]
II	21	.6821	14.41	.03360	<1	.04730	.828
	22	1.3617	21.31	.04160	<1	.06390	.888
	25	.8438	13.15	.10290	1.60	.06416	.643
	26	1.7976	40.48	.05373	1.21	.04441	.890
	28	1.0449	19.50	.09570	1.79	.05358	.713
	29	1.9621	37.40	.04860	<1	.05246	.908
	30	1.4455	42.27	.06550	1.92	.03420	.840
	31	.7077	17.22	.07550	1.84	.04110	.677
	32	1.1774	27.14	.09235	2.13 *	.04338	.746
	33	1.3498	30.78	.06262	1.43	.04385	.837
	34	.9287	29.94	.04840	1.56	.03102	.820
	35	1.4321	55.38	.06115	2.37 *	.02586	.849
III	41	1.4245	41.48	.04835	1.41	.03435	.877
	42	1.1684	30.19	.08530	2.20 *	.03870	.760
	43	1.3666	27.42	.04111	<1	.04983	.890
	44	1.4714	26.90	.07153	1.31	.05470	.830
	45	1.7140	48.16	.06465	1.82	.03559	.864
	46	1.7115	41.24	.08080	1.95	.04150	.835
	47	1.0260	33.93	.06615	2.19 *	.03024	.784
	48	.7070	17.30	.06329	1.55	.04087	.718
	49	1.3221	38.30	.10067	2.92 †	.03452	.752
	50	.8365	10.04	.07016	<1	.08333	.732
	51	1.6241	18.65	.07817	<1	.08708	.901
	55	.7492	21.22	.04599	1.30	.03530	.793
	56	.9996	20.48	.04950	<1	.04880	.855
IV	61	1.8374	42.09	.04167	<1	.04365	.915
	62	1.4495	31.88	.06278	1.38	.04547	.847
	63	1.8331	95.87	.02588	1.35	.01912	.946
	64	1.2025	25.63	.06452	1.38	.04691	.815
	66	1.7505	37.76	.03339	<1	.04636	.928
	67	1.8842	76.25	.04548	1.84	.02471	.910
	69	1.4084	61.66	.04692	2.05	.02284	.879
	70	1.0347	64.31	.03014	1.87	.01609	.893
	71	1.1056	20.60	.02310	<1	.05367	.921
	72	1.2080	42.54	.02663	<1	.02840	.917
	73	1.3959	48.63	.03958	1.38	.02871	.895
	74	1.4304	47.55	.04005	1.33	.03008	.897
	75	1.9071	46.58	.02222	<1	.04094	.955

[a] All *F* values are significant at less than .0005 level; *df* for Ss 1–18, 5 and 15, for Ss 21–75, 6 and 24.
[b] *df* for Ss 1–18, 10 and 15, for Ss 21–75, 18 and 24.
[c] Intraclass correlation coefficient: MS behaviors — MS behaviors × semesters / MS behaviors + (no. of semesters — 1) MS behaviors × semesters.
* Significant at less than .05 level.
† Significant at less than .01 level.

TABLE 10. *Sums of arcsin transforms of proportional frequency data for individual children*

GROUP	*S*	DEP	NUR	AGG	CON	ACH	AW	FA	R [a]
I	1	7.82	1.60	3.61	8.48		2.11	2.84	1.92
	2	10.29	1.62	2.70	4.99		2.17	4.59	2.88
	3	10.28	2.73	1.26	5.53		2.83	3.46	2.43
	4	7.78	2.06	3.63	6.54		3.04	4.71	2.20
	5	8.91	1.91	4.54	5.33		2.46	4.39	1.84
	7	9.68	1.18	3.45	5.87		2.33	3.96	2.00
	8	10.21	1.92	4.01	3.71		3.25	4.24	1.54
	9	9.41	1.33	2.95	6.36		2.10	4.37	1.57
	10	10.24	3.57	2.40	4.99		1.83	3.46	2.36
	12	10.17	1.09	2.88	5.89		2.83	3.48	1.85
	13	8.79	1.56	4.16	5.87		1.89	4.95	1.79
	15	8.88	1.26	3.50	5.42		2.38	4.23	1.87
	16	9.91	2.51	1.37	5.07		2.64	5.17	2.18
	17	8.94	1.78	3.07	6.16		2.13	4.90	2.40
	18	10.29	2.69	2.14	5.47		2.88	3.51	1.37
II	21	9.00	3.56	6.40	8.09	4.92	2.47	5.90	2.79
	22	11.55	4.19	3.42	7.64	3.08	2.07	6.18	3.25
	25	9.51	3.89	4.12	8.30	6.35	2.22	4.69	3.25
	26	13.06	2.80	3.12	7.31	4.20	2.24	4.64	2.71
	28	11.12	3.21	6.14	6.57	4.09	2.38	5.25	2.97
	29	13.24	3.42	1.78	7.40	3.34	2.67	5.15	2.94
	30	11.26	4.23	2.49	8.33	6.38	1.94	3.47	2.37
	31	10.64	3.87	4.36	6.37	5.25	3.78	5.92	2.60
	32	10.57	3.20	3.83	9.09	4.77	2.72	4.21	2.67
	33	11.11	3.73	3.89	9.14	4.03	2.42	3.87	2.69
	34	10.02	3.41	4.63	7.28	6.47	2.29	5.90	2.26
	35	12.07	2.69	5.35	7.45	5.12	2.51	3.30	2.07
III	41	11.91	3.14	2.36	5.21	7.61	2.80	5.48	2.38
	42	11.49	2.33	3.54	5.28	6.71	3.29	5.41	2.52
	43	12.35	2.99	3.79	5.78	6.34	2.63	4.80	2.86
	44	12.52	3.19	2.52	4.03	6.90	3.76	5.40	3.01
	45	12.79	3.01	2.46	6.44	6.47	2.34	4.09	2.42
	46	12.42	2.94	3.01	5.50	7.82	1.93	3.59	2.62
	47	9.81	3.44	4.00	6.62	8.88	2.34	4.22	2.23
	48	9.37	3.13	5.28	7.77	6.88	3.17	4.43	2.60
	49	11.85	2.06	7.17	4.51	5.56	3.18	4.02	2.38
	50	10.57	3.42	2.74	5.68	6.58	4.38	5.50	3.71
	51	12.18	2.31	2.77	3.67	8.43	3.96	4.31	3.79
	55	8.78	2.98	5.15	7.30	8.51	3.25	4.18	2.41
	56	10.98	3.41	5.43	7.53	5.76	2.52	4.54	2.84
IV	61	12.52	1.61	2.67	4.80	8.41	3.58	3.68	2.68
	62	11.82	1.77	4.90	4.77	7.87	2.73	4.25	2.74
	63	13.03	1.72	3.97	4.95	7.50	2.63	3.98	1.78
	64	10.85	2.42	3.45	4.68	8.83	3.80	4.59	2.78
	66	10.93	1.52	2.97	3.06	10.29	4.92	3.69	2.77

TABLE 10. (*Continued*)

GROUP	*S*	DEP	NUR	AGG	CON	ACH	AW	FA	*R*[a]
	67	12.25	1.98	1.67	3.76	8.90	3.76	4.89	2.02
	69	11.62	1.74	3.88	4.50	8.47	3.91	4.45	1.94
	70	9.64	2.27	4.10	7.61	8.51	3.13	4.41	1.63
	71	10.67	2.03	4.93	4.31	8.53	3.76	4.86	2.97
	72	10.81	2.50	4.24	7.56	7.41	2.40	4.19	2.17
	73	12.08	1.34	4.84	5.30	6.73	3.46	5.02	2.18
	74	11.48	2.84	2.74	4.52	8.63	2.78	5.46	2.23
	75	11.83	1.77	3.25	2.95	9.90	3.62	3.66	2.60

[a] Least significant range value at .05 level.

given the totals over semesters of arcsin transforms for the six or seven behavior categories for each child, together with the least significant range value at the .05 level.

An individual behavior profile is characterized by differentiation in both form and substance. As of this time, no way of expressing the latter beyond mere qualitative or schematic description presents itself. For example, one can say of the profile for *S* 21 that Dependency is significantly greater than Friendship-Affiliation, Autonomous Achievement, Nurturance, and Avoidance-Withdrawal; that Control-Dominance is significantly greater than Autonomous-Achievement, Nurturance, and Avoidance-Withdrawal; that Aggression is significantly greater than Nurturance and Avoidance-Withdrawal; and, finally, that Friendship-Affiliation is significantly greater than Avoidance-Withdrawal. And this behavior hierarchy can be schematized in the conventional manner, as follows:

DEP CON AGG FA ACH NUR AW

However, a number of means of quantitatively denoting the degree of differentiation in form suggest themselves. The first is the size of the *F* value for behaviors. For the 38 children in groups II, III, and IV, for all of whom there are seven-point profiles, the *F* value ranged from a high of 95.87, for *S* 63, to a low of 10.04, for *S* 50. The profiles of these two children are given in FIGURE 4. The

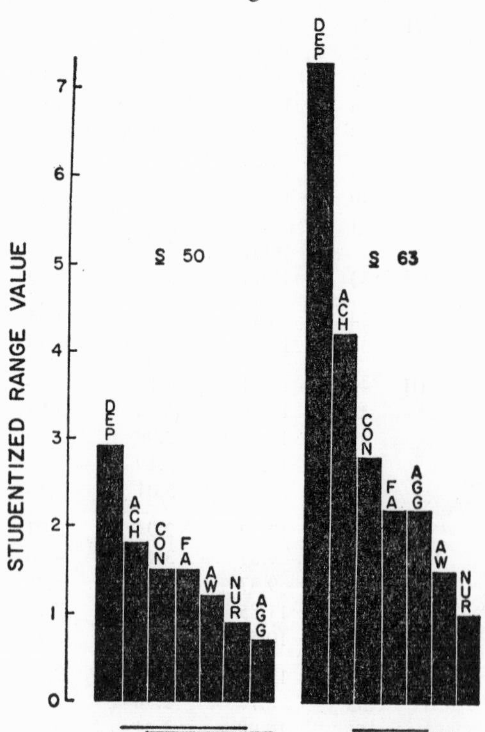

FIGURE 4

Individual behavior profiles: *S*s 50 and 63, lowest and highest *F* values for behaviors, respectively. Common underlining indicates no significant differences between categories.

differences in form between the two patterns are so striking as to require no comment.

A second possible index of differentiation in profile conformation is simply the total number of significant differences among behaviors. For a six-point profile, the number of possible differences is 30; for a seven-point profile, the corresponding number is 42. For *S* 21, the example given above, the total number of significant differences was 20. The range in values of this index (N), again only for the subjects in groups II, III, and IV, was from a high of 30 (*S*s 35, 63, 67, 69, and 70) to a low of 12 (*S* 31). The profiles of *S* 35, one of the highs, and *S* 31 are portrayed in FIGURE 5.

The variance (V) of the distribution of number of significant differences between a given behavior category and all other categories provides a third measure of differentiation. Again returning to *S* 21, the array with the N for each behavior is

DEP	CON	AGG	FA	ACH	NUR	AW
4	3	2	2	2	3	4

and the variance, .81. The highest V in groups II, III, and IV was 3.57 (*S* 31); the lowest, .48 (*S* 55). *S* 31 also had the lowest number of significant differences between categories, and his profile has already been given (FIGURE 5). The second highest V value was 3.48 for *S* 26. His profile was therefore selected for comparison with that of *S* 55 in FIGURE 6. A high V value seems to characterize those profiles in which one category is particularly salient.

Rank-difference correlation coefficients,

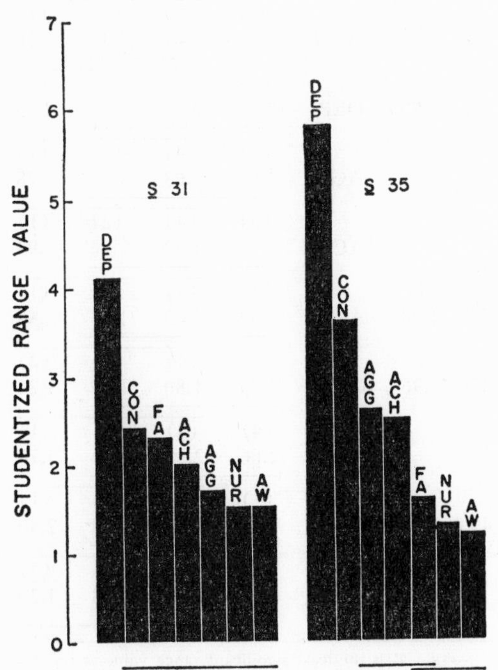

FIGURE 5

Individual behavior profiles: *S*s 31 and 35, lowest and highest N values, respectively; *see* text. Common underlining indicates no significant differences between categories.

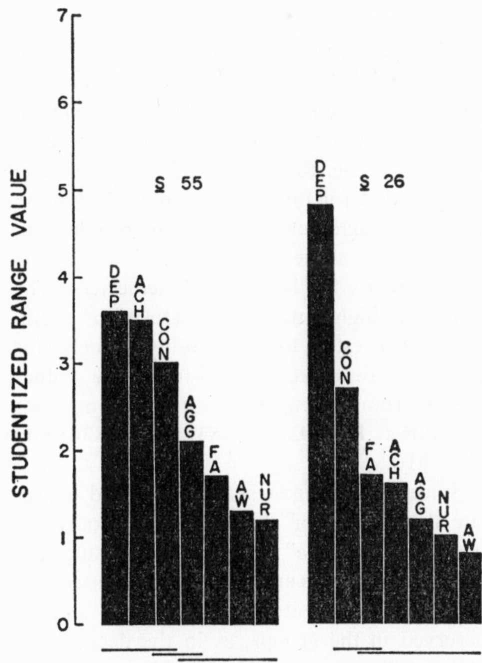

FIGURE 6

Individual behavior profiles: *S*s 55 and 26, lowest and (second) highest V values, respectively; *see* text. Common underlining indicates no significant differences between categories.

computed with the correction factor (Edwards, 1954) because of the large number of tied ranks in the distribution of N, between the three indexes of differentiation for the 38 children are given below:

	N	V
F	.79 †	−.11
N		−.39 *

* $p < .02$.
† $p < .01$.

As a measure of differentiation in profile, N would seem to add little information to that provided by *F*. However, V provides a dissimilar rank ordering, as has already been suggested by the illustration of extreme cases; its relation to N is not very substantial—although significant—and is negative, as would be expected.

Time Variations in Individual Behavior Profiles • That each child has a singular profile of social behavior takes on added significance if that profile can be shown to be constant over time. Returning to TABLE 8, it can be seen that for only nine of the 53 children were there significant changes in profile over the period of some two years, as indicated by significant *F*s for behaviors *x* semesters. The generally high intraclass correlation coefficients also testify to the stability of behavior profile in these young children. The values ranged from .643 to .972 with group medians as follows: I—.902; II—.832; III—.830; and IV—.910.

Studentized range tests were applied to isolate the sources of change in the profiles of the nine "unstable" subjects. The results are diagrammed in TABLE 11. In some cases, the change is an accentuation of a trend already observed in the groups, as in the decrease in Dependency in *S*s 7, 15, 18, 32, and 35; or the increase in Achievement in *S*s 32, 35, 42, and 47. In one instance, profile instability reflects a change that is counter to that of the groups, the *increase* in Dependency in *S* 49. Three of the children (*S*s 7, 9, and 47) experienced an increase in Control-Dominance, a trend of little significance in the group analyses.

TABLE 11. *Changes over time in unstable individual behavior profiles*
(studentized range tests)

S	R	BEHAVIOR	SEMESTER TOTALS			
7	.92	DEP		(2) 3.84	(3) 3.18	(4) 2.66
		CON		(4) 2.38	(3) 2.19	(2) 1.30
9	.73	CON		(4) 2.57	(3) 2.26	(2) 1.53
15	.86	DEP		(2) 3.85	(3) 3.16	(4) 1.86
18	.63	DEP		(3) 3.74	(2) 3.72	(4) 2.82
		NUR		(4) 1.35	(3) .79	(2) .54
32	1.15	DEP	(1) 3.42	(2) 2.57	(4) 2.42	(3) 2.16
		ACH	(4) 1.94	(3) 1.41	(2) 1.16	(1) .26
35	.89	DEP	(1) 3.58	(2) 3.16	(3) 2.70	(4) 2.63
		AGG	(3) 1.67	(4) 1.63	(2) 1.27	(1) .78
		ACH	(3) 1.91	(4) 1.32	(2) .96	(1) .93
42	1.08	ACH	(4) 2.42	(3) 2.03	(2) 1.38	(1) .88
47	.96	CON	(3) 2.29	(4) 1.80	(1) 1.29	(2) 1.24
		ACH	(4) 2.66	(3) 2.38	(2) 2.14	(1) 1.70
49	1.03	DEP	(3) 3.65	(4) 3.02	(2) 2.78	(1) 2.40
		AGG	(1) 2.51	(2) 1.78	(4) 1.58	(3) 1.29

NOTE.—R is the least significant range value at the .05 level. Numbers in parentheses above totals denote semesters. Common underlining indicates no significant differences among semester totals.

Summary • These analyses have demonstrated the possibility of describing for each child a profile of social behavior which appears to be relatively stable for most children during the age period from 2 to 5 years.

Conclusions

THE time-sampling observation method, as utilized in this study, proved to be sufficiently sensitive to reveal the differential frequencies with which several social behaviors were manifested in young children and to discriminate between individuals with respect to the resulting behavior profile. In the light of this methodological precision, the stability of the profile for more than 80 per cent of the youngsters over a two-year period becomes all the more impressive. During a period in the life span when instrumental behavior is demonstrably changing, in response to modifications in individual capabilities and social expectations, and—more specifically in the nursery school setting—where children experience marked alterations in teachers and programs, a pattern of individual social behavior that is strikingly unchanging emerged. It is as if each child has his own *behavioral economy* which persists through time. Admittedly, he modifies his behavior but only in search of enduring goals. The findings support Anderson's conclusion of some years ago of the "consistency rather than the inconsistency of personality traits" (1948, p. 413). A review by Kagan and Moss (1961) adduces more recent evidence for developmental stability.

Many questions regarding antecedent, concomitant, and subsequent factors remain to be answered. When is this singular, stable pattern of behavior established? Early, it would be presumed, in view of its existence at 3 years. The longitudinal investigation by Birch, Thomas, Chess, and Hertzig (1962), which demonstrated individuality from the first months of life, confirms this presumption. To what degree will a profile, determined in these early years, persist into later childhood, adolescence, and even adulthood? The fact that only a few of the behaviors observed in the age period 3 to 6 years were predictive of related behaviors in early adulthood in the Kagan and Moss (1962) study does not provide much basis for anticipating marked persistence in behavioral economy over the long term; in fact, these investigators are of the opinion that "developments during the age period 6 to 10 induce important changes in the child's behavioral organization" (1962, p. 272). The resumption of study of subjects of the present investigation, when they are between 9½ and 10½ years of age, should provide some evidence regarding any such discontinuity.

Under what circumstances is profile singularity developed and stabilized in these early years? The "deviant" cases—the nine unstable profiles—present a special challenge: Are these slow- or late-developing youngsters who have yet to achieve a stable patterning of social behavior? Or, are there circumstances—biological or social, past or present—which prevent them from attaining this kind of individual integrity? Ongoing analyses of child-rearing attitudes and practices and of certain structural characteristics of the families of these children, together with a consideration of constitutional correlates, are designed to provide answers to some of these questions.

Whatever the outcome of these further investigations, the fact remains that the present study has captured something of the essence of the *individual* child—a pattern of social behavior which remains remarkably invariant in these early years during which both the child as an organism and his social environment are constantly changing.

REFERENCES

ALLPORT, G. W. *Pattern and growth in personality.* New York: Holt, Rinehart & Winston, 1961.

ANDERSON, J. E. Personality organization in children. *Amer. Psychologist,* 1948, **3,** 409–416.

BALDWIN, A. L. The study of individual personality by means of the intraindividual correlation. *J. Pers.,* 1946, **14,** 151–168.

BIRCH, H. G., THOMAS, A., CHESS, S., & HERTZIG, M. E. Individuality in the development of children. *Develop. Med. Child Neurol.,* 1962, **4,** 370–379.

BROVERMAN, D. M. Normative and ipsative measurement in psychology. *Psychol. Rev.,* 1962, **69,** 295–305.

CHILD, I. L. Socialization. In G. Lindzey (Ed.), *Handbook of social psychology.* Vol. 2. Reading, Mass.: Addison-Wesley, 1954. Pp. 655–692.

EDWARDS, A. L. *Statistical methods for the behavioral sciences.* New York: Rinehart, 1954.

EMMERICH, W. Continuity and stability in early social development. *Child Develpm.,* 1964.

GEWIRTZ, J. L. Succorance in young children. Unpublished doctoral dissertation, State Univer. of Iowa, 1948.

KAGAN, J., & MOSS, H. A. Personality and social development: family and peer influences. *Rev. educ. Res.,* 1961, **31,** 463–474.

KAGAN, J., & MOSS, H. A. *Birth to maturity.* New York: Wiley, 1962.

KENDALL, M. B. *Rank correlation methods.* London: Griffin, 1948.

MCCLELLAND, D. C. *Personality.* New York: Sloane Associates, 1951.

MAY, J. M. Extended and corrected tables of the upper percentage points of the studentized range. *Biometrika,* 1952, **38,** 192–193.

MERMINOD, A. (Ed.) The growth of the normal child during the first three years of life. *Modern problems in pediatrics.* Vol. 7. Basel: S. Karger, 1962.

SCHEFFÉ, H. A method for judging all contrasts in the analysis of variance. *Biometrika,* 1953, **40,** 87–104.

SEARS, R. R., WHITING, J. W. M., NOWLIS, V., & SEARS, PAULINE S. Some child-rearing antecedents of aggression and dependency in young children. *Genet. Psychol. Monogr.,* 1953, **47,** 135–234.

SMOCK, C. D. Singularity and stability of behavior profiles in doll play. *Child Develpm.,* 1964.

WALKER, H. M., & LEV, J. *Statistical inference.* New York: Holt, 1953.

MARJORIE P. HONZIK, JEAN W. MACFARLANE, *and* LUCILE ALLEN

*The Stability of Mental Test Performance Between Two and Eighteen Years**

IN AN earlier study, the constancy of mental test performance was reported for a group of normal children during their preschool years (Honzik & Jones, 1937). These children are now young adults, and it is possible to show the relative stability or lability of their mental test scores over the entire period of testing, 21 months to 18 years, inclusive. The contribution of the present study lies in the fact of repeated individual tests given at specified ages over a 16-year period to more than 150 children; and, second, in the fact that this group of children was selected so as to be a representative sample of the children born in an urban community during the late 1920's. Furthermore, since the Guidance Study has as its primary purpose the study of personality development and associated factors, it has been possible to note the relation of fluctuations or stability in rate of mental growth to physical ills, unusual environmental strains or supports, and to evidences of tension or serenity within the individual child.

The Sample

THE Guidance Study has been described in detail in previous publications (Macfarlane, 1938, 1939, 1943). Suffice it to say here that the two groups, which are referred to as the Guidance and Control Groups, constitute representative subsamples of the Berkeley Survey. The names of every third child born in Berkeley between January 1, 1928, and June 30, 1929, were included in the Berkeley Survey (Welch, 1929). A total of 252 children from the Berkeley Survey Group were asked to come to the Institute for their first mental test at the age of 21 months. At this age level, the group of 252 children was divided into two matched subsamples of 126 children on the basis of socio-economic factors (parents' national derivation, income, father's occupation, socio-economic rating, neighborhood, and mother's age and education). One of these subsamples (of the Berkeley Survey) has been called the "Guidance Group" because of the program of intensive interviews [held] with the parents and children; the second group, which has had physical examinations and mental tests but fewer and less intensive interviews and these at a much later age of the child, has been called the "Control Group." The children in both groups were given mental tests at the age of 21 months. At ages 2 and 2½ years, only the children in the Guidance Group were tested. Thereafter, the testing program was the same for the two groups.

Every effort was made to test the children as nearly as possible on or near their birthdays. Actually, from 72 to 95 percent of the children were tested within one month of their birthdates at the various ages up to and including 8 years (Honzik & Jones, 1937).

As was to be expected in a longitudinal study, a number of children were unable to come in for one or more of the mental tests. The most frequent cause of a missed test was the family being "out of town." However, a number of families lost interest or became uncooperative as their children grew older;

* REPRINTED with abridgment by permission of Marjorie P. Honzik, Jean W. Macfarlane, and the American Psychological Association from *J. exp. Educ.*, 1948, 17, 309–323.

one child was killed in an automobile accident. TABLES 1 and 2 show the number of children tested at each age level. It will be seen that at 18 years 153 of the 252 children were tested on the Wechsler-Bellevue.

. . .

The Testing Program

THE testing program followed in the Guidance Study is summarized in the following table:

AGES	TEST
21 months–5 years	California Preschool Schedule I or II
6 and 7 years	Stanford-Binet, 1916 Revision
8 years	Stanford Revision, Form L
9–15 years	Stanford Revision (either Form L or M)
18 years	Wechsler-Bellevue

During the preschool years, 21 months to 5 years, inclusive, each child was tested at successive age levels on the same test, either the California Preschool Schedule I or California Preschool Schedule II.[1] Beginning at age 9, a program of test alternation was begun which was designed to show the effects of a change in the form of the test on mental test constancy. . . . All the children in both groups were tested on either Form L or Form M of the Stanford Revision at age 9 years.

1 The published California Preschool Scale Form A (Jaffa, 1934) is composed largely of items from the California Preschool Schedule I, together with a few items from the California Preschool Schedule II. The test items for the California Schedules I and II include selections made by Dr. Adele S. Jaffa from several standardized tests, together with some original items first validated at the Institute. These scales have been normed by the Thurstone method of absolute scaling.

But at ages 12 and 14 years, only two-thirds of the groups were given mental tests; the remaining third of the groups was tested at ages 13 and 15 years. In presenting group results, the scores for ages 12 and 13 years have been considered together, as have scores for ages 14 and 15 years.

The I.Q.'s obtained on the Stanford tests and the Wechsler-Bellevue were converted into sigma or standard scores so that they would be in comparable form to the mental test sigma scores obtained between 21 months and 5 years. The means and standard deviations of the I.Q.'s which were used in computing the sigma scores are given in TABLE 1. The mean I.Q.'s for the combined Guidance and Control Groups shown in the last columns of the table were the ones used in computing sigma scores for individual children.

TABLE 1 also shows that, although these children were selected as a representative sample of urban children, their scores are considerably above the test norms. The average I.Q. on the Stanford-Binet at ages 6 and 7 years and on the Stanford Revision, Form L at 8 years varied from 118.3 to 118.7. During the age period 9 to 13 years, the average I.Q. was approximately 120. The highest average I.Q. of 123 was obtained for the test period 14 and 15 years; and the lowest I.Q. average (118.2) was earned on the Wechsler-Bellevue at 18 years.

The distribution[s] of the I.Q.'s . . . for age periods 6 through 18 years . . . are relatively normal at all ages at which the Stanford-Binet or Form L or M of the Stanford Revision were the tests given. But at 18 years, the distribution of I.Q.'s on the Wechsler-Bellevue suggests that this test lacks "top" or at least does not differentiate between the children earning the highest scores at the earlier ages. Bayley (1948) has another explanation for the decreased variability at maturity. She suggests that variability is greatest during the age periods when the children are acquiring the functions being tested and that variability becomes restricted with the approach to maturity of the particular processes being measured.

Group Trends in Mental Test Stability

PEARSONIAN coefficients of correlation between test scores earned at specified ages between 21 months and 18 years are shown in TABLE 2. These correlation coefficients are based on the scores of the children in the combined Guidance and Control Groups for all but two age levels (2 and 2½ years) when only the children in the Guidance Group were tested.

Correlations for adjacent ages indicate a fair degree of mental test constancy when the interval between tests is at a minimum. The range of correlations for adjacent ages varies from $r = .71$ (between ages 21 months x 2 years; 2 x 2½ years; 3 x 3½ years; and 5 x 6 years) to $r = .92$ for the ages 12 x 14 years on the Stanford Revision, Form L. However, the correlations decrease markedly with the interval between tests but tend to increase with the age of the children when tested.

Comparison of the correlation coefficients for three-year intervals shows clearly the increase in mental test constancy with age:

2 x 5	years	$r = .32 \pm .06$
3 x 6	years	$r = .57 \pm .05$
4 x 7	years	$r = .59 \pm .04$
5 x 8	years	$r = .70$
7 x 10	years	$r = .78$
9 x 12 or 13	years	$r = .85$
14 or 15 x 18	years	$r = .79$

The correlation between tests given at 2 and at 5 years ($r = + .32$) suggests a prediction which is not much better than chance, but the magnitude of the test-retest correlation increases markedly with age.

The importance of both age and interval between tests on the test-retest correlation is shown by the relation of these r's (of TABLE 2) to the age ratio (age at first test/age at second test), = .85 (Honzik & Jones, 1937).

The relation of test scores earned at four specified ages (21 months, 3 years, 6 years, and 18 years) to test scores earned at all other ages may be seen in FIGURE 1. In the upper left quadrant of this figure is shown the correlation of the 21-month test with scores at later age levels. We note a marked decrease in the size of these correlation coefficients with age, especially during the preschool years. However, the correlation between the 21-month and 2-year test ($r = .71$) indicates that the first test given the children at the age of 21 months was fairly reliable.

The results of the upper right quadrant, showing the correlation of the 3-year mental test scores with scores at other ages, should be compared with those of the upper left quadrant. The correlations of the 3-year test with scores at the adjacent ages 2½ and 3½ years are fairly high (r's are .71 and .73) but decrease to values which indicate poor prediction by 9 years ($r = .43$).

Since Stanford tests are frequently given to children in the first grade, the results given in the lower left quadrant should be of interest to educators. The 6-year I.Q.'s are fairly constant, but the correlation coefficients are not sufficiently high so that the possibility of marked changes in the I.Q.'s of individual children is precluded.

The fourth quadrant of this chart shows the increasing prediction with age of success on the Wechsler-Bellevue at 18 years. The writers are concerned that the correlations with the Wechsler-Bellevue are not higher. Restricted variability, regardless of its cause, is probably a contributing factor. Another factor may be the differences in the types of test items included in the Stanford and Wechsler-Bellevue tests.

. . .

Changes in Scores over Certain Age Periods

THE correlation coefficients in TABLE 2 indicate the group trends with respect to the constancy of mental test performance. It is also of interest to know the extent of the changes in sigma scores or I.Q. which are occurring in individual children. Furthermore, the question arises as to whether the correlation between mental test scores is largely determined by a relatively small proportion of the cases or by the group as a whole. In a previous study (Honzik & Jones, 1937), we published the distribution of changes in sigma scores which occurred between the 6- and 7-year tests ($r = .82$) for these children. This distribution was normal, with 80 percent of the group showing sigma score changes of .5 or less. However, there were six children whose scores differed on these two tests by 1.5 sigma (approximately 20 I.Q. points since the standard deviation for ages 6 and 7 years is approximately 13) or more. The average change in score between 6 and 7 years was .5 of a sigma (6.5 I.Q. points).

If changes in I.Q. of 20 points can occur between the 6- and 7-year tests, it would be reasonable to expect rather marked changes in scores over the entire test period, 21 months to 18 years. We have, therefore, prepared distributions of the range of sigma score changes for the entire 16-year period of testing. We find that the scores of three children have increased between 4 and 4½ sigma (roughly between 70 and 79 I.Q. points, assuming an approximate standard deviation of 17.5 I.Q. points); and the scores of two children have decreased a similar amount. . . . The most interesting aspect of these tremendous changes in scores is the fact that the changes are not made abruptly but consistently over a long period of time. However, the greatest changes do occur on the preschool tests. We have, therefore, prepared distributions showing the range of changes in sigma scores and I.Q.'s between 6 and 18 years. No child's sigma score changes as much as 4 sigma during the school years. But the scores of one child (case 764) changes 3 sigma; and those of four others between 2.5 and 2.9 sigma.

Since educators and clinical workers use I.Q.'s rather than standard scores, we have prepared a distribution of the range of changes in I.Q. during the 12-year period 6 to 18 years for the two groups, Guidance and Control:

I.Q. Changes Between 6 and 18 years	Guidance n=114 %	Control n=108 %	Total n=222 %
50 or more I.Q. pts.	1	–	.5
30 or more I.Q. pts.	9	10	9
20 or more I.Q. pts.	32	42	35
15 or more I.Q. pts.	58	60	58
10 or more I.Q. pts.	87	83	85
9 or less I.Q. pts.	13	17	15

. . . We are impressed not only by the extent of the changes in I.Q. during the school years but also by the fact that the results are so similar for the two groups, Guidance and Control. This finding suggests the reliability of these figures and that they would probably be duplicated under similar conditions of testing. Changes in I.Q. of 30 or more points of I.Q. are shown by 9 percent of the children in the Guidance Group and 10 percent in the Control Group. The I.Q.'s of over half of the children showed a variation of 15 or more points of I.Q. at some time during the school years, and a third of the group varied as much as 20 points of I.Q.

Although it is extremely important to point out the possibility of marked changes in scores in individual cases, it is equally important to emphasize that the scores of many children change only slightly with respect to the group from one age period to the next. And it is only when the changes are consistently in one direction, or the other, over a period of years that the range of variation becomes as great as 3 or 4 sigma (or over 50 I.Q. points).

Stability and Instability in the Mental Test Scores of Individual Children

MENTAL test sigma score curves have been drawn for all of the children in the Guidance Study. In this sample of 252 children, we have found individuals whose mental test scores have remained relatively stable at either a high, average, or low level over the entire period of testing (21 months to 18 years). Other children have shown highly inconsistent scores in their mental test performance. . . .

CONSISTENTLY LOW SCORES

Case 504, a girl, had a mother who attended college two years and a father who graduated from college. The child was defective at birth, which showed up not only in tests (her I.Q.'s varied from 67 to 53, sigma scores from -3 to $-4\frac{1}{2}$) but in her whole developmental history. Clinical diagnosis was microcephaly, probably secondary to prenatal injury early in M.'s pregnancy.

Case 945, a boy. This child's scores are nearly all between -1 and -2 sigma, but he has one I.Q. as high as 110 and one as low as 87. He comes from a minority group of relatively low economic status. His mother reached the tenth grade; his father finished high school. Additionally, his life has been characterized by the chronic emotional and economic strain and the divorce of his parents, by poor health of both parents and himself, by inadequate supervision, and episodes of acute anxiety which showed themselves in severe psychosomatic disturbances.

CONSISTENTLY AVERAGE TEST SCORES

Case 783, a boy earning consistently average scores, presents the least variability in our group with respect to test scores (I.Q. 120 to 125, after the preschool years). What factors lead to this stability of performance? His health history shows, as an infant, impetigo, severe bronchitis, a critical thymus disturbance, and chickenpox. As a preschool child, he had frequent colds, obstructive adenoids, infected tonsils (removed at 7). During his elementary school years, he had a chronic nasal discharge, a systolic murmur. His adolescent years showed poor dental hygiene, acne. At age 18 he had mumps, measles, and scarlet fever. But in spite of this history, he was energetic when well and interested in athletics.

The family situation was markedly substandard. Eight people, sometimes nine or ten, lived in four rooms, the boy sleeping in his parents' room until 11. The father was irregularly employed, insecure, drank too much, and when drinking, got into trouble (fights and women). The mother was mature and steady but had a hernia, chronic endocarditis, and worked away from home and, frequently, worked far beyond her strength. The mother did not finish high school; the father had two years of college. Two sibs of the boy attended the University; one graduated.

The boy was a bed-wetter until 18, had an acute stammer from 9 to 12, was and is a chronic nailbiter. His school grades were considerably below his tested I.Q. He was ashamed of his home, his father, and since he had strong social affiliative interests (which his home precluded) and athletic interests (which his health and small stature interfered with), there was never a time in his history that he was not confronted with extreme frustrations.

The question is again asked: Why his stable test scores, since other children with less disturbing histories showed such ups and downs? The question is raised and, unfortunately, not answered. One hypothesis is that because of chronic strain, internal and external, he persistently functioned on tests below his potential and at a level which he could do without effort. Did he fail to vary, as other disturbed children, because he was never free of tension so that, unlike them, he never had the chance to have a high score and show his real potential?

Case 976, showing consistently average and fairly stable test scores, is a girl of immigrant parents whose mother had schooling until 16 and whose father had schooling until age 12. The father provided a very substantial income and status to his family with his prestige-giving business success. Her mother, lonely in a new country, overprotected her daughter, especially in her early years. The mother slept in her daughter's room until she was 9. This girl's two highest scores (I.Q. 137) occurred at age 9 (following tonsillectomy ending a long period of chronic infection) and at 14 (during a period of more freedom from home, and more social opportunity and success). Her lowest score after her preschool years occurred at 18 after the death of her father.

RELATIVELY CONSISTENT HIGH SCORES

Case 423 presents a high-scoring girl whose mother is a normal school graduate and whose father obtained a post-graduate university degree. Her highest test score was obtained at 6. Her scores continued high, but sagged during late adolescence. She is attractive, artistically talented, and socially successful. She got very high grades in the elementary and junior high school years. Her lowest test scores are at ages 9 and 10, a period of fatigue and poor posture and a period during which she strained to excel, and at year 18 where her sigma score showed a drop. Her high school years were characterized by much less interest in intellectual success, which she regarded as unfeminine and interfering with getting good dates; and her motivation in all test situations was markedly below that of her early years. Scholastic mediocrity was consciously sought and obtained, serving not only her date objective, but her emancipatory revolt against parents who placed a very high value on grades and a very low value on her boy friends.

Case 524 is the daughter of parents who both had graduate university training and who presented their children with a self-contained and a rich family-centered recreational program but with little outside social life. This girl showed continuously high scores, although there were frequent shifts of as much as .8 of a sigma over two-year periods and I.Q. variations from a low of 137 to a high of 162. Her most outstanding handicaps were tongue tie, corrected early; strabismus corrected at 11½; and more or less chronic reserve. Sociometric findings appraised her as being the most quiet and reserved in her class. Her main interests were less in persons than in reading and writing. Her highest score was obtained at 13, just after menarche and at a time when she was doing excellent school work (greatly approved by her education-oriented family, including aunts, uncles, and a grandmother who had been active educators). Social participation, which was always a strain for her, was particularly restricted at this time.

STEADILY DECREASING MENTAL TEST SCORES

Case 935 is a girl, an only child, who did well on tests at 21 months (I.Q. 120) but lost I.Q. points steadily at the rate of about 5 or 6 points per year, reaching an I.Q. of 64 (Wechsler-Bellevue) at 18 years. This is a decrease of 4½ sigma. School reports after the second or third grade showed consistent failures. Intensive physical tests, including encephalograms, disclosed no discoverable physical factors or disease processes. The estimated I.Q.'s of the parents are around 80 to 85, grammar school education. The mother reports that she, as a girl, was "held over" several times. Chronic emotional and economic strain characterized the home after the early preschool years. Estimates of intelligence on the Rorschach and Thematic Apperception Test indicated average intelligence or only slightly below average. Her fantasy life is apparently richer than her overt test performance or school performance. The question is unsettled as to whether this is a case of mental deficiency or possible hebephrenia.

Case 764 is an example of a gradual lowering of I.Q. from 133 to 77, and sigma scores from +1 to −3. She is an only child, born when the mother was 44, the father, 37. The estimated I.Q. of the mother is 65 to 70. The father is a skilled mechanic. The parents went to school until age 14.

Obesity began in late preschool years and increased steadily until medical advice was finally followed at age 14 (height 5 ft. 2 in., weight 160 lbs. at 13). Weight was normal at 17. There were, however, no I.Q. variations in relation to these physical changes. She was always over-indulged by the mother, who lived to feed her and keep her young, and who was always complaining that her daughter never gave her enough affection.

CASES WITH INCREASING SCORES

Case 553 is a boy whose mental test scores increased from a preschool sigma score of −2 to later sigma scores of +2.4 in spite of a bad physical history. He is small-statured, thin, with very poor musculature, and presents a history of early ear infections and chronic bronchitis from infancy—headaches (early glasses), stomach pains (appendectomy); he has had three operations and three serious accidents. He has had only one six-month period in his life free of illness. In spite of a frail frame, which has suffered many serious indignities, an early strained family situation, and relatively low mental test scores in his early preschool years, his tested ability steadily increased until 9, from which time he has maintained high and fairly stable scores. His mother is a normal school graduate; his father completed high school. His greatest security lies in his intellectual interests and achievements, but he has made good social adjustments and an amazingly good adjustment to his handicaps.

Case 567. The early preschool history of this girl (the period of her lowest test scores) was characterized by the critical illnesses of her mother and brother and the emotional and financial strain that these entailed. Further, the girl had very poor muscle tonus, fatigue posture, and was very shy and reserved. At 6½ years she had pneumonia. From 10 on, while still reserved, she had many supports in her life—music, athletic success, summer camps, the honor roll at school. Eighteen years marks her first year in college and away from home and her first really completely satisfying social life, which resulted in great expansiveness. Both parents are college graduates who did advanced work in their fields.

HIGHLY VARIABLE SCORES

Case 715, a girl whose I.Q. varies from 121 to 165, presents a history that was characterized by intermittent but severe eczema and asthma throughout the entire testing period. Ages 3 to 7 constituted a particularly bad period; age 9, where there was a drop in I.Q. of 12 points, was a period not only of asthma and poor vision but of acute economic insecurity and family uneasiness. At age 10, during her highest test period, she was taking two cc. of adrenalin daily to keep her asthma under control.

Added to health strain, social strain became more acute for her at 12 when she entered junior high school and continued through high school. It was a period of overweight, disfiguring eczema, and marked mother-daughter strain. Not only did the girl belong to a racial minority group, but she was not at one with them because of her marked intellectual interests, unshared by others in her racial age group, at school or in the neighborhood. Her mother is a high school graduate; her father had three years in college.

At the time of the 18-year test she was very much below par as she was recovering from an acute period of asthma.

Case 946, a girl, has varied in I.Q. between 142 (preschool) and 87. Her sigma scores have varied from +1½ to −2; her preschool years were clearly higher than later years. Her lowest score (I.Q. 87, sigma −2) occurred at 9 years, a period of acute body concern and excessive modesty. Immigrant parents of grammar school education, both unstable and involved in chronic, acute marital tension, were divorced when the girl was 7. This child was acutely uneasy around her young stepfather for the first years of her mother's new marriage. Much internal as well as external turmoil has characterized her life.

In selecting mental test curves to include in this study, the writers were impressed by the fact that the children whose scores showed the greatest fluctuations were children whose life experiences had also fluctuated between disturbing and satisfying periods. Two such cases are 715 and 946. . . .

There is only one further generalization that seems justifiable on the basis of mental test curves of only 14 children, and that is the fact that the records of all eight children showing consistent trends have final mental test scores which are similar to their parents' ability, as judged by their education, and socio-economic rating. Of the four children whose scores either decreased markedly or were consistently below the average for the group, three children were from homes which were low in the socio-economic scale and had parents with less education than the average for this Berkeley sample. One common factor in the decreasing scores of cases 935 and 764 may be the stimulating effect of affectionate parents on their only children in the early years. These parents with less than average ability could not continue to offer intellec-

TABLE 1. *Means and standard deviations of I.Q.'s for children in the guidance study*

AGE IN YEARS	TEST	GUIDANCE GROUP n	Mean	S.D.	CONTROL GROUP n	Mean	S.D.	TOTAL * n	Mean	S.D.
6	Stanford-Binet	109	118.8	11.6	102	118.3	13.5	211	118.6	12.6
7	Stanford-Binet	104	119.6	14.3	104	117.0	11.8	208	118.3	13.1
8	Stanford Revision Form L	100	119.4	17.4	99	117.9	17.0	199	118.7	17.2
9	Stanford Revision									
	Form L	36	126.1	20.7	54	119.0	19.7			
	Form M	64	117.5	16.7	40	123.4	13.9			
	Total Form L and M							194	120.7	18.2
10	Stanford Revision									
	Form L	65	118.3	18.0	42	123.7	15.0			
	Form M	33	121.6	17.8	50	121.1	19.5			
	Total Form L and M							190	120.8	17.9
12	Stanford Revision									
	Form L	35	114.9	15.3	57	121.4	15.3			
	Form M	34	125.1	16.9	8	126.9	19.4			
13	Form L		....		28	115.4	17.7			
	Form M	29	121.8	20.1		....				
12 or 13	Total Form L and M							191	120.3	17.4
14	Stanford Revision									
	Form L	28	128.2	16.8	23	118.8	17.9			
	Form M	32	117.0	17.6	35	127.6	13.5			
15	Form M	30	124.2	15.8	20	121.5	17.3			
14 or 15	Total Form L and M							168	123.2	16.9
18	Wechsler-Bellevue	80	118.4	12.0	73	117.9	11.0	153	118.2	11.6

* These means and standard deviations were used in computing the sigma scores for individual children.

TABLE 2. *Correlations between test scores given at different ages*

TEST		Age	n	CALIFORNIA PRESCHOOL SCHEDULE I OR II 2	2½	3	3½	4	5	STANFORD-BINET 6	7	STANFORD REVISION FORMS: L 8	L 9	M 9	L 10	M 10	L 12	L (12 or 13)	M (12 or 13)	L 14	M (14 or 15)	W-B 18
California Pre-school Schedule I or II		1¾	234.	.71	.62	.52	.48	.38	.39	.27	.29	.27	.26	.17	.22	.19		.19	.13	.07	.21	.07
		2	113		.71	.69	.60	.46	.32	.47	.46	.43	.45	.29	.37	.37	.49		.26	.21	.34	.31
		2½	114			.73	.64	.57	.46	.37	.38	.37		.32	.36					.26	.31	.24
		3	229				.71	.58	.57	.57	.55	.49	.53	.32	.36	.55		.36	.42	.35	.37	.35
		3½	215					.76	.71	.64	.60	.50	.59	.49	.59	.60		.51	.52	.49	.46	.42
		4	211						.72	.62	.59	.61	.59	.60	.66	.62		.48	.63	.54	.44	.42
										.71	.73	.70	.68	.71	.75	.67		.62	.68	.61	.62	.56
Stanford-Binet		6	214								.82	.77	.80	.67	.71	.76		.74	.65	.67	.70	.61
		7	208									.83	.82	.80	.77	.78		.71	.82	.73	.76	.71
Stanford Revision Forms:	L	8	199										.91	.93	.88	.88	.85	.85	.82	.85	.81	.70
	L	9	90													.90		.90		.87		.76
	M		104												.88				.79		.91	.66
	L	10	107														.87	.87		.85		.70
	M		83																.91		.87	.76
	L	12	92																	.92		.76
	L	(12	120																		.89	.78
	M	or 13)	71																		.88	.84
	L	14	51																			.73
	M	(14 or 15)	117																			.79

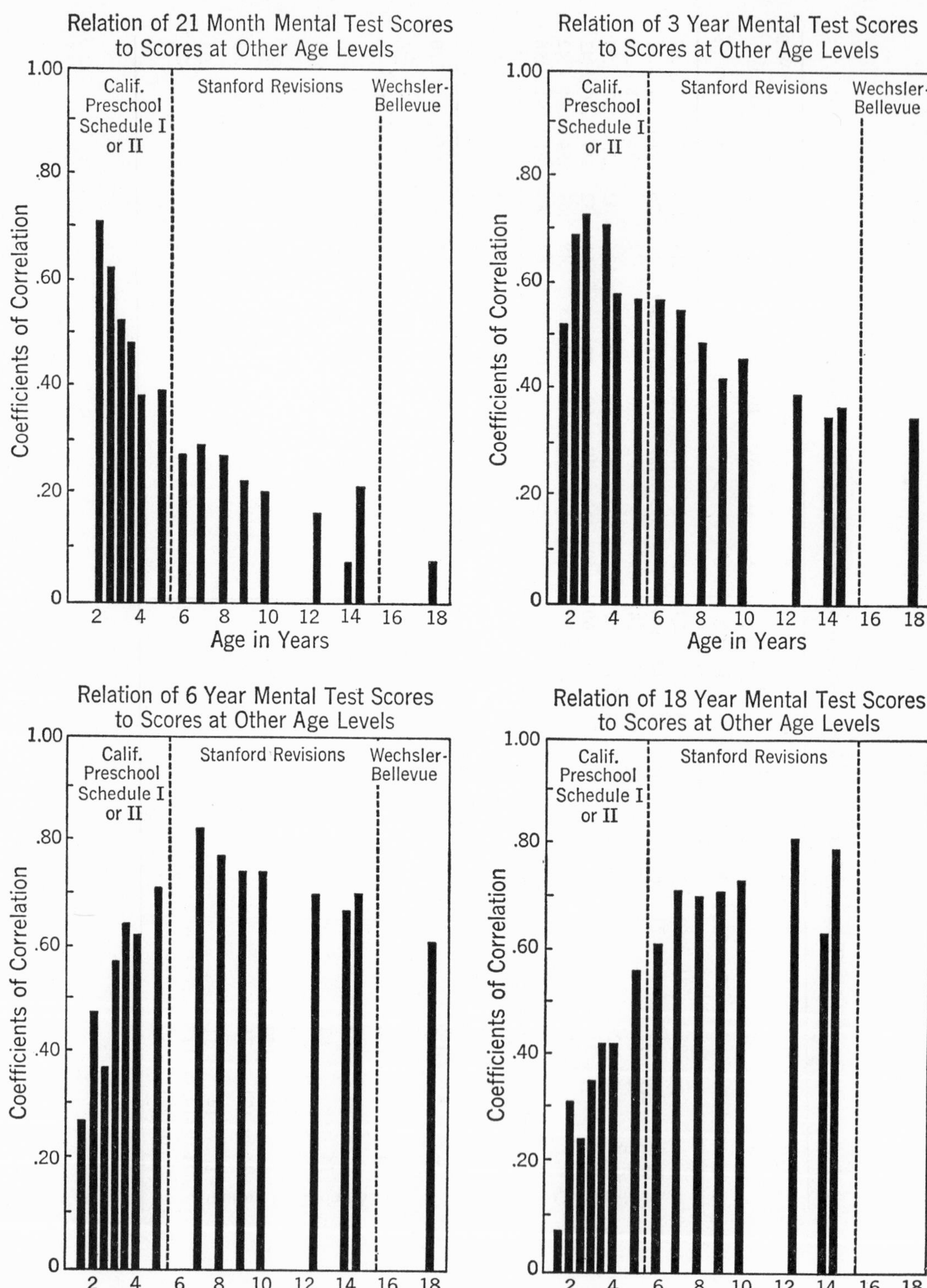

Relation of 21 Month Mental Test Scores to Scores at Other Age Levels
Relation of 3 Year Mental Test Scores to Scores at Other Age Levels
Relation of 6 Year Mental Test Scores to Scores at Other Age Levels
Relation of 18 Year Mental Test Scores to Scores at Other Age Levels
Calif. Preschool Schedule I or II
Stanford Revisions
Wechsler-Bellevue
Coefficients of Correlation
1.00
.80
.60
.40
.20
0
Age in Years
2
4
6
8
10
12
14
16
18

FIGURE 1

tually stimulating environments as their children grew older, nor can the hereditary factors with which they were endowed be discounted. The microcephalic youngster with low scores was the child of parents with above average intelligence. This case should probably be considered the result of an intra-uterine disturbance unrelated to hereditary or post-natal environmental factors.

On the other hand, the four children with increasing or consistently high scores had parents with more than average education (seven of the eight parents were college graduates). Superior hereditary and environmental factors were unquestionably contributing to the mental test records of these children.[2]

Summary and Conclusions

A GROUP of 252 children, who comprise a representative sample of the children living in an urban community, were given mental tests at specified ages between 21 months and 18 years. These data have been analyzed to show the extent of the stability of mental test performance for this age period. The results may be summarized as follows:

1. Mental test constancy for the age period 21 months to 18 years is markedly dependent upon the age at testing and the interval between tests. That is, group prediction is good over short age periods, and mental test scores become increasingly predictive after the pre-school years.
2. Test-retest correlations are as high for children tested on different forms (L or M) of the 1937 Stanford Revision as for children tested on the same form over the same age periods.
3. Distributions of the extent of the changes in I.Q. for the age period 6 to 18 years show that the I.Q.'s of almost 60 percent of the group change 15 or more points; the I.Q.'s of a third of the group change 20 or more points; and the I.Q.'s of 9 percent of the group change 30 or more points. The I.Q.'s of 15 percent of the group change *less* than 10 points of I.Q. The group averages, on the other hand, show a maximum shift in I.Q. over this age period of from 118 to 123.
4. Some individuals show consistent upward or downward trends in I.Q. over a long period, resulting in changes of as much as 4½ sigma or 50 I.Q. points.
5. Inspection of the mental test curves of the individual children included in this paper indicates that changes in mental test scores tend to be in the direction of the family level, as judged by the parents' education and socio-economic status. (Group findings showing an increasing relationship of family status to the children's test scores were presented in an earlier study [Honzik, 1940].)
6. Children whose mental test scores showed the most marked fluctuations had life histories which showed unusual variations with respect to disturbing and stabilizing factors. However, there were other children whose scores remained constant despite highly disturbing experiences.

In conclusion, it should be re-emphasized that, whereas the results for the group suggest mental test stability between 6 and 18 years, the observed fluctuations in the scores of individual children indicate the need for the utmost caution in the predictive use of a single test score, or even two such scores. This finding seems of especial importance since many plans for individual children are made by schools, juvenile courts, and mental hygiene clinics on the basis of a single mental test score. Specifically, it could be noted that a prediction based on a 6-year test would be wrong to the extent of 20 I.Q. points for one out of three children by the age of 18 years, and to the extent of 15 I.Q. points for approximately six out of ten children.

2 A more intensive and extensive study of factors related to the mental test curves of individual children is planned. The findings given here on only 14 children should be considered suggestive.

REFERENCES

BAYLEY, NANCY. Factors influencing the growth of intelligence in young children. *Yearb. Nat. Soc. Stud. Educ.*, 1940, **39**, 49–79.

BAYLEY, NANCY. Consistency and variability in the growth of intelligence from birth to eighteen years. *J. genet. Psychol.*, 1948, **75**, 165–196.

BRADWAY, KATHARINE, P. I. Q. constancy on the Revised Stanford-Binet from the preschool to the junior high school level. *J. genet. Psychol.*, 1944, **65**, 197–217.

GOODENOUGH, F. L. Studies of the 1937 revision of the Stanford-Binet Scale: I. Variability of the I.Q. at successive age levels. *J. educ. Psychol.*, 1942, **33**, 241–251.

GOODENOUGH, F. L., & MAURER, K. M. *The mental growth of children from two to fourteen years.* Minneapolis: Univer. Minnesota Press, 1942, Pp. 130.

HONZIK, MARJORIE P. The constancy of mental test performance during the preschool period. *J. genet. Psychol.*, 1938, **52**, 285–302.

HONZIK, MARJORIE P. Age changes in the relationship between certain environmental variables and children's intelligence. *Yearb. Nat. Soc. Stud. Educ.*, 1940, **39**, 185–205.

HONZIK, MARJORIE P., & JONES, H. E. Mental-physical relationships during the preschool period. *J. exp. Educ.*, 1937, **6**, 139–146.

JAFFA, ADELE S. *The California Preschool Mental Scale (Form A)*. Syllabus Series No. 251. Los Angeles: Univer. California, 1934. Pp. 66.

MACFARLANE, JEAN W. Studies in child guidance: I. Methodology of data collection and organization. *Monogr. Soc. Res. Child Develpm.*, 1938, **3**, 1–254.

MACFARLANE, JEAN W. The guidance study. *Sociometry,* 1939, **2.**

MACFARLANE, JEAN W. Study of personality development. In R. G. Barker, J. S. Kounin, & H. F. Wright, *Child behavior and development: a course of representative studies.* New York: McGraw-Hill, 1943.

TERMAN, L. M., & MERRILL, MAUDE A. *Measuring intelligence.* Boston: Houghton Mifflin, 1937. Pp. 461.

WECHSLER, D. *The measurement of adult intelligence.* Baltimore: Williams & Wilkins, 1944. Pp. 258.

WELCH, F. M. The Berkeley survey: a study of the socio-economic status of four hundred Berkeley families in years 1928–1929. Unpublished manuscript, Univer. of California, Institute of Child Welfare, 1929.

J. M. TANNER

The Regulation of Human Growth*

THE most striking and perhaps most fundamental characteristic of the growth of an animal is that it is self-stabilizing, or, to take another analogy, "target-seeking." Children, no less than rockets, have their trajectories, governed by the control systems of their genetical constitution and powered by energy absorbed from the natural environment. Deflect the child from its natural growth trajectory by acute malnutrition or a sudden lack of a hormone and a restoring force develops so that as soon as the missing food or hormone is supplied again the child catches up towards its original curve. When it gets there it slows down to adjust its path onto the old trajectory once more.

There was a time when this self-correcting and goal-seeking capacity was thought to be a very special property of living things, but now that we understand more about the dynamics of complex systems consisting of many interacting substances we realize that it is not, after all, such an exceptional phenomenon. Many complex systems, even of quite simple lifeless substances, show such internal regulation simply as a property consequent on their organization. Indeed the activity of the rocketeers has made us all too dismally familiar with the general notions of cybernetics and equifinality. Animal geneticists and auxologists, in particular Waddington and his colleagues at Edinburgh (see Waddington, 1957), have in the last decade introduced this approach into their ways of thinking, and amongst developmental psychologists Piaget at least (see Piaget in Tanner & Inhelder, 1960) has endeavoured to do the same. But though new models and a new mathematical symbolism are powerful aids to thought they do not of themselves tell us anything about the mechanisms of regulation that are at work. We know very little as yet about how these intricate growth patterns are organized. It is to this ignorance that I wish to draw your attention.

Let me begin by illustrating how regular is the growth of a healthy, well-nourished child. The upper section of FIGURE 1 shows the measurements of height of a boy in the Harpenden Growth Study taken every six months from age 4 to 10 by a single observer, Mr. R. H. Whitehouse. The circles represent the measurements, and the solid line is a simple mathematical curve of the form $h = a + bt + c \log t$ (where h is height and t age) fitted to them. None of the measurements deviates more than 4 mm from this line, although the experimental error of measuring height may be 3 mm even in experienced hands. The lower section of FIGURE 1 shows the same data plotted as six-monthly velocities; the continuous curve is the first derivative of the fitted curve in the upper section. This child shows a slightly better fit than average, but is by no means exceptional; the curves of many others in the Harpenden Growth Study are very similar. A curve of this form fits height data very well from about six months to around 10 years. If there were any periods of acceleration common to most children during this time, then they would be shown by the deviations of velocity from the fitted curves being mostly positive at that age, and negative before and after. When we average the deviations for 19 boys and 13 girls each fitted from $4\frac{1}{2}$ years to 9 years we find

* REPRINTED with abridgment by permission of the author and the Society for Research in Child Development from *Child Develpm.*, 1963, 34, 817–847.

no age at which these averages depart significantly from zero (see TABLE 1). In other words we can find no satisfactory evidence of a midgrowth or juvenile spurt in height occurring at 6 or 7 to 8.

At adolescence a different curve is needed, but Deming (1957) has shown and we have confirmed that the Gompertz function, which is a sigmoid curve with four parameters, fits just as well at that time as the simple curve does earlier (FIGURE 2).

There is no magic in these curves, which are simply graduation devices. The parameters, so far as we know, represent no particular physiological entities. They could be replaced by other equally well-fitting equations with equally few parameters. But the fact that 16 to 20 measurements taken at intervals of three to six months can be so accurately fitted by curves with only three or four parameters shows that growth, both before and during adolescence, is a very regular process.

TABLE 1. *Deviations from velocity predicted by individual's fitted curve for height measurements, for each year or half-year of age (i.e., "excess velocity" over that predicted)*

A. 19 boys and 13 girls, H.G.S., one measurer; curves fitted for minimum of age 5 to 9 years at half-year intervals, maximum age 3 to 10 years. Mean excess velocity in cm/year.

AGE PERIOD	5–5½	5½–6	6–6½	6½–7
19 BOYS	−0.17	−0.14	0.05	−0.16
13 GIRLS	−0.11	−0.18	−0.15	+0.24 [2]
AGE PERIOD	7–7½	7½–8	8–8½	8½–9
19 BOYS	+0.37 [1]	−0.07	−0.11	+0.04
13 GIRLS	+0.08	+0.05	−0.24	+0.07

[1] S.E. 0.21.
[2] S.E. 0.47.

B. 36 boys and 31 girls, C.S.C.; curves fitted for period six months to 8 years at one-year intervals after 2. Mean excess velocity in cm/year.

AGE PERIOD	4–5	5–6	6–7	7–8
36 BOYS	+0.11	+0.09	−0.12 [1]	+0.08
31 GIRLS	+0.02	−0.05	−0.05	+0.07

[1] S.E. 0.14.

Seasonal effect • A number of children show greater deviations from the fitted curve than does the child in FIGURE 1, but when they are investigated most of the deviations turn out to be regular, as in FIGURE 3. The fluctuations of velocity from 6½ onwards represent the effect that season of the year has on growth in height of many, but not all, children. (Small and irregular six-monthly fluctuations could be caused by measuring error: a low value on one occasion causing a low velocity, followed by a compensatory high one.) In FIGURE 3 deviations from the distance curve amount to 5 mm above and below it and the velocity of April to October growth averages no less than 1.6 cm/yr more than growth from October to April. But this seasonal rhythm is only superimposed on the basic regularity. In fact a small seasonal effect can be seen also in FIGURE 1, where the average May to November growth rate is 0.2 cm/yr more than the rate from November to May.

The cause of the seasonal effect is not known. Presumably the endocrine system is affected by light or temperature or some other climatic or just possibly some nutritional factor. The most likely endocrine mediators are probably the thyroid and the adrenal cortex, with thyroxine possibly accelerating growth and increased cortisol secretion possibly decelerating. We have no sure evidence however that a seasonal change in rate of secretion of either of these hormones takes place in man. Growth hormone could be another possibility and perhaps insulin a fourth. All we can say for certain is that there are marked individual differences in this response to seasonal change.

Illness • This is a simple example of the regulation of growth. Similar individual differences in the ability to regulate growth seem to occur in response to illness. We have fitted

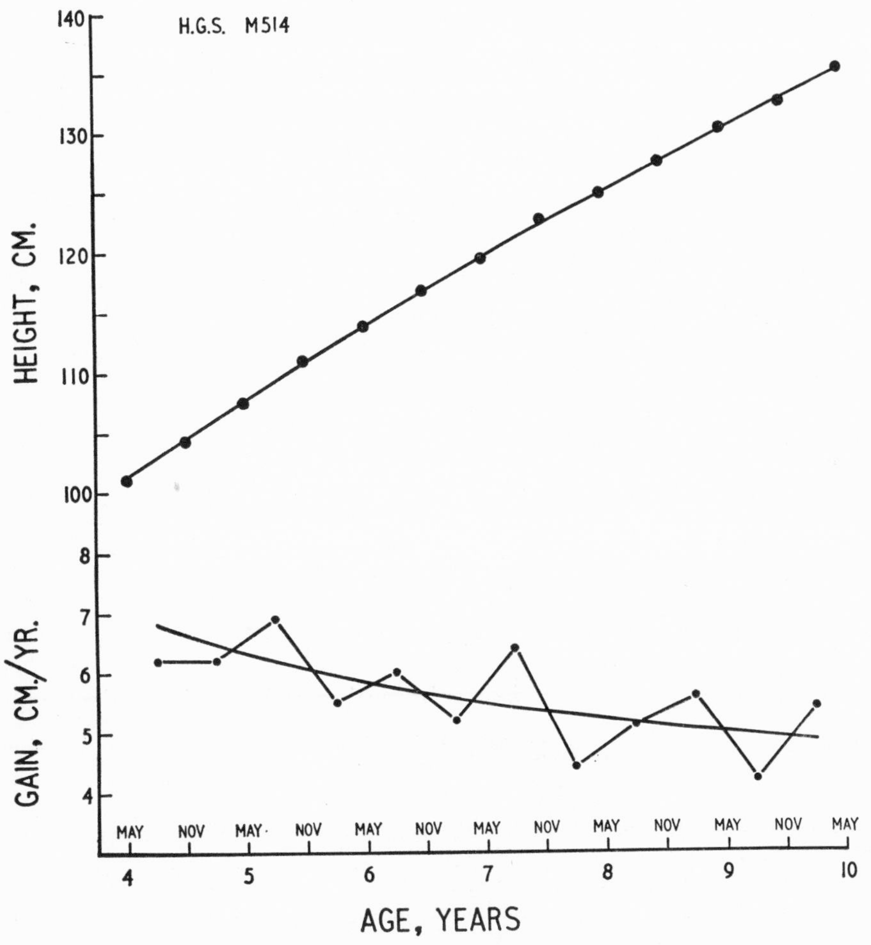

FIGURE 1

Growth of a boy in the Harpenden Growth Study measured every six months by R. H. Whitehouse.

Above: "distance" plot of height achieved at each age.

Below: velocity plot of average velocities each six months.

Solid lines: above, curve of form $Height = a + bt + c \log t$ ($t =$ age) fitted to individual's height-achieved points; below, the derivative of the fitted curve. (From Tanner, in F. Gross (Ed.), *Protein metabolism*. Berlin: Springer, 1962.)

curves to six-monthly height measurements of children who have suffered relatively minor illness, but omitted the first measurement following the illness. We then tested whether the post-illness measurement was significantly below the fitted non-illness curve. In the great majority of cases it was not; either the illness had had no effect or the catch-up had been complete within a few months. But in a few children the post-illness point was depressed, and these children were not apparently any sicker than the others, nor were they apparently eating less or behaving in any obviously different way in the uniform environment of the children's home where all were resident. Some children seem to be less

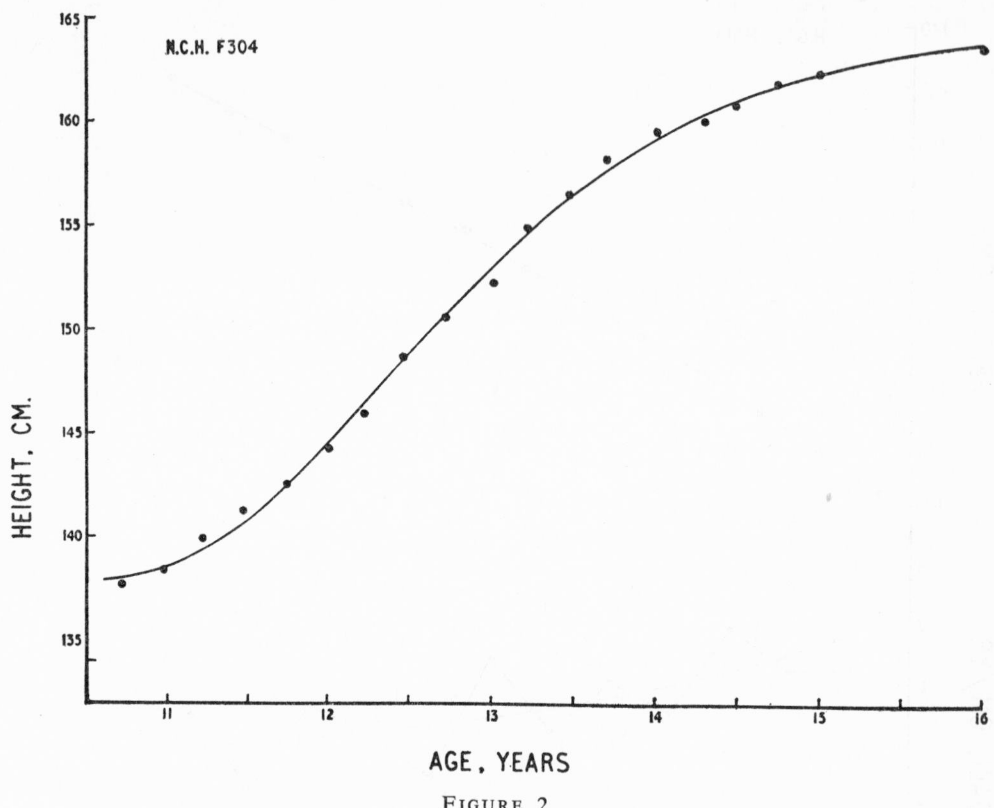

FIGURE 2

Growth of a girl in the Harpenden Growth Study measured at three-monthly intervals during adolescence by R. H. Whitehouse.

"Distance" plot of height achieved at each age.

Solid line: Gompertz curve fitted by maximum likelihood to individual's height-achieved points.

well regulated, or canalized, in Waddington's terminology, than others.

CATCH-UP GROWTH

More severe diseases, or acute malnutrition, cause a retardation in growth. In FIGURES 4 and 5 two instances of this are illustrated; three are from studies recently published with my paediatric colleagues Professor Prader and Dr. von Harnack (Prader, Tanner, & von Harnack, 1963). In each case a period of what we call catch-up growth follows restoration of the child's physiological state towards normal.

FIGURE 4 shows the effect on growth of a young child of two periods in which food intake was much reduced for psychological reasons. On the left is the curve of body length at successive ages ("distance" curve) and on the right are the average rates of growth at successive periods, plotted against the 50th percentile lines for length growth velocity (for details see Prader *et al.*, 1963). The velocity during each period of catch-up reached more than twice the average velocity for the chronological age; it was nearly twice average for the skeletal age, which was retarded in parallel with the retardation in length and caught up as the length caught up. The catch-up is apparently complete in that the child is quite normal in both length and velocity of length growth by age 5.

FIGURE 5 concerns a boy who was hypothyroid from his seventh year or before up to the age of 12 years, when thyroid administration was begun. In early childhood height

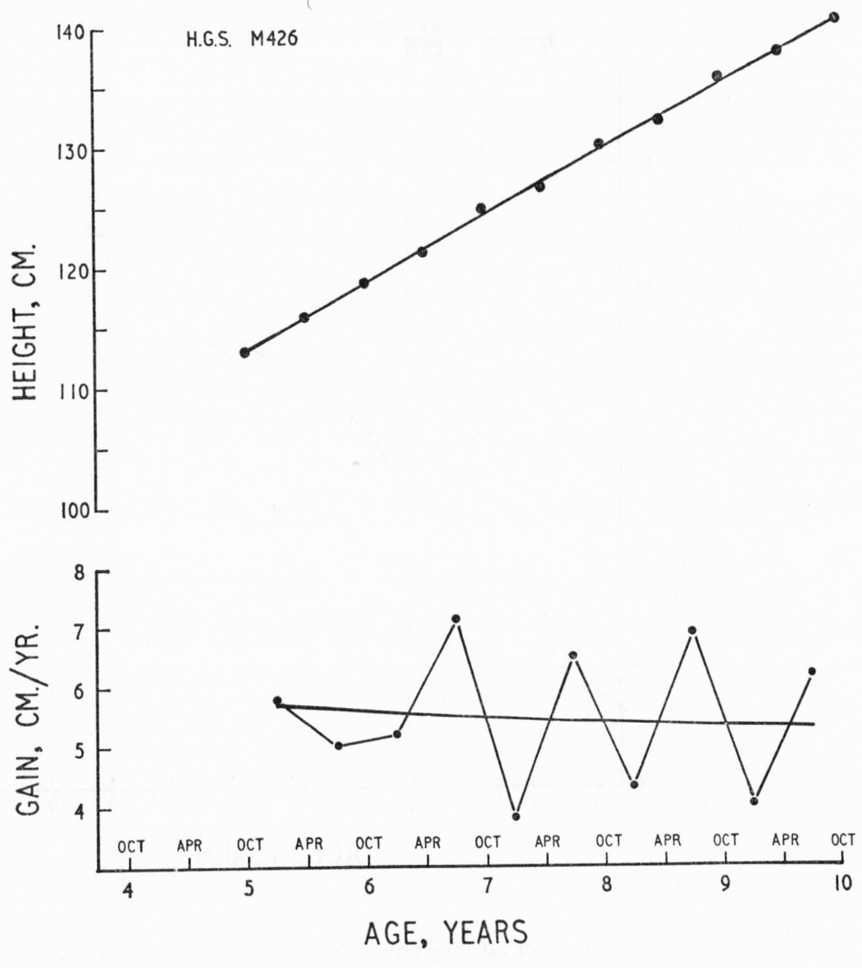

FIGURE 3

Growth of a boy in the Harpenden Growth Study measured every six months by R. H. Whitehouse.

Above: "distance" plot of height achieved at each age.

Below: velocity plot of average velocities each six months.

Solid lines: above, curve of form *Height* $= a + bt + c \log t$ ($t =$ age) fitted to individual's height-achieved points; below, the derivative of the fitted curve. Note the regular seasonal variation, Apr–Oct having a greater velocity than Oct–Apr. (From Tanner, in F. Gross (Ed.), *Protein metabolism*. Berlin: Springer, 1962.)

velocity had been average, but from 7 to 10 it dropped and from 10 to 12 actually became zero. During the first eight months after thyroid hormone was given the height velocity reached over twice average for chronological age. The boy's growth soon moved back to the normal pattern and he underwent an adolescent growth spurt which was average in intensity and took place at the nearly average skeletal age of 14 years. His chronological age was nearer 16, however. It seems that some of the years of hypothyroid arrest had been eliminated from his biological calendar so that he was still two years behind, but by 20, when his skeletal maturation was practically complete, he had caught up (presumably completely) in height.

. . .

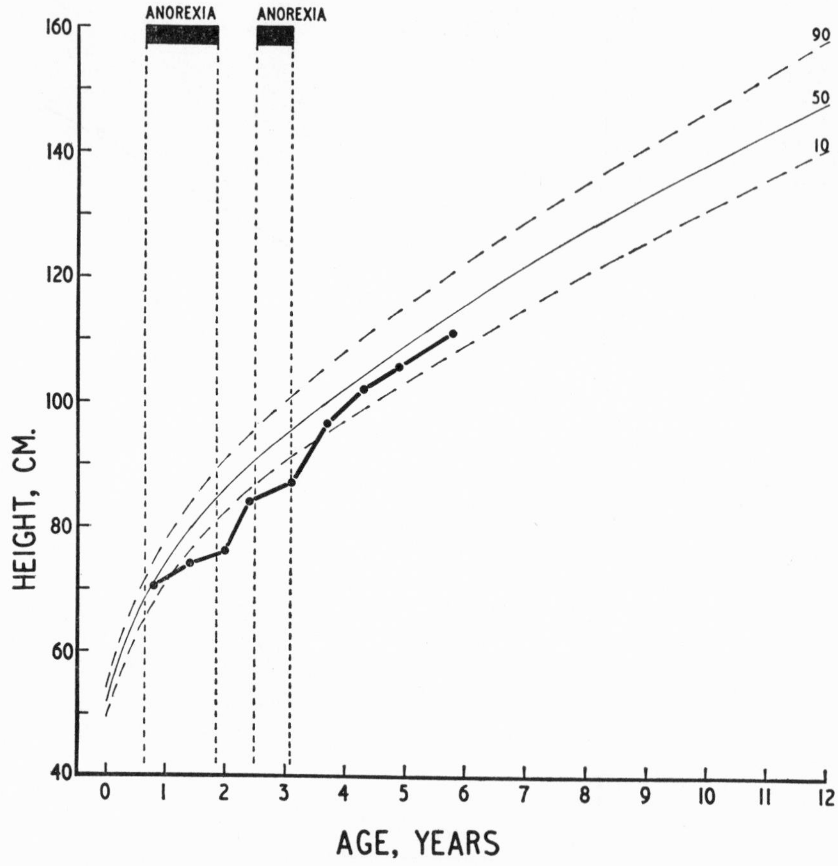

FIGURE 4A

Two periods of catch-up growth following episodes of anorexia nervosa in a young child. For explanation of charts see text. (From Prader, Tanner, & von Harnack, 1963.)

Birth catch-up • This capacity to catch up in growth seems to be used normally around the time of birth in man. There is evidence that the growth rate of the foetus, at least in weight, slows down during the last four weeks of pregnancy, as illustrated in FIGURE 6. The prenatal values are calculated from McKeown and Record's (1952) data on birth weights of live children born after a shorter gestation than average. In using them we are assuming that these early-delivered children's weights are the same as the weights of foetuses of the same age as yet still in the uterus; in other words, that amongst healthy singletons the early-born are not specially big or small children for their gestational age. Such an assumption may be challenged. But there is good evidence also of a catch-up occurring after birth, particularly in small babies. FIGURE 7, taken from the Ministry of Health (1959) partially longitudinal survey of some seventeen thousand babies, shows this well. Babies below the average weight gained more than the others, thus reducing the range of weight in the whole group. The catch-up finishes by about five months in this data and is distinctly more marked in boys than in girls (see Ministry of Health, 1959, Fig. III). Thus there is a negative correlation between birth weight and weight gain from birth to

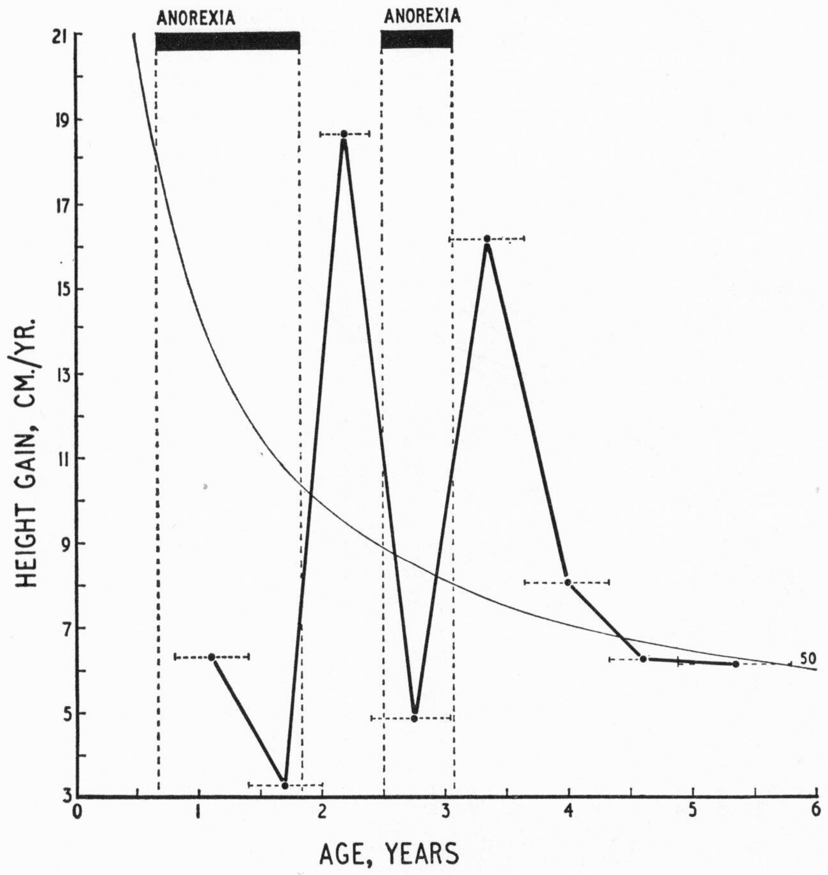

FIGURE 4B

three months, or from birth to six months of the order of about −0.15 (Thompson, 1955). The negative correlation is still present, though lower, by the time one year is reached. Norval, Kennedy, and Berkson (1951) give figures for the correlation of birth weight with the birth-to-one-year increment of −0.15 in boys and −0.05 in girls. The catch-up occurs also in length, indeed, probably to a greater extent than in weight. Simmons and Todd (1938) found it in the longitudinal data of the Brush Foundation and in 1938 remarked that

of particular interest are the negative coefficients between birth length and the birth to one year increment in length (boys −0.46, girls −0.01) and of the three month length with the three month to one year increment in length (boys −0.20, girls −0.05). It appears that during the first post-natal year our short babies gain in length more than our long babies and that this reversal occurs to a greater extent in the male than in the female.

Thompson (1956) found correlations of the order of −0.4 in both sexes between birth length and the length increment from birth to six months in some 4,500 babies in Edinburgh. By one year the correlation had somewhat dropped, but was still appreciable (average correlation −0.35).

The catch-up mechanism at birth is of much genetical importance. It seems to be the chief means by which variability in adult size is maintained in the population. Most of

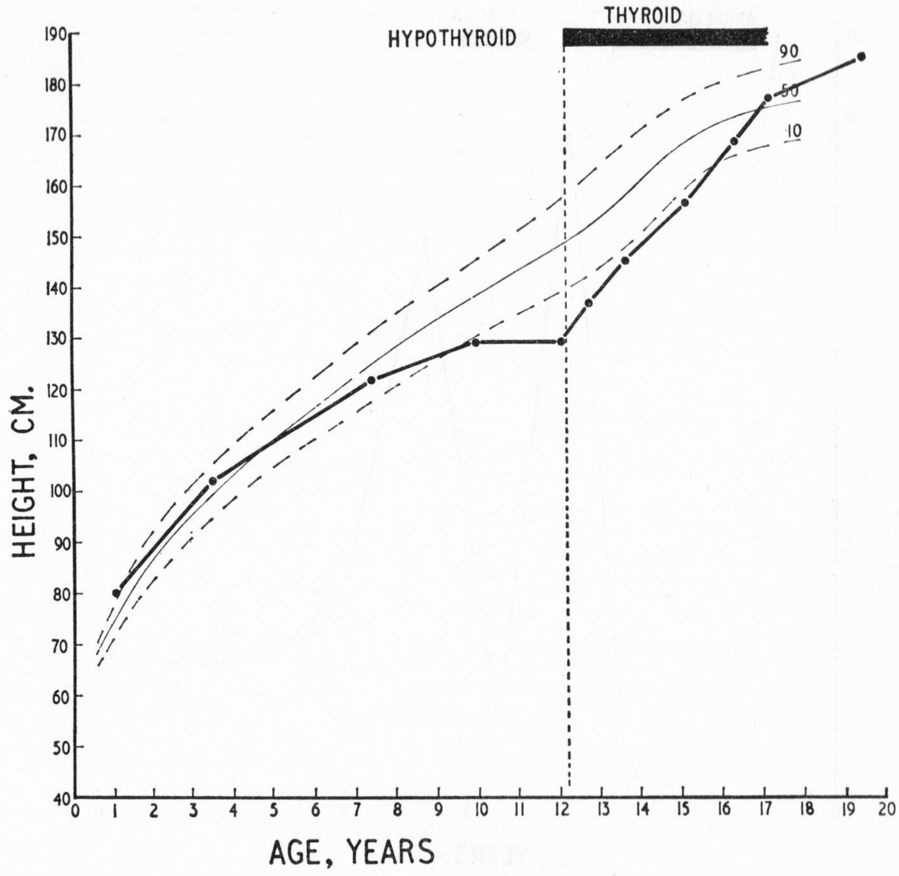

FIGURE 5A

Catch-up in a hypothyroid boy following treatment at 12 years old. For explanation of charts see text. (From Prader, Tanner, & von Harnack, 1963.)

the adult size variability is established by two years after birth, since by then the individual's adult size is to a large extent fixed (presuming adequate environmental conditions). The correlation coefficient between length of child at 2 years and length of the same child when adult, is nearly 0.8; it approaches 0.7 even at age 1. (Genetical differences in the time and intensity of the adolescent spurt account for the remainder of the adult variability.) Thus there would be many genetically large children developing in the uteri of small mothers and constituting a problem at the time of birth unless selection for assortative mating were very strong, a solution which would produce other genetically undesirable effects. The problem is solved by birth size being controlled almost entirely by uterine factors (Penrose, 1961), the correlation of birth length and adult length being only about 0.2. The catch-up after birth does the rest. Note that this is a true regulatory problem, for the form of FIGURE 7 makes it clear that only some of the small babies catch up. A proportion of them need little or no catch-up to reach and continue on their natural growth curves since they are genetically small; it is those aimed, so to speak, at largeness, who catch up to their proper track. The same phenomenon appears particularly clearly in cattle, where the size at birth of a calf born to a small-breed mother mated with a large-

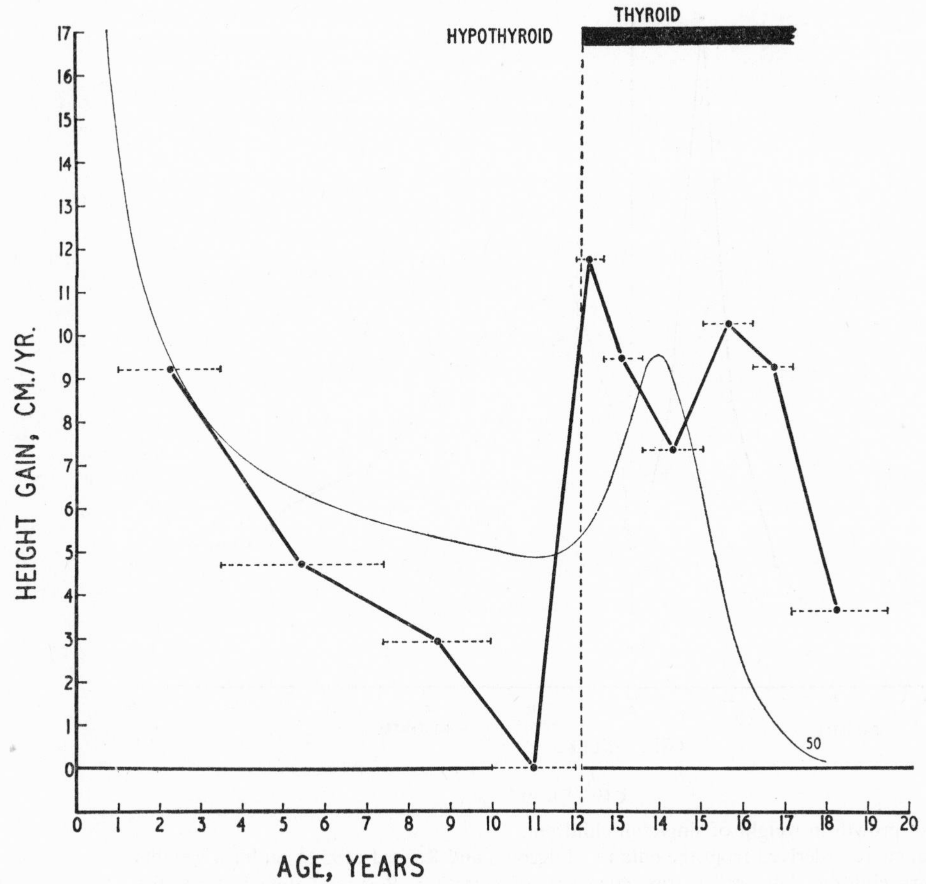

FIGURE 5B

breed father is considerably smaller than a calf of a large-breed mother and small-breed father. The two calves grow at different rates after birth so that by the time adult size is reached there is no longer any difference (Dickinson, 1960).

CONTROL OF CATCH-UP

In all the examples of catch-up growth the velocity of growth was rapid at first, became less as the child approached what we can reasonably assume was its pre-illness curve, and finally settled down to a normal value as the child regained the trajectory of his natural curve. A major problem that remains quite unsolved at present is the manner in which the organism knows when to stop the catch-up phase.

During a typical catch-up the whole organism grows rapidly and in at least approximately its proportionate manner. . . . It is difficult (though not impossible) to see how this could happen unless the stimulus to catch up is a systemic one circulating with the blood to all parts of the body. In everything that follows it must be remembered that we are dealing with growth in *size* and not in *shape*. So far as our present data goes shape in the human is little affected by a slow-down and subsequent catch-up of growth. Differential effects of malnutrition on limbs and trunk, for example, have never been proved to occur, though they have been suggested by analogy with some results on cattle. Growth in shape must clearly be regulated by peripheral mechanisms rather than the

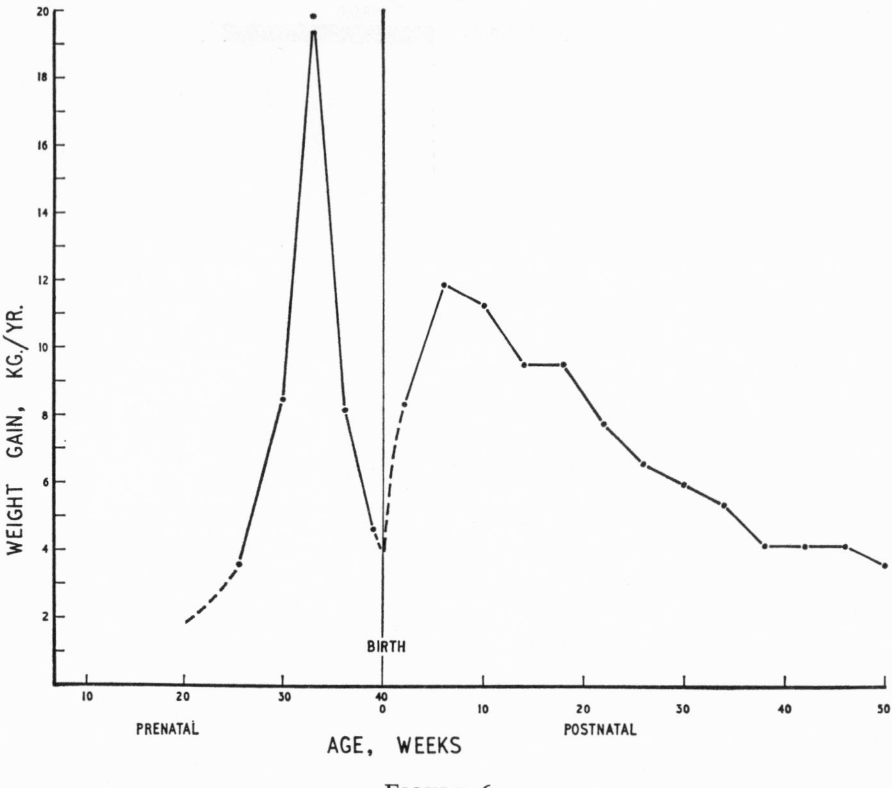

FIGURE 6

Velocity of growth in weight of singleton children.

Prenatal curve is derived from the data of McKeown and Record (1952) on birth weights of live-born children delivered before 40 weeks of gestation. Postnatal data is from the Ministry of Health (1959) mixed longitudinal data (their table VII).

Dotted line indicates the estimate of velocity immediately before and after birth, showing catch-up.

central mechanism for size postulated here.

We do not know what the catch-up stimulus is: growth hormone alone is not it, for one of the features of the catch-up is that skeletal maturity, retarded along with size, catches up also. Human growth hormone does not cause an increase in skeletal maturity when administered to hypophysectomized children (at least to those with bone ages of about 12), although it causes growth. Given to bone-age-delayed, insulin-sensitive dwarfs however (with bone ages of 4 to 10), it does cause advancement in bone age along with growth (personal observations). These dwarfs have apparently normal functioning of their ACTH and TSH mechanisms, and we must attribute the bone age result to an increase in one of these secretions (of a degree not detectable on present tests), or else to an unknown pituitary factor. We cannot identify ACTH with the catch-up factor because it does not cause growth in preadolescent children; indeed, in dwarfed children with evidence of ACTH deficiency, administration of ACTH to restore normal 17-hydroxycorticoid values does not result in either growth or skeletal age catch-up (Tanner & Clayton, unpublished). Thyroid hormone might possibly be the catch-up stimulus, but we cannot detect any increase in protein-bound iodine during growth hormone-dependent catch-up, and administration of thyroid causes only a

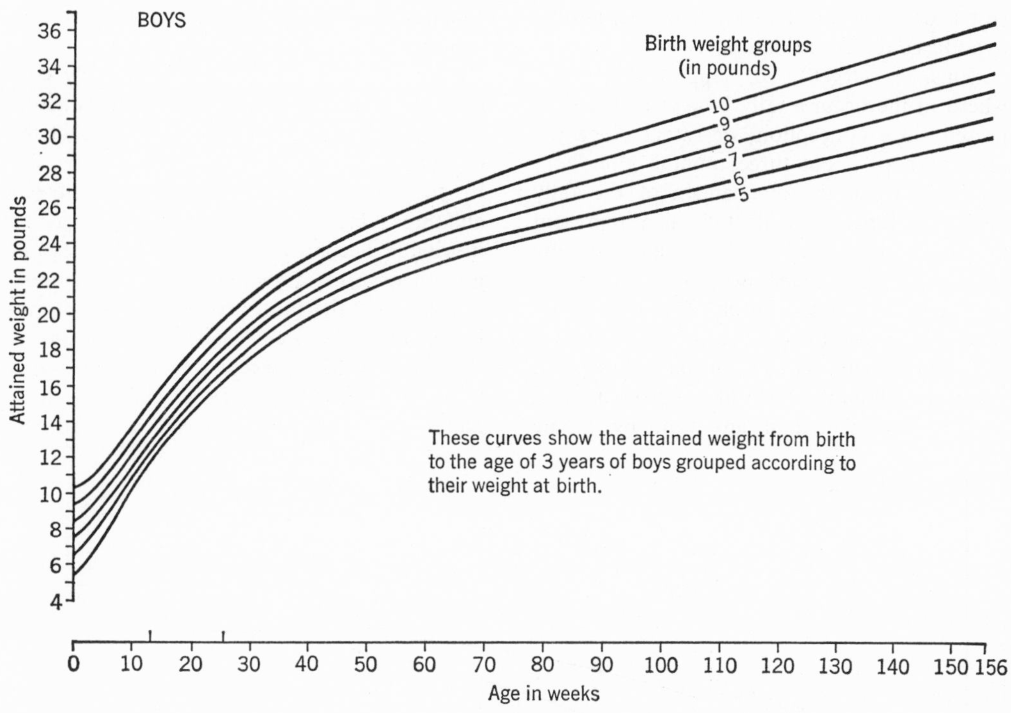

FIGURE 7

Attained weight from birth to age 3 of boys grouped according to birth weight. (From Ministry of Health, 1959.)

transient effect on growth unless there is a definite thyroid deficiency. On the whole it seems more likely that the catch-up factor is not a single substance, but a balanced response involving several hormones, all dependent on the pituitary.

The factor or factors must be released in response to a signal, and it seems likely that this signal acts either on the brain or the pituitary since its mode of operation is to cause a whole-body catch-up in response to a whole-body delay. Lack of growth of a limb, as in poliomyelitis, or hypertrophy of a limb, as in arterio-venous aneurysm, does not cause any catch-up or slow-down of the body as a whole (though in certain organs, such as the liver and kidney, local factors are additionally operative, causing hypertrophy of the corresponding organ alone following removal or disease of part of it).

The characteristics of catch-up require, it seems to me, that this signal represents the degree of mis-match between the actual size (or, for the sake of clarity, actual height) of the organism and the size (or height) required at that age by the hypothetical built-in or "target" growth curve. As the target curve is approached, the mis-match diminishes and the catch-up slows down. For the mis-match to be read both actual size and target size must somehow be represented in the organism. At present we do not know how either representation is made. It is possible that the mis-match is a peripheral phenomenon and occurs in all cells in all tissues, the cells themselves each carrying the code for their own maturity. The catch-up in treated hypothyroidism might indeed be explicable on this basis. But it seems an unlikely hypothesis for explaining most catch-ups and for explaining the normal control of growth in size, which is our ultimate objective. I should like to suggest a possible and, I believe, more plausible hypothesis for investigation.

Consider "target" size. Suppose that somewhere in the brain a tally is kept of the time passed since conception, or rather since the age (perhaps about three months after conception), when the mechanism of the tally begins to function. This tally can represent the target curve, for both are fundamentally series of signals made against a continuing time base. Suppose, purely for simplicity's sake, that the tally consists of a steady increase in the amount of a substance in certain nerve cells; then the form of the growth curve may be represented at any time by (some function of) the concentration of this substance (see FIGURE 8).

Now as to actual size—it is scarcely conceivable that the body can represent its actual extension in space. Suppose, instead, that the organism measures its actual height or size by the concentration of some form of circulating substance produced by cells as an inevitable accompaniment to the process of growth or protein synthesis. In this supposition I follow the most provocative and stimulating ideas of Paul Weiss (see Weiss & Kavanau, 1957), except that he envisages these substances—which he calls anti-templates—as numerous, tissue-specific, and act-

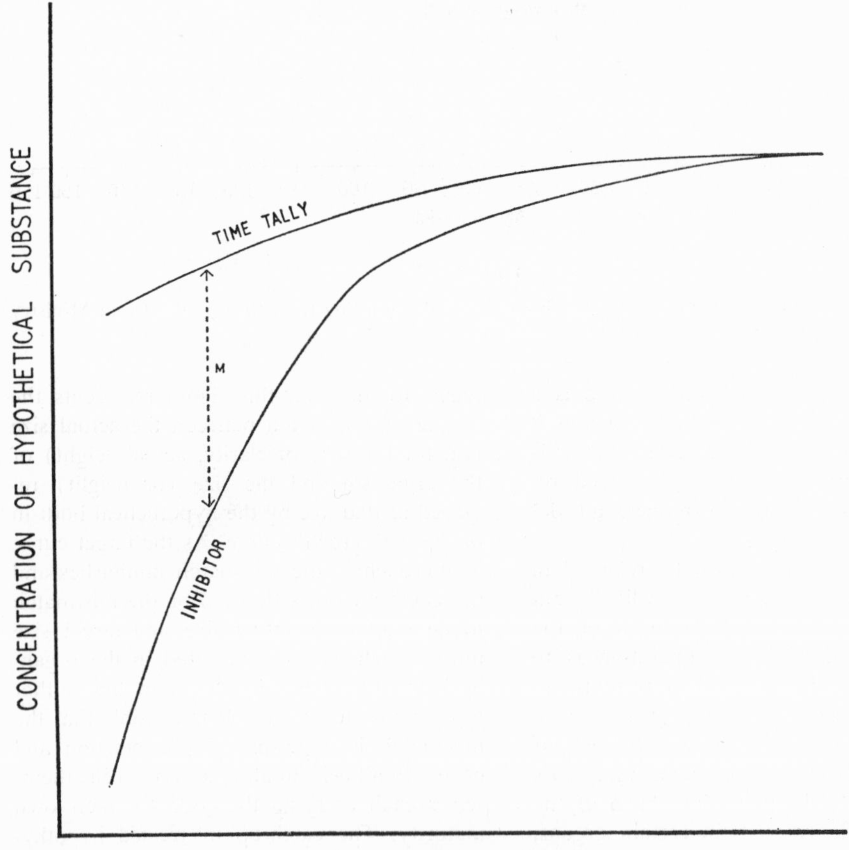

FIGURE 8

Hypothetical relations underlying supposed growth-controlling agents (see text). The quantity *m* represents the mis-match signal.

ing directly on peripheral cells, whereas I prefer to think primarily of a single substance acting at the brain level. In the simplest model then, the concentration of this substance (which we will call the "inhibitor") would be proportional to the size of the organism. Its actual concentration can be measured against the concentration expected on the basis of the time tally and the discrepancy can be used as the mis-match signal for release of the growth-stimulating factor. If, for simplicity's sake, we suppose that the time tally consists of a steady increase in the number of receptive sites for the growth-inhibitor substance, then the mis-match signal would consist of the number of unoccupied sites.

The tally need not, of course, represent clock time; on the contrary, it will represent the maturation rate for each individual organism. The rate of tally, and rate of change of that rate, will be an individual, presumably inherited characteristic.

The growth inhibitors are purely hypothetical substances. Neither their origin nor their site of action is known. Weiss supposes that each type of tissue produces inhibitors as it grows and that these diffuse out into the blood and inhibit the growth of the same tissue elsewhere in the body by local action at the cellular level. This is doubtless a valid model for lower animals. It may also be valid for certain aspects of shape in mammals. One might even suppose, at least a priori, that the general correspondence of development throughout the whole body of a given individual of a tissue such as muscle or bone (see Tanner, 1964) might be brought about in this way. But in the control of mammalian growth, certainly in size and probably even in bone and muscle, it seems more likely that the inhibitors act centrally. Furthermore it seems unlikely that many tissues produce tissue-specific inhibitors (though the kidney and liver may). Clearly the limbs contribute nothing important, for children with poliomyelitis, or even limbs entirely missing, grow perfectly normally in the rest of their bodies: they do not hypertrophy due to lack of inhibitors. Thus bone muscle and fat do not seem to be the source of inhibitor production. The liver is the obvious choice, but it is very difficult to provide evidence for this since damage to the liver diminishes the ability to metabolize substances essential for growth and hence may result in a slowing down of growth, even if inhibitor production is also diminished. Teng, Daeschner, Singleton, Rosenberg, Cole, Hill, & Brennan (1961) have reported that in childhood hepatomas growth slows down and on their removal a catch-up occurs. Though it is not the most obvious and likely explanation, the hepatoma *could* have been producing excess inhibitors. A case has recently been reported by Davis (1962) of a girl who had a liver disorder of unknown origin and suffered from lipodystrophy and much accelerated growth. This could be interpreted as lack of inhibitor, but of course other explanations are also available. The kidney seems an unlikely but possible site, and the thymus and lymph nodes are an attractive possibility on immunological grounds, but thymectomized mice in fact grow less and not more than normal.

We may reasonably think that the same mechanism underlies the form of the normal velocity curve of growth, wherein a baby grows faster than a 9-year old. Suppose, again for simplicity, that the tally accumulates at a constantly decreasing rate as illustrated in FIGURE 8. Suppose also that the inhibitors develop in proportion to the sites of synthesis used up in the cells as they pack in more protein, each turn of the RNA wheel, as it were throwing off a molecule of inhibitor. Then the inhibitor concentration would rise in an exponential fashion, fast at first and slowly later. The mis-match (m) between these two concentrations would be large at first and decrease after the manner of the growth velocity curve. In this simple model the concentration of growth-stimulating factor is directly proportional to the mis-match, and the velocity of catch-up is supposed to be directly proportional to the concentration of growth-stimulating factor. (Really one or other of these relationships might well be logarithmic.)

As FIGURE 9 shows, the model represents

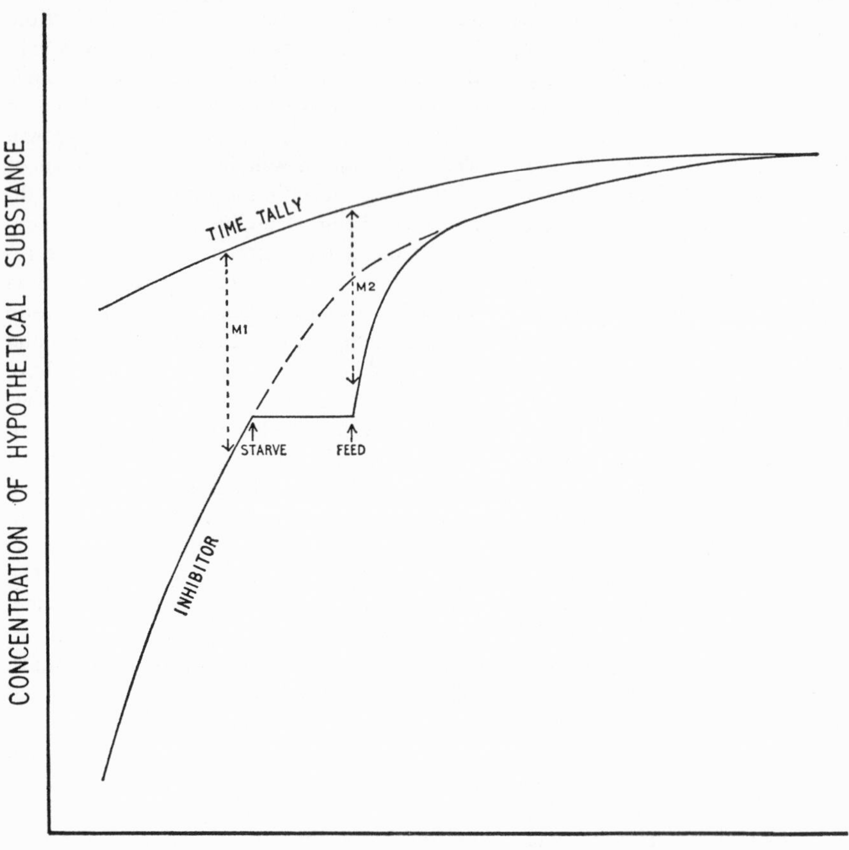

FIGURE 9

Velocity expected in catch-up growth, assuming control system of FIGURE 8. Catch-up velocity is proportional to the mis-match m_2, which is greater than the mis-match when starvation began and equal to the mis-match at an earlier age, as represented by $m_1 = m_2$.

the chief feature of catch-up correctly. The catch-up velocity seems usually to be not only greater than the velocity expected at the age of catch-up, but also greater than the velocity expected at the age at which growth stopped (see Prader *et al.*, 1963). The model predicts that the mis-match and hence the catch-up velocity will be the velocity appropriate to a younger age than this, how much younger depending on the relative curvatures of the time tally and inhibitor lines. The model also predicts that catch-up growth, following a given time of growth arrest, will be more intense at young ages than at older ones. This is generally thought to be the case, although our own data give no direct evidence for it.

We should not press such a crude model too far, but one cannot help noticing that the relation between the time tally curve and the inhibitor curve resembles that between the growth of the central nervous system and the growth of the rest of the body. Perhaps one of the reasons that the central nervous system develops ahead of the remainder of most of the body is that the time tally is located there. It would be logical if the earliest developing part of the organism carried the programme for the growth of the remainder.

Of course, this model may be quite wrong and, if not quite wrong, is certainly much oversimplified. The true situation is without doubt more complex; for example, we have assumed that the tally continues unaltered, even under circumstances which stop the rest of the organism from growing altogether. This is somewhat unrealistic. Catch-up is probably incomplete if the period of growth arrest by starvation, say, is prolonged. To explain this we may assume that the time tally is somewhat affected by the starvation, though to a much lesser extent than the rest of the body. It may fail to resume its old rate at refeeding, or it may return to its old rate but without a catch-up. Alternatively we can assume that catch-up depends not only on mis-match but also on the time tally's velocity (or its integral or total amount).

On purely cybernetical grounds we may expect at least two complications. To combat sluggishness in the response to the mis-match (under normal conditions) it is likely that the rate of change of the mis-match, rather than its absolute amount, would be taken as the signal for release of the growth-stimulating factor. Secondly we may expect multiple feedback pathways from tissues to centre, rather than a single feedback, in order to ensure stability of the system. This is what cyberneticists call reliability through redundancy, and we may expect it to complicate our physiological analysis here as elsewhere in analyses of feedback in the body.

We have so far ignored the existence of the adolescent spurt and dealt with growth as though it gradually ceased at the end of its exponential preadolescent curve, as it does in fishes and reptiles. In primates, particularly, there is a secondary growth system superimposed on this basic one, causing a new increase of growth rate to occur just when the impetus of the basic system is nearing its end. This secondary system, be it noted, is not a necessary condition for growth to cease, even in man. Children who suffer gonadal or gonadotrophic failure at adolescence may not close their epiphyses, but their growth gradually ceases all the same (see e.g., cases C X and C XII of Bayer & Bayley, 1959). Rats never close their epiphyses and reptiles do not have epiphyses to close. Evidently it is the dwindling of the mis-match signal which causes growth to slow down; finally the signal becomes vanishingly small, and the organism remains in a steady state of equilibrium. There is no reason to suppose that the adolescent growth cycle is organized in a different manner from the basic cycle, but it uses different substances. Its time tally and its inhibitors must be distinct from those of the basic cycle, just as its growth-stimulating factor is also distinct. But it is linked to the basic cycle in that its beginning occurs when the basic cycle has reached a certain point in its evolution.

Linkages such as these occur between many systems during growth and we must try to form some idea of how they may work. We know that adolescence is initiated when a restraining influence from the hypothalamus on the pituitary is removed. We think that under normal circumstances certain cells in the hypothalamus mature and that when they reach a certain stage of maturity they cease sending inhibitory impulses to the pituitary. This may be because they themselves no longer respond to the small amount of sex hormones or similar substances thought to be circulating in the blood even before puberty. Control over the hypothalamic cells is only reasserted when sex hormone levels rise much higher following adolescence (see Werff ten Bosch, 1959). It is tempting to identify the hypothalamus as the site of the time tally. Harris and Jacobsohn (1952) showed that when the pituitary gland of an adult rat was replaced by grafted pituitaries of newborn rats of the same strain, these newborn pituitaries assumed adult function and secreted gonadotrophins as soon as the vascular connection of the graft was complete. This is long before the donor rat would have reached puberty. It is therefore the hypothalamus which carries the information as to maturity.

. . .

Simple linkage alone does not seem able to account for the postponement of puberty after starvation. Though the facts here may be a little questionable, it seems that if a period of starvation occurs at the normal time of puberty, puberty is delayed, and that on refeeding puberty does not occur at once (as demanded by the simple linkage model), but only after a certain amount of catch-up growth has occurred. We could account for this by assuming that the switch mechanism is dependent not only on the velocity of the tally reaching a critical value *L*, but also on the mis-match reaching a certain value m_1. (See FIGURE 10.) In this case ordinary catch-up would occur until the mis-match reached m_2, equal to m_1. As the scanty experimental and clinical data make it seem probable that in fact puberty occurs before the catch-up velocity has actually fallen the whole way to the usual preadolescent velocity, we may think that the relationships are quantitative and that a further lowering of the tally velocity after *L* is passed makes possible a higher mis-match, the combination of the two being the quantity required to reach a threshold value. A two-factor linkage such as this seems more typical of events in growth than a single-factor one, in that it permits greater variability amongst a number of in-

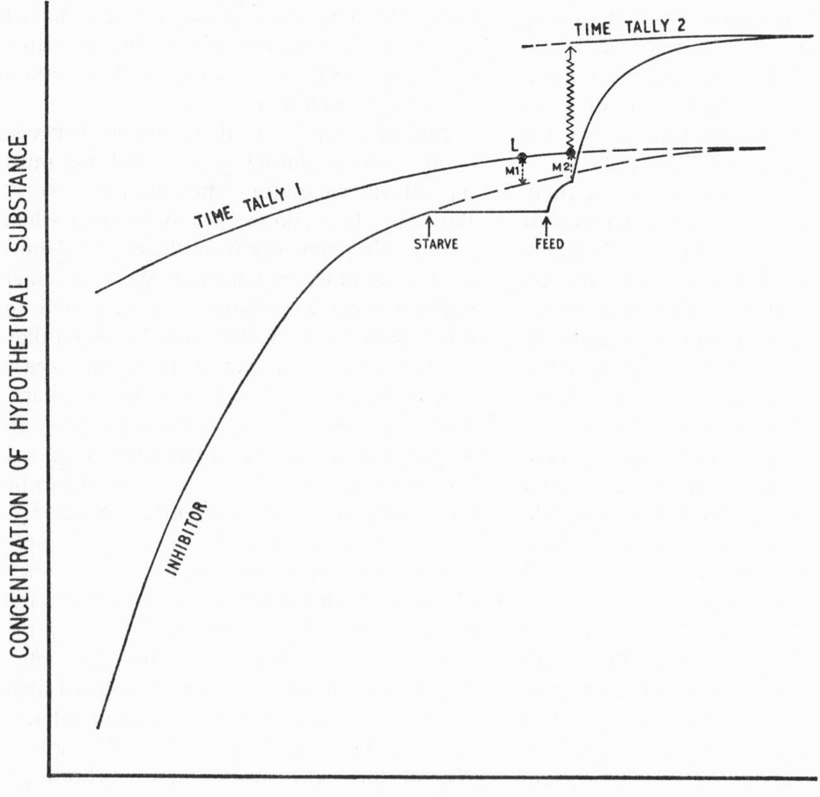

FIGURE 10

Hypothetical linkage of two systems under conditions of temporary starvation. The distances marked m_1 and m_2 are supposed equal. See text.

dividuals. In this sense it is a "looser" coupling. Actually the recent results of McCance (1962) on starvation and refeeding in pigs agrees with a fairly simple direct linkage, for puberty occurred in the starved and then fed pigs much before the body had caught up to its usual puberty size.

The model must be capable of explaining the disorder of precocious puberty. In some cases pubertal changes occur early, at a nearly normal size for chronological age; the children then finish their growth as very small adults. Essentially the same can be brought about in rats by destruction of an area in the hypothalamus; in an experiment of Donovan and Werff ten Bosch (1959), vaginal opening occurred at 33 days instead of 40, but the growth in body size was not accelerated. In this case we may suppose that *L* has been drastically moved back along the tally curve, that is, that the linkage takes place at a higher tally velocity than normal. Physiologically, it may be that the inhibitory impulses to the pituitary are steadily diminishing as the velocity of the time tally diminishes (i.e., as the maturity of the cells increases). If some of the inhibitory cells are destroyed, then the total effective inhibition diminishes, and the threshold is reached at an earlier point on the tally curve.

Other cases occur in which the child grows excessively fast from an early age, at first without any signs of puberty. He reaches puberty early however—very early as regards chronological age and somewhat early as regards size. The simplest supposition about the growth regulation of such a child is that the form of the tally curve is distorted so that its velocity is at first abnormally large. This would give rise to an abnormally large mismatch at the beginning of growth and hence to the accelerated growth. The point *L* would occur early in chronological time, if it reflects the same critical velocity as usual in the time tally. In this form of precocious puberty, therefore, puberty would occur early without any shift in time tally threshold. The disorder could equally be explained by underproduction of inhibitors, except that then, if we follow the linkage hypothesis above, we would not expect to get puberty till after the normal time and at a very large size.

DISORDERS OF REGULATION

Though the regulatory system normally acts with considerable precision, the syndrome of precocious puberty shows that it can sometimes become disordered. A most striking example of experimentally produced disturbance has been given by the work of Kennedy, McCance, and Widdowson in rats. Malnutrition was produced in rats from birth to 21 days by taking two litters born on the same day and redistributing the young so that one mother nursed only three rats and the other mother nursed twelve to fifteen. By 21 days the rats of the three-rat litters weighed two to three times as much as those of the twelve-rat litters and were considerably longer. At 21 days all the rats were weaned and thereafter allowed to eat as much as they liked. The small rats at once showed a catch-up, but it was insufficient to bring them up to the size of the large ones. Evidently the malnutrition had had some permanent effect, and they grew along a different growth curve from their well-fed littermates. It seems that their tally mechanism had been damaged, or reset along a flatter curve.

The rat is born relatively much earlier in its development than man. Its birth to 21-day period corresponds in most respects to the period of foetal life in man from about four postmenstrual months onwards, and it seems probable that the human equivalent of these experimental animals are those rather rare dwarfs who are born with an abnormally low weight.

The most likely explanation for these findings is that permanent damage has been caused to hypothalamic centres, or—which amounts to the same thing—that a necessary stimulus for hypothalamic development has been omitted at a critical period.

We have a model for this in the regulation of reproduction by the hypothalamus. In the rat the hypothalamus holds in its structure the information as to the sex of the animal in the same way as it holds the information as to the animal's maturity. When the pituitary from an adult male rat is transplanted into a hypophysectomized adult female and makes connection with the female hypothalamus, it produces gonadotrophins which follow the female cycle and support female sex behaviour. When a female pituitary is transplanted to a position below the male hypothalamus, it follows the pattern of male gonadotrophin secretion (Harris & Jacobsohn, 1952). The work of Barraclough and others has made it seem probable that this differentiation of hypothalamic structure is caused by the small amounts of male or female sex hormone secreted by the young rat's gonads before puberty, at about the fifth day after birth. The differentiation can be upset by injection of the opposite sex hormone. Thus, a single injection of about 1 mg. of testosterone propionate into a female rat at 5 days so alters the hypothalamus that after puberty the female pattern of gonadotrophin release is permanently replaced by a male pattern which causes constant vaginal oestrus and sterility. At the same time a centre in the anterior hypothalamus which is concerned in mating behaviour in females is also damaged or suppressed so that no mating occurs even when sex hormones are given in a manner which restores receptivity in spayed, but otherwise normal, rats (Barraclough & Gorski, 1962). On the contrary, injection of testosterone after puberty causes male sexual behaviour (Harris & Levene, 1962). Conversely, young males treated with oestradiol benzoate at 5 days produce female gonadotrophic cycles at puberty; and if their testes are replaced with grafted ovaries, these actually produce corpora lutea. Five days after birth in the rat is a critical period for the transfer of information from prepubertal gonad to hypothalamus. Opposite-sex hormone injections have little effect either before one to two days after birth or after seven to eight days after birth.

We may imagine that some similar sort of system carries the information as to maturity. Indeed some linkage between the systems is present, for females are ahead of males in maturity, in the rat skeleton from about the 18th day after birth (Tanner & Hughes, unpublished). The cells which inhibit the pituitary up till puberty lie in the anterior hypothalamus in the rat, in the same area as those controlling mating behaviour. Kennedy (1957) has shown that lesions in the ventromedial area, which cause or release excessive food intake in adult rats, have apparently no effect in young weanling rats who have normally a very high food intake. But their regulatory system has nevertheless been damaged, and when they reach the age at which their food intake should fall it fails to do so.

There is thus considerable collateral evidence pointing to the hypothalamus as the site of the hypothetical time tally. The site of action of the inhibitors is much more in doubt, but the hypothalamus is again perhaps most likely, with the mis-match signal generated as differences in excitatory state between two groups of neurones, resulting in the passage of a growth-stimulator releasing factor (compare corticotrophic releasing factor) to the pituitary. I repeat that this is speculation, but not fantasy.

FACTORS AFFECTING THE REGULATORY SYSTEM

The regulatory system is evidently built in to the organism and we would expect its characteristics, such as precision, speed of response, and so forth to be mainly genetically determined. Such indeed is the case. Two factors are known which affect the system: heterozygosity and sex. In animals hybrids seem to be better regulated, or canalized, than inbred strains, at least in a number of instances. Hybrid mice for example vary less than inbred in weight and in tail length either in a normal or a hot environment (Harrison, Morton, & Weiner, 1959). Nothing is as yet known about this in the human. The effect of sex however is becoming well documented in man (see Tanner, 1962, p. 127). Girls are apparently less easily thrown off their growth curves by adverse circumstances than boys. Greulich (1951) first drew attention to this, after studying the effects on growth of wartime hardships in Guam and of the atomic bombing in Hiroshima and Nagasaki. The same sex difference seems to occur in response to malnutrition in rats.

CONCLUSION

We have apparently ended rather far into physiological and genetic technology, but I think this an appearance only. One reason that I chose to speak about regulation in growth was because it is a general problem. By this I mean that formal, model solutions may be applicable not only to the problems of physical growth but in several different fields. It is an old and entirely justified complaint that the great majority of so-called interdisciplinary studies of child growth fail in their endeavour to link the psychology and physiology of development. The mistake was to suppose that the child was the integrating factor; that when psychologists and physiologists applied their techniques not to different children but to the *same* child, that integration would follow. An integral view can be obtained only when both groups use a common, and because common, more fundamental language than their present ones, and I have a feeling that that language in so far as child development is concerned will be cybernetics.

Summary

AN ANIMAL'S growth is self-stabilizing, or "target-seeking," in the sense that the animal has a strong tendency to return to its natural growth curve after being deflected from it by disease or starvation. Illustrations of the regularity of growth in height of children are given, showing the excellent fit of simple curves to longitudinal data before and during adolescence. Seasonal variation in growth rate about these curves is also illustrated.

Examples are given of "catch-up" or compensatory growth occurring in children at the end of periods of starvation, hypothyroidism, Cushing's syndrome, and growth-hormone-responsive dwarfism. It is pointed out that in healthy children a catch-up occurs frequently during the first six months after birth; genetically large babies are thus able to reach their growth curves after having been restrained when developing in the uterus of a small mother.

A hypothesis concerning the regulation of catch-up growth and of the normal velocity of growth is then presented. Since during the catch-up the whole organism grows in a proportional manner, it is thought likely that the control of size resides in a central mechanism. To explain how the organism "knows" when to stop the rapid catch-up velocity, it is supposed that in the brain there is a time tally mechanism which represents the normal growth curve by means of maturation changes occurring in certain nerve cells. The actual size of the organism is supposed to be monitored by means of an inhibitor substance produced proportionately to the increase of material in body cells. The mis-match between the time tally and the inhibitor concentration is then read and the velocity of growth is adjusted to be proportional to this mis-match. It is thought that this mechanism may underlie the normal velocity curve of growth (high velocity at first, low later) as well as catch-up growth.

Examples of how this simple model represents the known events of catch-up growth, of chronic starvation, and of precocious puberty are given. A second cycle is supposed to occur at adolescence, and the manner in which the linkage between the first and second cycles may be made definite, but relatively loose, is discussed. Work on the regulation of sex and maturity in experimental animals is quoted, indicating that the location of the time tally and of the reading of the mis-match may well be in the hypothalamus. It is stressed that this model is hypothetical only; if correct at all, it is certainly over-simplified. Nevertheless it might serve as a necessary basis for investigation in this neglected field.

REFERENCES

BARRACLOUGH, C. A., & GORSKI, R. A. Studies on mating behaviour in the androgen-sterilized female rat in relation to the hypothalamic regulation of sexual behavior. *J. Endocrin.*, 1962, **25,** 175–182.

BAYER, LEONA M., & BAYLEY, NANCY. *Growth diagnosis.* Chicago: Univer. Chicago Press, 1959.

DAVIS, J. Paper given at the International Congress on Paediatrics, Lisbon, 1962. (Unpublished.)

DEMING, J. Application of the Gompertz curve to the observed pattern of growth in length of 48 individual boys and girls during the adolescent cycle of growth. *Hum. Biol.*, 1957, **29,** 83–122.

DICKINSON, A. G. Some genetic implications of maternal effects: an hypothesis of mammalian growth. *J. agric. Sci.*, 1960, **54,** 379–390.

DONOVAN, B. T., & WERFF TEN BOSCH, J. J. VAN DER. The hypothalamus and sexual maturation in the rat. *J. Physiol.*, 1959, **147,** 78–92.

GREULICH, W. W. The growth and developmental status of Guamanian school children in 1947. *Amer. J. phys. Anthrop.*, N.S., 1951, **9,** 55–70.

HARRIS, G. W., & JACOBSOHN, D. Functional grafts of the anterior pituitary gland. *Proc. Royal Soc.* (Series B), 1952, **139,** 263–276.

HARRIS, G. W., & LEVENE, S. Sexual differentiation of the brain and its experimental control. *J. Physiol.*, 1962, **164,** 17–18.

HARRISON, G. A., MORTON, R. J., & WEINER, J. S. The growth in weight and tail length of inbred and hybrid mice reared at two different temperatures. *Philos. Trans.* (Series B), 1959, **242,** 479–516.

KENNEDY, G. C. The development with age of hypothalamic restraint upon the appetite of the rat. *J. Endocrin.*, 1957, **16,** 955–966.

MCCANCE, R. A. Food, growth and time. *Lancet,* 1962, **2,** 621–626; 671–676.

MCKEOWN, T., & RECORD, R. G. Observations on foetal growth in multiple pregnancy in man. *J. Endocrin.*, 1952, **8,** 386–401.

MINISTRY OF HEALTH (Great Britain). Standards of normal weight in infancy. *Min. Hlth Rep. Publ. Hlth No. 99.* London: H.M.S.O., 1959.

NORVAL, M. A., KENNEDY, R. L. J., & BERKSON, J. Biometric studies of the growth of children of Rochester, Minnesota. The first year of life. *Hum. Biol.*, 1951, **23,** 274–301.

PENROSE, L. S. *Recent advances in human genetics.* London: Churchill, 1961.

PRADER, A., TANNER, J. M., & VON HARNACK, G. A. Catch-up growth following illness or starvation; an example of developmental canalization in man. *J. Pediat.*, 1963, **62,** 646–659.

SIMMONS, K., & TODD, T. W. Growth of well children: analysis of stature and weight, 3 months to 13 years. *Growth,* 1938, **2,** 93–134.

TANNER, J. M. *Growth at adolescence* (2nd ed.) Oxford: Blackwell, 1962.

TANNER, J. M. Growth and constitution. In G. A. Harrison, J. M. Tanner, J. S. Weiner & N. A. Barnicot, *Human biology.* Oxford: Clarendon Press, 1964.

TANNER, J. M., & INHELDER, BÄRBEL (Eds.). *Discussions on child development.* Vol. 4. London: Tavistock Publications and New York: International Universities Press, 1960.

TENG, C. T., DAESCHNER, C. W., SINGLETON, E. B., ROSENBERG, H. S., COLE, V. W., HILL, L. L., & BRENNAN, J. C. Liver disease and osteoporosis in children: I. Clinical observations. *J. Pediat.*, 1961, **59,** 684–702.

THOMPSON, J. Observations on weight gain in infants. *Arch. Dis. Childh.*, 1955, **30,** 322–327.

THOMPSON, J. Infant Growth. *Arch. Dis. Childh.*, **31,** 382–389.

WADDINGTON, C. H. *The strategy of the genes. A discussion of some aspects of theoretical biology.* London: Allen & Unwin, 1957.

WEISS, P., & KAVANAU, J. L. A model of growth and growth control in mathematical terms. *J. gen. Physiol.*, 1957, **41,** 1–47.

WERFF TEN BOSCH, J. J. VAN DER. *Normale en abnormale Geslachstrijping.* Leiden: Univer. Leiden Press, 1959.

WIDDOWSON, E. M., & KENNEDY, G. C. Rate of growth, mature weight and life-span. *Proc. Royal Soc.* (Series B), 1962, **156,** 96–108.

WIDDOWSON, E. M., & MCCANCE, R. A. Some effects of accelerating growth: I. General somatic development. *Proc. Royal Soc.* (Series B), 1960, **152,** 188–206.